HANDBOOK OF CONCEPTUALIZATION AND TREATMENT OF CHILD PSYCHOPATHOLOGY

HANDBOOK OF CONCEPTUALIZATION AND TREATMENT OF CHILD PSYCHOPATHOLOGY

EDITED BY

HELEN ORVASCHEL
Nova Southeastern University, Florida, USA

JAN FAUST
Nova Southeastern University, Florida, USA

MICHEL HERSEN
Pacific University, Oregon, USA

2001

Pergamon
An Imprint of Elsevier Science

Amsterdam – London – New York – Oxford – Paris – Shannon – Tokyo

ELSEVIER B.V.
Radarweg 29
P.O. Box 211, 1000 AE
Amsterdam, The Netherlands

ELSEVIER Inc.
525 B Street
Suite 1900, San Diego
CA 92101-4495, USA

ELSEVIER Ltd
The Boulevard
Langford Lane, Kidlington,
Oxford OX5 1GB, UK

ELSEVIER Ltd
84 Theobalds Road
London WC1X 8RR
UK

First edition 2001
Second impression 2005
Third impression 2006

British Library Cataloguing in Publication Data
A catalogue record is available from the British Library.

Library of Congress Cataloging in Publication Data
A catalog record is available from the Library of Congress.

ISBN: 0-08-0433626

Working together to grow
libraries in developing countries

www.elsevier.com | www.bookaid.org | www.sabre.org

ELSEVIER   BOOK AID   Sabre Foundation
            International

Transferred to digital printing 2006
Printed and bound by CPI Antony Rowe, Eastbourne

Contents

Dedication

To the students we teach and
the patients they serve. *H.O.*

To my family: Nina and Brandon Campanile
To my family of origin: Betts, Verne, and Scott Faust. *J.F.*

To Jonathan and Nathaniel. *M.H.*

Contributors

Joan Asarnow

Department of Psychiatry
University of California, Los Angeles
Los Angeles, California, USA

Melanie Ballatore

Department of Educational Psychology
University of Texas
Austin, Texas, USA

Debora J. Bell-Dolan

Department of Psychology
University of Missouri, Columbia
Columbia, Missouri, USA

Donald A. Bux

Department of Psychiatry
University of Pennsylvania
Philadelphia, Pennsylvania, USA

Jill T. Ehreneich

Department of Psychology
University of Mississippi
Mississippi, USA

Jan L. Faust

Center for Psychological Studies
Nova Southeastern University
Ft. Lauderdale, Florida, USA

Adam B. Feder

Hollywood, Florida, USA

Ana I. Fins

Center for Psychological Studies
Nova Southeastern University
Ft. Lauderdale, Florida, USA

Edna B. Foa

Department of Psychiatry
University of Pennsylvania
Philadelphia, Pennsylvania, USA

Martin E. Franklin

Department of Psychiatry
University of Pennsylvania
Philadelphia, Pennsylvania, USA

Paul J. Frick   Department of Psychology
                          University of New Orleans
                          New Orleans, Louisiana, USA

Alan M. Gross   Department of Psychology
                          University of Mississippi
                          Mississippi, USA

Allison Hamff   Department of Educational Psychology
                          University of Texas
                          Austin, Texas, USA

Michel Hersen   School of Professional Psychology
                          Pacific University
                          Forest Grove, Oregon, USA

Delight Hicks   Winter Haven, Florida, USA
Carmichael

Stephen P. Hinshaw   Department of Psychology
                          University of California
                          Berkeley, California, USA

Kathleen A. Ingman   UCLA Neuropsychiatric Institute
                          Los Angeles, California, USA

Russell T. Jones   Department of Psychology
                          Va Polytech Institute
                          Blacksburg, Virginia, USA

Audra K. Langley   Neuropsychiatric Institute
                          University of California
                          Los Angeles, California, USA

Monique G. McCoy   Department of Psychology
                          University of Alabama
                          Tuscaloosa, Alabama, USA

Thomas H. Ollendick   Department of Psychology
                          Virginia Polytechnic Institute and
                          State University
                          Blacksburg, Virginia, USA

Michele L. Ondersma   Children's Hospital of Michigan
                          Detroit, Michigan, USA

Steven J. Ondersma	Merrill Palmer Institute Wayne State University Detroit, Michigan, USA
Helen Orvaschel	Center for Psychological Studies Nova Southeastern University Ft. Lauderdale, Florida, USA
Carrie Penn	Department of Psychology Va Polytech Institute Blacksburg, Virginia, USA
Mary J. Sanders	Department of Psychiatry Stanford University School of Medicine Stanford, California, USA
Lisa Selvig	Department of Educational Psychology University of Texas Austin, Texas, USA
Joyanna L. Silberg	Childhood Recovery Resources Sheppard Pratt Hospital Baltimore, Maryland, USA
Wendy K. Silverman	Department of Psychology Florida International University Miami, Florida, USA
Persephanie Silverthorn	Department of Psychology University of New Orleans New Orleans, Louisiana, USA
Nirbhay N. Singh	Department of Psychiatry Va Commonwealth University Richmond, Virginia, USA
Subhashni D. Singh	Department of Psychiatry Va Commonwealth University Richmond, Virginia, USA
Kevin D. Stark	Department of Educational Psychology University of Texas Austin, Texas, USA

Cyd C. Strauss   Clinical Psychology
                          University of Florida
                          Gainsville, Florida, USA

Lourdes Suarez   Medical University of South Carolina
                          Charleston, South Carolina, USA

David Tobin   Department of Psychiatry
                          Baystate Medical Center
                          Springfield, Massachusetts, USA

John F. Todaro   Brown University Medical School
                          The Miriam Hospital
                          Providence, Rhode Island, USA

Martha C. Tompson   Department of Psychology
                          Boston University
                          Boston, Massachusetts, USA

Carmen R. Valdez   Department of Educational Psychology
                          University of Texas
                          Austin, Texas, USA

Eric F. Wagner   College of Urban and Public Affairs
                          Florida International University
                          North Miami, Florida, USA

Holly B. Waldron   Department of Psychology
                          University of New Mexico
                          Albuquerque, New Mexico, USA

C. Eugene Walker   Department of Psychiatry and Behavioral Sciences
                          University of Oklahoma
                          Oklahoma City, Oklahoma, USA

William K. Wohlgemuth   Department of Psychology & Behavioral Science
                          Duke University
                          Durham, North Carolina, USA

Christine Zalecki   Department of Psychology
                          University of California
                          Berkeley, California, USA

Preface

The purpose of this edited text is to examine and illustrate the integration of conceptualization and treatment of child and adolescent psychopathology. The ability to accurately diagnose and treat those with mental health problems is both an art and a science. Such skill depends on a number of factors, including a wealth of nosological and theoretical knowledge and the ability to synthesize such knowledge into a comprehensive conceptual framework. It is this framework for or conceptual understanding of the presenting problem that guides treatment. Without such a guide, we believe that diagnostic understanding may be confused and interventions may be spurious.

The science of accurately diagnosing and treating is derived from empirical literature and theory, as well as understanding the relationship between the two. The artistic ingredient is the ability to utilize the science to understand the theoretical underpinnings of the diagnosis. With these considerations in mind, we have been fortunate in obtaining contributions from outstanding scholars who are active in both the science and practice of child and adolescent treatment.

The handbook is organized into seven sections. The first discusses issues of conceptualization and developmental considerations in treatment. Our intent was to begin by laying a foundation for the reader on the central thesis of integrating case conceptualization with treatment, as well as establishing the importance of development in the treatment of psychopathology in youth. Following part I are chapters on specific disorders and problems of childhood. Authors were asked to begin with a description of the clinical syndrome, followed by a conceptual framework for the pathology and a detailed treatment strategy related to the conceptual model. They were then to offer an alternative conceptual model, with a somewhat less detailed intervention that follows from the second model. The ensuing sections delineate treatment models and specific interventions for disruptive behavior disorders (Part II), mood disorders (Part III), anxiety disorders (Part IV), eating disorders (Part V), substance use disorders (Part VI), and a special topics section (Part VII) that covers firesetting, trichotillomania, elimination disorders, schizophrenia, sleep problems, and dissociative disorders. Overall, the Handbook is intended as an educational tool for graduate students and a resource for psychologists, psychiatrists, school counselors, social workers, and other mental health practitioners who treat children and adolescents and their families.

Clearly, such a comprehensive undertaking could not have been completed without the contribution and assistance of many individuals. First and foremost, we would like to thank our excellent contributors. The results of their efforts, commitment, and expertise have created a state of the art text that we believe will educate readers, at varied levels of training and from different disciplines, for years to come. We would also like to thank Diana Jones and Charlotte Dewhurst from Elsevier Publishing for their patience and dedication to bringing this project to fruition. We are also grateful for the support and tolerance of family and co-workers, who often received less time and consideration because our attention was diverted to this task. Finally, we express our gratitude to the many patients who taught us so that we may teach others.

Helen Orvaschel, Jan Faust, Michel Hersen
Fort Lauderdale, Florida and Forest Grove, Oregon
2001

Part I

Introduction

Chapter 1

General Issues in Conceptualization and Treatment

Helen Orvaschel, Jan Faust and Michel Hersen

Introduction

In a world filled with technicians, this text on conceptualization and treatment targets the professional. While the technician needs a "how to" book on techniques of treatment, the professional is better served by a "how to think" book. Rather than a list of intervention strategies, we offer a text on alternatives for how to view and understand psychopathology. The "how to" follows from the concepts used, rather than from fragmented application of techniques.

The inspiration for this book arose largely from our teaching experiences. While many students have basic knowledge in several theoretical domains and familiarity with a variety of intervention strategies, we encountered large numbers who were unable to link the two. The result is a treatment without form, an indiscriminate beginning, an uncertain trajectory, and an ambiguous end. Intervention devoid of a guiding conceptual framework risks an erroneous understanding of the problem, the treatment, or both. Since students' abilities to integrate diagnosis, conceptualization, and treatment often fell remarkably short, we wanted to begin to remedy these deficiencies by providing a comprehensive text of the most up-to-date and empirically supported treatment strategies for child and adolescent psychopathology. Rather than offer a series of recommended interventions, however, we hoped to impart the thinking behind these interventions, the conceptual formulation that led to the selection of a particular strategy, thereby conveying the integration of theory and treatment.

While a great deal is written about psychotherapy, and at least as much literature is available on theories of psychopathology, far less has been provided on efforts to integrate the two. This statement is not intended to equate theory with conceptualization, but rather to initiate a discussion on the need to join together the sometimes disparate areas of theory with treatment. Theory is generally comprised of facts, principles, observations and conjecture regarding their relationships in order to explain (in our case) normal and abnormal behavior. In other words, theory attempts to provide "scientific" concepts that explain causal relationships. "Schools of thought" may be a product of theory and, while not synonymous with conceptualization, are sometimes referred to as if they were. In our field we have such divergent "schools of thought" as psychodynamic, social, interpersonal,

Handbook of Conceptualization and Treatment of Child Psychopathology, pages 3–7.
ISBN: 0-08-043362-6

cognitive, humanistic, behavioral, existential, and the like. Each, in turn, contains numerous conceptual models derived from varying theoretical frameworks. For example, a cognitive school of thought may include conceptual models from the work of Beck or Ellis, while psychodyamic schools of thought can encompass traditional drive theory models or those of object relations or ego psychology.

While there are over 200 forms of psychotherapy, there are far fewer theoretical orientations. Consolidation of treatment methods may be advantageous and integration of treatment with theory would likely be useful in this endeavor. Nevertheless, a unitary, all encompassing theory of child psychopathology has been attempted in the past, but is not likely to have much of a future. Rather, the field of intervention would benefit from a more paradigmatic approach and this requires consideration of theoretical framework and conceptualization. A paradigm gains acceptance because it is better than its competitors at solving a particular problem. It does not have to solve all problems for this to be achieved, but it is necessary in a paradigm to agree on the nature of the problem (i.e., its definition and parameters) and how to evaluate a solution. Certainly, a paradigm serves as the archetype in order to provide direction, a way to move forward, but the model can be changed when dictated by necessity or alternative points of view.

Conceptualization derived from a theoretical perspective frames the clinicians' understanding of the presenting problem. For example, while most clinicians engage in diagnostic formulation, this matter is also dictated by a conceptual model. Diagnosis is the decision-making process used to assign someone to a nosologic class according to an established set of criteria, while classification is the ordering of these nosologic classes in relation to one another. Diseases are defined as either a physiological or psychological dysfunction, while illness is a subjective state of not being well. The nosology in the DSM identifies disease states, but many schools of thought view presenting problems according to a subjective state of well being or the lack thereof.

For existential schools of thought, diagnosis is not a relevant concept, inasmuch as the scope of therapy is exploration of a self-world construct. From this perspective, the individual who presents with anxiety is not seen as suffering from psychopathology that requires a label. For the existentialist, anxiety and depression are not symptoms but representations of the struggle within the individual to find meaning. Alternatively, psychodynamic models would encompass diagnostic formulation, but not necessarily from the prevailing nosologic system. Instead, the psychoanalytic clinician would focus on defense mechanisms and ensuing personality structures. Personality disorders would be noted, not according to the dictates of DSM-IV criteria; rather they would be based in the dynamic formulation guiding the therapist. For those with a strict behavioral outlook, diagnosis does not play a central role in treatment formulation. Rather, the behaviorist attends to specific problematic behavior and the contingencies that maintain it.

Clearly, the conceptual model used by the clinician determines whether a diagnostic formulation is necessary or appropriate. Moreover, the conceptual model as embedded in a paradigm dictates the type of nosology to be utilized. While our nosologic system provides the rules by which the field categorizes disorders or disease states into groups according to specified criteria, our various schools of thought do not agree on the appropriate taxonomic structure, or even if such classification is necessary. To the extent that we cannot agree on the criteria and boundaries of our nosology, nor whether a nosologic system should be utilized, communication between schools of thought is compromized and we remain preparadigmatic in our approach to intervention with psychopathology.

Beyond its impact on the "how or if" to diagnose, conceptual models make different assumptions about the etiology and nature of psychopathology (or the presenting problem), the factors that affect its presentation, and how to effect change. Does the individual seeking treatment have a problem with unresolved oedipal issues and the need to over-utilize primitive defense mechanisms or is this difficulty the result of poor sub-group boundaries within the family structure? Is the patient suffering from distorted cognitions, a lack of positively reinforcing experiences, anger turned inward, unsatisfying relationships with non-reciprocal expectations, an incongruent self-world construct, or a symbolic representation of a dysfunctional family system? By no means an exhaustive list, each of the aforementioned hypotheses offers an alternative for how to explain a presentation of depression.

A patient with panic attacks may be seen as misinterpreting physiologic cues, which in turn result in unrealistic thoughts about the consequences of the accompanying symptomatology. The ensuing anticipatory anxiety is so unpleasant that avoidant behavior is maintained by negative reinforcement. However, these same symptoms may also be viewed as a failure in the defensive structure, bringing unconscious material too close to consciousness. The anxiety and ancillary panic symptoms provide an alternative, albeit dysfunctional means of defending the individual from the unacceptable unconscious impulses. Alternatively, the adolescent with panic may provide her family with a focus for their concern, uniting them in efforts to deal with a "sick" child rather than attending to the marital disruption that is truly behind the presenting complaint. Each effort to explain or account for a particular condition is derived from a conceptual frame of reference and has theoretical and empirical underpinnings.

Arguments regarding which paradigm is the more valid in the above examples cannot, as yet, be resolved because there are no unifying criteria as to how to determine etiology, diagnostic validity, or even the meaning of symptomatic behavior. This dilemma makes conceptualization all the more critical, insofar as an appropriate intervention strategy must be derived as a function of the underlying assumptions about the pathology. That is to say, if I believe a behavior is maintained as a result of negative reinforcement, then exposure with reciprocal inhibition would be a valid intervention. If, on the other hand, I view the same behavior as a manifestation of unconscious conflict, a more logical treatment approach should include efforts to determine the underlying, internal discord, because attempts at resolution should result in symptomatic abatement. Intervention is dependent on ones understanding of the problem, its manifestation and maintaining variables. This understanding occurs in the context of prior knowledge, which is theory, and dictates course of action.

To intervene without an underlying theoretical framework is akin to building a house without a foundation. The conceptual model establishes how the therapy proceeds. Will the treatment be brief or open-ended with respect to duration? Cognitive strategies are designed generally to be executed in a time-limited manner while psychodynamic therapy is intended to be longterm and existential approaches take as long as they take. Behavioral interventions are heavily dependent on regular, on-going measurement of specific symptoms and behaviors but such assessments would not be part of strategic family therapists' procedures. Will the therapist examine dreams or explore dysfunctional beliefs? Will homework be assigned in the form of graded task assignments or will acceptance and reflection provide the tools for change? Will the treatment proceed with only the identified patient or will the family be expected to actively participate? Only a conceptual framework can begin to resolve these questions.

If, in fact, theory defines psychopathology and its components, establishes the domains appropriate for treatment, and determines the nature of psychotherapy, it thereby provides the underlying foundation that informs clinical practice. The conceptual model is essential in determining the therapist's role in the therapeutic process. The participation of the cognitive therapist is active and collaborative because collaborative empiricism is an important aspect of cognitive conceptualization. This is in sharp contrast to the analyst, whose role in some forms of psychoanalysis is to provide an ambiguous or blank slate upon which the patient may project or transfer characteristics from past relationships. The existential or client-centered therapist emphasizes a genuine, accepting relationship in order to provide a context for new learning and self-exploration, while in the systemic approach the therapist generally selects a focus for treatment and joins subgroups within the family in order to affect its structure.

There are theoretical assumptions inherent in various conceptualizations that can be contradicted by one another. For example, the behavior of the therapist is theoretically unconditional in client-centered and psychodynamic therapies, but implicitly conditional in behavioral and cognitive therapies because the therapist requests specific behavior of the patient. Such differences can present dangers to the integrity of the therapeutic process because the therapist's behavior may be incongruent with the purported model of treatment used. Of course, theoretical or technical eclecticism may result in a successful integration of approaches, but such success hinges on the clinician's understanding and conceptualization of the problem and careful consideration of the assumptions involved in these approaches, lest they be violated when incorporating more than one.

We began this discussion by indicating that far more has been written about treatment and about theory alone, than in combination. Does this mean that conceptualization is unnecessary for treatment, or superfluous to it? Of course, we would argue against such a supposition. While it is clear that many practitioners engage in psychotherapy without articulating a particular theoretical perspective, such a perspective is either inherent in the work, or the therapeutic process is devoid of coherent structure and process. How else would the clinician explain the selection of intervention strategies and the format within which the treatment has proceeded? The conceptual model certainly does not have to be the same for all disorders or, for that matter, different individuals with the same disorder. A model that is effective with one patient may be ineffective for another, even if the type of problem or disorder is the same. No treatment is effective for everyone, and absolute claims (across problem areas or individuals) about a treatment approach and the model from which it was derived are rare. Further, different models may be equally effective for the same problem. From this vantage, all experienced therapists are at least a little eclectic, and this may account for the frequent reports that level of therapist experience explains more treatment outcome variance than espoused theoretical orientation.

Theories of psychopathology are often a product of their time, as they are likely to reflect social attitudes, levels of scientific knowledge, and the extent to which a particular paradigm is accepted. The chapters that follow are not intended to represent an exhaustive inventory of appropriate treatments for the disorders covered. Rather, they are offered to provide the reader with insight into the conceptual model used by the authors, and the translation of this model as expounded by the formulation for a specific intervention strategy. To the extent that the task is successfully executed, the reader may surmise alternative formulations and construe additional treatments, better suited to the thinking or style of each individual clinician.

Chapter 2

Developmental Considerations in Treatment

Nirbhay N. Singh and Subhashni D. Singh

Introduction

A developmental perspective provides a framework for understanding the nature and course of specific childhood disorders, an essential basis for case conceptualization and long-term treatment. Knowledge of the developmental course of childhood disorders provides information about how symptoms of specific disorders vary across the life span, and how children's individual differences affect not only their developmental pathways but also their psychopathological pathways.

Clinicians need to have a good understanding of developmental processes because it enables them to differentiate normal and abnormal or psychopathological development in children at various ages and stages. Good case formulation of childhood disorders is based on an appreciation of patterns of continuity and discontinuity between variations within the normal range and specific childhood disorders. That is, it is not uncommon for children to display "normal" as well as abnormal behavioral patterns over time, depending on their biopsychosocial and cultural interactions. Knowledge of behavioral patterns enables clinicians to determine whether and what type of treatment is needed. Childhood disorders are never categorically distinct states; they have multifactorial etiologies that substantially overlap with variations in normal behavioral patterns. Being aware of the pathogenesis of specific childhood disorders provides a solid basis for developing treatments.

A developmental perspective is also important because it highlights the fact that the manifestation of childhood disorders varies with age. For example, attention-deficit/hyperactivity disorder is first evident in preschool years, depressive disorders increase in frequency during teenage years, delinquent behavior peaks in mid-teenage years, and the onset of schizophrenia occurs typically during late adolescence or early adult life. Often, these disorders may persist in adult life as well. Indeed, childhood disorders are a prerequisite for some disorders in adulthood; for example, conduct disorder is a prerequisite for antisocial personality disorders.

For all childhood disorders, it is essential that clinicians have an appreciation of how multiple influences combine to produce the presenting problems. This entails having knowledge of risk and protective factors, the child's transactions with layers of ecological contexts, effects of both nature and nurture, and the interplay of the brain, mind, body, and spirit. Linear models of treatment have rarely considered multiple factors when elaborating on the mechanisms involved in the

Handbook of Conceptualization and Treatment of Child Psychopathology, pages 9–38.

genesis and maintenance of various childhood disorders. Interactional and transactional models have been more inclusive of multiple factors, but even these models have paid little attention to the effects of service systems on the maintenance and treatment of psychological and psychiatric problems of childhood.

Children's transactions with their environment, broadly defined, influence their development. Sameroff (1993, p.6) has noted that children's development is a function of "the interplay between child and context across time, in which the state of one affects the next state of the other in a continuous dynamic process". Indeed, transactional processes influence not only psychological but also brain development; brain functions during the first year of life can be enhanced through physical touching, social interaction, and sensory stimulation (Greenspan, 1997). Thus, children actively create their own environments through bidirectional interactions with their caregivers.

What the children elicit from the environment and what the environment elicits from the children depends on their individual differences. In the transactional model, developmental outcomes are a function of the individual, his or her experiences, and his or her biological capacities. Thus, children's developmental outcomes (including psychopathology) cannot be fully understood without assessing the effects of the environment on them. For example, low birth weight of a baby may make the child's mother somewhat anxious. The mother's anxiety may result in the mother handling her baby rather cautiously, thereby reducing spontaneous and joyous interactions with her child. In response, the child's sleeping and feeding patterns are negatively affected, giving the mother the impression that her child has a difficult temperament. This decreases the pleasure that the mother gets in her interactions with her child, resulting in the mother spending less time with the child. This avoidance by the mother may result in reduced interactions with her child, thereby reducing incidental learning opportunities and resulting in a language delay.

Alternative outcomes may result from different kinds of responses from the mother, resulting in different developmental pathways for the child. For example, instead of being anxious, the mother provides additional love and affection to the infant. This added stimulation enhances the infant's biological and social development, resulting in closer bonding between mother and child. The child eats and sleeps well, and is thought by the mother to have a loving temperament. This increases the mother-child verbal and physical interactions, resulting in greater amounts of incidental teaching and learning, and the child has good language skills as the child grows up.

Understanding these transactional processes assists clinicians in providing early intervention and treatment of psychopathology at different developmental stages of the child. For example, in the first scenario, intervention can be directed at reducing the mother's anxiety so that it changes later mother-child interactions, or intervene with the child and improve his/her eating and sleeping patterns. Either of these interventions would change the developmental outcomes for the child. The transactional model of children's behavior provides the theoretical underpinning for designing intervention strategies that are appropriate at different levels of developmental regulation in the child. This approach would suggest that intervening just with the child might not be enough to change the developmental pathway for future behavior, both normal and pathological. Other regulatory systems that impact on the child's behavior will need to be assessed and understood before informed treatment decisions can be made. For example, treatment may include direct intervention with the child, providing parent training to improve the parents' ability to take care of the child, or focusing intervention on the biological disregulation when the child has a known organic disorder.

Conceptual Framework

Developmental theories underpinning clinical models of childhood psychopathology provide the basis for formulating testable hypotheses about the origins, maintaining variables, and treatment of specific childhood disorders. Although it is a comparatively new approach to understanding behavior in context, one of its attractions is that it provides a scientific basis for understanding normal and abnormal behavior.

Developmental psychopathology deals with multiple domains of a child's behavior, including the "ontogenetic, biochemical, genetic, biological, physiologic, cognitive, social-cognitive, representational, socioemotional, environmental, cultural, and societal influences on behavior" (Cicchetti & Cohen, 1995, p. 5). Sroufe and Rutter (1984) defined this approach as "the study of the origins and course of individual patterns of behavioral maladaptation, whatever the age of onset, whatever the causes, whatever the transformations in behavioral manifestation and however complex the course of the developmental pattern may be" (p.18). The Institute of Medicine's *National Plan for Research on Child and Adolescent Mental Disorders* endorsed and broadened this approach to include the investigation of the "emerging behavioral repertoire, cognitive and language functions, social and emotional processes, and changes occurring in anatomical structures and physiological processes of the brain" (National Advisory Mental Health Council, 1990, p.14).

There are certain basic assumptions in the field of developmental psychopathology. A primary assumption is that children engage in and move between "normal" and pathological modes of functioning. A secondary assumption is that the dynamic interaction among risk factors and protective factors determine both normal and pathological behavior. As children grow older, their developmental pathways undergo several adaptations and qualitative transformations within and among the biological, emotional, cognitive, and social domains. Whether these developmental pathways lead to normal or pathological behavior at any point in time is dependent on several factors. Among others, these factors may include the nature of the biological (e.g., infection, exposure to a toxic substance, malnutrition, or a hypoxic-ischemic event) or environmental insult (e.g., abuse), the dosage of the insult, its timing in terms of the age of the child, developmental vulnerability in terms of the interaction of the child's risk and protective factors, and the nature of the caregiving environment.

Cicchetti and Cohen (1995) proposed at least four principles that purport to explain the outcomes of children's behavior. The first principle is that the same outcomes are possible through a diverse set of developmental pathways (equifinality). A good example of equifinality is the finding that boys use different pathways to become delinquents (Loeber, *et al.*, 1991). The second is that specific developmental domains or dimensions operate differently depending on contextual factors. For example, childhood trauma may contribute differently to a child's adaptation, depending on family nurturance. The third is that children pass through critical developmental periods when their susceptibility to life experiences is greatly increased. Research has clearly demonstrated that critical periods exist for the shaping of biological, social, and psychological capacities. The final principle is that individual differences affect normal and pathological development.

Developmental psychopathology provides an overarching framework for understanding the diverse array of outcomes seen in children with the same disorders. It helps clinicians to understand how developmental domains and functions that modulate and integrate behavior affect emotional and behavioral disorders, and vice versa. Further, it alerts them to consider children's biological adaptability and protective factors, as well as sources of vulnerability, in their case formulation. Identifying and enhancing protective factors often provide the basis of a strength-based treatment approach.

Deciding What is Normal or Abnormal

While not all pathological behavior may fall along a normal-abnormal continuum, a child's behavior can be classified as "abnormal" only by comparison with normal functioning at different developmental levels. For example, behavior considered normal or adaptive at a certain age (e.g., 18 months) may be considered abnormal or psychopathological at a later age (e.g., seven years). Further, context may intersect with developmental adaptations because some childhood behavior patterns (e.g., hyperactivity) are often considered normal in some situations (e.g., playground) but not in others (e.g., in structured classrooms). Being able to detect emotional and behavioral problems within a developmental context is necessary for early intervention with those children who may need specialized psychological and psychiatric services.

In general, psychologists rely on standardized tests and direct behavioral observations to determine whether a child is displaying behaviors that can be considered deviant or in the "clinical range" when compared to demographically similar children. While these are reasonable approaches, there are a number of hazards as well. Regardless of the methods used to judge behavior along the normal-abnormal continuum, the judgment itself is influenced by a number of variables including the developmental level and demographic characteristics of the child (e.g., age, ethnicity, gender), context of the behavior (home, clinic, school), and informant characteristics (e.g., parents vs teachers vs clinicians) (Achenbach, *et al.*, 1987). Further, the normative samples used as the basis for developing standardized tests are rarely chosen randomly from the population to which the children are to be compared. This is a critical issue, especially with children who are not middle-class Caucasians (the typical "subject" used in many standardized rating scales). In the absence of a "gold standard" against which children can be judged as being normal or abnormal, clinicians can use a bootstrapping strategy suggested by Achenbach (1997) for this purpose.

Examples of Developmental Contexts: The Influence of Parent-child Interactions on Later Psychopathology

Parental Psychopathology

Parental psychopathology is a risk factor for many children, often compounding with other risk factors, such as substance abuse, child maltreatment, and exposure to violence. For example, maternal depression is a well-established risk factor that affects parent-child interactions. It leads to inadequate and often negative parenting that, in turn, leads to maladjustment and behavioral problems in the children. Maternal depression has been associated with parental unresponsiveness, inattentiveness, and the use of inadequate disciplinary methods (Gelfand & Teti, 1990). Further, low-income mothers who are moderately but not severely depressed are at increased risk for child abuse, including physical aggression (Zuravin, 1989).

It has been reported in recent research that low-income depressed mothers show three types of interaction patterns: (a) withdrawn-unavailable; (b) hostile-intrusive; and (c) mainly positive (Murray & Cooper, 1997), with the two negative interaction patterns having negative effects on the cognitive and emotional development of their children (Laucht, Esser, & Schmidt, 1994). Both mother and child contribute to the negative and positive interaction patterns. For example, transactional analyses of mother-child interactions suggest that as the withdrawn mother interacts less with her child, the child finds the interaction less rewarding (e.g., emotionally), and therefore initiates interactions less often with the mother. Similarly, the child may emit fewer affective reactions in response to the withdrawn or unavailable depressed mother, but more irritable reactions over time, thereby not reinforcing the mother's attempts to initiate positive interactions. These negative interaction patterns of children and their depressed mothers place the children at increased risk for problems in affect regulation (e.g., depression, subdued affect) and inappropriate aggression. As this example shows, parental psychopathology and its effects on parenting can have negative developmental consequences on the children.

Parent-child Attachment

There is substantial research on the importance of parent-child attachment as a powerful marker variable for later adjustment, as well as emotional and behavioral development of the child (e.g., Erickson, Korfmacher, & Egeland, 1992). Secure children are characterized as having experienced caretakers who have been consistently responsive to their cues and signals. These children have learned not only to implicitly trust that their caretakers will meet their needs, but also to have faith in their own ability to elicit this type of care. Early development of trust in their caretakers, as well as in themselves, influences secure children's expectations and behavior in later relationships with other adults. Research suggests that secure children grow into individuals who have a strong foundation for resolving subsequent developmental issues (Erickson, Sroufe, & Egeland, 1985; Lewis, Feiring, McGuffog, & Jaskir, 1984; Sroufe, 1983).

In general, secure attachment in infancy serves as a protective factor, and anxious or insecure attachment as a risk factor for later development. Insecure attachment has been classified as avoidant, ambivalent/resistant, and disorganized/disoriented. When compared to their peers who were judged to have secure attachment in infancy, preschool children who had avoidant attachment in infancy demonstrate higher levels of hostility, unprovoked aggression, and negative interactions with other children. When these children grow up, they continue to demonstrate avoidance, as well as low self-reliance in distressing situations. They tend to be emotionally distant and behave in socially negative ways. This often results in negative interactions with parents, peers, and teachers. For example, children who had avoidant attachment in infancy are viewed more negatively and subjected to harsher discipline by their teachers than those who had secure attachment (Sroufe, 1989). Also, they are rejected by their peers. Children with ambivalent or resistant attachment in infancy grow up showing behavioral inhibition and a lack of assertiveness during preschool years, and social withdrawal and poor peer interaction skills in early school years. Those labeled as having disorganized or disoriented attachment during infancy tend to show higher rates of aggressive, hostile, and coercive behavior during school-age years than their peers who had secure attachments during infancy (Lyons-Ruth, 1996).

The treatment implications of adaptive and maladaptive parenting are clear. Recognition and early intervention of maladaptive parenting arising out of parental psychopathology are key factors as they have the potential to preempt future childhood disorders, child maltreatment, delinquency, and aggressive behavior. Given that parent-child transactions change over time, and different risk and protective factors come into play as the child grows older, a systems approach involving multiple types of interventions may be appropriate. Intervention with the target child only may not be enough, as the transactions may involve multiple players, including peers, parents and teachers. Thus, an interactional, holistic approach may be necessary.

Protective and Risk Factors

There are a large number of factors that interact with children's development, and they either protect and enhance or risk and compromise their normal developmental processes. Although these protective and risk factors fall along a continuum of possibilities, they have a transactional relationship among themselves as well as with children's developmental processes. In effect, it is the balance of the effects of the protective and risk factors that are most obvious in terms of the normal variations in children's behavior or psychopathology. Children who grow up in conditions that are at risk for producing pathological behavior but, in essence, experience sustained protective processes are the ones who exhibit resiliency.

Protective Factors

Three sets of protective factors impinge on children's developmental processes. These include child, parental, and contextual protective factors. Child protective factors can be general or associated with each developmental stage. For example, general protective factors would include genetic inheritance, personality characteristics, good physical and mental health, above-average intelligence, and a good-natured temperament. Other protective factors are important at given developmental stages; that is, they are mediated by the child's developmental level. For example, lack of feeding and sleeping problems are important protective factors in infancy, and getting along with peers, good communication skills, good academic performance, social skills, and emotional stability are strong protective factors in middle childhood.

As noted above, secure attachment is a good parental protective factor because it indicates a positive, loving, and supportive parent-child relationship. Other critical parental protective factors include parental support of their child during stressful situations, firm rules regarding expected child behaviors, parental monitoring of the child, consistency rather than chaos in the home, supportive extended family, extended family caregiving, stable parental relationship, parents and older siblings as models of competence and good coping skills, family religious faith, and well educated parents (Masten, Best & Garmezy, 1990; Werner & Smith, 1992).

Contextual protective factors can also mediate risk for children. For example, a positive stable relationship with adults other than parents (e.g., grandparents, teacher, mentor, adult family friend) has been shown to enhance normal developmental processes even in the presence of other risk factors (e.g., inadequate parenting). Other factors include high socioeconomic status of family (i.e., middle-class or higher), access to health, mental health, and social services, parental employment, acceptable housing, family involvement in religious practice, enrollment and positive experiences at good schools, adequate financial resources, and a safe neighborhood.

Some of these protective factors are powerful enough to overcome the negative effects of risk factors. For example, a warm, stable and positive relationship with other adults can overcome the negative effects of a chronic risk factor such as being raised by a parent with severe and persistent mental illness. The negative effects of a stressful and chaotic family environment can be overcome by positive experiences at a good school. Further, although each of these factors is listed separately within and between groups (i.e., child, parents, and broader context), all of the protective factors have a transactional relationship with each other as well as with all risk factors.

Risk Factors

As with protective factors, there are three general groups of conditions that create developmental risk for children. These include vulnerabilities in the child, inadequate parenting, and socioeconomic and systemic factors.

Many biological conditions place children's normal development at risk, including genetic syndromes (e.g., fragile X, Prader-Willi syndrome, Lesch Nyhan syndrome, Down syndrome), familial risk factors for psychiatric disorders (e.g., ADHD, mood disorders, schizophrenia), exposure to tertogens in utero (e.g., toxic substances, such as alcohol and cocaine, or specific infectious diseases in the mother), prematurity and low birth weight, anoxia, birth complications, and chronic diseases. Other child vulnerabilities include difficult and behaviorally inhibited temperament or characteristic emotional responses. Children's temperament has been classified in a number of ways, but one that is generally accepted includes the following: (a) level of motor activity; (b) regularity of sleeping, eating, and eliminating; (c) withdrawal or approach in novel situations; (d) adaptability to changing environments; (e) sensitivity to environmental stimuli; (f) intensity of responses and energy level; (g) mood or disposition; (h) distractibility; and (i) attention span and persistence when engaged in activities (LeFrancois, 1995). Although temperament has traditionally been thought to be a biological substrate, it does influence and is influenced by a child's developmental process through its interactions with the environment. Thus, temperament is a product of the child's biological and environmental transactions.

Children with difficult temperament tend to be overly negative, highly sensitive, intensely reactive, and resistant to change. These children tend to have negative transactions with peers, parents and teachers, as they do not appear to have the ability to elicit positive attention from others. Those who are behaviorally inhibited are slow to warm up to new people and situations, but once they feel accepted, they are able to elicit positive attention from people. The degree to which they are behaviorally inhibited corresponds well with their risk status. For example, those demonstrating higher levels of behavioral inhibition tend to develop anxiety disorders by the time they reach middle childhood (Hirshfeld, *et al.*, 1992).

Temperament is also considered a risk factor if there is a lack of a goodness-of-fit between the child's temperament and the mother's personality. When a child's temperament elicits warm and loving parental reactions, there is little need for negative parent-child interactions as would be the case with a child with a "difficult" temperament. This suggests that child and parent outcomes are bidirectional, as each influences the other, and that the nature of the influence changes with each developmental stage that the child passes through.

There are a number of potential parental risk factors that have long-term consequences for children. Parental risk factors relate not only to parent-child interactions (e.g., maltreatment, lack of warmth and responsiveness), but also to parental vulnerabilities (e.g., single parenthood in the absence of extended family support, parental unemployment, family disruption or divorce, low maternal educational status, large family size [four or more children], parental psychopathology, and substance abuse). Parents who are at high-risk have reduced ability to mediate or buffer children's stresses during critical developmental periods, thus leaving the children more vulnerable to intrinsic and environmental risk factors, and psychopathology. This vulnerability is heightened by age, as younger children are inherently less able to cope with negative life events, such as witnessing domestic violence. For example, preschool children are not only traumatized by witnessing domestic violence but, in the absence of parental buffering of these stresses, they develop emergency coping strategies, such as aggression and emotional numbing, that may prove to be maladaptive as the child grows older. When parents are unable to teach their young children adaptive coping strategies, and the family has few protective factors that may overcome the negative effects of the risk factors, it makes the children more vulnerable to later psychopathology.

In addition to child and parental risk factors, community and socioeconomic risk factors also contribute to the well being of children. These risk factors are external to the family but may have serious outcomes for parents and children. Age of the children is important in terms of effects and consequences of exposure to community risk factors, as younger children need more parental mediation than older children. These risk factors include: poverty; inadequate or lack of access to medical and mental health care, health insurance, and social services; parental unemployment, homelessness or frequent change of residence and schools; inadequate child care; exposure to racism, discrimination, and community violence; poor schools; exposure to environmental toxins; and dangerous neighborhoods.

Many of these socioeconomic and community risk factors lead to feelings of helplessness and hopelessness in parents because they feel that they have no control over their own lives and that the quality of their lives will only get worse. Often these feelings, and the experience of living in chronic poverty, prove to be so dehumanizing that there is a loss of parental self-esteem and hope. Substance abuse and maternal depression is high in these families, further compromising their ability to provide "good enough" parenting (Winnicott, 1965). Fathers who lose their jobs tend to become more aggressive, negative, and punitive with family members, especially children. Further, families with numerous socioeconomic risk factors engage in less monitoring of their children's activities and behavior than other families. This lowers parental expectations of their children, often leading to negative effects on the children themselves. These children have more externalizing behavior problems in childhood and lower classroom competence when compared to their peers whose activities are closely monitored by their parents. While some parents can and do provide some buffering for the negative effects of socioeconomic and community risk factors, often the cumulative effects of these risk factors are so great that the overall outcome is still negative for the children.

Finally, there are transactional-developmental variables that increase children's risk for later psychopathology. Young children, especially those under six years of age who have not acquired adequate appraisal strategies because of their immature cognitive processing abilities, are more vulnerable to acute or enduring internal or external stressors because of their developmental status. They have not developed adequate coping mechanisms and, therefore, are unable to marshal enough internal or external resources to overcome adversity. For example, those over five years of age are better able to cope with natural disasters (e.g., earthquakes, hurricanes) than those under five.

Children who appear to have a favorable protective vs. risk factors balance may be at risk for psychopathology if life circumstances increase their vulnerability and reduce their coping ability. For example, children in poverty may be resilient enough to withstand the daily hassles of life but may not be able to cope following the death of a loved one. They are likely to shows signs and symptoms of apathy and depression. In other cases, children may learn passive ways of coping with events that occur repeatedly because they feel ineffective in their ability to engender a positive change. These children exhibit learned helplessness in the face of adversity. For example, children exposed to repeated physical and emotional abuse from an early age often show no emotional responsivity to the events and later may show signs of dissociation. For these children, no active coping mechanisms have worked, and the stressors are too great to be offset by whatever protective factors are available to them.

Young children who have been exposed to traumatic events and have not had the benefit of processing these events with a nurturing adult may develop coping mechanisms that prove to be maladaptive, as they grow older. For example, preschool children witnessing spousal abuse at home often become hypervigilant and are easily aroused when there is a hint of aggression. For such children, loud voices, stern commands, and postures that can be construed to be threatening are predictive of subsequent abuse. Repeated witnessing of spousal abuse has required the child to repeatedly use his or her coping and defense mechanisms, and these mechanisms become rigidly established as the child grows older. If this child senses abuse in a situation that, in reality, is not likely to be abusive, he or she is likely to mobilize his or her rigid coping and defense mechanisms even if the stressor is minor. Thus, such a child may attack another if the other child raises his or her voice, or takes a posture in play that appears to be threatening. Such children have not learned to discriminate between situations that require the use of their coping mechanisms and those that do not. Finally, because the risk and protective factors transact among themselves, multiple risk factors often overwhelm children's protective factors. Further, the dose of the risk and protective factors has to be considered in terms of the developmental level of the children because the same dose will have a different impact as the children grow older.

Assessment of risk and protective factors alert clinicians to the need for early intervention that is focused not only on decreasing the risk factors, but also on increasing and capitalizing on the available protective factors inherent in the child, family, and the broader community context. These protective factors are often categorized as strengths that can form the basis for intervention.

Analyzing Risk and Protective Factors: A Case Illustration

This case describes a family that was close to dissolving because of the severe strain purportedly caused by an adopted child. The parents' own marital problems exacerbated the chaotic family dynamics and increased the emotional tension already palpable in the family. An analysis of risk and protective factors was used in a developmental context to inform and guide evaluation and treatment.

Presenting Problems and Assessment

Ben was a seven-year-old boy whose presenting problems included toileting accidents, temper tantrums, unprovoked physical aggression towards other children, anxiety, eating from trash cans, restlessness and disruptiveness in class and at home, and very short attention span. He was overweight by about 15 to 20 pounds, and heavily medicated for behavioral problems. He had breathing problems as well. Ben had been under psychiatric and psychological care for most of his short life.

Ben had been adopted as a baby by a couple unable to have children of their own. The father was very outgoing, and liked fishing and hunting, working out at a gym, and spending time with his male friends. The mother was very controlling, obsessive about cleanliness and order in her house, and wanted a perfect child. Both were working parents and shared the care of the child. However, because of work circumstances, it was the father who had to respond to the child when problems occurred during the day.

By the age of two, it was clear to the parents that Ben had delayed developmental milestones and he was subsequently diagnosed with various childhood psychiatric disorders, including autism. As Ben's behavior deteriorated, his parent's interactions with him also deteriorated. His father became abusive to Ben and his mother, both emotionally and physically. His mother often threatened to kill Ben and then kill herself. Both parents used emotional threats to make Ben behave in the manner they wanted. His mother was often depressed and anxious. She also had other family concerns, including the health and well being of her parents.

Before the current evaluation, Ben's mother had sought medical, psychiatric, and psychological help from virtually all available sources but was not happy with the outcomes. Ben's father blamed the child for ruining his life, as the father could no longer engage in any of the activities that he had enjoyed before Ben's adoption. Ben's mother loved him but used emotional and verbal threats for compliance. Often she expressed love and anger toward Ben at the same time.

Risk and Protective Factors
An analysis of the risk and protective factors suggested the following:

Ben's past risk factors:
1) Developmental delay;
2) Witnessing family violence and emotional abuse;
3) Experiencing physical violence from father;
4) Experiencing verbal and emotional abuse from mother;
5) Mother's depression and anxiety precluded close and warm maternal interactions;
6) Impaired coping mechanisms for physical, emotional, and verbal abuse; and
7) Mixed messages of love from parents.

Ben's past protective factors:
1) Both parents love Ben and want to do the best for him, as evidenced by their unending search for "successful" treatment for his problems.

Home and school observations, as well as interviews with parents, Ben, and school staff, showed the following:

Ben's current risk factors:
1) Parents have reached breaking point in their marriage, with father threatening to leave because of Ben;
2) Father is constantly critical of Ben;
3) Father is emotionally, verbally, and physically abusive to Ben and his mother;
4) Parents are inconsistent in their parenting style with Ben; and
5) School is threatening not to provide education to Ben because of his aggressive and other behaviors.

Current protective factors:
1) Parents seek further assistance in managing Ben's behavior at home and school;
2) Parents willing to be involved in new treatment regimen.

Transactional Analysis

A transactional analysis suggests that Ben's interactions with the layers of ecological contexts that surrounded him as he grew up gave rise to his emotional and behavioral problems. His aggression, impulsivity, short attention span, anxiety, and hyperarousal are consistent with what we would expect from children who have experienced or witnessed physical, verbal, and emotional abuse. Although he did not fully meet the DSM-IV criteria for PTSD (American Psychiatric Association, 1994), a broad-based, holistic assessment suggested that he was showing signs and symptoms of PTSD.

Ben's emotional and behavior problems could be interpreted in several plausible ways, depending on the breadth of the assessment process. Our assessment was based on a historical, holistic, and transactional approach (Singh, 2000a, 2000b). Previous assessments and psychiatric diagnoses had reached different conclusions, and therefore taken different therapeutic approaches than suggested by our approach. For example, at age two, his emotional and behavioral problems were seen as being consistent with a child having a developmental delay. This conclusion was based on an assessment of only the child, with no reference to the layers of ecological contexts in which the child was being raised. Several other assessments followed, each focused on the child. The final diagnosis was that Ben had attention-deficit/hyperactivity disorder, and given his behavior problems, he was on a psychopathological pathway to conduct disorder. In the absence of knowledge regarding Ben's transactions with his ecological contexts at different developmental levels, it is easy to arrive at a diagnostic workup that may fit one or more of the childhood psychiatric disorders. The critical test of the assessment and diagnosis process is whether they lead to therapeutic options that change Ben's developmental pathway from psychopathology to more normal development, and enhance his quality of life as well as that of his parents. The advantage of using a transactional approach is that it provides a more holistic picture of the child within his ecological context, and alerts the clinician to interactive factors that have affected his development, and changed his developmental pathway to what is evident today. This approach highlights the need for not only intervening with the child, but also with his significant others in the various contexts where his problems are most evident.

An Example of Developmental Considerations in Psychopathology: Attention-Deficit/Hyperactivity Disorder (ADHD)

ADHD is a lifelong disorder and knowledge of its developmental course assists clinicians in designing effective interventions at different stages in the life of an individual with ADHD. Although infant temperament is a predisposing factor for ADHD (Barkley, 1989), the minimum age of onset when a clear diagnosis can be made is about three years of age (Barkley, 1996). A majority of children with ADHD do not outgrow the symptoms during adolescence and adulthood. Given the interaction of the developmental course of the disorder and the children's personal characteristics, as well as their continuous transactions with the environment, the manifestation of the core characteristics of the disorder (i.e., inattention, impulsivity, hyperactivity, behavioral disinhibition) differs across children at the same age, as well as children at different ages.

Toddler and Preschool Children

Toddlers who are temperamental, have high levels of activity, and are thought by their parents to be non-compliant, are at high risk for ADHD by the time they are preschoolers. Although not all infants with these characteristics develop characteristics of ADHD, many who do seem to share these traits. In the typical scenario, these toddlers engage in excessive crying in infancy, and have colic, feeding problems, and sleep disturbances. They are difficult infants to bond with, and their excessive crying, colic, and feeding problems form the basis of insecure mother-child attachment, and slowly lead to negative mother-child transactions. These mother-child transactions become increasingly negative as the infants grow into toddlers and warm positive interactions decrease, less positive affection is shared between the mothers and their children, and the children show increasing non-compliance to parental requests. This results in stressful mother-child relationships, and the children engage in other behavior that parents perceive to be problematic.

This kind of interactional process takes place until parents (or clinicians) recognize and alter the environmental context so that "normal" development of the children can occur. The interactions between mother and child are bidirectional, and changes in both must occur for the children's development to proceed along normal behavioral pathways. Infants with difficult temperaments have a tendency to develop childhood psychiatric problems, including ADHD (Papalia & Olds, 1992). Intervention at this stage is often aimed at increasing the goodness of fit between the child's temperament and the mother's parenting style because a poor fit is likely to increase maladaptive functioning in the child. Further, a poor fit increases the mother's feelings of anxiety and inadequacy in handling the child because she sees the child as being demanding and difficult. When intervention produces a better fit, the mother reacts in a more accepting and warm manner, and is reinforced by the infant's responsiveness and more acceptable temperament. Overall, the mother-child transactions take a more positive developmental pathway, and future behavior problems are averted.

Precursors of ADHD in Toddlers and Preschool Children
There is evidence that children aged three to four years are increasingly referred for assessment and treatment of hyperactivity (Weiss & Hechtman, 1986). These are children whose behavior falls outside the normal range of motor activity for children at this developmental level. Further, their overactivity, non-compliance, and related behavior are not acceptable to childcare staff, preschool teachers, or to their parents. Although these children are too young to meet the criteria for one or more of the DSM-IV subtypes of ADHD, they exhibit serious problems with attention, hyperactivity, impulsivity, and non-compliance. The three subtypes of ADHD can be diagnosed in children four to six years of age based on structured diagnostic interviews of parents and teacher ratings on DSM-IV checklists (Lahey, *et al.*, 1998).

ADHD symptoms transact with normal developmental processes and change the developmental pathways for children diagnosed with the disorder. According to parental reports, about a third of the children with hyperactivity have a number of behavior problems even during the first year of life. These behavior problems are thought to be developmental correlates of ADHD, and include excessive crying, sleep problems, delays in vocalization, feeding problems, and physical anomalies. It is not that such behavior is evident only in infants who grow up having ADHD, but rather that it is often more difficult to deal with in these infants. For example, "hyperactive" infants do not respond well to the usual parental calming methods of rocking, cuddling, and comforting, and continue to cry for no apparent reason. Repeatedly failing to soothe the crying infant changes the typically warm and fuzzy mother-child interactions to one that is increasingly negative, as the mother gets more and more frustrated with the crying infant and her own inability to control this behavior. The mother-child interactions worsen even more when the infant has related problems with feeding and sleeping. The developmental process for the child is further compromised if the mother-child attachment and bonding is weakened, the mother is highly stressed, or if the mother herself has psychopathology.

Studies indicate that mothers of toddlers who are likely to grow up and have signs and symptoms of ADHD, typically have negative feelings toward their children, less frequent interactions with them when compared with mothers of children who do not have ADHD, and are not very affectionate with their children. These mothers have high stress levels and low self-esteem, and a stressful mother-child relationship. Because of their own issues, these mothers tend to view their toddlers as having worse problems than they objectively have.

By the time they reach preschool years, these children engage in excessive activities, display non-compliance, and often have difficulties in toilet training. They are impulsive, and constantly shift their attention during free play. Their peers reject them as playmates. All of these factors affect their developmental pathways, and unless appropriate intervention is provided, they continue to show further signs of the core symptoms of ADHD. It is during this period of the children's development (i.e., between three and six years) that parents are at their worst stress levels. Compared with mothers of normal children, mothers of preschoolers with ADHD have lower self-esteem, more depression, and higher stress. Sometimes, abusive or inadequate parenting may occur because the children's temperament and behavioral characteristics at this stage of their development interact with the stress level of the parents. These interactions are likely to produce more significant problems at a later developmental stage.

Often parents and clinicians will find it difficult to detect a difference between the behavior of a normally developing child and those of a child who may end up having ADHD. Wenar (1994) has suggested that preschoolers who are likely to have ADHD display behavior that is frenzied and unfocused, and interferes with learning and problem solving. Further, their oppositional behavior takes the form of temper tantrums. Others have noted that the non-compliance and overactivity of these children are predictive of adjustment problems in elementary school (Campbell, *et al.*, 1986). Often these children have adverse home situations that further affect their developmental pathways.

Parents describe their preschool children with ADHD as "excessively restless, temperamental, meddlesome, and disruptive... frequently shift from one activity to another... destroy toys by tinkering repeatedly with them... and bedwetting at night" (Safer & Allen, 1976, p. 44). Further, Barkley (1989) described preschool children with characteristics of ADHD as non-compliant, defiant, overactive, and mischievous. Parents of these preschool children find limit setting to be a very frustrating, unrewarding, and thankless experience, especially as it elicits strong resistance from the children. As a result, the children engage in more temper tantrums and non-compliance, which results in the parents becoming more demanding and disapproving of their children's behavior. This sets up a negative parent-child interaction pattern that may eventually develop into an aggression coercion cycle (Patterson, 1982).

There is an emerging literature on the cognitive correlates of ADHD symptoms in preschool children, a finding that is also true for other childhood disorders (e.g., learning disabilities, conduct disorders). For example, 80 percent of a sample of preschool children who had speech delays, as well as hyperactivity and inattention, were later diagnosed with ADHD (Ornoy, Uriel, & Tennebaum, 1993). Large-scale followup studies of children with speech and language impairments have reported that these children have higher rates of both learning disabilities and ADHD when compared to their peers who did not have these impairments in early life (Cantwell & Baker, 1992).

Observations in preschool settings of four to five-year-old children with symptoms of ADHD show that they engage in fewer play activities, less functional motor play, are less competent in social interactions, and display less attention and cooperation during group activities when compared with children without such symptoms (Mash & Johnston, 1982). These children were also found to be more non-compliant when compared to their peers.

The developmental findings of infants, toddlers, and preschool children suggest that precursors of the core symptoms of ADHD appear early in a child's life. However, not all or even a majority of the children displaying these precursors later fulfill the diagnostic requirements for ADHD. Indeed, it behooves clinicians to be wary of labeling toddlers and preschoolers as showing signs of ADHD because no more than about ten percent of them may end up being ADHD (Campbell, 1990; Palfrey, Levine, Walker, & Sullivan, 1985). However, while these early precursors of the symptoms of ADHD may not persist in most children, whether they develop into problematic behavior as the children grow older will depend on many factors, including quality of parenting practices, interactions with caretakers and preschool staff, and self-regulation by the children.

Treatment Strategies for Precursors of ADHD

Symptoms in Toddler and Preschool Children

Four types of interventions are generally used with toddlers and preschool children who are suspected to be at risk for ADHD, including parent training, structured preschool programs, social skills and self-control training, and medication (Blackman, Westervelt, Stevenson & Welsch, 1991). Typically, medication is not the treatment of first choice in this population, given their age and the difficulties in making a firm diagnosis of ADHD.

Parent Training. There are a number of general as well as specific interventions that have been found useful. The interventions can have a developmental (e.g., increasing parent-child attachment) or a management focus (e.g., contingency management). Interventions designed to enhance parent-child relationships tend to emphasize parental attentiveness, responsive care, warm and loving physical contact, and verbal stimulation. Increasing parental use of one or more of these caregiving variables contingently increases the child's responsiveness to the parents, and enhances parent-child bonding and attachment. Other programs focus on teaching parents how to develop or enhance emotionally supportive, non-judgmental relationships with their children, and how to make their perceptions of and reactions to their children's behavior more positive.

Generic parent management programs have been designed to teach how parents can increase their children's compliance, set behavioral rules for their children, and to improve parent-child interactions. Although these programs are not designed explicitly for parents of children with ADHD, they do increase the competence of the parents in managing the behavior of their children. These programs are particularly useful for parents whose children with ADHD may also have coexisting disorders, such as conduct disorders. Those that focus on parents of children with ADHD, have the expanded aim of helping parents understand the nature of ADHD and how ADHD affects their children's behavior, and how to use contingency management techniques to help their children behave in more positive and socially acceptable ways (e.g., Goldstein & Goldstein, 1990). There are also a number of structured parent training programs that have been developed, including Barkley's (1987; 1997) parent training for defiant children and Forehand and McMahon's (1981) parent training for non-compliant children. In addition, parents of children with ADHD can receive much needed social support through parent support groups, such as C.H.A.D.D. (Children and Adults with Attention-Deficit Disorders; Fowler, 1992).

Structured Preschool Programs. Preschools are not designed to cater to the needs of children who exhibit high levels of activity, impulsivity, and aggression. Indeed, children exhibiting such behavior are often "kicked out" of preschools (Barkley, 1990). Instead of expulsion, the solution is to help the preschool staff become better informed about ADHD and to change their perceptions about how children with ADHD behave. Like these children's parents, preschool staff need to learn behavior management techniques so they can control the children's disruptive, aggressive, and non-compliant behavior. There are a number of model projects on classroom management for preschool children with ADHD that show much promise (Chesapeake Institute, 1993), and can be tailored to increase the capacity of preschool staff to handle these children.

Psychopharmacological Interventions. Medication is not a good option for young children with ADHD as their response to stimulants is variable, and they have a greater propensity to show adverse side-effects of these drugs. Further, there is very limited drug research with this population and our knowledge of the effects of drugs on them is very sketchy. What little we know suggests that medication reduces off-task behavior and increases their rate of compliance to maternal commands, but also increases irritability and solitary play. Our current under-standing is that the hazards outweigh the benefits of medication for this popula-tion. Thus, only when all proven alternative therapies have failed, should medication be considered for preschool children with very severe symptoms of ADHD. Even then, it should be used together with psychosocial treatments.

Middle Childhood

The middle childhood years, between the ages of six and twelve, are critical in the development of children with ADHD. This is the period during which their behavior patterns firm up, and are more easily differentiated from their normal age peers in terms of the core symptoms of ADHD, including inattention, impul-sivity, and hyperactivity, as well as non-compliance. It is during these years that these children will seamlessly move in and out of acceptable and unacceptable behavior patterns, displaying developmentally normal and abnormal behavior. If left untreated at this stage, these behavior patterns develop into psychopathologi-cal pathways, and along the way some children may also develop serious second-ary problems, such as oppositional defiant or conduct disorders.

Signs and Symptoms of ADHD in Middle Childhood

At this stage of their development, children with ADHD have deficits on objective measures of self-regulation, inhibition, attention, and executive control. They have school adjustment problems, including failure to complete assigned tasks, disrup-tive behavior in the classroom, and problems in socializing with normal age peers. In addition, many have learning disabilities, comorbid anxiety, and mood disor-ders (Biederman, Newcome & Sprich, 1991). They have difficulty in accepting responsibility and need constant supervision. Their behavior is often immature. They engage in temper tantrums at the lower age range and increasingly in aggres-sion as they grow older. Chaotic family life exacerbates their vulnerability to behavior problems and childhood disorders, such as depression. All of this has a negative impact on their school achievement, feeds into their low self-esteem, and increases their behavior problems. They engage in risk-taking and dangerous behavior to gain attention. A supportive, structured home life buffers them from some of the risk factors, and lessens their symptoms of the disorder.

Children with secure attachment patterns in early childhood tend to maintain harmonious relationships with their parents during middle childhood. These children see parents as authority figures, and this belief generalizes to other adults they interact with, such as teachers. Parents can maintain their authority figure status as long as they provide quality parenting that is warm, loving, and accept-ing of the child.

During middle childhood, those with ADHD put a heavy burden on parent-child relationships as their symptoms of poor inhibitory control, inability to regulate behavior, and impulsivity begin to manifest overtly in the form of non-compliance with parental requests. These children begin to place similar stresses on their teachers, resulting in parents experiencing further stress due to their children's academic performance and behavior problems at school. Other second-order effects on parents, especially mothers, begin to appear at this stage, including maternal depression, self-blame, social isolation and eventually marital discord.

Increasingly, during this stage of their development, children with ADHD move in and out of normal development and psychopathology. They strain family good will by arguing and fighting with siblings, engaging in temper tantrums when asked to pull their weight around the house or to perform simple household chores. Their children's immaturity and lack of responsibility in taking care of themselves and their school work (e.g., homework) is the source of much parental anger and angst. In some families these difficulties are risk factors for physical and emotional child abuse (Barkley, 1990). Astute clinicians assess this potential risk factor when gathering developmental and family data, as it indicates the nature of intervention necessary to enable the parents to revert to a more positive relationship with their children.

Parenting style often dictates the outcome of long-term parent-child relationships. Authoritative parenting has been found to be nurturing and responsive to the needs of children more than any other parenting style (e.g., authoritarian, permissive, and uninvolved). Each of these other parenting styles has a different effect on children, as well as different effects on boys and girls (Baumrind, 1977). There is an interactive effect among the type of attachment, parenting style, the family's cultural and ethnic determinants of child-rearing practices, and the developmental characteristics of children with ADHD.

Parenting is not an etiological factor for ADHD, but it does contribute substantially to children's development, both negative and positive. For example, when children with ADHD begin being disruptive, aggressive, non-compliant, and overactive, some parents respond by being intrusive and controlling. In response, the children escalate their behavior, and induce the parents to be more intrusive, controlling, and punitive. This escalating cycle of behavior strains parent-child relationships, and may eventually contribute to the development of secondary conduct-related problems in the children. Further, it must be noted that mothers are more likely to be caught in this cycle than fathers. Fathers are not only bigger and more intimidating to children at this stage of their development; they are also more likely to use physical punishment than mothers. Further, mothers and not fathers are typically the primary caretakers and, therefore, bear the brunt of parental responsibility in their children's upbringing.

Other parental characteristics may also impinge on the children's development. For example, parental psychopathology increases the problems faced by children with ADHD (Weiss & Hechtman, 1993). For example, it has been found that many mothers and fathers of children with conduct disorders (with or without ADHD), typically have antisocial personality and substance abuse disorders, with mothers also having somatization disorders. Parental antisocial disorders increase the likelihood that children with ADHD will also have conduct disorders. Depression is common in mothers who have children with ADHD, and this depression is more pervasive in these mothers when compared with those whose children have learning disabilities, and other psychopathologies, such as anxiety, affective, and developmental disorders. Given the interaction of parental psychopathology and children's development, it behooves clinicians to assess for parental psychopathology before treatment of the child.

Family stress has a negative impact on children, including emotional outbursts, sadness, depression, low self-esteem, poor school performance, and shame. Family stressors include divorce, abuse, neglect and poverty. Many children from divorced families, for example, become demanding, non-compliant with parental wishes and teacher directions, and hostile in their dealings with parents and peers. Even marital discord has been found to affect children adversely. For example, there is a strong correlation between marital discord and behavior problems in boys. There is also a correlation between marital discord and children with ADHD but this relationship is stronger if the children also have coexisting conduct disorder. Research in this area suggests that parental problems, such as marital discord, exacerbate and maintain ADHD in vulnerable children, and the children's behavior problems exacerbate parental problems.

Family stressors affect the behavior of children with ADHD in an interactive manner, often worsening their secondary symptoms such as non-compliance and aggression. The continuing developmental outcomes of family and other stressors on children depend to a large extent on the balance of risk and protective factors for each child. Risk factors, such as insecure attachment and family stress, cannot be assumed to have direct causal pathways to negative outcomes because of the ongoing transactions that occur among risk factors, protective factors, and layers of ecological contexts. However, the resilience research clearly suggests that psychopathology is more likely with each additional risk factor that children have to overcome.

Middle childhood is a critical period for the development of self-regulation and self-control (Papalia & Olds, 1992). Children learn the standards by which they are judged by their parents and society. They learn that meeting these standards will result in positive regard not only by their parents but also by their peers and other adults. Children learn how to live up to these standards not only by self-regulation but also through interaction with their social ecology. Lack of self-regulation or of positive interaction with parents, teachers, and society may result in loss of self-control, and the development of behavior problems. Given that middle childhood is the time during which children increase their use of teasing, bullying, swearing, and fighting with others, children need more self-control rather than less. Children with ADHD are either the recipients or instigators of such behavior and, in both cases, they need better self-control if they wish to be accepted by their peers.

Research over the last decade indicates that children with various childhood disorders exhibit executive control problems which may include problems with flexibility, planning, inhibition, and self-monitoring (Denckla, 1994). Beginning in middle childhood, deficits in executive control functions assume increasing importance in children with ADHD, and especially with those who have coexisting learning disabilities or conduct disorders. These deficits affect academic as well psychosocial functioning in these children. Measurement of executive control functions has proven rather difficult as it appears that both neuroanatomical and psychodevelopmental constructs are being used to understand the underlying mechanisms involved in executive control. Given the interactional nature of executive control functions, it is difficult to clearly measure the impact of each function. Although our knowledge of executive control functions is currently rather limited, what we do know thus far indicates that there is a complex relationship between executive dyscontrol and ADHD in children. Some of this research does indicate that executive control functions may indeed provide meaningful explanations why children with ADHD have problems with self-control, self-regulation, and problem solving.

Developmentally, this is also the time that attentional processes come into their own. Children learn to be more focused, deliberate, and adaptive. They learn to regulate their attentional processes, and demonstrate sustained attention when the task demands it (Berk, 1989). Attention gets more focused as children age, as is demonstrated by the research on incidental learning, which increases until the age of eleven and then declines. By about eleven years of age, children are better able to attend to relevant information and ignore irrelevant information. This may explain why some children with ADHD who are academically successful up to this age have problems when more sustained attention is needed for academic excellence.

School adjustment difficulties are evident even in the first grade for children with severe ADHD characteristics. As they progress through middle childhood, they have serious difficulties at school in terms of completion of academic tasks, disruptive or non-compliant behavior in the classroom, and poor relationship with normal age peers. Boys, in particular, evidence school failure, academic underachievement, and learning difficulties. Children with ADHD who are aggressive and non-compliant have more school adjustment problems than those who do not have these behavior problems.

When children do not do well at school because of their ADHD and coexisting disorders or behavior problems, it increases parental frustration and stress. Not only do the children require an inordinate amount of monitoring and supervision to do their homework, but also parents frequently have to deal with school staff who are not very understanding of the difficulties that parents of children with ADHD face. Teachers often are unable or unwilling to make accommodations for children with ADHD in their classrooms that may enable such children to cope better with the academic demands placed on them. These school problems contribute to the already strained parent-child relationship, and increase the conflictual relationship that parents of these children may already have with the school. In turn, the school may see these parents as being difficult, uncooperative, and demanding. This cycle almost invariably ends up with the parents blaming the school and the school blaming the parents for the child's behavior and lack of academic progress (Taylor, 1994). The negative interaction cycles between home and school need to be taken into account when developing home-school intervention programs for these children.

Numerous other developmental changes occur during this period that impact on children's developmental pathways, including cognitive functioning, emotional development and expression, social skills and perspective taking. These and other developmental processes interact with children's personal characteristics and the environment, and affect the course and severity of ADHD in children. Conversely, ADHD affects the developmental challenges of middle childhood.

Treatment Strategies for Children with ADHD

Various interventions have been devised and tested for treating children with ADHD who are between the ages of six and twelve years. These have included parent training, teacher training, academic interventions with the children, social skills training, and medication. There has been no shortage of intervention approaches and, while most do not have randomized clinical trials proving their efficacy, many have been shown to be effective with small samples. Further, although there is a small cottage industry of books and manuals designed to provide assistance to parents and teachers for caring and teaching children with ADHD, most have not been tested with children who have ADHD and comorbid disorders.

Parent training. Some families would have received parent training when their children were preschoolers showing signs of developing ADHD. For these parents, a booster parent training program would be in order. For those parents whose children were diagnosed during middle childhood, and have had no formal behaviorally-based parent training for increasing compliance and reducing behavior problems in their children, one of the three programs discussed earlier would be appropriate (i.e., Barkley, 1997; Forehand & McMahon, 1981; Patterson, 1976). Barkley (1997) developed an eight to 10-session parent training program that aims to improve parents' ability to manage their children, increase their knowledge of ADHD and behavior principles, and reduce their children's non-compliance. Forehand and McMahon's (1981) parent training programs are designed for a minimum of 10 sessions, and aim to teach parents how to decrease their children's non-compliance, teach them about social learning theory as it relates to children's behavior control, and to shape the parents' expectations of their children. Patterson's (1976) program is designed for a minimum of five training sessions, and aims to teach parents and children how to reduce coercive behavior patterns. All of these programs have been tested and found effective in their aims.

Variations of parent training programs have been developed that are broader in scope, and can be best described as family system interventions. These programs are often designed to include multimodal treatments for family stressors and methods for minimizing risk factors that exacerbate children's core symptoms of ADHD. Structured family systems approaches to parent training include, "(1) improvements in parenting skills; (2) improvements in family functioning; and (3) the development of rationales supporting the importance of each of the parenting and family system skills developed" (Cunningham, 1990, p. 434). These programs are typically about 15 sessions and may include booster sessions as indicated.

As with parents of preschoolers at risk for developing ADHD, parents are encouraged to join parent support groups, such as the local C.H.A.D.D. chapters.

These support groups provide parents with information about community resources as well as emotional support from others who have had similar experiences with their children, the school system, and social service systems. Some parents may also need individual counseling, depending on whether they are at risk for developing or exacerbating their own mental health conditions.

Teacher Training and Classroom Interventions. As with parents, there are many programs that aim to teach teachers better methods for controlling children's disruptive and non-compliant school behavior. These programs are not as well structured as parent training programs or tested in large studies. However, the same basic behavioral principles and behavior management techniques are taught, with added information on the nature and course of ADHD in children. Unfortunately, most of these training programs are not designed to inform teachers of the developmental and psychopathological pathways that children traverse as they go through school, and how teacher interactions with these children may either increase the risk or provide a buffer for serious symptoms of ADHD and other problem behavior.

Teachers have been taught how to increase work productivity, and decrease disruptive and off-task behavior in children using behavioral techniques (e.g., classroom token economies, response cost, time-out procedures, and positive and negative management contingencies). There is a plethora of research studies showing that, when used appropriately, teacher-based behavioral management systems are effective in the classroom.

Academic Problems. Children with ADHD often require additional help in the classroom, such as extra instructional opportunities, so that they can keep up with academic demands of school. There are a number of models of classroom assistance that can be used with these children (see Jones, 1989; Goldstein & Goldstein, 1990; Zentall, 1995), and all of these emphasize that teachers may need to modify tasks and classroom structure to better fit the needs of children with ADHD. For example, to increase sustained attention and effort, teachers can use briefer lessons and shorter assignments; to increase motivation, teachers can reduce the redundancy in the lessons and make the assignments more interesting and novel; and, to increase executive functions, teachers can have a more structured classroom that is highly organized. In addition, a number of classroom-level interventions have been used to increase academic performance of children with ADHD. Space precludes their discussion but interested readers may consult Jones (1994), Reif (1993), and Levine (1993; 1994).

Medication. Medication has been the mainstay of ADHD treatments by family physicians. In effect, medication has well-established, short-term efficacy for this disorder. Stimulants, the major class of psychotropic medications used to treat children with ADHD, are effective in improving sustained attention, impulse control, activity level, disruptive behavior, compliance, work completion, and work accuracy (Barkley, 1990; Wilens & Spencer, 2000). Other drugs are also used when the first-line treatment with psychostimulants are ineffective, or if children have coexisting disorders, such as depression and conduct disorder (Popper, 2000). These drugs include Bupropion and most tricyclic antidepressants for managing the core behavioral symptoms of ADHD and, to a lesser extent, for cognitive symptoms. Other drugs, such as alpha2 adrenergic agonists, are moderately effective in reducing hyperactivity and impulsivity. Some of the newer drugs being researched, such as reboxetine and atomoxetine, show a good deal of promise but we need more data on them with regard to efficacy and safety. Given our emphasis on developmental variables and children's interactions with layers of ecological contexts in giving rise to their current disorder(s) and behavior, it is useful to remember that medication typically forms an important, but only one aspect of a comprehensive treatment for children with ADHD.

Multimodal Treatments. There have been increasing calls for multimodal therapies given that children with ADHD not only display the core symptoms of this disorder but also exhibit behavioral and academic problems as well. The largest and best-controlled multimodal treatment study has been completed recently (i.e., Multimodal Treatment Study for ADHD; MTA Cooperative Group, 1999a, 1999b). This was a randomized clinical trial involving 579, seven- to nine-year-old children with ADHD who were treated for 14 months in one of four groups: community comparison; behavioral treatment; pharmacological intervention, and combined pharmacological and behavioral treatment. Initial published results suggest that the results are very complex and depend on the domains that were assessed (i.e., symptoms of ADHD vs. impairment), settings (i.e., home vs. school), and informant (parents vs. teachers). Medication was most effective in treating the symptoms of ADHD. However, the combined medication and behavioral treatment was more effective when compared with medication alone in terms of the functional impairments of the children. Medication alone was superior to behavioral treatment alone on parent and teacher ratings of inattention and teacher ratings of hyperactivity. However, there was no difference between the two treatments for observed classroom behavior, parent and teacher rated social skills, parent rated parent-child relationships, peer sociometric ratings, and academic achievement. Parents preferred interventions that included behavioral treatments when compared with the medication alone group, and they mostly preferred the combined medication and behavioral treatment. While this study appears to have produced a wealth of information, it is clear that treatment outcome was not straightforward. Further, a limitation of the study was that other components of multimodal interventions, such as family systems, enhancement of protective factors, and cultural components were not included.

Conclusions

If developmental factors are considered in the treatment of children, they are an exception rather than the rule. There has been little incentive for clinicians, as well as researchers, to integrate developmental psychology and child therapies, such as child psychotherapy, because published treatment studies have been able to demonstrate beneficial effects without resorting to developmental constructs. However, the point can be made that incorporating developmental factors that may be related to treatment effects can enhance the effectiveness of current child therapies.

Developmental factors may correlate strongly with treatment effects. For example, research has shown that children and adolescents benefit from cognitive behavior therapy (CBT). However, given that cognitive processes are involved, it is likely that age would be a factor in CBT treatment outcome. In a meta-analysis of 64 CBT treatment outcome studies, Durlak, Fuhrman, and Lampman (1991) reported that although children and adolescents benefited from CBT, the effect sizes varied with age. The effect size was 0.57 for children ages five to seven, 0.55 for children ages seven-eleven, but 0.92 for those ages 11-13. Clearly, age is an important moderating variable in CBT, but whether it has a similar impact on other types of therapy remains to be investigated. Further, age is a rather gross variable as it encompasses diverse developmental factors (e.g., cognitive, social, contextual), each of which may differentially affect treatment outcome.

Another consideration is that some child therapies may not be as effective as they could be because developmental factors have not been taken into account when formulating the specifics of the treatment. For example, social skills training programs inherently involve abstract reasoning. While abstract reasoning is evident in adolescence, when formal operations are fully developed, many social skills training programs for preadolescent children involve a good deal of abstract reasoning. Including abstract reasoning in therapies for children who are developmentally unprepared for it may, in fact, reduce the effectiveness of these therapies.

A related example involves sophisticated language requirements in some therapies, such as CBT and psychodynamic treatments that encourage the child to describe various feelings. For some treatments, such as for internalized conditions (e.g., anxiety and depression), children are often required to describe their feelings in terms of physiological arousal and psychological state so that an individualized treatment plan can be developed. The cognitive capacity and language limitations of the children being treated often determine the precision with which a therapist is able to develop a treatment program. Further, the language requirements of the treatment program (e.g., "self-talk" components of CBT programs for anxiety, impulsivity, depression, and aggression) differentially affect treatment outcome depending on the age and language sophistication of the children. Thus, a developmental perspective on treatment suggests that a broader, holistic approach is needed as opposed to linear models of treatment that are much in vogue today.

Linear models of treatment focus almost exclusively on the individual and his or her presenting problems. Typically, the process involves history taking, assessments of specific presenting problems, case formulation, and development of child interventions. With respect to the linear model, the emphasis is on understanding the child's presenting problems and then developing a treatment to control or ameliorate them. Transactional models are broader, and include assessment of multiple factors that may bear on the child's presenting problems. Thus, parental and school factors are considered in the case formulation. However, neither of these general approaches accounts for the effects that service delivery systems may have on the child. Thus, if the child is at school, the effects of the school system on children's presenting problems need to be factored into case formulation. Similarly, if the child is an inpatient at a psychiatric hospital, then the effects of being at the hospital and the effects of the hospital system have to be considered in the case formulation. Further, in addition to the presenting problems, the strengths of the child, the qualities of his or her caretakers or providers, and the impact of the system have to be assessed and considered in the case formulation. A child functions well when there is a good fit among the three (the child, caretakers/providers/teachers, and the layers of systems). Assessment of the goodness-of-fit amongst the three components indicates where the fit is weak or fragile, and the case is formulated to strengthen the fit. The case formulation takes into account the strengths and weaknesses of the three components, and identifies the solutions by considering the changes that can be made in all three components. It is a holistic approach that is inclusive of the whole child, care providers, and the supporting systems (Singh, 2000a, b).

This model requires the comprehensive assessment of (a) the child, (b) the service or care providers, and (c) the system or layers of systems. Assessments include the strengths and problems associated with each component, rather than just the problems or disorders exhibited by the individual. The focus of intervention is on increasing the strengths of all three components, thereby encouraging a positive cultural change, and on decreasing the child's problem behavior or disorders through individualized treatment programs. This model assumes that children will have correct DSM-IV diagnoses, rational pharmacotherapy, and appropriate psychosocial interventions derived from the assessed needs of the child. Further, it assumes that the strengths of the child form the basis for all interventions, and that all interventions are designed to facilitate an enhanced quality of life rather than just the amelioration of the problem or disorder. It also assumes that the strengths of the people who provide care for the child (e.g., parents, teachers, inpatient staff) have been assessed, enhanced, and woven into the interventions for the child. Finally, it assumes that the strengths of the system (e.g., family culture at home) or layers of systems (e.g., classroom and school systems, ward management systems, hospital systems, school and hospital policies, funding mechanisms for service needs) have been assessed and used to enhance the child's treatment.

References

Achenbach, T. H. (1997). What is normal? What is abnormal? Developmental perspectives on behavioral and emotional problems. In S. S. Luthar, J. A. Burack, D. Cicchetti, & J. R. Weisz (eds), *Developmental Psychopathology: Perspectives on Adjustment, Risk and Disorder*. Cambridge, UK: Cambridge University Press. 93–114.

Achenbach, T. H., McConaughy, S. H., & Howell, C. T. (1987). Child/adolescent behavioral and emotional problems: Implications of cross-informant correlations for situational specificity. *Psychological Bulletin, 101,* 213–232.

American Psychiatric Association. (1994). *Diagnostic and Statistical Manual of Mental Disorders* (4th ed.) Washington, DC:. American Psychiatric Association.

Barkley, R. A. (1987). *Defiant Children: A Clinician's Manual for Parent Training.* New York: Guilford Press.

Barkley, R. A. (1989). Attention-deficit hyperactivity disorder. In E. J. Mash & R. A. Barkley (eds), *Treatment of Childhood Disorders.* New York: Guilford Press. 39–72.

Barkley, R. A. (1990). *Attention-deficit Hyperactivity Disorder: A Handbook for Diagnosis and Treatment.* New York: Guilford Press.

Barkley, R. A. (1996). Attention-deficit/hyperactivity disorder. In E. J. Mash & R. A. Barkley (eds) *Child Psychopathology* New York: Guilford Press. 63–112.

Barkley, R. A. (1997). *Defiant Children: A Clinician's Manual for Assessment and Parent Training.* (2nd ed.). New York: Guilford Press.

Baumrind, D. (1977). Some thoughts about childrearing. In S. Cohen & T. Chomisky (eds) *Child Development: Contemporary Perspectives.* Itasca, IL: Peacock.

Baumrind, D. (1989). Rearing competent children. In D. Damon (ed.), *Child Development Today and Tomorrow.* San Francisco: Jossey-Bass.

Berk, L. E. (1989). *Child Development.* Boston: Allyn & Bacon.

Biederman, J., Newcombe, J., & Sprich, S. (1991), Comorbidity of attention-deficit hyperactivity disorder with conduct, depressive, anxiety, and other disorders. *American Journal of Psychiatry, 148,* 564–577.

Blackman, J. A., Westervelt, V. D., Stevenson, R., & Welsch, A. (1991). Management of preschool children with attention-deficit hyperactivity disorder *Topics in Early Childhood Special Education, 11,* 91–104.

Campbell, S. B. (1990). The socialization and social development of hyperactive children. In M. Lewis & S. Miller (eds), *Handbook of Developmental Psychopathology* New York: Plenum Press. 77–92.

Campbell, S. B., Ewing, L. J., Breaux, A. M., & Szumowski, E. K. (1986). Parent-identified behavior problem toddlers: Followup at school entry. *Journal of Child Psychology and Psychiatry, 27,* 473–488.

Cantwell, D. P., & Baker, L. (1992). Association between attention-deficit hyperactivity disorder and learning disorders. In S. Shaywitz & B. Shaywitz (eds), *Attention-Deficit Disorder Comes of Age: Toward the Twenty-first Century.* Austin, TX: Pro-Ed. 145–164.

Chesapeake Institute (1993). *Education of Children with Attention-deficit Disorder.* Washington, DC: U.S. Department of Education.

Cicchetti, D., & Cohen, D. J. (1995). Perspectives on developmental psychopathology. In D. Cicchetti & D. J. Cohen (eds), *Developmental Psychopathology: Theory and Methods.* NY: Wiley. *1,* 3–20.

Cunningham, C. E. (1990). A family systems approach to parent training. In R. A. Barkley, *Attention-deficit Hyperactivity Disorder: A Handbook for Diagnosis and Treatment.* New York: Guilford Press. 432–461.

Durlak, J. A., Fuhrman, T., & Lampman, C. (1991). Effectiveness of cognitive-behavior therapy for maladapting children: A meta-analysis. *Psychological Bulletin, 110,* 204–214.

Denckla, M. B. (1994). Measurement of executive function. In G. R. Lyon (ed.) *Frames of Reference for the Assessment of Learning Disabilities: New Views on Measurement Issues.* Baltimore: Paul Brookes. 117–142.

Erickson, M. F., Korfmacher, J., & Egeland, B. (1992). Attachments past and present: Implications for intervention with mother-infant dyads. *Development and Psychopathology, 4,* 495–507.

Erickson, M. F., Sroufe, L. A., & Egeland, B. (1985). The relationship between quality of attachment and behavior problems in preschool in a high-risk sample. In I. Bretherton & E. Waters (eds), Growing points in attachment theory and research. *Monographs of the Society for Research in Child Development, 50* (1-2, Serial No. 209). 147–166.

Forehand, R., & McMahon, R. J. (1981). *Helping the Noncompliant Child: A Clinician's Guide to Parent Training.* New York: Guilford Press.

Fowler, M. (1992). *C.H.A.D.D. Educator's Manual: An In-depth Look at Attention-deficit Disorders from an Educational Perspective.* Fairfax, VA: CASET.

Gelfand, D. M. & Teti, D. M. (1990). The effects of maternal depression on children. *Child Psychology Review, 10,* 329–353.

Goldstein, S., & Goldstein, M. (1990). *Managing Attention Disorders in Children.* New York: Wiley-Interscience.

Greenspan, S. I. (1997). *The Growth of the Mind.* New York: Addison–Wesley.

Hirshfeld, D. R., Rosenbaum, J. F., Biederman, J., Bolduc, E. A., Faranone, S. V., *et al.* (1992). Stable behavioral inhibition and its association with anxiety disorder. *Journal of the American Academy of Child and Adolescent Psychiatry, 31,* 103–111.

Jones, C. (1989, November/December). Managing the difficult child. *Family Day Caring,* 6–7.

Jones, C. (1994). *Attention Deficit Disorder: Strategies for School Age Children.* San Antonio, TX: Psychological Corporation.

Lahey, B. B., Pelham, W. E., Stein, M. A., Loney, J., Trapani, C., *et al.* (1998). Validity of DSM-IV attention-deficit/hyperactivity disorder for younger children. *Journal of the American Academy of Child and Adolescent Psychiatry, 37,* 695–701.

Laucht, M., Esser, G., & Schmidt, M. H. (1994). Parental mental disorder and early child development. *European Child and Adolescent Psychiatry, 3,* 124–137.

LeFrancois, G. R. (1995). *An Introduction to Child Development* (8th ed.). Belmont, CA: Wadsworth.

Levine, M. (1993). *Developmental Variation and Learning Disorders.* Cambridge, MA: Educator's Publishing Service.

Levine, M. (1994). *Educational Care: A System for Understanding and Helping Children with Learning Problems at Home and at School.* Cambridge, MA: Educator's Publishing Service.

Lewis, M., Feiring, C., McGuffog, C., & Jaskir, J. (1984). Predicting psychopathology in six-year-olds from early social relations. *Child Development, 55,* 123–136.

Loeber, R. M., Stouthamer-Loeber, Van Kammen, W., & Farrington, D. P. (1991). Initiation, escalation and desistance in juvenile offending and their correlates. *Journal of Criminal Law and Criminology, 82,* 36–82.

Lyons-Ruth, K. (1996). Attachment relationships among children with aggressive behavior problems: The role of disorganized early attachment patterns. *Journal of Clinical and Consulting Psychology, 24,* 64–73.

Mash, E. J., & Johnston, C. (1983). Parental perceptions of child behavior problems, parenting self-esteem and mothers' reported stress in younger and older hyperactives and normal children. *Journal of Consulting and Clinical Psychology, 51,* 86–99.

Masten, A. S., Best, K. M., & Garmezy, N. (1990). Resilience and development: Contributions from the study of children who overcome adversity. *Development and Psychopathology, 2,* 425–444.

MTA Cooperative Group. (1999a). 14-month randomized clinical trial of treatment strategies for attention-deficit/hyperactivity disorder. *Archives of General Psychiatry, 56,* 1073–1086.

MTA Cooperative Group. (1999b). Moderators and mediators of treatment response for children with attention-deficit/hyperactivity disorder. *Archives of General Psychiatry, 56,* 1088–1096.

Murray, L. & Cooper, P. (1997). *Postpartum Depression and Child Development.* New York: Guilford Press.

National Advisory Mental Health Council (1990*).* *National Plan for Research on Child and Adolescent Mental Disorders.* Rockville, MD: National Institute for Mental Health.

Ornoy, A. Uriel, L., & Tennebaum, A. (1993). Inattention, hyperactivity, and speech delay at 2–4 years of age as a predictor of ADD-ADHD syndrome. *Israel Journal of Psychiatry and Related Sciences, 30,* 155–163.

Palfrey, J. S., Levine, M. D., Walker, D. K., & Sullivan, M. (1985). The emergence of attention deficits in early childhood: A prospective study. *Developmental and Behavioral Pediatrics, 6,* 339–348.

Papalia, D. E., & Olds, S. W. (1992). *Human development* (5th ed.). New York: McGraw-Hill.

Patterson, G. R. (1976). *Living with Children: New Methods for Parents and Teachers.* Champaign, IL: Research Press.

Patterson, G. R. (1982). *A Social Learning Approach to Family Intervention: Vol. 3. Coercive family process.* Eugene, OR: Castalia.

Popper, C. W. (2000). Pharmacological alternatives to psychostimulants for the treatment of Attention-Deficit/Hyperactivity Disorder. *Child and Adolescent Clinics of North America, 9,* 605–646.

Reif, S. (1993). *How to Reach and Teach ADD/ADHD Children.* West Nyack, NY: Center for Applied Research in Education.

Safer, D. J., & Allen, R. P. (1976). *Hyperactive Children.* Baltimore: University Park Press.

Sameroff, A.J. (1993). Models of development and developmental risk. In C. H. Zeanah, Jr. (ed.), *Handbook of Infant Mental Health.* New York: Guilford. 3–13.

Singh, N. N. (2000a, April). *Holistic Approaches to Building on Strengths.* Keynote address presented at the Building on Family Strengths Conference. Portland, OR.

Singh, N. N. (2000b, March). *Plan of Life Service Delivery System: Stretching the Current Service System.* Presented at the Mississippi Juvenile Rehabilitation Facility, Brookhaven, MS.

Sroufe, L. A. (1983). Infant-caregiver attachment and patterns of adaptation in preschool: The roots of adaptation and competence. In M. Pelmutter (ed.), *Minnesota Symposium on Child Psychology.* Hillsdale, NJ: Erlbaum. *16,* 41–83.

Sroufe, L. A. (1989). Relationships, self and individual adaptation. In A.J. Sameroff & R. N. Emde (eds), *Relationship Disturbances in Early Childhood.* New York: Basic Books. 70–94.

Sroufe, L. A. & Rutter, M. (1984). The domain of developmental psychopathology. *Child Development, 55,* 17–29.

Taylor, J. (1994). *Helping your Hyperactive/Attention Deficit Child.* Rocklin, CA: Prima.

Weiss, L., & Hechtman, L. (1986). *Hyperactive Children Grown Up.* New York: Guilford.

Weiss, L., & Hechtman, L. (1993). *Hyperactive Children Grown Up: ADHD in Children, Adolescents, and Adults.* (2nd ed.). New York: Guilford.

Wenar, C. (1994). *Developmental Psychopathology: From Infancy through Adolescence.* New York: McGraw Hill.

Werner, E. E., & Smith, R. S. (1992). *Overcoming the Odds: High Risk Children from Birth to Adulthood.* Ithaca, NY: Cornell University Press.

Wilens, T. E., & Spencer, T. J. (2000). Stimulants and attention-deficit/hyperactivity disorder. *Child and Adolescent Psychiatric Clinics of North America, 9,* 573–603.

Winnicott, D. W. (1965). *The Maturational Process and the Facilitating Environment.* London, UK: Hogarth Press.

Zentall, S. S. (1995). Modifying classroom tasks and environments. In S. Goldstein (eds), *Understanding and Managing Children's Classroom Behavior.* New York: Wiley. 356–374.

Zuravin, S. J. (1989). Severity of maternal depression and three types of mother-to-child-aggression. *American Journal of Orthopsychiatry, 59,* 377–389.

Part II

Disruptive Disorders

Chapter 3

Oppositional Defiant Disorder

Persephanie Silverthorn

According to the Diagnostic and Statistical Manual-IV (DSM-IV), Oppositional Defiant Disorder (ODD) is characterized by a pattern of negativistic, hostile, and defiant behavior (American Psychiatric Association, 1994). During childhood, boys are more frequently diagnosed with ODD, but during adolescence this ratio becomes more equal and approximately as many girls as boys are diagnosed with the disorder (American Psychiatric Association, 1994; Frick and Silverthorn, 2001). The prevalence of ODD varies by age, with the rate estimated to be between four and nine percent in preschoolers, six to twelve per cent in school age children, and up to 15 percent in adolescence (Frick & Silverthorn, in press).

ODD is diagnosed when at least four of the following symptoms are often present for more than six months: "often loses temper; argues with adults; often actively defies or refuses to comply with adults' requests or rules; often deliberately annoys people; often blames others for his or her mistakes or misbehavior; is often touchy or easily annoyed by others; is often angry and resentful; is often spiteful and vindictive" (American Psychiatric Association, 1994). In addition, the child must show clinically significant impairment in functioning in order to warrant a diagnosis (American Psychiatric Association, 1994). Children with Attention Deficit/Hyperactivity Disorder are frequently diagnosed with ODD, and children with ODD often have comorbid Learning Disorders, emotional disorders (depression and anxiety), and Communication Disorders (American Psychiatric Association, 1994; Frick & Silverthorn, 2001).

In determining whether ODD is present, it is important to make a careful differential diagnosis. ODD is often characterized as a milder form of Conduct Disorder (CD), and considerable debate has existed about whether these two disorders are separate and unique or if ODD is simply a milder form of CD. However, the evidence supports a developmental and hierarchical relation between these two disorders, with ODD typically preceding CD. That is, while a majority of boys who develop CD had ODD when younger (82 percent in one four year study), less than half of children with ODD (47 percent) progress on to the more serious CD (Lahey, et al., 1995). Also, the developmental link between ODD and CD seems to only hold for children who develop CD prior to adolescence. Those individuals exhibiting adolescent-onset CD are less likely to have had ODD before CD (Hinshaw, Lahey, & Hart, 1993). Therefore, one of the most important tasks

Handbook of Conceptualization and Treatment of Child Psychopathology, pages 41–56.
Copyright © 2001 by Elsevier Science Ltd.
ISBN: 0-08-043362-6

in diagnosing ODD is to ensure that CD is not present. When symptoms warrant both diagnoses, CD supersedes the diagnosis of ODD (American Psychiatric Association, 1994).

Another important task in determining if ODD is present is to consider developmental features. Because the developmental periods of preschool and adolescence are typically characterized by transient oppositional behavior, diagnoses of ODD during these time periods should be made with caution (American Psychiatric Association, 1994). In addition, it is specifically noted in DSM-IV that "a criterion [is] met only if the behavior occurs more frequently than is typically observed in individuals of comparable age and developmental level" (American Psychiatric Association, 1994). Thus, because during certain time periods, children and adolescents are more likely to have non-diagnosable oppositional behaviors, it is important to ensure that the behaviors in question occur more frequently and are more severe than those manifested by children of the same chronological and mental age. To ensure symptom severity falls outside the range of typical behavior fluctuations the required frequency for diagnosing varies by symptoms. For example, it has been suggested that to make an ODD diagnosis some behavior needs to occur only within the last three months (spiteful or vindictive, blames others for his/her mistakes), some at least twice per week (touchy or easily annoyed, loses temper, argues with adults, defies or refuses adults' requests), and others at least four times per week (angry or resentful, deliberately annoys others) (Angold & Costello, 1996).

Treatment Strategies for ODD

There are several reasons why it is important to intervene quickly to reduce the symptoms of ODD. First, as noted, ODD frequently precedes the diagnosis of CD, particularly in children under ten (Lahey, *et al.*, 1995), although this does not appear to apply for boys with an adolescent-onset CD (Hinshaw, *et al.*, 1993) and may not apply for girls with CD, who appear to follow a different pathway to the development of CD (Silverthorn & Frick, 1999). Children on the pathway which includes early onset of ODD followed by a childhood-onset of CD are at particular risk for continued antisocial and delinquent behavior throughout adolescence and adulthood. Second, although several efficacious treatments exist for CD, attrition rates are often high, ranging from 30 percent to 59 percent, and treatments are much more effective for younger children than for older children (Brestan & Eyberg, 1998). For these reasons, it is important to intervene as quickly as possible, when children are younger and symptomatology is less severe, before behavior worsens and/or becomes more entrenched, making treatment less likely to succeed.

As noted, evidence suggests that ODD is a separate diagnostic category, not simply a milder form of CD. However, "the distinction between oppositional defiant disorder and conduct disorder... has been honored more by its non-observance than its observance" (Lahey, *et al.*, 1994). That is, most investigations tend to combine the two diagnoses under the heading "conduct problems," and few researchers have attempted to investigate the efficacy of treatments for individuals diagnosed with ODD and not CD. Nevertheless, there are several treatment strategies available for ODD. Not surprisingly, most are similar to treatments for CD.

Within the last decade, several large meta-analytic studies have been conducted for child and adolescent treatments, and the effects suggest that by the end of treatment, 76 percent to 81 percent of children and adolescents in the treatment groups made improvements when compared with control (no-treatment) children (Weisz & Hawley, 1998). Several different types of treatment have been found to be efficacious according to meta-analysis, including cognitive-behavioral (parent-training, problem-solving skills training) and family therapies (Weisz & Weiss, 1993; Weisz & Hawley, 1998).

Although there are many treatments available for children with ODD, according to "29 years, 82 studies, and 5,272 kids," only two treatments were designated as "well-established," both of which utilized parent-training models designed for young children (e.g., up to six or eight years old) (Brestan & Eyberg, 1998). In addition to the two treatments designated as well-established, ten treatment programs were designated as "probably efficacious" (Brestan & Eyberg, 1998). Four of these treatments are also based on parent-training models, with another four based on cognitive-behavioral skills training models (see also, Frick, 1998). Kazdin & Weisz (1998) simultaneously evaluated empirically supported treatments, and similar to Brestan & Eyberg (1998), reported that the two most efficacious interventions for conduct problems and oppositional behaviors are parent-training models and cognitive-behavioral skills training models (including problem-solving skills training; see also Frick, 1998). Importantly, treatments based on both models have shown positive effects lasting one to three years after treatment or longer (Kazdin, 1997; Kazdin & Weisz, 1998). Thus, researchers agree that the most effective and empirically supported treatments for ODD are based on parent-training models, with cognitive-behavioral skills training models also showing probable efficacy.

Parent Training Models

Parent training programs are among the most researched treatment programs for conduct problems, and there are several models available for different ages which have received empirical support. The more popular programs are delineated in the following books and tapes: *Helping the Noncompliant Child* (Forehand & McMahon, 1981), *Parents and Adolescents* (Patterson & Forgatch, 1987), *Defiant Children: A Clinician's Manual for Parent Training* (Barkley, 1987), *Living with Children* (Patterson & Gullion, 1968), *Parent-Child Interaction Therapy* (Hembree-Kigin & McNeil, 1995), and Webster-Stratton's videotaped parent training program (Webster-Stratton, 1994) (see also Brestan & Eyberg, 1998; Frick, 1998).

Parent training programs operate under the assumption that parental behavior, such as inconsistent and ineffective discipline strategies, contributes to the development and/or maintenance of oppositional and defiant behavior. The theory is that changing the contingencies in a child's environment will lead to changes in the child's behavioral repertoire. Thus, all of the programs have numerous steps in common.

First, all programs attempt to explain the rationale of the program to the parent(s). While this may be obvious, in practice, parents can feel that they are criticized or blamed for the child's behavior when the intervention offered is a family-based, parent-training model rather than an individual child focused intervention. Given the high attrition rate for therapy, perhaps 60 percent or higher (Brestan & Eyberg, 1998), it is important that the parent be invested in the treatment procedure. Thus, it is important to convey in a non-judgmental manner that parent involvement will be necessary for any program's success. One technique that may be effective in reducing the perception that a clinician is blaming the parent by suggesting parent training is to explain that children with difficult temperaments (as children with ODD and ADHD often have) typically need additional structure, and even the most effective parent will benefit from learning specialized techniques. In addition, many clinicians explain before the interview and assessment that in their particular practice, they routinely see the whole family rather than just the child. By explaining this policy ahead of time, the parent may not feel personally attacked when the clinician eventually suggests parent training.

The second step for nearly all parent training programs is to increase the number of positive interactions between the parent and child. Many of the programs ask the parent to interact with the child in a play task while the parent attends to and praises the positive behavior and ignores selected negative behavior. The rationale for this step is to (a) encourage the child to engage in positive rather than negative behavior, and (b) to interrupt the coercive cycle which often emerges between an ODD child and his or her parent. As is explained to the parent during this initial session, when a child engages in expected, positive behavior, they cannot be simultaneously engaged in negative behavior. However, in practice, "selling" this step to a parent is often difficult. Frequently, parents are frustrated with their child's behavior by the time they initiate therapy, and they expect that the clinician will offer immediate solutions for managing their child's negative behavior. When the clinician instead instructs that the parent play with the child, many are understandably frustrated. Nevertheless, regardless of parental protest, it is important that the parent begin with increasing positive interactions before attempting to eliminate the negative behavior.

Third, parent training programs focus on increasing parental effectiveness and decreasing children's negative behavior. While the specifics vary between programs, nearly all parent training methods focus on teaching the parent to provide effective commands and instructions, be consistent, and properly use discipline techniques, such as time out, removal of privileges, and the five-minute work chore. Parents of oppositional and defiant children are often inconsistent in their discipline and ineffective in their commands; thus, remedying these deficiencies is necessary to decrease the child's negative behavior. In addition, for most of the parent training models, the third step also includes introducing contingency management programs to provide structure and additional incentives for compliant behaviors. Throughout the treatment program, parents are given weekly homework assignments and are encouraged to problem solve in-session with the therapist.

Taken together, these steps are usually effective in reducing or eliminating oppositional and defiant behavior. However, parent training programs require a strong commitment from parents, and many are unwilling or unable to give it. Ideally, for parent training to be effective, all regular custodians of the child should be involved with treatment; parent training is less effective when only one parent participates. In addition, a child with oppositional and defiant behavior may not live with a parent, although these programs may be effective with custodial grandparents (Silverthorn & Durrant, 2000). Furthermore, Kazdin (1997; Kazdin, *et al.*, 1992) has suggested that attrition rates are higher for treatments requiring a parent component than for programs which focus on the child. For these reasons, another popular method for treating ODD is cognitive behavioral skills training.

Cognitive Behavioral Skills Training

The second method for treating ODD is cognitive behavioral skills training. These programs include problem-solving skills training (Kazdin, *et al.*, 1987; Kazdin, Siegal, & Bass, 1992), anger control training with stress inoculation (Feindler, Marriott, & Iwata, 1984), anger coping program (Lochman & Wells, 1996), and self-instructional training (Kendall & Braswell, 1985; see also Brestan & Eyberg, 1998; Frick, 1998). The rationale is that the oppositional and defiant behavior is maintained by limited or absent problem solving abilities and from inaccurately interpreting social situations. Several programs require that the skills be taught in a group format; however, these skills can be administered on an individual basis.

While the specifics vary by program, the most important component for most is the teaching of problem solving skills. This consists of teaching the child to use a multiple-step problem solving strategy. Although the number of steps depends on which program is used, the general strategy is to (a) identify the problem and eventual goal, (b) develop multiple solutions, (c) chose one of the solutions based on anticipating the consequences of the actions, and (d) evaluate the success of the solution chosen. The child is taught to use these problem solving techniques in response to a number of different academic and interpersonal (e.g., with parents, teachers, peers; at home and at school) situations.

Another component frequently used is standard cognitive behavioral training to change distorted and maladaptive cognitions. Similar to adult programs, children are taught to identify the thoughts which lead to particular feelings. Typically, this component centers on teaching children to differentiate between thoughts and feelings and then learn to identify and label particular feelings. Children are then taught to identify cognitive distortions and taught a series of skills to change their maladaptive thought processes.

Another component for several of the cognitive behavioral skills training programs is social skills training. Typically, this involves a series of role-play activities in which the child uses problem solving skills in a variety of interpersonal situations. In each session, the therapist and child engage in a number of practice runs which include modeling, corrective feedback, and social reinforcement. The child is given a homework assignment to use the skills away from a therapeutic context and to report the results in the next session. In addition, children are taught perspective taking skills, which are designed to help with their interpersonal cognitive deficits in which they mistakenly attribute hostile intent to neutral situations. Furthermore, some programs include an active parent component, in which the parent watches all or part of the sessions and is encouraged to foster the use of problem solving skills outside the sessions.

A final component for some programs is to help the child identify their own physiological, internal cues which can alert them to arousal states. Specifically, many oppositional and defiant children are unaware of internal changes which indicate they are becoming aroused (e.g., increased heart rate, clenched fists, shallow breathing, flushed cheeks). The purpose of this component is to help the child become aware of antecedent physiological signals which would cue them to use problem solving skills.

Research suggests that while cognitive behavioral skills training is effective, it is less effective than parent training programs and does not necessarily generalize to other situations (see Frick, 1998 for a review). Therefore, several programs advocate the use of both parent training and cognitive behavioral skills training in a combined treatment program (Henggeler & Borduin, 1990; Henggeler, *et al.*, 1998; Kazdin, *et al.*, 1992). Research has suggested that these combined programs are more effective than either treatment alone (Kazdin, *et al.*, 1992).

Case Example

Elizabeth Arthur is a ten-year, seven-month old female who was referred for a comprehensive evaluation by her parents. The primary concern was Elizabeth's reading achievement. According to her mother, Elizabeth's grades are "really bad," and although she appears to be able to do the work at home, she does not perform well at school. A second area of worry was with Elizabeth's oppositional and defiant behavior, which is present both at home and at school. Finally, Ms. Arthur also expressed concern that Elizabeth has attentional difficulties.

Elizabeth spends half her time with her biological mother and half her time with her biological father. Elizabeth's parents were divorced three years ago, although they share joint custody, and Elizabeth's mother is currently remarried. Elizabeth has five adult step-siblings from her father's previous marriage, none of whom live with her father. Ms. Arthur has two years of college and works as a receptionist at a local dentist office. Mr. Arthur has an eleventh grade education and works as a manager in a furniture store.

According to maternal report, Elizabeth was born following a full-term pregnancy. Ms. Arthur reports that she had high blood pressure during pregnancy and smoked three packs of cigarettes a day throughout her pregnancy. Ms. Arthur also reports significant stress during her pregnancy due to the presence of continual nausea and her five step-children, all of whom were living with her at the time. All developmental milestones are reported to be within normal limits. Elizabeth is also reported to have mild allergies; however, no other medical or health problems were reported. Elizabeth has never been evaluated by a mental health professional for emotional or behavioral problems.

Elizabeth is in the fourth grade at Lorne St. Elementary School. She was previously in a reading resource room in the first and second grades but was removed by her mother at the beginning of the third grade. She had performed poorly in every grade and is reported to be failing thus far this semester. In addition, Elizabeth is having significant behavioral problems in her classes. Elizabeth has been getting into trouble for inattention, failing to complete her schoolwork, and talking back to teachers. According to Ms. Barkely, the school counselor, Elizabeth's behavior is often varied and unpredictable. Elizabeth appears inattentive and talkative one day (interacting well, albeit loudly, with peers), and then acts "moody" the following day, fighting with other students and talking back to teachers. In general, she is disruptive, draws attention to herself, daydreams, and fails to complete her work. Several teachers noted that Elizabeth has a significant problem with not completing her in-class and take-home school work, which has negatively impacted her grades.

At home, Elizabeth exhibits much of the same defiant and inattentive behavior that is reported at school. In general, she is argumentative and fails to follow adult requests. In addition, she often throws temper tantrums when she does not get her way. Furthermore, Elizabeth has extreme difficulties completing her homework due to both inattention and non-compliance. According to Ms. Arthur, the discipline Elizabeth receives depends on whether she is at her father's or her mother's house. In general, both parents use a variety of discipline methods in an attempt to control Elizabeth's behavior, including time out, removal of privileges, reasoning, and spanking. Ms. Arthur reports that she often begins by reasoning with Elizabeth, and when that does not work, she may use one of the other methods. Often, she will simply ignore the behavior; however; when another strategy is necessary, she will typically use time out or removal of privileges. She reports rarely being consistent with her application of discipline. Most often she feels guilty about punishing the child and will reinstate the privileges earlier than announced. Mr. Arnold reports that he also uses many of the same techniques, but reports being much more consistent in responding to a misdeed. However, he reports more difficulty with enforcing the discipline strategy that he has administered. Specifically, even when he attempts to implement a strategy, such as removal of a privilege, he will enter Elizabeth's room to find that she is engaging in the forbidden activity.

During the assessment session, Elizabeth initially had difficulty leaving with the examiner to participate in testing. Ms. Arthur spoke with her and persuaded her to begin testing. After that, Elizabeth appeared to have no difficulties and although she questioned what her mother was doing, she chose not to visit her mother when this was offered. Elizabeth appeared worried about whether she would "fail" the test. She worked hard on items that she said were "not like school work." However, on harder items, she would give up and say she was finished even if the task was not completed. She had difficulty elaborating on her answers and would say "I don't know." Elizabeth was aware of failure and would become quiet, slump in her chair, and rest her head on the table as items became more difficult. No motor, hearing, or speech problems were noted and Elizabeth wore her glasses for the testing session.

On the WISC-III, Elizabeth obtained a Full Scale IQ score of 83 (13th percentile) with there being a 95 percent probability that her true score falls in the range of scores from 76 to 90. This score indicates current intellectual functioning in the Low Average Range. She obtained a Verbal Scale IQ score of 84 (14th percentile), indicating verbal comprehension in the Low Average Range. Within this area, her abilities are equally developed. Elizabeth obtained a Performance Scale IQ score of 83 (13th percentile), indicating perceptual organizational abilities in the Low Average Range. Her skills are equally developed in this area as well, with the exception of an absolute and personal strength on a task which measures psychomotor speed. Elizabeth appeared to enjoy this task since it was "not like a school task."

Elizabeth scored in the Low Average to Average Range on measures of academic achievement. Specifically, she obtained an age standard score of 85 (16th percentile) on the Reading Cluster of the Woodcock-Johnson Tests of Achievement-Revised, which indicates reading achievement in the Low Average Range. She obtained an age standard score of 98 (45th percentile) on the Math Cluster, which is in the Average Range. Elizabeth's achievement scores are commensurate with the estimate of her intellectual abilities.

Elizabeth's emotional and behavioral functioning was assessed through structured interviews conducted with her mother and teacher, and through rating scales completed by her mother, teacher, and Elizabeth herself. Elizabeth's teacher reported a high number of symptoms related to hyperactivity, inattention, and impulsivity. Many of these symptoms were confirmed by Elizabeth's mother. Specifically, Elizabeth's teacher reported problems with hyperactivity, such as difficulty remaining seated and fidgeting. Difficulties with attention included being easily distracted, needing frequent reminders, stopping and starting her schoolwork, not completing her schoolwork, and not listening. Impulsive behavior included blurting out answers and making careless mistakes. Elizabeth's mother endorsed most of these symptoms and added that Elizabeth experiences difficulty with restlessness and trouble following through with tasks. These symptoms are consistent with a diagnosis of Attention-deficit Hyperactivity Disorder (ADHD).

A diagnosis of ADHD is supported by results of rating scales filled out by Elizabeth's teacher, mother, and father which indicate that this behavior is more severe than would be expected for a child of Elizabeth's age. Further support for a diagnosis of ADHD is Ms. Arthur's report that most of this behavior appeared when Elizabeth was six years old. Finally, teacher report indicates that this behavior is causing significant problems for Elizabeth in school. Academically, Elizabeth's functioning has been adversely affected because she turns in hastily completed, inaccurate work or fails to complete her work.

A second problematic area that was reported via structured interview with Elizabeth's teacher and mother was defiance and oppositional behavior. Teacher and maternal reports indicate that Elizabeth talks back, breaks rules, bothers others on purpose, blames others for her mistakes, and is angry and resentful. This behavior occurs almost every day and has caused problems for Elizabeth in school and at home. Although this is common in children with ADHD, the occurrence is frequent and severe enough to be consistent with a diagnosis of Oppositional Defiant Disorder (ODD). A diagnosis of ODD is supported by the rating scale completed by her teacher that indicates these problems are more severe than is usual in a child her age and by maternal report that this behavior has been occurring since the third grade.

A diagnosis of ODD was further supported by rating scales completed by Elizabeth's teacher and mother, and results of the sociometric exercise that indicated that Elizabeth is having difficulties with her peers. Fifteen percent of her peers indicated that they liked her least, twenty percent indicated that she fights most, and ten percent indicated that she was the meanest. These percentages are high for a female child this age. It is likely that Elizabeth's difficulties with peer relationships are due to the behavior associated with both ODD and ADHD.

Diagnostic status:
Attention-deficit Hyperactivity Disorder, Combined Type (314.01)
Oppositional Defiant Disorder (313.81)

Conceptualization

In this case, Elizabeth is clearly exhibiting sufficient defiant behavior to qualify for a diagnosis of ODD. This behavior is present both at home and at school, where it is interfering with her academic and social functioning. Her academic failure, peer difficulties, and oppositional behavior place her at risk of more severe conduct problems as she enters adolescence. Thus, her behavior clearly needs immediate intervention.

In order to effectively treat her oppositional and defiant behavior, it is important to conceptualize the etiological and maintaining factors involved in this behavior. In this example, her ODD is conceptualized as secondary to her ADHD and is believed to be maintained by her parent's inconsistent discipline practices. Chronologically, her inattention, impulsivity, and hyperactivity have been present since first grade, while her oppositional and defiant behavior only began in the third grade. As is often the case, undiagnosed ADHD can lead to several negative consequences, such as academic failure, peer difficulties, and problematic relationships with teachers. This appears to have happened in Elizabeth's case, where her symptoms of ADHD appear to have contributed to her ongoing academic failure. In addition, children with ADHD, particularly undiagnosed ADHD, often feel that they are unfairly "picked on" and can become angry and defensive as a result. Thus, in this example, it is believed that as a result of her frustration with the symptoms of ADHD and interpersonal difficulties, Elizabeth began engaging in oppositional and defiant behavior.

Although children with ADHD are at greater risk of ODD, other factors are typically present in order to maintain this behavior. This clearly can be seen by her parent's reactions to her behavior. As described by her mother, Elizabeth's parents would use a number of techniques to attempt to control her behavior, which often varied depending on whether she was at her mother's or her father's house. Regardless of location, however, both parents would inconsistently use all disciplinary methods. In addition, when a punishment was applied, neither would see that the strategy was enforced; her mother would remove the punishment out of guilt, whereas her father would not monitor her closely enough to see that she refrained from the forbidden activity. As a result of these inconsistent disciplinary methods, Elizabeth learned that she could engage in a variety of negative behavior with few consequences. When punishments were applied, Elizabeth knew they would rarely last the expected length of time.

Treatment

Given that Elizabeth's behavior is conceptualized as being maintained by her parents' lack of consistent discipline, it was decided that the primary treatment modality would be parent training. However, there were other factors contributing to the initiation and maintenance of her behavior. Therefore, there were several additional treatment recommendations that needed to be addressed before parent training could be effective.

(1) Stimulant Medication
Given the severity of Elizabeth's behavior and its impact on her school and social functioning, a consultation with a pediatrician for a trial of stimulant medication was recommended. Research has shown stimulant medication to be effective in helping ADHD children to complete schoolwork. It has also been shown to have a positive impact on peer relationships. Because difficulty with sustaining friendships has been found to strongly predict a variety of later psychological problems, this would be a crucial preventative measure. In this case, the pediatrician felt that Elizabeth's ADHD symptomology was severe enough to warrant stimulant medication, and she was placed on 25mg of Ritalin twice a day.

(2) Tutoring
Elizabeth was showing school failure to such a significant degree that it was highly unlikely to be remedied by medication alone. Thus, tutoring was initiated to help Elizabeth improve her grades and to make up the material she had not learned due to her inattention, impulsivity, hyperactivity, and defiance. Immediately after the assessment was completed, Elizabeth began receiving tutoring sessions from a female high-school student in her neighborhood. They met twice a week at Elizabeth's home for two hours each meeting.

(3) Classroom Behavior Management

It was unlikely that Elizabeth's difficulties in school would show an immediate reduction simply as a result of the medication and tutoring. Thus, it was recommended that her teacher implement a behavioral program in the classroom. This program involved constructing a checklist of specific behavioral goals, including (a) complying with instructions, (b) speaking in a polite tone of voice to teachers and peers, and (c) keeping to herself while seated. Elizabeth's teacher evaluated her behavior before recess, before lunch, and before she went home for the day. Elizabeth's parents were given a copy of her behavior chart daily.

When implementing a behavioral program, several factors must be addressed if the program is to be effective. First, it is important that the behavior to be monitored is discrete and operationally defined. Also, the behavior needs to be the kind she can correct (speaking politely) rather than what she is expected *not* to do (not talking back). Second, the reinforcement periods must be reasonable for the age of the child (e.g., four times a day for a younger child, twice a day for an older child). In Elizabeth's case, because she was 10 years old and in the fourth grade, the evaluation period was divided into three periods: from the beginning of school to recess (8:00am to 10:00am), from recess to lunch (10:15am to 12:00pm), and from the end of lunch to the end of school (12:15pm to 3:15pm). Because Elizabeth was relatively well-behaved during lunch, it was decided that lunch would not be part of her evaluation period.

Third, the child must be allowed some room for error. Too many parents and teachers expect 100 percent compliance from their child, forgetting that (a) this is not reasonable, and (b) this reduces the incentive for a child to behave once a mistake has been made. Therefore, it is recommended that the percentage required to earn the reward be set relatively low in the beginning (60%–70%). In Elizabeth's case, she had the opportunity to earn nine points a day (three categories evaluated three times a day) and 45 points a week. In the beginning, she needed to earn six points a day for her daily reward and 30 points a week for her weekly reward.

Fourth, it is important that the rewards used be ones that are specific to the behavior program and not ones that would be normally available. In addition, the rewards should be reasonable and should not be ones that could be considered "bribes." Therefore, reasonable classroom reinforcers could be time on the computer (if this not normally available) or time spent with the teacher (if this is feasible). Rewards from home may include time spent with the parent or extra television time. Rewards such as food or money are discouraged, although a good weekly prize may be a visit to a particular restaurant or a pizza party, provided that this would not occur regardless of the behavior program.

Finally, for a behavior program to be effective, the reinforcement must be consistently administered as promised. However, as has been noted several times, it was conceptualized that the primary contributing factor for the maintenance of Elizabeth's non-compliance was parental inconsistency. Thus, it was doubtful that her parents would be able to consistently implement any reward that Elizabeth earned. In addition, her father expressed frustration that Elizabeth only needed to earn 67 percent of the available points to earn a reward; he felt that this was too lenient. In contrast, Elizabeth's mother felt that Elizabeth should not be denied extra television time or computer time based on her school performance. For these reasons, it was decided that Elizabeth's reinforcement would be implemented at the school. In general, it is preferred that all reinforcers be administered at home by the parent(s). However, it was clear that parent training needed to be initiated and effectively implemented before the reinforcer could be transferred from being administered by Elizabeth's teacher to her parents.

(4) Parent Training

The main component in Elizabeth's treatment is parent training. Elizabeth's parents are divorced; however, since they have joint custody, it was decided that both parents needed parent training if the treatment was to be effective. Thus, it was decided that each parent would bring Elizabeth to treatment every other week, so that each parent was receiving two sessions a month, with Elizabeth receiving four.

For both parents, the initial session focused on describing parent training and listing in detail what would occur over the next several months. Each parent was informed that he/she would first learn to interact with Elizabeth in a more positive manner, learn the skills of praising and attending, and begin ignoring certain behavior ("pick and choose their battles"). Then, they would learn to give effective commands and begin initiating contingency management programs (similar to the one at school) for use in their homes. Finally, they would learn time out and other discipline techniques.

Once parent training began, each parent was repeatedly told the importance of consistency. Reinforcement schedules were described, and Elizabeth's parents learned that they could make the behavior more entrenched if they eventually gave in to her demands or failed to follow through on their actions. Information obtained during the assessment suggested that both parents would have their own difficulty with consistency. Ms. Arnold frequently suffered from guilt when punishing Elizabeth, and often stopped the punishment earlier than anticipated. Thus, extra time was spent attempting to alleviate her guilt and on problem-solving with her to determine what could be done to decrease the probability that she would "give in" and remove the restriction. Mr. Arnold, on the other hand, failed to consistently apply discipline strategies because he failed to monitor Elizabeth's activities. Thus, extra time was spent helping him organize his schedule and his home so that he could be more diligent in monitoring Elizabeth.

Initially, Elizabeth resisted attempts to provide structure and organization, and increased her oppositional and defiant behavior. Her parents had been warned that this might occur and were able to adhere to the parent training regimen without much difficulty. The contingency management programs were nearly identical for both homes, and both parents were able to maintain roughly the same schedule for Elizabeth. Although the incentives varied by home (computer at her father's home, television at her mother's), each parent made a concerted effort to provide as similar a program as possible. Eventually, once her parents became proficient at maintaining consistency, the school contingency management program was able to be reinforced at home. Eight months after the initiation of treatment, Elizabeth's behavior were markedly improved both at home and at school.

Alternative Conceptualization

In the last section, it was repeatedly stated that the primary conceptualization was that while Elizabeth's ODD originated as a result of her ADHD and academic failure, it was maintained though her parents ineffective and inconsistent discipline, and once the proper contingencies were consistently applied, the oppositional and defiant behavior would be reduced. However, an alternate conceptualization is that Elizabeth's impulsiveness, poor decision making, and social-cognitive deficits were maintaining her oppositional behavior and contributing to her peer difficulties. From this perspective, Elizabeth's problems were instead due to cognitive deficiencies in problem-solving skills and social attributes. Thus, if her oppositional and defiant behavior were to be reduced, she would have to learn to modify her thinking and control her impulsiveness.

Alternative Treatment

Given this alternative conceptualization, the most effective treatment to reduce Elizabeth's oppositional and defiant behavior would be to implement cognitive behavioral skills training. Similar to the treatment described above, Elizabeth would still be referred to a pediatrician and receive tutoring. However, instead of emphasizing changes in contingencies in her home and school environment, the focus here would be on providing effective problem solving skills to help her execute non-oppositional choices and to improve her peer interactions.

In this situation, group therapy was not available; therefore, Elizabeth met individually with the therapist once a week. Treatment initially focused on making a problem-solving workbook. Initially, Elizabeth was taught the problem solving skills using standard vignettes. However, she was soon asked to bring in situations from school and home in which a negative interaction had occurred. In these real-life situations, she was encouraged to generate alternative solutions and to hypothesize what might have happened if she had chosen a different strategy. She was also given homework in which she was asked to use problem solving skills in real life situations. Although her parents did not watch any of the sessions, the therapist met with Elizabeth and a parent every other session (each parent once a month) to describe the current goal and to enlist the aid of her parents in reinforcing the newly acquired skills.

After several weeks of developing her problem solving skills, treatment began to focus on recognizing internal physiological cues which would alert her that she was getting angry. Elizabeth reported that she frequently felt her face become flushed and would find herself clenching her hands. She was then taught several relaxation skills to use when she began to feel those symptoms. Use of these relaxation skills were then incorporated into the alternative solutions she generated as part of her problem solving skills.

Next, treatment began to focus on identifying and modifying Elizabeth's distorted cognitions. Through didactic procedures, she was taught that distorted cognitions frequently lead to negative feelings and maladaptive responses. In her workbook, she began to learn to identify and label feelings. Then, she began using a three-column sheet to record situations, thoughts, and feelings. Eventually, she began using a five-column sheet, where she also recorded an alternative cognition and her subsequent feeling.

The final step in treatment was to help Elizabeth practice the skills she was learning. Sessions began to focus on role-play situations in which Elizabeth brought in real-life problems. In these sessions, she and the therapist acted out problem solving techniques and appropriate responses to negative situations. The therapist modeled behavior traits when necessary, provided feedback for Elizabeth's responses, and provided social reinforcement. In addition, session time was spent focusing on perspective taking and providing a non-hostile interpretation of ambiguous stimuli. Five months later, Elizabeth's behavior had improved both at home and at school, although she continued to have some peer difficulties at school.

Summary

In this chapter, the diagnosis of Oppositional Defiant Disorder was discussed, as well as two effective and popular methods for treating this disorder. The case example was illustrative of typical ODD in which the child had several comorbid conditions (ADHD, poor academic functioning, poor peer relations) and was potentially at risk of developing increasingly severe antisocial behavior. Thus, it was important that appropriate and effective interventions be implemented. In both conceptualizations, it was believed that the symptoms of ODD originated from the ADHD and concomitant academic failure. However, in the first conceptualization, it was hypothesized that the symptoms of ODD were being maintained by ineffective and inconsistent parental discipline strategies. Thus, treatment focused on initiating parent training and helping both parents to begin using effective contingency management techniques in an attempt to reduce the child's oppositional and defiant behavior. In the second conceptualization, the child's behavior was thought to be maintained by impulsiveness and cognitive deficits in problem solving skills. Based on this conceptualization, the logical treatment was cognitive skills training, which would teach problem solving techniques. In each example, the treatment followed from the conceptualization.

It is believed that a proper conceptualization is of utmost importance in determining the most effective treatment. There are numerous interventions available, only some of which are effective. However, even the most effective treatments can fail to reduce symptomatology without proper conceptualization of the problem.

Clinicians should conceptualize the initiating and maintaining factors for the observed symptoms, as well as any pertinent contextual factors. Only within this overall framework should they choose an empirically supported intervention.

References

American Psychiatric Association (1994). *Diagnostic and Statistical Manual of Mental Disorders* (4th ed.) Washington, DC: Author.

Angold, A., Costello, E. J. (1996). Towards establishing an empirical basis for the diagnosis of Oppositional Defiant Disorder. *Journal of the American Academy of Child and Adolescent Psychiatry, 35,* 1205–1212.

Brestan, E. V., & Eyberg, S. M. (1998). Effective psychosocial treatments of conduct-disordered children and adolescents: 29 years, 82 studies, and 5272 kids. *Journal of Clinical Child Psychology, 27,* 180–189.

Frick, P. J. (1998). *Conduct Disorders and Severe Antisocial Behavior.* New York: Plenum Press.

Frick, P. J. & Silverthorn, P. (2001). Psychopathology in children and adolescents. In H. E. Adams (ed.) *Comprehensive Handbook of Psychopathology* (3rd ed.). New York: Plenum Press. pp. 879–919.

Hinshaw, S. P., Lahey, B. B., & Hart, E. L. (1993). Issues of taxonomy and comorbidity in the development of conduct disorder. *Development and Psychopathology, 5,* 31–49.

Kazdin, A. E. (1997). Parent management training: Evidence, outcomes, and issues. *Journal of the American Academy of Child and Adolescent Psychiatry, 36,* 1349–1356.

Kazdin, A. E., & Weisz, J. R. (1998). Identifying and developing empirically supported child and adolescent treatments. *Journal of Consulting and Clinical Psychology, 66,* 19–36.

Lahey, B. B., Applegate, B., Barkley, R. A., Garfinkel, B., McBurnett, K., *et al.* DSM-IV field trials for oppositional defiant disorder and conduct disorder in children and adolescents. *American Journal of Psychiatry, 151(8),* 1163–1171.

Lahey, B. B., Loeber, R., Hart, E. L., Frick, P. J., Applegate, B., *et al.* (1995). Four-year longitudinal study of Conduct Disorders: Patterns and predictors of persistence. *Journal of Abnormal Psychology, 104,* 83–93.

Lahey, B. B., Loeber, R., Quay, H. C., Frick, P. J., & Grimm, J. (1994). Oppositional defiant disorder and conduct disorder. In T. A. Widiger, A. J. Francis, H. A. Pincus, R. Ross, M. B. First, & W. Davis (eds) *DSM-IV Sourcebook.* Washington, DC: American Psychiatric. *3,* 189–209.

Silverthorn, P. & Durrant, S. L. (2000). Custodial grandparenting of the difficult child: Learning from the parenting literature. In B. Hayslip & R. S. Goldberg-Glen (eds) *Grandparents Raising Grandchildren: Theoretical, Empirical, and Clinical Perspectives.* Springer. pp. 47–64.

Silverthorn, P., & Frick, P. J. (1999). Developmental pathways to antisocial behavior: The delayed-onset pathways in girls. *Development and Psychopathology, 11,* 101–126.

Weisz, J. R., & Hawley, K. M. (1998). Finding, evaluating, refining, and applying empirically supported treatments for children and adolescents. *Journal of Clinical Child Psychology, 27,* 206–216.

Weisz, J. R., & Weiss, B. (1993). *Effects of Psychotherapy with Children and Adolescents.* Newbury Park, CA: Sage Publications.

Weisz, J. R., Weiss, B., & Donenberg, G. R. (1992). The lab versus the clinic: Effects of child and adolescent psychotherapy. *American Psychologist, 47,* 1578–1585.

Parent Training

Barkley, R. A. (1987). *Defiant Children: A Clinician's Manual for Parent Training.* New York: Guilford.

Forehand, R., & McMahon, R. J. (1981). *Helping the Non-compliant Child.* New York: Guilford.

Hembree-Kigin, T. L., & McNeil, C. B. (1995). *Parent-child Interaction Therapy.* New York: Plenum.

Patterson, G. R., & Forgatch, M. (1987). *Parents and Adolescents Living Together. Part 1: The Basics.* Eugene, OR: Castalia.

Patterson, G. R., & Guillon, M. E. (1968). *Living with Children: New Methods for Parents and Teachers.* Champaign, IL: Research Press.

Webster-Stratton, C. (1994). Advancing videotape parent training: A comparison study. *Journal of Consulting and Clinical Psychology, 62,* 583–593.

Cognitive Problem Solving Skills Training

Feindler, D. L., Marriott, S. A. A., & Iwata, M. (1984). Group anger control training for junior high school delinquents. *Cognitive Therapy and Research, 8,* 299–311.

Kazdin, A. E., Esveldt-Dawson, K., French, N. H., & Unis, A. S. (1987). Problem-solving skills training and relationship therapy in the treatment of antisocial child behavior. *Journal of Consulting and Clinical Psychology, 55,* 76–85.

Kazdin, A. E., Siegel, T. C., & Bass, D. (1992). Cognitive problem-solving skills training and parent management training in the treatment of antisocial behavior in children. *Journal of Consulting and Clinical Psychology, 60,* 733–747.

Kendall, P. C., & Braswell, L. (1985). *Cognitive-behavioral Therapy for Impulsive Children.* New York: Guilford.

Lochman, J. E., & Wells, K. C. (1996). A social-cognitive intervention with aggressive children: Prevention effects and contextual implementation issues. In R. D. Peters & R. J. McMahon (eds) *Preventing Childhood Disorders, Substance Abuse and Delinquency.* Thousand Oaks, CA: Sage. pp. 111–113.

Other Treatment Programs

Henggeler, S. W., & Borduin, C. M. (1990). *Family Therapy and Beyond: A Multisystemic Approach to Treating the Behavior Problems of Children and Adolescents.* Monterey, CA: Brooks/Cole.

Henggeler, S. W., Schoenwald, S. K., Borduin, C. M., Rowland, M. D., & Cunningham, P. B. (1998). *Multisystemic Treatment of Antisocial Behavior in Children and Adolescents.* New York: Guilford.

Chapter 4

Conduct Disorder

Paul J. Frick[1] and Monique G. McCoy

Characteristics and Causes

General Description

Conduct Disorder (CD) is one of two Disruptive Behavior Disorders defined by the Diagnostic and Statistical Manual of Mental Disorders, 4th Edition (DSM-IV: American Psychiatric Association, 1994). The definition of CD refers to a persistent pattern of behavior in which the basic rights of others and/or major societal norms or rules are violated. The symptoms used to operationally define this pattern of behavior fall into four categories: aggression to people or animals, destruction of property, deceitfulness or theft, and serious violation of rules. The DSM-IV also makes a distinction between two subtypes of CD. In one subtype, the Childhood-onset Type, children start showing antisocial and aggressive behavior before age ten, usually as the culmination of a process beginning early in life with oppositional behavior following which the child progresses into more and more severe types of conduct problems over time (Lahey & Loeber, 1994). The Adolescent-onset Type of CD, in contrast, is defined by a later development of CD symptoms (on or after age 10) without signs of severe aggressive and antisocial behavior before this time. In addition to the different patterns of onset, these two subtypes of CD also have very different outcomes. The childhood-onset group is more likely to continue to show serious antisocial and criminal behavior into adulthood than the adolescent-onset group, whose problematic behavior is much more likely to be limited to the adolescent period (Frick & Loney, 1999).

This breakdown of CD into childhood-onset and adolescent-onset subtypes illustrates a very important concept for understanding and treating children with CD. Specifically, it illustrates the fact that children with CD constitute a very heterogeneous group with major differences among those with the disorder in their clinical presentation, clinical course, and underlying causes of behavior. Given this diversity, it is not surprising that, in addition to the DSM-IV approach, there have been many other methods for dividing children with CD into more homoge-

[1] Work on this chapter was supported by grant R29 MH55654-02 from the National Institute of Mental Health.

Handbook of Conceptualization and Treatment of Child Psychopathology, pages 57–76.
Copyright © 2001 by Elsevier Science Ltd.
All rights of reproduction in any form reserved.
ISBN: 0-08-043362-6

neous subtypes (see Frick & Ellis, 1999 for a review of these approaches). For example, a distinction has been made based on whether the child (a) is capable of sustaining social relationships and tends to commit antisocial behavior with other deviant peers (socialized or group type), or (b) is not capable of sustaining social relationships and tends to commit antisocial acts alone (undersocialized or solitary type). Distinctions have also been made based on whether or not the child shows primarily aggressive or primarily non-aggressive symptoms of CD. Some approaches to subtyping children with CD have been based on the co-occurrence of other disorders, such as the presence of Attention Deficit Hyperactivity Disorder or an anxiety disorder.

One of the more promising approaches to dividing children with CD into subtypes is based on the presence of callous and unemotional traits. These traits have been used to define psychopathy in adults and are characterized by pathological egocentricity, an absence of empathy, an absence of guilt, superficial charm, shallow emotions, an absence of anxiety, and the inability to form and sustain lasting and meaningful relationships. The presence of these traits seems to designate a very severe group of children within the Childhood-onset Type of CD (Frick, 1998; Frick & Ellis, 1999). For example, children with CD and callous and unemotional traits, tend to show a greater variety of antisocial behavior (including aggression), they have a higher rate of police contacts at a young age, and they have a stronger family history of criminal and antisocial behavior than other children with CD but without these traits. Furthermore, the most severe and violent juvenile offenders (i.e., violent sex offenders) tend to show high rates of these callous and unemotional traits.

Epidemiology and Clinical Course

The prevalence of CD depends on a number of factors including the type of symptoms leading to the diagnosis, the age group studied, and the gender of the child. To illustrate changes across different age groups, the prevalence of CD is estimated as being present in only about two to four percent of school-aged children with a dramatic rise in prevalence during adolescence to about six to 12 percent (McGee, Feehan, Williams, & Anderson, 1992). This rise in prevalence is due to the addition of the Adolescent-onset Type of CD in adolescence. Embedded in these estimates are important differences in the prevalence of CD for boys and girls that also changes across development. Overall, boys tend to show higher rates of CD than girls. However, this sex ratio is moderated somewhat by age with school-aged boys outnumbering girls with CD by about a ratio of four to one, whereas in adolescent samples this ratio drops to about two to one. Also, it is clear that the male predominance of CD is much greater for aggressive and violent antisocial behavior and much less for non-aggressive behavior or for relational aggressive behavior (e.g., excluding children from play groups, spreading rumors about children to have them rejected by others) (Crick & Grotpeter, 1995).

There have been a large number of prospective longitudinal studies illustrating the short and long term course of CD and these studies have documented fairly substantial stability in this disorder (see Frick & Loney, 1999 for a review). For example, over a four-year year period, between 45 percent and 50 percent of children with CD can be rediagnosed with the disorder. Longitudinal studies following children with CD into adulthood have found that between 43 percent and 64 percent of boys and approximately 17 percent of girls with CD have been arrested for criminal behavior by adulthood, and about 31 percent of boys and 17 percent of girls can be diagnosed with an antisocial disorder as an adult. Importantly, a substantial degree of stability is accounted for by a small proportion of children with CD. For example, the stability of CD is dramatically reduced when the 5 percent of children with the most persistent pattern of CD are excluded from the stability estimates (Moffitt, 1993). Variables that predict which children with CD are most likely to continue to show antisocial behavior in adolescence and adulthood include displaying a large number and multiple types of CD symptoms in multiple settings, developing CD symptoms at an early age (before adolescence), and having a co-morbid diagnosis of Attention Deficit Hyperactivity Disorder (Frick & Loney, 1999).

Comorbid Disorders

In addition to affecting the course of CD, the presence of co-occurring disorders has a number of other important clinical implications for understanding and treating children with CD. ADHD is by far the most common co-morbid diagnosis, with rates of ADHD ranging from 65 to 90 percent in clinic-referred children with CD. As mentioned previously, the presence of ADHD predicts a poorer outcome for children with CD. In addition, the presence of ADHD leads to more severe behavior problems and predicts earlier and more severe substance use in children with CD. Although ADHD is the most common co-occurring disorder, children with CD also show high rates of learning disabilities, high rates of emotional disorders (e.g., depression and anxiety), and high rates of substance abuse. The presence of these many co-morbid conditions often necessitates a very comprehensive clinical assessment for children with CD, and comprehensive treatment approaches that not only focus on the primary symptoms of CD but also address the co-occurring problems in adjustment.

Causal Theories

A number of different factors, both within the child and within his or her psychosocial context, have been associated with CD. For example, several aspects of a child's family environment have been consistently associated with CD (Frick, 1994). These include high rates of parental psychopathology, especially substance abuse and antisocial disorders, high rates of divorce and marital conflict, and use of ineffective parenting practices (e.g., low parental involvement, poor monitoring and supervision, and harsh or inconsistent discipline practices). Children with CD also tend to be rejected and isolated by peers and, as a result of this peer rejection, they often do not experience the socialization of prosocial peers that is crucial for developing non-aggressive and non-aversive means of interacting with others. Also, this rejection by prosocial peers places a child at risk for associating with other antisocial and rejected peers. Another aspect of a child's psychosocial context that has been related to CD is living in economically impoverished circumstances that limit a child's chances of advancing educationally, occupationally, or socially.

In addition to these important aspects of a child's psychosocial context, there are individual vulnerabilities within the child that have been associated with CD. For example, research has documented a number of neurological correlates to CD related to poor impulse control and to irregularities in the functioning of the autonomic nervous system (Lahey, McBurnett, Loeber, & Hart, 1995). The autonomic irregularities may underlie some of the unique temperamental features found in children with CD, such as their preference for thrill and adventure seeking activities and their reward-dominant response style in which their behavior is more responsive to cues to reward than to punishment. Also, children with CD are more likely to show a number of neurocognitive deficits. These deficits include a lower overall IQ, in addition to more specific cognitive deficits, such as deficits in their verbal abilities and in their executive functioning. Finally, children and adolescents with CD often show social information-processing deficits, such as a hostile attributional bias or deficient social problem-solving skills, that make them more likely to respond aggressively in interpersonal contexts.

One way of viewing these many factors which are correlated with CD is from a "cumulative risk" perspective in which the development of CD is regarded as a function of the number of risk factors to which a child is exposed. Alternatively, children with CD may develop their severe pattern of antisocial and aggressive behavior through a number of causal pathways, each with a somewhat unique set of causal processes. As a result, various subgroups of children with CD may differ in the causes of their behavior problems. For example, research has illustrated that childhood-onset and adolescent-onset patterns of CD have very different correlates that could suggest the operation of different causal mechanisms (Frick, 1998; Moffitt, 1993).

Children with a childhood-onset type of CD exhibit higher rates of cognitive and neuropsychological dysfunction and higher levels of family dysfunction than the adolescent-onset group. As a result, the childhood-onset group is viewed as a more characterological disturbance involving the "juxtaposition of a vulnerable and difficult infant with an adverse rearing context that initiates... a transactional process in which the challenge of coping with a difficult child evokes a chain of failed parent-child encounters" (Moffitt, 1993, p.682). In contrast, children in the adolescent-onset group do not show as many of the individual and familial vulnerabilities that are characteristic of the childhood-onset group. Instead, this group shows a personality pattern characterized by high levels of rebelliousness and rejection of traditional status hierarchies. As a result, this type of CD is viewed as more of an exaggeration of the normative developmental process of separation and individuation that characterizes adolescence (Moffitt, 1993).

Research also suggests that the subtype within the childhood-onset category defined by the presence of callous and unemotional traits may also show a unique constellation of causal factors (Frick, 1998). That is, children with callous and unemotional traits not only show a more severe pattern of behavior, as mentioned previously, but they also show several other characteristics that differentiate them from other children within the childhood-onset type of CD. For example, children with callous,unemotional traits are more likely to show autonomic irregularities, a thrill and adventure seeking or fearless temperament, and a reward dominant response style than other children with childhood-onset CD. However, they are *less* likely to be impaired intellectually and their behavior is *less* strongly associated with dysfunctional parenting practices. Therefore, this group seems to show a temperament defined by low behavioral inhibition that is characterized physiologically by a higher threshold of reactivity in their autonomic nervous system functioning and behaviorally by low fearfulness to novel or threatening situations and poor responsiveness to cues to punishment. This temperament can negatively influence the development of guilt and empathy in children (see Kochanska, 1993 for seven different theories to account for this link) and may make them less susceptible to parental socialization attempts.

The division of CD into the childhood-onset and adolescent-onset types and, the further division of the childhood-onset type into those with and without callous and unemotional traits, appear to be quite helpful for explaining some of the diversity within the CD diagnosis. However, all of these approaches to classifying and subtyping CD have substantial limitations when attempting to account for the development of CD in girls (Silverthorn & Frick, 1999). Girls with CD often show an adolescent-onset to their antisocial behavior, as reflected by the increase in prevalence of CD in adolescence compared with a decrease in the male predominance of the disorder in the same age group. However, girls with CD, despite the later onset, have many characteristics that make them more similar to boys with a childhood-onset CD. Although research on CD in girls is limited, they appear to show a very stable form of CD with poor adult outcomes, they exhibit high rates of neuropsychological and cognitive deficits, and they often come from very dysfunctional family backgrounds. As a result, Silverthorn and Frick (1999) have described the developmental pattern in girls as being a "delayed-onset" trajectory to illustrate that these girls are likely show temperamental and environmental vulnerabilities throughout development, similar to boys with childhood-onset CD, but they do not manifest overt antisocial and aggressive behavior until adolescence.

Treatment Research

Overview of Outcome Studies

A recent review of published treatment outcome studies that used psychosocial treatments for children and adolescents with CD documented 82 studies involving over 5,272 children (Brestan & Eyberg, 1998). The size of this literature far surpasses published research on the treatment of most other childhood disorders. Unfortunately, despite the size of this literature, there are several sobering statements that can be made about the effectiveness of the current treatment technology. First, even for those treatments that have proven to be effective, the greatest degree of improvement seems to be in the treatment of younger children (before age eight) with less severe types of conduct problems (e.g., oppositional, non-compliant). Although this finding highlights the need to focus on the prevention of CD in young children who are beginning to show problematic behavior, it also suggests that there is a need for better interventions for older children and adolescents with more severe conduct problems. Second, the generalizability of treatment effects across settings tends to be poor. That is, treatments that are effective in changing a child's behavior in one setting (e.g., mental health clinics) often do not bring about changes in the same child's behavior in other settings (e.g., schools). Third, improvements brought about in the behavior of children with CD are often difficult to maintain over time. This seems to be particularly true of older children with severe conduct problems and for children from very dysfunctional family environments. Albeit with these limitations, there have been four treatment approaches that have proven to be effective in treating a large number of children with CD in controlled outcome studies.

Effective Treatments for Conduct Disorder

The first intervention that has proven effective in controlled outcome studies is the use of contingency management programs. These programs (a) establish clear behavioral goals of positive behavior to increase (e.g., appropriate expression of anger, prosocial interactions with peers, respectful comments to adults) and negative behavior to decrease (e.g., aggression, non-compliance with adults, rule-breaking behavior), (b) a system of monitoring a child's progress towards these goals (e.g., point or token system), and (c) a system of positive and negative consequences to encourage progress towards meeting these goals. These contingency management programs are based on the theory that a child has not been taught to modulate his or her behavior appropriately due to faulty contingencies operating in his or her natural environment. Therefore, these interventions are designed to provide a corrective environment (i.e., very structured expectations and consistent consequences) to help a child or adolescent learn to modulate behavior in response to environmental demands. These interventions have been used to reduce problem behavior in many different settings, including a child's home, or classroom, and in residential treatment centers.

The second treatment that has proven to be effective for many children with CD is Parent Management Training (PMT). PMT programs are based on a wealth of research showing an association between inadequacies in a child's rearing environment and the development of CD. Most of these programs were developed from a social learning tradition that emphasized the importance of what the child is taught in the home (i.e., how he and she is socialized) for the development of conduct problems. A critical focus of PMT programs is to teach parents how to develop and implement very structured contingency management programs in the home. However, the reason that PMT programs are included separately from contingency management techniques is because they focus on a number of other family processes related to CD as well. They also focus on improving the quality of parent-child interactions (e.g., having parents more involved in their children's play, improving parent-child communication) and helping parents to change other aspects of the home environment (e.g., timing and presenting requests, developing clear and explicit rules and expectations, monitoring and supervising children in a developmentally appropriate manner) that can help to reduce the aggressive and antisocial behavior displayed by children with CD.

The third type of intervention that has proven effective in treating children with CD are cognitive-behavioral approaches designed to overcome deficits in social cognition and deficits in social problem-solving experienced by children and adolescents with CD. These cognitive approaches place primary importance on how a child processes social information (e.g., impulsively or with a tendency to attribute hostile intent) and how he or she uses this information to determine an appropriate behavioral response for understanding a child's susceptibility to antisocial and aggressive behavior. For example, the Anger Coping Program developed by Lochman (1992) helps children to use self-instructional statements (e.g., "Stop and Think!") to inhibit automatic, impulsive, and aggressive responses in interpersonal situations. Children are also guided through a number of perspective-taking tasks designed to overcome perceptual biases in social interactions (e.g., hostile attributional biases). Children are taught anger control techniques which involve recognizing physiological signs of angry arousal and using these signs as cues to inhibit angry responses. Further, they are instructed to initiate a multi-step problem-solving process that considers non-aggressive alternatives to solving interpersonal conflicts.

The final intervention that has proven effective in the treatment of children with CD is the use of stimulant medication. As mentioned previously, a substantial proportion of clinic-referred children with CD also show ADHD. The impulsiveness associated with ADHD may directly lead to some of the aggressive and other poorly regulated behavior of children with CD. Alternatively, the presence of ADHD may indirectly contribute to the development of CD through its effect on children's interactions with peers and significant others (e.g., parents and teachers) or through its effect on a child's ability to perform academically. Therefore, for many children and adolescents with CD, reducing the ADHD symptoms is an important treatment goal. One of the more successful treatments for ADHD is the use of CNS stimulants, with Ritalin (MPH) the one most commonly used. The effectiveness of stimulant medication for reducing conduct problems in children with both ADHD and CD has been shown in several controlled medication trials.

Comprehensive and Fexible Approaches to Treatment

Each of the four treatments described in the previous section target basic processes that research has shown to be important in the development of CD. They were each embedded in a theoretical model that focused on one type of causal process, either faulty conditioning, poor social learning experiences, faulty social cognition, or neuropsychological vulnerabilities. However, these treatments have ignored two important characteristics of CD that were discussed previously. First, these treatments ignore the fact that CD is multi-determined. For most children and adolescents, CD is the end result of a complex interaction of many different types of causal mechanism. As a result, interventions that target only one type of process are likely to have limited effectiveness. Second, there appear to be many different causal pathways through which children and adolescents can develop CD. As a result, intervention programs that are not tailored to the specific processes involved in the development of conduct problems for an individual child are also likely to be limited in their effectiveness.

In recognition of these limitations, a number of treatment approaches have attempted to simultaneously target multiple processes that could lead to CD. One example of such a comprehensive approach to treatment is the Families and Schools Together (FAST Track) Program that was developed by the Conduct Problems Prevention Research Group (CPPRG, 1992). The FAST Track program was designed to intervene early in children's development of CD using a coordinated package of multiple interventions. FAST Track integrates five core intervention components designed to promote competence in the family, child, and school in a coordinated and integrated fashion. First, the FAST Track program includes 22 sessions of an enhanced PMT intervention conducted in a group format. This intervention includes the standard PMT components designed to help parents develop and use appropriate parenting skills and to facilitate positive parent-child interactions. In addition, the standard PMT intervention was enhanced with components (a) to help parents foster their children's learning, (b) to help parents develop positive family-school relationships, (c) to help parents promote anger control skills and problem-solving strategies in their children, and (d) to encourage parents to use similar self-control strategies themselves. Second, the FAST Track program involves a home-visitor/case management component. A case manager visits the family home(s) biweekly to help parents practice skills learned in the PMT groups. The case manager also responds to any problems in implementing these skills in the home. Third, the FAST Track program includes a cognitive-behavioral intervention that combines features of social skills training programs that focus on friendship and play activities with more traditional cognitive-behavioral interventions that help children improve their anger control and interpersonal problem-solving skills. Fourth, the FAST Track program includes an academic tutoring component that was designed to promote reading skills using a phonics-based program. Fifth, the FAST Track program includes classroom intervention that helps teachers develop contingency management programs to effectively manage disruptive behavior in the classroom.

The comprehensive nature of the FAST Track program recognizes the multi-determined nature of CD by providing a coordinated intervention that addresses the multiple needs of children with this disorder. However, there is no systematic attempt to match treatment components to the individual needs of the children and families. A similar treatment structure is provided to all children and families, which is not consistent with emerging research on the different causal pathways through which children develop CD. Multi-Systemic Therapy (MST) (Henggeler & Borduin, 1990) is a comprehensive approach to treatment of CD that was explicitly designed to be flexible in its implementation so that treatment could be tailored to the needs of the individual child and his or her family. Rather than being a single type of therapy or specific set of interventions, MST is an *orientation* to treatment.

MST was developed as an extension of a family systems orientation to psychological intervention. In systemic family therapy, problems in children's adjustment, such as conduct problems, are viewed as being embedded within the larger family context. In fact, the primary pathology leading to CD is viewed as being within the family environment and not within the child. MST expands this notion to include other contexts, such as the child's peer, school, and neighborhood contexts, all of which can and should be a potential focus of intervention. Therefore, MST explicitly recognizes the potential importance of using multiple interventions targeting change at many different levels when designing a treatment plan, rather than focusing solely on the individual or family level, as in other treatment approaches reviewed here previously. This broad systemic view seems to fit current research on CD as being caused and maintained by multiple causal processes. To determine an appropriate treatment plan, MST involves an initial comprehensive assessment that seeks to understand the level and severity of the child or adolescent's presenting problems and to understand the systemic context of these problems. After this assessment, the information is used to outline an individualized treatment plan based on the specific needs of the child and his or her family.

MST has proven to be quite successful at treating children and adolescents with CD in several different types of settings. The success of MST illustrates that successful treatment of CD does not involve simply selecting one "best" intervention (e.g., PMT), even if the intervention is comprehensive (e.g., Fast Track), and implementing it for all children and adolescents with the disorder. Rather, MST utilizes a variety of treatment approaches to address the various factors contributing to the child's antisocial behavior and this is tailored to the needs of the individual child. As a result, it is more consistent with research suggesting that the processes which cause or maintain CD may differ across children and adolescents who have the disorder.

MST is an exemplar of a flexible and comprehensive approach to treatment of CD. Although it was developed as an extension of family systems theory, knowledge and adherence to systemic orientation to intervention may not be a necessary condition for its success in treating children with CD. For example, developmental theory also recognizes the importance of considering multiple interacting causal processes in the development of any type of psychopathology, including CD. However, while recognizing the critical importance of contextual factors, it places equal emphasis on dispositional factors (e.g., temperamental vulnerabilities) that may place a child at risk for conduct problems. These factors are often considered less important in treatments developed from a systemic orientation.

Therefore, a flexible and comprehensive approach to treatment can be guided by several different theoretical orientations. However, there appear to be three critical features that are important in designing intervention programs that are consistent with current research on the characteristics and causes of CD (Frick, 1998). First, to select the most efficacious set of interventions for a child or adolescent with CD, a clinician must understand the basic nature of CD and the multiple causal processes that can be involved in the development of this disorder. Without such an understanding, a clinician will have difficulty making decisions on the most important targets of intervention. Second, a flexible approach to treatment requires that there be a clear, comprehensive, and individualized case conceptualization to guide the design of a focused and integrated approach to treatment. A case conceptualization is a "theory" as to what are the most likely factors involved in the development, exacerbation, and maintenance of conduct problems for a child or adolescent. Hence, the research on CD is applied to each individual with the disorder. Third, successful intervention for children and adolescents with CD typically involves multiple professionals and multiple community agencies working together to provide a comprehensive and integrated intervention utilizing empirically established treatment approaches whenever possible. These three ingredients critical to the successful treatment of a child or adolescent with CD is illustrated by the following case example.

Clinical Case Example

Referral and Background Information

Jacob was ten years old and midway through his fourth grade year when he was referred by his mother to a university-based outpatient mental health clinic for a comprehensive psychological evaluation. According to Jacob's mother, he was having significant problems at school, both behaviorally and academically. He had been suspended from school many times since the beginning of the fourth grade for arguing with teachers, fighting with other children, and failing to complete his work. Furthermore, he was failing most of his academic subjects. His school was considering placing Jacob in an alternative school for children with severe behavioral problems if his school behavior did not improve.

His mother reported that she had been concerned about Jacob's behavior since kindergarten. He had trouble learning basic academic skills, he had great difficulty staying in his seat and following class rules, and he frequently was engaged in fights with other children. These problems continued into the first grade where his teacher reportedly was concerned that he may have Attention Deficit

Hyperactivity Disorder. He was tested by a private agency specializing in diagnosing learning disabilities and was found to be below age norms in reading, mathematics, and handwriting skills. He was diagnosed with a learning disability and began receiving bimonthly tutoring sessions at the agency. According to Jacob's mother, Jacob's behavior problems escalated in the second grade which she partly attributed to his teacher who was "unduly cruel to him." However, his behavior also worsened at home where he had frequent fights with children in his neighborhood. Jacob failed the second grade but was allowed to continue on to the third grade after attending summer school. In the third grade, Jacob began receiving special education services for children with learning disabilities, and this continued into the fourth grade.

At the time Jacob was referred for a psychological evaluation, he was living with his mother and father, and two sisters, ages 13 and 16. His father owned a construction company and his mother was employed part time as a school janitor. His parents had divorced ten months before the evaluation. According to Jacob's mother, the divorce followed "four years of frequent verbal arguments" that were frequently witnessed by the children. The conflict was so intense that Jacob's older sister reportedly threatened to run away from home if they did not divorce. However, after the divorce his parents reportedly began to "work their differences out" and had reunited after six months of separation.

Psychological Testing

Based on the referral information described above, Jacob underwent a comprehensive psychological evaluation, assessing his learning, his behavioral and emotional functioning, and his family context. As part of this evaluation, he was given a standardized intelligence test (Wechsler, 1991) where his overall intellectual ability was estimated as being somewhat below age norms, with a full scale intelligence score of 84 (14th percentile). On this testing, his verbal and non-verbal abilities were equally well-developed. More importantly, however, his scores on standardized measures of academic achievement (Woodock & Johnson, 1989) were consistent with this estimate of his intellectual abilities. His age standard scores across the academic subjects ranged from 80 (9th percentile) in math to 86 (17th percentile) in reading. These scores suggested that Jacob's academic skills were below others of his age but were at a level that would be predicted given his below average intellectual abilities.

Jacob's emotional and behavioral functioning were assessed through a clinical interview conducted with Jacob's mother and through structured diagnostic interviews (Shaffer, *et al.*, 1992) and behavior rating scales (Reynolds & Kamphaus, 1992) completed by Jacob, his parents, and his teacher. Jacob's mother reported that the first problems to emerge were problems of inattention and overactivity that were present as early as age four but became much more noticeable in the first grade. The problems of inattention and overactivity appeared to be a significant source of his problems in the fourth grade, as well. For example, his parents and teachers all agreed that he often forgot things, was easily distracted, was very disorganized, and had difficulty finishing things. Furthermore, Jacob's teachers attributed much of his poor academic performance to his failure to complete work and to careless mistakes in his work. Examples of his overactive and impulsive behavior included difficulty awaiting his turn in group activities, often interrupting others when they are speaking, talking excessively, and being very fidgety and restless. On standardized behavior rating scales, the problems of attention, impulsivity, and overactivity were all rated by his parents and teachers as being significantly above an age normative range. Overall, Jacob's longstanding history of inattentive, hyperactive, and impulsive behavior, that appeared to be interfering with his school adjustment, and that was more severe than would be expected for his age, was consistent with a diagnosis of Attention Deficit Hyperactivity Disorder, Combined Type.

The assessment of Jacob's emotional and behavior adjustment also revealed a long-standing and severe pattern of conduct problems as well. These problems seemed to have started as oppositional and defiant behavior in early school years. For example, on the structured interviews, his mother reported that in the first grade Jacob frequently would talk back to his teacher and would throw temper tantrums if he did not get his way. However, since the first grade his conduct problems appeared to have been increasing in number and severity. According to both his parents and teachers, Jacob frequently got into physical fights with other children and sometimes bullied small children. They also reported that he had been caught cheating in his school work and had been disciplined for using foul language. Jacob himself admitted to this behavior, and added that he had engaged in several acts of vandalism, had stolen money from family members, and stolen candy from a store. In the year before the testing, Jacob reportedly had two very severe anger outbursts, during which he had knocked his closet door off its hinges and had damaged the ceiling in his room by throwing things. Also within the past year, he had started a fire in his neighborhood for which he had received a "warning" from the police. The severity of all of these conduct problems was evident on the standardized behavior rating scales and supported a diagnosis of Conduct Disorder, Childhood-Onset Type.

An assessment of Jacob's family environment revealed that his mother was very frustrated with Jacob's behavior and was unsure of the best way to handle him. When he misbehaved, either at home or at school, she reportedly tried to remove privileges such as not allowing him to watch television, not allowing him to play outside, or sending him to bed early. However, she admitted that she often did not try to enforce these punishments because "they just led to further arguments" with Jacob. She also reported spanking Jacob about once a week with a belt in an effort to control his behavior. Jacob's mother reported that, before their divorce and remarriage, she frequently argued with Jacob's father about discipline and how to deal with Jacob's misbehavior. However, she indicated that these arguments had been much less frequent since their remarriage because his father reportedly worked "six or seven days a week" and was not home often. When his father was home, Jacob's behavior reportedly was much improved.

One final area of concern which emerged from this evaluation was that Jacob's behavioral difficulties appeared to be significantly affecting his peer relations and his self-concept. Jacob's mother reported that he had difficulty making friends and was frequently left out of social activities. She reported that Jacob often came home crying because of his rejection by peers. Jacob's teacher confirmed his problematic peer relations and reported that it was because he was often very negative and aggressive with peers, causing his classmates to avoid him. On a self-report rating scale, Jacob recognized his problems relating to peers and admitted to having a poor self-concept which involved a negative view of his competencies in a large number of areas.

Case Conceptualization

The results of the psychological evaluation clearly indicated that Jacob had a history of behavioral problems that had been negatively affecting his academic, social, and emotional adjustment for an extended period of time. Consistent with the history of many children with childhood-onset CD, his behavior problems started in early elementary school with problems of inattention, impulsiveness, and hyperactivity consistent with a diagnosis of ADHD. It is likely that his behavior represented a temperament that made him very difficult to discipline consistently and effectively. This was combined with a family environment that involved a high degree of family conflict and a father who was only minimally involved in Jacob's socialization due to work demands, all of which seemed to further impair his parents' ability to manage his behavior effectively. Hence, Jacob's parents presented as very inconsistent and negative in attempts to deal with Jacob's behavior.

Jacob's behavior problems progressed into increasingly more serious aggressive and antisocial behavior. In early school grades, the conduct problems consisted primarily of negative (e.g., temper trantrums) and defiant (e.g., refusing teachers' requests) behavior but in later school grades the aggressive (e.g., fighting and bullying) and antisocial (e.g., stealing, cheating, vandalism) emerged and they were evident by age ten. This history of conduct problems was consistent with a diagnosis of childhood-onset CD. Jacob's poor school performance appeared to be largely a consequence of his behavior. Also, his pattern of negative behavior resulted in Jacob being rejected from his peer group and this exclusion led him to miss out on the socialization provided by prosocial peers. Jacob appeared to be distressed by his behavior and the consequences it had on his academic and social adjustment.

Treatment Approach

Based on this conceptualization, a treatment strategy was outlined for Jacob and his family that simultaneously targeted many of the problem areas that seemed to have contributed to the development of his conduct problems or seemed to be contributing to their maintenance and/or increasing severity over time. Described previously as being typical for children with CD, the intervention involved multiple professionals implementing a coordinated intervention.

First, Jacob was referred for consultation with a physician to consider initiating a trial of stimulant medication. This referral was considered an important first step because Jacob's problems of impulse control seemed to be a major contributor to his behavior problems, especially his aggression toward peers. Furthermore, his academic performance seemed to be negatively affected by his inability to sustain his attention and complete work, as well as his impulsiveness which led to many careless mistakes. As a result, a successful trial of medication could lead to a reduction in some of the major areas of impairment experienced by Jacob. Also, it is possible that if Jacob was better at focusing attention and was less impulsive, he could be more responsive to the other interventions that were part of his treatment plan.

Second, Jacob and his family were referred to a clinical child psychologist to provide a family-based intervention. Some specific goals of this intervention were to evaluate the current level of marital conflict in the home and to work toward reducing both it and its effects on Jacob. Also, it was recommended that this intervention should focus on increasing Jacob's father's involvement in the home and in activities with his son. A critical goal of this intervention was also to help Jacob's parents work together to consistently and positively manage Jacob's behavior using one of the standardized PMT programs described previously. This would involve setting clear goals and expectations for Jacob, developing a system for monitoring whether he was meeting the goals, using both positive and negative consequences for motivating Jacob to improve his behavior and to improve parent-child communication, and for helping his parents to better monitor and supervise his activities.

Third, referral to the psychologist also focused on consulting with Jacob's teacher to help her develop more effective behavioral management programs to improve Jacob's behavior in the classroom and to foster more effective communication between Jacob's school and his parents. One possibility recommended for meeting this treatment goal was the establishment of a structured home-school note system for Jacob. This system would involve Jacob's parent(s) and teacher working together to (a) set several clear goals for Jacob's school behavior (e.g., stayed on task, was respectful towards teachers, was respectful towards classmates), (b) have his teacher evaluate his performance on his behavior periodically through the day, (c) have this note reviewed by his parents each night, and (d) have an incentive system for improvements on these behavioral goals provided by his parents.

Fourth, the referral to the psychologist also focused on work with Jacob to develop better anger control strategies, to learn to inhibit impulsive behavior in general, and to develop more effective skills for interacting with same-aged peers. As reviewed previously, these are skills typically taught in many of the cognitive-behavioral programs that have been used in the treatment of children with CD.

Most of these programs have been implemented in a small group format but, unfortunately, there were no such groups available to which to refer Jacob. Therefore, it was recommended that the consultation with the psychologist involve the teaching of these skills within the context of individual psychotherapy. Also, once Jacob's impulsive behavior was reduced through a combination of cognitive-behavioral intervention and stimulant medication, and once his ability to relate to peers improved somewhat, Jacob could be encouraged to participate in structured group activities with peers (e.g., sports, scouting) outside school to allow him to interact with peers in a setting in which he might be more successful.

Fifth, it was recommended to Jacob's parents that they obtain a one-on-one tutor for Jacob outside school to help him learn academic skills that he had missed in the classroom due to his behavioral difficulties. Furthermore, this tutor could help Jacob to learn organizational strategies to prevent him from losing assignments, to develop study strategies that increased his preparedness for tests, and to develop a systematic approach to completing homework that did not involve extended periods of time requiring sustained attention (e.g., break homework down into parts and take short breaks after completing each part).

Alternative Conceptualizations

The treatment plan outlined above was based on a conceptualization of Jacob's conduct problems as coming from a transactional process of a child with a difficult temperament (e.g., impulsive and below average intelligence) interacting with a less than optimal rearing environment. The intervention targeted all aspects of this transactional process including the temperamental factors (e.g., medication, tutoring) and family functioning (PMT, reducing family conflict), as well as factors that seemed to have developed as result of this transactional process, such as conduct problems (e.g., behavior management systems, anger control training), problematic interactions with peers (e.g., cognitive behavioral interventions for social problem-solving), and low self-esteem.

This conceptualization fit quite well with the research presented earlier in the chapter on the mechanisms that appear to be involved in the development of childhood-onset type CD (Moffitt, 1993). Fortunately, Jacob appeared to fit the impulsive pattern of CD within the childhood-onset type. This was fortunate because a number of interventions have been developed and proven effective in changing the processes that seem to underlie this pattern of CD, and these were incorporated into the treatment plan outlined previously. We assessed for the presence of callous and unemotional traits based on parent and teacher reports using behavior rating scales (Frick & Hare, in press), but Jacob did not seem to show high levels of these traits. He seemed significantly distressed by his behavioral and social difficulties, whereas children with callous and unemotional traits are often not as distressed over their behavioral problems (Frick, 1998).

His high level of emotional distress and low self-esteem did present an alternative conceptualization to explain Jacob's conduct problems, however. It was possible that Jacob's stressful family environment, (e.g., high level of familial conflict) and his father's lack of involvement in the home, which could be interpreted by Jacob as a form of rejection, could have resulted in an emotional disorder. Jacob reportedly often cried, had a pessimistic outlook toward the future, and had a low self-esteem (e.g., he frequently stated that "he couldn't do anything right"). He did not show discrete episodes of depressed mood that would be consistent with a Major Depressive Disorder. However, both the standardized rating scales and structured interviews indicated a significant number of anxious and depressive symptoms. In the conceptualization presented above, these signs of emotional distress were interpreted as "effects" of the chronic behavioral disturbance and the problems in his social relationships caused by this disturbance.

However, an alternative conceptualization includes these symptoms of emotional distress as the result of his internal distress and poor self-concept. Jacob's aggression and anger could have been a way of expressing his emotional distress by focusing his anger outwards towards others, rather than inwards towards himself, and as a way of inappropriately gaining a sense of mastery over his environment (e.g., controlling social situations as the aggressor), albeit in a maladaptive way. An underlying emotional disorder as a cause of a behavioral disturbance is central to many psychodynamic conceptualizations of childhood behavior disorders, including CD.

This insight-oriented case conceptualization would lead to a very different treatment plan than the one outlined previously, indicating the need for a more traditional approach to psychotherapy in which Jacob would, with the help of a therapist, work through his emotional conflicts (e.g., perceived parental rejection, poor self-concept) so that he would no longer need the conduct problems as a way of coping with them. This type of conceptualization is an important alternative to consider in that insight-oriented psychotherapy remains one of the most commonly used forms of intervention for children and adolescents with CD.

Although individual psychotherapy was recommended as part of the previous treatment plan, it was (a) not given primary importance in the overall intervention approach and (b) it was not focused on gaining insight into intrapsychic conflicts but was focused instead on helping Jacob to develop more effective anger control strategies and better interpersonal problem-solving skills. The first conceptualization was chosen over the latter one for two main reasons. First, there were several pieces of information from Jacob's case history and psychological testing that suggested his emotional symptoms were secondary to his behavior problems and not the primary underlying cause. Jacob's behavioral problems seemed to have predated the development of the anxious and depressive symptoms, with the behavioral problems being present as early as ages four and five. In contrast, the emotional symptoms did not develop until the third and fourth grades, only after the behavioral problems had been causing impairments in Jacob's psychosocial functioning for a significant period of time. Also, the emotional symptoms appeared to be directly related to the behavioral problems. For example, Jacob's crying episodes typically occurred after peer conflicts at school and focused on Jacob feeling rejected by his peers. Second, and more practically, insight-oriented approaches to treatment of children with CD have not proven to be effective in reducing the behavior associated with this disorder in controlled outcome studies, although they have not been subjected to many such tests of their effectiveness (Kazdin, 1995). Therefore, one would have to be very cautious in using such unproven interventions without a compelling rationale for rejecting alternatives that have been proven to achieve at least some limited success.

Summary

The case presented above was designed to illustrate the central importance of conceptualization in designing an effective intervention strategy for children with CD (Frick, 1998). Although this could be argued for most forms of psychological disturbance, the importance of case conceptualization appears especially important in the treatment of CD for several reasons. First, the diagnosis of CD provides quite limited information for guiding interventions because there are so many different causal pathways, each involving somewhat different causal processes. As a result, treatment does not involve selecting the most effective treatment for CD and using it to treat all children with the disorder. Instead, it involves tailoring the treatment to the unique causal processes involved in the development of CD for each child. Second, because of the multiple causal processes that can underlie CD and because of the large number of areas in which a child with CD can be impaired, children with CD often require a comprehensive assessment of many areas of functioning. A clear case conceptualization is necessary to weave this assessment information into a clear "theory" as to the primary causes of a child's problems and thereby pointing the way to the most important targets of intervention (Kamphaus & Frick, 1996). Third, this case study illustrated that the treatment of CD typically involves targeting multiple problem areas, using several different forms of intervention, and involving multiple professionals. A clear case conceptualization shared by all professionals involved in the treatment helps to implement such a comprehensive intervention in a coordinated and complementary fashion.

Another important contribution of a well-formulated case conceptualization that is illustrated in the case study is its usefulness for integrating research into clinical practice. Many mental health professionals endorse a scientist-practitioner approach to clinical intervention. However, the focus of this approach is often solely on using empirically-supported treatments; that is, using treatments that have proven effective in treating a certain type of problem in controlled outcome studies. Another critical aspect to a scientific approach to clinical intervention, however, is the use of basic research on psychological disorders to design better interventions or to modify existing interventions based on advances in our understanding of a disorder. The critical role of case conceptualization in this process is illustrated in the case study presented previously. This conceptualization attempted to fit the information from Jacob's history to the research reviewed earlier in the chapter on the multiple causal pathways through which children develop CD. His case seemed to fit quite well with boys in the childhood-onset type of CD who do not show callous and unemotional traits, thereby providing a link between basic research on CD with the development of a treatment plan for an individual child.

In summary, case conceptualization is critical for designing effective treatments for children with CD. It should be the cornerstone of clinical endeavor and a bridge between the research literature on CD in children and adolescents, and the design of treatment plans for them as individuals. In the past, when clinical interventions for disorders were typically developed from single theoretical orientations (e.g., psychodynamic, behavioral), individualized case conceptualization was not as complex a process and required primarily only a sound background in a single theoretical orientation to intervention. As research has accumulated showing that no single orientation is sufficient to account for all psychological disorders or even for any single disorder, as illustrated by the many different types of causal processes that can underlie CD, the case conceptualization process has become much more complex. However, a recognition of this complexity is necessary to obtain a true integration of science and clinical practice and to make clinical interventions responsive to advances in research. Given the amount of research that has highlighted the complexity involved in understanding the development of CD, this disorder provides an excellent example of the importance of case conceptualization for designing interventions that are sensitive to advances in research.

References

American Psychiatric Association (1994). *The Diagnostic and Statistical Manual of Mental Disorders*. 4th ed. Washington, DC: Author.

Brestan, E. V., & Eyberg, S. M. (1998). Effective psychosocial treatments of conduct-disordered children and adoelscents: 19 years, 82 studies, and 5,272 kids. *Journal of Clinical Child Psychology, 27*, 180–189.

Conduct Problems Prevention Research Group (1992). A developmental and clinical model for the prevention of conduct disorder: The FAST Track Program. *Development and Psychopathology, 4*, 509–527.

Crick, N. R., & Grotpeter, J. K. (1995). Relational aggression, gender, and social-psychological adjustment. *Child Development, 66*, 710–722.

Frick, P. J. (1994). Family dysfunction and the disruptive behavior disorders: A review of recent empirical findings. In T. H. Ollendick & R. J. Prinz (eds), *Advances in Clinical Child Psychology* New York: Plenum. *16*, 203–222.

Frick, P. J. (1998). *Conduct disorders and severe antisocial behavior*. New York: Plenum.

Frick, P. J., & Loney, B. R. (1999). Outcomes of children and adolescents with conduct disorder and oppositional defiant disorder. In H. C. Quay & A. Hogan (eds), *Handbook of Disruptive Behavior Disorders*. New York: Plenum. 507–524.

Henggeler, S. W., & Borduin, C. M. (1990). *Family Therapy and Beyond: A Multisystemic Approach to Treating the Behavior Problems of Children and Adolescents*. Pacific Grove, CA: Brooks/Cole.

Kamphaus, R. W., & Frick, P. J. (1996). *The Clinical Assessment of Children's Emotion, Behavior, and Personality*. Boston: Allyn & Bacon.

Kochanska, G. (1993). Toward a synthesis of parental socialization and child temperament in early development of conscience. *Child Development, 64*, 325–347.

Lahey, B. B., & Loeber, R. (1994). Framework for a developmental model of oppositional defiant disorder and conduct disorder. In D. K. Routh (ed.) *Disruptive Behavior Disorders in Childhood.* New York: Plenum.

Lahey, B. B., McBurnett, K., Loeber, R., & Hart, E. L. (1995). Psychobiology of conduct disorder. In G. P. Sholevar (ed.) *Conduct Disorders in Children and Adolescents: Assessments and Interventions.* Washington, DC: American Psychiatric Press. 27–44.

Lochman, J. E. (1992). Cognitive-behavior intervention with aggressive boys: Three-year follow-up and preventive effects. *Journal of Consulting and Clinical Psychology, 60*, 426–432.

McGee, R., Feehan, M., Williams, S., & Anderson, J. (1992). DSM-III disorders from age 11 to age 15 years. *Journal of the American Academy of Child and Adolescent Psychiatry, 31*, 50–59.

Moffitt, T. E. (1993a). Adolescence-limited and life-course persistent antisocial behavior: A developmental taxonomy. *Psychological Review, 100*, 674–701.

Silverthorn, P. & Frick, P. J. (1999). Development Pathways to antisocial behavior: The delayed-onset pathway in girls. *Development and Psychopathology, 11*, 101–126.

Suggested Reading List

Assessment Techniques used in the Case Study

Reynolds, C. R., & Kamphaus, R. W. (1992). *Behavior Assessment System for Children (BASC).* Circle Pines, MN: American Guidance Service.

Shaffer, D., Fisher, P., Piacentini, J. C., Schwab-Stone, M., & Wicks, J. (1992). *National Institute of Mental Health Diagnostic Interview Schedule for Children: Version 2.3.* New York: Columbia University.

Wechsler, D. (1991). *The Wechsler Intelligence Scale for Children.* (3rd ed). San Antonio: The Psychological Corporation.

Woodcock, R. W. & Johnson, M. B. (1989). *Woodcock-Johnson Psychoeducational Battery-Revised.* Allen, TX: DLM Teaching Resources.

Overview of Basic Research on Conduct Disorder

Frick, P. J., & Ellis, M. L. (1999). Callous-unemotional traits and subtypes of conduct disorder. *Clinical Child and Family Review, 2*, 149–168.

Moffitt, T. E. (1993a). Adolescence-limited and life-course persistent antisocial behavior: A developmental taxonomy. *Psychological Review, 100*, 674–701.

Patterson, G. R., Reid, J. B., & Dishion, T. J. (1992). *Antisocial boys.* Eugene, Oregon: Castalia.

Quay, H. C., & Hogan, A. E. (1999). *Handbook of Disruptive Behavior Disorders.* New York: Plenum.

Routh, D. K. (1994). *Disruptive Behavior Disorders in Childhood.* New York: Plenum.

Clinical Assessment

Kamphaus, R. W., & Frick, P. J. (1996). *The Clinical Assessment of Children's Emotion, Behavior, and Personality.* Boston: Allyn & Bacon.

Treatment Outcome

Brestan, E. V., & Eyberg, S. M. (1998). Effective psychosocial treatments of conduct-disordered children and adoelscents: 19 years, 82 studies, and 5,272 kids. *Journal of Clinical Child Psychology, 27,* 180–189.

Kazdin, A. E. (1995). *Conduct Disorders in Childhood and Adolescence. (2nd ed.)* Thousand Oaks, CA: Sage.

Focused Treament Approaches

Barkley, R. A. (1987). *Defiant children: A Clinician's Manual for Parent Training.* New York: Guilford.

Bierman, K. L., & Greenberg, M. T. (1996). Social skills training in the FAST Track program. In R. DeV. Peters & R. J. McMahon (eds) *Preventing Childhood Disorders, Substance Abuse, and Delinquency* (pp. 65–89). Thousand Oaks, CA: Sage.

Forehand, R. & McMahon, R. J. (1981). *Helping the Noncompliant Child: A Clinician's Guide to Parent Training.* New York: Guilford.

Greenhill, L., & Osman, B. P. (1991). *Ritalin: Theory and Patient Management.* New York: Liebert.

Hembree-Kigin, T. L., & McNeil, C. B. (1995). *Parent-child Interaction Therapy.* New York: Plenum.

Kelly, M. L. (1990). *School-home Notes.* New York: Guilford.

Lochman, J. E., & Wells, K. C. (1996). A social-cognitive intervention with aggressive children: Prevention effects and contextual implementation issues. In R. DeV. Peters & R. J. McMahon (eds) *Preventing childhood disorders, substance abuse, and delinquency* (pp. 111–143). Thousand Oaks, CA: Sage.

Patterson, G. R., & Forgatch, M. S. (1987). *Parents and Adolescents Living Together.* Eugene, OR: Castalia.

Comprehensive Treatment Approaches

Conduct Problems Prevention Research Group (1992). A developmental and clinical model for the prevention of conduct disorder: The FAST Track Program. *Development and Psychopathology, 4,* 509–527.

Frick, P. J. (1998). *Conduct Disorders and Severe Antisocial Behavior.* New York: Plenum.

Henggeler, S. W., & Borduin, C. M. (1990). *Family Therapy and Beyond: A Multisystemic Approach to Treating the Behavior Problems of Children and Adolescents.* Pacific Grove, CA: Brooks/Cole.

Chapter 5

Attention-Deficit Hyperactivity Disorder

Stephen P. Hinshaw and Christine Zalecki[1]

Introduction

The past decade has witnessed considerable focus on attention-deficit hyperactivity disorder (ADHD) in children and adolescents (as well as adults), attended by ever-increasing numbers of scientific investigations, plentiful attention from the media, and a host of contentions and controversies. Among the key questions that have emerged are the following: Is ADHD a valid diagnosis? Is it a "real" condition, or a label that adults with overly high expectations give to children for displaying normal-range problems? Has it been overdiagnosed, or (alternatively) has scientific recognition of its symptoms and severe impairments, along with advances in assessment, finally led to appropriate rates of diagnosis? Have pharmacologic treatments – most notably, stimulants like Ritalin – been overprescribed? Do such medications provide legitimate intervention options? What is the role of psychosocial treatment strategies, and how should they supplement or supplant medications? Finally, what is the nature of ADHD, and how does the field's understanding of underlying mechanisms lead to the conceptualization and selection of appropriate treatments?

Addressing all these is beyond the scope of this chapter, so a focus on the last question, pertaining to the nature of ADHD and implications for treatment will be presented. In highlight, it is apparent that (a) the fundamental nature of ADHD is still open to question and (b) although some conceptual rationale exists, effective psychosocial treatments for ADHD are based largely on practical, empirical considerations. To set the stage for the case material, a description of the core features of ADHD, emphasizing subtypes of this condition, its overlap (comorbidity) with other psychiatric disorders, the substantial impairment in key functional domains that it engenders, and current theorizing as to etiology and underlying mechanisms are provided. This material is followed by the conceptual underpinnings of both behavioral and medication-based treatment approaches. Despite the current volume's emphasis on psychosocial intervention strategies, pharmacologic treatments merit discussion, given the widespread use of stimulant medications for treating ADHD and the substantial evidence for benefits from pharmacologic

[1]Work on this chapter was supported by grants R01 MH45064 and R01 MH50461.

Handbook of Conceptualization and Treatment of Child Psychopathology, pages 77–104.
ISBN: 0-08-043362-6

strategies. Consequently, the primary case report describes a child who has benefited from combination treatment (medication plus intensive psychosocial intervention); a second report portrays a child who responded to psychosocial treatment alone. We conclude with discussion of limitations of current treatment formulations and strategies and with speculation about the types of treatments that may most likely prove beneficial for ADHD in future years.

Clinical Description and Background Information

Because of space limitations, coverage in this section is at an overview level. For more detailed information regarding ADHD-related issues, see Barkley (1998), Hinshaw (1999; 2000), and Tannock (1998).

Description and Diagnosis

Nearly everyone can visualize a child with ADHD. The prototypic individual has difficulty paying attention during class lessons or homework sessions, acts impulsively (e.g., blurting out answers before questions have been completed or performing risky activities without consideration of consequences), and fidgets or moves about recklessly in his or her environment. Children with such features are difficult to manage, leading to conflicts with parents, teachers, and peers.

Several studies of both community and clinical samples reveal that the core symptoms form two distinct factors: (a) inattention and disorganization vs. (b) hyperactivity and impulsivity. At a level of categorical diagnosis, the criteria for ADHD in the fourth edition of the *Diagnostic and Statistical Manual of Mental Disorders (DSM-IV)* mandate developmentally extreme symptoms in either or both of these areas, which are of early onset (before the age of seven years), longstanding (at least six months' duration), pervasive (displayed in multiple situations), and impairing. That is, a child with ADHD is distinguished from his or her peers on the basis of the extremity of attentional and behavioral problems, the persistent nature of such difficulties, their display in multiple settings, and the problems that they produce in key domains of daily functioning.

It should be noted that difficulties with allocating sustained attention to academic tasks, inhibiting behavior in the face of temptation for immediate gain, and refraining from excess motor behavior are nearly ubiquitous in childhood, particularly in structured educational settings. Thus, differentiating ADHD from normal-range activity level, from insufficient or disorganized classrooms, or from chaotic home environments is indeed a clinical challenge. Critics, in fact, contend that ADHD has been overdiagnosed in the 1990s. Yet substantial evidence supports the validity of ADHD, on the basis of such important features as diagnostic reliability, coherence of the syndrome, cross-cultural manifestations, and evidence for clear impairment – if appropriate assessment and diagnosis are performed. These crucial endeavors involve (a) collecting information (utilizing well-normed instruments) from parents and teachers who see the child on a daily basis; (b) ensuring that the symptom patterns are developmentally extreme, cross-situational, and impairing; (c) obtaining a thorough history, to examine the long-standing nature of the underlying difficulties; and (d) ruling out the substantial number of other problems or conditions that can mimic or accompany ADHD (e.g., response to child abuse; temperamentally high activity level in absence of clinical-range ADHD; numerous sensory or neurological conditions). Additional information on assessment can be found in the recommended readings referenced at the end of the chapter.

The subtypes of ADHD noted in DSM-IV pertain to the predominant types of symptoms that are displayed. Children with extreme levels of inattention (but not hyperactivity/impulsivity) are categorized in the predominantly Inattentive type; those with high degrees of hyperactivity/impulsivity (but not inattention) are placed in the predominantly Hyperactive/impulsive type; and those with impairing symptoms in both domains comprise the Combined type. It is likely that most individuals referred for clinical services fit into the Combined type, meaning that treatment efforts must contend with both (a) inattention and its sequelae and (b) the many problems that pertain to impulsive and hyperactive functioning. Despite their different presentations, all three ADHD subtypes have been shown to demonstrate scientific and clinical validity.

As recently as two decades ago, the field believed that ADHD (or its terminologic counterparts "hyperactivity" or "hyperkinesis") was a transient disorder, limited to childhood. Yet prospective research has shown clearly that ADHD persists through adolescence in a majority of cases and through young adulthood in a plurality. Importantly, the visible symptoms of motoric restlessness and over-activity do tend to fade over time; yet subjective restlessness often persists, and the consequences of continued inattention and difficulties with impulse control are cumulative. Thus, the developmental course of ADHD is typically not benign. It is quite conceivable, therefore, that effective intervention during a child's early years may help to prevent or attenuate a lifetime of difficulties. The overall prevalence of ADHD appears to be approximately three to five percent of the school-aged population (American Psychiatric Association, 1994), with boys more likely than girls to meet diagnostic criteria, particularly for the Hyperactive-impulsive and Combined types. Girls with ADHD are, in fact, an understudied population; treatment research with female samples is rare but extremely needed.

Comorbidity

Only rarely does ADHD exist unaccompanied by one or more additional disorders. That is, comorbidity – the presence of two or more distinct disorders – is the rule rather than the exception regarding ADHD. First, at least half of the time, ADHD is accompanied by high levels of aggressive symptomatology, which may qualify for diagnoses of oppositional defiant disorder (ODD) or conduct disorder (CD). Children with combinations of ADHD and such disruptive disorders are at markedly high risk: they have family histories that include ADHD, substance abuse, and antisocial problems; they display deficits in verbal skills; they experience extremely high levels of peer rejection; and they traverse a long-term course marked by substantial risk for continuing antisocial behavior patterns (Hinshaw, 1999). Treatment of such aggressive ADHD youngsters is thus a complex and difficult enterprise. Second, ADHD also shows significant overlap (up to one-third of cases) with "internalizing" disorders, marked by anxious, withdrawn, and depressive features. Recent evidence suggests that youth with ADHD plus significant anxiety disorders show relatively better response to psychosocial treatment strategies (without medication) than do those without this comorbidity, a point to which we return later in the chapter. Third, nearly 20 percent of children with ADHD also display a marked learning disability. In such cases, typical stimulant medication treatments facilitate some aspects of achievement but do not alter the underlying processing deficits that render learning, especially reading, problematic (e.g., phonologic processing skills, phonemic awareness). Overall, it is clear that treatment strategies for ADHD must frequently contend with associated conditions and disorders.

Impairment

When clinically significant levels of ADHD are present, the syndrome is associated with clear impairment in precisely those domains of functioning that are essential for competence in development.

ADHD is strongly related to *school problems and academic underachievement*, as evidenced by both lowered achievement test scores and such other indicators as retention, expulsion, special education placement, and dropout rates. Such academic problems are evident even in ADHD youth without comorbid learning disabilities. School-based intervention is therefore essential for contending with ADHD.

Family disharmony has been clearly shown, through high rates of discordant parent-child interactions, substantial parenting stress and distress, and higher-than-expected levels of marital dissatisfaction and divorce among families with an ADHD child. For the most part, such relational disturbances appear to follow from (rather than precede) the behavioral problems displayed by the child, revealing evidence for child effects on adults; yet negative family interchanges can and do fuel the persistence of ADHD and, particularly, aggressive-spectrum comorbidities. Meaningful interventions for ADHD must directly target home life and family interaction patterns, in order to break the negative transactional pattern that often emerges.

Perhaps the most devastating impairment relates to the strong tendency for children with ADHD to experience substantial levels of *rejection from their peers*. Indeed, ADHD children come to be rejected by agemates after extremely brief periods of interaction, and negative regard from peers is quite stable once it has formed. Because peer rejection has been repeatedly linked with poor long-term outcomes such as school dropout, delinquency, and mental health problems in adulthood, it is no wonder that ADHD is a persistent disorder. Peer rejection is nearly universal for children with comorbid ADHD and aggression; but even when aggressive behavior is not present, ADHD children are still highly likely to encounter significant peer disapproval. (The Inattentive type of ADHD is more clearly associated with peer neglect than with active peer rejection, which characterizes the Hyperactive/Impulsive and Combined types.) Overall, ADHD children's problems with social interactions and peer relations are a crucial target for intervention strategies.

Children with ADHD have a tendency to sustain *accidental injuries,* including those that can be quite severe. Thus, another challenge for designers of treatments is contending with and preventing the damaging effects of accidental injury, which (in the case of head injuries) may serve to compound ADHD-related symptomatology.

ADHD is associated with marked impairments in such *adaptive life skills* as motoric competence, performance of self-care skills, and overall independence. Despite normal-range IQ scores, many children and adolescents with ADHD have failed to attain the kinds of adaptive functioning necessary for successful performance in society. Promoting independent functioning is therefore an important treatment-related goal.

As the above summary highlights, in appraising the effects of treatments for youth with ADHD, it is necessary to go beyond the symptoms comprising the disorder to consider the often-devastating home, school, and peer-related problems and impairments that may be present. In other words, effective treatments for ADHD must supersede amelioration of symptom counts alone.

Risk Factors and Etiology

The most important message regarding the broad topic of causal factors related to ADHD is that there is no single etiologic sequence or pathway leading to this disorder; the syndrome is quite heterogeneous, both symptomatically and etiologically. A key hope for future research is that the various developmental pathways can be better characterized. Another important point pertains to the linkage between etiology and treatment conceptualization. Although many would contend that optimal treatments must be directed towards "ultimate" causal factors, we know from other forms of psychopathology (and, indeed, from many medical disorders) that effective interventions may take place far "downstream" from causal risk factors (if such are indeed known to exist). For example, cognitive therapy can successfully treat unipolar depression, even though cognitive distortions appear to follow from (rather than precede) depressive mood states. Thus, the clear evidence for biological risk factors in relation to ADHD does not rule out psychosocial interventions as a potentially important treatment modality.

A host of twin and adoption studies have shown extremely high estimates for the heritability of ADHD, in the neighborhood of .7 to .8. ADHD thus appears to be more heritable than schizophrenia or unipolar depression, approaching figures associated with bipolar disorder. Importantly, such heritability estimates pertain to dimensions of ADHD and not to a diagnostic category, per se. In other words, what appears to be inherited is a vulnerability to the spectrum of ADHD-related behavior rather than a "disorder," per se. Of course, heritability is defined as the proportion of individual differences in a trait attributable to genetic, rather than environmental, influences; it does not speak to the joint roles of genes and environment in shaping a given person's symptom picture or to the clear roles that environments can play in altering phenotypic expression of highly heritable traits.

An important clinical implication is that biological relatives of children and adolescents with ADHD are themselves quite likely to display subclinical or clinical manifestations of the disorder. Treatment of ADHD, which of necessity involves active family cooperation and collaboration, is therefore a continuing challenge when family disorganization, denial, and lack of follow-through are part of the genetic legacy of the disorder.

Other biological (but non-genetic) risk factors have been found to contribute substantially to ADHD. One salient example is low birth weight (defined as less than 2500 grams, or approximately 5.5 pounds), which has been demonstrated in rigorous, recent investigations to predict specifically to subsequent ADHD (see review of Tannock, 1998). Other prenatal and perinatal risk factors, including birth complications as well as maternal ingestion of tobacco, alcohol, and other psychoactive substances, predispose to later ADHD-related symptomatology.

Except for a key investigation of low-income, high-risk families, there is not clear evidence that family interaction patterns shape the core symptoms of ADHD. On the other hand, research in several laboratories (including our own) shows that parenting attitudes and practices are related to impairments (and strengths) in boys and girls with this disorder. That is, maternal negativity may foster comorbid antisocial behavior in boys with ADHD; and maternal authoritative parenting beliefs (warmth, structure, expectations for independence) is associated with positive peer regard in ADHD samples (see suggested readings at end of this chapter). In sum, despite the clearly biological underpinnings of ADHD-related symptomatology, family socialization appears to be critical regarding the types of aggressive and antisocial comorbidity – and the peer-related competencies – that are crucial for long-term outcomes.

Underlying Mechanisms

Although the search for the underlying nature of ADHD continues, several hypotheses and theories have recently gained ascendancy. At a neural level, frontal and frontal-striatal circuits have received the most consistent support in recent years, with implications for "executive" deficits in planned behavior and in the regulation of motor output. More explicitly psychological hypotheses abound (e.g., problems regarding oversensitivity to reward, poorly regulated arousal, difficulties in motivation, dysregulated emotional control, poor verbal mediation of behavior), but none has received unequivocal support. Barkley's (1997) unifying theory of ADHD has captured considerable interest in recent years. Omitting the Inattentive type, it posits that the fundamental deficit in Combined and Hyperactive-impulsive types of ADHD pertains to difficulties with basic inhibitory processes, such as those related to the need to suspend a previously rewarded or prepotent response. To the extent that it is accurate, this model implies that the core deficit of ADHD occurs at a basic neuropsychological level of inhibitory processing, which occurs temporally prior to (and, indeed, sets the stage for) such verbal processes as self-directed speech. One implication is that interventions attempting to teach self-regulation through verbal self-control may be occurring too late and too far downstream for clinical success. Indeed, the intuitive appeal of cognitively-based interventions for children and adolescents with ADHD has not been met with empirical support.

Summary So Far

ADHD involves longstanding, developmentally aberrant, and cross-situational difficulties in attention, impulse control, and overactivity. Its subtypes are focused around the "poles" of inattentive/disorganized vs. hyperactive/impulsive domains. Often occurring with comorbid conditions – most notably, antisocial-spectrum disorders, internalizing syndromes, and learning deficits – ADHD often yields significant impairment in those functional domains (school functioning, home life, peer relations, accidental injuries, adaptive behavior) that are essential for optimal development. Both heritable and non-genetic biological risk factors appear extremely salient; family socialization is critical regarding aggressive comorbidity and social functioning. Among a host of competing explanations, fundamental problems in inhibitory control appear central for the Combined and Hyperactive-impulsive types; but the field has not yet conclusively demonstrated knowledge of such underlying processes. The most important message is that, left untreated, ADHD is typically associated with a lifelong pattern of compromised functioning. Thus, promoting and developing effective treatment procedures is essential.

Treatment Descriptions

As noted at the outset, the description of psychosocial/behavioral approaches to ADHD is supplemented with a brief overview of medication-based treatments, because of both the high prevalence of pharmacologic intervention and the clear evidence for its success. The goal is to help the reader understand the necessity of considering both psychological and biological approaches to treating ADHD. Also noted is the problematic area of cognitively based interventions for ADHD – those conceptually and intuitively compelling treatments that, unfortunately, have not yielded evidence for providing benefit to this population (despite the established efficacy of cognitive-behavioral intervention for other child disorders, as described in other chapters in this volume).

Behavioral/Psychosocial Treatments

Children with ADHD lack behavioral compliance and control; they fail to display intrinsic motivation for task completion; they display low rates of rule-governed behavior; and they respond erratically under typical home and classroom conditions of delayed and inconsistent reward (Barkley, 1998). On these grounds, ADHD would appear to be tailor-made for intervention programs that feature regular and consistent reinforcers. Such reinforcement-based behavioral programming could, ideally, pave the way towards skill-building and behavior regulation, with the gradual development of intrinsic motivation in task performance. Indeed, such is the conceptual rationale for application of behavioral reinforcement procedures to the problems and impairments pertaining to ADHD.

Empirically, there is far more evidence backing the use of behaviorally oriented treatments for ADHD than there is for psychodynamic or play therapy approaches, which have received little, if any, empirical support for this population. Yet, given the long-entrenched nature of the child guidance movement in the United States, expressive therapeutic approaches are still utilized extensively. Whereas there may be some indication for interventions of this type to help with traumatic events experienced by some children with ADHD, play and expressive therapies have not been shown to effect change in the core symptomatology or the important ancillary domains (family, peer, school) pertinent to ADHD.

The four main types of behavioral treatment strategies for this population include (1) direct contingency management, (2) clinical behavior therapy, (3) cognitively based interventions, and (4) social skills groups (see Hinshaw, 2000; Hinshaw, Klein, & Abikoff, 1998; Pelham & Hinshaw, 1992). Each is described in turn.

In Direct Contingency Management, intensive reward and punishment procedures are instituted in specialized treatment facilities or demonstration classrooms. Under heavy schedules of administration, systematic reward and punishment (e.g., response cost, time out) procedures are implemented, based on observations of baseline performance and functional analyses of antecedents and consequences for existing behavior. Most instances of direct contingency management programs have been evaluated in accordance with single-case experimental methods, whereby behavior under periods of intensive contingencies is contrasted with less systematic reward and punishment. The gains showed by children with ADHD in such programs are often impressive; but (i) appraisal of behavioral improvement is typically made during periods of maximum contingencies and (ii) the generalization of such gains to less-heavily consequated time periods is often problematic (Hinshaw, *et al.*, 1998). In our case formulation below, we address the potential for clear, often dramatic improvement in social, academic, and behavioral functioning during periods of direct contingency management.

In Contrast, Clinical Behavior Therapy procedures typically involve consultation with parents and teachers regarding the establishment of behavioral programs at home and school. Usually guided by a structured curriculum of parent and teacher sessions, clinical behavior therapy works with these adults in the child's natural environment who can alter expectations, make basic accommodations, target behavioral and academic goals, and provide more consistent application of positive and negative contingencies. In a typical sequence of parent training, families learn to (a) direct positive attention to the child, (b) select target goals and collect baseline data, (c) implement reward programs, (d) utilize negative contingencies (time out, response cost), (e) work cooperatively with the school to reinforce academic and behavioral performance in the classroom, and (f) establish programs for behavior in public and with peers. Teachers, in turn, may learn to modify expectations and change seating arrangements; provide more frequent prompts and cues; establish a reward system; implement response cost; and coordinate a daily report card (DRC) with parents. For the DRC, parents and teachers first select academic and behavioral targets in the classroom, and the teacher then rates, each day, the child's attainment of these goals. The child carries the DRC home; if s/he has received a preselected percentage of positive teacher endorsements, the family provides additional reinforcement as part of the home reward program. The coordination between home and school, in terms of specifying target behaviors, providing mutual feedback, and rewarding (at home) progress in school, is the essential element of the DRC.

Considerable evidence exists for the clinical utility of clinical behavior therapy procedures for children and adolescents with ADHD (Hinshaw, *et al.*, 1998). On the other hand, effects are not typically as large or long-lasting as needed for the multiple, persisting impairments pertinent to this disorder.

Regarding Cognitive Approaches, a longstanding issue with respect to contingency-based programs for children is the limited extent to which gains have been shown to generalize across situations or maintain over time, once structured extrinsic reinforcement is faded. In the 1970s, a key rationale for adding cognitive components to behavioral contingencies for children was to foster just such "extensions" of treatment gains, by teaching the child to manage his or her own behavior through problem solving and verbal mediation. The regulatory deficits of what was then termed "hyperactivity" were claimed to be extremely well-matched for cognitive, self-instructional, problem-solving interventions (see review in Hinshaw, 2000).

In practice, cognitive treatments for children with ADHD have a more traditional "clinical" feel, in that the child (alone or in a group setting) meets with a therapist or pair of therapists. Through games and exercises, instruction is given in (a) self-instructions (fading from overt adult directions to the child's whispered self-talk, with internalized self-speech the final step); (b) problem solving steps to help with guidance through problematic academic or social interchanges; and (c) means of coping with errors. Although the premise is that these cognitively oriented strategies will facilitate greater generalization and maintenance of behavior change, evidence for the efficacy of such procedures with children diagnosed with ADHD has been quite negative (Hinshaw, 2000). One issue is that any clinic-based treatments for ADHD will have extreme problems in generalizing to the natural environment. Another is that self-regulatory speech may be too far "downstream" from the fundamental deficit of the child with ADHD to be of much help in behavioral regulation. On the other hand, when cognitive procedures such as self-evaluation and anger management are paired with direct contingencies, there is at least some evidence for short-term benefit with respect to social behavior (see Hinshaw, 2000, and recommended readings at end of chapter). Overall, in light of the negative evidence regarding exclusively cognitive, self-instructional interventions as applied to samples of children with ADHD, the focus herein is on more overtly behavioral approaches. It is noted, however, that extending contingency-based programs through fading of reward systems and through self-evaluation is an important clinical aim.

Briefly, **Social Skills Interventions** for youth with ADHD are addressed because of the clear impairments in peer relations pertinent to ADHD (see above) and because of recent empirical evidence that social skills-related treatments can produce meaningful improvement in this population (Pfiffner & McBurnett, 1997). Social skills interventions are typically conducted in groups, wherein counselor/ therapists discuss and model appropriate social behavior, have the children rehearse the skills under supervision, and provide direct rewards for improved social functioning. The curriculum of Pfiffner and McBurnett is instructive in this regard: it blends play activities, counselor modeling, individual and group contingencies, and active rehearsal, all in a systematic attempt to improve multiple aspects of peer-related behavior. Importantly, benefits from this social skills intervention were extended when a parent component was added to the treatment, in which parents learned about the children's skill development and actively rewarded improved social functioning at home. Training in anger management is also an important component of social skills treatments, so long as it includes active behavioral rehearsal under realistic social circumstances. Readers are encouraged to become familiar with relevant procedures, which involve an active blending of behavioral, cognitive, and anger management approaches.

Stimulant Medications

As highlighted earlier, considerable controversy has arisen during the past decade with respect to the use (or possible overuse) of stimulant medications for children and adolescents with ADHD. The voluminous research on this topic, coupled with the heated debates about the benefits and liabilities of pharmacologic treatments, require far more attention than can be given in these limited pages (for comprehensive reviews of stimulant-related issues and outcomes in the field, see Greenhill, 1998; Greenhill & Osman, 2000). Instead, a brief description of issues and findings is provided, given the frequent usage of medication-related treatments for ADHD and the clear evidence for their benefits in a majority of cases. Indeed, in many respects medication treatments for ADHD are the standard by which other interventions are compared, mandating such coverage in a chapter that otherwise focuses on psychosocial intervention strategies.

First, a large number of carefully controlled studies demonstrate that stimulant medications – usually methylphenidate (Ritalin) or dextroamphetamine (Dexedrine) – provide clear benefits for approximately 80 percent of children and adolescents with ADHD. Effects are found not only for the core symptoms of inattention, impulsivity, and hyperactivity but also for such ancillary domains as social behavior (including reduced aggression), classroom performance, and parent-child interactions. Effects typically appear quickly (within minutes of the initial dose), but careful titration and dosage adjustments are needed to ensure that the child is receiving the proper dosage level. As with psychosocial treatments, individual differences in treatment response are evident, with some youngsters showing minimal or adverse response, a majority showing clear benefit, and others revealing quite dramatic gains. Stimulants do not appear to act "paradoxically" in their anti-ADHD effects; rather, nearly all individuals (regardless of diagnostic status) show enhanced attention with low-dose stimulant treatment. Thus, a positive response to stimulants does not "guarantee" a diagnosis of ADHD, as the medication effects are nonspecific.

Overall, behavioral effects of stimulants appear stronger, in the short run, than comparable effects of clinical behavior therapy or even systematic contingency management. Despite the clear differences between (a) giving a child stimulant medications and (b) performing systematic behavioral intervention, a basic similarity is that, for both treatment modalities, the effects of treatment are short-lived: behavioral gains resulting from stimulant treatment usually dissipate quickly after the last dosage received (effects of a given dosage last only several hours), and gains noted from behavioral contingencies similarly tend to fade when the contingencies are no longer applied. Thus, both pharmacologic and psychosocial treatment strategies must contend with extending treatment benefits over time – an essential consideration, given the persistent nature of ADHD symptomatology and impairment.

Side-effects of stimulant medications range from minimal to severe, but the vast majority of youth are able to receive medication treatment without prohibitive side-effects. Despite clear benefits of stimulant medications for school activities and for social skills, it is not the case, of course, that medications alone can enhance academic achievement. Furthermore, whereas stimulants are decidedly helpful for reducing problematic social behavior, additional treatments are needed to enhance peer relationships overall. Amidst concern that taking medication for behavior control may give the child the "message" that she or he lacks personal control over self-regulation, recent evidence suggests that receiving medications does not cause the child to relinquish personal responsibility. Yet, assuring that the child maintains strong personal effort is essential. Finally, despite the demonstrated benefits of stimulant medications over periods ranging from months to a year or two, it is important to note that adolescent and adult functioning do not appear to be normalized by medication treatments alone. The impairments related to ADHD span multiple domains of functioning across years of development; and in many cases medications for symptom control will simply not be sufficient for ultimate competence.

Has stimulant medication become a substitute for skill teaching, moral education, or adequate schooling? Or, rather, is this pharmacologic regimen a needed treatment for a biologically based disorder? A full answer lies beyond the scope of these pages, but it is first clear that appropriate assessment is essential to eliminate the possibility that medications will be used to cure social ills or to substitute for good parenting and schooling. At the same time, the positive benefits of stimulant treatment cannot be dismissed; these medications, at present, are the most powerful (albeit incomplete) treatment modality that exists.

Combining Psychosocial and Pharmacologic Treatments

A crucially important question concerns the incremental benefits of combining effective behavioral or psychosocial treatments with medication-based interventions. Initially, it would seem that combining these regimens would yield additive or even multiplicative benefits, in that behavioral interventions should "take" more effectively in a child whose brain functioning is now better regulated and who is more fundamentally amenable to treatment. Initial research, in fact, revealed that combined treatment regimens yielded greater levels of improvement than single-modality interventions, even if the differences were not always statistically significant. But evidence for clear differences between medication-only and combination treatments is not always found. In fact, large-scale clinical trials have produced mixed evidence: a multimodality study by Hechtman and Abikoff found no significant increment from adding systematic behavioral and other psychosocial treatments to individually titrated medication. Additionally, the largest study in the field – the Multimodal Treatment Study of Children with ADHD (MTA) – appeared to show that combined treatment added little to medication regarding the outcome domain of ADHD symptom patterns. Yet (a) when such symptom patterns were examined categorically, in terms of "excellent" response, combined treatment clearly outperformed medication alone; and (b) multimodality treatment was the only intervention with more improvements than community treatment for the ancillary outcomes of internalizing comorbidity, family relations, academic achievement, and social skills. In addition, over the long run, it is conceivable that combination treatments may alter the developmental trajectory of ADHD more fundamentally than do medication regimens alone.

A key issue regarding such findings for children with ADHD (indeed, for children with any disorder) is that individual differences in treatment response are great. That is, the "average" treatment outcome across a group of subjects belies highly idiosyncratic response within individual children and families. Thus, some children may perform optimally with medication alone, at least in the short term; others may show little or no room for improvement with psychosocial intervention; whereas still others may need combination treatment to yield meaningful clinical gains. Importantly, despite the gains that can often be found with medication approaches, some youngsters have prohibitive side-effects, and certain families may not consider pharmacologic intervention. In many cases, therefore, psychosocial treatments must be able to stand on their own.

Further Summary

This section described behavioral and medication-related treatment strategies for children with ADHD and summarized "headline" findings from several decades of relevant research. With respect to behavioral interventions, direct contingency management can yield large effects for youth with this disorder, but usually in highly specialized settings and only so long as the contingencies are in effect. Clinical behavior therapy, involving hands-on consultation with parents and teachers, also yields improvement, but gains typically fall short of full clinical significance (Hinshaw *et al.*, 1998). Crucially, cognitive treatments designed to enhance mediation and problem solving have failed to yield positive effects for children and adolescents with clinical levels of ADHD. On the other hand, combining cognitive procedures with specific contingencies and extensive behavioral rehearsal may help to extend gains from behavioral programs alone; and rehearsal-based social skills training has recently shown promise. As for pharmacologic intervention, stimulant medication treatment provides a standard against which psychosocial treatments are typically compared, in terms of the prevalence of stimulant treatment and the evidence for strong behavioral effects. These effects are typically superior to those of behavioral intervention but last only as long as pills are ingested; combining behavioral with pharmacologic approaches may yield optimal benefits in several key domains of functioning. Finally, large individual differences in treatment response are the rule, mandating careful appraisal of interventions for each case.

Case Presentation and Conceptualization

We now present a case of a boy with ADHD who has participated in multi-modality treatment, which combines clinical behavior therapy, direct contingency management, and stimulant medication. Whereas such a combination-treatment approach makes it difficult to tease apart psychosocial vs. pharmacologic effects, it is consistent with the types of interventions that may be indicated for difficult-to-manage children with ADHD who display significant comorbidities. Furthermore, in this case the addition of systematic psychosocial interventions clearly incremented the effects of medication. Along with a description of the boy and his family, we conceptualize their many needs and detail the treatment strategies that were applied. As a counterpoint, we also present a brief, second case, in which psychosocial/behavioral interventions were utilized without medication.

Background Information

Robert is a boy of mixed ethnic heritage who was initially referred for treatment when he was nine years old. Along with two younger siblings, he lives with his parents in a lower-middle-class section of a large city. Robert had a healthy childhood, with no delays in terms of his development. He was first considered to have ADHD by school personnel when he was in kindergarten. His primary problems included overly active behavior, interactions with his classmates that were "too physical," and difficulties following directions from teachers. In addition, friendships were becoming problematic. During this time period, his parents reported that they believed his behavior to be typical for a boy of his age (that is, he was overactive and often defiant). Their concerns were focused more on his difficulties with nighttime bedwetting. Because of the school's appraisal, however, Robert's parents brought him to a pediatrician, who confirmed the diagnosis of ADHD and prescribed Ritalin. At that time, no other form of treatment was recommended to the family, and Robert's behavior in school showed some improvement. His dosage level was increased, over time, to ten mg, twice per day.

As with any childhood disorder, it is germane in a case discussion of ADHD to include a family history of behavior problems and psychopathology. Indeed, in this case, the family history is salient. Robert's father reported that although he was never formally diagnosed with ADHD, he suspects that he had the disorder as a child. He had, in fact, been diagnosed with a learning disability (LD) when he was in grade school; ADHD-related symptomatology may have been subsumed under the LD diagnosis. In addition, he has developed alcoholism. Although there is no history of physical abuse, when Robert's father was under the influence of alcohol, he behaved erratically and showed verbal hostility to his son. In terms of daily interactions, he also reportedly discouraged Robert's expression of feelings about his lack of friends, instead encouraging him to "toughen-up" in order to solve his social problems.

A history of alcohol abuse is also present in Robert's mother's family. From a young age, she needed to perform a fair amount of caretaking for her mother, because of drinking problems. Robert's mother reports that although she used to get quite involved in her husband's drinking issues, her attendance at Al-Anon meetings in recent years helped her to disengage. Importantly, through structured interviews and informal discussions, Robert's mother was found to be excessively involved in Robert's life. It was not uncommon, for example, for her to attempt to mend social ties for Robert by calling his classmates in an effort to resolve playground conflicts that had occurred during school. In addition, she frequently intervened in the conflicts between her husband and Robert, typically finding herself "siding" with Robert.

When Robert was referred to us for treatment at age nine, he was in the third grade and still receiving Ritalin. At school, he was reportedly having difficulties with disruptive behavior in class, overactivity, problems completing work, and oppositional behavior. At home, Robert had been acting aggressively toward his mother (for example, he had hit her on a few occasions), had destroyed property, and was oppositional and defiant when he was asked to do chores or complete his homework. Thus, the medication was not "holding its own" as a sufficient treatment modality for Robert. In addition, the biggest concern reported by Robert's parents pertained to the domain of peer interactions. He had been known to kick and fight with his classmates, having been sent home on one occasion after biting another student. His parents reported that he continued to have great difficulty in making friends and maintaining friendships; he was rarely invited to other children's houses to play. Robert attends a small parochial school. Although the relatively small classroom size may well be optimal for a child with attentional problems, all children in a given grade stayed with common classmates each year. Thus, there was no real possibility of making a "fresh start" once a negative reputation had been formed. Robert's reputation as a "troublemaker" and a difficult child, in fact, had begun in kindergarten.

Regarding assessment, extensive parent and teacher questionnaires were obtained, as well as a formal structured interview with parents, cognitive and achievement testing with Robert, and a complete history. Robert met criteria for ADHD (Combined type) plus Oppositional Defiant Disorder. Some symptoms of Conduct Disorder were evident, although Robert fell short of diagnostic criteria. While his IQ was within the average range, his achievement level for his age and grade was below average. Thus, academic skills were an important target area. In addition, pertinent observations of Robert during an open-ended interview indicated that he engaged in a fair amount of aggressive fantasizing and exaggeration. For example, when he was asked what the happiest thing is that he ever did, he responded "When I killed a girl in my class." When asked what the scariest thing that ever happened to him was, he responded it was when he was "Almost killed in a haunted house." His reporting of these and other aggressive fictitious events was done in a matter-of-fact and relatively emotionless manner. No other signs suggestive of thought disorder were apparent.

Overall, Robert is a child who began exhibiting symptoms of ADHD as well as significant oppositionality and aggression at a young age and who responded only partially to stimulant treatment. Indeed, his frequent resorting to defiant and oppositional behavior patterns to resolve problems, his longstanding rejection by peers, and his problems with academic achievement are all predictors of negative long-term outcome. Systematic intervention was clearly indicated to help him alter his developmental trajectory. Complicating the treatment picture is the family history. The childhood behavior problems and current alcohol abuse by his father not only suggest possible genetic contributions to Robert's overactive and aggressive behavior but also signal discordant family interaction patterns, including paternal modeling of anger, poor conflict resolution, and his mother's overinvolvement with Robert's difficulties.

Conceptualization

This case was conceptualized and the treatment strategy was planned from a behavioral/social-learning approach. The identified areas of impairment for Robert are quite typical for children with ADHD, including classroom performance problems, social problems, family disharmony, and general difficulties with adaptive functioning (e.g., following rules, coping with daily conflicts). In addition, significant oppositionality and aggression are a major concern for up to 50 percent of children with ADHD (particularly boys). Behavioral interventions have proven successful for these types of problems. Indeed, a social learning approach to intervention has several points in its favor. First, at a basic empirical level, behavioral approaches have shown clear benefit for children with ADHD, ODD, and CD (see earlier sections of this chapter), at least in the short run and at least as long as contingencies are in place. Such efficacy is in clear contrast to expressive therapies for these externalizing problems, which, despite their continued popularity, have not received much empirical support.

Second, as discussed earlier, recent conceptions of ADHD (e.g., Barkley, 1997) emphasize difficulties with impulse control and inhibitory processes as central to the disorder. For such children who lack intrinsic motivation for repetitive daily tasks and who respond poorly when given sporadic reinforcement, there is theoretical reason to believe that consistent and regular rewards for positive behavior, and expectable, non-emotional negative consequences for misbehavior, are precisely what is required to normalize functioning. The ongoing clinical challenge is to maintain and generalize treatment-related gains from direct contingency management and clinical behavior therapy to lasting benefits across multiple situations of life.

Third, a social learning approach is both functional and practical. Rather than assuming that altering underlying attentional problems will automatically translate into better classroom performance, peer relationships, and parent-child interactions, behavioral strategies target not only core symptoms of ADHD but also those functional impairments that may, in fact, be causing greater distress. Thus, target behavior is identified in precisely those areas of problem behavior and impairment that require direct intervention.

Treatment Strategy

Overview. In keeping with the above conceptualization, the psychosocial treatment strategy adopted for Robert was a multimodal approach that targeted his problematic, ADHD-related behavior (a) with peers, (b) in a classroom setting, and (c) with his parents. The strategy incorporated both direct contingency management, through an intensive summer treatment program (Pelham & Hoza, 1996), and clinical behavior therapy, whereby a therapist and paraprofessional worked with his parents and teachers in a cooperative and collaborative manner, training them in optimal behavior management (Pelham & Hinshaw, 1992). As with any behavioral treatment program, target behavior was individualized according to discussions with parents and teachers, and specific rewards were developed in accordance with Robert's own preferred activities and desired objects. Despite their use of empirically derived, generic principles of reinforcement, social learning strategies are both individually based and creatively implemented – a point often lost on those unfamiliar with such approaches.

In addition, Robert's treatment protocol included a pharmacologic component. Because it was unknown whether Robert's prior dosage level of methylphenidate was optimal, a titration was initially performed through which various dosages (as well as placebo) were tried, in double-blind fashion, and his response was rated daily by parents and teachers. Data revealed that he responded optimally to 20 mg per dose, a higher level than his previous dosing pattern. This increased dosage was then instituted on a regular basis, but soon his parents reported side effects of lethargy and "spaciness." He was reduced to ten mg b.i.d., with good results (see below). It is quite conceivable, in fact, that the concurrent behavior therapy procedures facilitated improvements at a dosage level that had formerly begun to lose its effectiveness.

Summer Treatment Program (STP). A major component of Robert's treatment was his participation in an intensive, eight week STP (Pelham & Hoza, 1996) that emphasized direct contingency management and social skills training. In a group of twelve boys of similar age, Robert engaged in classroom and computer activities, and outdoor sports events that were conducted by counselors who had been extensively trained in behavior modification strategies (and who were supervised by professional therapists who also served the role of conducting the parent training program described below). A point system (token economy) served as the primary basis for treatment. Under this system, Robert earned points for appropriate social behavior (e.g., helping peers), group participation (e.g., contributing appropriately to group discussions), and for sports skills (e.g., being able to recite rules of daily sports). In turn, points could be lost for disruptive social behavior (e.g., teasing peers), inappropriate group behavior (e.g., interrupting during group discussions), violating the rules of sports activities, and failing to follow counselors' directions. For more severe problem behavior, such as physical aggression and repeated non-compliance toward staff, a time-out was assigned in addition to point loss.

The points that were gained throughout the week could be exchanged for several privileges, some of which were assigned daily and others weekly. Children who showed marked improvement from one day to the next were assigned titles such as "High-point Kid" or "Most Improved Kid" and received special daily privileges (e.g., being team captain during sports). The weekly contingency was a field trip at the end of the week, whereby children who had shown improvement from week-to-week participated in an all-day trip (e.g., to a science museum, bowling, or to miniature golfing). During this field trip, the point system was not in place; the trip thus served both to reward children for appropriate behavior during the week and to see how well the program's camp behavior modification could generalize to a less structured setting.

Robert responded exceptionally well to the structured camp setting and its contingency program. Most importantly, he improved in his ability to interact with others and make prosocial contributions to both group and individual interactions. For example, his appropriate contributions to group discussions increased from an average of five contributions per day during the first week of camp to 23 during the last week. Other prosocial skills improved as well, including positive peer interactions (from three per day to nine per day) and instances of helping peers (one per day to seven per day). Throughout the summer he rarely received a time-out and was one of the few children who consistently earned the field trip privilege. He was often assigned the title of "High-point Kid," which he particularly enjoyed because of the positive attention he earned from staff and from other children.

Another key component was the daily social skills training that was implemented throughout the summer. Formal social skills training was performed several times throughout the day, whereby counselors would discuss and model a particular social skill (such as cooperation) and then have the children enact short role-plays that exemplified the skill (see Pfiffner & McBurnett, 1997, for an empirical investigation of a similar curriculum). The social skills training was also integrated throughout each day's activities, such that children were given positive reinforcement for exhibiting the skill.

A final component was the DRC (see description earlier in chapter). Unlike the STP point system under which children were all assigned points for the same general behavior, the DRC involves an individualized behavior modification tool in which targeted behaviors (at school or an STP) are rewarded at home by the parents. Given his baseline profile of strengths and weaknesses, Robert's DRC primarily contained targeted behaviors that were peer related, such as "no bragging to peers" and "compliment a peer." Throughout the day, Robert was verbally reinforced for exhibiting his DRC behaviors. At the end of the day the total percentage of DRC behaviors with a positive endorsement was tallied. Upon meeting a preselected percentage, he was allowed to select a reward at home that the family had agreed upon (e.g., being allowed to play a video game for a certain period of time). The DRC thus exemplifies coordination between daily behavior at camp or school and a home reward program, serving as a tool for teaching parents how to provide consistent reinforcement.

Classroom Intervention. A key goal following the STP was to generalize gains into his school setting during the academic year. Thus, Robert was treated within the context of a classroom intervention delivered by a paraprofessional classroom aide who had worked as a camp counselor at the summer program (Swanson, 1992). This counselor/aide, who worked alongside Robert's regular classroom teacher for three hours per day, continued to be supervised by the therapist conducting parent training and teacher consultation. Because Robert had responded extremely well to the highly structured STP, with its high rates of reinforcement, it was important to determine how well the gains could generalize to a more typical environment. Also, the classroom intervention targeted some of Robert's key areas of impairment – such as inappropriate classroom behavior, inappropriate social interactions with classmates, and difficulties completing schoolwork and homework – that the STP had only begun to address.

This program blends direct contingency management and clinical behavior therapy. That is, the aide both provided direct behavior management and reinforcement to Robert as necessary – beginning with frequent prompts and verbal rewards and then fading to a less-frequent schedule – and coached the regular classroom teacher in behavior management techniques (such as how to provide immediate and direct positive reinforcement). Also, along with the supervising therapist, the aide served as a consultant for Robert's parents and teachers, encouraging them to "take over" the more structured approach to behavior management modeled in the STP and in the aide program.

An essential component was the classroom DRC, similar to the DRC implemented during the summer program but differing in two important ways. First, whereas the target behaviors during the summer program DRC targeted peer-related behavior, the classroom DRC specified behavior that was more directly relevant to Robert's problems in the classroom. The reasons pertained to both Robert's substantial improvement during the summer in peer relations and to his considerable academic and behavioral problems during the regular school year. Second, whereas the summer camp staff and Robert's parents worked together to implement the summer camp DRC, during the school year his teacher was also included as an integral member of the treatment team.

Working together, the paraprofessional, the teacher, Robert's parents, and Robert himself chose various target behaviors for the DRC. These included the following: "remain seated properly," "work quietly without distracting others," and "be respectful of peers." At the beginning of the intervention, the paraprofessional provided scheduled reinforcement at 15 minute intervals, during which time he would briefly inform Robert how he had performed on the targeted behavior during the last interval. During the first two weeks of the program, in fact, Robert's weekly percentage average on his DRC did not drop below 88 percent; the reinforcement intervals were therefore increased to 30 minutes. As the treatment progressed and Robert continued to do well, the scheduled reinforcement intervals increased to 60 minutes, 120 minutes, and then the entire school morning, time periods far more easily monitored by a regular classroom teacher. Robert was eventually monitoring his own behavior and filling out his own DRC. Thus, in accordance with behavioral principles, Robert eventually began to implement self-monitoring and self-reinforcement. The goal of social learning interventions is not continual reliance on frequent external rewards but rather the shaping of self-regulation. In this sense, cognitive procedures (including self-monitoring and self-reinforcement) may serve to extend and generalize previously established gains. We caution, however, that adult "back-up" monitoring is still required for children who progress to self-monitoring phases of a behavioral program.

As in the STP, reinforcement for performance on the DRC was provided by Robert's parents at home. Through weekly team meetings (paraprofessional, teacher, therapist, and Robert's parents), troubleshooting was performed, towards the end of maintaining treatment continuity across school and home. The ultimate goal was for the school and family to be able to continue the classroom intervention without the assistance of the paraprofessional. Encouragingly, after Robert's paraprofessional aide left the classroom following the fall semester and Robert was completing his DRC on his own, his weekly DRC percentages never fell below 90 percent.

Parent Training. A third mode of treatment in Robert's psychosocial intervention involved structured parent training sessions attended by Robert's parents. In both group and individual sessions with the professional therapist, they learned to apply social learning and behavioral management strategies in order to modify Robert's behavior at home and to maintain consistency with the interventions he had received at the STP and in the classroom. Thus, the parent-training component directly exemplifies clinical behavior therapy, in which professionals serve to train adults in the child's natural environment to utilize social learning principles.

Although limited space does not allow a session-by-session account, highlights are provided of principles and strategies that were most relevant to Robert and his parents. For more detailed description of parent training for families of children with ADHD, see recommended readings at the end of this chapter.

In the initial parent training sessions, Robert's parents learned to provide positive attention and positive reinforcement to appropriate behavior at home. As with many families of children with ADHD, this family had grown accustomed to attending chiefly to Robert's inappropriate behavior. Explicit instruction was given to attend to positive behavior that may have previously been taken for granted (e.g., following directions). During these early sessions Robert's parents also leaned to identify antecedents that typically led to negative interactions with Robert and began to learn how to alter these negative interaction patterns. For example, Robert's parents learned that when they repeatedly asked or pleaded with him to do a particular thing (e.g., begin his homework), he would typically become defiant and attempt to bargain with them (e.g., he would tell his mother he would do his homework after he finished watching television and after she agreed to make him his favorite snack). Instead, Robert's parents learned to issue simple, direct commands that needed to be followed in order to avoid negative consequences (e.g., loss of privileges or, with repeated non-compliance, a time-out).

An overriding objective throughout the training sessions was for Robert's parents to select target goals for themselves and Robert and to learn how to implement contingencies and reward programs to achieve these goals. The first step was to identify a problematic behavior, collect baseline data for that behavior, and then select gradual and realistic goals for Robert. Indeed, having parents attempt to begin with the child's worst or most destructive problem behavior is usually doomed to failure. Robert's parents, for example, first learned to identify how long it took for Robert to begin doing his homework after they had asked him to do so. The data they collected suggested that Robert usually did not start his homework until an average of 30 minutes after they asked him to begin working; thus their first goal was that he begin within 25 minutes. A daily contingency program was also implemented, such that he received a small reward if he met his daily goal (e.g., extra time watching television that evening), and a larger reward if he met a weekly goal (e.g., a trip to a toy store on the weekend if he met his daily goal four out of five days during the week). With this program in place, Robert gradually responded and began to take less time to start working on his homework, at which time a new target goal and reward program was implemented (e.g., "begin homework within ten minutes of request"; "complete homework without complaining").

Robert's parents then learned how to implement negative contingencies (such as time-out). In this process, they learned the critical importance of monitoring their own emotional reactions (e.g., anger or frustration) in response to Robert's defiance and noncompliance. Thus, the program featured anger management strategies for the parents as well as means of maintaining an alliance between parents. An additional component was psychoeducational in nature, whereby Robert's parents were educated about ADHD, how to modify their expectations in relation to Robert's ADHD-related symptoms, and about what they could possibly expect in terms of the disorder's long-term course.

Treatment Termination and Summary

In summary, Robert's treatment focused on several areas of impairment, utilizing treatment professionals and paraprofessionals, parents, and teachers as members of a treatment team. In addition to receiving stimulant medication, he attended an eight-week summer program, during which he showed considerable improvement in terms of positive interactions in groups and with individual peers. Following this STP, his 12-week classroom intervention was supervised by a paraprofessional aide, who helped him, his teacher, and his parents learn how to utilize a DRC to monitor appropriate classroom and peer-related behavior. Also, his parents attended parent training sessions, during which they learned basic parenting, social learning, and behavior management strategies.

Robert showed an excellent short-term response to this multimodal regimen. At treatment termination, in fact, teacher ratings, parent ratings, and structured diagnostic interviews indicated that Robert no longer met criteria for ADHD, Combined Subtype, or ODD. Whether the gains are attributable to the psychosocial vs. medication components of treatment is largely indeterminate, but his substantial improvements with the same dosage of stimulant medication that previously had yielded only minimal gains suggests strongly the incremental benefits of the systematic behavioral contingencies (and, perhaps of the parents' increased cohesiveness).

A few months after termination of treatment, Robert's mother reported that he was doing well overall, with improved functioning maintained at home and at school. Yet, a two-year follow-up yielded a picture of a mixed longer-term response. On the one hand, Robert – who continues to receive psychopharmacologic treatment – is doing well in terms of his ADHD-related symptoms. On the other, he continues to have considerable difficulties with his peers. That is, his teachers no longer have problems with his disruptive behavior in the classroom; his ability to pay attention in class and complete his work has also continued to improve. Yet he is still severely rejected by his classmates and often expresses anger and hostility toward those whom he most wants to befriend. His parents have expressed concern that he suffers from an extreme lack of self-esteem and worry that his continued lack of social skills will lead to negative long-term consequences. They have recently started to bring him to see a therapist for individual therapy, in hopes that "having someone to talk to" will help him work through what they perceive as his despair at not having any friends.

Alternative Case Conceptualization

This case could alternatively be conceptualized from a family systems perspective. For example, in a family with (a) an alcoholic father, (b) a mother who has struggled with alcoholism in her family of origin and whose allegiances are currently torn between her husband and oldest son, and (c) a boy struggling to identify with a father who displays periodic dyscontrol, a therapeutic focus on modifying the boy's problem behavior might miss the central family dynamics that serve to perpetuate maladaptive interaction patterns in all members. From an extreme family-systems perspective, in fact, Robert is the "identified patient" in a family with fundamental structural and relational difficulties, taking on the familial dysfunction through his symptoms. As such, attempting to "fix" his problem behavior through reinforcement (or any individually focused intervention) perpetuates the belief that he is the "problem" while failing to address the fundamental dynamics and imbalances in the family system.

A more moderate perspective (and one closer to our own viewpoint) would posit that: (a) ADHD is a "real" condition, with both biological and relational components; (b) this syndrome responds to empirically supported pharmacologic and psychosocial treatments (the latter typically involving active family intervention); and (c) the limits of such behavioral treatment are apparent in a case such as Robert's, where the initial success of clinical behavior therapy procedures was not maintained or extended fully into the domains of peer interactions and family functioning. Within this viewpoint, the inclusion of family therapy in a truly multimodal treatment package may have ensured stronger gains and more last-lasting progress for the entire family.

Additional perspectives are provided by a family systems point of view. First, many might consider that any behavioral efforts devoted towards ameliorating Robert's problematic behavior would prove futile unless the father's alcohol-related problems were first managed. Indeed, consistency in behavioral response is crucial for parents who implement social learning principles; and it is hard to imagine that a parent struggling with out-of-control drinking would be able to deliver positive and negative consequences in a balanced, "in control" manner. Second, at a deeper level, it may well be that Robert's searching for male role models will continue to be skewed when his father's drinking promotes inconsistency and a tendency to "shut down" Robert's sadness regarding his lack of friends. Third, despite many differences in emphasis and approach, nearly all family theories posit that a strong alliance must be formed between those adults who play parenting roles. In the case of a family in which one parent displays alcoholism, it would be nearly impossible for a unified, united parental alliance to thrive. Indeed, in the case of Robert, his mother came to overidentify with and overinvest in Robert's problems (witness her calling classmates of Robert to "solve" peer-related issues). Structural family theorists and therapists may well claim that such skewed boundaries – or, from another perspective, such enmeshment – must be the central focus of therapy, rather than the dispensing of more consistent reinforcers to the "problem child."

Fourth, extending a family systems perspective to Robert's own psychological processes would emphasize the powerlessness that Robert often experiences. At home, his father's alcohol abuse, erratic behavior, and encouragement of "toughness" on Robert's part have made it difficult for Robert to feel at all safe in expressing emotions (such as anger or sadness). Furthermore, Robert's mother feels guilty for the treatment that Robert receives from her husband, and she compensates through overinvolvement. This posture maintains Robert's feelings of inefficacy and reinforces his belief that he does not have the power or the ability to change his social standing. Importantly, such powerlessness might well lead to fear and anxiety in relation to peers. That is, Robert has been rejected by peers throughout grade school and has therefore leaned to alternate, defensively, between either withdrawing or aggressing toward peers in an effort to ward-off inevitable rejection. Although he exerts some control over his environment at school by exhibiting either extreme of behavior, the negative response he inevitably receives from peers leads to feelings of isolation and solitude, reinforcing his feelings of worthlessness and powerlessness. Without support from his parents, he will continue to be unequipped to master peer interactions. Thus, from a family systems perspective, it is the parents who would need to confront (a) substance abuse issues, (b) their own relationship, and (c) appropriate boundaries with their children before lasting progress could be made in terms of Robert's problem behavior and social relations.

At the very least, then, this family should benefit from family therapy as a supplement to their other treatments, in which issues of parental alliance, substance abuse, and appropriate intergenerational boundaries would be addressed directly. In the long run, it is conceivable that such a focus would help, more fundamentally, with Robert's continuing problems in the peer domain and with his long-term adjustment.

Alternative Case

As a brief counterpoint to the case of Robert, who was treated with combined psychosocial and pharmacologic interventions, we present the case of a boy treated with psychosocial interventions only. This second child, Sam, and his family received similar STP, classroom, and parent training interventions as Robert. Sam's case indicates a positive response to psychosocial interventions without stimulant medication.

Background Information and Referral Issues

Sam is a Latino male who was referred for treatment when he was seven and in second grade. He had been identified from a very young age as being unusually active and inattentive. His parents reported that they first became concerned about him during infancy, at which time he was active and had difficulty sleeping. At age three, both Sam's parents and daycare providers noted that he was overactive, displaying difficulty with focusing on tasks. In kindergarten, Sam's teacher reported that he had difficulties listening, staying seated, and following directions. Subsequent teachers commented on this distractibility and disorganization, his failure to complete classwork, and his disturbing peers. Sam's parents brought him to his pediatrician, who recognized symptoms of ADHD and prescribed Ritalin. Sam continued to take Ritalin inconsistently until his referral. Sam's parents reported increasing discomfort at treating their young child with medication, expressing interest in intensive psychosocial treatment.

Following the completion of an assessment battery, it was determined that Sam met criteria for ADHD, Combined type. It is noteworthy that (a) considerable symptoms of anxiety were present, including obsessional thoughts and some manifest fears and (b) his clinical presentation was more consistent with that of a boy with the Inattentive type – that is, he appeared "spacy," distractible, and socially awkward (rather than aggressive). Indeed, much of the overactive behavior that he displayed was in the form of fidgeting rather than running around a classroom or the home.

Treatment Strategy

The psychosocial treatment strategy used to treat Sam was quite similar to Robert's. Whereas Robert's key areas of impairment were inattention, aggression, and social problems, Sam's symptoms were primarily related to inattention, overactivity, and disorganization. Therefore, intervention for Sam targeted these ADHD-related symptoms. During the early days of the STP, Sam was observed to be disorganized (e.g., he constantly misplaced and lost his belongings), "spacy" (e.g., during computer activities he would stare blankly out the classroom window), disengaged and unfocused while in group activities (e.g., during sports-related group discussions he would play with dirt or grass), overactive, and impulsive (e.g., he had difficulties waiting his turn and standing in line). As noted above, the STP point system rewards cooperation, on-task behavior, and group participation. Sam responded well to this highly structured program. His number of appropriate contributions to group discussions, for example, increased from an average of five per day during the first week to 13 per day during the last week. His ability to pay attention improved as well: Accuracy rates for "attention questions" (queries about what had just been said during a group discussion or group activity) increased from an average of 40 to 60 percent across the program.

Sam also showed marked improvement following a classroom intervention, during which a paraprofessional aide worked with Sam, his teacher, and his parents on designing and implementing a contingency program that rewarded Sam for improved performance on targeted goals and monitoring his DRC. Target behaviors for the DRC reflected his difficulties with staying focused and organized: "Stay on task," "follow directions," "keep desk neat," and "remain seated." For the entire twelve-week classroom intervention Sam did exceptionally well, achieving weekly DRC averages of 90 percent and above. He continued to maintain these high DRC percentages after the paraprofessional left his classroom, at which time he and his teacher worked cooperatively on completing his DRC to send home each day.

During parent training (see more detailed description above), his parents learned how to implement a contingency program that targeted completing his homework and chores and staying organized. Specifically, they learned how to provide a limited number of prompts for Sam to continue working, instead of continuing with their habit of nagging him. With direct and consistent reinforcement at home, Sam began to work more independently and in a more organized fashion. Importantly, his parents also reported that their overall relationship with him had improved as well.

At the termination of his treatment, Sam no longer met criteria for ADHD, Combined Subtype. His parents have reported that he has continued to develop better work habits at home, although they still report concern about his difficulties staying organized. His teacher has reported that his behavior in the classroom has continued to improve as well. She does report, however, that he can still get distracted when he is not provided with structure and that the DRC helps him to stay organized and focused. Longer-term follow-up is in progress.

Moderators of Treatment Response

In intervention research, moderator variables are defined as preexisting factors (e.g., client age or gender, comorbid diagnostic patterns, familial socioeconomic status or SES) that influence the pattern of response to a given treatment or treatment comparison. In other words, SES could be claimed to moderate outcome if the pattern of response to intervention conditions differed for middle-class vs. impoverished families. Recently, the large-scale MTA (a multisite clinical trial for children with ADHD; see earlier section) reported on findings pertinent to moderators of outcome. In brief, although several potential moderator variables (male vs. female status of the participants, prior treatment with medication, comorbidity with ODD or CD) did not markedly influence the study's overall patterns of outcome, comorbidity with an anxiety disorder did moderate treatment response. Specifically, with respect to the outcome domain of ADHD symptomatology, those children in the MTA with comorbid anxiety disorders (e.g., separation anxiety, overanxious disorder, multiple phobias), showed an enhanced response to the intensive psychosocial/behavioral treatment condition (which excluded medication). In fact, for such children the psychosocial-only treatment did not differ in outcome from medication management or a combination treatment involving

behavioral plus medication components. In contrast, for the non-comorbid participants, medication and combination treatments outperformed psychosocial/beha-
vioral treatment for ADHD-related symptoms. In short, the presence of an
anxiety disorder in the child yielded relatively stronger benefits for an exclusively
psychosocial approach to treatment.

In many ways, the case of Sam exemplifies such a finding. He presented initially
as an anxious, largely inattentive/disorganized child; as just described, his performance without medication was uniformly strong. Readers should consult the
findings of the MTA Cooperative Group (1999a, 1999b) in the Recommended
Readings section for more details regarding this provocative finding.

Final Thoughts

In this chapter we have provided an overview of ADHD, outlined the several
types of social learning/behavioral treatments for this disorder (direct contingency
management, clinical behavior therapy, cognitive-behavioral interventions, and
social skills training), briefly reviewed evidence for the benefits yielded by such
treatments (as well as by medications), provided two case examples utilizing intensive behavioral procedures, and considered an alternate, family systems perspective. Our main conclusion is that behavioral interventions for ADHD are viable
but, ultimately, far from a panacea. Indeed, in the short term and on average,
pharmacologic treatments produce stronger effects; and evidence for incremental
benefits of combination treatment is uneven. Individual differences in treatment
response are the rule rather than the exception; clinical practice needs to adopt an
empirical stance whereby intervention effects are systematically evaluated for each
case. Furthermore, as we have emphasized, both behavioral and medication strategies for ADHD are palliative rather than curative, in that their benefits persist
only as long as the treatments are actively applied. ADHD, in fact, is best conceptualized as a chronic condition (about which the field still lacks essential information regarding underlying mechanisms); the most apt treatment model may well be
one of rehabilitation and accommodation rather than "cure." As better information is obtained, in future years, about responsible processes and mechanisms,
there is clearly hope for the development of more specific and more powerful
treatments.

Finally, we note that two essential aspects of psychosocial intervention with the
population under consideration are *coordination and collaboration.* That is, in light
of the multiple problems and impairments displayed by children and adolescents
with ADHD across diverse settings (home, school, peer groups, leisure activities)
and the need, in many instances, for treatments to span educational, family-
related, social, and behavioral goals, consistency in service delivery and coordination of efforts is paramount. If services are fragmented and if teachers, doctors,
psychologists, and paraprofessionals do not coordinate efforts, it is virtually a
guarantee that intervention effects will be limited and spotty. The disorganization
inherent in ADHD must be countered by intensive organization and coordination

among those attempting to forge more consistent environments and more productive performance.

References

Barkley, R. A. (1997). *ADHD and the nature of self-control*. New York: Guilford Press.
Barkley, R. A. (1998). *Attention-Deficit Hyperactivity Disorder: A Handbook for Diagnosis and Treatment.*(2nd ed). New York: Guilford Press.
Greenhill, L. L. (1998). Childhood attention deficit hyperactivity disorder: Pharmacological treatments. In P. E. Nathan & J. Gorman (eds) *A Guide to Treatments that Work*. New York: Oxford University Press. 42–64.
Greenhill, L. L., & Osman, B. O. (2000). *Ritalin: Theory and Practice*. (2nd ed.). New York: Mary Ann Liebert.
Hinshaw, S. P. (1999). Psychosocial intervention for childhood ADHD: Etiologic and developmental themes, comorbidity, and integration with pharmacotherapy. In D. Cicchetti & S. L. Toth (eds) *Rochester Symposium on Developmental Psychopathology, Vol. 9 Developmental Approaches to Prevention and Intervention*. Rochester, NY: University of Rochester Press. 211–270.
Hinshaw, S. P. (2000). Attention-deficit hyperactivity disorder: The search for viable treatments. In P. C. Kendall (ed.), *Child and Adolescent Therapy: Cognitive-behavioral Procedures*. New York: Guilford Press. 88–128.
Hinshaw, S. P., Klein, R. G., & Abikoff, H. (1998). Childhood attention deficit hyperactivity disorder: Nonpharmacological and combination treatments. In P. E. Nathan & J. Gorman (eds) *A Guide to Treatments that Work*. New York: Oxford University Press. 26–41.
Pelham, W. E., & Hinshaw, S. P. (1992). Behavioral intervention for attention-deficit hyperactivity disorder. In S. M. Turner, K. S. Calhoun, & H. E. Adams (eds) *Handbook of Clinical Behavior Therapy*. (2nd ed) New York: Wiley. 259–283.
Pelham, W. E., & Hoza, B. (1996). Intensive treatment: A summer treatment program for children with ADHD. In E. D. Hibbs & P. S. Jensen (eds) *Psychosocial Treatments for Child and Adolescent Disorders: Empirically Based Strategies for Clinical Practice*. Washington, DC: American Psychological Association, 311–340.
Pfiffner, L., & McBurnett, K. (1997). Social skills training with parent generalization: Treatment effects for children with attention deficit disorder. *Journal of Consulting and Clinical Psychology, 65*, 749–757.
Swanson, J. M. (1992). *School-based Assessment and Intervention for ADHD Students*. Irvine, CA: K.C. Press.
Tannock, R. (1998). Attention deficit hyperactivity disorder: Advances in cognitive, neurobiological, and genetic research. *Journal of Child Psychology and Psychiatry, 39*, 65–99.

Recommended Reading

Assessment:
Hinshaw, S. P., March, J. S., Abikoff, H., Arnold, L. E., Cantwell, D. P., Conners, C. K., et al. (1997). Comprehensive assessment of childhood attention-deficiency hyperactivity disorder in the context of a multisite, multimodal clinical trial. *Journal of Attention Disorders, 1*, 217–234.

Mash, E. J., & Barkley, R. A. (1996). *Behavioral Assessment of Childhood* Disorders (3ʳᵈ ed) New York: Guilford.

Shaffer, D., Richters, J., & Lucas, C. P. (1998). *Assessment in Child and Adolescent Psychopathology*. New York: Guilford.

Etiology:

Breslau, N., Brown, G. G., DelDotto, J. E., Kumar, S., Ezhuthachan, S., Andreski, P. (1996). Psychiatric sequelae of low birth weight at 6 years of age. *Journal of Abnormal Child Psychology, 24*, 385–400.

Hinshaw, S. P. (1994). *Attention Deficits and Hyperactivity in Children*. Thousand Oaks, CA: Sage.

Whitaker, A. H., Von Rossen, R., Feldman, J. F., Schonfeld, I. S., Pinto-Martin, J. A., *et al.* (1997). Psychiatric outcomes in low-birth-weight children at age 6 years: Relation to neonatal cranial ultrasound abnormalities. *Archives of General Psychiatry, 54*, 847–856.

Family and Peer Influences:

Anderson, C. A., Hinshaw, S. P., & Simmel, C. (1994). Mother-child interactions in ADHD and comparison boys: Relationships to overt and covert externalizing behavior. *Journal of Abnormal Child Psychology, 22*, 247–265.

Erhardt, D., & Hinshaw, S. P. (1994). Initial sociometric impressions of ADHD and comparison boys: Predictions from social behaviors and from nonbehavioral variables. *Journal of Consulting and Clinical Psychology, 62*, 833–842.

Whalen, C. K., & Henker, B. (1992). The social profile of attention deficit hyperactivity disorder: Five fundamental facets. *Child and Adolescent Psychiatric Clinics of North America, 1*, 395–410

Additional Treatment Strategies:

Hinshaw, S. P., Henker, B., & Whalen, C. K. (1984). Cognitive-behavioral and pharmacologic interventions for hyperactive boys: Comparative and combined effects. *Journal of Consulting and Clinical Psychology, 52*, 739–749.

Hinshaw, S. P., Henker, B., & Whalen, C. K. (1984). Self-control in hyperactive boys in anger-inducing situations: Effects of cognitive-behavioral training and methylphenidatde. *Journal of Abnormal Child Psychology, 12*, 55–77.

Combination Treatment:

Pelham, W. E., & Murphy, H. A. (1986). Behavioral and pharmacologic treatment of attention deficit and conduct disorders. In M. Hersen (ed.) *Pharmacological and Behavioral Treatment: An Integrative Approach*. New York: Wiley. 108–148.

MTA Cooperative Group, (1999a). A 14-month randomized clinical trial of treatment strategies for attention–deficit hyperactivity disorder (ADHD). *Archives of General Psychiatry, 56*, 1073–1086.

MTA Cooperative Group, (1999b). Moderators and mediators of treatment response for children with ADHD: The MTA study. *Archives of General Psychiatry, 56*, 1088–1096.

Part III

Mood Disorders

Chapter 6

Childhood Depression

Kevin D. Stark, Melanie Ballatore, Allison Hamff, Carmen Valdez and Lisa Selvig

Description of the Clinical Syndrome

DSM-IV Diagnostic Criteria for Childhood Depression

The most common criteria used for the diagnosis of major depression in children are found in DSM-IV, the fourth edition of *Diagnostic and statistical manual of mental disorders* (American Psychiatric Association, 1994). According to DSM-IV, the defining symptoms of depressive disorders are equivalent across children, adolescents, and adults. There are three primary diagnoses of unipolar depressive disorders including major depression, dysthymic disorder, and depressive disorder not otherwise specified, each of which is briefly described here. The quintessential symptom of depressive disorders is a mood disturbance, either dysphoria, irritability, or anhedonia. The mood disturbance is accompanied by a number of co-occurring symptoms that vary across the three diagnoses. In the case of major depression, the mood disturbance must last for a period of at least two weeks and must be present more often than not. In addition, at least four of the following symptoms must be present:

1) Significant, unintentional weight loss or gain (in children failure to gain weight as would be expected);
2) Insomnia or hypersomnia;
3) Psychomotor agitation or retardation;
4) Fatigue or loss of energy;
5) Feelings of worthlessness or excessive guilt;
6) Diminished concentration or ability to make decisions;
7) Recurrent thoughts of death, suicide, or suicide attempt.

These symptoms must cause impairment or distress in social, academic, occupational, or other areas of functioning. In order to meet criteria for major depression, these symptoms may not have been caused by the physiological effects of a substance or medical condition, and may not be due to bereavement.

Dysthymic disorder is often described as a chronic, low-grade depression. The depressed or irritable mood must be present for more days than not and last for

Handbook of Conceptualization and Treatment of Child Psychopathology, pages 107–132.

at least one year. In addition to the mood disturbance, at least two of the five following symptoms must be present:

1) Poor appetite or overeating;
2) Insomnia or hypersomnia;
3) Low energy or fatigue;
4) Poor concentration or difficulty making decisions; and/or
5) Feelings of hopelessness.

When individuals exhibit some of the symptoms of major depression or dysthymia but does not meet their diagnostic criteria, a diagnosis of depressive disorder not otherwise specified may be appropriate. For example, if a youngster is reporting a mood disturbance along with a number of additional symptoms, but the disturbance has lasted for less than one year, then a diagnosis of depressive disorder n.o.s. may be appropriate.

Developmental Considerations in Diagnosis

Although depressive disorders in children, adolescents, and adults are diagnosed according to the same criteria, it is important to recognize that certain features and symptoms of depression may manifest themselves differently across the life span. Indeed, certain depressive symptoms are more typical at different ages (Cicchetti & Toth, 1998). Of significance is the fact that depression in children may often be overlooked or not properly assessed. This is not surprising, considering that disruptive externalizing behavior attracts more attention as well as affects other people in a child's life (Hammen & Rudolph, 1996). In addition, because children are more likely to suffer from co-occurring conditions, it is particularly important that clinicians carefully consider differential diagnoses when dealing with children.

The only modification for young men and women of adult criteria for depression in DSM-IV is recognition that irritability may be the primary mood disturbance during childhood or adolescence. This modification reflects the fact that children may be less able to express feelings of dysphoria. They may express emotional distress through irritability and frustration (Hammen & Rudolph, 1996). As opposed to verbalizing their feelings, children may do this through temper tantrums and a variety of externalizing behavior.

In addition to presence of an irritable mood, there are a variety of other characteristics related to depression in youth, some of which apply primarily to children, some to adolescents, or to both. Tables 6.1 – 6.4 provide information regarding features of depression that tend to occur with relatively more frequency in either childhood, adolescence, or adulthood. It should be noted that while there are differences in the frequency of features commonly observed in depressive disorders during childhood and adolescence, rates of most symptoms in children and adolescents appear to be relatively similar (Kovacs, 1996).

Table 6.1: Shared Symptoms and Features in Childhood and Adolescent Depression.

- Irritable mood (may be substituted for depressed mood)
- Depressive episodes tend to co-occur in conjunction with other disorders (i.e., disruptive behavior disorders, ADHD and anxiety disorders)
- Excessive worrying
- Social withdrawal
- Drop in school performance
- Problems with self-esteem
- Higher rates of suicidal ideation
- Lower rates of delusions

Sources: Chambers, *et al.*, 1982; Cole, 1990; DSM-IV, 1994; Fleming, *et al.*, 1989; Kovacs & Goldston, 1991; Mitchell, *et al.*, 1988.

What are the symptoms and features that tend to be shared by both children and adolescents? Lowered school performance may be expected when youths experience impaired ability to think and concentrate, decreased productivity, fatigue, and psychomotor agitation or retardation. Lowered self-esteem, excessive worry, and social withdrawal also are symptoms observed in pre-pubertal children as well as adolescents. Both groups tend to have higher rates of suicidal ideation (Mitchell, McCauley, Burke, & Moss, 1988). However, relative to adults, children and adolescents are less likely to experience delusions.

Table 6.2: Symptoms and Features Observed Primarily in Depressed Children.

- Irritable mood accompanied by temper tantrums
- More likely to show depressed appearance
- Unlikely to report subjective dysphoria and hopelessness
- Unlikely to evidence hypersomnia or insomnia
- Sleep disturbances more likely to include nightmares
- More likely to exhibit psychomotor agitation
- Exaggerated somatic complaints
- Fewer appetite disturbances
- May fail to gain expected amount of weight
- May be less cooperative and more apathetic
- Experience higher rates of auditory hallucinations
- More likely to suffer from Separation Anxiety Disorder
- More likely to have phobias
- Less likely to make a serious suicide attempt

Sources: Carlson & Kashani, 1988; Chambers, *et al.*, 1982; DSM-IV, 1994; Fleming & Offord, 1990; Kashani, Holcomb, & Orvaschel, 1986; Kovacs, 1996; Mitchell, *et al.*, 1988; Rehm & Sharp, 1996; Ryan, *et al.*, 1987.

Table 6.3: Shared Features and Symptoms Observed in Adolescent and Adult Depression.

- More likely to report subjective dysphoria and hopelessness
- More likely to evidence sleep disturbances (hypersomnia or insomnia)
- More likely to develop eating disorders
- Experience higher rates of weight loss
- More likely to suffer from substance abuse disorders
- Less likely to exhibit a depressed appearance
- Experience lower rates of auditory hallucinations

Sources: Carlson & Kashani, 1988; Chambers, *et al.*, 1982; DSM-IV, 1994; Fleming & Offord, 1990; Mitchell, *et al.*, 1988; Ryan, *et al.*, 1987.

Table 6.4: Symptoms and Features Observed Primarily in Depressed Adults.

- Evidence higher rates of anhedonia
- Evidence higher rates of diurnal variation
- Evidence higher rates of vegetative and melancholic features
- More likely to make serious suicide attempts
- More likely to experience early morning awakening
- Evidence increased psychomotor retardation
- Less likely to exhibit depressed appearance
- Less likely to have somatic complaints
- Less likely to have poor self-esteem
- Experience fewer feelings of guilt
- Experience higher rates of delusions

Sources: Carlson & Kashani, 1988; Chambers, *et al.*, 1982; Mitchell, *et al.*, 1988.

In comparison with depressed adolescents and adults, depressed children are much less likely to report subjective dysphoria and feelings of hopelessness (Ryan, et al., 1987). They are more likely to show a depressed appearance (Carlson & Kashani, 1988), exhibit psychomotor agitation, and have exaggerated somatic complaints (Ryan et al., 1987). In addition, children are more likely to suffer from separation anxiety disorder and phobias (Ryan, et al., 1987), as well as being more uncooperative and apathetic (Kashani, Holcomb, & Orvaschel, 1986). Although commonly seen in depressed adolescents and adults, children are much less likely to develop either sleep (Mitchell, et al., 1988) or appetite disturbances (Fleming & Offord, 1990). If depressed children do have sleep problems, it is likely to be due to nightmares (Rehm & Sharp, 1996). Instead of actually losing weight, children may simply fail to gain as expected. In addition, children are less likely to make serious suicide attempts (Birmaher & Brent, 1998).

Depressive disorders appear to present a somewhat different set of symptoms across developmental groups, but the core symptoms of depression are parallel across age groups. Therefore, although there are important differences in specific symptoms and features, the diagnosis of depression throughout the life span appears to encapsulate the same psychological entity (Kovacs, 1996).

Description of Two Treatment Approaches for Depression

The two approaches to treatment that have received the most empirical support for depressed individuals, cognitive-behavioral therapy (CBT) and interpersonal therapy (IPT), will be described in the following sections. When these two treatment approaches are properly implemented, they have more in common than they differ. In fact, it may be due to the manyshared components and the time-limited and active approach to treatment, that both interventions are effective. The senior author is a cognitive-behavioral therapist. Thus, descriptions that follow of CBT relative to IPT are more detailed. This is not meant to demean the alternative approach; rather, it is a reflection of the author's preferred mode of conceptualizing and treating depressed youths.

Cognitive Behavioral Therapy for Depressed Youths

Overview
Based on research and a model of childhood depression (Stark, Boswell-Sander, Yancy, Bronik, & Hoke, 2000), a cognitive behavioral treatment program for depressed youths has been developed (Stark, 1990). A therapist's manual that describes the intervention in a session-by-session format (Stark & Kendall, 1996) and children's workbook (Stark, Kendall, McCarthy, Thomeer, and Baron, 1996) have been published. Modifications are made to the standard procedure to address environmental disturbances such as parental psychopathology, physical or sexual abuse, substance abuse, marital discord, neglect, and abandonment. Based on a review of the treatment manuals of the existing empirically-based cognitive behavioral treatments for depressed youths, the treatment program described in this chapter appears to be prototypical.

   Emphases during the initial sessions of CBT are on developing the therapeutic relationship and assessment of the child and the primary environments in which he or she functions. A solid therapeutic relationship and an empathic understanding of the child are necessary for successful treatment. The therapeutic relationship is seen as an interpersonal milieu that in and of itself facilitates the learning of new ways of thinking about the self and relationships with others. The therapeutic relationship provides the child with new learning experiences about his or her social behavior and the therapist models appropriate interpersonal behavior. In addition, the interactions provide the therapist with an opportunity to assess the youngster's social behavior and the ways that he or she interprets social interactions. The therapeutic alliance facilitates acquisition and application of coping skills. While the therapeutic relationship is viewed as an important and necessary component of treatment, it is not sufficient for producing clinically significant change.

Formal and informal assessment procedures are used to acquire an understanding of the child's experience of his or her depressive symptoms. As we have discussed elsewhere, results of the assessment of relevant treatment constructs included cognitive, behavioral/social, familial, parenting style, and parental adjustment along with a medical exam guide treatment. The interested reader is referred to Stark, *et al.* (2000).

Significant others from within the child's primary environments are also participants in treatment through parent training, family therapy, and consultation. Intervention with the parents, family, and school is necessary to: (a) support the individual work being completed with the child; (b) encourage the development of new adaptive schema and rules for processing information; (c) encourage the use of coping skills in the extra-therapy environment; and (d) change environmental events that are contributing to the development and maintenance of the cognitive, interpersonal, and familial disturbances that underlie the depressive symptoms.

Treatment Program

During the first few sessions, the cognitive-behavioral therapist educates the child-client about depression and the model of depression. In particular, the child is taught that a relationship exists between mood, behavior, thinking, and brain chemistry. In addition, the youngster is educated about therapy and how to become a "good client."

During the second session, the child and his or her parents work with the therapist to generate a list of pleasant activities. The list consists of recreational, social, and other activities that the child enjoys. The parents support is secured in terms of transportation and sometimes expenses. Subsequently, a daily schedule is created and the child is instructed to self-monitor engagement in the pleasant activities. The list is expanded over the sessions as more "fun" activities are identified, and mastery activities as well as other desirable events and thoughts are added to the list. Mastery activities are added as a means of helping to structure and break down these tasks into manageable pieces. In addition, completion of these tasks reduces stress. Over the course of treatment, the child is asked to increase engagement in pleasant activities and to self-monitor and self-record in a workbook daily mood and engagement in pleasant events. The mood rating and frequency of pleasant events are graphed for each day, which helps children to see how mood and behavior are related. Activity scheduling appears to raise mood, and children can be taught to "do something fun" as a means of managing their depressive affect.

Problem Solving Set

Depressed youths often experience more stressors in their lives. Thus, it is important for them to have a general tool that they can use to guide their attempts to reduce and cope with stress. Problem solving is modeled by the therapist throughout treatment and directly taught to the child-client over sessions four to twelve.

During this time, the children learn a modified version of Kendall's (Kendall & Braswell, 1993) procedure. Due to the pessimism of depressed youths, a "psych-up" step has been added between problem identification and solution generation. The youngsters identify and use their own preferred self-statements for getting motivated to attack the problem. In addition to direct education, games are used to teach youngsters each of the six problem solving steps and how they are applied. After the children understand each step, and they can apply it to playing games (they are asked to think out loud whenever they take a turn), they begin to apply problem solving to hypothetical problems generated by the therapist. Then they apply problem solving to their own intrapersonal problems, and finally to their own interpersonal problems. The therapist coaches the children through the process and provides them with constructive feedback. It is especially important to help the youngsters to counter their negative thinking that short-circuits or prematurely terminates the process. Daily problem-solving diaries are included in the children's workbook and they are completed as therapeutic homework. These diaries help the children to master each of the steps, to compile a list of the problems faced between meetings, and to structure their attempts to independently solve problems.

Cognitive Interventions
The therapist is continually listening for examples of depressive thinking. Negative thoughts can be elicited using a variety of questions, and they are readily evident in the depressed youngster's descriptions of his or her daily experiences and expectations for the future. Based on the therapist's knowledge of the child, he or she must determine whether the negative, depressive thoughts reflect objective reality, or whether they are negatively distorted. Depressed youths tend to negatively distort their perceptions and memories. However, it is important to note that the schemas that guide the information processing of children are still forming and often reflect their realities. In these cases, negative thoughts may be an accurate reflection of the child's unfortunate situation. In other cases, negative thinking no longer is an accurate reflection of what is happening in their lives. Rather, it is an unrealistically negative (distorted) view of what is happening. Early in treatment, as rapport is being established, the therapist might decide to record the child's negative thoughts into his or her notes rather than try to restructure them. As therapy progresses, the therapist uses cognitive restructuring procedures to counter the distorted thoughts. After the therapist has modeled this process for the first 12 sessions, the children are taught to identify and restructure their own distorted thoughts and beliefs. Ultimately, the goal of CBT for depression is to build-up positive schema and weaken the negative counterparts.

Depressed children are taught various strategies for altering their maladaptive cognitions. With one exception, these treatment components are directly taught to children around the twelfth meeting so they can become more focused on negative material which would have exacerbated depressive symptoms early in treatment. Altering faulty information processing through self-monitoring of pleasant activities, desired events, and positive thoughts is the exception to this rule. It is included early in treatment because it is designed to redirect the youngster's attention from negative thoughts and feelings to enjoyable activities, desired events, and positive thoughts, which produces an elevation in mood and energy.

The consciousness of depressed children is dominated by negative automatic thoughts. As these thoughts are identified, cognitive restructuring procedures along with cognitive modeling and self-instructional training are used to directly alter them. Automatic thoughts are targeted by the therapist throughout treatment, and the youngsters learn how to identify and modify them on their own as therapy progresses.

When a depressed child is having an especially difficult time countering thoughts, self-instructional training can be used. Self-instructional training (Meichenbaum, 1977) is used to help children internalize any set of self-statements that guide their thinking and/or behavior. Any content of thoughts can be taught. This is especially useful with children who are experiencing a deficit in their verbal mediational skills; however, it can also be used to teach children thoughts they can use to counter negative thinking.

Depressed children evaluate their performances, possessions, and personal qualities more negatively than the non-depressed and their self-evaluations tend to be negatively distorted. One of the primary objectives of CBT for depression is to enhance the youngster's self-schema. Thus, a deeper level of change is the ultimate goal of CBT. During the final six sessions, children are taught to evaluate themselves more reasonably and positively when it is realistic to do so using cognitive restructuring procedures. During this process they learn to recognize their positive attributes, outcomes, and possessions. Self-monitoring of supportive evidence is used as a means of solidifying the new self-schema. Over the course of treatment, the therapist and children continually identify and review evidence that supports a positive self-schema. In some instances, the children's negative self-evaluations are accurate and they can benefit from change. In such instances, the goal of treatment becomes one of helping youngsters to translate personal deficiencies into realistic goals, and then to develop and carry out plans for attaining self-improvement. This process of working toward self-improvement is the final stage of treatment as the youngsters bring all of the previous coping strategies to bear on self-improvement.

Interpersonal Behavior

The relationship that develops between the child and therapist has therapeutic value. The youngster learns how to trust someone and how to deal in a healthy fashion with appropriate intimacy. In addition, through the acceptance provided by the therapist, the youngster learns that he or she is likable and worthy. As social disturbances become evident during the natural exchanges between the child and therapist, they are directly addressed through feedback and by teaching the youngster more adaptive behavior.

Our own research indicates that primary stressors experienced by youths are interpersonal in nature. Typically they involve conflict between the youngster and his or her parents or friends. Thus, the youngsters' relationships within the family and with peers are explored. When they are not adaptive or satisfying, they become one of the foci of treatment. From this perspective, an attempt would be made to change the interactions themselves as well as the thoughts and beliefs that underlie the behavior of each individual involved in the interactions. The target of the intervention varies greatly and includes maladaptive beliefs of an individual, coercive interchanges, structural variables, or social skills deficits.

Parents

Parents and teachers are seen as a central link between the child's acquisition of skills during therapy sessions and their application to the natural environment. Parents begin this training component at the same time as the child begins therapy. The parent training program is designed to foster a more positive family environment through teaching the parents how to (a) use positive behavior management techniques, (b) reduce conflict, (c) increase the child's role in the family decision-making process, and (d) improve their child's self-esteem.

One of the central components of the parent-training program is teaching parents to use positive behavior management procedures. To accomplish this objective, procedures have been borrowed from Barkley (1997). Initially, parents are taught to recognize and attend to positive affect and behavior through a series of role-play activities. When they can clearly recognize positive behavior as it occurs, can appropriately comment on it, and understand the notion of extinguishing undesirable behavior through non-attention, the parents are assigned the task of spending 15-20 minutes each day playing with their child. They are instructed to make it an enjoyable activity in which they strive to pay particular attention to their child's positive actions. These positive actions are socially reinforced and recorded in a diary by the parent throughout the week.

During the next few meetings, parents are taught how to use reinforcement techniques and informed of the impact reinforcement has on their child's mood and self-esteem. Once again, role-play activities are used to facilitate acquisition of these skills. Parents collaboratively work with the therapist to identify targets for change and to develop plans to use reinforcement procedures to produce change.

In addition to reinforcement techniques, parents are taught the value of praise. Specifically, praise helps children to boost self-esteem and can increase occurrence of desirable behavior. Thus, parents are instructed to praise their child a minimum of four to six times per day. Moreover, they are taught to be concrete, genuine, and specific when giving praise. They also are cautioned against using hyperbole and left-handed compliments with their child. During this time, as parents are increasing the use of praise, they are also asked to note how often they criticize their depressed child. The goal of this activity is to eventually reduce number of criticisms by one each day until they are eliminated.

Parents are then taught how to avoid getting caught in a coercive cycle. Parents are taught to give clear and effective directives, the time-out procedure, and use of natural consequences. Following such training, parents are given an additional homework assignment to monitor their effectiveness in implementing the new disciplinary procedures and to record any problematic situations for consideration at the next meeting.

Some of the difficulties in the relationship between depressed youths and their parents stem from the parent's inability to listen empathically. Through education, parents can learn how to express empathy. Families of depressed children often fail to engage in recreational activities. Thus, it is important to teach these families to have fun. Parents are asked to identify various low-cost/no-cost activities in which the family can participate. Problem solving is then used to facilitate the scheduling of such activities during the week. In addition to engaging in pleasant activities, parents are instructed to self-monitor the impact of these events on the family.

Interpersonal Therapy

Over the past few years, Mufson and colleagues have adapted IPT to the treatment of depressed adolescents (Mufson, 1993). The primary therapeutic goals of IPT are to decrease depressive symptoms and to improve interpersonal functioning. To accomplish these goals, the youngster and the therapist identify one or two problem areas from among the following: (a) grief, (b) interpersonal role disputes, (c) role transitions, (d) interpersonal deficits, and (e) difficulties in single parent families.

Treatment is divided into three phases, each of which consists of four sessions. During the initial phase, problem areas are identified, a rationale for treatment is provided, a formal therapeutic contract is written and signed, and the adolescent's role in therapy is defined. Some psychoeducation about the nature and impact of depression is provided to the youngster and his or her parents. The therapist works with the youngster and his or her parents to ensure that the child is socially engaged in the family, school, and with friends. Parents are asked to encourage their child to engage in as many normal activities as possible.

During the middle phase of treatment, the nature of each previously identified problem is clarified, effective strategies for attacking the problems are identified, and relevant plans are developed and implemented. When developing plans, there is an overarching ambition to improve interpersonal functioning. Youngsters are taught to monitor the experience of depressive symptoms and their emotional experiences.

To achieve these therapeutic objectives, the therapist utilizes exploratory questioning, encouragement of affect, linking affect with events, clarification of conflicts, communication analysis, and behavior change techniques such as role-playing. Throughout these sessions, the therapist provides the youngster with feedback about symptom change in an attempt to enhance "self-esteem." The therapist and youngster work as a team. Together, they assess accuracy of the initial formulation of problem areas and evaluate the impact of ongoing events occurring outside the sessions for their impact on depressive symptoms. The therapist evaluates the youngster's interpersonal style through their within-session interactions. With the youngster's informed permission, the family is encouraged to support the treatment goals.

The final phase of treatment, Sessions nine to twelve, comprise the termination phase. The primary objectives of this phase are to prepare the youngster for termination, and to establish a sense of personal competence for dealing with future problems. The youngster's feelings about termination are discussed and feelings of competence are engendered.

Case Example

Cathy is an eleven year-old girl who is in the sixth grade of a suburban middle school. Historically, she achieved at an above average level. However, her grades have slipped over the past few grading periods. She is well behaved and respectful of teachers and other school staff. She dislikes it when other students misbehave in class. She is unaware why this bothers her, but when it happens, she feels angry and anxious and tries to stop it by telling the teacher. Cathy has a few girlfriends, but she only sees them at school.

Cathy lives with her father, mother, and eight year-old brother. She is a third generation Mexican American. Her father is in middle management at a high tech company. Mr. Hernandez regularly works until 7:00 p.m. on weekdays, and until 3:00 p.m. on Saturdays. When he is at home in the evening, pages from work commonly interrupt his free time, and he "plugs in" at home to continue his work. He is a strong father who believes in a lot of discipline in the house and doesn't believe that he should take part in the day-to-day running of the household. He is warm and strict. Mrs. Hernandez has been a "stay-at-home-mom" since the birth of their second child. She has been grappling with a depressive disorder since adolescence. She experiences irritability as the primary mood disturbance. She tends to see misbehavior in her children when it has not occurred. In addition, she is less capable of giving her children emotional support, love, and affection. Due to excessive fatigue and a sleep disturbance, she spends much time resting. Consequently, Cathy is given caring responsibility for her younger brother. When her brother misbehaves, Cathy is held responsible. Her caregiving responsibilities prevent her from being able to participate in her own social and recreational activities. The mother's depressive symptoms have led to marital discord. This conflict has spilled over to the children. The parents argue with each other and then, due to irritability, react angrily toward their children. The emotional tone of the household is one of conflict. As Cathy approaches home after school, she can feel her mood drop in anticipation of conflict with her brother, her mother, and between her parents.

Cathy's aunt was instrumental in her parents pursuing a referral for treatment. Cathy's father was reluctant to get help, as he perceived her depressive symptoms as laziness. The initial contact was with a psychiatrist in private practice.

CBT Case Conceptualization

When conceptualizing Cathy's case from the CBT perspective, the therapist refers to current models of depression and then individualizes a model to fit her specific characteristics. The CBT model of depression is evolving as new research is reported. Current research that evaluates tenets of models of depression and other research that has implications for conceptualizing the disorder are integrated into, or change, the therapist's working model. Current cognitive-behavioral models of depression are stress diathesis models in which stress interacts with a diathesis within the child to produce and maintain a depressive disorder. From this perspective, there is no single diathesis; rather, it is recognized that multiple etiological pathways may exist. It is believed that depression is associated with disturbances in cognitive, interpersonal, familial and biochemical functioning as well as deficits in critical emotion regulation skills. Furthermore, a reciprocal relationship exists between these disturbances, and these disturbances reciprocally interact with stress. Thus, a disturbance in one area would affect, and be affected by, each of the other domains. For example, a biochemical disturbance would affect mood, vegetative functioning, and information processing and leave the youngster more vulnerable to the effects of stress. The disturbance in mood and information processing would feedback into, and impact on, the biochemical disturbance, and they would affect the youngster's behavior which in turn impacts relationships with others. The behavior and reactions of significant others may be misperceived due to distortions in information processing which lead to a confirmation of, or the activation of, dysfunctional schema. Once activated, these dysfunctional schema guide information processing. Depending on the age and learning history of the youngster, the schema may be more or less structuralized and thus open to, and shaped by, new experiences.

Since Cathy's mother is depressed, Cathy may have a genetic predisposition toward depression. This predisposition could have led to development of a neurochemical diathesis. Her depressed mother, the marital discord, and childcare responsibilities for her brother are chronic stressors. Due to her mother's tendency to see misbehavior when Cathy has not misbehaved, and her tendency to blame Cathy for her brother's misbehavior, she is frequently punished and a negative affective atmosphere exists in the home. Moreover, since her mother spends so much time "resting," and her father is over-involved in work, they have failed to engage Cathy in the types of interactions necessary to teach affect regulation skills. Attachment behavior is characterized by an insecure style and the internal working model is one of contradictions. Sometimes Cathy is smothered with affection and other times her parents are cold, distant, and hostile. Her interpersonal schema defines relationships as fraught with pain and unreturned love.

Children are active constructors of their environments both in terms of their actions and with respect to their perceptions of the environment. They try to make sense of, or derive meaning from, their interactions with the environment and especially from interactions with significant others. These experiences and interactions serve as learning experiences that lead to the development of the schema that eventually guide information processing. The message that Cathy perceives from repeated punitive interactions with her parents would be "I'm bad." In addition, lack of emotional availability of her mother and father along with the negative interactions would lead to the self-perception; "I'm unlovable." Since these messages are communicated often and they are accompanied by other learning experiences that communicate the same message, this self view has been internalized and structuralized as a core schema which guides her information processing. The other schemas that comprise the internal working model have become structuralized in a similar fashion and guide interpersonal behavior. Cathy's schema serve as filters that eliminate schema-inconsistent information and process schema-consistent information which further strengthens the developing negative sense of self and the rest of her internal working model. It is apparent that she makes a number of information processing errors including emotional reasoning, selective abstraction, minimization and maximization, and, all or nothing thinking. Cathy's consciousness is flooded with negative thoughts that represent a negative distortion in her thinking. Furthermore, such a negative style of thinking and other depressive symptoms as well as her "standoffish" behavior may be "putoffish" to peers, which leads to isolation. Given Cathy's learning history, it also is possible that the cognitive disturbance was the diathesis for the development of the depressive disorder.

Cathy is unlikely to get close to others as she expects to be hurt and rejected. Thus, Cathy's behavior reinforces her internal working model and prevents her from having schema inconsistent learning experiences. During times of stress, Cathy does not seek social support given her history of not getting support. Thus, she does not have access to the interpersonal warmth and security that comes from social support. In addition, she does not have access to consoling conversations with significant others that often produce a restructuring of beliefs about the situation and how it is likely to impact her life. The extent to which children feel supported, safe, and secure predicates their use of adaptive mood regulation strategies. Thus, Cathy fails to learn essential mood regulation skills.

It has been hypothesized that core schemas are formed through early learning experiences and communications within the family. We call this the cognitive interpersonal pathway. In the case of Cathy, schema that make her vulnerable to stress may develop as a result of interactions that are characteristic of an insecure attachment, negative evaluative statements directed at her from her parents, and her parents' over-reliance on punitive procedures which communicate the message that she is "bad" or "unlovable," the world is an unpleasant place, and caregivers hurt you. Cathy, through genetic predispositions and temperament, plays a role in constructing this environment. Furthermore, her behavior impacts the environment in a fashion that supports the developing schema.

It is within the family milieu that a child develops crucial attachment behavior, interpersonal skills, and the expectations that guide interpersonal relationships. In Cathy's case, she has learned an angry style of interacting and one in which rejection or a lack of support is expected. This rejection in turn leads to development of a sense of self that is comprised of a poorly developed positive self-schema and a more active negative self-schema, a negative world schema, and negative schema about interpersonal relationships as well as the self within these relationships. In addition, such rejection leads to withdrawal to her home, which reinforces the negative perceptions and behavior, and prevents her from having corrective learning experiences. The impact is further heightened through negative distortions in information processing and a deficit in mood regulation skills. Affect interacts with the previously mentioned variables in a reciprocal fashion. Cathy may experience dysphoria due to the perception of social or familial rejection, from the atmosphere of conflict and punishment within the family milieu, or from biochemical imbalances. Similarly, the mood disturbance impacts Cathy's information processing and behavior. Cathy lacks the skills necessary for moderating or changing her dysphoria and the stress in her life.

Stressful events have both a direct impact on biological functioning and an indirect effect through the individual's perceptions of stress and the potential harm that he or she may experience. Cathy, due to errors in information processing, believes that she does not possess the skills or abilities to effectively cope with stress. In addition, she perceives a wide variety of events as potentially harmful, which leads to greater stress. Social support is a buffer for the effects of stress, but due to her internal working model, she is not likely to seek social support or to receive it. Stress appears to impact the hypothalamic-adrenal system causing the adrenal glands to over-secrete hydrocortisone or cortisol. When stressed, hypothalamic neurons, regulated by norepinephrine neurons in the *locus coeruleus*, secrete corticotropin-releasing hormone, which stimulates the production of adrenocorticotropin (ACTH) by the pituitary. ACTH then stimulates the adrenal glands to produce cortisol. Stress-related hormones and neurotransmitters influence many aspects of cerebral functioning. This may lead to a disruption in the neurotransmitter system as well as producing many of Cathy's symptoms of depression.

Cognitive Behavioral Therapy

Cognitive behavioral therapy is guided by an assessment of the child, caregivers, and the primary environments within which the child functions. Referral for a physical examination is prudent to determine whether a medical condition may be underlying the child's depressive symptoms. In addition, the youngster's family is assessed to identify unhealthy structural parameters, interactions that lead to and maintain maladaptive schema, maladaptive parenting behavior, and parental psychopathology. The assessment process may involve use of formal instruments, but more often uses the clinical interview and observations to complete the hypothesis and testing process. It is important to emphasize that this is a fluid process that begins during the initial contact and continues throughout treatment. As disturbances are identified, relevant treatment procedures are chosen and implemented.

The child-client's level of cognitive development determines the methods used for engaging him/her in treatment and the extent to which behavioral and cognitive change techniques are used. With younger children, more play and other enactive methods are used as the medium for teaching the youngsters coping and emotion regulation skills and cognitive strategies. With older children and adolescents, a more traditional talk/interview format can be used. In general, the younger the child, the more reliance on the use of behavioral procedures for teaching coping skills and the greater the emphasis on parent involvement and parent training. When intervening at the cognitive level with young children, self-instructional training would be used to teach more adaptive thinking. With more introspective, insightful, and cognitively mature children, a more traditional cognitive restructuring procedure would be used.

Cathy is at an in-between age where it is important to be more explicit when teaching her how to identify and restructure depressive thoughts. She has the ability to introspect, self-monitor, and evaluate her own thoughts. Due to some initial mistrust, a combination of enactive procedures followed by the traditional interview format was followed for Cathy. The activities served as a non-threatening way to build trust and then later in treatment she seemed to enjoy the verbal interchanges.

An important consideration in development of the treatment plan is the mental health of the youngster's parents. In Cathy's case, her mother was depressed and her father was disengaged due to work demands. One of the goals of treatment was to get Cathy's mother into treatment. Another goal was to explore with her father possible ways to reduce the amount of time he worked and to increase his involvement in the family. Given the parents' reluctance to seek treatment for Cathy, it was important to establish rapport and some credibility with them, especially with her father since he was the primary decision-maker.

Mr. Hernandez's insurance company referred Cathy to a psychiatrist who requested that both parents be present for the initial evaluation. The psychiatrist diagnosed Cathy with a moderately severe case of major depressive disorder and her assessment revealed that Mrs. Hernandez also was experiencing an episode of major depression. The psychiatrist prescribed an anti-depressant that had provided Mrs. Hernandez with relief in the past, and since she responded well to it, Cathy was given a prescription for the same drug. The psychiatrist emphasized the importance of combining somatic with psychological treatments for both Cathy and her mother. She recommended that they contact one of the authors to work with Cathy and another psychologist to work with her mother. Mrs. Hernandez said she had already "successfully dealt with her past" in previous counseling so she needed no further treatment. During subsequent meetings to evaluate the impact and safety of the medication, the psychiatrist learned that Cathy's mother was experiencing intense guilt about her daughter's depressive disorder and thus avoiding involvement in Cathy's treatment. She continued to recommend that Mrs. Hernandez contact a psychologist and become involved in her daughter's treatment by at least taking Cathy to some of the sessions so that she could meet the therapist who was working with her daughter.

For the first four meetings, Mr. Hernandez brought Cathy to her therapy appointments. An attempt was made to engage him in Cathy's treatment from the beginning by meeting with him first to discuss his concerns. He was relieved to learn about the nature of cognitive behavioral therapy and liked the idea that his daughter was going to learn skills for coping with stress, her depressive symptoms, and negative thinking. He also was pleased that the therapist was going to set aside time each week to discuss the coping strategies that Cathy was learning and how the parents could help her to apply them. He was informed that Cathy would complete a symptom checklist (Stark, 1990) every week to track the impact of therapy. Mr. Hernandez understood and appreciated the idea of "accountability" for therapy. Since Cathy reported improvement over time on the checklists, he became invested in Cathy's treatment. Therapy sessions were typically divided into 40 minutes of individual time for Cathy, five to ten minutes of bridging time in which Cathy taught the therapeutic strategy of the day to the parent who brought her to the meeting, and the remaining ten–15 minutes was spent discussing how the parents could support Cathy's application of the skills outside of the meetings.

The first meeting with Cathy was devoted to establishing rapport, laying the foundation for a solid therapeutic relationship, providing her with an overview and the rationale for treatment, discussing her role in treatment, and completion of some formal assessment measures that would be used to guide treatment (Stark, *et al.*, 2000). Cathy was not forthcoming in the initial meetings, rather, she was quiet and provided minimal answers to questions. Thus, it was decided that more enactive procedures would be used to engage her in treatment. Confidentiality and the limits of confidentiality were discussed. The therapist noted that he typically met with parents for about 15 minutes at the end of each meeting to describe the skills that they had worked on and to help the parents learn how to help their child apply these skills. The therapist pointed out that he would not divulge what Cathy said during the meetings, and she was given the choice to remain in the room during this portion of the meeting or to go out in the waiting room and play.

Activity scheduling was one of the main foci of the second through fourth meetings. Cathy was not socially or recreationally active due to her childcare responsibilities and the belief that others would reject her. At the start of these meetings, Cathy was asked to rate her mood in general for the day, and her current mood, on a 0 to 10 Likert-type scale. Subsequently, she chose a game to play with the therapist. As the game was nearing completion, she was asked to once again to rate her mood at the moment. By comparing the present mood rating to the others, she was able to see that doing something enjoyable helped her to feel better. Subsequently, Cathy and the therapist generated a list of activities that she enjoyed doing. When her father joined Cathy and the therapist, he was asked to add to the list any activities he thought Cathy enjoyed. A schedule of pleasant activities was created for the week, and Mr. Hernandez was encouraged to help Cathy remember to follow the schedule and to assist her with transport and some money. Since many of the things that Cathy wanted to do involved Mr. and Mrs. Hernandez, he was asked to discuss with his wife her involvement in the plan and the possibility of joining the meetings. In addition, the importance of freeing Cathy from childcare responsibilities to engage in these activities was discussed.

During the third and fourth meetings, the pleasant activities schedule was expanded to include examples of pleasant things that happen (e.g., receive a compliment, get a good grade), positive thoughts, mastery activities (completion of household chores, school projects, etc). Cathy was asked to self-monitor occurrence of pleasant events on diary sheets provided in her workbook when they occurred (or as close in time as possible) and then to rate her mood for the day just before going to bed. After generating the list, Cathy was given practice at self-monitoring and self-recording while playing a game. Once again, Cathy, her father, and the therapist created a pleasant activity schedule for the week and used problem solving to identify impediments to following the schedule and to generate plans for overcoming these impediments. Before the end of the third meeting, Cathy's father asked her to play in the waiting room. After Cathy left, he expressed concerns about his wife as she was experiencing considerable guilt about their daughter's depressive disorder. He was encouraged to talk with his wife about the importance of joining him for Cathy's next meeting.

In addition to working on the pleasant events schedule during the fourth meeting, Cathy was directly taught the problem solving steps. Each step was written down on a dry erase board and defined by the therapist. Cathy recorded the steps in her workbook in her own words. Then, Cathy and the therapist played a game as a means of illustrating and practicing the application of the problem solving steps. The therapist modeled the process during each turn by thinking out loud, and he coached her through the process and provided her with feedback as she verbalized her thoughts while completing her turn. During the bridging portion of the fourth meeting, Cathy taught her father and mother the problem solving steps. Subsequently, she was encouraged to play in the waiting room while her mother was given an opportunity to get to know the therapist. During this time, Mrs. Hernandez voiced her concerns about causing her daughter's depressive disorder and felt some relief when the therapist noted that there was no way to determine what caused Cathy's depressive disorder, reminding her that even if she passed on a genetic predisposition to depression – she had no choice in this, that she obviously loved her daughter and did not intentionally do anything to harm her, and that she was doing the right thing by getting her daughter treatment and becoming involved in the treatment. She appeared to experience some relief from the discussion and agreed to regularly attend Cathy's meetings as well as a series of meetings between both parents and the therapist to work on methods for helping Cathy to apply the skills. It was noted that Cathy would benefit the most from therapy if her parents could model for her the use of the skills as well as other emotion regulation skills.

The primary focus of the fifth through twelfth meetings was on learning and applying problem solving. Until Cathy clearly understood the meaning and application of the steps, she applied problem solving to game play. Then, with the therapist's help, she began to apply problem solving to hassles in her daily life during the therapy sessions. As part of her between meeting homework, she wrote down problems that she faced in a "problem-solving diary" in her workbook. In addition, she noted in the diary the clues that told her that a problem existed. Problem identification was the focus of sessions four, five, and six. During sessions seven and eight, the emphasis was on getting and staying psyched-up for dealing with problems even if she faced multiple problems or was unsuccessful in her initial attempts to solve a problem. During sessions nine and ten, the emphasis was on solution generation. Sessions eleven and twelve were devoted to choosing the best plan, monitoring implementation of the plan, and self-reinforcement for trying to solve the problem or choosing another plan if the original plan seemed not to be working as desired. In addition to working on problem solving, Cathy continued to self-monitor engagement in pleasant events through the 12th meeting. During sessions, Cathy and the therapist graphed the number of pleasant events that she checked off each day and her mood for the day. This graph was used to identify especially mood enhancing activities, and she was encouraged to use such activities as a way to cope with sadness and anger.

During the sixth meeting, while Cathy was talking about trying to increase her engagement in recreational and social activities, she stated that doing this made her very uncomfortable and she didn't know who to invite to do things with her. With Cathy's informed consent (and the consent of her parents), the therapist contacted her teacher who said that Cathy had the skills for making and keeping friends, but that she was shy and sometimes alienated her peers by tattling on them. Both her discomfort with asking others to do things with her and the tattling became problems to be solved. Underlying the shyness was a belief that others were likely to hurt her feelings if she became close to them. This belief was supported by the distortion of overgeneralization and was restructured to be more realistic – some people act in hurtful ways, but their hurtful behavior doesn't mean anything about me, and I can stay away from them. As noted below, her parents' behavior also was changed to counter this belief. As part of the problem-solving plan, Cathy was asked to identify the girls in class who were nicest to her and she was instructed to spend more time with them at school. During these interactions, she was asked to determine which girl was nicest to her and who she would most like to invite to play with her outside school. Once she identified a girl, she spent more time with her at school and then started to call and e-mail her while at home. Since this continued to go well, she was encouraged to take the next step and ask her friend to do something outside school. To increase the probability of the girl agreeing to the invitation, Cathy's parents were encouraged to give Cathy the opportunity to invite the girl to do a highly desirable activity (go with her family to a water park for the day). Monitoring the enactment of this plan took a number of weeks. Cathy's reaction to the misbehavior of others also became the focus of problem solving. While discussing a recent example of misbehavior in the classroom, a maladaptive belief became evident: if others misbehave the adult will get angry and I will get into trouble. This belief was restructured to: if others misbehave I will stay out of it and let them get into trouble. She was asked to try this alternative belief out and see if it was true. In addition, through problem solving, she decided that the best plan was to ignore the misbehavior and get away from it if it was possible to do so.

Following the fourth individual meeting with Cathy, her parents began meeting with the therapist to help support the treatment. During the first of these meetings, the problems that Cathy's childcare responsibilities were causing were discussed. A plan was developed to release Cathy from these responsibilities. Mrs. Hernandez was feeling better as a result of the medication, and she could see how taking care of her brother was stifling Cathy's ability to follow through on the pleasant events schedule.

One of the objectives of the meetings with the parents was for them to acquire the same skills that Cathy was learning. It was hoped that this would help them teach Cathy how to apply the skills, and it was seen as a way to help Mrs. Hernandez with her depressive disorder. During the first few meetings, the emphasis was on engaging in recreational and social activities as a means of enhancing mood and coping with the stress of childrearing and work. During this discussion Mrs. Hernandez revealed the belief that she didn't deserve to do anything fun because she wasn't getting her housework completed nor was she being as good a mother as she desired. This belief was restructured so she could see that doing enjoyable activities would in fact fuel her energy level and that it was the depression that was causing her to feel so tired and thus unable to complete all her housework. She noted an improvement in her energy level as a result of the antidepressant and she could see that she would get more done if she also felt better from doing enjoyable things. So, she agreed to do more enjoyable activities on her own during the day while the children were at school. While this was initially difficult as she had drifted away from her friends and she didn't know many other "stay at home mothers," eventually, she was able to engage in both solitary activities that she enjoyed and activities with friends. During these meetings, the parents became aware of the fact that following the birth of their children they had stopped doing things together as a couple. They were encouraged to ask a relative to baby-sit for the children while they went out and enjoyed each other's company. They could see how doing this would help them feel better toward each other, model for the children the engagement in recreational activities and how to maintain a healthy marital relationship. They were instructed to note and set aside for future meetings any disagreements that came up before or during the "dates."

Another goal of the meetings on activity scheduling was to begin to change the affective tone of the household, get both parents positively engaged in recreational activities with their children, and to begin to set-up a more positive and active approach to parenting. Both parents were encouraged to take turns every other night doing something enjoyable with either Cathy or her brother. In other words, one night Cathy and her mother would do something enjoyable for 20 minutes while Mr. Hernandez and his son would do likewise. The following night the parents would switch children. This had the secondary effect of reducing Mrs. Hernandez's resentment toward her husband for leaving all the childcare responsibilities to her. Cathy began to look forward to evenings at home, which engaged the children in play, and decreased the likelihood that they would argue with each other or do something else that might create conflict.

During the second meeting with the parents, they were taught how to use problem solving as a means of dealing with problems the family faced and for resolving their own conflicts. One of the problems Mrs. Hernandez raised was the difficulty she had managing their son's behavior. During the exploration of the child's misbehavior and how his mother handled it, she revealed a belief that setting limits and delivering punitive consequences would damage his self-esteem and, in the long-run, lead to him resenting her and ruin their relationship. Through some education, and reviewing the practical evidence to date for the belief (e.g., their relationship was being damaged by the conflict his misbehavior was causing), she was able to change the belief which helped her to accept the idea of learning a new parenting style. At each subsequent meeting, the parents were asked to describe problems they faced and how they used problem solving alone or together to solve the problems.

Also during the second meeting with the parents, Mrs. Hernandez noticed that it was very difficult for her to let Cathy become more independent and to spend more time away from home. Through the downward arrow technique of questioning, another belief became apparent: if my children are independent and don't need me, then I am worthless. Cognitive restructuring was used to counter this and Mrs. Hernandez was encouraged to identify evidence that supported the belief that she was worthy, and in fact a better mother if she taught her children how to become independent and successful.

While Cathy was well behaved, as with any child, there were times when she would misbehave. In addition, while Mrs. Hernandez was depressed, she tended to see misbehavior in her children when it really did not occur nor warrant any discipline. Frequently, Cathy and her brother would get into arguments, which upset Mrs. Hernandez. To deal with this, during the third parent meeting, both parents were taught a more active and positive style of managing their children's behavior. The parents worked together to generate a list for their children of expected/desirable behavior and the corresponding reinforcing consequences (typically engagement in a recreational activity with a parent), and a list of inappropriate behavior and the consequences for each of them. This approach seemed to fit well with Mrs. Hernandez's belief that the parents needed to be fair at the same time as supporting Mr. Hernandez's desire to run a more "disciplined household." It appeared as though inconsistency, which stemmed from Mrs. Hernandez's depressive disorder, Mr. Hernandez's involvement in work at home, and a reluctance to be punitive, had contributed to the problem. Thus, consistency in the delivery of consequences was emphasized. The parents were taught to look for positive behavior and qualities in their children and to praise them. They were instructed to provide each child with at least four realistic compliments each day. It was noted that the more positive approach would contribute to development of a positive sense of self. However, it was also noted that a child develops a deep, lasting, positive sense of self through parents setting reasonable but high expectations for performance across domains and then letting the children go about achieving goals through their own efforts. The parents met three more times with the therapist to specifically work on behavior management issues, including effective use of time out, contingent removal of privileges, and work details as methods for decreasing undesirable behavior. Punitive procedures were discussed after a more positive environment was in place and the parents were using the positive behavior management strategies.

During sessions 13 to 18, Cathy was taught to recognize and restructure her depressive thoughts. She was taught to be a thought detective who found negative thoughts and then examined the evidence that refuted them versus the evidence that supported them, looked for alternative interpretations of the event, and performed experiments to test the validity of the thoughts. The most common thoughts were: no one likes me; if you upset adults they get mad at you and punish you; I'm unlovable; I'm bad; and, I am responsible for the behavior of others. The therapist helped Cathy to apply cognitive restructuring techniques to these thoughts, and ultimately the self-schema that she is unlovable and bad. She was asked to self-monitor evidence that supported alternative healthier thoughts and schema, and to notice and record negative thoughts. This was difficult for her to do, so she was asked to e-mail them to her therapist each day. In addition, during the 14th meeting, Cathy chose to adopt a more optimistic outlook as the area of self-improvement on which she wanted to work. Thus, therapy focused on teaching her to look at the positive side of things and to adopt a more internal, global, and stable attributional style. Cathy and the therapist explored her expectations for the future and did experiments to determine whether the negative or new positive expectations turned out to come true. This self-monitoring helped her to internalize a more optimistic view of the future. During the 17th and 18th meetings, the therapist began preparing Cathy for termination. They reviewed the symptom checklists, he applauded her efforts in producing the improvement, and he asked Cathy for her ideas about what led to these improvements. This discussion was used as an opportunity to review the skills and strategies that Cathy had used to produce the improvements. In addition, the therapist and Cathy discussed their feelings about no longer meeting.

Simultaneously, Mr. and Mrs. Hernandez met with the therapist and they began working on communication skills and empathy. They were taught to become active listeners to their children. Both skills were practiced during discussions between the parents. Then they were asked to apply the skills to the children outside the sessions. Implementing these skills countered Cathy's belief that she was unlovable as she felt understood and listened to. The parents were taught cognitive restructuring techniques and they were both asked to self-monitor for negative thoughts and to practice using cognitive restructuring on them. They were asked to help Cathy complete cognitive restructuring diaries. In these diaries, Cathy would note her negative thoughts and then, through the structure provided in the diary forms in her workbook, she would practice restructuring them.

The final meeting was with Cathy and her parents. During this time, Cathy's progress and the progress of the family were reviewed and the changes that led to improvements were discussed. Methods for dealing with future problems were discussed, and the family and therapist celebrated the improvements.

IPT: Case Conceptualization and Treatment Plan

Since one of the authors is a cognitive behavioral therapist and worked with Cathy and her family, more detail regarding this approach to treatment has been provided. This is not meant to diminish the potency or value of IPT. It was possible to pull from case notes when describing the CBT approach to treating this case. Keeping that caveat in mind, from the IPT perspective, Cathy's depression stems from the disruption in interpersonal relationships caused by the role disputes between Cathy and her mother, and lack of social relationships with peers that may arise from a social skills deficit. The primary therapeutic objective would be to improve Cathy's interpersonal functioning across school and home environments.

During the first meeting with Cathy, while establishing rapport and building a therapeutic relationship, Cathy and the therapist identified interpersonal role disputes with her mother and interpersonal deficits with peers as the areas on which to focus treatment. A formal therapeutic contract was written and signed, and Cathy's role in therapy was defined. Part of the second meeting was spent in a discussion about the nature and impact of depression on Cathy and her parents. During this discussion, it became evident that Cathy was not socially engaged at school, with her parents, or with friends. While meeting with her parents, they were asked to encourage Cathy to engage in as many normal social and recreational activities as possible.

To address the role dispute which was defined as Mrs. Hernandez's expectation that Cathy take care of her brother after school, the therapist encouraged Cathy to express emotions she felt while babysitting her brother, and about having to do this every weekday. Mrs. Hernandez also explained to Cathy that she had not been feeling well and that she had appreciated having a mature daughter who could help her out. She also stated that she was feeling better due to the medication and that she had more energy and thus could take over that responsibility. Cathy also communicated the disappointment she felt about not being able to do more recreational things with her parents. Cathy and her mother used problem solving to develop plans for doing more things together and as a family. During these discussions, both Cathy and her mother were encouraged to express their feelings about each other and how these feelings were linked to their behavior and things that had happened.

Cathy's teacher was contacted before the third meeting as a means of assessing Cathy's interpersonal behavior with peers. The teacher noted that she generally got along well with her peers but that she was shy and that her peers would get upset with her when she would tell the teacher on them if she thought they were misbehaving. The third through eighth meetings focused on acquisition of social skills and the building of relationships with peers. The therapist used exploratory questioning to help Cathy discover what was underlying her shyness and need to tattle on others. During exploration, it became apparent that Cathy expected to be rejected and this led to the shyness. In addition, she was afraid that the teacher would get mad at her and that she would be punished and this led to her tattling.

Cathy was asked to self-monitor her interactions with peers and this information was used during the sessions as an opportunity to explore the emotional impact of interactions on Cathy, and to develop new skills for interacting with peers. The therapist and Cathy role-played common social interactions at school and outside school as a means of helping Cathy to acquire the prerequisite social skills for building more and better social relationships. Cathy self-monitored the result of her attempts to apply new social behavior and how new reactions from others made her feel. She noted that her relationships were improving and that she felt better. The therapist provided her with positive feedback regarding both her improvements in symptoms and social behavior as a means of enhancing her self-esteem. Cathy's parents were encouraged to help her have opportunities to spend time with friends.

During sessions nine to twelve, the termination phase, the therapist began preparing Cathy for termination by reviewing what they had accomplished to date, what she was going to continue to work on, and discussing what it was going to be like for each of them to no longer meet. Cathy's efforts to improve her interpersonal relationships were discussed as the genesis of the change, and problem solving was used to predict and plan for future interpersonal problems.

Summary

CBT and interpersonal therapy for depression are remarkably similar. At a general level, both interventions share a problem-focused, time-limited approach in which the depressed child and the therapist work together to identify problems that contribute to depressive symptoms and then develop plans for overcoming these problems. Proponents of both treatment models accept that successfully resolving these problems will reduce stress and improve functioning which will produce a reduction in depressive symptoms and a sense of "self-efficacy" (Stark, 1990) or enhanced "self-esteem" (Mufson, 1993). Surprisingly, the process of symptom reduction and problem resolution is similar across the treatment programs.

In both forms of treatment, the child and the therapist form a team that is designed to collaboratively identify and solve problems. Within the IPT model, the roles of the child and therapist in this process are clearly defined and the child-client signs a contract stating that he or she will fulfil his or her role and responsibilities in therapy. Within CBT, specific expectations for the child-client and therapist are discussed, and youngsters complete a contract in which they agree to complete therapeutic homework. Within both programs, the youngster's interpersonal behavior within the therapeutic relationship is viewed as a symptom rather than as a sign of some underlying illness. Thus, the youngster's interpersonal behavior with the therapist and with others is assessed for its appropriateness and effectiveness and is the direct target of intervention.

Both interventions utilize engagement in social and recreational activities as a therapeutic tool to reduce depressive symptoms. In the CBT program, this procedure is called pleasant events scheduling and is approached very systematically.

The therapist helps the youngsters generate a list of low-cost, no-cost recreational activities that are "fun" and for which access is under the youngsters' control. Additional activities that are more costly and require parental support through transportation etc. are then added to the list. Each child develops a weekly schedule for engagement in pleasant activities and self-monitors engagement in these activities. Problem solving is used as a method for developing the plans that enable youngsters to actually engage in the activities. In addition, problem solving is taught to the youngsters as a method for revising plans when unexpected impediments to engagement in an activity arise. Youngsters are taught to use pleasant activities as coping strategies. In other words, when the youngster notices a change in mood, he or she would engage in an activity that has potent mood enhancing qualities. Parents are asked to both support their youngster's engagement in pleasant activities and to gently encourage their child to follow the pleasant events schedule.

Problem solving is a central component of both treatment programs. In IPT it is used as a means of enhancing interpersonal relationships and for developing plans that deal with problems that are the primary focus of treatment. Within CBT, problem solving is directly taught to the participants as a means of dealing with daily hassles, and more significant interpersonal and impersonal problems. One of the overarching goals of treatment is to help youngsters develop a problem solving philosophy toward life. Depressed youths can often recognize that a problem exists but become emotionally overwhelmed by it and fail to do anything about it. In CBT, youngsters are taught self-statements that help them remain motivated, or to become motivated, for solving problems.

Self-monitoring is a central component of both treatment programs. In IPT, youngsters are asked to self-monitor their depressive symptoms and feelings. During later sessions, youngsters are asked to monitor how extra-therapy events impact their experience of depressive symptoms. In the CBT program, youngsters are directly taught how to self-monitor thoughts, feelings, behavior, and extra-therapy events. In both programs, youngsters are asked to monitor their feelings on a daily basis. However, there is a subtle difference between the two programs. Initially, in CBT youngsters are taught to only self-monitor the experience of positive emotions. The rationale behind this is that they are being taught to change their focus from a predominantly negative one to a predominantly positive one. Later in treatment, after an improvement in mood has occurred, the focus changes to both positive and negative events as the youngster and therapist attempt to identify situations that lead to stress and an exacerbation of depressive symptoms.

Interpersonal relationships are the focus of IPT and CBT. Relationships with peers and family members are considered to be important determinants of depressive symptoms. The primary difference between the two interventions may be in the way that interpersonal problems are conceptualized and in the breadth of intervention procedures. Within CBT, interpersonal relationships, especially those within the family, are hypothesized to shape the developing youngster's sense of self, relationships, and the world. Important schemas are believed to develop through learning experiences within this interpersonal context. As the schemas develop and become structuralized, they begin to guide information processing. As a youngster enters an interpersonal relationship, schema regarding interpersonal relationships and the self (also referred to as the internal working model) are activated and guide information processing. These schemas may be consistent with the situation and would lead to accurate information processing and adaptive behavior. When schemas that are activated are inconsistent with the situation or simply maladaptive, then maladaptive interpersonal behavior would result. Similarly, it is within the family context that a youngster develops interpersonal skills. For a variety of reasons, a child may not develop effective social skills. Thus, an interpersonal problem may stem from a skill deficit as well as from a cognitive disturbance. Within CBT, the self-relevant cognitions and cognitions about relationships as well as the interpersonal skills required by the situation are assessed and become the focus of intervention. Relevant cognitions about interpersonal relationships, including the schema, automatic thoughts, expectations, and attributions of the individuals involved in the interactions, are all assessed as they impact the problematic interactions. Interpersonal conflict is a central component of IPT. It is not a central component of the child element in the CBT program. However, it is an element of the family therapy component as research indicates that families of depressed youths are characterized by elevated levels of conflict. Given what appears to be an intimate link between interpersonal and cognitive functioning in depressed youths and the need to intervene at both levels, it may be useful to re-label this therapeutic approach as cognitive therapy within the interpersonal context and to intervene in both domains to improve skills and to change interaction patterns that would support a depressive style of thinking.

There appear to be two primary differences in treatment approaches. First is in the guiding rationales for treatment. Second is that CBT is designed to enhance a youngster's self-schema and to help youngsters learn a healthier and more positive style of processing information. Participants are taught to identify negative automatic thoughts, errors in information processing and negative self-evaluations. Then, they are taught to use a number of cognitive restructuring techniques to alter these negative thoughts. The IPT program focuses on interpersonal conflicts and relationships. While research has clearly demonstrated that disturbances in interpersonal functioning exist in the families and friendships of depressed youths, it may be more useful to recognize the reciprocal relationship between the cognitive and interpersonal domains.

References

American Psychiatric Association. (1994). *Diagnostic and Statistical Manual of Mental Disorders.* (4th ed). Fourth Edition. Washington, D.C.: American Psychiatric Association.

Birmaher, B., & Brent, D. (1998). Practice parameters for the assessment and treatment of children and Adolescents with depressive disorders. *Journal of the American Academy of Child and Adolescent Psychiatry, 37,* 63S–83S.

Carlson, G., & Kashani, J. (1988). Phenomenology of major depression from childhood through adulthood: Analysis of three studies. *American Journal of Psychiatry, 145,* 1222–1225.

Chambers, W., Puig-Antich, J., Tabrizi, M., & Davies, M. (1982). Psychotic symptoms in prepubertal major depressive disorder. *Archives of General Psychiatry, 39,* 921–927.

Cicchetti, D., & Toth, S. L. (1998). The development of depression in children and adolescents. *American Psychologist, 53* 221–241.

Cole, D. A. (1990). The relation of social and academic competence to depressive symptoms in childhood. *Journal of Abnormal Psychology, 99,* 422–429.

Fleming, J. E., & Offord, D. R. (1990). Epidemiology of childhood depressive disorders: A critical review. *Journal of the American Academy of Child and Adolescent Psychiatry, 29,* 571–580.

Hammen, C., & Rudolph, K. D. (1996). Childhood depression. In E. J. Mash & R. A. Barkley (eds) *Child Psychopathology.* New York, NY: Guilford Press. 153–193.

Kashani, J.H., Holcomb, W.R., & Orvaschel, H. (1986). Depression and depressive symptoms in preschool children from the general population. *American Journal of Psychiatry, 143,* 1138–1143.

Kendall, P. C., & Braswell, L. (1993). *Cognitive Behavior Therapy for Impulsive Children* (2nd. ed.). New York: Guilford Press.

Kovacs, M. (1996). Presentation and course of major depressive disorder during childhood and later years of the lifespan. *Journal of the American Academy of Childhood and Adolescent Psychiatry, 35,* 705–715.

Kovacs, M., & Goldston, D. (1991). Cognitive and social cognitive development of Depressed children and adolescents. *Journal of the American Academy of Child and Adolescent Psychiatry, 30,* 388–392.

Mitchell, J., McCauley, E., Burke, P. M., & Moss, S. J. (1988). Phenomenology of depression in children and adolescents. *Journal of the American Academy of Child and Adolescent Psychiatry, 27,* 12–20.

Rehm, L. P., & Sharp, R. N. (1996). Strategies for childhood depression. In M.A. Reinecke, F.M. Dattilio, & A. Freeman, (eds), *Cognitive Therapy with Children and Adolescents.* New York, NY: Guilford Press. 103–123.

Reynolds, W. M., & Johnston, H. F. (1994). The nature and study of depression in children and adolescents. In W. M. Reynolds & H. F. Johnston (eds) *Handbook of Depression in Children and Adolescents.* New York, NY: Plenum Press. 3–17.

Ryan, N. D., Puig-Antich, J., Ambrosini, P., Rabinovich, H., Robinson, D., *et al.* (1987). The clinical picture of major depression in children and adolescents. *Archives of General Psychiatry, 44,* 854–861.

Stark, K. D. (1990). *The Treatment of Depression During Childhood: A School-Based Program.* New York: Guilford Press.

Stark, K. D., Boswell Sander, J., Yancy, M. G., Bronik, M. D., & Hoke, J. A. (2000). Treatment of depression in childhood and adolescence. In P. C. Kendall (ed.) *Child & Adolescent Therapy: Cognitive-behavioral Procedures.* New York: Guilford Press. 173–234.

Stark, K. D. & Kendall, P. C. (1996). *Treating Depressed Children: Therapist Manual for "Action".* Ardmore, PA: Workbook Publishing.

Stark, K. D., Kendall, P. C., McCarthy, M., Stafford, M., & Barron, R., *et al.* (1996). *ACTION: A Workbook for Overcoming Depression.* Ardmore, PA: Workbook Publishing.

Chapter 7

Dysthymia

Helen Orvaschel

Clinical Description

Diagnostic Criteria

Dysthymia is a major, non-bipolar, non-psychotic mood disorder, generally viewed as less severe than major depressive disorder (MDD). It is described in our current nosologic system as a form of chronic depression, with symptom free periods permitted for no longer than two months during the minimum duration specified. DSM-IV criteria require the presence of depressed mood more days than not, and at least two additional accompanying symptoms. These may include poor appetite or overeating, insomnia or hypersomnia, low energy or fatigue, low self-esteem, poor concentration or difficulty making decisions, and/or feelings of hopelessness, all of which result in significant distress and/or impaired functioning (American Psychiatric Association, 1994). While several of the symptoms overlap with (i.e., fatigue, insomnia) or are similar to (i.e., low self-esteem vs. worthlessness) those of MDD, there are notable differences between these two disorders. Anhedonia, psychomotor disturbances, and suicidalilty are listed as symptoms of MDD but are not part of dysthymia criteria, while the reverse is true for feelings of hopeless. The logic in these distinctions is not obvious, inasmuch as hopeless is often associated with MDD, and anhedonia and suicidality are certainly seen in dysthymia. Nevertheless, both the distinct and shared symptoms of dysthymia and MDD connote the intent to define the former as a less intense but clearly related syndrome.

Because of its more chronic, insidious presentation, dysthymia is more likely to be untreated and is sometimes viewed as characteristic of the individual suffering from it, rather than as an atypical or pathologic presentation. However, dysthymia may be quite impairing, is a risk factor for subsequent MDD, and is often comorbid with it. For those with early onset mood disorders (age < 21 years), and particularly for adolescents, dysthymia tends to precede MDD, increases risk of subsequent MDD threefold, and is highly comorbid with MDD (lifetime odds ratio of 3.4) (Lewinsohn, Rohde, Seeley, & Hops, 1991). Studies of children note that dysthymia has a protracted course (median length of 3.9 years), has the least favorable time to recovery compared with all other mood disorders (median

Handbook of Conceptualization and Treatment of Child Psychopathology, pages 133–148.
Copyright © 2001 by Elsevier Science Ltd.
All rights of reproduction in any form reserved.
ISBN: 0-08-043362-6

recovery time of 3.5 years), has an earlier age of onset than MDD, is as likely as MDD to be associated with recurrence, and provides a significant increased risk for developing MDD (Kovacs, Feinberg, Crouse-Novak, Paulauskas, & Finkel-stein, 1984a; Kovacs, Feinberg, Crouse-Novak, Paulauskas, & Pollock, *et al.*, 1984b; Kovacs, Obrosky, Gatsonis, & Richards, 1997). In addition, dysthymia superimposed on MDD is associated with shorter periods of remission and increased likelihood of relapse of MDD (Kovacs, *et al.*, 1984a). Taken together, the cumulative data on dysthymia in children and adolescents suggest a clinically significant psychopathologic state, capable of interfering with the mastery of edu-cational, interpersonal, and intrapersonal maturational milestones expected during this phase of growth.

Developmental Considerations

While no substantive differences in adult-based criteria are noted for children and adolescence, the two-year duration criterion was modified to one year, (ostensibly) in some recognition of the proportional difference in time a younger person has had available to develop psychopathology. The only other distinction between adults and non-adults mentioned in the DSM is that irritability may serve as a mood equivalent of depression for children and adolescents. The direct mention of irritability as a developmental distinction for younger dysthymics is interesting, inasmuch as irritability has long been noted as a hallmark feature of depressive mood disorders across all ages. Despite lack of a distinct literature supporting mood equivalence of irritability for children and adolescents over and above that of adults, its availability for use in the diagnosis of MDD and dysthymia is clinically appropriate. Other than the two variations noted, DSM-IV does not address developmental differences in criteria for mood disorders, generally, or for dysthymia, specifically. Nevertheless, developmental differences in diagnosis do exist.

Although somatic complaints are not criteria items and are not unique to dys-thymia, they are a frequent facet of child clinical presentations, particularly for younger children. Vegetative symptoms, on the other hand, are considerably less common in children as compared with adolescents or adults, while atypical features such as hypersomnia and a pattern of sensitivity to interpersonal rejection are more characteristic of adolescent presentations. Despite the fact that anhedo-nia is not a criterion item for dysthymia, it is frequently present in child and ado-lescent patients who often characterize it as feelings of boredom rather than a loss of or inability to experience pleasure.

Developmental distinctions should also be noted for assessment of mood distur-bance, per se. Whereas adults with MDD are expected to be depressed all or most of the day, and those with dysthymia are described by DSM as depressed most of the day, more days than not, younger children will rarely meet such stringent time requirements, even when taking into account the mood equivalence of irritability. While less true for adolescents, mood lability is typical of all young children and decreases as age increases. Therefore, assessing depressed mood or its equivalent (irritability) in younger populations should be done with an eye toward the age of the subject being assessed. For example, a seven year old who is depressed for three or four hours at a time, several days a week, is well in excess of what would be normatively expected for a non-depressed child of that age. Persistence of such behavior over the course of weeks, months, or even years is an indication of pathology and a mood disorder should be given serious consideration. The differential determination of MDD or dysthymia should be based on symptom presentation, level of severity, extent of impairment, and duration of presenting disturbance.

Associated Features

Similar to MDD, children and adolescents with dysthymia are frequently characterized by feelings of inadequacy, generalized anhedonia, and social withdrawal. However, the chronic and long-term nature of the condition is likely to result in particularly more detrimental consequences during this important maturational process. For example, long-term feelings of inadequacy that onset at so early an age may impact the development of cognitive schema regarding the sense of self as unworthy, unlovable, or ineffective and these schema may be lifelong. A consequence of extensive social withdrawal may be a failure to develop adequate social skills often acquired as a result of fundamental peer interactions during these critical developmental periods. Dysthymics are often viewed by their peers as sullen, moody, and pessimistic, and generally "no fun" to be around. Support for these assertions has been provided from data derived from the Oregon Adolescent Depression Project, which reported that those with past histories of dysthymia were likely to have less social support from friends and that many of their interpersonal difficulties persisted after recovery from the mood disorder (Klein, Lewinsohn, & Seeley, 1997).

Dysthymic children are likely to feel chronically lacking in energy, which in turn affects school productivity, and their willingness, or lack thereof, to participate in other school related activities, abetting their anhedonia and sense of ineffectiveness. Over time, concentration problems may diminish academic achievement, further impairing overall functioning, and exacerbating their (already) negative self-image. The associated irritability in this disorder causes these children to be viewed as cranky by peers as well as their own family, often resulting in parent child conflicts and family discord in addition to peer rejection.

Comorbid psychopathology is more often the rule than the exception in presentations of dysthymia. The most common comorbid disorders include MDD, anxiety disorders (particularly separation anxiety disorder in children younger than ten), oppositional defiant disorder (ODD), conduct disorder (CD), and substance disorders. While truly accurate prevalence data for dysthymia in the general child and adolescent population are lacking, estimates have placed the rates roughly between two and five percent, depending on the age of the groups studied.

It should be apparent from the clinical description and associated features of dysthymia that children suffering from this disorder are vulnerable to a plethora of difficulties with the potential for negatively impacting many facets of their existence in the near term and possibly throughout the course of their lives. Intervention should have as a goal, not only alleviation of immediate suffering, but modification of maladaptive patterns of behavior such that if left unchanged may cause impairments in functioning for years to come.

Treatment Strategies

Overview. Despite extensive research regarding the efficacy of psychotherapy for adults with MDD and more recent interest in adolescent depressives (Brent, Kolko, Birmaher, Baugher, & Bridge, 1999; Lewinsohn, & Clarke, 1999), it appears that the treatment of dysthymia has generated considerably less interest. In fact, no single psychosocial intervention has been established for the treatment of dysthymia, generally, and none has been systematically examined for child and adolescent populations, specifically. Some information on the treatment needs of dysthymics has accrued as a byproduct of research on MDD. For example, adolescents with double depression (MDD and dysthymia) and those who present with hopelessness reportedly require much more time in treatment before a response can be expected (Brent, et al., 1999). Research with children has suggested that externalizing conditions, such as ODD and CD, have been associated with a longer duration of dysthymia and, possibly, recovery and treatment resistance (Kovacs, et al., 1997). Despite such ancillary information, psychotherapeutic and medication recommendations for dysthymia are non-specific and have defaulted to those made for MDD, as is evident from the following statement regarding this disorder: "In the absence of published studies of psychotherapeutic or pharmacological treatment of children and adolescents, clinicians are advised to use interventions recommended for the treatment of youth with MDD" (American Academy of Child and Adolescent Psychiatry, 1998, p. 1238). In as much as psychotherapy for adolescent MDD has received second class treatment, with current interventions always a derivative of adult approaches (Mueller & Orvaschel, 1997), the above statement from the practice parameters for depressive disorders relegates dysthymia treatment to second class status, once removed.

An overview of treatment approaches used with child and adolescent MDD is not the focus of this presentation and is beyond its scope, particularly in as much as such work has been reviewed elsewhere (Lewinsohn, Clarke, & Rohde, 1994). However, lack of clear-cut guidelines for treatment of dysthymia in youth leaves the clinician with a "seat of the pants" approach to this serious psychopathological condition. Not only are specific treatment recommendations for this condition lacking, no empirical data are available on issues related to preferred modality of treatment (i.e., individual vs. group vs. family vs. their combination), targets of intervention (e.g., symptoms vs. school vs. social functioning), explicit treatment methods, preferred theoretical orientation, and the like.

In the absence of empirical data to the contrary, one could argue that group treatments are more cost effective than individual therapy and should therefore be the preferred modality. Groups may also provide specific benefits for younger populations, such as providing a venue for social skills training. It may also be viewed as less stigmatizing because of access to others with similar problems and sharing with others may result in some perspective, often lacking in youth. On the other hand, family treatment may be necessary because of frequency of family discord, need for improved communication, and the fact that problems in youth are difficult to separate from the family with whom they live. Similarly, the literature does little to steer the clinician to the "correct" theoretical orientation for the treatment of mood disorders. Should cognitive theory take precedence over psychodynamic options or is an eclectic stance the more logical choice. Because the focus here is on the presentation of treatment approaches derived from conceptual models, decisions regarding these issues must ultimately be based on the clinician's determination of practicality and feasibility, as well as how the problems are conceptualized.

Case Example

Description. Jennifer was a 15 year old white female attending tenth grade at a local high school. She resided with her biological parents and twelve year old brother. Her 42 year old mother, a bookkeeper, brought her to treatment. Her father, age 46 years, held an executive position in a pharmaceutical company. According to Mrs. G., she could not remember the last time Jennifer appeared happy and stated that the family viewed her as angry and hostile. Jennifer's parents decided to initiate treatment for her because they no longer assumed her behavior was a "phase of adolescence" that would pass. They also believed her problems were having a negative affect on the household and were beginning to impact her school work.

Assessment. The intake was comprised of separate K-SADS-E (Orvaschel, 1995) interviews, with Mrs. G and Jennifer, as well as a depression inventory completed by Jennifer. Diagnostic impressions were derived from summary ratings of information provided by both informants and all other available clinical data. A teacher report was not obtained because, as an adolescent, she did not spend much time with any particular teacher and the problems reported were primarily home based. Information on academic functioning was readily available from Jennifer and her parents.

The advantage of using a semi-structured interview format is that it allows a more comprehensive assessment of signs and symptoms of psychopathology, rather than an overemphasis on presenting complaints. Evaluation focused on both past and current disturbances and the systematic determination of chronology. Selection of a paper and pencil depression measure was based on the identification of a mood disturbance during interview; the use of an inventory allows quantification and measurement over time. Because many chronically depressed adolescents have been known to self-medicate with drugs and alcohol, a careful assessment of substance use was also ascertained. Finally, information on family psychiatric history and the family's interaction and functioning was obtained.

Jennifer appeared to be her stated age, was appropriately dressed, slightly over-weight, and rather sullen. Her mother stated that Jennifer is moody and has an "attitude" and that she doesn't have many friends. These characteristics had been true for the past three or four years, but during the past year and a half her grades dropped from As and Bs to Bs and Cs. She had also become argumentative at home, was easily provoked, and was less communicative than she had been. Jennifer admitted to a depressed and irritable mood that had been intermittently present for about four years. She also endorsed increased difficulty concentrating, fatigue, and feelings of inadequacy. Jennifer acknowledged that she often felt that things would never get better and she was increasingly withdrawn both from peers and family. Suicidal and homicidal ideation were denied. While reporting very brief experimentation with marijuana and alcohol, regular use of drugs, alcohol, and cigarettes was denied and no evidence of substance abuse was noted. Jennifer was oriented to person, place, and time; there was no evidence of past or current psychosis or cognitive dysfunction and no history of attention deficit hyperactivity disorder (ADHD) or CD. A history of childhood phobias was noted, but the fears were no longer salient or impairing. Criteria were met for ODD during the past year, including loss of temper, frequent arguments with adults, being easily annoyed, and often feeling angry. The latter two symptoms may well have been a reflection of the mood disorder. Based on the presence of chronic depressed mood, accompanying symptoms (concentration difficulties, fatigue, low self-esteem, and hopelessness), and impairment, Jennifer was diagnosed with dysthy-mia. In light of the presence of significant irritability, the potential for a bipolar disorder was considered but ruled out in the absence of any additional symptoms of mania. MDD was ruled out on the basis of the intermittent nature of the mood disturbance and absence of sufficient number of MDD symptoms.

Mrs. G. reported a normal, full term pregnancy with no complications. Jenni-fer's health and developmental history were described as unremarkable; milestones were met within normal limits, and a recent physical exam found her to be healthy. While described as sometimes hypochondriacal, no disabilities or physical impairments were present, and Jennifer was not on any medications. Onset of menarche was shortly after her twelfth birthday. While apparently interested in boys, she had not begun dating.

Jennifer began school at the age of five and this transition had been uneventful. Although she was never viewed as enthusiastic, she did not object to going to school, had no separation difficulties, was never disruptive in the school setting, and had been an above average student, except during the past year. Jennifer never had many friends and admitted to being withdrawn and socially uncomfor-table. She stated that she did not like herself and didn't see why anyone else would like her much, either. She reported feeling fat and unattractive and that she had "no personality." While acknowledging that she was "good at schoolwork," she did not think she was very smart and indicated that she was having a harder time keeping her mind on her studies, which is why her grades had declined during the previous year. She did not enjoy spending time with her family, whom she viewed as critical and annoying. She appeared to have few interests and was not having fun. Jennifer did indicate an interest in making more friends and participating in more activities with peers, but seemed at a loss as to how to accomplish this goal.

Primary Conceptualization

On the basis of the preliminary information provided by Jennifer and her mother, several conceptual models are suggested. Presence of negative schema evident in Jennifer's description of herself, the world, and her view of the future, in conjunction with her oppositionalism clearly indicate that a cognitive behavioral approach would be a suitable treatment modality. Alternatively, insinuation of family conflict alluded to in the intake may promote a family approach to the case (although additional information on family interaction would be needed to explicate such a model). Despite viability of the aforementioned conceptualizations, an alternative system was viewed as capable of providing a more encompassing explication of Jennifer's presentation. From the clinician's perspective, the most salient complaints presented were chronic, intermittent depressed mood and associated symptoms that began with the inception of adolescence and a long-standing history of interpersonal difficulties with exacerbation coincident to the onset of the mood disturbance. Accompanying oppositional difficulties and family discord were considered a consequence of the mood disorder, with an assumption that remission of the dysthymia would result in elimination of these concurrent problems. Therefore, an interpersonal conceptual model was believed to provide the most comprehensive elucidation of the mood disorder and was deemed the strongest candidate for effective resolution of the presenting problems.

Interpersonal psychotherapy (IPT) (Klerman, Weissman, Rounsaville, & Chevron, 1984) was developed initially as a specific, time-limited intervention for non-bipolar, non-psychotic, depressed adults and was subsequently modified for use with depressed adolescents (IPT-A) (Mufson, Moreau, Weissman, & Kerman, 1993). IPT takes no position on the etiologic nature of the mood disturbance (i.e., biologic, genetic, stress-diathesis), but considers that depression occurs in an interpersonal context. Development is seen as psychosocial in nature and social bonds are viewed as important to human function. While cognitive therapy focuses on dysfunctional belief systems, and behavioral therapy focuses on the loss of positive reinforcement, IPT focuses on dysfunctional interpersonal communication processes. The goal of IPT is to decrease depression by improving (the quality of) current interpersonal functioning.

Because IPT was designed as a time limited intervention, essential early tasks in the therapy include determination of a primary problem area and identification of behavior(s) that could benefit from change. IPT-A has five problem area categories (compared with four for adults) from which the patient and therapist collaboratively select one (or two) on which to work. The problem areas selected are based on the view that they are a primary contributing factor to the depression and help to establish treatment goals. Possible problem areas include grief, interpersonal disputes, role transitions, interpersonal deficits, and single-parent families, the latter being unique to the adolescent population.

If the problem area selected is grief, onset of depression is viewed as associated with the death of a significant person in the adolescent's life. Such grief is viewed as pathologic in nature by virtue of time (i.e., prolonged, delayed, chronic) and/or presentation (i.e., symptom type or severity of disorder). Goals of the treatment are to facilitate the mourning process and help the patient re-establish relationships that will compensate for that which was lost. One would obtain information on the patient's emotions surrounding the death and its overall impact, as well as assistance in coping with difficult affective components such as guilt, shame, anger, fear for the self, saying final good-byes, and the like. Consideration would be given to the adolescent's role in the family before and after the death, the nature of the relationship lost (e.g., resolving negative and positive aspects of the relationship), the remaining social and family support network, as well as the adolescent's maturity and coping skills.

Interpersonal Disputes may be seen as the problem area contributing to depression if the adolescent and significant others in his/her life have "non-reciprocal expectations" about the nature of their relationship. Before selecting this problem area, there must be evidence of conflict with the significant other(s) in relation to the onset of the mood problems. Understanding the nature of the interpersonal conflicts may suggest a strategy for treatment and possible resolution, so the extent of the disputes at presentation is "staged." The first stage is "renegotiation," defined as awareness of the problem (by one or both parties), the presence of arguments, and attempts to change the interaction by those involved. The task of therapy for this stage is conflict resolution with efforts to improve communication. The second stage is "impasse," where discussion and even fighting have stopped and been replaced by silent hostility. The treatment task may be to reopen unresolved issues by reinitiating communication. The third stage of a dispute is "dissolution." Here it is determined that the dispute cannot be resolved and the therapeutic tasks become similar to those of grief, because the relationship is ended and needs to be mourned and replaced. Interpersonal disputes in the first two stages require a discussion of expectations and resolutions that may lead to areas of agreement, exploration of negotiation strategies, resources for change, and modification of maladaptive patterns of communication.

Role Transitions may be a source of difficulty if it is determined that the adolescent has difficulty with life or role changes (e.g., move from childhood to adolescence, changes in the nature of relationships) that coincide with the onset of mood disturbance. These transition difficulties may originate with the adolescent or the parents, and threaten self-esteem or sense of identity or involve a loss of social support, demands for new social skills, or change in role definition. Treatment goals include assisting the adolescent to cope with needed changes, dealing with affect (i.e., anxiety, sadness, fear) regarding expected changes, defining new roles and assisting with growth opportunities, restoring self-esteem, and developing a new support system and skills needed for the transition.

Interpersonal Deficits are considered as problem area targets if the patient presents with a history of social impoverishment or social isolation. These cases tend to be more difficult to treat because of the chronic nature of the difficulties presented and because they are often associated with comorbid psychopathology and personality disorders. The goals of treatment are to reduce social isolation, improve social and communication skills, enhance social confidence and comfort, and assist in the establishment of fulfilling relationships.

Finally, selection of the **single-parent family** as the problem area is determined when depression is the result of difficulties caused by the single-parent structure of the family. The identified problem may be with either the absent or the custodial parent. Goals include an acknowledgement of the loss or family disruption, identification of feelings of rejection, anger, guilt, or other dysfunctional affect, reduction in pseudoparentification of the adolescent, and resolution of issues with the remaining parent. The adolescent may need to mourn loss of previous family life, gain acceptance of the permanence of the situation, redefine a role in the new family structure, and clarify expectations for a relationship with the custodial and non-custodial parent.

No more than two problem areas are selected for any given case, in order for treatment to remain focused and adhere to the twelve to 16 week duration originally intended. An interpersonal review is done in order to identify all social roles and their components and to determine if interpersonal difficulties are present that may be related to the onset of the mood disorder. Medication needs are evaluated, risk of suicidality is assessed, and the patient is educated regarding depression and the nature of IPT. The therapist serves as an active, supportive advocate who is non-judgmental and optimistic. Treatment progress is periodically reviewed and the focus is on current behavior, with reference to past patterns as they relate to ongoing issues.

Treatment. Following the diagnostic evaluation, the therapist met with Jennifer and her mother and discussed her understanding of the problems presented and the parameters of confidentiality. Jennifer agreed to return for individual treatment. Although IPT was designed as a three month intervention, those boundaries were established for MDD. Literature about the chronic nature of dysthymia and the presence of hopelessness suggested the need for flexibility regarding treatment duration in this situation. Treatment was also expected to take longer because of the problem area (ultimately) identified. In light of the need for flexibility, no treatment time frame was established at the onset, representing a departure from IPT procedure.

During the subsequent two sessions, the therapist provided Jennifer with information on the diagnosis of dysthymia and oriented her to the nature of IPT. She was advised that her symptoms fit an expected pattern and that the likelihood of treatment success was high. The potential usefulness of medication was also evaluated. Several factors played a role in this decision making process. Little evidence supports the efficacy of medication for dysthymia and no systematic literature is available for adolescent populations. Available data on less severe depression suggest that psychotherapeutic interventions are at least as effective as antidepressants. Since this was a first effort at treatment, a fair trial with IPT made more sense than a medication referral at that juncture. Jennifer and the therapist agreed that she would complete a depression symptom inventory every four weeks so that her treatment progress could be monitored; therefore, the prospect of medication could be re-evaluated if improvement was judged to be inadequate.

During the third and fourth sessions, social roles and their components were identified and problem areas were selected for intervention. Examining Jennifer's social roles allowed an exploration of her interpersonal contacts, including their frequency, the nature of activities, whether they were satisfactory, expectations of others, and how or what should be changed. It became evident that Jennifer had very infrequent contact with teens and spent too much time at home doing things her parents thought appropriate but she found irritating. Examining when she began to feel unhappy about her social interaction, Jennifer determined that the onset of adolescence coincided with the worsening of her mood and related symptoms. While she did not excel socially before adolescence, she did have friends and participated in peer related activities with some regularity. During the process of entering her teens, however, Jennifer felt less capable and comfortable with age appropriate activities and began to withdraw. On the basis of the information provided, the problem areas selected were interpersonal deficits and role transition.

The fifth through tenth sessions focused on discussions of social and communication skills. Efforts were made to provide reassurance and encourage exploration and experimentation with social interaction during and between sessions. The therapeutic relationship was used to assist in development of new, more age appropriate interpersonal skills and to improve interpersonal awareness and increase self-confidence and self-esteem. The therapist's supportive encouragement assisted in the formulation of strategies that might increase the number of peer contacts and improve the quality of Jennifer's social interaction. Time was spent discussing what Jennifer wanted from these peer relationships and what she expected peers wanted from her. Finally, a process was established that allowed implementation of approaches to problem resolution. That is, a series of social skills was explored, practiced, and acted upon in a variety of settings over the course of several weeks.

A little symptom reduction was evident from the fourth to the eighth session. This was pointed out to Jennifer so that she was aware of the relationship between her mood and activities to improve social contact. Jennifer's mother also acknowledged a slight improvement in her behavior at home. For the first three months, parental involvement in treatment was minimal. By the eleventh session, the therapist began to introduce issues central to role transitions and the part they may have played in the difficulties encountered. Discussions focused on normative development and the fact that individuals mature at different rates. Attention was also given to the role of parents in the encouragement of independence. Jennifer was able to examine her own readiness for the emotional and interpersonal demands of adolescence, as well as that of her parents. She noted that her parents encouraged her to stay close to home, emphasizing the dangers of teen interaction more than the advantages. She acknowledged that this reinforced her own fears and insecurities about her ability to cope with adolescence and spiraled her toward more social withdrawal and subsequent resentment toward family. As therapy progressed, she began to gain self-confidence. This led her to feel the need for more independence and she asked how her parents might be included in the treatment so that she could negotiate a new arrangement at home.

The 16th and 17th sessions included Jennifer and her parents. While IPT (A) is designed as an individual treatment, it does not preclude the participation of family members, albeit on a limited basis. Before the parents attended, Jennifer and the therapist discussed the objectives of the meetings and the negotiation strategies to be explored. Some time was also spent during these sessions educating Jennifer's parents about appropriate expectations for teenagers and the give and take of limit setting. The remaining time was devoted to helping Jennifer and her parents improve communication. While the above tasks were not completed in two meetings, their initiation facilitated ongoing attention to them by all parties, so that they became enduring objectives at home and were routinely explored in the therapy process.

By the 24th week, Jennifer had significantly reduced her depressed mood, was more energetic, less argumentative, and concentrating more effectively at school. She also made a new friend and was beginning to participate in some age appropriate social activities (i.e., she attended a school dance). An additional month was devoted to examining her new role and the advantages and disadvantages of her entrance into the world of young adulthood. There was recognition of the need for new skills and she was encouraged to examine her thoughts and affects about the transitional process. In the 30th week, the therapist introduced the prospect of termination during a discussion of Jennifer's improvement in symptoms and functioning.

In IPT, a discussion of termination generally is initiated two to four weeks before the end of treatment; however, adolescents often need more time for this process. Additionally, treatment duration was extended for this case, so the need for a more protracted termination process was assumed. Jennifer and the therapist met weekly for six more sessions and met every other week for the last four sessions. She was encouraged to express her feelings about the treatment and its impending end. Anxieties were normalized, as well as concerns about relapse and feelings of loss. Progress was evaluated and new skills were reviewed. Throughout the final ten weeks, Jennifer and the therapist continued to work on social and communication skills with peers and more effective interaction with parents, as well as issues regarding self-esteem and appropriate expectations. Jennifer's mother participated in parts of several sessions, but most parent-child negotiations took place at home. Treatment ended at the 40th week with reassurances that contact could be reinitiated if needed.

The resolution of dysthymia in this adolescent may be viewed as a result of remedying the patient's deficits in interpersonal relationships, which were exacerbated by her inability to transition into adolescence. While the adjunctive use of a social skills group could be considered in such cases, this was not necessary for Jennifer. Her motivation and commitment to the treatment, and her ability to form a strong working relationship with the therapist should be considered as positive factors in the therapeutic outcome, as was the cooperation of her parents.

Alternative Conceptualization and Treatment

Recognition of family issues in the treatment of psychopathology has a long history. When Jennifer was brought in for initial evaluation, her mother indicated that her behavior was negatively impacting the family. More extensive examination indicated that much time and energy was expended on Jennifer's "attitude" problems and her moodiness was often the focus of parental discussions. Mrs. G was the more critical of Jennifer, while Mr. G was viewed as withdrawn from the family and more involved with his work. She reported that her husband deferred to her on matters concerning their daughter, but was quick to criticize her as overprotective of both children. Jennifer believed that her mother favored her brother, Mark, while she had no one "on her side." Jennifer's mother discouraged her from participating in many school activities, stating she was trying to protect her daughter from difficult situations she encountered. Based on the information provided, a compelling argument could be made for a family approach to the treatment of Jennifer's dysthymia and ODD.

Many types of family therapy are available, with varying theoretical orientations and intervention techniques. For example, family treatment may include psychoeducation or support, methods considered particularly helpful with chronic psychopathologies like schizophrenia or bipolar disorder. Cognitive behavioral approaches to the family draw on basic principles of learning and emphasize communication and problem solving skills, while psychodynamic family therapists often target the interpretation of underlying family conflicts. However, treatments most frequently associated with family therapy are those of the strategic and structural schools of thought, both of which consider the family system as the object of intervention. The strategic therapist encourages a reorganization of the family with the intent of altering the dysfunctional nature of existing family communication patterns, assumed to be a function of unsuccessful efforts to resolve the problems of one or more members. The structural (or systemic) family therapist concentrates on the relationships of family members to each other and views psychopathology as a representation of problems within the family organization and inappropriate boundaries between individuals and subgroups.

Using a family treatment approach, the conceptual model that would have been selected for Jennifer is structural (systemic) family therapy (Minuchin, 1974). This type of treatment would require greater attention to the family structure and dynamics, as it would be assumed that Jennifer's dysthymia was a byproduct of the family's dysfunctional relationships rather than a disorder "belonging" primarily to her. As the family unit would be the target of treatment, all family members would be expected to attend sessions. A new manner of understanding "Jennifer's problems" must be established in the family context. Her symptoms can be viewed as system-maintaining devices that serve a function within the family structure. Dysfunctional family patterns have been established and become rigid and the therapist must assist "the group" to change these patterns of interaction.

During the initial phase of treatment, this therapist would join the family and establish herself as leader. In this family, the task would not be difficult as family leadership was not firmly in place and all parties looked to the therapist as having the expertise to solve their problems. This first step serves to immediately alter the structure of the family. The therapist would then establish goals, modifying the interrelationships of family members to each other in order to facilitate the achievement of these goals. The therapist saw Jennifer as a unifying force in the family because she helped Mr. and Mrs. G. to unite with concern for her emotional difficulties and opposition to her disruptive behavior. It was also one of the few times Mrs. G. viewed her husband as supportive rather than critical of her. In structural terms, Mr. and Mrs. G. did not form a cohesive parental subgroup. Mr. G. was withdrawn from the family and critical of his wife's parenting, leading her to feel lonely, isolated, and angry. She became both overinvolved and overcontrolling with her children, behavior that often results in poor socialization of children, as was the case with Jennifer. Jennifer's social withdrawal and subsequent dysthymia provided her mother with a companion in the home. Her oppositional behavior provided the parents with a reason for a united front against an unruly child, a form of triangulation.

In this family, isolation was characteristic of most of its members. Mrs. G. felt isolated from her husband while both Mr. G. and Jennifer felt isolated from the family, generally. Mark tried to be the peacemaker but only served to annoy Jennifer who viewed him as the favorite and the "good one". He, in turn, was dependent on the mother, but wanted very much to establish a closer relationship with his father. These family dynamics had been true for a very long time and it can be assumed that change would take months.

The therapist would attempt to alter family subsystems by unifying the parents and removing the diversionary use of Jennifer's problems. This could be done by assigning the parents specific tasks regarding the parenting of both children. For example, the more distant parent (Mr. G.) could be asked to take charge of the children for a week, with Mrs. G. providing support. Subsequently, they could be formed into a "subcommittee" during a meeting and given responsibility for establishing certain limit setting rules for the children. At the same time, both children would be organized into another subcommittee and assigned a task, such as planning a fun activity for just the two of them. The function of these exercises would be to further the therapist's goal of reuniting the parents and placing the children in their appropriate roles. If Mrs. G. began to feel less lonely, she could begin to disengage from her enmeshment with the children, which in turn would begin to allow Jennifer to venture into adolescence. The children's alignment with each other would also afford an opportunity to interfere with the coalition between mother and daughter, an inappropriate boundary. Reducing triangulation should help the parents initiate an examination of their issues as a couple, hopefully strengthening the marriage and thereby reducing isolation experienced by each. Efforts to make Mark and Jennifer a team should help establish them in child roles and give them some sense of commonality in the family, even if that commonality was initially established by getting them to temporarily unite against the parents. For example, Mark could be encouraged to occasionally misbehave, giving Jennifer the opportunity to be the peacemaker and the good one, altering the family's rigid perceptions of each child's role.

The process of family therapy would proceed until the family unit was restructured in a manner that encouraged healthier relationships. The strategies employed could include communication analysis, behavioral intervention, problem solving, as well as altering interactions and boundaries. In time, the parents would emerge as leaders of the family unit, preferably as a more unified couple who each tried to meet each other's needs. Together, they would help to encourage Jennifer's (and Mark's) independence and participation in age appropriate activities. Without the triangulation needs, Jennifer's behavior should improve and she would begin to feel a part of the family rather than apart from it. The resolution of Jennifer's dysthymia and ODD would be accomplished not by focusing on Jennifer's "so-called psychopathology," but by focusing on the functions served by her behavior within the family system. When the system was no longer dysfunctional, these pathologies would no longer be necessary and their resolution would occur as a natural outgrowth of the family therapy process.

Integration of Treatments and Conceptual Models

The conceptual models elucidated for Jennifer involved different treatment modalities (individual vs. family) and targeted different issues. In either case, how the therapist understood the presenting problem dictated the mode of intervention, how it would proceed, and the role the therapist would play. The interpersonal approach recognizes the role of social interaction as central to the emotional well-being of the individual. From this perspective, interpersonal problems may cause, exacerbate, or be the result of a mood disorder. When the type of interpersonal difficulty is identified as relevant to the onset of the disorder, it is targeted for remediation. The therapist acts as the patient's advocate, establishes a supportive but collaborative therapeutic relationship, and guides the interpersonal emphasis of the treatment. This view is in contrast to a structural family model that perceives boundaries and hierarchical roles as paramount to the healthy functioning of families and their individual members. In a structural approach, the family is the unit of intervention. The therapist joins the family unit as a leader, assumes responsibility for the goals of treatment, and engages in a process of altering the family structure in order to achieve these goals.

Both types of intervention (IPT and structural) may at times use similar techniques in treatment, but the treatments are themselves not technique driven. Instead, specific methods (i.e., directive or non-directive exploration, communication analysis, therapeutic modeling, role-playing, and the like) are used to facilitate the objectives established for the focus and outcome of treatment, as determined on the basis of the conceptual model used to understand the nature of the presenting problem. Treatment progress is evaluated according to standards established for the specific model and proceeds until a determined outcome is achieved. The desired outcome, however, is dictated by the clinicians' underlying theoretical perception of what constitutes health or normalcy and how to assess the meaning of an unhealthy or dysfunctional presentation.

References

American Academy of Child and Adolescent Psychiatry (1998). Practice parameters for the assessment and treatment of children and adolescents with depressive disorders. *Journal of the American Academy of Child and Adolescent Psychiatry*, 37(Supp), 63S–83S.

Brent, D. A., Kolko, D. J., Birmaher, B., Baugher, M., & Bridge, J. (1999). A clinical trial for adolescent depression: Predictors of additional treatment in the acute and follow-up phases of the trial. *Journal of the American Academy of Child and Adolescent Psychiatry*, 38, 263–271.

Klein, D. N., Lewinsohn, P. M., & Seeley, J. R. (1997). Psychosocial characteristics of adolescents with a past history of dysthymic disorder: Comparison with adolescents with past histories of major depressive and non-affective disorders, and never mentally ill controls. *Journal of Affective Disorders, 42*, 127–135.

Klerman, G. L., Weissman, M. M., Rounsaville, B. J., & Chevron, E. S. (1984). *Interpersonal Psychotherapy of Depression*. New York: Basic Books.

Kovacs, M., Feinberg, T. L., Crouse-Novak, M. A., Paulauskas, S. L., & Finkelstein, R. (1984a). Depressive disorders in childhood I. A longitudinal prospective study of characteristics and recovery. *Archives of General Psychiatry, 41*, 229–237.

Kovacs, M., Feinberg, T. L., Crouse-Novak, M.A., Paulauskas, S. L., & Pollock, M., *et al.* (1984b). Depressive disorders in childhood II. A longitudinal study of the risk for a subsequent major depression. *Archives of General Psychiatry, 41*, 643–649.

Kovacs, M., Obrosky, S., Gatsonis, C., & Richards, C. (1997). First-episode major depressive and dysthymic disorder in childhood: Clinical and sociodemographic factors in recovery. *Journal of the American Academy of Child and Adolescent Psychiatry, 36*, 777–784.

Lewinsohn, P. M., Clarke, G. N., & Rohde, P. (1994). Psychological approaches to the treatment of depression in adolescents. In W. M. Reynolds and H. F. Johnston (eds) *Handbook of Depression in Children and Adolescents*. Plenum Press, New York.

Lewinsohn, P. M., Rohde, P., Seeley, J. R., & Hops, H. (1991). Comorbidity of unipolar depression: I. major depression with dysthymia. *Journal of Abnormal Psychology, 100*, 205–213.

Lewinsohn, P. M., & Clarke, G. N. (1999). Psychosocial treatments for adolescent depression. *Clinical Psychology Review, 19*, 329–342.

Minuchin, S. (1974). *Families and Family Therapy*. Cambridge, MA: Harvard University Press.

Mueller, C., & Orvaschel, H. (1997). The failure of adult interventions with adolescent depression: What does it mean for theory, research, and practice? *Journal of Affective Disorders, 44,* 203–215.

Mufson, L., Moreau, D., Weissman, M. M., Kerman, G. L. (1993). *Interpersonal Psychotherapy for Depressed Adolescents.* New York: Guilford Press.

Orvaschel, H. (1995). *Schedule for Affective Disorders and Schizophrenia for School-age Children-epidemiologic – Version-5 (K-SADS-E).* Nova Southeastern University, Ft. Lauderdale, Fl.

Part IV

Anxiety Disorders

Chapter 8

Separation Anxiety Disorder

Cyd C. Strauss and John F. Todaro

Description of Separation Anxiety Disorder

Separation anxiety disorder (SAD) is the only anxiety disorder identified in the Diagnostic and Statistical Manual of Mental Disorders, Fourth Edition (DSM-IV; American Psychiatric Association, 1994) as occurring primarily in childhood and adolescence (i.e., onset before age 18). The defining feature of SAD is an unrealistic and excessive fear of separation from home or from major attachment figures. This anxious reaction must be beyond that expected for a child's developmental level; separation anxiety is normal and common from approximately six months of age until two to three years of age, peaking around 18 months. For a diagnosis of SAD, the child must experience three of eight criteria defined by the DSM-IV. These criteria include:

1) recurrent excessive distress when separation from home or attachment figures occurs or is anticipated;
2) excessive and persistent worry about loss or harm befalling major attachment figures or fear of abandonment;
3) unrealistic and persistent worry that a calamitous event will separate the child from a major attachment figure, such as fear of getting lost or kidnapped;
4) school refusal or persistent reluctance to go to school in order to stay with major attachment figure or at home;
5) persistent and excessive fear and avoidance of being alone or without attachment figures at home or in other settings, often resulting in "clinging" or "shadowing" attachment figures;
6) persistent reluctance to sleep alone or away from home;
7) repeated nightmares involving the theme of separation; and
8) physical complaints, such as headaches, stomach aches, or nausea that occur upon separation or when separation is anticipated.

For a diagnosis of SAD, symptomatology must be present for at least four weeks, and onset of the disorder must occur before the child is 18 years old (American Psychiatric Association, 1994).

The literature presents consistent findings regarding the onset, precipitants for, and course of SAD. Onset of SAD may occur as early as preschool years; onset

Handbook of Conceptualization and Treatment of Child Psychopathology, pages 151–173.
Copyright © 2001 by Elsevier Science Ltd.
All rights of reproduction in any form reserved.
ISBN: 0-08-043362-6

during adolescence is rare (Last, *et al.*, 1987). According to Klein and Last (1989), onset may be acute or chronic and often occurs after a major stressor, such as the death or illness of a relative, moving to a new school, or moving into a new neighborhood. Onset also has been reported to occur after prolonged vacations or absences from school (e.g., summer vacation, physical illness resulting in missed school) and at certain developmental transitions (e.g., entry into elementary or junior high school). Without intervention, the course of SAD is variable, with symptomatology alternating between periods of exacerbation and remission according to life stressors and developmental transitions (Klein, *et al.*, 1989).

Separation anxiety is among the most common disorders for which children are referred to clinics specializing in anxiety disorders (Last, *et al.*, 1987). Across studies, prevalence of SAD in the general population has been estimated at approximately one to four percent of children and adolescents (Andersen, *et al*, 1987; Bowen, *et al.*, 1990; Kashani, *et al.*, 1988). Rates of SAD also have been estimated in pediatric populations, with approximately four percent of children and adolescents meeting diagnostic criteria for this disorder (Costello, 1989). The prevalence rate of SAD appears to be greater in young children than in adolescents in both the general population (Kashani & Orvaschel, 1988, 1990) and in clinical samples (Last, *et al.*, 1987).

It is common for children and adolescents with SAD to have various coexisting childhood disorders. Specifically, children with SAD often describe having specific fears, such as fears of the dark, bumblebees, or ghosts; these fears may or may not be of phobic proportion (Last, 1989). Approximately one-third of children with SAD have concurrent generalized anxiety characterized by general worrying and/or tension (formerly diagnosed as overanxious disorder in DSM-III-R; American Psychiatric Association, 1987), with generalized anxiety most commonly observed to be secondary to the primary problem of separation anxiety (Last, Hersen, *et al.*, 1987; Last, Strauss, & Francis, 1987). Furthermore, approximately one-third of children with a diagnosis of SAD display a coexisting major depression (Last, *et al.*, 1987). Finally, 22 to 24 percent of children diagnosed with SAD experience a coexisting attention deficit disorder, zero to nine percent carry a concurrent diagnosis of conduct disorder, and 14.3 to 27.2 percent have a coexisting oppositional disorder (Last, *et al.*, 1987).

Several studies have examined specific diagnostic symptoms that occur in children and adolescents with SAD. Approximately 75 percent of clinic-referred children who were diagnosed with SAD showed the diagnostic criterion of school reluctance or avoidance (Last, *et al.*, 1987). Furthermore, somatic complaints often accompany school reluctance/avoidance, in which the child complains of symptoms such as headaches or stomach aches before attending or while in school. Somatic complaints also occur in other situations where separation from an attachment figure is anticipated. Indeed, up to 78 percent of clinic children and adolescents diagnosed with SAD report somatic complaints (Last, 1991).

In terms of developmental considerations, studies have demonstrated that the symptoms and nature of separation anxiety vary depending upon the age of the child. Comparing children between the ages of five and eight years ("young" SAD children), children between the ages of nine and twelve years ("middle" age group), and children between the ages of 13 and 16 years ("adolescents"), young children are significantly more likely to present with more total symptoms of SAD than are children in the middle age-group. No such differences have been observed between the adolescent group and the other two groups. In addition, different patterns of symptoms tend to occur in each age group of children with SAD. Two patterns of symptoms have been found in young children with separation anxiety: (1) "worry about harm befalling an attachment figure" and "worry that a calamitous event will separate the child from an attachment figure" is one frequently observed pair of symptoms; and (2) "worry about harm befalling an attachment figure" and "reluctance or refusal to go to school" often coexist in this young SAD group. The most common concurrent symptoms for middle children are "excessive distress upon separation" and "withdrawal, apathy, sadness, or poor concentration when separated," with 50 percent of this group displaying these two symptoms simultaneously in one study.

Moreover, SAD seems to be diagnosed more commonly in young children. In one large study of SAD children, the percentage of children found in each group declined with age, such that 44 percent of the sample were in the young group, 36 percent were in the middle group, and 20 percent were adolescents (Francis et al. 1987). This early occurrence of SAD in childhood contrasts with the age at intake observed in two other most common anxiety disorder subtypes leading to referral to a child outpatient clinic, i.e., overanxious disorder (per DSM-III-R; now diagnosed as generalized anxiety disorder in DSM-IV) and a phobic disorder of school. However, it must be noted that prior studies have examined *age at intake* to determine the prevalence of the disorder in different age groups. In contrast to the supposition that separation anxiety primarily is present in younger children, it may be that children with SAD are *referred* for evaluation at a younger age than other anxiety-disordered youngsters, although these subtypes may be equally common among the different age groups in the general population. Epidemiological studies conducted in non-referred samples and follow-up investigations of clinically-referred anxious children will enable greater understanding of SAD symptomatology in children.

Case Description

Sara is a twelve-year-old Caucasian girl who was referred by her mother for evaluation and treatment of anxiety. Sara resides with both biological parents and her two younger sisters, ages nine and three years, in North Central Florida. She attends the sixth grade at a parochial school. The primary reason for referral was Sara's severe anxiety concerning sleeping alone at night. Each night, Sara had problems falling asleep due to her concerns about being apart from her parents during the night. She noted that it took several hours for her to fall asleep nightly. She also was unable to spend the night at friends' homes due to her anxiety.

In addition to Sara's reluctance to go to sleep without being near her mother and/or father, she displayed frequent worries about harm befalling her parents, overconcern about harm to herself so that she would not see her parents again, fearfulness about being home alone, and repeated complaints about multiple somatic concerns when apart from her parents. Somatic complaints included frequent dizziness, stomach aches, and headaches. Sara called her mother from school almost daily complaining of physical symptoms, requesting that her mother pick her up from school. As a result, Sara missed one to two days of school each week. Sara similarly had difficulty being apart from her parents to visit with friends at their homes.

Sara and her mother indicated that these problems with anxiety began approximately one year before the initial therapy visit. They noted, however, that Sara had started the "habit" of going into her parents' bedroom nightly when she was four-years-old. At that time, Sara slept on the floor next to her parents' bed. The reason the parents initiated treatment at this time was that anxiety about separation increasingly was interfering with Sara's school attendance and causing Sara greater discomfort.

Evaluation of Sara's difficulties consisted of administration of a structured clinical interview with the mother and child individually, using the Schedule for Affective Disorders and Schizophrenia – Epidemiologic version (K-SADS; Orvaschel, *et al.*, 1982). Based on the structured interview, Sara met diagnostic criteria for a DSM-IV diagnosis of SAD. Completion of self-report measures further revealed that Sara demonstrates high levels of state and trait anxiety, as measured using the State-Trait Anxiety Inventory for Children (Spielberger, 1973). She also endorsed fears on the Fear Survey Schedule for Children Revised (Ollendick, 1983) consistent with her self-reported separation anxiety; her factor score on the Fear of danger and death was elevated relative to a normative sample of girls. Specific items rated as producing "a lot" of fearfulness for Sara included her fears of death, getting lost in a strange place, having to go to school, exposure to germs or getting a serious illness, and not being able to breathe. The mother also completed self-report measures of her own levels of anxiety and depression, which indicated that she similarly experienced high levels of trait anxiety; in contrast, the mother did not endorse symptoms of depression. Due to the mother's description of anxiety on self-report questionnaires, a structured clinical interview was administered to her to evaluate anxiety symptomatology more completely. This interview revealed that the mother did not meet diagnostic criteria for any specific anxiety disorders, although she did appear to experience sub-clinical levels of generalized anxiety and social phobia. In particular, the mother noted that she always had felt she had been a worrier since childhood. She indicated that at the time of referral she spent approximately one hour per day worrying about her family's health, her role as a parent, responsibilities at work, and finances. She also reported signs of social anxiety, in that she noted feeling anxious when initiating social contacts with others, resulting in some avoidance of group social activities. She also reported becoming anxious about others' possible critical evaluation of her. The mother had not received any cognitive-behavioral interventions or pharmacotherapy for her anxiety.

Cognitive Behavior Therapy for SAD

Cognitive behavior therapy (CBT) is one of the most common and effective treatments utilized for SAD. CBT for SAD consists of three main components: graduated exposure to feared or avoided situations, training in relaxation procedures, and instruction in rehearsal of coping self-statements. The aim of the graduated exposure approach is gradually to increase the child's or adolescent's independent activities, such as attending school or going to friends' homes without anxiety. Relaxation training is taught to help the child/adolescent cope with physiological aspects of anxiety, such as increased heart rate, shortness of breath, dizziness, or nausea, during exposure exercises and also to implement the lessons between sessions while in the real world. Cognitive rehearsal of coping statements also is used to facilitate the child's graduated approach to feared or avoided situations.

In-vivo Exposure

The first treatment component of CBT, graduated in-vivo exposure, involves having the child engage in activities previously avoided in a gradual or stepwise fashion. Initially, a Fear and Avoidance Hierarchy is developed using input from both the child and the parent(s). The hierarchy incorporates feared situations ranging from those that elicit mild levels of anxiety to those provoking extreme anxiety or panic. In instances in which the child both avoids school and other situations involving separation from the parent, two separate hierarchies are constructed. The treatment hierarchy typically consists of approximately ten items; each item explicitly states the activity to be practiced. The hierarchy is developed by including items that vary the feared/avoided situation based on dimensions of significance to the individual child, such as duration apart from the parent, distance from the caretaker, and presence (or absence) of other individuals. Items then are arranged in order from those eliciting minimal anxiety to those evoking maximal discomfort by having the parent and child rate each item on a Likert scale (e.g., 1-10) regarding the degree of anxiety or distress experienced in each situation.

The next step in the graduated exposure procedure is to implement the hierarchical exposure through use of homework assignments. Each homework assignment is negotiated among the child, parent(s), and therapist. It is important to note that the child needs to feel in control of the pace at which he or she progresses. Frequency of practice during the week is dependent on the nature of the particular item, but the child is encouraged to practice as often as possible (typically ranging from once a week to three times per week). The child keeps a record of the date of the practice and provides a Likert rating of anxiety experienced during the assigned exposure. Progression to the next hierarchy item occurs only after the child successfully approaches preceding items with little or no anxiety on at least two consecutive occasions and habituation has occurred.

Whereas the adult empirical literature has established efficacy of graduated *in-vivo* exposure therapy in the treatment of agoraphobia and other specific phobias (Barlow & Beck, 1984), there has been less systematic evaluation of this behavioral procedure in alleviating fear associated with separation. Single-case studies (e.g., Ayllon, *et al.*, 1970; Kennedy, 1965) and several controlled investigations (Blagg & Yule, 1984; Hagopian & Slifer, 1993; Last, *et al.*, 1998) have provided preliminary evidence to support the effectiveness of in-vivo exposure to reduce separation anxiety symptoms or separation-related school refusal. In the first of these studies, Blagg & Yule (1984) demonstrated that prolonged in-vivo exposure (i.e., flooding) was superior to inpatient hospitalization and individual psychotherapy plus home tutoring in the treatment of school refusal. Hagopian & Slifer (1993) showed in a controlled case study that school avoidance in a six-year-old girl diagnosed with SAD could be treated successfully using graduated exposure combined with positive reinforcement for successive approximations of independent school attendance. In this latter study, the child received rewards for remaining in the classroom for gradually longer durations while fading the mother's proximity and time spent in the school. Interestingly, Last and colleagues (1998) found that graduated in-vivo exposure was equally effective at reducing school refusal in children with school phobia as an educational, supportive control condition. The authors concluded that psychosocial treatments are effective in returning children to school and alleviating anxiety regardless of whether children participated in a structured cognitive-behavioral treatment approach or a more traditional psychotherapeutic approach. Overall, these studies suggest that a graduated in-vivo treatment approach shows promise in treating separation anxiety symptoms, but more studies clearly are needed to establish its efficacy.

Relaxation Techniques

Relaxation techniques also are used to assist the child with SAD to cope with anxiety. The child is trained in deep muscle relaxation (Jacobsen, 1938), using a technique modified for children and adolescents (Ollendick & Cervy, 1981). Children learn a maximum of three muscle groups each session and practice these skills twice daily at home. Children also select a pleasant imagery scene, such as eating in ice cream or playing on the beach, to enhance relaxation (Graziano & Mooney, 1980). As with cognitive coping statements, relaxation procedures are utilized to facilitate approach behavior during homework assignments on the hierarchy; these relaxation skills can be used during imaginal exposure as well.

Cognitive Component

The second component, cognitive therapy approaches, also can be useful in the treatment of SAD. Using cognitive therapy procedures, the underlying assumption is that the child's maladaptive thoughts, beliefs, attitudes, and self-statements lead to or maintain anxiety-related behavior. The child's maladaptive self-statements, displayed when anxious, are identified first. Subsequently, more adaptive coping statements are generated that can be used when anticipating or confronting anxiety provoking situations. Such statements for SAD children may include those that stress the child's capability of being independent (e.g., "I can do this on my own."), the fact that their parents will be safe while apart, and self praise (e.g., how brave the child is when he/she is alone). These cognitive self-statements are rehearsed within treatment sessions and then are practiced in the child's environment when confronted with anxiety provoking situations. In particular, these cognitive self-statements are used to assist the child when approaching items on the treatment hierarchy, thus reducing anticipatory anxiety or anxiety experienced during homework tasks.

Mansdorf & Lukens (1987) provided preliminary evidence for the efficacy of cognitive behavioral techniques in a study of two children presenting with school phobia (one also displayed SAD symptomatology). Through use of cognitive techniques, both children improved by the fourth weekly session of treatment. Follow-up assessments continued for three months after the children reached criterion, with no signs of relapse. Additionally, Ollendick, *et al.*, (1991) successfully eliminated nighttime fears and other SAD symptomatology in two children through the use of cognitive therapy combined with reinforcement. Interestingly, addition of reinforcement (e.g., earrings, trips to the mall, verbal praise) was a critical factor in treatment success; indeed, cognitive techniques in the absence of contingent reinforcement produced only slight improvement with one child and no improvement in the second child.

Cognitive-behavioral Case Conceptualization

Evaluation of Sara's presenting complaints revealed that she displayed anxiety symptomatology consistent with a DSM-IV diagnosis of SAD, including excessive and persistent worry about harm befalling her parents, worries about harm to herself that could result in her not seeing her parents again, difficulty sleeping alone at night and away from home, frequent somatic complaints, and distress upon separation from home and attachment figures. She also displayed reluctance to stay at school, often calling her mother with complaints of stomach aches or headaches in hopes of returning home to be with her mother.

Sara's separation anxiety problems were conceptualized using the tripartite model of anxiety, recognizing each of the three components of anxiety: behavioral, physiological, and cognitive components. In terms of the behavioral component of anxiety, anxious behaviors primarily consisted of Sara's avoidance of situations involving separation from her parents and home. Such behaviors included reluctance or refusal to sleep alone or away from home, to remain at school, and to go to friends' homes alone. The physiological symptoms of anxiety described by Sara and her mother included Sara's somatic concerns about stomach aches and headaches, as well as her autonomic arousal (e.g., accelerated heart rate, shortness of breath, sweaty palms) when separated from her parents. The cognitive component consisted of maladaptive patterns of worries, including catastrophic interpretation of physical symptoms and an overestimation of the likelihood of harm befalling her parents or herself while apart. A more detailed conceptualization of Sara's anxiety symptomatology using the tripartite model follows.

In terms of the behavioral component of anxiety, Sara avoided a range of situations involving separation from her parents that began after a summer camp experienced one-year before initiation of treatment. At that time, Sara was away at overnight camp and experienced elevations in anxiety levels, somatic concerns, and worries about her parents. Upon her return from summer camp, Sara began sleeping in her parents' room nightly. This increased level of separation anxiety after a transition in Sara's life (first time away at camp) has been observed with other children and adolescents with SAD.

A history provided by Sara and her mother revealed the child had, before this summer camp experience, slept with her parents several nights weekly, since she was a young child. By their account, it seems that Sara had never learned the skills needed to fall asleep on her own. In addition, the parents' bedroom likely contained stimuli that became paired or conditioned with falling asleep, that were not present in her own room. As Sara became older, she reportedly developed cognitions that something "scary" could occur if she were in her room alone, such as fearing that someone could break into the house and that she would be unable to get help in time. This type of worry is not uncommon in young children normally, but with reassurance and repeated exposure to sleeping alone without negative outcomes this fear ordinarily extinguishes. Due to Sara's intermittent avoidance of sleeping alone, her fearful cognitions persisted and extinction did not occur.

In addition to Sara's avoidance of sleeping alone, she also displayed avoidance of other situations involving separation from her parents (e.g., going to friends' homes, remaining at school for the full school day). Avoidance of such anxiety provoking situations resulted in her short-term alleviation of anxiety symptoms, but likely led to the maintenance or exacerbation of her separation fears in the long-run. By avoiding such situations, Sara was unable to learn that her catastrophic fears would not occur and that her anxiety would diminish if she remained in these situations.

In terms of physiological symptomatology, Sara reported a long-standing history of somatic complaints, including headaches and stomach aches. Sara's physiological symptoms were affected by her maladaptive pattern of cognitions; she often "catastrophized" their meaning. For example, Sara's interpretation of headaches was that her brain might be swelling or that she might have a brain tumor. Increased heart rate was viewed by Sara as indicating that she may be having a heart attack. Such hypervigilance concerning somatic symptoms may have followed the initial development of anxious feelings and the concurrent elevations of physiological symptoms associated with anxiety, including increased tension, heart palpitations, shortness of breath, and so on. Sara's interpretation of such physiological arousal also was faulty, i.e., rather than correctly perceiving her increased arousal as indicative of heightened anxiety levels, she interpreted them to indicate life-threatening conditions. The cognitive model of anxiety suggests that anxious individuals have a tendency to perceive exaggerated levels of threat, danger, and fear (Beck & Emery, 1985). Sara likely learned this pattern of fearful interpretation of somatic symptoms from her mother, who similarly worried excessively about health issues and modeled such faulty thinking.

Additionally, in terms of the cognitive component of anxiety, Sara displayed other patterns of cognitive distortions that exacerbated her anxiety levels. She frequently anticipated that she or her parents would be harmed or killed when separated, fearing that her parents would be injured in a car accident, that her parents would be the victims of a robbery or other crimes, or that she would be kidnapped so that she might not see her parents again. This "fortune-teller error" or overestimate of the probability of a negative outcome created considerable anxiety for Sara. Her tendency to catastrophize and overestimate a negative or dangerous outcome had become an automatic pattern that occurred in anticipation of or during each situation involving separation.

In order to address Sara's SAD symptomatology, a cognitive-behavioral treatment approach was planned for Sara to address the three main components of her anxiety. The three components involved graduated in-vivo exposure exercises, training in relaxation techniques, and instruction in cognitive coping strategies. The treatment utilized to treat Sara's separation fears is outlined below.

Cognitive-behavioral Treatment for Sara

During the first treatment session, instruction in progressive muscle relaxation skills was begun using the procedure developed for use with children and adolescents. Sara learned three muscle groups each session and practiced these skills twice daily at home. She also chose and imagined a pleasant scene, imagining herself flying over the neighborhood, to facilitate relaxation. Sara kept a daily record of her relaxation practice sessions, including the date and time of relaxation practices and ratings of tension levels before and after each relaxation procedure.

While learning relaxation techniques, Sara was asked to keep a daily diary at home of situations that induce anxiety, subjective anxiety associated with these situations, and cognitions that precede or accompany anxiety. These records were used to identify Sara's beliefs that may have been contributing to her problems with separation anxiety. Daily monitoring of Sara's cognitions revealed that she frequently "scanned" her body for symptoms of anxiety or possible illness, which resulted in escalation of her anxiety level. She also engaged in "catastrophic" thinking, such as "What if I am having a heart attack?" or "Maybe my brain is swelling" when trying to fall asleep at night or while at school. Based on Sara's daily records, Sara learned to rehearse positive coping statements that could substitute for maladaptive cognitions, such as "These are only symptoms of anxiety. They will pass. Let me take deep breaths and relax" or "I know that I am being silly. My brain is not swelling. I am fine." Sara practiced rehearsing more appropriate cognitions and became very proficient at identifying maladaptive thoughts and replacing them with more realistic and adaptive cognitions. Over the course of treatment, Sara reported that these adaptive thoughts, rather than her fearful cognitions, became automatic for her.

Systematic desensitization using graduated in-vivo exposure was a third, but central, treatment component for Sara. Cognitive self-statements and progressive-muscle relaxation were used to help Sara cope with each item of the graduated exposure procedure, as well as to eliminate worries regarding her mother's safety and to reduce general tension. Sara practiced confronting feared situations on her hierarchy between sessions and recorded her anxiety level (0-8 Likert scale) during each confrontation on a record form provided by the therapist. Sara was reassured that she was in control of the rate at which she proceeded in confronting items on the hierarchy. The therapist and parents provided encouragement and praise throughout treatment in efforts to reinforce Sara's approach behavior.

More specifically, Sara's fearfulness regarding sleeping alone initially was addressed. A treatment hierarchy was developed that consisted of Sara sleeping alone in her own bed for increasingly more nights each week; thus, each subsequent item on the hierarchy provoked increasing levels of anxiety. That is, Sara's first goal was to sleep alone four of the seven nights of the week. After successfully sleeping by herself for four nights, Sara then was able to sleep by herself for five of the seven nights of the week, and so on.

Coping strategies were utilized to help Sara fall asleep each night, including utilizing her progressive muscle relaxation skills and reading for 15 minutes before turning out the light. If Sara was unable to fall asleep within 15 minutes once the light was turned off, she resumed reading for another 15-minute period. This strategy was used until Sara was able to fall asleep. The parents agreed to provide small rewards (e.g., a trip to the ice-cream shop) for sleeping in her own bed the previous night. Sara also negotiated with her parents for weekly rewards (e.g., going to a nice restaurant with her mother, a shopping trip to the mall) for successfully meeting her goal of sleeping alone for the specified number of nights on the hierarchy that week.

The graduated exposure approach combined with use of coping strategies and provision of rewards for successes was implemented until Sara and her mother reported that Sara was successfully sleeping by herself nightly without anxiety. This approach was utilized for six weeks (i.e., Sara sometimes remained at a goal for more than one week due to the fact that she was not yet ready to move to the next step on the exposure hierarchy) and Sara was then able to sleep by herself nightly without experiencing anxiety. She continued to use her relaxation techniques, rehearsal of positive self-statements and reading to help her fall asleep, although these strategies were needed less and less over time. The nightly rewards were discontinued after Sara was sleeping alone nightly for two consecutive weeks, and the weekly rewards were no longer provided after four weeks of successfully sleeping by herself each night.

A second treatment hierarchy was developed that included a range of situations that provoked Sara's anxiety about separation. Items on this hierarchy included the mother leaving her alone at home for gradually longer periods, going to friends' homes for increasingly long durations, attending extracurricular activities with friends, sleeping overnight at friends' homes, and attending school without going to the office and calling home concerning somatic symptoms (so that the mother would pick her up and take her home from school). During weekly sessions, Sara, her mother, and the therapist again mutually agreed on the specific homework task(s) that Sara would practice during the week. Sara did not progress to the next level on the hierarchy until her anxiety on the previous hierarchy item had decreased to a low level or was absent (i.e., a rating of 0 or 1 on her 8-point Likert scale) during two consecutive practices of an item. Sara's second hierarchy of combined anxiety-provoking situations was as follows:

Anxiety provoking situation	Subjective units of distress (SUD) ratings
Mom leaves Sara home alone for 10 minutes.	2
Mom leaves Sara home alone for 20 minutes.	4
Mom leaves Sara home alone for 30 minutes.	5
Sara goes to a friend's home for one hour.	5
Sara goes to a friend's home for 1½ hours.	5
Sara does not go to the office at school to call home, unless she has a fever or is vomiting.	6
Sara goes to a friend's home for two hours or longer.	6
Go to a football game with friends.	7
Sleep overnight at Sara's grandparents' home.	8
Sleep overnight at a friend's home.	8

Sara again used her relaxation and cognitive coping skills to facilitate her approach to each item on the hierarchy. After the fourth week of implementing this hierarchy, she was able to remain home alone for half of a day without concern about her mother. She then reported success at not calling home from school, which required frequent practice of her coping self statements (e.g., "My stomach may hurt mildly right now, but I know I will feel better soon. It is probably just anxiety that will pass"). During this phase of therapy, the mother also was instructed not to pick Sara up from school if she called, unless there was clear overt evidence of illness (fever, vomiting). The mother readily complied with this recommendation from the therapist. Sara reported little difficulty with items on the hierarchy pertaining to going to friends' homes for gradually longer periods. It seems that once earlier items on the hierarchy were achieved, Sara felt little anxiety about going to friends' homes. After two weeks of practicing going to a friend's house for one hour and then one and a half hours, she initiated going to a friend's home for a full day on her own and experienced no anxiety doing so. Next, Sara attended a football game with friends and reported mild anxiety while on this outing. She scheduled additional activities with friends and gradually became more comfortable going with friends to the mall, to movie theaters, and so on. Finally, Sara attempted to sleep over-night away from home, first with relatives and then with friends. This step on the hierarchy required approximately four weeks of practice and Sara ultimately was able to sleep away from home with low levels of anxiety. Over the course of therapy, Sara continued to practice earlier items on the hierarchy in efforts to maintain her success and low levels of anxiety. For example, once she was able to remain alone at home for brief periods, her homework assignments included practice of staying alone at home while adding new hierarchy steps. At termina-tion of treatment, Sara and her mother reported that Sara was experiencing little or no anxiety in the range of situations on the treatment hierarchy. Somatic symptoms had reduced significantly in frequency, from several times daily to occurring once or twice monthly. Catastrophic thinking similarly was infrequent and was managed with her cognitive coping skills. Sara no longer met criteria for a DSM-IV diagnosis of SAD.

Behavioral Family Therapy for SAD

An alternative treatment for SAD discussed more recently in the child anxiety treat-ment literature is the behavioral family treatment (BFT) of SAD. Unlike traditional CBT for SAD which focuses mainly on the individual, BFT focuses on both family-child and teacher-child relationships. BFT is not intended to substitute for CBT in treating SAD; instead, this approach utilizes parents and teachers to enhance imple-mentation of traditional CBT strategies. In this capacity, parents and teachers can serve as surrogate therapists in managing the child's SAD symptomatology in the child's natural environment. BFT, therefore, has a multi-system focus that involves the child, parents, and teachers as active participants in treatment.

Although there are relatively few reported studies which have investigated the effectiveness of BFT for SAD, there is some evidence to suggest that involving members of the family in the treatment may enhance traditional CBT interven-tions. For example, Barrett, Dadds, *et al.* (1996) evaluated effectiveness of three interventions for SAD (CBT, CBT plus family anxiety management, and wait list control) in a sample of 79 children diagnosed with SAD, overanxious disorder, and/or social phobia. The family component consisted of training parents in four skills: (1) contingency management skills, including reinforcement of adaptive coping behavior and ignoring excessive anxious behavior displayed by the child; (2) anxiety management skills for coping with their own feelings of anxiety; (3) modeling skills for demonstrating adaptive coping behavior to their children; and (4) general problem solving skills to foster greater family cohesion and main-tenance of treatment gains. In this study, CBT strategies for SAD included psychoeducation about anxiety, in vivo exposure, and cognitive restructuring. Families receiving CBT plus family anxiety management (CBT + FAM) were found to have fewer children who met diagnostic criteria for each anxiety type compared with both the CBT and wait list groups at six and 12 month follow-up assessments. The combined CBT + FAM treatment, therefore, provided the child as well as the family with an arsenal of skills from which the family unit could maximize opportunities for treatment success.

Researchers have also involved teachers in psychosocial treatments for SAD. As described above, Blagg and Yule (1984) compared three interventions for SAD: behavioral treatment ($n = 30$), hospital inpatient treatment ($n = 16$), and home tuition and psychotherapy ($n = 20$). In the behavioral treatment, parent and teacher discussions were organized to encourage treatment consistency (e.g., use of positive reinforcement in response to courageous behavior displayed by the child) and treatment expectations (e.g., gradual return to school) across both the home and school environments. A significantly greater proportion of children receiving the behavioral treatment (93 percent) were reported to demonstrate successful treatment outcomes compared with both other treatments (hospital inpatient, 37.5 percent; home tuition and psychotherapy, 10 percent). Although it is unclear from these findings which of the several components in the behavioral treatment condition contributed to the positive outcome, parent and teacher involvement may have played a significant role in affecting therapy success.

Given the results of these studies, there appears to be some empirical support for the use of families, as well as teachers, to augment traditional cognitive behavioral strategies for SAD. This multi-system approach allows treatment to be comprehensive, encompassing a number of individuals and environments which impact SAD symptomatology.

The BFT of SAD consists of three components: psychoeducation, contingency management, and parent anxiety management and modeling. A more detailed description of each component follows below.

Psychoeducation

The psychoeducational component of the BFT of SAD involves educating children, parents, and teachers about separation anxiety, precipitating and maintaining factors, and the impact of SAD on familial and academic functioning. In age-appropriate terms, the clinician describes SAD symptomatology, the tripartite model of anxiety (i.e., behavioral, physiological, cognitive), and factors that may influence the onset and course of SAD.

Parents and teachers are also educated regarding how their behavior may impact the anxiety of the child. Specifically, parents and teachers come to understand that they serve as emotional models for the child. For example, if parents handle stress by avoiding those stressful situations, then the child will learn to avoid stressful situations as well. Therefore, how they demonstrate coping to the child may have a lasting impact on how the child manages his/her own separation anxiety. Similarly, parents and teachers gain awareness of the impact that their responses to SAD symptoms may have on the presentation of those symptoms. For example, parents and teachers may inadvertently reinforce separation anxiety, by regularly supporting fearful behavior (e.g., crying, whining) or by allowing the child to avoid anxiety provoking activities/environments (e.g., school, visiting friends). This psychoeducation will serve as a foundation to assist parents and teachers toward an understanding of SAD, which is intended to help them to manage SAD more effectively.

Contingency Management

Contingency management is the second component of BFT for SAD. In this component, both parents and teachers play important roles in managing SAD symptoms. There are three primary skills which parents and teachers learn during the contingency management component of BFT: (1) providing positive reinforcement following adaptive coping responses or courageous behavior, (2) ignoring fear-based verbal or non-verbal behavior, and (3) limiting avoidance of feared activities/environments.

The first skill in contingency management is utilizing positive reinforcement procedures when the child demonstrates adaptive coping or courageous behavior. Before the skill is taught, however, it is important to educate parents and teachers regarding how positive reinforcement procedures impact behavior in general. Specifically, parents come to learn that they can influence the frequency of adaptive behavior by immediately responding to the behavior in a positive manner. Parents and teachers are educated about how to select appropriate reinforcers that will increase the frequency of adaptive coping and/or courageous behavior. Reinforcers may take the verbal form (e.g., labeled praise) or non-verbal form (e.g., additional privileges). Once the parents and teachers have demonstrated an understanding of these issues, parents and teachers then learn how to identify coping and courageous behavior, such as utilization of positive self-statements or attempting to sleep alone at night. Parents may initially be resistant to these procedures for fear of manipulating their child's behavior; however, through education, parents and teachers are taught that these procedures allow the child to learn how to manage their anxiety and encourage the use of adaptive coping responses.

The second skill used in contingency management is the practice of ignoring anxious behavior displayed by the child. Similar to the first skill, parents and teachers are educated about how ignoring can affect anxious behavior. Specifically, parents and teachers learn that by simply not attending to anxious behavior, the occurrence of reassurance seeking and other anxious behavior can be reduced. In this way, the child does not receive attention or reinforcement for anxious behavior, such as crying, whining, and expressions of somatic complaints. Over time, such behavior will reduce in frequency and be replaced by other more adaptive behavior.

The final skill parents and teachers learn in this phase of BFT is how to limit avoidance behavior exhibited by the child. As a result of the child's separation fears, the child tends to avoid certain activities or environments for fear that some harm may befall the child or parent while apart. Parents and teachers come to learn that avoidance may be exhibited in many forms, including refusal to go to school, refusing to sleep alone at night, or refusing to visit with friends. This pattern of avoidance behavior is detrimental to the child since he/she never learns how to deal with fears and, consequently, continues to experience interference in daily functioning (e.g., limited social relationships, interruptions in academic performance). Contingency management, therefore, provides parents with a method to limit gradually opportunities for avoidance by encouraging approach behavior. By encouraging the child to participate in such activities through the use of both positive reinforcement for approach behavior and ignoring anxious verbalizations, the child is then actively engaged in an exposure exercise, allowing for separation fears gradually to become less distressful.

Parent Anxiety Management and Modeling

The third component of BFT for SAD is based on research reporting that parents who suffer from anxiety frequently raise children who also experience anxiety. From a behavioral family perspective, parents serve as emotional models for their children and can have a significant influence on their children's emotional behavior. Parents come to understand that how they manage their own feelings of anxiety likely influences how their children cope with their own anxiety. Therefore, if parents are taught how to manage their own anxiety effectively, they become good coping models for their children. Due to time constraints, this component of the intervention provides a brief, introductory course in the self-management of anxiety, and is not intended to be a comprehensive treatment for clinically-significant levels of parental anxiety. In fact, if parents present with clinically significant levels of anxiety, it is recommended that a referral be made for the parent(s) to receive CBT to address their own difficulties with anxiety.

There are two aims for this parent-anxiety management and modeling component of the intervention: (1) to teach parents how to manage their own feelings of anxiety, and (2) to teach parents how to demonstrate adaptive coping for the child. In most cases, this component of the intervention occurs over the course of three to five sessions. In order to achieve the first aim, parents are instructed in the use of a brief relaxation procedure. Relaxation strategies may take the form of deep breathing exercises or more structured progressive muscle relaxation. Both strategies target symptoms of physiological arousal commonly experienced by individuals with anxiety. In addition, parents are also instructed in how to use positive self-statements when confronted with stressful situations. Positive self-statements facilitate the coping process by reorganizing the individual's internal dialogue to promote support and encouragement while confronting their feelings of anxiety. As the parents develop these coping strategies and learn to limit their own avoidance of anxiety-related activities or environments, they can then serve as better models to the child for how best to manage anxiety.

In order to promote greater mastery of coping skills and generalization of treatment effects, parents are involved in treatment as models. In this capacity, parents serve as surrogate therapists, teaching their child how to cope with anxiety. There are a number of advantages to using parents as models in treatment. For instance, given that parents and their children have an established rapport, parents can facilitate anxiety treatments by using their trust and closeness with the child to facilitate home-based exposure exercises which initially will be distressful to the child. Also, given that parents most often have much greater contact with the child than treatment providers, they can provide more opportunities for between-session practice. Finally, by serving as models, the parent-child bond can be enhanced and greater degree of trust between the parent and child can be achieved.

Behavioral Family Therapy Case Conceptualization

From the information provided in the case description, Sara appears to be experiencing clinically significant levels of separation anxiety which meet diagnostic criteria for SAD. Given some of the family information (e.g., inappropriate management of Sara's SAD symptoms, poor modeling of adaptive coping by members of family), it seems that Sara's SAD symptoms can be targeted with a treatment program that incorporates a broader intervention beyond individual psychotherapy alone. Although a CBT intervention would help Sara in desensitizing her separation fears and learning how to cope better with her anxiety, the larger family system seems to have played an integral role in the onset and maintenance of Sara's problems. Therefore, without proper attention to family issues, Sara's separation fears may not be successfully remedied using a CBT intervention alone. A CBT plus behavioral family intervention seems appropriate in this case.

A behavioral family therapy perspective suggests that Sara's difficulties are influenced by the family system. A definitive causal link between Sara's separation fears and the family is not clear from the information provided; however, some hypotheses can be made. For instance, Sara's mother's description of her parenting style can be characterized as somewhat overprotective, since she rarely encouraged Sara to play with her friends alone or participate in sleepover parties. This overprotective parenting style may have inhibited the development of independent, courageous behavior. Also, Sara's mother described suffering from her own levels of anxiety which, over time, may have been observed by Sara. These early observations of her mother's anxiety and methods for managing anxiety may have demonstrated to Sara how to exhibit and manage anxious behavior under times of stress. As Sara grew older and the stress of having to attend school without the comfort of her mother, Sara's anxious reactions may have been a reflection of those expressed by her mother. Finally, the role of genetic/biological influences on the onset of Sara's separation fears can not be ignored. From the case description, it appears that Sara's family history is significant for anxiety problems. However, the preponderance of evidence in support of highly influential environmental factors, such as ineffective management of Sara's anxious behavior and frequent modeling of anxious behavior by Sara's parents, appears to be more compelling in Sara's case and needs to be targeted in treatment.

The case description also provides a number of examples demonstrating the role of the family in maintaining Sara's SAD symptomatology. Sara's mother noted that the parents: (1) had allowed Sara to sleep in her room when Sara had became anxious alone in her room at night, and (2) had allowed Sara to stay home from school one to two times per week in an effort to comfort Sara's separation fears. Essentially, these strategies served to reinforce Sara's use of avoidance as a coping strategy for managing her separation fears. By allowing Sara to avoid these stressful situations, her parents demonstrated that avoidance is an effective coping strategy in the short run for dealing with fears associated with sleeping alone at night and attending school alone.

From the standpoint of treatment, this family would benefit from instruction in parent management skills for handling Sara's SAD symptoms. Additionally, Sara's mother would also benefit from some brief training in managing her own level of anxiety followed by instruction in modeling adaptive coping behavior to Sara. In this way, a comprehensive approach to the treatment of Sara's SAD that targets some of the maladaptive coping patterns used by the parents and the child can be provided. A description of the BFT designed for Sara and her family is presented below.

Behavioral Family Therapy for Sara and her Mother

The intervention developed for Sara and her family took place over the course of ten 90-minute sessions. Due to Sara's father's inability to attend regular psychotherapy sessions, BFT sessions were conducted with either Sara's mother alone or, in the case of one session, with Sara's mother and teacher. Each 90-minute session began with approximately 30 minutes of describing and explaining the implementation of a specific BFT skill. The remaining 60 minutes in each session involved practicing the skill with the therapist via role-play exercises. At the end of each session, homework assignments were given in order to encourage use and practice of newly learned skills with Sara in the home environment.

Psychoeducation (Session one)

The first session of BFT involved providing the rationale for BFT to Sara's mother. One 90-minute session was devoted to providing Sara's mother with an overview of familial influences on Sara's separation anxiety and strategies used in BFT. Sara's mother also was provided with a number of additional readings for her to peruse on her own to increase her knowledge and understanding of SAD and the family's role in managing Sara's difficulties with anxiety.

Contingency Management (Sessions two – four)

The next three sessions focused on contingency management training. Initially, Sara's mother was taught how to identify SAD symptomatology. The tripartite model of anxiety was presented followed by specific examples of physiological, cognitive, and behavioral symptoms of SAD. Sara's mother was asked to generate some of her own examples of SAD symptoms that Sara had commonly exhibited. Sara's mother indicated that her child often endorsed a number of physical complaints when anxious, including dizziness and stomach aches. She also noted examples of fearful cognitions, such as "someone may hurt [me] when [I] am asleep" and that "mom might get into an accident while she is out." Finally, Sara's mother described numerous examples of avoidance behavior ranging from Sara not wanting to sleep alone at night to refusing to go to school without her mother. In order to increase Sara's mother's skill in identifying SAD symptomatology, she was instructed to keep a daily record of physiological, cognitive, and behavioral examples of SAD symptoms Sara had exhibited over the course of the next week.

In session three, Sara's mother learned how to reinforce adaptive coping skills and courageous behavior. For Sara, courageous behavior was described as going to school without calling her mother during the school day, visiting with friends alone, and/or sleeping in her room alone at night. Whenever Sara was able to display courageous behavior, she was to be given a reinforcer. Sara's mother was taught that reinforcers need not be expensive or material items but, rather, they could be tangible items or expressions that are deemed desirable by a child. A number of examples were offered, such as labeled praise (e.g., "I like the way you were able to sleep in your room last night on your own."), tangible rewards (e.g., an ice cream, a new board game), or social reinforcement (e.g., hug, kiss). Once a reinforcer was selected, it was emphasized that it be administered immediately following any instance of courageous behavior in order to increase the likelihood that Sara would continue to display that behavior in the future. In addition, Sara's mother was instructed to reinforce her child for using coping skills she had learned in her individual CBT sessions. For instance, Sara's mother was taught to reinforce any form of adaptive coping, including the use of relaxation skills, reciting positive self-statements, or engaging in previously avoided activities. Reinforcers, as noted above, were to be administered immediately after Sara used her coping skills.

The fourth session consisted of instructing Sara's mother in the use of ignoring, in her efforts to extinguish anxious behaviors. Sara's mother was taught to ignore Sara's expressions of anxiety and, instead, to direct her child to engage in the feared activity. This skill was somewhat difficult for Sara's mother to implement, since she often felt bad about not attending to her child's whines or calls for attention. As a result of the mother's reluctance to utilize ignoring, a modified approach was devised that allowed the mother to acknowledge Sara's feelings, but reduced the attention provided following anxious behavior. For instance, when responding to Sara's complaints that her stomach was hurting before leaving for school, Sara's mother was encouraged to say "I know your stomach hurts, but we need to go to school now." In this way, Sara's mother felt more comfortable that she was able to address her child's complaint, while, at the same time, not allowing her to engage in avoidance behavior. Over time, Sara's mother became more proficient at using ignoring as a means of decreasing Sara's anxious behavior and, by the end of treatment, seemed to feel more comfortable with not attending to most whines or requests to avoid that were expressed by Sara.

Parent-teacher Meeting (Session five)

To ensure that the school system was aware of Sara's difficulties with anxiety and the treatment plan, a conference was scheduled that included the parent, teacher, and therapist. This meeting had two primary aims: (1) to educate Sara's teacher about SAD and the treatment plan developed to help address Sara's difficulties with anxiety, and (2) to involve Sara's teacher in the intervention by instructing her in the use of contingency management techniques in the classroom to enable her to better manage Sara's SAD symptomatology. Sara's teacher had some prior education in SAD and its impact on the child, which facilitated the education process. The teacher was provided with some clear examples of physiological, cognitive, and behavioral symptoms that Sara frequently exhibited at school. In response, the teacher was instructed both to reinforce signs of courageous behavior and to ignore signs of anxious behavior. This instruction was very similar to that covered with Sara's mother, but was significantly condensed due to time constraints. At the end of this session, Sara's teacher seemed comfortable with her role and later complied with suggestions for better managing Sara's anxiety. Sara's teacher was encouraged to contact the therapist if she had any further questions about her role in Sara's treatment.

Parent Anxiety Management and Modeling (Sessions six – nine)

During these sessions, Sara's mother was instructed in the use of a number of anxiety management techniques to cope with her own stress and anxiety. Session five involved teaching Sara's mother how to use a relaxation procedure to better manage stress. Sara's mother indicated that she preferred to use deep breathing exercises rather than the progressive muscle relaxation procedure, since she had learned this skill during her pregnancy as a means of managing pain. Once Sara's mother demonstrated good use of deep breathing in session, she was assigned daily homework assignments to be performed twice a day for twenty minutes each session (total of 40 minutes per day). Initially, she practiced using these skills in stress-free situations; once proficient in achieving a relaxed state in nonstressful circumstances, she gradually implemented deep breathing exercises in increasingly more stressful situations. With time, Sara's mother learned how to use deep breathing as a means of managing her own anxiety at home, at work, and in other settings.

In sessions six and seven, Sara's mother also received training in how to use positive self-statements to cope with distressing thoughts. Her general worries seemed to focus on two areas of life: managing daily stressors (e.g., being on time for appointments, household chores) and being a good parent for Sara. First, Sara's mother was coached in generating positive self-statements to help her cope with stressful daily responsibilities. She described a number of daily stressors, such as attending to household chores, managing the family's finances, and meeting deadlines at work. According to Sara's mother, these stressors all shared the same theme of feeling overwhelmed by a large task. As a means of coping with her thoughts associated with feeling overwhelmed, Sara's mother was instructed to recite a brief positive statement, such as "If I break this activity down into smaller steps, I can get through this." Second, in order to manage worries associated with parenting, a number of positive self-statements were developed. For example, when feeling anxious about her ability to manage Sara's SAD symptoms, Sara's mother was instructed to state to herself that "I can do this. I am a good parent." These statements allowed Sara's mother to cope with the negative thoughts, which had caused her a great deal of distress.

The final skill presented to Sara's mother was modeling. Sessions eight and nine focused on teaching Sara's mother the importance of demonstrating relaxation skills and positive self-statements as coping mechanisms to Sara. Modeling was presented as a multi-step procedure, beginning with Sara's mother pointing out the stressful situation to Sara (e.g., I am going to work even though I feel nervous). Next, Sara's mother was taught how to articulate and demonstrate a coping plan to her child. For example, Sara's mother indicated that she would state "I feel nervous about all that I have to do today at work, so I need to use my breathing exercises to help me relax." She would then demonstrate the use of breathing to Sara and state how her deep breathing would help lower her levels of anxiety. In addition, Sara's mother also stated that she modeled the positive self-statements to Sara, such as "I am a good worker and I can get all of my work done." This procedure worked very well by using Sara's mother as a surrogate therapist in demonstrating how to manage anxiety. It also ensured that Sara had multiple opportunities to observe the correct way to implement adaptive coping strategies in stressful situations.

Overview (Session ten)

This final session was used to review all of the skills learned in the first nine sessions. This session also allowed Sara's mother to bring up problems experienced while implementing the intervention in the home environment.

Summary

SAD is a disorder of childhood and adolescence characterized by significant levels of anxiety experienced upon separation from home or from individuals to whom the child is attached. Difficulties with separation from attachment figures are common, occurring in approximately one to four percent of children and adolescents

(Andersen, *et al.*, 1987; Bowen, *et al.*, 1990; Kashani & Orvaschel, 1988). Preliminary research investigating psychosocial treatments for SAD have suggested that Cognitive-Behavioral Therapy (CBT) and Behavioral Family Therapy (BFT) approaches can be effective in reducing SAD symptomatology in children and adolescents.

CBT for SAD is the most commonly utilized psychosocial intervention for this anxiety disorder. Based in the tripartite conceptualization for anxiety, the child with SAD is seen as experiencing three sets of anxiety symptoms: behavioral, physiological, and cognitive. CBT targets each of these components by employing specific strategies for alleviating the distress and dysfunction associated with each component. These strategies, including exposure-based exercises (behavioral component), relaxation techniques (physiological component), and positive self-statements (cognitive component), have been discussed and applied to the treatment of separation anxiety symptoms displayed by a twelve-year-old adolescent named Sara.

In particular, a comprehensive CBT intervention was designed for Sara. A large emphasis of Sara's treatment involved in-vivo exposure exercises to help her desensitize her fears of being separated from her parents and going to school alone. In addition, Sara was provided with instruction in relaxation strategies and training in positive self-statements to assist her in managing anxiety during exposure exercises within sessions as well as between sessions in her natural environment. Altogether, Sara appeared to benefit from her CBT intervention by resuming a more adaptive lifestyle accompanied by significantly lower levels of separation anxiety.

A BFT treatment also was designed for Sara and her family. A BFT perspective suggests that separation anxiety is influenced by natural contingencies occurring in home and school settings. In these environments, parents and teachers play significant roles in the maintenance of separation anxiety and avoidance behavior by attending to and regularly supporting these symptoms. Therefore, from a BFT conceptualization, treatment for SAD must involve a broader focus, including parents and/or teachers, as well as the child, in treatment.

In this case, a ten-session BFT intervention was designed for Sara, her mother, and her teacher. In particular, Sara's mother was provided with a number of skills, such as psychoeducation about parental influence on their child's anxiety, contingency management, personal management of anxiety, and modeling of adaptive coping behavior. In addition, Sara's teacher was involved in treatment, by educating the teacher about SAD symptoms and by having the teacher alter contingencies in the classroom after anxious and brave behavior. These efforts provided the teacher with a better understanding of Sara's difficulties and offered some training in the management of symptoms in a manner consistent with BFT treatment. Over time, Sara's mother became very proficient in identifying Sara's SAD symptoms and responding to them appropriately. She also became quite good at managing her own levels of anxiety, thus being a good coping model for Sara. Overall, Sara's difficulties with separation anxiety diminished.

Both CBT and BFT interventions are rooted in behavioral theories of anxiety. Although there have been no reported studies comparing the effectiveness of CBT versus BFT treatments. Barrett, *et al.*, (1996) offered evidence suggesting that the combination of these treatments was more effective than CBT alone. Therefore, the most beneficial therapeutic intervention for SAD at this time appears to involve using CBT for the child, while also involving members of the child's home and school systems to facilitate the child's acquisition of coping skills and approach behavior.

Changes in economic aspects of clinical practice with an emphasis on reducing costs may not be consistent with this combined approach. One recommendation to promote efficiency can be to overlap CBT and BFT interventions within the same 90-minute therapy sessions, the first 60 minutes being spent with the child and remaining 30 minutes being spent with the parents. Alternatively, the child and parents may both be present during certain portions of therapy (e.g., psychoeducation, relaxation training, instruction in cognitive self-statements) to encourage efficiency and acquisition by instructing both the child and the parent at the same time. In this way, treatment would be more economical for the family, while allowing it to be comprehensive.

References

American Psychiatric Association. (1994). *Diagnostic and Statistical Manual of Mental Disorders* (4th ed.) Washington DC: Author.

Anderson, J. C., Williams, S. M., McGee, R., & Silva, P. A. (1987). DSM-III disorders in preadolescent children: Prevalence in a large sample from the general Population. *Archives of General Psychiatry, 44,* 69–76.

Ayllon, T., Smith, D., & Rogers, M. (1970). Behavioral management of school phobia. *Journal of Behavior Therapy & Experimental Psychiatry, 1,* 125–138.

Barlow, D. H. & Beck, J. G. (1984). The psychosocial treatment of anxiety disorders: Current status, future directions. In J. B. W. Williams & R. L. Spitzer (eds) *Psychotherapy Research: Where are We and Where should We Go?* New York: Guilford. 26–69.

Barrett, P. M., Dadds, M. R., & Rapee, R. M. (1996). Family treatment of childhood anxiety: A controlled trial. *Journal of Consulting & Clinical Psychology, 64,* 333–342.

Beck, A. T., & Emery, G. (1985). *Anxiety Disorders and Phobias: A Cognitive Perspective.* New York: Basic Books, Inc.

Blagg, N. R., & Yule, W. (1984). The behavioural treatment of school refusal: A comparative study. *Behaviour Research & Therapy, 22,* 119–127.

Bowen, R. C., Offord, D. R., & Boyle, M. H. (1990). The prevalence of overanxious disorder and separation anxiety disorder: Results from the Ontario child health study, *Journal of the American Academy of Child & Adolescent Psychiatry, 29,* 753–758.

Francis, G., Last, C. G., & Strauss, C. C. (1987). Expression of separation anxiety disorder: The roles of age and gender. *Child Psychiatry & Human Development, 18,* 82–89.

Graziano, A., & Mooney, K. (1980). Family self-control instruction for children's nighttime fear reduction. *Journal of Consulting and Clinical Psychology, 48,* 206–213.

Hagopian, L. P. & Slifer, K. J. (1993). Treatment of separation anxiety disorder with graduated exposure and reinforcement targeting school attendance: A controlled case study. *Journal of Anxiety Disorders, 7,* 271–280.

Jacobsen, F. (1938). *Progressive Rrelaxation.* Chicago, Ill: University of Chicago Press.

Kashani, J. H. & Orvaschel, H. (1988). Anxiety disorders in mid-adolescence: A community sample. *American Journal of Psychiatry, 145,* 960–964.

Kashani, J. H. & Orvaschel, H. (1990). A community study of anxiety in children and adolescents. *American Journal of Psychiatry, 147,* 313–318.

Kennedy, W. A. (1965). School phobia: Rapid treatment of fifty cases. *Journal of Abnormal Psychology, 70,* 285–289.

Klein, R. & Last, C. G. (1989). *Anxiety Disorders in Children.* London: Sage.

Last, C. G. (1991). Somatic complaints in anxiety disordered children. *Journal of Anxiety Disorders, 5,* 125–138.

Last, C. G., Hanson, C., & Franco, N. (1998). Cognitive-behavioral treatment of school phobia. *Journal of the American Academy of Child & Adolescent Psychiatry, 37,* 404–411.

Last, C. G., Hersen, M., Kazdin, A. E., & Finkelstein, R. (1987). Comparison of DSM-III separation anxiety and overanxious disorders: Demographic characteristics and patterns of comorbidity. *Journal of the American Academy of Child & Adolescent Psychiatry, 26,* 527–531.

Last, C. G., Strauss, C. C., & Francis, G. (1987). Comorbidity among childhood anxiety disorders. *Journal of Nervous and Mental Disease, 175,* 726–730.

Mansdorf, I. J., & Lukens, E. (1987). Cognitive-behavioral psychotherapy for separation anxious children exhibiting school phobia. *Journal of the American Academy of Child & Adolescent Psychiatry, 26,* 222–225.

Ollendick, T. H. (1983). Reliability and validity of the revised Fear Survey Schedule for Children (FSSC-R). *Behaviour Research and Therapy, 21,* 685–692.

Ollendick, T. H. & Cerny, J. A. (1981). *Clinical Behavior Therapy with Children.* New York: Plenum Press.

Ollendick, T. H., Hagopian, L. P., & Huntzinger, R. M. (1991). Cognitive-behavior therapy with nighttime fearful children. *Journal of Behavior Therapy & Experimental Psychiatry, 22,* 113–121.

Orvaschel, H., Puig-Antich, J., Chambers, W., Tabrizi, M. A., & Johnson, R. (1982). Retrospective assessment of prepubertal major depression with Kiddie-SADS-E. *Journal of American Academy of Child Psychiatry, 4,* 392–397.

Spielberger, C. D. (1973). *State-Trait Anxiety Inventory for Children (STAI-C).* Palo Alto, CA: Mind Garden.

Chapter 9

School Phobia

Wendy K. Silverman and Delight Hicks Carmichael

Description of the Disorder

Introduction

School phobia is frequently overlooked in edited volumes of child psychopathology and its treatment. Although we are not entirely certain why this happens, it probably has to do, in part, with school phobia *not* being included as a separate or distinct diagnostic category in current psychiatric nomenclature (e.g., DSM-IV; American Psychiatric Association, 1994). Because the organization and content of most edited volumes are usually reflective of the diagnostic classification schemas that are in use, in most child psychopathology/treatment edited volumes, there is no separate chapter on "School Phobia." The topic is often not mentioned at all. If it is mentioned, its coverage is woven through various chapters, such as those on anxiety and conduct disorders. Although such coverage is better than no coverage, it is limiting because it does not allow a full discussion of the complexities involved in the conceptualized treatment of the problem of school phobia.

We therefore think it is fortunate that the editors of the present volume were guided by the growing recognition that school phobia *is* a serious, frequently debilitating, and prevalent problem of childhood, and not by the current classification scheme. In terms of the problem being serious and debilitating, extensive school absence interferes, for example, with children's social and educational development, and has long-term consequences including an increased risk of anxiety disorders in adulthood (e.g., agoraphobia), social maladjustment, and employment difficulties. In terms of the problem being prevalent, school refusal affects about five percent of all school-age youngsters, spread fairly evenly across boys and girls (Kearney & Silverman, 1996).

Use of the term "phobia," reflects the terminological and conceptual confusion that has plagued the problem of excessive school absenteeism since it was first introduced as a phobia in 1941 by Johnson, Falstein, Szurek, and Svendsen. Most investigators currently working in the area, however, have come to view school phobia as a subset of School Refusal Behavior (SRB). As a consequence, the more comprehensive term, SRB, has come to be preferred over school

Handbook of Conceptualization and Treatment of Child Psychopathology, pages 175–190.

phobia (Burke & Silverman, 1987; Kearney & Silverman, 1996). We recognize that even this term has its difficulties, as it may be taken to imply a conscious decision on the part of the child to refuse to go to school – a perspective that is clearly not appropriate to all cases (Wicks-Nelson & Israel, 1997). Despite this difficulty, we prefer the term "School Refusal Behavior" over School Phobia, and therefore we use the former term subsequently in this chapter.

Similarly, we prefer the term School Refusal Behavior over the term "Truancy." Truancy is usually characteristic of children who are absent from school on an intermittent basis, usually without parental knowledge. As discussed in this chapter, children with SRB are absent for extended durations, such as consecutive days, weeks, or months, and usually with parental knowledge. Truancy also is usually associated with other disruptive child behavior problems (e.g., conduct problems) as well as poor academic performance. Although we hasten to add that this latter distinction also has been a matter of controversy, in light of the considerable comorbidity that has been found for anxiety and conduct disordered problems in children (Russo & Beidel, 1994).

The Clinical Picture

The word that best describes the clinical picture of SRB is "heterogeneous." There is no one picture of the "school refusing child." Some children who display SRB fail to attend school fully and completely. Other children may initially attend school in the morning but call their parents to be picked up early; frequently because they have somatic complaints (e.g., nausea, headaches). Another group of children displaying SRB may attend school and even manage to stay there all day. However, it is a chore each morning to get these children to school because of severe problem behavior (e.g., temper tantrums, crying, pleading). Another group of children with SRB is similar to the latter in that they attend school, but they experience unusually high levels of distress most of the time there, leading to regular pleas to remain home in the future. These are not distinctive patterns of SRB, however, and it is not uncommon for children to display more than one pattern at a given time. Nor is it uncommon for children to "move in and out" of varying patterns over time.

The heterogeneity of SRB also is apparent in terms of extensiveness of the problem behavior, mode and age of onset, and premorbid functioning of the child. These characteristics are captured well by the subtypes of SRB that have been frequently referred to in the literature as either "Neurotic," "Acute," or "Type I" vs. "Characterological," "Chronic," or "Type II" (Kennedy, 1965). Neurotic, acute or type I SRB refer to the sudden onset of school refusal in a young child who has previously performed well in school and has no prior history of maladaptive social/intellectual functioning. Characterological, chronic, or type II SRB refer to the gradual onset (over several months or years) of school refusal in an older child who appears to have emotional, social, and intellectual difficulties (past or present). SRB that is characterological, chronic, or type II tends to have a poorer prognosis than SRB that is neurotic, acute, or type I.

The heterogeneity of SRB also is manifested in terms of diagnostic picture. Recent research has systematically documented the clinical features of children who display SRB by evaluating them with structured diagnostic interviews and deriving DSM (Diagnostic and Statistical Manual) diagnoses. For example, Last & Strauss (1990) investigated DSM-III-R anxiety disorder diagnoses in 63 school refusing youth (ages seven to 17). The most common primary diagnosis was separation anxiety disorder (n = 24), followed by social phobia (n = 16), and specific phobia (n = 14). Children with SRB also frequently display multiple diagnoses (i.e., comorbidity) (Kearney, et al., 1995). The main implication of these findings is that several of the clinical features that characterize SRB are the same as those featured in a given SRB case (e.g., excessive avoidance if criteria for phobic disorder are met, etc.).

Further, for children who meet criteria for a particular DSM diagnostic category, even more heterogeneity may exist. For example, for children with SRB who meet primary diagnosis for specific phobia only, at first glance "school' might be considered a circumscribed and specific stimulus. In fact, however, "school" covers several different types of specific stimuli, including the hallway, classroom, gymnasium, pool, fire alarm, school bus, animal, or piece of equipment, etc. (Kearney, et al., 1995). Identifying the specific phobic object or event thus becomes an important point to consider when assessing SRB in children with a primary diagnosis of the condition.

Heterogeneity among children with SRB also is apparent in terms of the presence and types of somatic symptoms or complaints that they may report. Although somatic symptoms or complaints are frequently the main reason why parents feel that they need to keep their children at home rather than force attendance, not all children report such symptoms. For example, in a sample of adolescent school refusers (n = 44) who were comorbid with anxiety and depression, many but not all reported somatic complaints (Bernstein, et al., 1997). Perhaps more important was the finding that specific types of somatic complaints varied across the sample, and included autonomic (e.g., headaches, sweatiness, dizziness) and gastrointestinal (e.g., stomach aches) symptoms. These findings highlight the importance of inquiring about somatic complaints (presence/absence and type) among children with SRB.

Treatment Approaches

As with any child's emotional or behavioral problem, how one conceptualizes the problem of SRB is likely to be influenced in part by theoretical orientation (e.g., psychodynamic, behavioral). A psychoanalytically/dynamically oriented clinician, for example, would generally focus on the parent–child relationship and its contribution to fear of separation as well as school refusal. Influenced in part by Johnson, et al. (1941), this clinician would likely conceptualize SRB as a consequence of a severe anxiety response that occurs upon separation by both mother and child. Such separation anxiety is likely to be viewed as being cultivated through mutual dependency on the part of the mother and child, and that the child has come to fear that something bad may happen either to him/herself or to his/her mother during separation. In the latter instance, the child may have aggressive wishes toward the parent that the child's fears will be fulfilled (Wicks-Nelson & Israel, 1997).

Even though conceptualizations of the problem of SRB are influenced by theoretical orientation and, as a consequence, will vary in accordance with the theory held, there is one thing that is unlikely to vary among clinicians, no matter what the orientation. Namely, the majority of clinicians of all theoretical orientations stress the importance of getting the child back to school. Therefore, in general, they take an active approach in returning the child to school (Kearney & Silverman, 1996; Wicks-Nelson & Israel, 1997).

In fact, most of the *evidence-based approaches* target improvement in school attendance as the main goal. School attendance is, therefore, the primary outcome measure in treatment research literature, with additional indices of improvement (i.e., the "evidence") being scores on self-rating scales of fear, anxiety, or depression, and parent behavior rating scales. Some researchers/clinicians may be completely satisfied with this view of "evidence," some will be only partially satisfied, and some may be completely dissatisfied. Nevertheless, because of the growing interest in using treatments that have been shown to have some efficacy, evidence-based treatment approaches are discussed in the remainder of the chapter.

The sections that follow provide conceptualization and treatment strategies for two evidence-based treatment approaches. The first approach can be referred to as an "Exposure-based Transfer-of-Control Treatment Approach," the second approach as a "Functional Prescriptive Treatment Approach."

Exposure-based Transfer of Control Treatment

Conceptualization. The transfer of control treatment approach (Silverman & Kurtines, 1996a, 1996b, 1997) explicitly recognizes that SRB, similar to anxiety disorders in children, is complex, multi-faceted, and multi-determined. As a consequence, it focuses on delineating the links between the types of interrelated maladaptive processes or symptoms (e.g., avoidant behavior, distorted thinking, relational) that are associated with SRB and the types of therapeutic procedures and strategies (e.g., behavioral, cognitive, relational) that can be used to modify processes or symptoms.

The approach holds that effective long-term psychotherapeutic change in children involves a gradual "transfer of control," generally from therapist to parent to child. The therapist is viewed as an expert consultant who possesses knowledge of the skills and methods necessary to produce therapeutic change, and who then transfers use of these skills and methods to the parent, and subsequently, from parent to child. In treating SRB in children, the primary focus of the transfer of control is on controlling occurrence and successful implementation of key change producing procedures. The approach further assumes that a critical task of the treatment is allowing for the adequate transfer of control from the therapist to the child.

Key Change Producing Procedure. Exposure is the key therapeutic ingredient or change producing procedure here. This is because a large and growing body of research evidence shows that exposure to the feared object or situation is important for reducing fears and avoidant behavior (Silverman & Kurtines, 1996b). Although there are varying views among theorists and investigators as to why exposure works, all of these views involve in various ways the modification of behavioral, cognitive, and affective processes. The forms of direct therapeutic exposure used in the treatment involve the child confronting anxiety-provoking objects or events (in vivo and imaginory) in a gradual manner.

Facilitative Strategies. Also involved in the treatment is a variety of therapeutic strategies for facilitating occurrence of exposure. These involve use of both behavioral and cognitive strategies. The first, *contingency management*, is based on behavioral processes of change and emphasizes the training of parents in the use of appropriate contingencies to facilitate the child's exposure or approach behavior toward feared objects or situations. A key element of contingency management is contingency contracting. The second, *self-control*, is based on cognitive processes of change. Self-control emphasizes the training of the child in the use of appropriate cognitive strategies to facilitate exposure or approach behavior toward school-related fearful objects or situations. A key element of self-control training is cognitive restructuring and self-reward. Evidence has documented efficacy of both of these facilitative strategies to reduce phobic disorders in children and adolescents, including children with SRB (Silverman, *et al.*, 1999a).

Using a Transfer of Control Approach for Implementing an Exposure-based Intervention. The transfer of control approach provides guidelines for the administration of behavioral and cognitive strategies. The approach is built on the links that exist between key maladaptive processes of SRB (i.e., behavioral, cognitive, affective), related contextual processes (e.g., relational) that give rise to and/ or maintain these processes, and the key change producing procedure (i.e., exposure) and related therapeutic facilitative strategies (e.g., contingency management and self-control training) that have an impact on these maladaptive processes.

As noted, in treating children with SRB, the primary focus of transfer of control is on "controlling" the occurrence, and successful implementation of the key change producing procedure – child exposure or approach behavior. Hence, the transfer of control involves first the training of parents in contingency management and in using these skills to encourage the child's exposure (parent control). This is followed by a gradual fading of parental control while the child is taught to use self-control strategies to encourage his/her own exposure (child control). Consequently, parental (or external) control is gradually reduced while the child learns cognitive self-control strategies in contexts specific to his or her anxiety problems. Although a transfer-of-control approach is not explicitly discussed in recent articles that have reported on the efficacy of cognitive behavior therapy for SRB in children (King, *et al.*, 1998; Last, *et al.*, 1998), we believe a case could be made for such a transfer occurring in cognitive behavior therapy. This view awaits empirical verification, however.

Another important part of transfer-of-control is "relapse prevention," in which strategies are presented to handle and prevent recurrence of avoidant behavior. Relapse prevention is viewed as important to help ensure a complete-final transfer of control so that in the event of relapse both the child and parent will be able to successfully manage the event, especially if they are no longer being seen by the therapist.

In some cases with transfer of control, the therapist may find it is either sufficient or necessary to work with single and direct lines only. For example, in the case of a young child and competent parent the therapist may find it useful to work directly with the parent, i.e., a line from therapist to parent (Silverman, *et al.*, 1999a). Similarly, in the case of an adolescent and a competent parent the therapist may find it useful to work directly with the adolescent, i.e., a line from therapist to adolescent (Silverman, *et al.*, 1999a). In yet other circumstances (e.g., when the parent suffers from psychopathology) the therapist might find it useful to devise another pathway of control to the child, such as through the peer group (i.e., group treatment) (Silverman, *et al.*, 1999a) or to "clear up" the blocked pathway by treating the parent along with the child (i.e., dyadic treatment) (Cobham, *et al.*, 1999; Ginsburg, *et al.*, 1995). In addition, in certain settings, such as in school, the therapist may find it necessary to work with a single and direct line (i.e., a line from therapist to child), because parents are usually unavailable for participation in school-based treatments.

The therapeutic stance of the transfer of control approach has three basic dimensions: *problem-focused and present-oriented, structured, and directive.* The problem-focused and present-oriented dimension is rooted in the therapist's desire to achieve a very specific goal: to have the child return to school. The structured and directive dimensions are more rooted in the specific nature of the population and problem. Specifically, the transfer of control approach provides a "natural" structure of how therapy is conducted in that it guides the sequence of the change producing procedures (from therapist to parent to child), thereby rendering a structured approach more useful. A therapeutic stance that is directive rather than non-directive is adopted because of the nature of the problem: SRB tends to be linked to external antecedent conditions, and the most effective change producing procedure involves exposure to the conditions that elicit the avoidant response. The therapeutic stance is consequently directive because the most effective change producing procedure involves systematic and direct arranging of exposures to school-related, fearful/anxious producing stimuli.

Case Illustration

Description

David was a twelve-year old Caucasian male in the seventh grade, who had been showing intermittent school attendance from the very beginning of the school year. In the beginning, the days he missed were due to a number of somatic complaints including severe nausea and terrible headaches that he experienced in the mornings at home. He also began missing more school days immediately after extended or holiday weekends. As the school year went on, David's school attendance worsened to the point that, when he presented to our clinic, he had not attended a single day of school for 32 consecutive days. David was referred by his pediatrician who had ruled out an organic basis for David's somatic symptoms and complaints.

David's parents were divorced and he lived with his mother and his younger sister. David presented by indicating that he did not want to attend the school because it was such a "bad" school. He spoke of deteriorating conditions of the school building, the terrible teachers who "did not teach," and the other kids who did not care about learning but were just into making trouble, smoking cigarettes, and being generally obnoxious. David was very firm in stating that he was not "afraid" or "anxious" about attending school. He admitted though that attending school was difficult for him. He spoke particularly of feeling uncomfortable when he needed to "do things in front of other kids," as well as just generally "hanging out" with others. Although the school was "terrible," he recognized that he needed to get himself back in school. This recognition on David's part likely contributed to his willingness to cooperate in the assessment and, as will be seen, to become an active collaborator with the therapist (the first author) in working on returning to school.

It was further apparent that although David's mother had long had difficulty in managing her son's behavior, with the advent of David's SRB, her ability to handle her son had deteriorated. David appeared to be "the boss" in the relationship and the mother had little knowledge of how to gain control over his behavior, particularly with respect to his SRB.

Assessment. David and his mother were given child and parent versions of the Anxiety Disorders Interview Schedule-Child and Anxiety Disorders Interview Schedule-Parent (Silverman & Nelles, 1988). They also completed a number of paper-and-pencil measures including child and parent versions of the Revised Children's Manifest Anxiety Scale and the Fear Survey Schedule for Children – Revised. The ADIS-C/P contains a section specific to SRB in which the respondents are asked to indicate what it is about school that "makes it difficult for the child to go." Both David and his mother endorsed a number of items on the "list" that is supplied, including the other kids, the teachers, and speaking in class. In addition, to presenting with SRB, diagnostic criteria were met for Social Phobia. Elevated scores also were obtained on the questionnaire measures. Based on the assessment results, David and his mother were invited to participate in the treatment program. Both he and his mother agreed and displayed high interest and motivation in beginning the sessions.

Overview of Treatment

In this case of David, it was believed important to help the mother gain control over some of David's SRB and also help David to learn how to better control or handle difficult school situations, particularly those that pertained to social evaluative ones. Separate child and parent meetings, followed immediately by a conjoint meeting, were therefore conducted to help achieve a transfer of control from the therapist to parent to child. David and his mother were seen by the therapist for about 20 minutes each, and the conjoint meeting was about another 15 minutes. The treatment ran for 13 weeks and focused on first, the conceptual basis of the treatment including the transfer of control notion and the importance of exposure. Second, the multi-faceted nature of SRB (e.g., avoidance behavior) was described as a way to present the rationale for behavioral and cognitive strategies. Third, a hierarchy was derived and out-of-session exposure tasks were described. Fourth and fifth were the teaching and application of contingency management and cognitive self-control training. The last part of the treatment was relapse prevention.

Treatment's Conceptual Basis. David's treatment was presented as a joint and collaborative effort between therapist, child, and parent. As a consequence, the importance of David and his mother understanding the nature of SRB and the rationale underlying its treatment was emphasized. Also emphasized was the transfer of control notion to help enhance the mother's and child's understanding that ultimate success would be up to each of them. Within this frame, the therapist emphasized that there was nothing magical about the treatment program. For treatment to work, both the mother and David must practice all that they learn – just as they would any other skill. The therapist also explained that David would not necessarily be "cured." Rather, he would learn skills needed to make it easier for him to attend school.

Next, the importance of exposure or approach behavior was emphasized. David and his mother were told that when individuals stay away from (or avoid) school, their avoidance is maintained because they do not have the opportunity to learn ways to successfully master difficult situations associated with school, and that particular situations may not lead to the horrible consequences that they believe will occur. To help learn this, it is necessary to approach or deal with school-related situations. Numerous examples of this view were given, including the popular notion of "getting back on a bicycle after falling off," which was readily understood.

It also was explained that when the exposures are done, it will be important to ensure that elevated levels of arousal or discomfort are experienced by David. The importance that David face this arousal and discomfort and not leave the situation until these feelings are reduced was stressed. It was explained that such reduction will occur, if he allows for it (i.e., by staying in that situation and with that experience).

Multifaceted Nature of SRB. In presenting the program's conceptualization of SRB and its treatment, it was explained to David and his mother that the boy's SRB was apparent not just in terms of non-attendance, or avoidance, but also in his physical or somatic complaints and symptoms, and his negative views about the school. It was further explained to David that his avoidance of school involved school situations that had a social component, particularly where David would be faced with the prospect of being evaluated by others or having to interact with his peers.

To help explain this the therapist posed questions to both the child and parent. Examples included: "When you think about having to go to school, what thoughts do you have?," "What do you feel like doing when you know it is time for school?," "How does your body react when it is time for school?" The therapist also prompted, as necessary, to facilitate David's understanding (e.g., "What are you more likely to do when it is time to go to school – stay closer or run away?" and "What are you thinking?").

Hierarchy. Several of the early sessions were spent in developing a hierarchy for gradual, in vivo exposure tasks. Both David and his mother were informed that David would learn how to handle going to school by "doing" exposures, i.e., "facing school situations." They were told that the program took a gradual approach to exposure, thereby creating step-by-step success experiences.

David's hierarchy consisted of fifteen specific situations that ranged from only slightly fearful to extremely fearful. These focused on a variety of school-related situations in which David indicated he could not currently place himself. Although the expectation was conveyed that David was to progress up the hierarchy, it was also made clear that he was the one who ultimately determined rate of progress. The point about eliciting arousal or discomfort and handling it successfully with each exposure was emphasized again.

In devising the hierarchy, it was necessary to first elicit and rank the information obtained. The therapist and David first "brainstormed" to generate a list of all the different situations or facets of school that rendered school a "difficult place to be." Once this list was generated, the next task was to rank order the items. David was asked to identify the two items on the list that represented the extreme anchors for the two ends of the hierarchy (i.e., which is the most difficult, which is the least?). He had no difficulty in doing this. Then, using a scale from 0 (not at all scary/never stay away from) to 8 (very, very scary/always stay away from), he rank-ordered the remaining items (or the steps of the hierarchy) that fell in between.

The hierarchy developed included the following items from least to most difficult: driving by the school, drive by school when school is not in session, drive by school when school is in session, sit in car in front of school when school is not in session, sit in car in front of school when school is in session, stand in front of the "common" area at the start of the school day (i.e., where the students gather while they are waiting for the first period to begin), do the latter plus talk to some other kids, walk to first class while talking to another kid, sit in classroom, stay in classroom.

A final consideration involved in constructing David's hierarchy was that cooperation and/or assistance of school personnel was viewed as necessary. The therapist contacted the school counselor and explained the program's goals and strategies, and determined that the cooperation of the school would be forthcoming.

Out-of-session Exposure Tasks. To introduce tasks that were assigned each week, it was explained that given that the therapist met only one hour a week with David and his mother, and given that there remained 167 hours in the week, it was important that they practice out-of-session aspects of what they learn in session. Many of these would involve out-of-session exposures, given the importance of exposures in the treatment. These assignments would involve "doing exposures" that begin at the low end of the hierarchy and increase in difficulty as David's treatment progressed. The emphasis was on David making his best attempt at a step on the hierarchy, though again, the importance of inducing an aroused state or discomfort and 'staying with" that feeling was emphasized. This was necessary before the next step on the hierarchy could be taken.

Contingency Management. As adapted for use in the treatment of SRB, this is designed to transfer control from therapist to parent and to facilitate graduated exposure of the child to school by using behavioral contingency management procedures. Emphasis is placed on teaching parents behavioral strategies to facilitate child exposure along each step of the hierarchy. Specific learning principles and procedures taught to David's mother included positive reinforcement, shaping, extinction, contingency contracting, following through, and consistency. While this was happening, time with David was spent on refining the hierarchy, and on devising and refining the "reward list." This was followed by writing specific contracts between parent and child that detailed the child exposure task (i.e., steps on the hierarchy) and the reward that went with it (i.e., an item on the reward list) as a consequence of successful completion by the child. Because David did not interact with his peers very often, rewards that would continue his non-socializing with other children were discouraged (e.g., computer games), in favour of rewards from activities that David could carry out with his sister or his mother (e.g., going to a movie).

Self-control. After successful child exposures, self-control training was started. The focus was on teaching David cognitive strategies such as self-observation, self-talk (identifying and modifying), self-evaluation, and self-reward. Kendall's (1994) technique of employing stick figures with "thought bubbles," like those seen in comic strips, was adopted to help depict different types of self-talk and their role in maintaining David's SRB. For example, David was asked to think of situations that made it difficult for him to attend school and to fill in bubbles that showed scary or anxious thoughts. David was also taught how to question his thoughts and modify them to render them less maladaptive. The therapist also served as a model and encouraged questioning aloud, such as "Is that really likely to happen?," "Has it actually happened before?," and "What if it does?" The aim of such questioning was to help David realize that constructive alternatives were available even in the worst of situations.

David was also taught the modified STOP acronym where S stood for School (rather than "Scared" as it does in working with children who present with anxiety disorders), T stands for Thoughts, O stands for Other thoughts or Other things I can do to handle school, and P stands for Praise myself for successfully handling my exposure to school situation (e.g., "I did it!").

The therapist played an active role in helping David to identify or generate alternative, coping thoughts. He asked David a series of questions pertaining to such issues as reality checking (e.g., "have I ever forgotten what to say and if so, how often?"), decatastrophizing (e.g., "will I die or be paralyzed forever?"), and problem-solving (e.g., "what if I do forget what to say, what can I do in that situation?").

Part of David's self-control training also involved helping him to recognize the link between his somatic symptoms and complaints and "school." This was done in the early phases of treatment when David was asked to keep a daily diary, where he was to self-observe and self-monitor his bodily reactions, and in particular, when he was experiencing somatic symptoms. Such monitoring indicated that these reactions occurred most often at bedtime and in the mornings, when most children are preparing for school. Reactivity associated with David's monitoring was apparently helpful as David's reporting of somatic complaints and symptoms decreased as the weeks went on.

Relapse Prevention. Two main concepts were presented during the relapse prevention phase. First, the importance of continued practice or of continuing child exposure, and second was how to interpret and construe "slips." Given the importance of continued exposure, it was emphasized that the more David continues to engage in it, the less likely it is that he will have a relapse. This is because much of what David has accomplished is due largely to his exposure exercises, and like any accomplishment "if you don't use it, you lose it." Examples were provided from other skills that David may have learned in his life, such as sport or an instrument, and how if he did not continue to practice he would lose the skill needed for success.

Second, it was explained that no matter how much David practiced and continued to engage in exposure, a "slip" is likely to occur. It was emphasized that this is a common occurrence. The example was given of a person on a weight loss program who may have successfully lost 20 pounds but then eats a piece of cake at a party. This example was discussed and it became evident to both David and his mother that an adaptive interpretation of this event was: "This is a single event. It does not mean that everything is blown or ruined. And I need to pick myself back up and get back on the positive track I was on." Emphasis also was placed with the mother on her role in handling slips and how many children are prepared to look to their parents and take the cues from them in interpreting falls from grace.

Outcome and Prognosis

By the end of the tenth session, David had regularly attended school for one month with no absences. Before the twelfth session, David's mother called the therapist and indicated that David was having trouble going to school after an extended school holiday. Following a session emphasizing relapse prevention strategies, David was able to return to school full-time. At the end of treatment David no longer met diagnostic criteria for social phobia and all scores on the child- and parent-rating scales showed significant improvement. Such improvement was maintained at a one-year follow-up assessment. The prognosis for continued improvement is viewed to be positive in light of David's and his mother's high levels of motivation, their willingness to become actively involved in the treatment and their high levels of compliance.

Functional Prescriptive Treatment Approach

An alternative approach to treating SRB is via a prescriptive treatment approach (Burke & Silverman, 1987; Kearney & Silverman, 1996). Evidence for the efficacy of this approach for treating generalized anxiety in children has been provided by Eisen and Silverman (1993; 1998) and, a *functional* prescriptive treatment approach has been shown to have efficacy for SRB (Kearney & Silverman, 1990; 1999). This approach emphasizes the identification of several "motivating variables." Upon accurate identification of a particular child's motivating variable, a specific prescriptive treatment is assigned and implemented.

Kearney and Silverman (1993, 1996) suggested that SRB may be maintained by at least one of the following functions in children:

1) avoidance of stimuli provoking specific fearfulness or generalized anxiety escape from aversive social or evaluative situations;
2) escape from aversive social or evaluative situation;
3) attention-getting behavior (analogous to traditional externalizing symptoms of separation anxiety, such as tantruming);
4) positive tangible reinforcement (analogous to truant behavior, or preferring to stay home and play, or avoiding school for reasons other than fear or anxiety).

The former two variables refer to school refusal behavior controlled by negative reinforcement while the latter two are controlled by positive reinforcement.

Treatment is thus based on a functional model of assessment of the child's fears and incorporates appropriate treatment strategies of one of four functional categories:

1) systematic desensitization/relaxation training;
2) social skills training, modeling and cognitive restructuring;
3) shaping and differential reinforcement of other behavior;
4) contingency management.

Treating David – II

Assessment. David and his mother would complete the same assessment materials as in the previously described treatment approach (i.e., semi-structured interviews, questionnaires). In addition, however, both mother and child would complete the School Refusal Assessment Scale for Children (SRAS-C/P; Kearney & Silverman, 1993), a 16-item questionnaire designed to identify the motivating conditions surrounding school refusal behavior in youth. The SRAS-C/P assesses children's and parents' perspectives on maintaining variables of school refusal behavior and Kearney and Silverman (1993; 1996) have provided guidelines about how the measure can be used to determine prescriptive treatments.

In David's case, based on a combined mean score on the SRAS-C and SRAS-P, David's primary maintaining variable for his school refusal behavior would likely be escape from aversive social and evaluative situations, including speaking in class and talking with his peers. David would be prescribed a treatment that focused on enhancing his social skills via therapeutic modeling and skills training as well as on reducing his fear of negative evaluation via a cognitive restructuring treatment program. David would practice these skills in increasingly difficult school/social situations.

David would be seen in individual child focused treatments for about 50 to 60 minutes. Before beginning treatment, baseline information would be obtained. Baseline information would focus on David's approach to school (a) during normal school days which included social interactions and public performances and (b) on weekends when he was less socially engaged. The latter would provide additional evidence of his avoidance of social interactions as well as a comparison for progress. This would provide evidence that David displayed anxiety and somatic complaints in and outside school when in social situations. Anxiety would presumably increase when he felt he was being evaluated in some manner.

Social Skills Training and Modeling. Emphasis would be placed on training David in social skills so he would have increased confidence in his ability to deal with social situations. Before initiating any training, David's social strengths and weaknesses would be identified. This would be accomplished by simply engaging in interactions with David in the clinic and perhaps by bringing in other individuals to talk with David. Videotaping the interactions and asking David "what he thought" would be particularly useful in helping to identify strengths and weaknesses, as well as to facilitate David's own awareness about these issues. A training format might then be used which would include such strategies as demonstration, coaching, and practice with feedback. More specifically, first, the social skill would be described, discussed, and demonstrated. Second, David would practice the skills with the therapist who would assign tasks during the week for David to practice his skills with other children. Practice would continue until David had mastered the skills. Third, the therapist would critique or coach David, emphasizing the positive, good aspects of his behavior, as well as areas for improvement. At each treatment session, social skills assignments would be reviewed, with appropriate feedback and rewards provided.

Cognitive Restructuring. Emphasis would be placed on David's fears of negative evaluation, in terms of his beliefs about what his peers think of him, how he tends to look or do "foolish" things, etc. The therapist would function as a model of coping skills and self-talk as well as provider of feedback and praise for David's performance. Many of the same cognitive strategies discussed under self-control would be applicable, including teaching David how to question his thoughts and modify them to render them less maladaptive. Encouraging the asking of questions such as, "Is that really likely to happen?," "Has it actually happened before?" and "What if it does?" would be encouraged as well to help David realize that constructive alternatives are available even in the worst of situations.

Summary

The two treatment approaches discussed in this chapter have supporting evidence that they "work" in reducing SRB and in returning children to school. Given that most clinicians, regardless of orientation, view "returning the child to school" as a central goal of any treatment, the approaches under discussion would seem worth considering in treating SRB – either as the "frontline" treatment or as an adjunct to other modes of psychotherapy (individual, family, pharmacotherapy, etc.).

Both the transfer-of-control approach and the functional-prescriptive-treatment approach involve the use of cognitive and/or behavioral strategies. However, the transfer-of-control approach focuses on identifying the "lines of control" (e.g., from therapist to parent, from therapist to child, or from therapist to parent to child) and the use of behavioral (e.g., contingency management) and/or cognitive (e.g., self-control) to devise lines of control to help facilitate the occurrence of the key change producing procedure (i.e., exposure to school situations). Diagnoses obtained via semi-structured interviews are viewed as helpful mainly in terms of helping to identify specific content for in-session and out-of-session exposures. In David's case, for example, because he had a diagnosis of social phobia, his exposures also involved those that pertained to social situations.

The functional prescriptive treatment approach, as noted, also involves the cognitive and/or behavioral strategies but the ones that would be selected in a given case would be "prescribed" in accordance with the motivating conditions that surround a child's SRB. In helping to determine a child's motivating conditions, the School Refusal Assessment Scale (Child and Parent Versions) would be useful to administer. In the case of David, results of the assessment would be likely to indicate that the motivating condition surrounding his SRB was escape from aversive social and evaluative situations. As a consequence, his prescriptive treatment served to reduce this escape by providing him with improved social skills and to reduce his fear of negative evaluation treatment through cognitive restructuring.

Despite the efficacy demonstrated for the two approaches discussed in this chapter, the relative efficacy of either approach is not yet known. Examining this issue represents an important future step as we further work on improving our conceptualizations and treatments of child psychopathology.

References

American Psychiatric Association (1994). *Diagnostic and Statistical Manual of Mental Disorders*. Washington, DC.: American Psychiatric Association.

Bernstein, G. A., Massie, E. D., Thuras, P. D., & Perwein, A. R. (1997). Somatic symptoms in anxious-depressed school refusers. *Journal of the American Academy of Child and Adolescent Psychiatry, 36*, 661–668.

Burke, A. E., & Silverman, W. K. (1987). The prescriptive treatment of school refusal. *Clinical Psychology Review, 7*, 353–362.

Cobham, V. E., Dadds, M. R., & Spence, S. H. (1998). The role of parental anxiety in the treatment of childhood anxiety. *Journal of Consulting and Clinical Psychology, 66*, 893–905.

Eisen, A. R., & Silverman, W. K. (1993). Should I relax or change my thoughts?: A preliminary study of the treatment of Overanxious Disorder in children. *Journal of Cognitive Psychotherapy: An International Quarterly, 7*, 265–280.

Eisen, A. R., & Silverman, W. K. (1998). Prescriptive treatment for generalized anxiety disorder in children. *Behavior Therapy, 29*, 105–121.

Ginsburg, G. S., Silverman, W. K. & Kurtines, W. M. (1995). Family involvement in treating children with phobic and anxiety disorders: A look ahead. *Clinical Psychology Review, 15*, 457–473.

Johnson, A. M., Falstein, E. I., Szurek, S. A., & Svendsen, M. (1941). School phobia. *American Journal of Orthopsychiatry, 11*, 702–711.

Kearney, C. A., Eisen, A. R., & Silverman, W. K. (1995). The legend and myth of school phobia. *School Psychology Quarterly, 10*, 65–85.

Kearney, C. A., & Silverman, W. K. (1990). A preliminary analysis of a functional model of assessment and treatment for school refusal behavior. *Behavior Modification, 14*, 340–366.

Kearney, C. A., & Silverman, W. K. (1993). Measuring the function of school refusal behavior: The School Refusal Assessment Scale. *Journal of Clinical Child Psychology, 22*, 85–96.

Kearney, C. A., & Silverman, W. K. (1996). The evolution and reconciliation of taxonomic strategies for school refusal behavior. *Clinical Psychology: Science and Practice, 3*, 339–354.

Kearney, C. A., & Silverman, W. K. (1999). Functionally-based prescriptive and nonprescriptive treatment for children and adolescents with school refusal behavior. *Behavior Therapy*, 673–696.

Kendall, P. C. (1994). Treating anxiety disorders in children: Results of a randomized clinical trial. *Journal of Consulting and Clinical Psychology, 62*, 100–110.

Kennedy, W. A. (1965). School phobia: Rapid treatment of 50 cases. *Journal of Abnormal Psychology, 70*, 285–289.

King, N. J., Tonge, B. J., Heyne, D., Pritchard, M., Rollings, S., *et al.* (1998). Cognitive-behavioral treatment of school-refusing children: A controlled evaluation. *Journal of the American Academy of Child and Adolescent Psychiatry, 37*, 395–403.

Last, C. G., Hansen, C., & Franco, N. (1998). Cognitive-behavioral treatment of school phobia. *Journal of the American Academy of Child and Adolescent Psychiatry, 37*, 404–411.

Last, C. G., & Strauss, C. C. (1990). School refusal in anxiety-disordered children and adolescents. *Journal of the American Academy of Child and Adolescent Psychiatry, 29*, 31–35.

Russo, M. F., & Beidel, D. C. (1994). Comorbidity of childhood anxiety and externalizing disorders: Prevalence, associated characteristics, and validation issues. *Clinical Psychology Review, 14,* 199–221.

Silverman, W. K. & Kurtines, W. M. (1996a). *Anxiety and Phobic Disorders: A Pragmatic Approach.* New York: Plenum Press.

Silverman, W. K., & Kurtines, W. M. (1996b). Transfer of control: A psychosocial intervention model for internalizing disorders in youth. In E. D. Hibbs & P. S. Jensen (eds) *Psychosocial Treatment of Child and Adolescent Disorders: Empirically Based Strategies for Clinical Practice.* Washington, DC: American Psychological Association. 63–82.

Silverman, W. K. & Kurtines, W. M. (1997). Theory in child psychosocial treatment research: Have it or had it? A pragmatic alternative. *Journal of Abnormal Child Psychology, 25,* 359–367.

Silverman, W. K., & Nelles, W. B. (1988). The Anxiety Disorders Interview Schedule for Children. *Journal of the American Academy of Child and Adolescent Psychiatry, 27,* 772–778.

Silverman, W. K., Kurtines, W. M., Ginsburg, G. S., Weems, C. F., Rabian, B., et al. (1999a). Contingency management, self control, and education support in the treatment of childhood phobic disorders: A randomized clinical trial. *Journal of Consulting and Clinical Psychology, 67,* 657–687.

Silverman, W. K., Kurtines, W. M., Ginsburg, G. S., Weems, C. F., Lumpkin, P. W., et al. (1999b). Treating anxiety disorders in children with group cognitive behavior therapy: A randomized clinical trial. *Journal of Consulting and Clinical Psychology, 67,* 995–1003.

Wicks-Nelson, R., & Israel, A. C. (1997). *Behavior Disorders of Childhood, (3rd ed.).* Upper Saddle River, NJ: Prentice-Hall.

Chapter 10

Social Phobia

Thomas H. Ollendick and Kathleen A. Ingman

Defining the Condition

An age-related increase in social evaluative fears is part of normal development in children as they approach adolescence (Ollendick, *et al.*, 1989). As discussed by Albano (1995), the development of specific cognitive skills, such as the ability to examine and interpret situations from another's perspective, can be both a blessing and a curse to the developing adolescent. As children approach adolescence, peer relationships become increasingly important and children begin to place value on what their peers may think of them. Thus, transient episodes of social anxiety are not uncommon and are part and parcel of normal development.

For a small percentage of children and adolescents, however, social anxiety causes extreme distress and interference and does not remit over time. For these individuals, social anxiety may lead to detrimental outcomes such as depression, school refusal, conduct problems, and substance abuse. If left untreated, social phobia can lead to persistent problems with anxiety and depression in adulthood (as reviewed by Beidel & Turner, 1998).

Social phobia, as defined by DSM-IV (APA, 1994), is characterized by a marked and persistent fear of social or performance situations in which embarrassment or humiliation may occur. Frequently, when exposed to possible scrutiny by others, the child fears that he or she might do something or act in a way that will be humiliating or embarrassing. For children and adolescents with social phobia, exposure to social or performance situations frequently provokes an immediate anxiety response that is excessive or unreasonable. In children, this anxiety response may take the form of crying, tantrums, freezing, clinging to a familiar person, and inhibited interactions. Older adolescents and adults may experience panic-like symptoms when confronted by anxiety-provoking social situations. Other behavioral manifestations of social anxiety may include stuttering, poor eye contact, mumbling, nail biting, and trembling voice (Beidel & Turner, 1998). Although behavioral avoidance is commonplace among socially phobic adults, socially phobic children often do not have the option of avoiding feared situations. Therefore, children may show a decline in school performance, school refusal, and avoidance of age-appropriate social activities. Children who do attempt to avoid

Handbook of Conceptualization and Treatment of Child Psychopathology, pages 191–210.

anxiety-provoking situations may be mistakenly diagnosed as oppositional since they refuse to do as they are asked (Francis & Ollendick, 1990).

Adolescents with social phobia often report anxious cognitions concerning escape from the situation, negative evaluation, failure, humiliation, embarrassment, inadequacy, and self-criticism. Alternatively, some individuals report that when confronted by an anxiety-provoking situation, they are flooded by so many thoughts that they are unable to think clearly and focus at all (Beidel & Turner, 1998). Negative cognitions are much less common in younger children. In fact, many researchers have hypothesized that for children who have not yet reached Piaget's formal operations stage, consideration of the future (and catastrophic thinking) may not be possible. Although adolescents and adults typically recognize their fears as irrational, younger children often do not. In fact, younger children may not be able to identify the nature of their anxiety at all and, at least in some instances, deny fear or anxiety.

The average age of onset for social phobia is considered to be mid-adolescence (APA, 1994), coinciding with the normal vulnerability to social embarrassment seen in adolescents. However, a number of authors have reported diagnoses of the disorder in prepubertal children as young as age eight (Albano & DiBartolo, 1997; Beidel & Turner, 1998). It is important to note that for a child to receive a diagnosis of social phobia, the anxiety must occur in peer settings, and not just in interactions with adults. In addition, the child must be capable of social interactions, which differentiates socially phobic children from children with pervasive developmental disorders or nonverbal learning disabilities.

A list of situations that are commonly avoided by children and adolescents is presented in Table 10.1. It should be noted that while many children might exhibit generalized social fears to many different social situations, some children and adolescents may fear only one or very few specific types of social situations, such as public performances. The generalized subtype has been reported to be of

Table 10.1: Commonly Feared Situations for Children and Adolescents with Social Phobia.

Giving oral reports	Answering the telephone or doorbell
Taking exams or quizzes	Attending after-school activities
Calling a classmate for missed homework or assignments	Initiating or joining in conversations with peers
Asking the teacher for help	Situations requiring assertiveness, such as saying no to someone
Walking through the school hallways	
Working on a group project	Dating
Performance-based activities such as gym class and music lessons	Having a picture taken
	Ordering food in a restaurant
Speaking to persons in authority	Using public restrooms
Calling and inviting a friend to do something	Going to parties
	Writing on the blackboard

Adapted from Albano (1995) and Beidel and Turner (1998).

greater severity and chronicity than the specific subtype. In addition to social eva-luative anxiety, many socially anxious children may display deficits in social skills such as poor eye contact and low, muffled speech. Furthermore, they may lack enthusiasm for typical age-appropriate interests because mainstream social activ-ities and social reinforcement are lacking in their everyday lives (Albano, 1995).

Children with social phobia, especially those of the generalized subtype, typi-cally present with comorbid conditions. Selective mutism and test anxiety seem to be particularly frequent in children with social fears. In addition, other anxiety disorders, depression, and even externalizing behavior problems such as opposi-tional defiant disorder and conduct disorder are not uncommon (Albano, 1995; Beidel & Turner, 1998). Generally, it is rare to see a child presenting only with social phobia.

Approaches to Treatment

Empirically supported treatments for social phobia in children and adolescents pri-marily involve the use of behavioral or cognitive-behavioral strategies. One such treatment for use with pre-adolescent children is Social Effectiveness Therapy for Children (SET-C), developed by Beidel and Turner (1998). SET-C is a twelve-week program (24 bi-weekly sessions) that focuses on group social skills training and individualized exposure therapy. The child meets with a therapist to focus on graduated exposure to feared situations during one weekly session, and with a small group of children that focuses on social skills training during the other weekly session.

During the individualized exposure sessions of SET-C, a therapist first works with the child and parents to construct a fear hierarchy. With the help of a Subjective Units of Distress Scale (SUDS), the child and therapist identify and rank feared situations in a hierarchical fashion. Once the hierarchy is con-structed, the therapist begins with items that are low on the hierarchy (i.e., less anxiety-provoking) and presents one or two of them to the child each week. The child is asked to engage in the situation during the session until distress has dissipated. Role-play and behavioral rehearsal are used if necessary. Items addressed during the session are assigned as homework for further practice during the week. As items that are lower on the hierarchy are mastered, the therapist works up the hierarchy and presents situations that are increasingly feared by the child. For items that are difficult to recreate during the session (i.e., situations that are specific to school), the therapist may create simulated situations or, more typically, enlist the help of the child's parents or a teacher in implement-ing the exposure strategy. The goal of the exposure process is for the child to engage in the highest item on the hierarchy with a minimal amount of fear and distress.

As mentioned above, SET-C also includes a group social skills training (SST) component. The goal of SST is to teach children specific skills and allow them to practice these skills under therapist supervision. Skills that are addressed in the

SET-C program include initiating and maintaining conversations, listening, joining groups, giving and receiving compliments, and assertiveness. Generally, one skill area is taught each week using the following procedures: instruction, modeling, behavioral rehearsal, feedback, and positive reinforcement. Beidel and Turner include a peer generalization component in the SST part of their treatment program. More specifically, they recruit a group of non-anxious peers who serve as helpers and provide opportunities for social learning. After each SST session, the children with social phobia and the peer helpers go on an outing together. This outing allows the children with social phobia to practice the skills they have learned in the SST group and interact with non-anxious children in a natural setting.

Beidel and Turner's SET-C protocol relies primarily on behavioral strategies. Other researchers have used cognitive restructuring procedures in addition to behavioral strategies in their treatments of social phobia. One such treatment is the *Cognitive-Behavioral Group Treatment for Adolescent Social Phobia* (CBGT-A) developed by Albano and colleagues (described in Albano & DiBartolo, 1997). This protocol was developed for use with adolescents for whom cognitive techniques may be developmentally appropriate strategies. Like SET-C, the CBGT-A program includes social skills training and graduated behavioral exposures. In addition to these components, the CBGT-A includes training in cognitive restructuring and problem-solving skills. The purpose of cognitive restructuring is to replace negative, anxiogenic thoughts with more rational ones. Adolescents in the group are instructed to identify negative automatic thoughts, question the evidence for their negative predictions, and generate more realistic and rational responses to their negative thoughts. Adolescents are also taught problem-solving skills, including how to identify a problematic situation, set a realistic goal for the situation (defined in an operational manner), brainstorm solutions and plans, compare all possible alternatives, choose and implement the best alternative, and reinforce themselves for doing so. Typically, therapists model the new skills in session and monitor group participants as they practice the skills in role-play scenarios. Adolescents are encouraged to practice the new skills in natural situations as homework.

The CBGT-A program is designed to be implemented over 16 weekly sessions. The first eight sessions constitute a skill-building phase during which cognitive restructuring, problem-solving, social skills, and assertiveness are taught and mastered. The second half of treatment (sessions nine through 16) focuses on graduated behavioral exposures. As in the SET-C program, individualized fear hierarchies are generated for each adolescent and adolescents take turns engaging in simulated exposures during the session. The adolescents are prompted to use the skills acquired during the first phase of treatment to help manage their anxiety. Each adolescent is also assigned items from his or her hierarchy to practice during the week as homework.

Although both the SET-C and CBGT-A programs include the involvement of parents in treatment, neither program places emphasis on the role that the family plays in maintaining the child's anxious behavior. Fortunately, Howard and Kendall (1992) have developed a family-focused cognitive-behavioral treatment for childhood anxiety disorders. Although no socially phobic children were included in the initial evaluative study of the treatment (Howard & Kendall, 1996), the protocol is designed for treatment of all childhood anxiety disorders and can easily be adapted to focus on social evaluative fears. Howard and Kendall's program is designed to be individualized for each child with consideration of the child's level of cognitive development, family structure, and the family's abilities to help the child master new situations.

In general, Howard and Kendall use cognitive-behavioral strategies adapted from Kendall's (1990) *Coping Cat Workbook*. Similar to the CBGT-A program, the skills taught include recognizing anxious feelings and somatic reactions, identifying anxious cognitions, developing problem-solving steps to cope with anxiety, self-evaluation, and self-reward. Behavioral strategies (similar to those used in the SET-C and CBGT-A programs) such as relaxation training, modeling, role-play, in vivo exposure, and contingent reinforcement are also included.

Howard and Kendall added a family-based component that includes assessment of family functioning and family style, expression of negative affect, problem negotiation, respect for the child's experience, normalization of the child's anxiety, and family participation in the sequence of learning tasks and assignments. The treatment program is divided into two segments. The first eight sessions center on exploring the interpersonal nature of the child's anxiety, increasing flexible thinking about the problem, and teaching active strategies to change the child's and family's reactions to the child's anxiety. Sessions nine through 16 focus on practicing anxiety management skills in situations where the child has displayed anxious behavior. These practice sessions also provide opportunities to structure family members' involvement. The specific situations used for the practice sessions are individually designed. Thus, social evaluative situations could be used to tailor the treatment for children with social phobia.

The remainder of this chapter will focus on a sample case of a child with social phobia. The case will be conceptualized from two different perspectives. Following each conceptualization, a detailed treatment plan that incorporates components of the above treatments is provided.

Case Example

Jason is a ten-year-old white male who lives with his biological parents (mother, age 41; and father, age 46), and brother (age 16). Jason's mother is a social worker and Jason's father is a small business owner. Jason is currently enrolled in the fourth grade at a public elementary school.

Jason was referred to an outpatient mental health clinic for psychological evaluation by his school psychologist, who requested clarification of behavioral problems observed by Jason's parents, teachers, and himself. Specifically, these observers noted a pattern of anxious and oppositional behavior that occurred frequently at school and periodically at home. The primary concerns of Jason's teachers involved "withdrawal," "fear of failure," and a lack of friendships with other children his age. Moreover, Jason's teachers reported that he frequently refused to cooperate with their requests to work jointly with other children. Jason had cried on several occasions when pushed to do so. In spite of the fact that Jason refused to participate in group learning activities, Jason performed exceedingly well academically and they noted that he often read or studied by himself in the school library during recess and lunch. He was viewed as a "loner."

At home, Jason's parents reported that he behaved "normally" around family members including his brother but that he often became teary or defiant when the family planned to go on an outing where there would be other children his age. When forced into such situations, Jason either interacted primarily with his parents and other adults, or with children much younger than himself. They noted that Jason suffered from frequent stomachaches and often missed school as a result. They reported that Jason did not have any friends his own age. They attributed Jason's social isolation to his high intelligence, rationalizing that he was much smarter than other children his age and that he was bored by their activities and interests. They indicated that Jason had been socially isolated since they moved to their current home from another state two years ago. However, they also noted that he had always seemed shy and wary of interactions with other children, preferring to be by himself and to play alone.

Jason refused to meet alone with the clinician during his first visit to the mental health clinic. Thus, a clinical interview was conducted while his mother sat quietly in the corner of the room. During the interview, Jason rarely looked at the therapist and talked in a barely audible voice. He reported that he was frequently teased by other children at school because he was a "nerd." He said that he preferred to play on his own since the other children were "stupid" or "mean." He stated that he often felt "bad" or "sick" when the teacher required him to work in a group, when he had to talk in front of the class, during recess and gym class, in the school cafeteria, and on the bus. He also said that he sometimes felt sad when the other children excluded him from their activities. In addition to anxiety in social situations, Jason reported that he worried about his academic performance and felt that since he was the smartest child in his class, he had to receive the highest grades. Jason also said that he worries that something bad will happen to his parents or his brother.

Jason completed the *Social Phobia and Anxiety Inventory for Children* (SPAI-C; Beidel, Turner, & Morris, 1995) and the *Children's Depression Inventory* (CDI; Kovacs, 1978). Jason's responses on the SPAI-C indicated that he was experiencing significant anxiety and distress in most social situations with peers his age. The results of the CDI indicated that Jason was suffering from mild symptoms of depression. Based on results of the clinical evaluation, Jason was diagnosed with Social Phobia and Generalized Anxiety Disorder. A diagnosis of a depressive disorder was not viewed as appropriate since Jason's symptoms of depression did not appear to be severe enough to warrant it.

Case Conceptualization

From a behavioral perspective, Jason's difficulties may be caused in part by a lack of age-appropriate social skills. If he lacks adaptive social skills, his attempts at normal social interactions with peers will be unsuccessful. Negative feedback from his peers serves as a punisher and decreases the frequency of his behavior. Avoidance of social situations decreases his anxiety and is therefore negatively reinforcing. Unfortunately, avoiding social interactions only adds to his skills deficits since he has little opportunity to practice or observe others. Jason's oppositional behavior can be viewed as a symptom of his avoidance. Social interactions have become so aversive (and avoidance so reinforcing) that he is willing to disobey his parents and teachers regardless of the consequences.

In addition, it is evident that Jason's social phobia and generalized anxiety are a reflection of a long-standing history of shyness and behavioral inhibition. He has, according to his mother, "always been a shy child who found it difficult to interact with other children." Moreover, he never seemed to "enjoy" being with or around other children, preferring to be alone instead. This history, along with his recent move to his current home, seemed to exacerbate his behavioral tendencies leading to his current isolation. Thus, treatment should focus on improving Jason's social skills and breaking the cycle of anxiety, avoidance, and reinforcement.

Treatment Plan

Because of his age and the nature of his symptoms, a behaviorally oriented treatment adapted from Beidel and Turner's SET-C was selected. Thus, the primary components of Jason's treatment included SST and graduated exposures. The goal of SST was to reduce Jason's social skills deficits. It was anticipated that once Jason's social skills improved, he would have more reinforcing interactions with his peers and the frequency of his social behavior would increase. The graduated exposures were designed to break the cycle of anxiety and avoidance. If Jason was encouraged to systematically place himself in anxiety-provoking situations and stay in them until his anxiety decreased, he would gradually become less fearful of them and thus less avoidant. Since it was hypothesized that much of Jason's oppositional behavior was motivated by his desire to avoid anxiety triggers, an exposure-based treatment would increase his overall compliance at home and at school as well.

Since Jason was treated in a small clinic, the group setting that Beidel and Turner recommend for SST and peer generalization was not feasible. Therefore, these essential components of their treatment protocol were modified for use in individual therapy. In general, Jason met with the therapist alone for most of the sessions. His parents were involved during some sessions, however, and the therapist met with them briefly at the end of each session to discuss Jason's progress and his homework assignments. The therapist also maintained regular contact with Jason's teachers for the same purpose.

First Session

During the first session, the therapist met with both Jason and his parents to provide information about anxiety and explain the rationale for treatment. It was important that they understood the importance of the graduated exposures in particular. Because exposing Jason to feared situations would cause anxiety and discomfort, Jason and his parents needed to fully commit to this aspect of treatment. Ending exposure sessions prematurely could have the adverse effect of ultimately increasing, rather than decreasing, Jason's anxiety.

In addition to gathering support for the treatment plan, the first session provided an opportunity for the therapist to establish rapport with Jason. Since Jason had refused to meet with the therapist individually during the intake session, it seemed that time needed to be set aside to earn Jason's trust and establish a good working relationship with him. Therefore, the therapist met with Jason individually at the end of the session to discuss his goals and play a game.

Second Session

The second session was devoted to creating an anxiety and avoidance hierarchy that would be used in subsequent sessions for the graduated exposures as well as a weekly assessment measure. The therapist met with Jason individually for this session. The therapist and Jason discussed specific situations that made him anxious and wrote them down on index cards. It was important that each situation be operationally defined in very specific terms (i.e., reading a prepared speech in front of the class for two minutes). In addition to a description of the anxiety-provoking situation, Jason provided ratings of his anxiety level in each situation, as well as an estimate of his typical avoidance of each situation (on a scale of 1 to 9, lowest to highest). Special attention was given to ensuring that situations falling

Table 10.2: Jason's Anxiety and Avoidance Hierarchy.

Feared situation	Anxiety	Avoidance
Having a group of friends over to my house for a party	9	9
Playing with a group of kids on the playground during recess	8	9
Playing with one kid on the playground during recess	7	9
Work on a group project with other kids during class	7	6
Read out loud in front of the class	7	5
Tell someone to stop kicking my chair	6	4
Having the teacher call on me when I don't know the answer	5	2
Calling a classmate on the phone to ask about the homework	4	6
Raising my hand during class and asking to go to the bathroom	3	2
Raising my hand in class when I know the answer	2	4
Playing with my cousins at a family party	2	3
Asking a classmate if I can borrow a pencil	2	1

Anxiety and avoidance ratings are made on a 1 through 9 scale with 1 being no anxiety/avoidance and 9 being extreme anxiety/avoidance. The ratings shown here represent Jason's anxiety and avoidance at the onset of treatment.

on every point of the avoidance and distress continuum were included. When there appeared to be gaps in the hierarchy, existing items were modified slightly to make them more or less anxiety-provoking. For example, "reading a prepared speech in front of the class for two minutes" could be made more anxiety-provoking by changing the time or nature of the speech: "giving a spontaneous (unprepared) speech to my class for two minutes." Once approximately ten situations had been identified and rated, they were recorded in hierarchy form, as shown in Table 10.2. Prior to the next session, the hierarchy was typed on a form with the anxiety and avoidance ratings for each item left blank. In subsequent sessions, Jason was given a copy of this form and asked to rate his current amount of anxiety and avoidance for each item.

Third Through Twelfth Sessions

These sessions were generally divided into two parts. The first half of the session focused on social skills training, while the second half of the session was reserved for behavioral exposures.

Social Skills Training. In general, one specific social skill was targeted for each session (see Table 10.3 for a list of skill areas addressed in Jason's treatment).

First, the therapist instructed Jason on how to perform the skill. Specific steps were written down in a notebook. For example, when learning how to greet people, the steps were as follows: (1) identify an appropriate person to greet (perhaps someone you already know or would like to meet); (2) select an appropriate time (avoid interrupting the person if he/she is busy, avoid talking during class, etc.); (3) make eye contact, smile, and say hello. After discussing these steps, the therapist modeled the skills for Jason. Modeling included examples of how to perform the skill both correctly and incorrectly. After several examples, Jason practiced the skill himself, first with the therapist, and then with other staff in the clinic. The therapist provided feedback when necessary, along with plenty of verbal reinforcement. Different scenarios were practiced, including several where the other person's response was not favorable (i.e., they did not respond).

Table 10.3: Social Skills Training Content Areas Addressed in Jason's Treatment.

Initiating conversations
Listening skills
Skills for joining groups
Establishing and maintaining friendships
Sharing, cooperating, and taking turns
Giving and receiving compliments
Refusing unreasonable requests
Social perspective taking

Jason was given homework each week that required him to practice the new skills. For the skill of greeting someone, Jason was asked to say hello to two people he already knew each day plus introduce himself to one stranger each day. At the end of the session, Jason taught the new skill to his parents, and they agreed on an appropriate reward that he would receive each day after completing the assignment.

Behavioral Exposures. Starting with the item at the bottom of his hierarchy, Jason was exposed to one or two hierarchy items each week. During the session, Jason engaged in each behavior continuously (or in some cases repeatedly) until his anxiety decreased. Jason was prompted to rate his anxiety each minute, and the therapist recorded these ratings. Since Jason's hierarchy items were all activities that occur outside the session, simulated scenarios were used instead. This was accomplished by enlisting the participation of clinic staff who would act as peers, teachers, etc. When Jason's anxiety response habituated, the scenario would be modified to be more anxiety-provoking until habituation occurred again. For example, when Jason no longer felt anxious about asking to borrow something (when the person complied with his request), the scene was changed to asking to borrow something and being turned down. An example of Jason's anxiety ratings during an exposure session is provided in Figure 10.1. It should be emphasized that it was critical that the exposures continue until Jason's anxiety decreased so his anxiety response habituated and he experienced success. Jason was rewarded for his successful completion of each session with verbal praise and a pleasant activity of his choosing.

As with the social skills, Jason was instructed to continue exposing himself to the hierarchy item during the week for homework. This homework was extremely

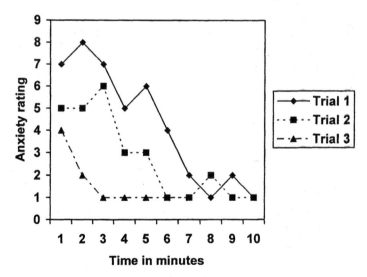

Figure 10.1: Jason's Anxiety Ratings During an In-session Exposure Exercise.

important as it provided Jason with an opportunity to decrease his anxiety in actual in vivo situations, rather than simulated ones. Jason's parents and teachers were kept informed of his homework assignments so they could help arrange the needed scenario if necessary. For example, when practicing answering questions in class, Jason's teacher intentionally called on him more than usual. Again, Jason was rewarded for the successful completion of each homework assignment. Once Jason had adequately desensitized himself to each item, a slightly higher hierarchy item was targeted.

Compliance. As is often the case with children, Jason was initially reluctant to become involved with treatment for his problems. Once he felt more comfortable with the therapist, however, he disclosed that he wished to have more friends at school and to not have embarrassing outbursts in front of other children. Thus, he was able to identify goals that motivated him. In addition to being self-motivated, it was important that Jason have some external reinforcers that would give him an extra push during difficult exposure sessions and homework assignments. Jason, his parents, and the therapist created a list of rewards that Jason could earn each week by participating during the sessions and completing homework assignments. The list included very small reinforcers that Jason would receive after completing each assignment (i.e., favorite dessert, 15 minutes of favorite video game, etc.) as well as bigger reinforcers that Jason could earn by completing all his assignments for the week, or by reaching the top of his hierarchy (going to a movie, receiving a new Nintendo game, etc.).

At several points during treatment, Jason failed to complete his homework assignments. When this occurred, the therapist reviewed with Jason his goals for treatment as well as the rewards he selected for completion of his homework. In addition, the therapist discussed potential obstacles to homework completion with Jason and his parents during each session. For example, when Jason was asked to practice telling others to stop kicking his chair, it seemed likely that Jason might return the next week and say that no one did that to him over the course of the week, therefore, he could not practice it. To avoid this problem, other assertiveness situations were discussed and assigned for homework as well.

An additional problem that may interfere with therapy occurs when parents fail to follow through with their commitments to provide rewards or help with exposure exercises. In the case of providing rewards, Jason and his parents worked together to develop a system for monitoring his progress and implementing rewards. Each week, Jason wrote down his homework assignments on a chart that was kept in the family kitchen. Each day at dinner time, he marked whether or not he completed the assignments for the day and, if so, whether his parents gave him his reward. In the case of larger rewards such as outings, Jason's parents would schedule a time when they could take him on the outing. When Jason needed his parents' assistance in engaging in exposure exercises (i.e., when he had friends over), the therapist helped Jason and his parents negotiate an arrangement (i.e., what day he would invite them for, how long, etc.).

Peer Generalization. Beidel and Turner include a peer generalization component in their SET-C protocol. More specifically, anxious children go on outings each week with non-anxious peers following group treatment sessions. While this is no doubt helpful in that anxious children can observe non-anxious peers and practice new skills, it seems impractical for many clinical settings. In place of these more formal social outings, Jason's parents helped arrange opportunities for Jason to interact with his peers. Initially, they arranged family gatherings where Jason could play with cousins and family friends who were less threatening to him. As his skills improved and his anxiety decreased, they enrolled Jason in several after-school activities such as Boy Scouts and karate classes. In addition, they made it a priority to allow Jason to have friends over to their home whenever possible.

Final Session 13

In the final session, Jason and the therapist reviewed all that he had learned and summarized his progress. Although Jason's anxiety had decreased significantly (as indicated in his self-report as well as the reports from his parents and teacher), he still experienced mild anxiety from time to time. In addition, he occassionally worried about non-social things such as grades and other family members. The therapist instructed Jason on how to continue to practice the skills he learned and expose himself to feared situations. In addition, the therapist reviewed with Jason and his parents how they could distinguish between normal fears and more problematic anxiety.

Alternative Case Conceptualization

In addition to the individually focused behavioral conceptualization offered above, Jason's case can also be effectively viewed from a more family-based cognitive-behavioral perspective. During the intake, Jason's mother described herself as a "worrier" when it comes to her family. She also stated that she was shy and reserved herself, and that Jason takes after her. Such comments suggest that Jason may have learned his anxious behavior from his mother, and that perhaps his anxiety is maintained by his mother's overprotective parenting style. If she restricts his activity he may lack opportunities to experience mastery in new situations.

Moreover, both of Jason's parents place high value on academic achievement. This emphasis may also contribute to Jason's overall anxiety level. Jason may have adopted his parents' high expectations and as a result places an inflated amount of importance on doing well at school. To ensure his success, he spends an inordinate amount of time studying rather than engaging in social activities with other children his age. Thus, he lacks opportunities to learn social skills and behaves in a way that his peers view as "nerdy" or "weird" which places him in further isolation.

Jason's cognitions about himself may also contribute to his anxiety. Because he values success very highly, he has frequent maladaptive thoughts about his own failure. When put in a social situation, he assumes that he will be laughed at or rejected by other children. In addition, he feels that he must always know the correct answers in class, and therefore does not raise his hand for fear that he could be wrong and would feel embarrassed. Finally, the behavioral causes described in the first conceptualization also apply to this more complex, family-centered, cognitive-behavioral conceptualization.

Alternative Treatment Plan

The following treatment plan is adapted from Howard and Kendall's (1992) cognitive-behavioral family therapy for anxious children. The following general family-focused strategies are employed:

1) initial observation of family interaction to assess the level of family functioning and family style;
2) parents' participation in setting goals and negotiating individual commitment to trying alternative responses to anxiety-provoking situations;
3) parents' participation in a sequence of learning tasks and assignments (tailored to fit the family's hypothesized role in the maintenance of the child's difficulties);
4) session interactions that encourage expression of negative affect and differences, problem negotiation, and respect for the child's opinions and experience;
5) normalization of the child's anxiety and understanding of the child's symptoms in the wider context of how relationships within the family and between the family and other systems are negotiated;
6) exploring parental beliefs, expectations, and attributions and their relationship to the child's anxiety.

In addition to the family-focused strategies, Howard and Kendall's treatment also uses general child-focused cognitive-behavioral strategies including affective education, self-observation of anxious reactions, relaxation, graduated learning, coping modeling, role-play rehearsals, and homework assignments.

First Session

The first session would include Jason, his parents, and his brother. The therapist would use the first session to provide the family with basic information about the treatment program, develop rapport, and learn about the interpersonal context of Jason's anxiety. The therapist would provide information about the treatment strategies and help the family develop an incentive program for Jason. Specifically, Jason would earn points for participating in treatment and completing homework assignments. During the first session Jason and his family would identify several rewards for which the points could be exchanged.

The bulk of the session would be a discussion between the therapist and the family about Jason's anxiety. The purpose of the discussion would be to establish rapport, normalize the experience of anxiety and avoidance, and gather information about the role that family members play in maintaining Jason's anxiety. Topics for conversation might include whether other family members experience anxiety, who is most aware of Jason's anxiety, who reassures Jason the most, how family members cope with their own and Jason's anxiety, and how each family member will have changed by the end of treatment. Depending on the success of this conversation in gaining information, family members might be asked to role-play a scenario in which Jason becomes anxious. The therapist could then see first-hand how each family member reacts to his anxiety.

For homework, Jason would be asked to pretend to be anxious (when he is not actually anxious) one time over the course of the week. The family would be asked to figure out when this happens and bring their guess to the next session.

Second Session

During this session, the therapist and family would negotiate an agreement about therapy goals. Each member of the family would be asked how he or she will know that Jason's anxiety is no longer a problem. Differences would be negotiated until a compromise is reached.

The therapist would introduce several ideas that are intended to encourage more flexibility in thinking about anxiety-provoking situations. First, feelings often seem to come and go without our control. Second, feelings are our own and not always caused by something outside. This is why we each might have a different reaction to the same event. Third, we share our feelings both by what we say and how we act, and different people have different ideas about what feelings should be shared. Finally, different feelings have different physical expressions. This last idea could be illustrated by having family members act out different feelings and guess by attending to facial expression, posture, and movements. Because of Jason's relatively young age, he may have trouble recognizing and labeling feelings and therefore extra time should be spent on this part of the session.

The therapist would inform Jason's parents and brother that they will serve as role models to help Jason learn to cope with his anxiety. They would each be asked to choose one area where they experience anxiety and would like to cope better. They could then learn anxiety management skills along with Jason and serve as examples for him. For homework, Jason would be asked to pretend not to be anxious at least once when he really is. The rest of the family would then try to guess when he does this.

Third Session

The session would start with a review of the homework assignment and the topics that were covered in the last session. The discussion would then shift to how feelings are expressed in families. This might include questions about how each family member knows when another is worried, angry, etc., and how they feel about each other's emotions. The therapist would try to establish links between each family member's emotions and behavior.

The therapist would then introduce the idea that somatic responses signal anxiety. Each family member would identify what somatic cues help them recognize their anxiety. This discussion would be important because being able to recognize when Jason is frightened or anxious would be the first step of a four-step plan for him to manage his anxiety. For homework, each family member would be asked to keep a journal and record at least two anxious experiences and the relevant somatic changes that they noticed.

Fourth Session

After a review of the homework assignment, relaxation training would be introduced. The family would be told that many of the somatic feelings associated with anxiety involve tension. Family members would then engage in an exercise where they alternate between acting like a robot or a rag doll. This exercise would help illustrate for Jason and his family the difference between tension and relaxation. Following this exercise, a relaxation procedure would be introduced. The family would be asked to close their eyes and take deep breaths. At this point, the family would be coached on diaphragmatic breathing. Jason would be informed that deep breathing is one technique he can use to manage his anxiety. Once diaphragmatic breathing is mastered, the therapist would lead the family in a progressive muscle relaxation exercise. Jason would be given an audio tape of this relaxation exercise so that he could use it for practice at home.

Following the relaxation exercise, the therapist would emphasize that by practicing relaxation Jason can learn to better recognize when he is tense. The therapist would then role-play an anxiety-provoking scenario and model appropriate coping by talking about somatic responses and demonstrating how to use breathing and relaxation. Following the therapist's lead, Jason would role-play his own scenario. For homework, Jason would be asked to practice the relaxation exercise. Other family members would be encouraged to practice with him.

Fifth Session

In this session, cognitive restructuring would be introduced. First, the therapist would describe the concept of self-talk and how it is a part of the anxious experience. Jason would be told that recognizing his anxious thoughts is the second part of his four-step plan. The family would be given cartoons with empty thought bubbles. They would take turns filling in possible thoughts for the cartoon characters. Initially, the cartoon would involve non-anxious stimuli, but then ambiguous and finally anxious stimuli would be presented in the cartoons. The therapist would model how responding with alternative thoughts can change the person's behavior and the outcome of the situation. Then Jason and his family would practice generating alternative thoughts for various scenarios.

The therapist would role-play the use of alternative thoughts to cope with an anxiety-provoking situation. The therapist would then coach Jason to do the same in his own role-play, with his parents and brother as actors in the role-play. For homework, Jason would be asked to write down his thoughts during an anxious situation. In addition, he would continue to practice his relaxation exercise. Before the next session, the therapist would generate an anxiety and avoidance hierarchy for use during exposure procedures (see Table 10.2, p. 198).

Sixth Session

The therapist would review the anxiety and avoidance hierarchy with the family and ask Jason to rate each situation. This would allow the therapist to make adjustments in the hierarchy if necessary and help Jason develop a less monolithic view of anxious situations. The therapist would then draw a chart on the chalkboard with three columns: situations, feelings, and thoughts. Jason would fill in the chart with situations that cause him anxiety and relevant feelings and thoughts that he has in those situations. The therapist would then add a fourth column for actions, and possible alternative actions would be listed there.

The therapist would summarize the two coping strategies that Jason has learned: recognizing his feelings and recognizing anxious self-talk. The therapist would emphasize that these are the first two steps to dealing with a difficult situation. Then the therapist would introduce actions as a third coping strategy. More specifically, a discussion would follow where Jason would be taught how to develop a plan for coping with his anxiety. He would practice generating a variety of behavioral options for each situation and then practice choosing and enacting the best one. The therapist would role-play use of these skills first, and then coach Jason and his family during their own role-plays. For homework, the family would be asked to practice the three coping steps in anxiety-provoking situations.

Seventh Session

The session would begin with a review of the relaxation procedure. The therapist would lead the family through a relaxation exercise, and Jason would be given a recording of the exercise to use at home. The remainder of the session would focus on the final step for coping with anxiety: self-rating and self-reward. Jason would be told to reward himself every time that he attempts to use the anxiety management strategies that he has learned. The fact that it takes lots of practice to perfect these skills would be emphasized. Jason would be instructed on how to evaluate his own performance. Because of Jason's tendencies toward perfectionism, special attention would be paid to establishing realistic standards of performance. The new skills of self-evaluation and self-reward would be practiced using role-plays. For homework, Jason and his family would be asked to each pick one situation where they feel anxious, use the coping strategies, and pay special attention to self-rating and self-reward.

Eighth Session

At the start of the eighth session, the therapist would give the family an overview of what they should expect for the remainder of treatment. They would be told that exposing Jason to the situations on his hierarchy that make him anxious will be the focus for the next seven sessions. The therapist would emphasize that all family members will be involved, and in many cases will be asked to change the way they respond to Jason's anxiety. It is also possible that the therapist would need to meet with Jason or his parents alone in future sessions to address these issues.

The remainder of the session would involve exercises where Jason and his family could practice the steps they have learned. Family members would act out scenarios that cause them anxiety, and Jason would coach them through each situation. Then the roles would be switched and Jason's family would have the opportunity to coach him through a situation. For homework, Jason would teach the coping skills he has learned to another family member or significant adult who has not attended the session.

Ninth Session

The therapist would begin the session by reviewing Jason's parents' choice of situations in which they wish to act more effectively as a way of helping Jason overcome his anxiety. They would each develop their own hierarchy of steps. Items on the hierarchy might include managing their own anxiety when Jason faces difficult situations. If this is the case, then they could practice this while Jason is engaging in the exposures.

The therapist would reorient the family to the change in treatment strategy. It would be explained that the remaining sessions will focus on practicing what has been learned so far. This practice would occur both in and out of the therapy sessions and with and without the therapist's help.

The therapist would then lead Jason and his family through an in vivo exercise. An item from low on the hierarchy would be chosen. The situation would be enacted with the use of props to make it as realistic as possible. Jason would be asked to rate his anxiety level in the situation. Jason's family members would be asked to rate their own levels of anxiety and to comment on their own expectations and reactions. Jason would use the four skills he has learned to manage his anxiety. Regardless of the success of the exercise, the therapist would encourage Jason to reward himself. The entire exercise would then be repeated several times, with the therapist and various family members acting as helpers.

As the therapist notices the reactions of other family members (i.e., anxiety, interruptions, distractions), these reactions could be addressed directly during the session by speaking with the family member or by asking Jason to direct his family in how they can best assist him. Other family members could also be enlisted to reassure the distressed member or draw attention away from Jason. Alternatively, Jason and his parents could switch roles, with Jason acting as the parent and his parents acting as anxious children. By practicing a variety of responses to Jason's anxiety, family members would learn to cope better in difficult situations and any family patterns that maintain Jason's anxiety would be broken.

The session would conclude with a progressive muscle relaxation exercise. For homework, each family member would be asked to practice a situation from his or her hierarchy.

Tenth Through Fifteenth Sessions

Each session would begin with a review of the homework assignments. Then a scenario would be presented and Jason would be asked to rate his anxiety. The therapist would role-play how Jason might manage his anxiety in the situation. As in session nine, Jason would practice managing the situation in an in vivo exposure. Family members would practice how they would respond to Jason's anxiety and the skills they have learned for helping him cope. During each session, one or two scenarios would be enacted. The therapist would choose situations that provoke increasing levels of anxiety as Jason develops mastery over his anxiety. As in session nine, the exposure situations would also be assigned as homework.

Final Session 16

The final session would review skills that Jason and his family have learned and discuss the progress they have made. Attention would be paid to how the family could help Jason maintain his newly acquired skills.

Conclusions

Case conceptualizations serve several functions (Shirk & Russell, 1996). They direct attention to pathological mechanisms that contribute to presenting problems and orient the therapist to change processes that can alleviate the child's problems. In the above case, the focus of treatment depended on the nature of the specific mechanisms that were identified as causing and maintaining the boy's difficulties. The initial conceptualization consisted of primarily behavioral and social learning factors that caused and maintained his social anxiety. Thus, the treatment plan centered on social skills training and behavioral exposures that corrected the maladaptive learning cycle. When the conceptualization of the boy's problems shifted to include family and cognitive factors, the treatment plan was altered to address these issues.

In addition to assisting in treatment planning, case conceptualization can provide a useful framework for evaluation of treatment progress. Essentially, case conceptualizations are tested through the application of relevant treatment procedures. In our case example, if the boy had not responded well to social skills training, this might have cued the therapist to consider the possibility that he did not actually suffer from a social skills deficit. Perhaps he already possessed the requisite social skills but was acutely anxious about using them in social encounters. If so, an approach incorporating specific anxiety-reduction procedures would have been more appropriate. Likewise, if in the alternative treatment plan the family did not exhibit any behavior that might contribute to or maintain their son's anxious behavior, then the conceptualization would need to be altered to focus on the boy as an individual or on other systems, such as his school.

Perhaps most importantly, case conceptualization provides the therapist with a framework for decision making within the session. Considered from a cognitive-behavioral perspective, the boy's failure to adequately cope with his distress during an exposure exercise could be attributed to the fact that he has not adequately mastered cognitive coping skills. If this were the case, then the therapist might interrupt the exposure exercise to review the skills that were taught. Alternatively, if failure to cope with anxiety were viewed from a primarily behavioral perspective, the therapist would continue the exposure with the knowledge that the boy would habituate to the anxiety-provoking stimulus eventually. Interrupting the exposure would only reinforce his anxious behavior as it would allow him to avoid the situation.

In sum, case conceptualization serves to guide the therapist in the understanding, assessment, and treatment of a given child and his or her family and social context. Without an adequate conceptualization, treatment will likely falter. Moreover, it should be stressed that conceptualization must be highly individualized; not all cases of social phobia will respond to the same set of interventions.

References

Albano, A. M. (1995). Treatment of social anxiety in adolescents. *Cognitive and Behavioral Practice, 2,* 271–298.

Albano, A. M., & DiBartolo, P. M. (1997). Cognitive-behavioral treatment of obsessive-compulsive disorder and social phobia in children and adolescents. In L. Vandecreek, S. Knapp, & T. L. Jackson (eds) *Innovations in Clinical Practice: A Source Book.* Sarasota, FL: Professional Resource Press. *15,* 41–58.

American Psychiatric Association. (1994). *Diagnostic and Statistical Manual for Mental Disorders.* (4th ed.). Washington, DC: Author.

Beidel, D. C., & Turner, S. M. (1998). *Shy Children, Phobic Adults: Nature and Treament of Social Phobia.* Washington, DC: American Psychological Association.

Beidel, D. C., Turner, S. M., & Morris, T. L. (1995). A new inventory to assess childhood social anxiety and phobia: the social phobia and anxiety inventory for children. *Psychological Assessment, 7,* 73–79.

Francis, G., & Ollendick, T. H. (1990). Behavioral treatment of social anxiety In E. L. Feindler & G. R. Kalfus (eds) *Adolescent Behavior Therapy Bandbook.* New York: Springer Publications. 127–145.

Howard, B. L., & Kendall, P. C. (1992), *Cognitive-behavioral Family Therapy for Anxious Children: Therapist Manual.* Philadelphia, PA: Child and Adolescent Anxiety Disorders Clinic, Temple University.

Howard, B. L., & Kendall, P. C. (1996). Cognitive-behavioral family therapy for anxiety-disordered children: a multiple-baseline evaluation. *Cognitive Therapy and Research, 20,* 423–443.

Kendall, P. C. (1990). *Coping Cat Workbook.* Ardmore, PA: Workbook Publishing.

Kovacs, M. (1978). *Children's Depression Inventory (CDI).* Unpublished manuscript, University of Pittsburgh School of Medicine.

Ollendick, T. H., King, N. J., & Frary, R. B. (1989). Fears in children and adolescents: Reliability and generalizability across gender, age, and nationality. *Behaviour Research and Therapy, 27,* 19–26.

Shirk, S. R., & Russell, R. L. (1996). *Change Processes in Child Psychotherapy.* New York: Guilford.

Chapter 11

Treatment of Childhood Generalized Anxiety Disorder/ Overanxious Disorder

Jill T. Ehrenreich and Alan M. Gross

Children displaying Generalized Anxiety Disorder (GAD), or its diagnostic precursor, Overanxious Disorder (OAD), experience an excessive amount of worry or anxious apprehension that cannot be reliably linked to a specific object or situation. The number, severity and frequency of worries identified by GAD children serve to distinguish them from both normal children and those suffering with other types of anxiety disorders (Tracey, et al., 1997). GAD children often demonstrate worries regarding a wide range of fear objects: future events, the appropriateness of past behavior, social concerns, competence, performance, school, health, personal safety or even just the "little things" that may present a daily challenge (Weems, et al., 1997). Additionally, somatic signs of motor tension, such as stomach aches, headaches, sleep disturbance, restlessness or fatigue are common complaints among children with generalized anxiety. It has also been hypothesized that GAD children maintain a state of cognitive vigilance for signs of threat in their environments, often resulting in measurable task performance decrements. These children may be exceedingly self-conscious, seeking endless reassurance from parents or other authority figures, while extracting only temporary relief from the comfort presented to them. While GAD children are typically regarded as very well-behaved, their good behavior is associated with an eagerness to please adults that results in the application of labels such as "perfectionist" or "overly mature." Despite, or perhaps partly due to their typical well-mannered demeanor, generally anxious children may be neglected by their peers, particularly when they present symptoms of comorbid depression.

GAD is regarded as the most common of the anxiety disorders. Both young children and adolescents may suffer from GAD, with prevalence rates estimated between two and ten percent of the general population, depending upon the type of sample and stringency of criteria considered (Werry, 1991). GAD can begin at any age, and while older children and adolescents tend to report more anxiety symptoms, the type and severity of GAD symptoms described are similar for both children and adolescents (Tracey, et al., 1997). The ratio of male to females with GAD remains fairly equal until adolescence, after which, females become disproportionately represented in the population. While prevalence rates for specific

Handbook of Conceptualization and Treatment of Child Psychopathology, pages 211–238.
Copyright © 2001 by Elsevier Science Ltd.
All rights of reproduction in any form reserved.
ISBN: 0-08-043362-6

ethnic groups remain unknown, GAD does seem to be overrepresented among middle to upper income children in clinical samples.

The rate of remission among generally anxious children is quite high, with the majority of symptoms disappearing or decreasing sharply in severity within two years of initial presentation. However, for an unspecified minority of children, GAD may persist in a chronic state through adulthood (Werry, 1991). The full range of potential complications which may aid the chronicity of GAD is beyond the scope of this discussion. However, some additional factors which may be linked to severity of GAD symptom presentation include: comorbid diagnoses (particularly depression or additional anxiety disorders), school refusal, parental stress or psychopathology, and familial dysfunction.

Treatment Approaches

Despite a long history of theoretical interest from a diverse group of psychology luminaries, including Freud, Pavlov, Skinner, and Wolpe, generalized anxiety, particularly in children, remains chronically understudied. This paucity of research is readily apparent from examination of treatments specified for children with GAD. In fact, few treatments have been proposed for generalized anxiety specified as a target for intervention, and only two treatment strategies, cognitive behavioral procedures (Kendall, 1994) and cognitive behavioral treatment with family anxiety management (Barrett, 1993) attained "probably efficacious" status in a recent review of empirically supported treatments for children with anxiety disorders. No anxiety-focused interventions were classified as "well established" in this review (Ollendick & King, 1998). Despite this general lack of empirical validation for use with GAD children, a number of both behavioral and cognitive-behavioral approaches have been traditionally utilized, individually and in combination with one another, with this population.

Behavioral Treatments

Exposure Techniques. Though it may take one of several formats, all types of prolonged exposure involve asking the child to confront fear-evoking stimuli, either imaginary or in vivo. The rationale behind such a procedure is that, if exposure to a feared situation is of a sufficient intensity and duration, the child will eventually acclimatize to the setting, hence reducing or eliminating previous fear or worries regarding that situation. The basic scenario for exposure involves constructing a hierarchy of feared situations, ranked from least-frightening to most-frightening, then imagining each situation in turn until the most distressing stimulus has been confronted (Barrios & O'Dell, 1998). With *in vivo* procedures, the child encounters the actual feared stimulus, as opposed to pictures or imagined representations of that stimulus.

While exposure techniques are fundamental to most behavioral and cognitive-behavioral treatment packages for anxiety, some considerations must be taken into account when using exposure. For instance, the child must possess the capacity to distinguish between threatening and non-threatening stimuli, a discrimination which may be difficult for young anxious children, or children with unfocused, generalized fears, to discern. Further, the therapist must be mindful of the child's tolerance for aversion, as applying an exposure paradigm which is exceedingly frightening may only serve to reinforce the child's fears (Kendall, Chansky, Freidman, Kim, Kortlander, Sessa, & Siqueland, 1991).

Systematic Desensitization. Systematic desensitization is, in essence, a product of combining exposure techniques and responses incompatable with anxiety. There are three essential steps in systematic desensitization:

1) training the child in muscle relaxation techniques (relaxation typically involves learning to repeatedly tense then relax specific muscle groups or learning to relax those muscle groups on cue);
2) constructing a hierarchy of feared situations;
3) exposing the child to each feared stimulus, starting with the least-feared and progressing to the most-feared, while the child is in a relaxed state (Morris & Kratochwill, 1998).

Systematic desensitization relies on the premise that fear of certain stimuli and situations is learned via the pairing of those stimuli with an anxious physiological state. Thus, the resultant anxiety may be *un-learned* by presenting those stimuli again in the presence of a physiologically relaxed state.

Modeling. All types of modeling are based on an observational learning paradigm (Bandura, 1986), in which the child observes a model interacting appropriately with feared stimuli. Observation of this model may occur live in front of the child, utilizing a filmed or slide presentation of the model, through the child imagining the model behaving appropriately in feared situations, or by first observing the live model enacting the adaptive response, then by practicing those adaptive responses him/herself (Barrios & O'Dell, 1998). Support for the adoption of adaptive behavior is given through therapist feedback, guided instruction, and reinforcement for the enactment of appropriate responses. The goal of modeling is for children to reduce anxiety and learn new, more appropriate methods of responding in fearful situations. Modeling may prove most effective with older children and when the child is similar to the model in age, fear level, and experience with feared stimuli (Barrios & O'Dell, 1998).

Contingent Reinforcement. To treat generalized anxiety utilizing contingent reinforcement, the therapist must control the environmental contingencies that follow a child's interaction with feared stimuli. By manipulating the environment so a child is reinforced for appropriate interaction with feared stimuli, or for systematically progressing toward interaction with anxiety-provoking situations, the therapist is theoretically increasing the probability of the appropriate behavior occurring again in the future. While research on the utility of contingency management with GAD children is non-existent, this procedure has proven effective with other types of anxious behavior, such as school phobia.

Cognitive-behavioral Procedures

Self-control. Self-control techniques combine instruction in the use of adaptive cognitive behavior with specific therapeutic assistance in adoption of a modified behavioral pattern (Morris & Kratochwill, 1998). Cognitive behavior is adjusted as the therapist assists patients in altering their thoughts about an upcoming stressor or an anxiety-provoking situation that is ongoing. Cognitions are regulated through the adoption of a more positive set of self-statements regarding competent performance in the feared situation. In addition, the therapist aids in adjusting a patient's perception of the potential threats anticipated in the feared situations. New behavioral patterns that involve use of a muscle relaxation paradigm, or imagined techniques, such as creative visualization, when approaching feared stimuli, are introduced to the child. While most investigations of self-control techniques have generally supported their utility with a variety of childhood anxiety difficulties, more research is currently needed to establish whether these techniques are appropriate for a GAD child population.

   Cognitive-behavioral Procedures for Anxious Children. Kendall's (1994) cognitive-behavioral treatment (CBT) for anxious children is a 16-Session, manualized program which emphasizes a variety of information processing adjustments and behavioral techniques which aim to reduce children and young adolescents' maladaptive or excessive arousal to feared situations. This program has demonstrated success over a wait-list control group in a recent analysis of CBT efficacy (Kendall, *et al.*, 1997). The overarching goal of CBT is to instruct children in recognizing the maladaptive or excessive anxious arousal, and allow the recognition of this arousal to serve as a cue to initiate anxiety management techniques (Kendall, *et al.*, 1991).

   CBT treatment involves two phases. The first phase emphasizes identification of the child's particular responses to anxiety, the use of relaxation techniques and coping self-talk in anxiety-provoking situations, as well as use of self-reward contingent upon appropriate behavior in such situations. These concepts are then summarized for the child using the acronym FEAR (Kendall, *et al.*, 1992): Feeling Frightened? Expecting bad things to happen? Attitudes and actions that will help? Results and rewards?

   The second phase involves performance-based practice opportunities, in which the therapist serves as a model for each skill introduced, then invites the child to participate with the therapist in the activity. Next, the child is encouraged to practice these techniques in a non-threatening, therapeutic environment. The child continues to practice this new, adaptive coping behavior, both in the imagination and in vivo, as the situations presented become increasingly stressful, until the child has demonstrated mastery of these skills in a number of anxiety-related situations.

   Cognitive-Behavioral Therapy with Family Anxiety Management. Barrett (1993) combined the proven utility of Kendall's (1992) CBT treatment for children with an additional component, family anxiety management (FAM), a 12-Session family intervention designed to empower parents and child to work together as an "expert team" in managing anxiety. CBT and FAM treatments are provided to the "expert team" concurrently, with approximately 30 minutes of Session time spent on CBT and 40 minutes on family therapy. Further, CBT + FAM treatment has demonstrated even greater results than CBT alone in clinically anxious samples. Barrett, *et al.* (1996) found that only 16 percent of children treated with CBT + FAM met diagnostic criteria for an anxiety disorder at post-treatment, compared with 43 percent of the CBT alone group, and 74 percent of the wait list control group. At both six month and annual follow-up assessments, CBT + FAM still demonstrated greater maintenance of treatment gains than CBT alone.

FAM, also known as *The Friends Program* (Barrett, *et al.*, 1997), is a manualized treatment program that emphasizes process methods, such as the open sharing of information, and joint determination of Session content, with an effort to identify and reinforce skills which individual team members may find helpful to the therapeutic process (Barrett, *et al.*, 1996). FAM has three primary goals for treatment: First, parents are taught to reward courageous behavior while simultaneously extinguishing inappropriate anxiety responses. This first goal is achieved through the application of simple contingency management skills such as a variety of descriptive praise, planned ignoring, and natural consequences. Second, parents are instructed in how to increase awareness of their own emotional difficulties, particularly their anxiety-related behavior in stressful situations. Parents are then encouraged to model problem-solving and other appropriate responses to such stressors. Finally, parents are given further training in problem-solving and communication skills that will enable them to maintain treatment gains by working together as a team. Some of the topics covered during this final phase of FAM therapy include: learning methods of reducing interparental conflict over child-related issues, maintaining parental consistency in responding to child anxiety, the establishment of casual daily discussions in which appropriate listening skills are practiced, and the scheduling of a weekly problem-solving meeting to discuss effective family and child management (Barrett, *et al.*, 1996).

Case Example

Presenting Problem

Stella, an eleven- year-old African-American female, was initially referred by her mother, Ms. L, to a community mental health center. Stella was in the fifth-grade at a local elementary school and lived with her mother, younger sister, and maternal grandmother in a small, Southeastern town. Although Ms. L reported that Stella had a history of "worry spells," the severity and frequency of Stella's somatic complaints and self-reported worries had increased greatly since Stella, her sister, and mother moved in with her maternal grandmother, approximately one year before referral. The family's move was necessitated by the acute illness of Stella's maternal grandmother, who suffered from diabetes-related complications. Ms. L reported that since the family moved from a large Southeastern city, approximately 60 miles away, Stella had made few friends. Ms. L indicated that Stella's main worries concentrated around her health, her weight, the health of her family, and school-related issues. Stella reportedly requested reassurance regarding the health of family members before leaving her home for any extended period of time. Stella also regularly asked her mother to contact her father, Mr. L, who resided in their former hometown, for reasons such as inquiring about "how he is today." Ms. L indicated that when she attempted to ignore Stella's requests for reassurance, Stella increased the emotionality of her requests, until a family member complied and/or comforted her. Ms. L also indicated that Stella was having difficulties sleeping at night, often remaining awake for two to three hours past her bedtime. Stella complained to her mother that she was getting "fat," but was within normal weight limits for her age. Approximately one to two days per week, Stella requested that her mother allowed her to stay home from school due to headaches, stomach aches or nausea. Routine medical examinations did not find a medical etiology for these complaints. Since that time, Stella had not been allowed to stay home from school. However, Ms. L reported that school health workers then began contacting her, "at least once a week," to inform her that Stella was complaining of illness. Despite these somatic complaints, Stella's grades remained impressive. Ms. L characterized Stella as "an A or B student." Stella's most recent report card consisted of three As, two Bs, and one C (in handwriting). Stella reportedly cried for over an hour after learning that she would receive a C on this report card. Her teacher reported that Stella requested additional handwriting assignments in an attempt to improve this grade. Her teacher also complained that Stella's constant reassurance-seeking regarding her health and academic performance was disruptive to the classroom. Moreover, her teacher stated that Stella rarely spoke to anyone but her in the classroom and that, as a result, other students appeared to ignore Stella.

History

Stella, the daughter of a high school teacher and an assistant store manager, experienced no complications at birth. Ms. L was in generally good health, aside from occasional asthma difficulties, during her pregnancy. Stella reportedly met all developmental milestones ontime, save for the development of speech which began at about 22 months. Since that time, speech had developed normally, and Stella had no present speech or cognitive delays.

Ms. L reported that she and her former husband were divorced when Stella was five years old, during the summer before Stella beginning kindergarten. Ms. L indicated that Stella's fears markedly increased around this time, especially when her father moved out of the family home. In particular, Stella requested to see her father daily, claiming to be concerned that he would leave town without her. If she was not granted this request, she would cry or tantrum until her mother relented. Stella also had a difficult time making the transition to kindergarten, despite the fact that she had attended a preschool, uneventfully, for the two years before beginning kindergarten. Ms. L stated that Stella would routinely cry and scream when she was brought to class. Her kindergarten teacher indicated that this behavior would persist for up to 45 minutes after Ms. L left the classroom. Moreover, Stella would cry easily at home, particularly when her mother was unable to reassure her or pay immediate attention to her behavior. At that time, Mr. L began volunteering in Stella's classroom for a few hours a day, approximately two to three times per week. Immediately after this began, Stella's mood improved. Though she still cried easily, Stella adjusted to her kindergarten classroom and often discussed how happy she was with the opportunity to immediately show her father her outstanding schoolwork. In the absence of her father, Stella's kindergarten teacher reported that she was less gregarious, but still improved over her prior behavior. Stella also eventually made two close girlfriends, with whom she remained in daily contact until her move.

Though Stella's apparent anxiety and mood difficulties abated over the next six months, Ms. L stated that her ex-husband continued to "baby" Stella by coming to see her whenever she requested, buying her unnecessary gifts, and failing to discipline Stella when needed. In fact, Ms. L stated that both before and after the divorce, she was solely responsible for the discipline of her daughters. Ms. L relayed that her ex-husband felt his daughters were well-behaved and did not require punishment. Ms. L stated that she often felt guilty when attempting to discipline her children. Moreover, Ms. L indicated that feelings of guilt might have contributed to her difficulties in ignoring Stella's demands for reassurance.

Approximately one year before referral, Stella's maternal grandmother was hospitalized and required extensive rehabilitation. Though Ms. L stated that she felt tremendously guilty and nervous about uprooting her daughters, her mother's care took precedence over concerns she harbored about Stella's adjustment abilities. Ms. L initially took a three-month leave-of-absence from her teaching job to care for her mother full-time, who was in a wheelchair and required assistance with many basic care routines. Ms. L indicated that this was Stella's first experience observing such a serious illness. Moreover, when Ms. L returned to work, Stella began assisting in many of her grandmother's care routines. While Stella reportedly enjoyed the opportunity to help care for her grandmother, she stated that some of her grandmother's health problems were, "scary and gross." Stella also expressed concern over when, how and where her grandmother was going to pass away. In addition, she asked her mother, several times, about where they would live, if her grandmother died.

Ms. L reported that both Stella and Mr. L made a "big fuss" over the move, during which time he threatened to fight Ms. L for custody of the girls. Stella also requested that she be allowed to live with her father, rather than move with her mother and sister. However, after some discussion of the matter, it was determined that Ms. L would retain primary custody of both girls. Ms. L indicated that Stella seemed very disappointed when she was told that she would have to move with her mother and sister, but refused to discuss the matter with anyone but her father. After the move, Stella continued to speak with her father daily, and she traveled to see him and her friends approximately every other weekend.

Stella's weight concerns reportedly began following a doctor's visit, when a nurse commented on how much weight Stella had put on over the last year. In fact, Stella was slightly underweight during the previous year, though Stella insisted that the nurse and others thought she was too heavy. Further, Ms. L found Stella's "obsession" about her 'C' in handwriting to be in great contrast to her formerly proud attitude about her schoolwork. Before receiving the C, Stella reportedly made a deliberate effort to bring her excellent academic performance to the attention of both her parents. However, Ms. L stated that recent conversations with Stella revealed little pride in her school work, and instead revolved around Stella's concerns about how she could improve her academic performance.

Ms. L indicated a strong desire to assist her daughter in overcoming her anxiety. She reported a willingness to try anything, short of medicating her daughter, to aid in her recovery. Mr. L indicated by telephone that he was also committed to helping his daughter overcome her difficulties and would attempt to participate in therapy Sessions, as his work schedule permitted.

Assessment

The assessment process was initiated at the first interview. During this Session, the clinician met first with Ms. L. The clinician obtained relevant historical data and a general description of the presenting problem. Developmental information was solicited, as well. At the end of this first Session, both Stella and her mother were given several questionnaires to complete and return before their next Session. Included among these questionnaires were both self-report and parental report instruments assessing anxiety symptomotology, anxiety sensitivity, depressive symptomotology, self-concept, negative cognitions, parental affect, and general child behavior problems. Following the initial interview, Ms. L called and stated that Stella's father would be participating in the therapy process. Mr. L also called to reiterate this information. Mr. and Ms. L, Ms. and Stella then returned to complete separate administrations of the child and parent versions of the Anxiety Disorders Interview Schedule, *DSM-IV* revision (ADIS-C and ADIS-P; Silverman & Nelles, 1988). After review of these assessment instruments, it was determined that Stella qualified for a primary diagnosis of Generalized Anxiety Disorder (severity rating of 6).

During the child interview, Stella demonstrated an appropriate range of affect. She was well-groomed, and of approximately normal height and weight for her age. She appeared somewhat nervous, looked around the room frequently, and twice asked the therapist if she could leave the room to tell her parents that she loved them. Stella also expressed concern over whether her performance in the interview was acceptable. She acknowledged that the move had been very difficult for her, and admitted that she worried often. When asked to elaborate on what she worried about, Stella was unable to describe her specific fears, save some concerns about her grandmother's well-being and whether she would be allowed to return to her former hometown. She did report numerous somatic complaints, including headaches, nausea, and general fatigue. She stated that these feelings of distress were often worse immediately before she left for school and before taking tests. She stated that she was very concerned that her new classmates did not like her, and began crying when asked whether she had made any new friends at school. She also described herself as "chubby and kind of ugly," and claimed to be currently on a diet to lose excess weight.

Questionnaire data revealed that Stella's anxious apprehension had a strong physiologic component, though she also demonstrated several cognitive and behavioral facets of anxiety. She scored in the clinical range on several measures of anxiety, particularly on those questionnaires which assessed "anxiety proneness" or reactions to anxiety sensations. Stella indicated frequent use of negative self-statements, a moderate level of social anxiety, low self-esteem, and a mild level of depression. Questionnaire data revealed that Ms. L suffered from moderate range depression, and mild generalized anxiety, while Mr. L had experienced symptoms of alcohol abuse, panic disorder, and moderate depression. Further, parental ratings of Stella's behavior indicated difficulties with somatic complaints, anxiety/depression, and current social problems. This information was consistent with Stella's GAD diagnosis.

Case Conceptualization

After review of Stella's behavioral history, current complaints, and assessment information, her presenting problems were conceptualized as a partial product of inconsistent or inappropriate parental usage of contingency management skills, complicated by poor parental cohesion. Although both parents exhibited a strong commitment to managing Stella's anxious behavior, they had done so in a disparate and inconsistent manner. For example, Ms. L had frequently reinforced Stella's reassurance-seeking by failing to consistently ignore Stella's inappropriate demands for her attention. In fact, Stella appeared to have increased the severity and frequency of her demands for attention, partially via Ms. L's reinforcement of her reassurance-seeking behavior. Mr. L also powerfully reinforced this behavior by providing a fairly consistent pattern of unqualified reinforcement for his daughter's reassurance-seeking. Inappropriate reinforcement delivery had also resulted in the establishment of an association between Stella's presentation of somatic complaints and escape from the demands of the school environment. This association may have been inadvertently strengthened by forcing Stella to go to school after no medical etiology could be established for her physical problems, since presentation of somatic complaints in the school environment again resulted in occasional escape from this aversive situation. Mr. L had personally modeled an anxious pattern of behavior, as indicated by his own struggles with panic, as well as a history of pre-emptively reassuring his daughter at both home and school. Ms. L also provided Stella with a model of fearful and avoidant behavior, as exemplified by her occasional failure to discipline the child because of her own self-reported guilt feelings and anxiety. Finally, Mr. and Ms. L had frequently and vividly displayed not only poor parental cohesion, but an open hostility toward one another which served as an impediment to the mounting of a consistent plan for managing Stella's behavior.

Stella also presented individual anxiety difficulties such as poor management of reactions to physiological anxiety sensations, frequent use of negative self-state-ments, a paucity of coping responses when anxious, and an overall lack of appropriate self-reinforcement. Stella appeared to have a fundamental difficulty in appropriately labeling her physiologic responses to fearful stimuli, as indicated by her self-report of frequent headaches, stomach aches and nausea without known medical etiology. Moreover, Stella did not appear to associate her somatic responses with her fears about her grandmother's health, her father, her weight, or perceived imperfections in her schoolwork, although they occurred contiguously in time. Assessment measures confirmed Stella's high degree of phy-siologic reactivity to fear. Questionnaire data revealed that Stella experienced a very high number of self-reported negative cognitions and a low level of self-esteem. Stella's negative self-statements appeared to center around fears about what will occur in the future, negative self-evaluation, perfectionist standards of performance, increased worry about what others (particularly her father, teacher, and classmates) were thinking, and concerns about failure. The report of Stella, her parents, and teacher indicated that she failed to generate many alternative coping solutions, other than withdrawal from an anxiety-provoking scenario (i.e., school or new social scenarios) or reassurance-seeking (i.e., regarding her grand-mother or father), when experiencing anxiety. Finally, Stella set extremely high standards for her own success in school and social situations. She did not appear to perceive herself accurately, as indicated by the distortions in self-reported body image.

Treatment Selection

Stella's case required a treatment which could address parental behavior manage-ment difficulties, the adversarial relationship between Stella's parents, as well as Stella's individual issues with anxiety. Cognitive-Behavioral Therapy with Family Anxiety Management (CBT + FAM; Barrett, 1993) treatment was selected because it provided the necessary behavioral and cognitive components to adequately confront all of these problems As previously indicated, CBT + FAM is a manua-lized treatment approach which taught Mr. and Ms. L new contingency manage-ment skills such as extinguishing fearful/complaining behavior, reinforcing appropriate coping behavior, and parental modeling of brave approach behavior in their adult lives (Barrett, 1999). In addition, parental cohesion was specifically addressed via three parental support sessions, specifically aimed at assisting Mr. and Ms. L in encouraging one another to use learned contingency management skills, be consistent, and work together to solve child behavior problems. Finally, CBT + FAM addressed Stella's individual needs by teaching and encouraging her and her family to utilize four new skills:

1) Improved awareness of physical reactions to anxiety-related sensations;
2) Recognition and evaluation of self-statements made when anxious;
3) Development of new coping methods, such as muscle relaxation and thought substitution, for responding to anxious feelings;
4) Determination of more appropriate self-evaluation standards and increased usage of self-reward.

Treatment Procedures

Assessment results were discussed in a feedback session before the initiation of treatment. Although parental difficulties were introduced as a potential contributing factor in the maintenance of child anxiety, this was done in the course of identifying the concept of CBT+FAM's "team" work approach to anxiety management. This treatment method avoids identifying any one source of causation for problem behavior, but rather emphasizes the development of a shared perception of problems and treatment responsibilities. This process was begun during assessment feedback, as all members of the team (child, parent, and therapist) were given the opportunity to discuss assessment information and jointly determine a course for treatment. The team determined that Stella and her parents would participate in nine, one-and-a-half-hour "team" sessions with both Stella and her parents, given individual time with the therapist to discuss that session's treatment goals. It was also determined that at least three parental support sessions would take place after every third team session, to reinforce contingency management skills, as well as discuss joint parental problem-solving strategies.

Therapy sessions were divided into child, parent, and joint parent-child segments. Unless otherwise indicated (e.g., parental support sessions), each parent segment mirrored the child segment in content. By using this approach, the parents not only learned new contingency management skills, but also became aware of the specific treatment techniques utilized, in order to encourage and model their usage in the home environment. During each session, primary treatment goals were introduced, suggestions on application of these treatment procedures were made, and methods of self-monitoring between sessions were introduced.

Session One

Goals:
1) Review of specific treatment procedures, particularly the "team" concept;
2) Introduction to the concept of anxiety, emphasizing normalization and adaptive function of anxious behavior;
3) Initiation of self-monitoring homework, specifically a jointly-formed hierarchy of feared situations;
4) Address any parental concerns and expectations for therapy.

Stella and her parents appeared on-time for their first session. In a joint therapy segment, the agenda for treatment was examined by viewing Stella's copy of the *Coping Cat Notebook* (Kendall, 1994). The general subject matter introduced in each session was discussed. Since Mr. L felt that he might have to miss an occasional session due to work conflicts, the importance of Ms. L discussing with him any missed session information was emphasized. Mr. L was also encouraged to participate in any family activities introduced during missed sessions.

An example of the "team" concept was reviewed by utilizing the metaphor of a sports team. The therapy "team" was likened to a sports team in which the child acted as the captain, since the effort of the child was most vital to the performance of the team. The parents were suggested as very important team players, since they knew the child best. Meanwhile, the therapist was introduced as a player who had some specific techniques for helping the team perform optimally. Stella was encouraged to examine other parallels between her treatment "team" and a sports team to reinforce this concept.

The construct of anxiety was discussed as central to the therapy process by suggesting that Stella and her parents all had things in their lives that they wished to feel happier or less worried about. The therapy process was referred to as a positive and productive method of achieving this goal. Further, the three of them were reinforced for disclosing situations in which they wished to feel happier or less worried. The concept of worrying was normalized for Stella by suggesting that all children feel scared sometimes and that Stella was very brave for learning how to handle her fears. Stella's parents were given a more detailed model of anxiety, including possible biological influences, such as an increased sensitivity to fear sensations. This sensitivity was discussed as a potentially positive skill, if Stella could learn to utilize appropriate coping skills in response to such sensations. Further, learning influences and Stella's needs for attention were discussed, emphasizing how Stella's parents have tried to protect their sensitive and fearful child through inconsistent or inappropriate reinforcement, rather than blaming Mr. or Ms. L for Stella's anxiety problems. Other influences, such as the relationship between avoidance and anxiety, modeling influences, and accidental reinforcement of anxious behavior were briefly discussed with Stella's parents. Additional parent questions or concerns about the concept of anxiety or the therapeutic process were also discussed at this time.

Several homework assignments were introduced as exercises in team cohesiveness, as well as a method of increasing awareness and of monitoring Stella's particular fears. Suggested activities included working together to create a fear hierarchy for Stella, in which feared situations were written down in the order of easiest to deal with to most difficult to confront. Stella's parents were also encouraged to work together to create a list of fearful or reassurance-seeking behavior that they wished to eliminate by a planned ignoring of that behavior. Finally, Stella was asked to share a happy time that she experienced every day of the next week with at least one of her parents. In return, her parents were invited to share a happy time they remembered from their day.

Session Two

Goals:
1) Introduction to the concepts of thoughts and feelings, in preparation for exchanging negative thoughts for more positive ones;
2) Discussion of positive parenting skills, as well as initiation and rehearsal of behavior correction procedures;
3) Review homework, emphasizing identification of enjoyable situations discovered during the course of the previous week.

This second session began with a review of the previous week's homework assignments, with team members praised by the therapist for their active participation. Stella appeared to particularly enjoy discussing "happy times" with her parents. This feedback led into a discussion of how feelings are related to both thoughts and physical manifestations of emotion:

Therapist: What part of discussing happy times with your parents did you enjoy the most?

Stella: I liked it best when daddy would tell me about the nice people he met at work and then I would tell him about how well I did on my handwriting.

Therapist: What happens to your face when you feel happy about your schoolwork?

Stella: I don't know. I guess I smile when I think about how well I did.

Therapist: That's true Stella, I saw you smile just now when you were discussing the nice things your dad said about your handwriting assignments. Do you think that your face makes different kinds of expressions when your feeling other things, too?

Stella: Yeah, I frown when I'm sad about grandma being sick.

Therapist: What kinds of things are you thinking about when you feel sadness about your grandma?

Stella: That maybe she'll die, because doctors can't always fix things that are wrong with people. And that maybe mommy or I will get diabetes, too, because when K (sister) got chicken pox, I also got chicken pox and then I was sick for a week. Momma said you can't get diabetes like chicken pox, but I don't know. Do you think I might get diabetes?

Therapist: I think it's pretty normal to feel worried about people when they get sick, and I'm really glad you share how you feel sad and worried when you think about your grandma being ill.

A set of *Coping Cat Notebook* exercises for identifying feelings and thoughts in particular situations, plus review of facial expressions that frequently occur in the context of different emotions were assigned as homework for the next week to reinforce accurate emotion labeling. For the next week, Stella and her parents were asked to concentrate on using this activity to identify only positive thoughts and feelings.

Feared situations detailed by Stella and her family were also reviewed in this session. Family members discussed how they each behave in such situations. Meanwhile, Stella was encouraged to denote the benefits of overcoming these fears. Stella and her parents were informed that overcoming fears was much like learning to ride a bike, a step-by-step process that you can get better at with daily practice. Regular completion of homework assignments was cited as one type of daily practice that could help the family improve their anxiety management skills.

The interaction detailed above between the therapist and Stella was also reviewed for Stella's parents as an example of ignoring attempts for reassurance, as the therapist did when Stella inquired about whether she would contract diabetes. Stella's parents also discussed the list of fearful events they wished to stop, such as escaping school-related demands via complaining about physical ailments. The therapist and Stella's parents role-played a scenario in which Stella demanded to be allowed to stay home from school due to illness. Appropriate, planned ignoring and, if necessary, use of a brief time-out procedure were rehearsed.

The concept of specific labeled praise was introduced to Stella's parents in this session. Stella's parents were encouraged to attend to non-avoidant or approaching behavior, as well as positive evaluations of herself and others. Mr. and Ms. L. were asked to give examples of praise that they might use with Stella. Further, practice at this praising behavior was reinforced by requesting that the parents select four or five types of behavior they most wished to praise before the next session.

Session Three

Goals:
1) Discussion and reinforcement of the family's attempts to identify thoughts and feelings associated with happy moments during the week. Also, reinforcement for any attempts to cope with negative emotions should be identified;
2) Introduction to the exposure paradigm, and its relation to changing negative evaluations of anxiety-provoking situations;
3) Explanation of how body signals function as an adaptive warning system when anxious;
4) Introduction of relaxation techniques as a method of coping with these body signals;
5) Discussion of how modeling of anxious behaviors in adult lives may assist in the development and maintenance of child anxiety.

All family members attended this Session. Homework from the previous week was reviewed, with the therapist emphasizing the family's successful completion of

Coping Cat exercises. Stella was able to relay a few attempts at appropriately coping with her grandmother's illness, including two open and frank discussions about death with her grandmother and her pastor. All family members agreed that these were important and positive methods of confronting and coping with Stella's fears about dying. All family members were praised for these efforts, and the therapist emphasized that simply trying to cope properly with fears, rather than attempting to be perfect, was the goal of such activities.

The therapist discussed how the family was nearing completion of the first portion of their FEAR Plan (in the context of CBT + FAM, where F = feeling good, E = expecting good things to happen, A = action, R = review and reward). The components of the **F or feeling good** section were reviewed for Stella and her parents. These segments included: (a) thinking happy thoughts; (b) doing something that makes you feel happy; and (c) learning to relax the body. The interrelations between these concepts were discussed.

The therapist explained how certain body signals, like headaches or rapid breathing might serve as a normal signal of anxiety. Each "team" member was then encouraged to talk about what kinds of body signals they felt when anxious. Next, a rationale and procedure for daily, brief muscle relaxation exercises were introduced to the family. It was explained to the child and her parents that Stella, along with one of her parents, were to practice this muscle relaxation paradigm for five to ten minutes a day. It was determined that Stella and her mother would practice this activity together after school each day.

The "team" then moved on to a review of the exposure hierarchy that was created following Session One. The family was encouraged to discuss openly what coping skills the family had previously employed to overcome these fears. In particular, the family addressed strategies that were previously effective, which were not, and why. The therapist and Stella's parents agreed that the most effective strategy for assisting Stella in exposing herself to feared situations, given her high need for attention, was to reinforce proactive, approach behavior. The parents role-played utilizing verbal praise as a reinforcer for assisting Stella in coping with the first item on her fear hierarchy (eating normal size portions of food at meal times). Specific usage of cognitive coping skills and muscle relaxation when confronted with this feared stimulus was practiced with Stella in session. Finally, the rationale and procedures for exposure therapy were discussed thoroughly with Stella and her parents. Specific parental concerns about not being able to assist Stella with the feared stimulus in the school setting were addressed by emphasizing home practice of the exposure scenario, as well as Stella utilizing self-monitoring of her eating behavior in school.

In the parental segment of the third Session, Stella's parents were encouraged to continue their excellent use of labeled praise. They were also educated about how both positive and negative modeling can affect the behavior of others around them. Stella's parents were encouraged to discuss how they each behaved in anxiety-provoking situations. Mr. and Ms. L were reminded that they were not to blame for Stella's anxious behavior, though both parents agreed that more appropriate modeling in anxiety-provoking situations could only benefit Stella's mental health.

As a homework assignment for the following week, Stella and her parents were asked to discuss, each day, one difficult event that occurred during their day. Further, each family member was asked to share how he/she felt about this event, and what he/she thought during the event. Family members were encouraged to work together over the next week to develop positive solutions for coping with these difficult events, concentrating on what kinds of positive cognitive appraisals may be utilized in dealing with the situation.

Parental Support Session One

The first parental support session served to introduce the purpose of these additional training sessions to Stella's parents. Moreover, the therapist and Stella's parents were able to clarify some specific concerns regarding the physical distance between Mr. L and Stella. Specifically, he was concerned that Ms. L was handling the bulk of Stella's daily coping activities (i.e., relaxation, review of Stella's exposure activities, discussion of coping with difficult situations, etc.). Ms. L concurred that because of her physical guardianship of Stella, as well as the compatability of her work schedule with Stella's school schedule, she was in fact handling the bulk of these "team" activities with Stella. Mr. and Ms. L agreed that it was best for Stella to continue practicing daily relaxation activities with her mother, though Mr. L agreed to practice these exercises with Stella during their visits. Further, Mr. L agreed to contact Stella by phone every other evening for the sole purpose of reviewing her progress with exposure and discussing coping skills in relation to daily difficulties. Both parents were praised for their continuing active interest in improving Stella's response to anxiety. Stella's parents were also encouraged to continue sharing any difficulties with consistent usage of praise and planned ignoring, although both parents claimed that they were adequately applying these skills, thus far.

Several problem-solving scenarios that have previously caused problems between Mr. and Ms. L were introduced by the therapist, including disagreements over discipline procedures and arguing in front of their children. Both parents were encouraged to discuss more appropriate methods for handling their disagreements. The therapist and Stella's parents determined that it was vital to remain calm when a disagreement occurred, support the other parent in their use of discipline techniques (even if one parent wished to adjust that discipline strategy at a later date), and discuss problem-solving strategies only after their individual anger had past and each parent was relaxed. The parents appropriately role-played responses to a disagreement over discipline. Furthermore, both parents were asked to continue providing support to each other for consistent use of behavior management techniques over the next few weeks.

Session Four

Goals:
1) Review the impact that thoughts have on feelings, with an emphasis on the idea that control over behavior is obtained via conscious positive thought;

2) Presentation of a more detailed rationale for anxiety management;
3) Review progress on exposure paradigm and discuss challenges/skills involved with handling the next feared situation on hierarchy.

This session was attended by only Ms. L and Stella, as Mr. L had a work conflict. Ms. L was reminded of the importance of sharing Session information with Mr. L and encouraging continued joint support of anxiety management activities. Stella reported that she continued to enjoy the therapy process, especially the additional contact with her parents. She reported some frustration about not being able to go home from school when she had headaches this week. However, she said she had only experienced one major headache and one smaller one, both of which had improved during later relaxation exercises with her mother. Ms. L also reported some benefit from relaxation, but indicated even greater benefit from listening to her daughter's difficult daily situations and sharing her own with Stella. Ms. L admitted that she initially felt uncomfortable about this activity, but now found it to be a rewarding way to spend some individual time with Stella. Stella also reported that she believed herself to be of substantial benefit to her parents in generating alternative positive thoughts to use when feeling anxious or sad. The therapist utilized this discussion to introduce the importance of the next component in the FEAR model, **E or expecting good things to happen**. Stella was reminded that her *Coping Cat* activities for the week would all be used to help her concentrate on this new component. The therapist and Stella discussed this concept extensively and role-played a scenario in which the therapist was stuck in a tree and scared of climbing down. Stella was asked to help the therapist generate positive ways to think about the situation, and how to estimate the likelihood of being able to climb down the tree alone. Ms. L also reviewed this exercise and was reminded of the importance of using conscious positive thoughts to overcome anxiety-provoking scenarios.

The therapist, Stella and Ms. L also reviewed a more detailed rationale for anxiety management. The therapist presented this information to Stella in the following manner:

Therapist: From what you are saying, Stella, it seems like you sometimes have trouble getting relaxed in really nerve-wracking situations, like when you're getting ready to take a test or when grandma has to go to the doctor. This next part of therapy is designed to help you pick out those things that make you feel anxious, to become more aware of how your body reacts when you are around those things, and learn new, healthy ways of telling yourself and others about your concerns. You know, being anxious, as we've discussed before, is a normal feeling. We all become upset about some things. The important thing to do now is to work on preparing for dealing with our stress, learning to relax, and most importantly, practicing new ways of coping during our everyday life. By doing those things, you can learn to handle anxious feelings in a way that is not too upsetting for you.

Ms. L was given a more detailed presentation of the steps involved in anxiety control, though the overall concepts reviewed were the same. As a homework assignment, family members were encouraged to keep a diary of body hints, thoughts, feelings, and behavior which occurred during daily difficult situations.

The therapy "team" also discussed the challenges involved with progressing to the next step on Stella's fear hierarchy, which involved taking tests or having oral evaluations in class. The team discussed what kinds of coping skills would be appropriate to utilize in the classroom. It was determined that Stella would utilize new breathing and muscle relaxation skills, as well as positive thoughts related to evaluation outcomes when her anxiety-level was increased by these situations this week.

Session Five

Goals:
1) Review homework materials, with particular attention to identification of body hints, as well as anxiety-related thoughts, feeling, and behavior;
2) Reinforcement of relaxation and positive self-talk skills;
3) Discussion of specific plans for preventing anxiety in challenging situations;
4) Continuation of exposure paradigm.

Following a review of the week's homework assignments and the home use of relaxation therapy, it was determined that all of the "team" participants were making sufficient progress and effort in the program, thus far. So the primary focus of this session was on the introduction and adoption of a new skill, positive self-talk. The therapist began this process by reviewing the relationships between thoughts, feelings, and behavior. The therapist emphasized to Stella's parents how a connection between irrational thoughts and anxious behavior might occur. Mr. and Ms. L were encouraged to discuss recent incidents in which they became anxious. The therapist then assisted in identifying the irrational assumptions at work in their thoughts about the incident described. Stella's parents each attempted to identify positive self-talk that could have been used in each of these incidents. For example, Ms. L described a situation in which the principal of the school where she is employed recently reviewed her job performance. Although Ms. L had only experienced generally positive feedback from her employers in the past, and had done nothing which would suggest any negative feedback would be forthcoming, she reported feeling a great deal of dread about even going to work on the day of her evaluation. Alternative self-statements which were suggested for Ms. L included:

1) I am a competent worker;
2) I am a good teacher;
3) My boss has provided fair and positive feedback to me in the past, today will be no different.

All family members were encouraged to continue the practice of identifying positive self-talk by individually preparing a self-talk routine that could be implemented when anxious feelings surface. The family members decided, as a group, that after identification of an anxiety provoking situation, each would initiate positive self-talk by asking themselves at least one of the following questions: "How can I make myself feel good?" or "Given what I am worried about, what kinds of good things might happen?"

The therapist then reviewed the next portion of the FEAR model, **A or actions**. This concept was introduced during the discussions of positive self-talk indicated above. As each family member rehearsed the self-talk routine for their individual stressors, the therapist inquired whether they could each generate solutions for making their situations less fearful. Family members were encouraged to write down these solutions. After these solutions had been verbalized, the therapist asked participants to determine how they would feel if they were to implement that solution. Finally, family members were asked to choose a solution that would be beneficial to them, as well as lessening the fearful content in the described scenarios. Practice and rehearsal in both positive self-talk and action plan identification were assigned as homework for the week. Additionally, the next step in Stella's fear hierarchy was introduced (i.e., talking to other children at school). Potential obstacles, as well as specific relaxation and positive self-talk skills associated with this task were identified by Stella and her parents.

Session Six

Goals:
1) Review of progress to date;
2) Discussion of realistic expectations and self-reward;
3) Selection of a positive coping role-model;
4) Introduction of a maintenance and therapist fading plan;
5) Continuation of exposure paradigm.

It was clear by the start of this sixth session that Stella was making significant therapeutic gains. She and her family had taken a remarkable interest in encouraging Stella to make positive coping choices in her personal life, as well as in their own. However, some problems were still noted by Ms. L in consistently ignoring Stella's reassurance-seeking behavior, which had seemingly lessened in intensity, but not frequency. Mr. L stated that he also was having some difficulty recognizing when Stella was reassurance-seeking. Thus, it was determined that consistent management of this behavior would be a primary target of Parental Support session 2. All family members seemed to be benefiting from relaxation activities, positive self-talk exercises, and action plans, though Mr. L reported some continuing personal difficulties in approaching feared situations. Stella and her parents agreed that the therapy process had been beneficial, and all family members wished to continue their anxiety management behaviors.

The therapist initiated a discussion of realistic expectations and self-reward. The therapist introduced this concept as the last segment of the FEAR program, that being **R or review and reward**. Participants were encouraged to identify psychological rewards, such as positive self-talk, as well as more tangible reinforcers, like enjoyable activities. All "team" members were encouraged to present situations in which they were not perfect, but still deserving of reward. For example, the therapist noted a situation in which she was nominated for a prestigious award, but lost the award to an equally qualified nominee. The group was then asked to volunteer positive statements which the therapist could use to reward herself, despite the loss. This procedure was then repeated, with each participant contributing a scenario in which reward identification might be challenging.

In the child segment of this session, a discussion of positive coping models was initiated. Stella was asked to identify someone she admired (real or fictitious) and decide how that person might handle some of the anxiety-provoking scenarios on Stella's fear hierarchy. Stella chose the TV character "Moesha" as her role model. When asked how Moesha might cope with the idea of making friends at a new school, even though she was frightened, Stella volunteered the following:

Stella: Moesha is really brave. She isn't afraid of talking to anyone.
Therapist: Do you think Moesha might be afraid of what the new kids will think of her?
Stella: She might be a little afraid inside, but I think she would still try to talk with them and see what they were like.
Therapist: Do you think that you could approach the children at your new school the way Moesha might do it?
Stella: Yeah, that's a good idea. I could try to be brave like Moesha.

Stella's parents were also asked to consider how brave coping models might interact in situations they feared. All family members were invited to consider how their coping model would handle their daily difficult situation and write that solution down to discuss in the next session. Family members were also instructed to keep track of the FEAR segments utilized for dealing with each of the difficult situations encountered during the next week. Finally, expectations and anticipated complications in confronting the next portion of Stella's fear hierarchy (i.e., openly discussing medical concerns about her grandmother) were addressed.

Parental Support session Two/Three

Parental support Session Two generally covers "casual discussions," a structured method of setting a time aside each day to discuss both child management issues and general household concerns, while parental support Session Three typically covers "problem solving discussions," a more in depth manner of communicating when coping with more severe child problems. These concepts were difficult for Mr. and Ms. L, since they possessed many communication barriers and a lingering hostility toward one another that made even simple discussion challenging. The therapist introduced the concept of a weekly parental phone conversation to discuss child behavior management issues as a variant of the "casual discussions" plan. Crisis phone calls were suggested as a variant of the problem-solving discussion plan. A paradigm for respectful and casual, feedback-centered discussions was presented and role-played successfully by both parents in this session. Stella's parents were encouraged to practice their casual, respectful discussions over the next week, with the understanding that the only topic under consideration during these discussions would be child behavior issues.

Also during this Session, the therapist addressed concerns about the consistency of ignoring Stella's reassurance-seeking by modeling planned ignoring and role-playing scenarios similar to those in which Stella had sought reassurance in the past. These role-plays were conducted with both parents individually and in a combined activity. Both parents seemed to benefit from this exercise and were praised for their continuing efforts to consistently deliver appropriate methods of behavior management.

Two weeks later, in parental support Session Three, the therapist introduced the format for any and all crisis calls. By this format, both parents agreed to conduct crisis calls at mutually convenient time, when both parents were calm and could discuss the issue without interruptions from children. The parent presenting the crisis would attempt to identify the problem as specifically as possible, and deal with one problem at a time. Together, both parents would suggest potential solutions. Then, parents would discuss these potential solutions, choose one particular solution to implement, plan a strategy for implementation, and agree to review this solution again at a later date. Given Mr. and Ms. L's previous success at role-playing, it was no surprise that they were able to master this skill with minimal practice, in session.

However, practice at giving one another constructive, positive feedback was more tenuous. Mr. and Ms. L had difficulty finding specific, positive thoughts to express to one another, and had to be prompted several times with therapist-derived suggestions. After some review of constructive feedback skills, plus reiteration of the goal of constructive feedback (i.e., to make the other person feel comfortable about your opinions, while assisting them in changing their behavior for the better), the L's appeared to improve in this process. The therapist encouraged Stella's parents to practice constructive feedback skills during their weekly, casual discussion phone call.

Sessions Seven to Nine

Goals:
1) Review and continued rehearsal of FEAR plan;
2) Detailed presentation of maintenance plans;
3) Reinforcement of continued self-monitoring;
4) Continuation of exposure paradigm;
5) Plan a final reward party to occur during the last Session.

Over these final "team" sessions, the primary goal of therapy was to rehearse and reinforce Stella's continually improving anxiety management skills. Rehearsal of FEAR plan strategies utilized during the previous week was the first order of business at each of them. The therapist also introduced a therapy maintenance plan in which the use of self-monitoring was gradually phased out, new behavior skills were still discussed by the family at home, and a plan for intervention was identified in case a significant worsening of Stella's progress was noted following therapy termination. Stella's parents, Stella and the therapist determined that, given her excellent progress, a three-month follow-up appointment would be sufficient for reinforcement of these plans. During the final session of "team" therapy, all participants were rewarded with certificates of achievement and Stella was asked to audiotape a vignette describing her progress in therapy to date, as a reward for her substantial improvement over the last few months. Stella expressed a great deal of pride on this taped vignette, which included the following statement, "I used to be afraid of lots of things, so I would run and ask someone to help me. But I think I can help myself now, because I can relax and I can think of other ways to deal with scary thoughts."

Alternative Case Conceptualization

An alternative conceptualization of Stella's case would be to consider her difficulties as generally child-specific problems. By concentrating on the issues presented by Stella alone, we can still mount an effective and empirically valid treatment approach. From this perspective, Stella's case would be considered as a constellation of individual behavior problems, including inappropriate responses to somatic sensations, complicated by an overabundance of negative cognitions, unreasonably high standards for reward, and ineffective coping strategies. The inappropriate reinforcement strategies employed by Stella's parents in managing her fearful and avoidant behavior would be considered as secondary to her individual difficulties managing anxiety sensations.

Treatment Selection

Based upon the assessment data collected and case conceptualization constructed, the treatment program selected for Stella was derived from Kendall, *et al.*'s (1992) *Cognitive-Behavioral Therapy for Anxious Children* (CBT). This treatment plan primarily focused upon eradicating Stella's anxiety symptomotolgy, via individual therapy sessions with the child. Each of the four basic skill areas for which Stella received CBT training corresponded to a particular problem area revealed during her assessment. CBT training emphasized instruction of:

1)   Awareness of physical reactions to anxiety-related sensations;
2)   Recognition and evaluation of self-statements made when anxious;

3) Development of appropriate coping mechanisms for dealing with anxiety sensations;
4) Self-evaluation and reward.

The secondary goal of treatment was to gain Stella's parents unilateral support, and participation, in her therapy. It was noted that recent disagreements between Mr. and Ms. L regarding Stella's living situation, discipline, and other family-related issues occurred during the period of time in which Stella's anxiety levels had increased dramatically. The CBT program involved Stella's parents in the treatment process through the use of at least one required parent meeting, which occurred before the fourth treatment session with the child. This meeting outlined Stella's goals for therapy, and progress in therapy, thus far. Parental concerns and expectations about the effectiveness of therapy were addressed. The therapist also used this session to discuss how the L's frequent disagreements and own psychological health impacted Stella's anxiety levels. Moreover, both parents were encouraged to become involved with the therapy process, beginning in the following session, by learning and assisting Stella with relaxation skill practice.

CBT Treatment Procedures

Most of the procedures involved in CBT alone have already been described as specific components of the CBT+FAM treatment program. The material introduced in CBT (and the associated manual for children, *Coping Cat Notebook*) individual sessions is essentially the same as the material presented in CBT+FAM, excluding the parent-focused contingency management skills and support sessions. However, CBT alone presents the material in a more detailed, didactic and practice-heavy manner during its 16 session course. The first eight are focused on the learning and initial practice of new skills, while the second eight center upon structured and repetitive practice of the skills learned during initial sessions. Table 11.1 delineates the specific skills and goals detailed by the therapist in each CBT session.

Table 11.1: Skills and Goals Emphasized in Cognitive-Behavioral Therapy (CBT) Sessions.

Session number	Skill emphasized	Session goals
1	Introduce treatment program to child	1. Build rapport 2. Orientation to program 3. Encouragement of child participation and verbalizations in sessions

Table 11.1: Skills and Goals Emphasized in Cognitive-Behavioral Therapy (CBT) Sessions (cont.).

Session number	Skill emphasized	Session goals
2	Identification and normalization of different feelings	1. Continue rapport building and review homework 2. Introduction of concept that different feelings have different physical expressions. 3. Normalization of fears and anxiety 4. Begin construction of a fear/anxiety-provoking situations hierarchy 5. Introduction of a journal to record child's experiences with anxiety
3	Recognition of somatic responses to anxiety	1. Review journal and homework assignments 2. Discuss specific somatic reactions to anxiety 3. Practice recognition of somatic responses to anxiety via modeling and role-play 4. Practice of somatic signal recognition in more stressful scenarios 5. Practice in using somatic responses as cues for increasing anxiety 6. Recording body reactions to anxiety in journal for one full day
Additional session with parents	Parental cooperation in treatment program	1. Provide parents with additional information about treatment plan 2. Give parents an opportunity to discuss concerns about child's behavior 3. Provide examples of situations in which child becomes anxious and his/her specific reactions to fear 4. Give parents specific ways to become involved in treatment
4	Introduction of relaxation as a method for reducing somatic responses to fear	1. Provide child with feedback regarding parent session 2. Review diary assignments 3. Discuss idea that somatic feelings are associated with muscle tension 4. Introduce idea of relaxation and specific relaxation therapy paradigm 5. Elicit suggestions about ways relaxation may be incorporate into daily life 6. Practice relaxation via modeling, role-play and *in vivo* participation 7. Reinforce need for daily relaxation exercise by assigning practice as homework assignment

Table 11.1: Skills and Goals Emphasized in Cognitive-Behavioral Therapy (CBT) Sessions (cont.).

Session number	Skill emphasized	Session goals
5	Recognition of the role self-talk plays in anxiety	1. Review relaxation practice from preceding week 2. Introduce concept of self-talk and relationship to anxiety 3. Detail role of self-talk in experiences specific to child 4. Rehearse self-talk skills via modeling, role-play and *in vivo* practice
6	Modification of anxious self-talk into coping self-talk	1. Review use of relaxation and self-talk 2. Introduce active modification of feelings and self-talk when anxious 3. Develop a problem-solving plan for intervening with anxious thoughts 4. Practice problem-solving under conditions of minimal anxiety 5. Continue practicing problem-solving in increasingly anxiety-provoking scenarios
7	Introduction of appropriate self-evaluation and reward for performance and coping skills	1. Review use of problem-solving and relaxation skills 2. Introduce concepts of self-rating and self-reward 3. Practice making self-ratings and self-rewarding when successful through use of imagined scenarios
8	To review the FEAR plan and practice its usage in non-stressful situations	1. Introduce FEAR acronym (*F*eeling frightened? *E*xpecting bad things to happen? *A*ttitudes and actions that will help? *R*esults and rewards?) 2. Encourage child to carry a wallet-sized copy of FEAR acronym with them to refer to when needed 3. Apply FEAR skills in non-stressful situations 4. Review all major concepts introduced in first 8 sessions 5. Post-session: Prepare several situations which may provoke mild anxiety in child, for use in sessions to assist in imaginary and *in vivo* practice
9	Practice FEAR plan in low anxiety scenarios	1. Utilize imaginary practice with mildly anxiety provoking situations 2. Begin in vivo practice in low anxiety situations 3. Practice relaxation exercises
10	Continue practice of coping skills via in-session practice	1. Discuss coping skills utilized during past week 2. Practice coping skills in session using imaginal exposure 3. Rehearse use of anxiety management through *in vivo* exercises 4. Post-session: prepare scenarios which may provoke moderate anxiety for practice in Session 11

Table 11.1: Skills and Goals Emphasized in Cognitive-Behavioral Therapy (CBT) Sessions (cont.).

Session number	Skill emphasized	Session goals
11	Utilize coping skills learned in situations which produce moderate anxiety	1. Reward appropriate coping skills demonstrated between sessions 2. Practice coping skills that cause moderate anxiety via imaginal exposure 3. Practice these same skills *in vivo*
12	Continue practice of FEAR skills in situations that produce moderate anxiety	1. Continue in vivo practice of FEAR plan in situations that evoke moderate anxiety 3. Ask child to create a poster or other reminder of FEAR plan to hang in child's room
13	Initiate use of coping skills in situations that provoke high levels of anxiety	1. Review self-monitoring of FEAR plan usage 2. Begin practice of coping skills, using imaginal exposure, in highly anxiety provoking situations
14	Begin *in vivo* practice of FEAR plan in high anxiety situations	1. Review journal entries detailing coping skills use 2. Practice use of FEAR plan *in vivo* with scenarios that evoke high levels of anxiety 3. Increase length of time between sessions to two weeks, to decrease dependence on therapy for anxiety management
15	Continue *in vivo* exposure to situations that produce high levels of anxiety	1. Review self-monitoring activities during two week interval between sessions 2. Rehearse *in vivo* exposure exercises in scenarios that produce high levels of anxiety 3. Continue two week interval between sessions
16	Review and summarize training program, emphasizing maintenance and generalization of new skills	1. Review self-monitoring activities during inter-session interval 2. Tape a video in which the child creates a narrative describing their progress and experiences in therapy 3. Schedule a follow-up session for child and parents to review assessment data and bring closure to the therapy process

Source: Kendall, *et al.*, 1992

Summary

GAD is a profoundly understudied disorder, with only a handful of treatment-relevant studies examining this phenomenon in terms of its current diagnostic incarnation. Both CBT and CBT + FAM are empirically validated cognitive-behavioral approaches to treating this disorder in youth. While these two approaches share many of the same techniques, they also provide a unique demonstration of the relationship between case conceptualization and treatment selection. Specifically, they represent two very different perspectives on the degree of parental involvement necessary in child anxiety treatment. CBT certainly attempts to involve parents in the treatment process, by including them in a Session dedicated to their education about treatment. However, CBT + FAM involves the entire family in the management of child anxiety through all stages of treatment, thereby acknowledging the roles that family members play in the maintenance of anxiety-related behavior. Thus, the amount of family involvement noted in the assessment of child GAD makes a difference in the selection of an empirically validated treatment methodology. Furthermore, although they employ the same treatment constructs, CBT + FAM appear to be the more appropriate selection for a case that is conceptualized as involving more behavioral targets for intervention, since it provides specific parent training in contingency management skills. CBT would be more appropriate for a child whose case is conceptualized as presenting predominantly cognitive symptoms as the major impediments to healthy child development. Thus, the problematic generalized anxiety symptomotology identified by the therapist is vital to the successful application of appropriate GAD treatment techniques.

References

Bandura, A. (1986). *Social Learning Theory*. Englewood Cliffs, NJ: Prentice-Hall.

Barrett, P. M. (1993). *Management of Childhood Anxiety: A Family Intervention Programme*. Unpublished.

Barrett, P. M. (personal communication, February 9, 1999).

Barrett, P. M., Dadds, M. R., & Rapee, R. M. (1996). Family treatment of childhood anxiety: A controlled trial. *Journal of Consulting and Clinical Psychology, 64*, 333–342.

Barrett, P. M., Lowry-Webster, H., & Holmes, J. (1997). *Strategies for the Prevention of Anxiety in Youth: The Friends Program Workbook*. Queensland, Australia: Griffith University, Griffith Early Intervention Project.

Barrios, B. A., & O'Dell, S. L. (1998). Fears and anxieties. In E. J. Mash & R. A. Barkley (eds) *Treatment of Childhood Disorders* (2nd ed) New York, NY: Guilford Press. 249–337.

Kendal. P. C. (1994). *Coping Cat Notebook*. Ardmore, PA: Workbook Publishing.

Kendall, P. C., Flannery-Schroeder, E., Panichelli-Mindel, S. M., Southam-Gerow, & M., Henin, A., *et al.* (1997). Therapy for youths with anxiety disorders: A second randomized clinical trial. *Journal of Consulting and Clinical Psychology, 65(3)*, 366–380.

Kendall, P. C. Chansky, T. E., Freidman, M., Kim, R., Kortlander, E., *et al.* (1991). Treating anxiety disorders in children and adolescents. In P.C. Kendall (ed.) *Child and*

Adolescent Therapy: Cognitive-behavioral Procedures. New York, NY: Guilford Press. 131–164.

Kendall, P. C., Kane, M., Howard, B., & Siqueland, L. (1992). *Cognitve-behavioral Therapy for Anxious Children: Therapist Manual*. Ardmore, PA: Workbook Publishing.

Morris, R. J., & Kratochwill, T. R. (1998). Childhood fears and phobias. In R. J. Morris & T. R. Kratochwill (eds) *The Practice of Child Therapy*. Needham Heights, MA: Allyn & Bacon. 91–131.

Ollendick, T. H., & King, N. J. (1998). Empirically supported treatments for children with phobic and anxiety disorders: Current status. *Journal of Clinical Child Psychology, 27(2)*, 156–167.

Silverman, W. K., & Nelles, W. B. (1988). The anxiety disorders interview schedule for children. *Journal of the American Academy of Child and Adolescent Psychiatry, 27*, 772–778.

Tracey, S. A., Chorpita, B. F., Douban, J., & Barlow, D. H. (1997). Empirical evaluation of *DSM-IV* generalized anxiety disorder criteria in children and adolescents. *Journal of Clinical Child Psychology, 26(4)*, 404–414.

Weems, C. F., Silverman, W. K., La Greca, A. M., Rudolf, J., & Cutler, A., *et al.* (1997). *What Do Children Worry About?: Worry and its Relation to Anxiety Disorders in Children and Adolescents*. Miami, FL: Poster session presented at the annual meeting of the Association for the Advancement of Behavior Therapy.

Werry, J. S. (1991). Overanxious disorder: A review of its taxonomic properties. *Journal of the American Academy of Child and Adolescent Psychiatry, 30(4)*, 533–544.

Chapter 12

Post Traumatic Stress Disorder in Children and Adolescents: Conceptualization and Treatment

Jan Faust

Classification

The diagnostic classification of Post Traumatic Stress Disorder (PTSD) emerged from the post-war era stipulating that soldiers exposed to grossly inhumane acts of violence developed severe anxiety symptoms. In recent years such symptomatology has been noted in adults exposed to extreme stressors other than war, such as rape, natural disasters, terrorism, and automobile accidents. Still more recently, children have been observed to develop constellations of symptoms consistent with the Diagnostic and Statistical Manual of Mental Disorders (DSM) classification system, and features of the disorder that may be uniquely expressed by children are more explicitly stated in recent versions of the DSM (American Psychiatric Association – APA- 1994, 2000). Differences between adult and childhood onset PTSD have been better delineated over the years.

In the more recent version of the DSM, there are two primary components of PTSD. First, the individual's exposure to a traumatic event either directly or indirectly (e.g., witnessed) and such events involve actual or threatened death, serious injury, and/or impairment of the physical integrity of self and/or other (APA, 1994, 2000). Irrespective of the type of trauma, such exposure produces intense fear, helplessness or horror in the individual. The DSM-IV includes a provision for children that these reactions may be expressed by disorganized or agitated behavior.

The second major diagnostic feature includes three clusters of symptoms that reflect exposure to the traumatic event, including:

1) re-experiencing the traumatic event;
2) persistent avoidance of stimuli associated with the trauma including numbing of general responsiveness; and
3) persistence of symptoms of increased arousal.

Within each of these clusters of symptoms the DSM delineates specific symptoms that comprise each category (APA, 1994, 2000).

DSM-IV symptoms, which are specific to children, include the definition of

Handbook of Conceptualization and Treatment of Child Psychopathology, pages 239–265.
Copyright © 2001 by Elsevier Science Ltd.
All rights of reproduction in any form reserved.
ISBN: 0-08-043362-6

"traumatic" event to include developmentally inappropriate sexual contact without threatened or actual violence or injury. Further, a child's fear, helplessness, and horror may be manifested by disorganized or agitated behavior. In addition, DSM-IV allows for re-experiencing the traumatic event by children to be manifested in repetitive play with trauma themes, and while the content of nightmares for adults needs to be trauma specific, for children, frightening content without such themes satisfies this subcategory. In addition, children via behavioral reenactment of the trauma may manifest flashbacks typically observed in adults. For example, it is not unusual for traumatized sexually abused children to engage in sexual activity with other children (APA, 1994, 2000).

Finally, in order to meet diagnostic criteria for PTSD, symptoms must be evident for more than one month and must cause significant distress or disruption in social, occupational, and academic and/or other functioning (APA, 1994, 2000).

Theoretical Conceptualizations

All treatment modalities are based upon theoretical models that explain the behavior observed; consequently, upon intake and preliminary evaluation, it is important for the clinician to understand the behavior and diagnostic entity based in a theoretical framework. This is accomplished via formulation of a conceptualization of the symptoms with which the child presents. The conceptualization is the foundation or blueprint which guides treatment. Treatment is based upon the theoretical framework (conceptualization) that the clinician develops for the child and his/her diagnostic presentation.

Although the literature examining treatment effectiveness for PTSD is scant, in general, research on childhood PTSD treatment has lagged significantly behind that of adult work. In reviewing the literature, it is evident that two treatments are used more frequently than others for the treatment of PTSD. Both family systems and cognitive behavioral treatments appear promising in the treatment of adults with PTSD, and more recently preliminary evidence suggests both to be useful in treating children with PTSD.

Family Systems Conceptualization

Family Systems Therapy (FST) – A body of literature has focused on a family systems approach in the treatment of PTSD. Much of the family systems PTSD therapy research has utilized adult subjects, primarily war veterans. And many of the papers published on use of FST have relied on case study as the method of scientific observation. Sexual abuse is one of the most frequently cited traumas for children, and the child abuse literature has supported the use of FST in its treatment, although most of the research does not discriminate among diagnostic groups. There is one study wherein researchers empirically studied the effectiveness of FST in the treatment of sexually abused children with PTSD. Findings indicate that FST significantly reduced anxiety symptoms and depressive symptoms from pre to post treatment, in these children (Faust, *et al.*, 1999).

One of the most important premises of FST is that behavior problems and psychological symptoms *are not caused* in a linear fashion but rather are caused and/ or maintained in a circular manner. This means that the direction of causality cannot be said to run from one source directly to another but rather the problems evolve multidirectionally. For example, a therapist who has a linear approach to conceptualization may suggest that a child's behavior problem is the result of his/ her parents' positively reinforcing her behavior (i.e., A, the parents, cause or maintain B, the child's non-compliant behavior). The therapist who views problems as a circular system would not only look to the parents' behavior in determining problem manifestation but would also try to determine how the child elicits responses from his/her parents which determine the behavior in which she ultimately engages. Further, the circular thinking therapist would attempt to determine how other family subsystems (and other non-family systems such as schools) impact the child and his/her parents' exchanges as well as how these exchanges in turn impact the family subsystems (and external systems).

FST therapists attempt to alter the family system in various ways to achieve the ultimate goal of symptom reduction/elimination. Two types of FST include structural family therapy and strategic family therapy. With respect to the former, structural family therapists suggest that the family is a system that functions in specific social contexts. The system operates upon a series of transactional patterns (Minuchin, 1974). Transactional patterns are automatic (via repetition) methods by which family members interact with one another. These patterns of relating and interacting are systemically inherited, as they are often passed down from preceding generations; hence, their etiology is often not identifiable. One of the purposes the familial transactional patterns serve is in the assignment of roles to one another. Further, the responsibilities and power ascribed to each role are also determined via these transactional patterns.

From a structural FST perspective, family member exchanges also help dictate the boundaries among and between family members as well as subsystems within the families. The boundaries help to regulate and modulate the amount and kind of contact family members have with one another as well as with others outside the family system (Minuchin, 1974). Hence, the boundaries also serve to determine the responsibilities and power attached to the roles. According to Minuchin (1974), the boundaries help protect the uniqueness and autonomy of each individual within the family, each subsystem (dyads, triads, etc), and the family as a whole. Structural family therapists believe that the roles family members are assigned, including their responsibilities and boundaries between other family members, determine each individual's behavior including the amount of power within the system. For example, for adaptive family functioning, there needs to be a clear boundary between parents (the executive dyad) and the children, with the former roles having more power and responsibility than the latter. Problems are manifested in individuals when family boundaries, roles, and interactions among family members no longer support the family structure.

In applying structural family therapy in conceptualizing PTSD reactions, it is not unusual in families with a traumatized child for the child to have been assigned a role with more power than he/she can cognitively, emotionally, and behaviorally manage. Furthermore, by assigning the child a role with an inappropriate amount of power, the boundaries change between family members. For example, children who have been sexually abused have often been assigned a parent role and are in charge of their own protection, which not only makes them more vulnerable to abuse but also heightens their feelings of being in danger (not safe and protected). Hence, this heightened sense of vulnerability and danger makes these children susceptible to intense fear reactions (PTSD). In addition, as is the case with incest, if the child is assigned the mother role, the boundary between mother and father becomes more diffuse and less connected. This change in roles and responsibilities places the "mother" child at risk of victimization by the father (father surrogate), while the boundary between that child and siblings becomes more distant. With respect to the latter, the child in the mother role is unable to align herself with her siblings who could offer some support and age appropriate protection. The goal of structural FST is to modify the family structure and interactions by altering intrafamilial alliances (e.g., boundaries, power), including transactional patterns of relating.

In addition, strategic family therapists hail from a family systems perspective and hence also believe that problems do not evolve in a linear manner but rather are circular in development. Further, while less concerned with family structure, strategic family therapists are more concerned with communication. Symptoms are viewed as communication of a problem in the system; hence strategic family therapists attempt to determine the maladaptive and repetitive patterns of relating and communicating in the entire system that is contributing to the maintenance of symptoms. Behavior that is presented by the identified patient is a function of intrafamilial communication. Behavior change is contingent upon altering communication patterns at many different levels, including meta communication. Meta communication refers to covert, indirect methods of sending messages perhaps via body language, omissions of content, mores and customs passed down over generations, double binding messages and the like. Strategic family therapists address those intrafamilial communications that are responsible for symptomatic behavior. They are less concerned with a complete family structure overhaul, intervening only in that part of the system that seems to need alteration because of communication and problem solving difficulties. In fact, strategic family therapists are not concerned with hierarchical distribution of power (e.g., parents as most powerful and children as least powerful) as are the structural family therapists.

Since strategic family therapists are concerned with family problems that emerge at all levels of communication, intervention reflects the content, level and process of communication. Strategic family therapists believe that families become snared in the same ways of communicating and problem solving. Hence, these therapists attempt to mobilize families to solve problems differently in ways in which families have never considered. This may require the therapist to "shake up" the family system with the delivery of a message that causes the family to view the problem differently – therapists' communication of a new way to view the problem. In order to communicate to the family a new way to solve the problem, strategic family therapists may "do" something differently. For example, it is not unusual for abused children to be blamed for both the abuse and their symptoms. Hence, the communication around the abuse is that the child was responsible in some way for it. So, if the dependent child is responsible for her own abuse, the metacommunication is that she cannot keep herselve safe, nor can the parents, who are ultimately in charge. The goal is to intervene with these circular patterns of communication/behavior by developing new behavior and communication patterns to replace the old ones. This does not require understanding of the origin of the problems, but rather strategic family therapists have families "doing" things differently. Hence the goal is not to overhaul the entire system but to enable the system to engage in exchanges that change behavioral patterns of relating.

Since both Structural Family Systems therapy and Strategic Family Therapy are embedded in systems theory (both adhering to the notion that symptoms are a function of circular systemic interactions), they are not incompatible and can be integrated. In applying FST to trauma, trauma symptoms emerge in individuals in response to the manner by which the family communicates and interacts around the traumatic event. In fact, research indicates that families of traumatized children and adults have greater familial conflict, are less supportive and more isolated, and have problems with communication as well as the assignment of age appropriate tasks and responsibilities. Inevitably the traumatized person in such a family system feels vulnerable and at-risk leading to a PTSD reaction. In the case of sexual abuse as a traumatic event, the ill-defined boundaries, lack of support, family disorganization and high conflict between parent and child ultimately lead to problems in the roles each family member assumes and the manner in which they carry out the attached responsibilities. The parent fails to treat the child in an age-appropriate manner thereby allowing the child equivalent power to that of the parents. Hence, the child may then feel responsible for her own parenting, including safety and protection. This causes her to feel susceptible to imminent harm and thus PTSD symptoms persist. These messages are also communicated directly and indirectly (metacommunication).

As described previously, the maladaptive patterns of interacting and communicating (e.g., poor family role assignments and boundaries, family conflict, family disorganization, and family members lack of support) in families of children with PTSD revolve around issues of safety, protection, and age appropriate role assignment. The goal of FST therapy is to redesign the family's patterns of interactional transactions in order to develop more functional patterns of relating (e.g., increase family organization and support) and communicating (decrease conflict). These changes in relating increase family communications such that the IP learns that he/she is safe and that the family will be able to protect him/her currently and in the future. Cloe Madanes, a prominent figure in her contribution to the development of strategic family therapy, has developed a working theory on the etiology of abuse in families. Madanes postulates that all people are motivated first by the wish to dominate, second, by a need to be loved, and third, by a desire to love and protect others (Madanes, 1990). She believes that these needs and desires can bring out exceptional qualities in an individual but also can induce more disruptive behaviors including possessiveness, domination, and violence. Such human motivations and needs explain the occurrence of abuse and its context as well as illuminating development of symptom presentation in children (e.g., PTSD). Symptoms from this perspective develop in the context of maladaptive communication and enactment of domination, maladaptive communications about protection (and resulting protective failures), and dysfunctional love. Trauma symptoms persist in the fear of self-harm (not feeling protected) as well as a violation of the spirit. These trauma symptoms are exacerbated by the secretiveness of the abuse and the meaning that such secretiveness carries as it resonates throughout the family system.

Family System Therapy Intervention for PTSD

FST intervention involves in-session assignments and maneuvers (e.g., such as reframing the problematic behavior as helpful and removing the identified patient (I.P.) from the "hot seat"), at-home tasks, and strategic choreography and interventions (e.g., paradoxical instructions), which are orchestrated to restructure family patterns of relating by addressing both verbal and non-verbal methods (including metacommunication) of communicating among family members. These interventions for the child with PTSD focus on altering the family system's methods of relating and communicating around issues of safety and protection and concomitant issues. This would include strengthening the parent(s') protective hierarchical role via redistribution of power. With respect to child sexual abuse as a trauma in particular, there is an emphasis on rewriting how abuse is spoken of in the family system. Typically in families it is not unusual for individuals to never speak about the abuse directly which enables the abuse to continue over the years and to be passed down from generation to generation. In applying both Minuchin's (1974) model of structural family therapy and Cloe Madanes' (1990) model of strategic family therapy to children who have been sexually abused and exhibit PTSD, the goal includes restructuring the family system's boundaries, coalitions, and the hierarchical distribution of power, including role assignment as well as addressing the episode(s) of sexual abuse from the motivations of the offender's domination, need for love, and the need to love and protect others. With respect to these motivations, the focus is on reorganizing the parent responsibility and power of protection for abuse by placing such responsibility and power for protection with the caretakers (offending parent and non-offending parent). Further, the non-offending parents are enabled to access their own power so that they can feel empowered and revel in confidence in the ability to protect their own children. Hence, the care taking role of the non-offending parent is strengthened.

In adhering to principles of FST, it is important that everyone who lives in the household, including those who have a close physical and/or emotional proximity to the child, attend sessions. Since it is believed that everyone is active in intrafamilial relational patterns then everyone has an impact upon the development of and maintenance of one another's behavior. By not including everyone in each session, a significant disruption in family communication can occur, and PTSD symptoms are allowed to continue. Interestingly, it is often the case that the individual complaining about the family member most "resistant" to treatment is usually the most resistant person him/herself. It has been observed that those voicing a willingness to participate while simultaneously accusing another of not being "willing to participate" is protecting the family from an important aspect of change. Perhaps there is ongoing abuse, or the PTSD is directly influenced by the most resistant and the complainer's interactions; therefore, there is need for the PTSD to continue. Often the parents will want to "protect" the non-abused younger siblings by stating that they do not feel it is appropriate for the younger child to attend therapy because: (a) they know nothing about the abuse, and/or (b) it is inappropriate for them to be exposed to this information. The therapist must explain first that children are extremely knowledgeable and are susceptible to many modes of communication about the abuse, even without having a good grasp of language (non-verbal children can read non-verbal language like code). Second, there is evidence for the veracity of this fact because abuse is passed down generationally. It is not a genetic transmission; it is an interactional transmission, which occurs when there are family secrets. Without rectifying such abuse communications and interactions around these secrets, abuse becomes a family moré and is integrated into the very fiber of the family, much like other morés and customs.

FST therapists can enhance family session attendance through a number of maneuvers including calling the most resistant person in the family and enlisting him/her via his/her great insight into the problem and/or appealing to the special position held with the IP (such that he/she has unique power to aid in the resolution of the problem/puzzle). One can also carefully use leverage in the case of an ongoing child protective services case and/or court ordered case. This is not to say that the therapist uses such leverage as blackmail ("come to therapy or else I will tell the judge") but rather, "we can write a letter on your behalf for successful participation in treatment."

When the family arrives at the initial sessions, the first step in the FST treatment protocol includes joining with the family, which is similar to establishing rapport or a therapeutic alliance. Once established, the therapist must immediately remove blame from the victim for the child abuse; this is initially accomplished through having each family member tell the therapist and the family his/her understanding of the abuse. One of the most important maneuvers at this point in treatment is to block *any* blame for the abuse with the child. Blame may be direct (the non-offending parent completely blames the child while exonerating the offending spouse) or subtle ("why didn't you tell me you were being abused").

Next, if blame of the victim has not been verbalized by any family member thus far (and hence has not needed to be blocked), the therapist must openly **relay** to the family that responsibility for the abuse rests with the perpetrator no matter what the conditions were of the abuse. It is clearly and openly articulated that the victim/survivor is not responsible for the abuse and the concomitant symptoms. Although Madanes (1990) has ordered the steps in treatment, the order may be changed as determined by the needs of the IP (identified patient) and his/her family. Overall, the steps for this treatment include:

1) A forthcoming description of the abuse by each family member with the therapist blocking any attempts by family members to alter the perceptions or content of each family member's own perceptions of the abuse;

2) Exploration with the family as to each family member's beliefs as to why abuse is wrong;

3) Discussion of the most significant reason the abuse is wrong, which is the spiritual pain ("pain in the heart") it causes for the victim. According to Madanes (1990), family members offer a number of reasons why the abuse is wrong but fail to mention the most important reason, which is the spiritual pain it causes the child victim. She describes this pain as "pain in the heart." Even if the family members initiate discussion of the spiritual pain it caused the child, it is very important for the therapist to openly discuss this pain and emphasize that this is the most important reason as to why the abuse was wrong;

4) Discussion of spiritual pain the abuse has caused other family members. While the majority of the children we see in our program are not to be reunified or have contact with the abuser, there are many cases where reunification of the abuser with the child is not only inevitable but also planned. Following Madanes' protocol with respect to abuser contact/reunification, she stipulates that the perpetrator must have some individual sessions with the family therapist and also complete the content of those steps involved in numbers 5,7–10, as listed here. During the individual sessions with the perpetrator, Madanes' places emphasis on accessing vulnerable feelings in the perpetrator so that he/she can experience the pain of the child victim (cf: Madanes, 1990);

5) Having the non-offending parent and others who should have known about the abuse apologize for not knowing about the abuse and not being able to protect the child from the abuser. Additionally, this would include having these non-offending relatives and others apologize for not having the lines of communication open to help prevent the abuse. With respect to the latter, it is important for children to know the adults are receptive to hearing anything the child has to tell them. This apology is the most delicate and difficult aspect of treatment integration. In addition, it is our clinical experience that it is also the most important part of treatment with respect to symptom resolution and healing. Madanes has the perpetrator apologize and sets this up through a number of individual sessions between therapist and perpetrator. In many of our cases, reunification with the perpetrator is not planned, or anticipated, nor is it in the best interests of many of the children we see; however, irrespective of the role the perpetrator will play in the child's life, an apology is imperative from the non-offending caretaker and others who should have known the

abuse was occurring (either through observation or for failure to be accessible to the child communicating his/her abuse).

In our program, we meet alone with the non-offending adults who are targeted for delivering the apology in order to explain the meaning of the apology for the child victim and the family. In addition, if the parent is resistant to the idea at first, this resistance is not voiced in front of the child which can exacerbate that child's sense of self-blame and responsibility for the abuse. In presenting the apology treatment component to the parent, we have found the following to be the most effective for parent compliance: the therapist states to the non-offending parent: "Even if there were no possible way for you to have known about the abuse, children put their parents on a pedestal and on some level children believe their parents have a crystal ball and should know everything. We have observed this phenomenon in cases where the non-offending non-custodial parent has lived thousands of miles away." The apology needs to be truly empathetic, heartfelt, and sincere; it cannot be rote or intellectualized. One way to obtain a heartfelt deeply emotional apology is to help the parent(s) access feelings of deep emotion (Madanes, 1990). Usually painful emotions are the most prominent emotions parents can readily access for their children. An example of accessing such deep emotions would include having parents relate a time (other than the abuse) they cried about their child out of worry, concern or fear, such as in the case when their young child underwent surgery, or was lost in a store, or when they may have lost custody temporarily due to divorce. There are some professionals, not versed in this form of therapy, who express concern that requiring the apology from the non-offending parent is akin to blaming a parent who might be a victim him/herself. Our belief is that the child does not perceive the apology as blame of the parents; rather, it is experienced as the ultimate validation of the horrendous act the child endured. Society places so much emphasis on having children apologize for their misdeeds that such apologies hold even greater importance for them than for adults (Faust, 2000). Thus, children from a very young age are taught to apologize and, as a result, learn that apologies hold special meaning in rectifying "wrongs." In addition, for the parent to apologize attests to parental strength, and this communicates to the child that the parent is strong enough to provide protection against future abuse (thereby increasing the child's sense of safety and reducing PTSD symptoms). At the beginning of treatment when a parent expresses excessive guilt for the child's abuse, this guilt must be addressed first in the protocol as it will interfere with family progress (the apology phase will be too painful for the excessively guilt-ridden non-offending parent);

6) Individual session is held with the child that puts the abuse in context of the child's complete life. It is during this session that the therapist enables the child to determine that he/she is not defined by the abuse. The child is neither victim nor survivor as this defines the child in relationship to the abuse. Rather, it is explained that the abuse was an **event** that occurred in the child's life. It was an event among numerous other events in the child's life. The

therapist reduces the abuse to hours and minutes over the course of the child's entire lifetime (Madanes, 1990). For example, for an eight-year-old girl who was abused three times by her babysitter while her parents were at the movies, the therapist might say: "Your parents were gone a total of four hours each time this babysitter sat you. If he molested you from the time your parents left until the time they returned, it would be a total of twelve hours of your life he hurt you. While the abuse was horrible, it was twelve hours of your life and you have lived over 70,000 additional hours during which time you weren't abused, during which time you attended birthday parties, went snow skiing, danced with your friends." The therapist must be careful not to minimize the abuse; he/she must indicate that it was horrible but the point is it does not define the child. What does define the child is all the other multitude of wonderful experiences he or she has had and his/her special personality;

7) Discussion of the consequences of abuse if it happens again, including a safety plan (i.e., guardian angel protector). This includes development of a safety plan, both for now and for long-term protection. An important aspect of this plan is the selection of a guardian angel or a protector who did not and could not have had knowledge that the abuse was happening (or at least such possibility of knowledge was remote) and with whom the lines of communication between child and guardian are open and actively encouraged. Particularly caring and devoted school guidance counselors, guardian ad liteums, family friends, and out-of-state relatives not related to the perpetrator can be utilized;

8) Reparation from abuser AND non-offending parent(s). This involves an offer and implementation of some form of reparation to the child from the perpetrator and non-offending caretakers. Reparation has both symbolic meaning and very real positive consequences for the child. Perpetrators are instructed by the child via the judge to donate money on a monthly basis to the child's college fund with the understanding that while the perpetrator took something away from the child (e.g., part of his/her spirit) during his/her childhood, he/she is offering to mend this for the future by contributing to the child's spiritual peace, as a young adult (college). By having the perpetrator do this monthly (or even weekly) he/she is forced to remember, with great frequency, the pain and damage he or she has done to the child. Families may also write to judges requesting that the perpetrator contribute to the local children's shelter for abused and neglected children, or to perform some community service (which does not involve contact with children) but contributes to the betterment of society. Sometimes adjudication has been previously delivered or charges are rescinded and it is difficult to engender compliance from the judicial system to enforce the reparation of the offender. Having the family write the letter to the judge or to a State Attorney has a dramatic impact for positive resolution of symptoms, despite the fact that the probability of reparation deliverance is low. Non-offending primary caretakers are also advised to give reparation as part of their sorrow for not knowing about the abuse. Examples of reparation include having parents or guardians give their children cell phones, beepers, or bedroom phone extensions as symbolic of

opening the lines of communication – the lines they wished they had originally opened so the abuse would never had happened. Similarly, non-offending mothers may take martial arts with their children in order to demonstrate their strength at "fixing" the problem and protecting the child from future harm;

9) Restoration of love among family members. Many non-offending parents place varying degrees of blame on the child for the abuse. The blame and anger the non-offending parents hold for the child interferes with their ability to love and nurture the child which is a barricade to open healthy communication of love, support, protection and acceptance. In order to restore the love, family members must reminisce, about loving times they had with the child. Non-offending parents will be encouraged to access their feelings during the birth of their child and describe the many characteristics of the newborn and the tremendous loving and protective feelings they held for him/her. We will also have them describe delight they experienced during the developmental milestones the child obtained (the first step, words, etc.). The therapist must help the parents access these soft, warm, loving feelings since many parents have built a protective wall around their soft vulnerable feelings, which interferes with their ability to be emotionally available to as well as protective of the child.

10) Enabling non-offending parents to forgive themselves (guilt reduction). It is during this treatment phase that non-offending family members' guilt must be addressed. Overwhelming guilt feelings in younger siblings of the victim are also observed. Guilt is particularly a problem with non-offending mothers and should be addressed through a series of tasks and maneuvers, including "ordeals." With respect to the latter, examples include that every hour the mother engages in self-blame for her child's abuse she needs to donate $10.00 to the local children's shelter. In the case of extrafamilial child abuse, the non-offending father may actively "acquire" the guilt from his non-offending wife through a series of steps. As mentioned above, if the guilt is overwhelming, it will have to be addressed much earlier in the protocol.

PTSD Family Systems Case Example

Case Conceptualization
The following case example illustrates the systemic family therapy conceptualization of a sexually abused child with PTSD. A variety of assessment measures were utilized at intake including the Child Behavior Checklist, Schedule for Affective Disorders and Schizophrenia for Children (KSADS), unstructured interview, behavioral observations, self-report measures, and personality assessment measures.

Emily, a six-year, three-month old Caucasian female, was brought by her parents for psychological services as a result of her disclosure of sexual molestation. Disclosure originated after Emily attempted to "French kiss" her father the evening of a neighborhood social event. Mr. Smith set a limit with his daughter as to that method of kissing and asked her where she had learned the behavior.

According to the Smiths, she had indicated "Monica". In fact, Emily had told 14-year-old Monica Jones that at the social gathering a 16-year-old boy, Edward, had molested her on two separate occasions. The most recent abuse occurred the same day of the social function. Monica told Emily she should tell her parents and that Monica would also tell her father, a law enforcement official, "because he would know what to do." Emily was satisfied with this plan. Mr. Jones informed Mr. Smith of the molestation the very same evening of its occurrence and after Monica had told him about Emily's abuse. Mr. and Mrs. Smith decided to wait until the next day to approach the molestation episode with their daughter. The next morning, however, Emily spontaneously approached her mother and told her that she learned to kiss "that way" from Edward.

The first time the molestation occurred was at a neighbor's house during a birthday party a month before the current episode which occurred at the Smiths' home, in their den. Emily indicated to the psychologist that the first time, Edward laid on top of her, "rubbing his body on me" and that he touched her breasts and vagina. During this molestation episode, she indicated that he touched her body parts through her clothing and the second time, he put his hands up her underwear and rubbed the skin of her vagina and that "it hurt." Mrs. Smith also said that Emily stated that Edward kissed her vagina and put his tongue in her mouth during this second episode of molestation. Emily told both her mother and psychologist that she tried to get-up but that he would not get off of her, and she could not move. She indicated that she was extremely frightened. Emily's five-year-old sister, Jennifer, reported that she remembers seeing Emily "fighting" Edward to get him off of her. Jennifer became visibly anxious when discussing the molestation and had a difficult time focusing on the psychologist's questions regarding her sister's abuse. Mr. and Mrs. Smith acknowledged Jennifer's anxious behavior as unusual.

The parents reported that they had noticed changes in Emily's behavior, which would have coincided in time with the first molestation. These changes were (DSM-IV, A Cluster) intense agitation, including inability to sit still and perceiving the world as a dangerous place, (B Cluster), nightmares, marked distress anytime the Smith's spoke of going over to the friend's house where the abuse occurred, (C Cluster) refusal to visit the house where the molestation occurred even though Edward did not live there, refusal to go into the den where the molestation occurred even though this avoidance prevented her from utilizing the computer for fun and schoolwork, avoidance of discussing the specifics of the abuse when asked by the psychologist and family members, loss of interest in all of her extracurricular activities (dance, music, and organized swimming), loss of interest in playing with her sister and her friends, preferring to be in the family room watching T.V., with a parent nearby and (Cluster D) frequent sleep disruptions, intense anger, and defiance. Criteria of duration of symptoms for at least a month and for the disturbance causing significant distress in her social, educational, and familial functioning were also met. Because one month had passed since onset of symptoms, PTSD was the most appropriate diagnosis as opposed to Acute Stress Disorder, which has a short window of expression. In addition, Emily met diagnostic criteria for Separation Anxiety Disorder as evidenced by her fear that harm may come to her parents, not having a perceived future, worry that something might happen to herself, shadowing her mother while at home, and mild school refusal. While it is our clinical experience that Separation Anxiety Disorder is fairly common in children who have PTSD, particularly stemming from abuse, Emily's separation anxiety symptoms predated the abuse. Since discussion of separation anxiety disorder is not the focus of this chapter, it will not be reviewed in detail here. The reader is advised to review Chapter 8.

It was evident that Emily was experiencing PTSD and that she continued to feel vulnerable and at risk for harm even upon the arrest of the perpetrator. It is likely that the family was communicating messages of vulnerability and danger. Upon exploring the structure of the system further and its modalities of communication, the family delivered subtle but powerful messages of Emily's blame for the abuse. Further, parental and child boundaries were diffuse. Although Emily hailed from a very loving family, her parents were afraid to impose or set limits and establish appropriate boundaries lest she reject her parents (not love them). Emily's parents were afraid of being perceived as the "bad guys" by establishing and following through with appropriate limit setting. Here it is evident that the Smiths' need to be loved interfered with their ability in establishing appropriate boundaries, assuming parental power, and delivering appropriate communications about the need for and expression of love. Emily assumed and was given too much executive (parental) power for her very young age of six. This reduced her to feelings of being in danger, and trauma symptoms persisted. Further, it was evident during this observational phase, while the Smiths' marriage was intact, they often disagreed on how to approach the issue of abuse with the children as well as parenting methods in general. This conflict and poor problem solving fractured the executive subsystem of the hierarchy (i.e., parental subsystem), further exacerbating Emily's feelings of vulnerability. Finally, a significant amount of shame about the abuse was communicated within the system. This was evidenced by the Smiths' desire to keep the sexual abuse a secret and to not talk about it with five-year-old Jennifer, who was present during abuse episodes. By attempting to keep the abuse a secret, a myriad of messages were communicated and Metacommunicated throughout the family system. One of the most salient messages was that somehow Emily contributed to or was responsible for the sexual abuse. That is, the Smiths were shamed by the abuse and communicated via its secrecy that such shame came from a sexual encounter their daughter initiated, at least in part. Further, for their daughter to "hear" that she was somehow responsible for such an overwhelming act of violence, was such a strong message of Emily's power –power which was not only beyond that of any six-year-old's capability but beyond that of any adult as well. Hence this family structure supported the development and maintenance of PTSD symptoms.

Treatment Application and Integration

It was decided that Emily and her family would be seen in Systemic Family Therapy for treatment of PTSD. Family therapy seemed particularly appropriate, not only given the family system's dynamics as described above, but also because

Emily presented with the additional Separation Anxiety Diagnosis, Emily's younger sister was present during the molestation, and her parents were in the near vicinity while the molestation occurred.

   The Smiths were informed that their daughter's healing could occur much faster if all family members attended sessions. While the Smiths were agreeable, they expressed reservations about having the younger daughter attend, given her age. It was explained to the Smiths that she had witnessed the molestation and was aware that Emily had experienced something malevolent. It was likely that Jennifer had a number of feelings about what she witnessed and heard, and it would only be to her benefit to have these feelings addressed in family therapy. At this time, discussion of the negative effects of insidious family secrets being passed down from generation to generation were reserved for later in treatment. The Smiths agreed to attend family therapy, and the first session was spent building trust between the family and the therapist. This included a series of man-euvers wherein each person had an opportunity to talk, become validated, and share non-threatening aspects of their lives. There was no pressure to discuss the abuse. Having firmly established a working relationship, at the next session, each family member was asked to discuss his or her understanding of what happened to Emily. It was ideal to begin with Jennifer, as this would allow the therapist and parents to discern the actual quantity and accuracy of information Jennifer had about Emily's molestation. Jennifer stated that Edward hurt Emily and touched her private parts. She began to cry. Through the discussion, it was evident that Jennifer had not only accurate knowledge but also, had cognitively elaborated on the information, until it overwhelmed her. In addition, Jennifer felt guilty for not being able to protect her older sister. The Smiths were incredulous and had "no idea" of the extent that Jennifer was impacted by Emily's abuse. Emily was given the choice of discussing the abuse or not, since there is to be no pressure on the victim, lest she feel revictimized. Emily opted to discuss the abuse, perhaps as a way of protecting her little sister. During the girls' disclosure of their understanding of the abuse, their parents, despite being sensitive, loving, and caring, could not prevent themselves from questioning them about the reason they did not tell them that Edward was hurting Emily. The therapist had to block these questions because, while the parents were in pain and concerned about the children, such questions implied that Emily (and her sister) were responsible for stopping the abuse (and hence for its onset and continuation). These questions were subtly blaming; this was explained to the family. By blocking the Smiths' subtle accusations (e.g., "Why didn't you tell us Edward was molesting you?") and educating them as to the effects of the subtle blame, the Smiths understood how such blame contributed to the girls feeling responsible for Emily's abuse. After everyone in the family discussed their understanding of the abuse and cor-rections were made between reality and intrapersonal interpretation of the events, everyone was asked why abuse is wrong, and the therapist offered the most important explanation as to the detrimental effect of abuse. She explained that abuse is wrong for many reasons, but the most important one was because of the spiritual pain it causes the victim. After this was emphasized and discussed at length, the therapist indicated that it is also wrong for the spiritual pain it causes the other family members. With the therapist's guidance, each family member was able to identify how the abuse affected him/her spiritually and the ways it caused such deep emotional pain.

The next step in this protocol involved the therapist meeting alone with Mr. and Mrs. Smith and priming them for the apology. It is interesting to note that parental guilt about their child's abuse can have many different effects on the parents. Some parents become highly defensive initially stating: "I'm not going to apologize for my child's abuse since I had no way of knowing." Others are so guilt ridden that they cannot begin to discuss apologizing without becoming overwhelmed by emotion (see above for discussion of several methods by which to approach the two extreme manifestations of guilt). For the Smiths, their level of guilt was within the two extremes; hence, they were receptive to the concept of the apology. Further, since they had ready access to their feelings during the role play, they were able to present the apology with great sincerity. The Smiths, therefore, were ready to present their apology in the family session. Thus, each parent apologized separately (while together in a family session) to both daughters. First the Smiths apologized to the direct victim, Emily, and then they apologized to Jennifer as well. Emily attempted to "let her parents off the hook" by stating that it was "okay," but the therapist intercepted and said that it was *not* okay. The Smiths took the therapist's lead and emphasized their heartfelt sorrow for their daughter's abuse. The apology discussion ensued for two sessions, to ensure that Emily could allow her parents to take responsibility for the abuse. This reduced the likelihood that Emily would maintain any self- blame for her abuse. Additionally during this session, Mr. Smith told his daughters for the first time that he had actually confronted Edward and his parents about the molestation and that Mr. and Mrs. Smith had filed charges against the perpetrator. The father's behavior appeared to have had a profound affect on the girls, as they brightened and their anxiety in session dissipated. In fact, Emily expressed that a sense of moral "rightness/justice" had been attained by her father's legal actions. She appeared to feel vindicated, as evidenced by her behavior in session (smug smile, etc.) In the next two sessions, the therapist met alone first with Emily and then with Jennifer. Although Jennifer was not the direct victim, she still was a victim as she observed the abuse, and it was her sister who was violated in her own home. The abuse was described contextually for the girls and reduced to hours and minutes of their lives. Since the abuse occurred on two occasions over the course of two hours (at most), Emily and the therapist discussed the abusive episodes as events, emphasizing that they did not define who she was as a person. The therapist said that she had been alive for more than 53,000 hours, during which time she had many wonderful hours of fun, including birthday parties, trips to Disneyland, dance and music recitals, and swimming competitions that she had won. It was these activities that reflected who she was as a person and that she spent many more hours of her life engaged in these activities than the abusive ones. A similar strategy was employed during the individual session with Jennifer; it was at this session that the therapist obtained a complete understanding about the extent to which the molestation affected Jennifer. Indeed, the miniscule of perceived power that a four year old has was obliterated instantaneously with her sister's abuse.

After individual sessions, the family met to discuss familial consequences should abuse reoccur, since abused children are more vulnerable to repeated episodes of abuse. The most severe consequences include legal removal of the child and permanent placement with entrusted guardians. While Madanes (1994) has leverage in her community's judicial system to enact this plan, many states are not so progressive. As a result, a modified plan is employed, including identification of a safe person with whom the child can share any communication. This safe person is informed of his/her role in the child's life, for the rest of the victim's childhood and perhaps beyond. The family must actively support this decision; one way of exhibiting their support for their child's use of a guardian angel is by structuring several activities between victim and guardian throughout the year (e.g., movies, shopping, park, etc.). This enables the parents to model their encouragement of the child's utilization of the guardian angel, thereby opening the lines of communication. The guardian during these meetings should actively encourage the child to discuss anything he or she wishes. In Emily's case, it was decided that Jessica and her law enforcement father would be the children's guardians, since as soon as they learned of the abuse they interceded and since Emily initially contacted Jessica. The therapist hesitated to appoint Jessica as the guardian since she is a minor and not responsible for protecting a child from another's abuse. However, Emily felt comfortable discussing the abuse with her, so we made it clear that Mr. Jones was the guardian but Jennifer could facilitate discussion, working as part of a team. It was also clarified that the meetings with Jennifer should be held with Jessica and her father together.

During the reparation phase the therapist instructed the family that symbolic reparation be made by Edward. The family decided that Edward should make a long-term contribution to Emily's college fund as well as an ongoing donation to an organization that supports abused children. Emily's response to this idea was similar to her response to her father's confronting and filing legal charges against Edward: she appeared to feel vindicated. In fact she said "this makes it right." Amazingly she also spontaneously endorsed Edward's need for help, suggesting that he receive some therapy. Reparation by Emily's parents was also discussed. It was decided that Mr. Smith would install a phone with intercom capabilities in Emily's room and Mrs. Smith, Emily, and her sister planned to enroll in karate. This was particularly important, as it was evident that Emily and Jennifer both perceived their mother as weak and passive.

The next step was to address the restoration of love which, for this family, was not difficult to accomplish, as they did not appear to have lost their ability to experience and express healthy love. However, we spent this session reminiscing about the children's birth, developmental progression through stages, and many wonderful fun times the family had together. The family exhibited a sense of humor which they were able to utilize in the context of the loving feelings they held for one another. Finally, it was important for the therapist to address the parents' guilt. Jennifer's guilt and sense of responsibility for her sister's abuse was addressed early on since it was extremely distressing for her and since in many ways she was victimized as well. Mr. Smith's guilt was partially alleviated through the action of confronting Edward and his family. This also empowered him, strengthening his efficacy and thereby heightening his sense that he is able to protect his family. Mrs. Smith still struggled during these last sessions with guilt; hence the therapist believed that she could reduce it through a ritual or task. It did seem that her guilt waned as she enrolled in karate; in order to capitalize on the effects of action, the therapist instructed her to do an extra deed for Emily and Jennifer whenever she found herself worrying about her responsibility for Emily's abuse. Such deeds included cleaning Emily's room for her, making an extra special snack, writing an extra special note for the girls' lunches etc. In addition, Mrs. Smith suggested that she was planning to begin a church fundraiser for the local charity for abused children; the therapist capitalized on this by suggesting that whenever she engaged in self-blame she should go to the den and work on the plan for the fundraiser.

By the completion of treatment, both girls were symptom free (including elimination of both Jennifer's PTSD and Separation Anxiety symptoms) and their parents' guilt was greatly reduced. Further, Mr. and Mrs. Smith felt empowered which enabled them to maintain the adaptive family boundaries and facilitate constructive family communication.

Cognitive Behavioral Conceptualization

An alternative conceptualization for PTSD acquisition and treatment includes a cognitive-behavioral (CBT) model. Scientists have recently begun to investigate the efficacy of CBT with children who meet DSM-IV criteria for PTSD. Since child therapy outcome research has lagged significantly behind adult research, it is not surprising that child CBT trauma models have evolved from adult trauma research. This is particularly evident in the PTSD and child maltreatment area (e.g., sexual abuse). Edna Foa and her colleagues have published studies demonstrating the efficacy of graduated exposure in treating adult rape victims (Foa, *et al.*, 1991). They based their PTSD conceptualization on both learning theory and a semantic (information processing) paradigm. Such theoretical principles include both classical and operant conditioning and the cognitive interpretation involved in learning. First from a classical conditioning perspective, by temporal association, previously neutral trauma stimuli become associated with the direct traumatic event (unconditioned stimuli) that innately produces fear responses. These neutral stimuli become conditioned stimuli for the PTSD fear response; therefore a multitude of neutral stimuli, which are paired not only with the unconditioned stimulus but also with other conditioned stimuli, evoke fear. Hence, higher ordered conditioning and stimulus generalization occurs. This elucidates the reason that people with PTSD respond anxiously to a multitude of stimuli. Then operant conditioning occurs because as individuals successfully avoid the traumatic stimuli, they have learned to terminate the unpleasantness associated with the conditioned stimuli. Hence, this explains why those with PTSD frequently avoid many different stimuli since avoidance is reinforcing. Learning theory does not explain, however, acquisition of unique features of PTSD, such as the startle response and dissociative behavior. It is believed that how abused children cognitively interpret and integrate the traumatic experience/stimuli, including their efficacy (control) over such stimuli, explains the unique features of PTSD. This then accounts for the child's perception and cognitive meaning assigned to and associated with the trauma-related stimuli determine trauma responses. This cognitive processing of the trauma and related stimuli can influence the fear response. In fact, researchers have determined that perceived threat might be a better predictor of PTSD than actual threat, thereby explaining the generalization of the fear response. Hence, this generalization explains observed fear responses to seemingly non-related trauma stimuli. For example, an adolescent who was raped in the home of some teens has a fear response (changes in physiology, subjective discomfort and avoidance behaviors) to barbeque and to fast food restaurants. In tracing her associations and cognitive understanding of such unrelated fear, she was able to identify running past a fast food hamburger restaurant as she was escaping her attackers and seeking help. While she was fleeing, she believed her life was still under threat.

This theory offers explanation for children exhibiting a more adverse PTSD response to intrafamilial abuse than extrafamilial abuse. If abuse occurs in the home by a caretaker, then the child is likely to associate many environmental stimuli (including a variety of components of parenting) with the trauma and the perceived threat of abuse. Additionally, children abused by a primary caretaker often feel less self-efficacy (less control) than those children abused by someone external to the family system. This lends support for the importance of the cognitive interpretation of abuse as important to development of symptoms. In fact, there is some evidence that the meaning children ascribe to abuse by a familial perpetrator is often more negative than with perpetrators outside the home.

By targeting any stimuli that elicit the fear response via systematic exposure/ desensitization, anxiety should extinguish across situations. Systematic desensitization, a form of reciprocal inhibition, is employed to extinguish the fear response as well as to counter anxiety with relaxation. Extinction occurs by repeatedly presenting the conditioned stimuli ranked in a fear hierarchy without pairing them with the unconditioned stimuli. In addition, relaxation counters the anxiety response. Hence, the link between trauma related stimuli and the fear response are disconnected. In addition, since the child is not allowed to escape or avoid the unpleasantness of the trauma stimuli without confronting the feared stimulus and engaging in an adaptive coping strategy (relaxation), non-adaptive avoidance is not reinforced. Finally, children are taught adaptive self-statements in order to alter their cognitive understanding and perception of the trauma stimuli. It is through such cognitive restructuring that children are able to heighten their mastery of fears and self-efficacy in general, which in turn enables them to reinterpret the traumatic events in a more adaptive manner. For children, caretaker involvement is critical to successful treatment, as caretakers are able to reinforce adaptive coping outside the therapy session where children are likely to encounter trauma related stimuli more frequently.

Cognitive Behavioral Therapy Intervention for PTSD

CBT for the treatment of PTSD is composed of three primary components:

1) Relaxation training and coping skills instruction;
2) Imaginal and analogue systematic desensitization, and graduated exposure;
3) Patient education, and behavioral parent education with an emphasis on contracting.

The first component is designed to give children active coping skills by which to directly reduce anxiety and disrupt the connection between anxiety and the reinforcing qualities of avoidance. Such skills taught by the therapist and employed by children also serve to heighten the patients' level of self-efficacy and locus control, since it is a strategy that they can actively engage in themselves in order to master their fear and anxiety. During this initial phase of treatment, very specific relaxation skills are taught and once completed, the development of a fear hierarchy ensues. Relaxation techniques include diaphragmatic breathing and progressive body muscle relaxation (including the tense-relax procedure so a child can differentiate between a state of arousal and one of relaxation), such as that delineated by Jacobson but modified by others for use with children. In particular, we prefer Koeppen's relaxation protocol (1974) as it attaches imagery to each of the muscle groups. Such modification heightens children's understanding of the procedure as well as their interest through the use of imaginative anchors. For example, instead of requesting the participant to make a fist and squeeze as tightly as he or she can, the child is asked to make a fist as if squeezing an orange to make orange juice. After the therapist instructs a child in full body relaxation, he/she helps the child to formulate a pleasant, safe, relaxing imaginary scene to attach at the completion of the relaxation protocol. Children from our geographic location typically develop beach or park scenes. Children have on occasion selected their bedroom as the most safe and relaxing place, which is useful as long as abuse did not occur in any of the bedrooms in the house. In cases where children were abused in their room and develop their relaxing image to be set in their room, we have encouraged them to develop different scenes so as to reduce the risk of their relaxing scene eliciting anxiety. Transition from total body relaxation to the relaxing scene involves having the child imagine he/she is walking down ten steps, with the instructions that with each step they take they are becoming more and more relaxed. Then they imagine they enter their special place where the scene is presented. Once the children finish this segment, the therapist guides them back upstairs, still in their imagination. As they "climb" the steps, they are instructed that they are becoming more and more alert but that they will remain calm and relaxed throughout the day. The benefit of attaching the imagery to the relaxation is easily discerned in its applicability and generalization. Once there have been enough pairings between relaxation and imagery (associationism), merely imagining the scene will induce relaxation. This is why it is important for the therapist to record a cassette tape of the relaxation procedure and to have a child listen to the tape on a daily basis for awhile.

Once the therapist instructs the child in relaxation, then he/she will need to initially develop a fear hierarchy with the child and parent separately. Often because of the avoidance component of the PTSD, the child will not be able to give details of feared stimuli for the hierarchy. Caretakers may be helpful in filling in the gaps as well as child protective service agents, police reports, and court documents. The hierarchy includes both those items which the child cognitively fears (he/she can verbalize) as well as those stimuli that are actively avoided. The child and parent independently rate the child's degree of fearfulness for each item on the hierarchy. Next, the child and therapist work together without the parent present during which the child is exposed to the feared stimuli imaginally, with the therapist describing the feared stimuli. These feared items are presented from least to most feared and avoided. Children are encouraged to apply relaxation techniques as fear mounts during the procedure. If fear becomes too overwhelming, they are requested to signal the therapist by raising a finger. After exposure to each item on the hierarchy the child is asked to rate the degree of fearfulness. Depending on the age of the children, they are asked to rate their degree of fear on a fear thermometer, with anchor points of one to five, one to eight or one to ten. On occasion, a developmentally young child will be unable to use these formatted Likert scales so the therapist will ask the child if he/she was not afraid, somewhat afraid, or a lot afraid. Succeeding items on the fear hierarchy are not presented until the fear ranking is a one on the preceding item.

In addition to the desensitization procedure, adaptive self-statements are taught to facilitate coping both as the child engages in the desensitization as well as when confronted with the feared stimuli outside the therapy sessions. Many of these children make distorted self-statements as a function of the abuse as well as their environmental models. So, in conjunction with the desensitization procedures, session time is devoted to having the child identify and challenge maladaptive self-statements, especially those related to the abuse and their fears. We will then help the child structure adaptive cognitions in order to replace the maladaptive self-statements.

As well as aiding the development of a fear hierarchy, the primary caretakers are also included in the treatment as they are instructed in methods to facilitate the child's use of coping skills, including the use of adaptive self-statements and to reward the child's adaptive behavior. The caretakers are also taught to help extinguish maladaptive fear responses. For example, the parent may be asked to ignore a specific aspect of a fear response while simultaneously having them reward or reinforce more adaptive responses (differential reinforcement of alternate behavior). The parent is instructed in use of reinforcers, including tangible rewards, verbal, and non-verbal. They are also taught when to administer such rewards. Instruction of reinforcement and extinction procedures is completed in both an informal and formal structured format. With respect to the latter, parents are instructed in the art of developing a written behavioral contract. Instruction of the parenting techniques includes dissemination of information (including written handouts), therapist modeling and demonstration, and shaping in session when caretaker and child are present. The last item in the treatment protocol includes child and parent instruction in body boundaries and methods to facilitate personal safety.

Cognitive Behavioral Therapy Case Example

Case Conceptualization
Dakota Harris, a ten-year, nine-month-old female who is in the fifth grade, was referred for services with symptoms of anxiety, including nightmares, worry and over concern about the feelings of others, sensitivity, and avoidance of discussing an alleged sexual molestation, fear about her peers discovering that she had been molested and some inattentiveness (daydreaming) and distractibility.

Dakota's mother reported that her computer teacher (Mr. Dodge) rubbed her private parts, including her buttocks and thighs and pressed up against her. Dakota also affirmed this and pointed to her vaginal area as well. It was reported that he rubbed her private parts under her outer clothes and through her underwear. Dakota's mother stated that Dakota first reported this at school to a school counselor, in response to a sexual harassment information discussion session at school.

Abusive attacks by Mr. Dodge were said to have occurred three to four times when Dakota was in fourth grade. Although Dakota had some contact with Mr. Dodge in third grade, she became much more involved in computers in the fourth grade and was a lab tech. She also participated in the computer club. According to Dakota's parents (Mr. and Ms. Harris), there were seven abuse criminal cases from Dakota's school with respect to Mr. Dodge's behavior. Mr. and Ms. Harris said that in 1994 there was an allegation of inappropriate behavior or contact by Mr. Dodge with a different child, and the school conducted its own investigation. Dakota's parents said that the school "swept it (their findings) under the rug" and sent a letter to Mr. Dodge to "cease and desist."

According to Ms. Harris, changes in Dakota's behavior since the abuse included heightened distractibility (Dakota moved her desk to a corner of her classroom so that she could focus better), and disorganization which appears to have impacted her academically as her grades have dropped significantly from before the abuse (Cluster A – DSM IV), increase in daydreaming, nightmares (e.g., Mr. Dodge chasing her in her dreams) and extreme distress when confronted by cues that were reminiscent of the trauma. With respect to the latter, Ms. Harris reported that Dakota "fell apart" when viewing a picture of Mr. Dodge (Cluster B – DSM IV), withdrawal and loss of interest in previous pleasurable activities (Dakota who is ranked as a national figure skating champion wanted to quit ice skating stating it was no longer fun, and she had no interest in attending the space museum where she and her father volunteered), and avoidance of stimuli (computer room and discussion of the events) associated with the abuse topic (Cluster C), and increased, irritability, sleep disruption and sensitivity (Cluster D). With respect to the latter, Dakota would personalize her class's disruptive behavior particularly when the teacher disciplined the class for the disruption. In addition, Mrs. Harris reported that Dakota had experienced an increase in rigidity and need for predictability over the past year. "She doesn't go with the flow and is prone to becoming frustrated and irritable quickly. She was much more flexible when she was younger." Dakota's grades were also lower the year of the abuse than before, according to her parents. From fourth to fifth grade, she was earning Cs and low Bs; prior to and before the abuse she earned As and Bs. Further, Mrs. Harris said that Dakota was preoccupied with her peers at school finding out about the abuse and this was causing her much anxiety. Ironically, shortly after the publicity about Mr. Dodge's behavior at school, one boy asked Dakota "What would you do if Mr. Dodge touched you?" Dakota said nothing in response to the question. In addition, according to her parents, Dakota no longer wears dresses or skirts to school, and she has difficulty talking/interacting with non-familial adult males.

Dakota's parents reported the possibility of two legal actions, a criminal action and civil suit. According to her parents, these legal actions cause Dakota much anxiety because she will have to see Mr. Dodge. According to Mrs. Harris, Dakota knows the judicial calendar better than her parents, and will often ask her parents for updates regarding possible modifications in the calendar (such as the addition of depositions).

In meeting with Dakota initially, she confirmed the above difficulties; interestingly, she indicated that she shared much of the responsibility for the abuse. In exploring this further, Mr. Dodge had elevated her to lab assistant and would give her treats that other children did not receive. Because he was "so nice" on many occasions, she believed that she had done something to warrant the abuse. In addition, she felt guilty about reporting the abuse since he "got in trouble," and he had been prone to give her treats and favors. One of the prevailing cognitive struggles for Dakota was her worry that he was mad at her.

Clinical Formulation

Given the history of symptom presentation, it was evident Dakota was experiencing Post Traumatic Stress Disorder. Many of her anxiety symptoms were initially conditioned by the association between the molestation and the myriad of stimuli present during the abuse. Her fear responses were directly classically conditioned (fear of Mr. Dodge stimuli) and included an element of higher order conditioning (fear of many different school rooms and experiences, including when there was perceived "danger" associated with school events such as when Dakota's class was being noisy and her teacher would discipline them). Many of these fear responses were then operantly conditioned through her avoidance. Dakota avoided rooms, peers, and situations at school, which was reinforcing (due to relief of anxiety) and then generalized to her avoidance of other activities, including ice skating and space museum work. Her cognitive interpretation of the abuse (the information processing component) included a view that her world was unpredictable and that she was in danger. She was able to verbalize her feelings of irritability and heightened sensitivity in response to feeling her environment was not safe or predictable. She was able to realize that this is why she had memorized the court calendars and would remind her parents of impending court dates or legal events (depositions, etc.). She also held two competing interpretations of the molestation which caused her great anxiety. On the one hand she realized that Mr. Dodge's abusive behavior was very wrong. On the other hand, she believed she was responsible for the abuse as, at times, Mr. Dodge was a "nice guy." From cognitive dissonance theory, inability to negotiate two conflicting thoughts causes great distress and requires the individual to either choose one over the other or to remain in a state of cognitive disequilibrium (which causes anxiety).

In applying CBT in the treatment of Dakota, the first step was to establish a therapeutic working relationship with her. Relationship building consisted of nondirective interaction, including reflection, play activities, and taking walks around the grounds of the office building. The first step after establishing rapport was to teach Dakota progressive muscle relaxation. We utilized Koeppen's procedure and had her develop her relaxing scene to attach to the end of the procedure. Dakota selected her mother's giant bed and a special soft quilt that her grandmother had made as her relaxing place. She described the room as cool but not chilly and dim but not dark. She indicated that when she imagines this space that she would like the T.V. to be on low with a Disney movie playing while she lies on the bed with the quilt. She also indicated that she would not like to have anyone else present in the room while she is there. A relaxation tape was made with those views attached, and Dakota and her parents were instructed to play the tape once per day.

The next step in treatment involved development of a fear hierarchy. Dakota became readily engaged in therapy but due to avoidance, which was one of her primary PTSD symptoms, she did not independently offer information about the abuse. In meeting separately with Dakota's parents, specific information from them as well as the police report enabled the therapist to develop a fear and avoidance hierarchy. This hierarchy was ranked from least to most fearful for Dakota. As she became anxious during the rating, the relaxation procedure was delivered to reduce her anxiety. Her hierarchy from least to most fearful included seeing the school room where Mr. Dodge molested her, thinking about Mr. Dodge and other teachers asking her to stay after school, imagining Mr. Dodge asking her to come to his desk, thinking about Mr. Dodge touching her arm, remembering Mr. Dodge touching her stomach, Mr. Dodge putting his hands on top of her underwear, Mr. Dodge putting his hands down her underwear and touching her vagina, seeing Mr. Dodge's picture in the literary magazine and on videotape, imagining seeing Mr. Dodge in the courtroom, testifying against Mr. Dodge in the courtroom with Mr. Dodge present.

The next phase of treatment included imaginal desensitization. However, when addressing that part of the fear hierarchy wherein Dakota was fearful of seeing Mr. Dodge's picture in the annual literary magazine and on videotape, analogue in vivo desensitization was conducted by having Dakota's mother bring in the school's literary magazines from the preceding three years as well as a videotape of him interacting with some of the school children at the school's annual picnic. Concurrently with the desensitization procedure, Dakota's maladaptive cognitions were addressed, which included her assumption of blame for the abuse and fearing that Mr. Dodge and her peers would be mad at her for "telling." While it took several sessions to successfully challenge these, such resolution of cognitive dissonance often takes longer, but Dakota already had an idea that as nice as Mr. Dodge had been he was responsible for his abusive behavior. Her worry about Mr. Dodge's anger was a particularly important cognition with respect to her higher items on the fear hierarchy (e.g., seeing Mr. Dodge in the courtroom). A list of adaptive self-statements was compiled and typed on a sheet that she took home with her. Examples of such statements with respect to her fear of Mr. Dodge's anger included: "So what if he is angry at me. HE is the one responsible for touching me." "Even though he may be angry, I am safe in the courtroom, Ms. Woods (her attorney), the Judge, my parents, and the bailiff will protect me. I am in control and he can't hurt me anymore." Dakota was assigned homework that involved practicing relaxation utilizing the relaxation tape. Further, she was asked to use the adaptive self-statements when confronted with feared stimuli. Her parents were also included in the homework as ancillary coaches.

Dakota's parents were instructed in providing small rewards for her daily listening of the relaxation tape. They were also instructed in behavioral contracting and how to use similar principles in shaping Dakota's behavior with respect to successful coping. For example, whenever Dakota discussed the court calendars with her parents, they were told to give her one informative sentence and then to ignore (extinguish) any other anxious checking of dates. They were also instructed to encourage (reinforce) her in using adaptive self-statements concerning court (and other feared situations). Similarly, her parents were told that they would be instrumental in not allowing Dakota to avoid feared stimuli as this would serve to reinforce maladaptive coping and hence her fear.

Dakota's response to treatment was excellent; the most important outcome of the protocol included elimination of PTSD symptoms. However, with addition of more positive coping strategies, including an alteration of self statements, Dakota's behavioral approach to her environment also changed positively. She presented with an aura of renewed self-confidence and calm assertiveness, attributable to a change in locus of control by heightening self-efficacy. Through use of realistic adaptive self-statements, Dakota became self-empowered.

Integration of the Two Different Models

In many cases two different therapy models may be utilized for the same case; but this is NOT ALWAYS the case. The therapist must make sure that he/she is not violating theoretical assumptions of either model. For example, it is not possible for the same therapist to conduct both behavioral and psychodynamic therapy with the same patient. This is because the psychodynamic theoretical assumption of projection and use of transference via a completely neutral unconditional therapist is violated when that same therapist engages in directive behavioral therapy which is often based on contingencies (and hence is conditional). Before determining if one can integrate treatment from two different theoretical models, one must first consider differences between the two models as well as unique characteristics of the patient and associated circumstances.

Differences Between CBT AND FST Models for PTSD

The principal difference between CBT and FST for the treatment of PTSD symptoms resides with the intervention target. With CBT the therapist aids the extinction of the fear response and increases the individual's coping resources. Therefore, when either external or internal stimuli elicit a child's anxiety response, the patient directly responds with a strategy/behavior designed to minimize anxiety, if such responses have not already been extinguished through exposure training. In family therapy, however, the environment/context is changed, which alters both the milieu directly and the individual's perception of it. The entire family is targeted for reduction of fear responses through better delineation of family roles and boundaries, and improved communication regarding protection and safety, as well as enhanced communication overall. As a result, via family systemic therapy, perceived threat in the environment is removed and the child feels safe. PTSD symptoms are thus eliminated

Integration of FST and CBT

It is possible to integrate both FST and CBT for PTSD without violating theoretical assumptions of either, since the former focuses on family context and milieu and the latter focuses on enhancing the individual coping response of the patient. In fact, it is likely that by focusing both on the context in which the trauma occurred and/or in which the child resided during the traumatic event, as well as on individual coping resources, recovery may be enhanced. There are a number of ways in which to integrate these treatments. Sometimes the therapist begins with CBT so as to reduce resistance of the family. By working one-to-one with the child (including the caretakers as assistants in aiding the child through behavioral contracting, etc), parents have an opportunity to work with the therapist as well as observe results of treatment. This heightens the parents' trust of the therapist. Such trust heightens amenability to FST. An alternative integrative approach is to split the sessions so that part is devoted to individual CBT and the rest to FST. Finally, on occasion, additional individual sessions are reserved from the FST protocol described above and expanded to include exposure therapy and cognitive restructuring. Similarly with respect to direct amalgamation of models, the parent training package of CBT can be dovetailed with restructuring of the family system. These components fit nicely together since in many cases parents need to reclaim their executive head of household (top of the family hierarchy) and the parent component of the CBT package helps to empower the parents, allowing them to set appropriate limits and boundaries (the ability to exercise such power). The one serious threat to successful integration of both FST and CBT is the therapist's alliance with the patient. In CBT the therapist has a working alliance with the patient in order to meet the goals of the therapy contract, whereas with FST, alliances with family members shift during and across sessions. The therapist must pay particular attention to this balance and should warn child patients that while he/she will always be on their side, during family therapy this may not appear to be true, as the therapist needs to alter familial interactions. With respect to the FST protocol for PTSD emanating from abuse, there is more direct therapist alliance with the child surrounding the abuse than with other issues, since pressure is removed from the child to disclose and the focus is to remove child responsibility for the abuse. The alliance issue may be more problematic, however, when the therapist attempts to restructure the family and improve communication about non-abuse issues. It is my recommendation that before attempting integration of both FST and CBT the therapist has acquired adequate experience in implementing each without incorporating the other.

Summary

This chapter presented two different theoretical models, family systems therapy and cognitive behavioral therapy, for the conceptualization and treatment of post traumatic stress disorder in children and adolescents. Each model was discussed with respect to theoretical foundation and corresponding intervention. In addition, application of each model with respect to conceptualization and treatment was demonstrated via case example. Finally, differences between the models and the ability to integrate both in conceptualization and treatment was reviewed.

References

American Psychiatric Association (1994). *Diagnostic and Statistical Manual – IV*. Washington DC: American Psychiatric Association.
American Psychiatric Association (2000). *Diagnostic and Statistical Manual – TR*. Washington, D.C.: American Psychiatric Association.
Faust, J. (2000). Integration of family and cognitive behavioral therapy for sexually abussed children. *Cognitive Behavioral Practice, 7(3)*, 361–368.
Faust, J., Ransom, M., Weiss, D., & Phelps-Doray, D. (1999). *Comparison of Two Treatments for Sexually Abused Children with PTSD*. Paper presented at the annual meeting of the American Psychological Association: Boston, MA.

Foa, E. B., Rothbaum, B. O., Riggs, D. S., & Murdock, T. B. (1991). Treatment of post-traumatic disorder in rape victims: A comparison between cognitive-behavioral procedures and counseling. *Journal of Consulting and Clinical Psychology, 59,* 715–723.

Foa, E. B., Steketee, G., & Rothbaum, B. (1989). Behavioral/cognitive conceptualizations of post-traumatic stress disorder. *Behavior Therapy, 20,* 155–176.

Koeppen, A. S. (1974). Relaxation training for children. *Elementary School Guidance and Counseling, 9 (1), 14–21.*

Madanes, C. (1992). *Sex, love, and violence.* A paper presented at the annual meeting of the American Association of Marriage and Family Therapy. Miami Beach, Fl. Madanes, C. (1990), *Sex, love, and violence.* New York: W.W. Norton & Company.

Minuchin, S. (1974). *Families and Family Therapy.* Cambridge, Mass: Harvard University Press.

Chapter 13

Obsessive Compulsive Disorder

Debora Bell-Dolan and Lourdes Suarez

Description of Clinical Syndrome

Obsessive compulsive disorder (OCD) is one of the least common anxiety disorders in children and adolescents. However, the intrusive obsessive thoughts and associated compulsive behavior characteristic of this disorder creates a debilitating condition in which the severity and time-consuming quality of this behavior can cause significant impairment in every aspect of a child's life, including economic, social, and psychological functioning. Epidemiological studies estimate that 0.3 percent of ten to eleven year-old children (Rutter, *et al.*, 1970) and one percent of adolescents suffer from this disorder (Flament, *et al.*, 1988). However, this may be a conservative estimate of the disorder given the secretiveness of its symptoms (Flament, *et al.*, 1988).

The symptoms of OCD in children and adolescents are similar to those found in adults. Obsessions refer to "persistent ideas, thoughts, impulses, or images that are experienced as intrusive and inappropriate and that cause marked anxiety or distress" (American Psychiatric Association, 1994, p. 418). The most common obsessions in children and adolescents involve concerns about germs or contaminants, fears that harm will come to self or others, scrupulosity (excessive religiosity or scrutiny of one's thoughts), and "forbidden" thoughts, such as aggressive or sexual thoughts (March, *et al.*, 1995; Swedo, *et al.*, 1989). Children and adolescents often attempt to suppress such anxiety-arousing obsessions by engaging in compulsive behavior. For example, a child with contamination obsessions might engage in hand-washing every time he/she feels threatened by the thought of being contaminated by disease-producing germs. Compulsions are these "repetitive behaviors or mental acts the goal of which is to prevent or reduce anxiety or distress" (American Psychiatric Association, 1994, p. 418). Similar to adults, common compulsions of children and adolescents involve washing and cleaning, repeating or redoing, checking, touching, counting, ordering/arranging, and hoarding (March, *et al.*, 1995; Swedo, *et al.*, 1989). Obsessions and compulsions seem to wax and wane over time, and are often exacerbated by psychosocial stress (American Psychiatric Association, 1994).

To warrant a diagnosis of OCD, the youngster may suffer from either obsessions or compulsions, although most have both symptoms. Even though most

Handbook of Conceptualization and Treatment of Child Psychopathology, pages 267–287.

adults with the disorder recognize that the obsessions or compulsions are unreasonable or excessive, this diagnostic requirement is not necessary for children and adolescents with OCD. In addition, obsessive and/or compulsive symptoms must "cause marked distress, be time-consuming (take more than one hour a day), or significantly interfere with the person's routine, occupational or academic functioning or usual social activities or relationships" (American Psychiatric Association, 1994; p 423). Finally, obsessions or compulsions that focus on other DSM-IV Axis I diagnoses, such as preoccupation with food in the presence of an eating disorder, hair pulling associated with trichotillomania, guilty ruminations from depression, or preoccupation with drugs in the presence of substance abuse disorder, would not warrant a separate diagnosis of OCD.

Developmental Considerations

Although OCD has a typical onset in late adolescence or early adulthood (American Psychiatric Association, 1994), the mean age of onset for childhood OCD has been reported to range between nine and 12.8 years (Flament, et al., 1988; Swedo, et al., 1989). In contrast with other childhood anxiety disorders, the onset of OCD has been found to occur earlier in boys, with a mean age of nine years, whereas girls were more likely to have an age of onset of eleven years (Swedo, et al., 1989). The overall male to female ratio of this disorder changes with age, becoming roughly equal in adolescence (Flament, et al., 1988)

Developmentally normal children often exhibit ritualistic behavior similar to that characteristic of OCD. In particular, around the ages of three and four years, children frequently develop bedtime rituals or want things to be done in a certain way; however, such behavior is normative and transitory. Most of the time it can be understood in the context of the developmental skill being mastered in that particular period. For example, children mastering independence and control may insist on doing a task differently from how their parents have taught them to do it, which to the parent may seem rigid or compulsive. However, normative obsessive-compulsive behaviors can be discriminated from OCD on the basis of content, timing, and severity (Leonard, et al., 1990). In general, normal obsessive-compulsive behavior occurs early in childhood, is exhibited by a large number of children, and is associated with the mastery of developmental issues. On the other hand, OCD manifests itself later in development, has a "bizzare" quality, and produces considerable dysfunction and distress (March, et al., 1995).

Childhood OCD seems to follow a chronic course. In young children with OCD, it is not uncommon for the principal symptom to change over time (Swedo, et al., 1989). That is, a child may have a washing ritual for two years, but then develop a checking ritual. OCD symptoms frequently increase in number during childhood, but then decrease in late adolescence or early adulthood (Rettew, et al., 1992). Most studies report that half of the total number of persons diagnosed with OCD in childhood or adolescence continue to suffer from OCD symptoms into adulthood. Although well-controlled treatment outcome studies for childhood OCD are scarce, the available treatments for OCD, including cognitive-behavioral, psychopharmacological, and family therapies have been shown to be beneficial and cost-effective ways of dealing with OCD in children and adolescents.

Treatment Approaches

Treatment for childhood OCD provides relief from its debilitating and often stigmatizing symptoms. In this section, two of the most commonly used treatment approaches for children and adolescents with OCD will be described. First, cognitive-behavioral therapy, which is the individual treatment of choice for childhood OCD, will be presented. Second, family involvement, a common and widely used intervention with childhood disorders, will be described as an adjunct to the individual treatment of childhood OCD.

Cognitive-Behavioral Psychotherapy. CBT is described in the literature as the treatment of choice for children and adolescents with OCD. Theoretically, CBT procedures fall within the social learning framework, which uses both behavioral and cognitive information to modify maladaptive functioning. The fundamental principles of cognitive approaches follow the claim that cognitive activity, which can be monitored and altered, affects behavior. Thus, the desired behavior change can be achieved through cognitive change. In addition, behavioral approaches rely heavily on behavior change to affect cognitive mechanisms and related emotional and physiological reactions. Such principles are at the core of cognitive-behavioral therapy for OCD. In particular, cognitive-behavioral treatment of childhood OCD employs behavioral strategies, such as exposure and response prevention, as well as cognitive interventions to alter anxious emotional, physiological, and behavioral responses. Cognitive-behavioral approaches to the treatment of OCD have been described by several authors. One excellent resource is March and Mulle's (1998) book, *OCD in Children and Adolescents*. This treatment manual offers a useful session-by-session guide to clinicians in the treatment of childhood OCD and provides the opportunity for empirical evaluation of treatment efficacy. The main components of cognitive-behavioral treatment, with some specific examples from March and Mulle (1998), are provided below.

Exposure and Response Prevention. The central behavioral intervention for OCD involves some form of exposure and response prevention (E/RP). Exposure occurs when a child encounters the feared object or thought. Exposure-based treatment is based on the premise that a child's anxiety is not realistic and is maintained by his or her avoidance of the feared stimulus and of the actual consequences of contacting that stimulus. For example, the child who fears contamination may avoid touching other children because of the obsessive thought that other children will transmit fatal germs. The child also may handwash compulsively as a "protection" against these germs. The presence of other children and the possibility of physical contact elicit anxiety; thus, the avoidance of this situation increases comfort. Unfortunately, this becomes a self-maintaining pattern whereby the child's avoidance reinforces anxiety, which leads to continued avoidance. The avoidance also prohibits the child from challenging his or her beliefs about germs and contaminants. Exposure-based treatments are therefore intended to disrupt the anxiety-maintaining cycle of avoidance by forcing contact with the feared situation while prohibiting the child from engaging in the "protective" compulsive ritual. Over time, as the child touches other children and does not contract fatal germs, the symptoms of anxiety, including physiologic symptoms, maladaptive beliefs, and avoidance behavior, decline.

Exposure can occur gradually, as in graded exposure or systematic desensitization, or it can occur all at once, as in flooding. With graded exposure, the child is exposed to the feared stimulus in gradual steps, moving to the next step only after habituation to the current step. In other words, the child will face and master small fears before moving to larger ones.

In general, graded exposure is recommended for children and adolescents because it helps to make the treatment predictable, controllable, and successful (March & Mulle, 1998). Flooding, on the other hand, involves exposure to the highest anxiety-provoking stimulus and can also be performed imaginally or in vivo. Because flooding begins with a highly anxiety-provoking stimulus, habituation during the exposure session may take longer than with graded exposure. However, the total number of sessions may be reduced. Despite this potential advantage, children may have less tolerance for anxiety than adults and thus resist treatment. In addition, their parents, seeing the child's distress, may remove the child from treatment prematurely, before the distress has abated. Therefore, because of practical and ethical concerns associated with treatment that is so distressing, flooding is usually not recommended with children and adolescents.

In graded exposure, the steps of exposure are based on a fear hierarchy generated by the child. Several fear-producing stimuli are ranked from least to most anxiety-provoking to generate a stimulus hierarchy that serves to organize the exposure sessions. The ranking of anxiety-provoking stimuli is obtained by estimating the amount of distress that each situation will elicit if exposed to it. This distress index is referred to as a Subjective Units of Discomfort (SUD) scale. A fear thermometer, where SUD scores ranging from one to ten are displayed pictorially, can be a particularly useful tool for estimating SUDs with younger children. Ideally, the child's fear stimulus hierarchy should contain at least one anxiety-provoking situation per SUD level.

Effective exposure often depends on response prevention, which is the process of blocking rituals or avoidance behavior. For example, a child who fears that the house is going to be robbed and frequently checks the front door, would have to refrain from ritualized checking until the anxiety is diminished. Whereas exposure aims at reducing anxiety and obsessional thoughts, response prevention diminishes or eliminates compulsive behavior. Particularly with children, complete response prevention may be an over-ambitious goal. Instead, children may alter the duration or form of the compulsive behavior or may increase the time lapse between an obsesssive thought and the compulsive behavior. For example, a child with a checking compulsion may wait 30 minutes before checking to see that the windows are locked, may check the windows in a different order, or may limit him/herself to 15 versus 30 minutes of checking. Gradually, the delay can be increased, the duration decreased, and the form changed enough to break the obsession-compulsion connection.

Guided by the stimulus hierarchy, exposure/response prevention (E/RP) to each consecutive stimulus is performed imaginally and/or *in vivo*. In imaginal exposure, the child reconstructs a mental image of being in contact with the feared object (e.g., he/she can imagine touching a doorknob and not washing his/her hands). This form of graded exposure is usually implemented before *in vivo* exposure. However, in cases where in vivo exposure is logistically impossible, imaginal exposure may be the only technique used. After completing imaginal exposure successfully; that is, the child's anxiety is reduced as reflected by low SUDs scores, he/she can proceed to the in vivo E/RP task for that stimulus. In in vivo exposure, the child has direct physical contact with the feared stimulus. For example, the child with contamination fears would have to touch or hold the object that he/she believes may have germs or be contaminated.

Although no empirical evidence exists regarding the required or optimal frequency and duration of exposure sessions with children and adolescents with OCD, traditional clinical practice with adults provides some helpful guidelines. With adults, imaginal and in vivo exposure sessions typically require 90 minutes to two hours. However, with children, March and Mulle (1998) suggest that duration may not be important, only that the child completes the task. During this period, the anxiety induced by exposing the child to the feared object is expected to diminish gradually. A SUDs rating of two or lower for several minutes may be an indication that anxiety has attenuated (March & Mulle, 1998). It can also be helpful to establish a "manageable" level of anxiety during the initial assessment and hierarchy development. The child indicates the maximum SUDs level that he or she can tolerate and still function effectively. Typically, a level of two or three, this child-defined manageable SUDs level can be used as the target anxiety level during exposure sessions. Using such a child-defined level can accommodate differences in children's usage of the SUDs rating scale, and also conveys to the child the notion that a total cessation of anxiety may be a less realistic goal than management of the anxiety. Exposure sessions are typically recommended to occur daily. In outpatient treatment, this can be accomplished with weekly therapy sessions and daily between-session homework assignments.

Anxiety Management Training. AMT includes a variety of coping techniques designed to facilitate exposure/response prevention tasks and help children deal with the anxiety during these sessions. AMT techniques typically involve a combination of relaxation training, breathing techniques, and cognitive restructuring.

Usually, breathing techniques are introduced before any other anxiety management tool. Diaphragmatic breathing has been used successfully with children. Using this technique, the child is taught to breathe with his/her diaphragm rather than the shallow breathing that often accompanies anxiety. With appropriate application of this breathing technique, the child's stomach pushes outward as he/

she inhales and inward as he/she exhales. This technique may be demonstrated with children by placing one hand on the stomach and the other one on the chest, while observing and feeling the movement of their bodies as they breath in and out. The child with OCD may use this technique before and during the E/RP task as needed to cope with the physical aspects of anxiety.

Deep muscle relaxation, where the child learns to tense and relax large muscle groups in a sequential manner, is also useful for reducing the physiologic anxiety symptoms. Children can be directed, using instructions or imagery (e.g., tensing the neck by imagining being a turtle pulling his/her head into the shell), to tense various muscle groups, and then to relax. Usually, the child is taught this relaxation technique beginning with the neck muscles, followed by arms, hands, stomach, legs, and finally the feet. This procedure can then be repeated working from the feet back to the head. Diaphragmatic breathing can be inserted before and after deep muscle relaxation and children may use both in this manner as preparation for E/RP tasks and to cope with the anxiety during these sessions.

Finally, children can learn cognitive strategies to cope with maladaptive thoughts about OCD, promote adaptive thoughts about their ability to deal with the feared situations and the obsessive thoughts, and to increase motivation to comply with E/RP tasks. One specific cognitive technique described by March and Mulle (1998) involves "talking back" to OCD. Using this technique, the child argues with OCD by constructing assertive statements, such as "Go fly a kite." Such statements emphasize that the child's OCD is separate from the child him/ herself and reinforces the idea that the child has power to refute or resist the obsessions and compulsions. When the child's own negative cognitions interfere with becoming assertive or "talking back" to OCD, self-talk may be introduced. Using self-talk, children can learn to cope with OCD by replacing negative self-talk with positive self-statements. For example, if the child's negative self-statements before the exposure task are "I won't be able to do it," then he/she can think instead "This task will be hard, but I will use my anxiety tools to deal with it." Positive self-statements should be realistic but optimistic, focusing on the child's ability to approach feared tasks and manage anxiety. These self-statements can also focus on the illogical nature of the obsessions and compulsions. Finally, self-praise can be useful in helping children to feel good about their efforts and to motivate continued exposure. Thus, anxiety management techniques may be used in conjunction with E/RP to successfully treat the core compulsion and obsession symptoms of childhood OCD.

Family Involvement

Although children and adolescents with OCD typically receive individualized treatment, the family is often involved at some point during this process. Family involvement may consist of providing education about OCD to parents and other family members, enlisting parent support to facilitate therapeutic strategies, such as exposure homework assignments, preventing parent involvement in the child's

OCD behavior, and dealing with parental anxiety symptoms. To date there has not been systematic evaluation of the impact of parental involvement in the treatment of OCD. However, most clinicians and researchers agree that it is important for most child and adolescent clients (Lenane, 1991; March, *et al.*, 1995).

Lenane (1991) has offered several recommendations for the extent of family inclusion in the treatment of OCD. Families who appear to function relatively well, engage minimally in the child's OCD behavior, and are receptive to suggestions about changing how they relate to their child may require infrequent contact and minimal family intervention. On the other hand, when one or both parents are extensively involved in their child's OCD behavior, are resistant to therapist suggestions about decreasing their involvement, and have conflicts over how to treat their child with OCD, more intensive family therapy may be needed.

Psychoeducation. Because child clients with OCD are usually brought in by their parents for treatment, initial sessions often include a brief education about the nature and causes of OCD to provide the parents with a framework for understanding their child's problem. For example, in their treatment manual, March and Mulle (1998) stress the importance of providing a neurobehavioral framework for the disorder. In this way, OCD is viewed as a neurological disorder for which neither the child nor the parents are to blame. Making OCD the problem rather than the child, identifies the specific target of treatment and is more likely to procure parental understanding and assistance later in treatment.

Parent Support of Treatment. Frequently, parents are asked to support their child's between-session work, such as by helping the child to complete homework assignments or rewarding the child's efforts to reduce OCD symptoms. Two contingency management techniques are frequently included as part of the family's involvement in order to reinforce treatment gains. First, parents may be instructed to use extinction or ignoring to remove potentially reinforcing consequences of the child's OCD behavior. For example, with a child who seeks reassurance from his/her parents about locking doors, parents may be asked to refrain from offering reassurance. In addition, positive reinforcement in the form of tangible rewards or praise may be beneficial to encourage exposure and increase self-esteem in children with OCD. Rewards can be used routinely during or between sessions to recognize treatment gains (March, *et al.*, 1994). Punishment and negative reinforcement, however, are contraindicated in the treatment of childhood OCD.

Family Therapy. In most cases of childhood OCD, family therapy is not necessary. However, in cases where family dysfunction prevents the application of cognitive-behavioral interventions for the child's OCD symptoms, it may be appropriate. Unfortunately, there are no specific clinical guidelines in the literature for family therapy in the context of childhood OCD. Borrowing from other treatment programs for child anxiety disorders, the following techniques may be useful as part of family therapy for childhood OCD. In particular, Silverman and Kurtines (1996) suggest various techniques to improve the parent-child relationship, including parenting skills training, parent-child communication training, and parent-child problem-solving training. In the case of OCD, parents with limited knowledge about child management techniques may be taught appropriate contingency management skills and deterred from using punishment when the child exhibits OCD behavior or does not comply with E/RP tasks. As part of parent-child communication training, parents and children with OCD may be trained to communicate in a non-threatening way about their emotions and needs. Finally, parent-child problem-solving training may assist families in resolving conflict as it relates to the child's OCD symptoms.

In cases where one parent's anxiety symptoms interferes with treatment of the child's OCD, family therapy that focuses on the parent's anxiety management may be useful. Treating parent anxiety symptoms involves using the same cognitive-behavioral techniques (e.g., exposure, relaxation, self-talk) described above in the treatment of childhood OCD. Silverman and Kurtines (1996) suggest that if both the child and the parent exhibit the same type of anxiety symptoms, they can do the exposure tasks together and then share a rewarding activity.

In general, family involvement in the treatment of childhood OCD appears to be a useful treatment approach, although it still lacks empirical support. However, the degree of family involvement seems to be related to the needs of each individual case. Considering the current state of the literature on child treatment of OCD, family involvement may be most beneficial as an adjunct to cognitive-behavioral treatment.

Case Description

Jack was a twelve-year-old boy referred for outpatient treatment of increasingly debilitating OCD. At the time of referral, Jack lived with his parents, Mr. and Mrs. Sprague, and his nine- year-old sister, Julie. Jack attended sixth grade at Smithton Elementary School, where he was in regular classes and was earning satisfactory grades.

Jack's parents reported a three-year history of Jack's OCD symptoms, with significant worsening over the past several months. At intake, Jack reported obsessive thoughts about germs and contamination, which he dealt with by avoidance of touching "unclean" items and by compulsive handwashing. Unclean items included other people and most items touched by other people, especially his family members or teachers. Thus, Jack would avoid touching his sister and parents, and they followed Jack's "rules" about not touching him. Jack's teachers were not informed of his OCD, although they did realize that he became irritable if touched.

In addition to people, Jack avoided touching items that had recently been touched by another person, including taking papers from his teachers, or a dinner plate from his mother. Jack reported that if he absolutely had to handle an item touched by someone else, it was easier if there was some time delay between when they touched the item and when he touched it, Thus, in school Jack arranged to sit at the end of a row so that when papers were passed down the row, a peer could place the paper on Jack's desk and Jack would not have to pass anything on right away. At home, his mother would place his plate on the table rather than handing it to him. Recently, the "safe" delay had lengthened so that Jack was having to wait an hour or more before touching "unclean" items. Consequently, he was having trouble completing schoolwork, eating meals, and helping with household chores. Jack's avoidance of touching and his compulsive handwashing also interfered with his social relationships such that Jack had stopped participating in team soccer and baseball and frequently played alone at recess rather than joining in group play on the jungle gym or basketball court. Because he could not avoid touching entirely, Jack was also requesting a bathroom pass to wash his hands at school several times a day and was spending an average of one to two hours per day washing his hands at home. Not surprisingly, Jack's hands had become raw, chapped, and sore.

Questionnaire assessment confirmed that Jack's OCD symptoms were in the severe range. He scored a 33 on the Children's Yale-Brown Obsessive Compulsive Scale (CY-BOCS) and a ten on the NIMH Global Obsessive-Compulsive Scale (March, 1998). He also reported that SUDs ratings for many normal daily activities were in the moderate to severe (5–10) range, with a SUDs level of less than three being defined by Jack as "manageable."

Jack's parents reported noticing odd touching and handwashing habits for the past three years. They denied any other behavior, mood, or thought problems. Jack's mother reported that she worries more than other people, but has never received treatment for anxiety problems. Jack's father admitted some perfectionistic tendencies and also reported that his grandfather and an uncle had some "odd habits' similar to Jack's touching and handwashing. However, he was not certain if his relatives were ever diagnosed or treated.

Case Conceptualization – Neurobehavioral

Jack's OCD can be explained well using a neurobehavioral framework. First, it is likely that Jack had a predisposition to OCD as evidenced by his family history of similar problems. His age also corresponded to the average age of onset for the disorder. The development of the symptoms Jack displayed seem to relate to an episode of illness and hospitalization approximately three-and-a-half years earlier. When Jack was eight years old, he contracted influenza and then pneumonia. His illness was severe enough for Jack to be hospitalized for three days to treat dehydration and breathing difficulties. Jack's mother reported that during the hospitalization, she worried that Jack would be exposed to additional germs, although she did not recall discussing this excessively in front of him. However, because Jack began talking about contamination and germs shortly afterwards, it is possible that Mrs. Sprague modeled the worry statements that became Jack's obsessive thoughts. Additionally, the good hygiene procedures that were modeled and encouraged in the hospital may have provided the basis for Jack's compulsive handwashing.

Thus, although OCD may be considered a neurobehavioral disorder with a genetic etiologic component, learning was presumed to play a role in the expression of Jack's symptoms. Additionally, the disorder was hypothesized to be maintained by environmental factors. For example, Jack's avoidance of situations in which he might touch contaminated items was reinforced by his failure to contract a serious illness from touching and by the decline in his uncomfortable anxiety state and obsessive thoughts. When avoidance was not possible, Jack's excessive handwashing was reinforced by these same consequences. Of note is that the reinforcement of touch avoidance and handwashing by Jack's avoidance of serious illness is more of a superstition than an actual contingent relationship; touching papers, a dinner plate, or a baseball touched by others is unlikely to lead to illness in a healthy boy. However, this does not matter – as long as the behavior is perceived to be reinforced by the absence of a negative consequence, the contingent relationship between the two events is untested and therefore still believable. This is especially true for children, who may not understand the illogical nature of the belief that avoidance or compulsive behavior will prevent the feared outcome.

Interestingly, Jack's obsessive thoughts about germs and contamination and his compulsive hand-washing did bear some logical relationship to each other – some illnesses could be passed through touch and prevented with handwashing. However, as is typical for OCD, some of Jack's obsession-compulsion connections were illogical. For example, when Jack witnessed family members touching "unclean" objects, he would become anxious and would soothe his anxiety through handwashing. Jack reported not worrying that family members would pass germs along to Jack, but simply that handwashing would "protect" the family member and would help reduce Jack's discomfort.

Treatment Strategy

Cognitive-behavioral approaches are commonly considered the treatment of choice for OCD, and because of the hypothesized relationship of Jack's OCD symptoms to modeling and to negative reinforcement of the avoidance and compulsive behavior, cognitive-behavior therapy was deemed appropriate.

Psychoeducation

As an initial step, the therapist used psychoeducation to explain OCD and its hypothesized etiology and maintenance to Jack and his parents. This was useful in helping to explain how Jack's beliefs about the connections between touching things, serious illness, and handwashing were excessive and illogical. March (1998) recommends describing the neurobehavioral disorder as similar to a bad microchip in the brain that emits incorrect or excessive messages (obsessive thoughts) that trigger compulsive behavior. This analogy was used to emphasize that the disorder was not simply a volitional behavior on Jack's part, but that it also did not have to be a major part of his life, because treatment could help to "reprogram" his brain and behavior. This psychoeducational phase of treatment also elucidated the impairment that OCD was causing in Jack's life, especially the interference in activities that Jack had previously enjoyed, like playing baseball. This was helpful in providing the motivation necessary for Jack to engage in the next phase of treatment. Finally, the therapist explained the rationale and proposed course of treatment. Specifically, the therapist explained that Jack would learn how to recognize the incorrect messages emitted by the bad microchip, and how to ignore or "talk back" to these thoughts and to "prove them wrong" so he could do the things he had been avoiding without feeling an overwhelming need to run away or wash his hands. The therapist also explained that Jack would be in charge of identifying specific thoughts and situations to be addressed in treatment and of the rate of treatment progress. Thus, an expectation of therapist- client collaboration and active client involvement was fostered.

Exposure and Response Prevention

Session One. The major focus of treatment was E/RP. Because of ethical concerns regarding flooding, graduated exposure with both imaginal and in vivo components was used. The first task was to generate an exposure stimulus hierarchy to include a variety of anxiety-provoking situations. The goal was to identify at least ten situations, one for each level of the 1–10 SUDs rating scale that Jack had learned to use during assessment. Jack's hierarchy is presented in Table 13.1. Jack generated several items for each SUDs level, which facilitated his mastery of the multiple anxiety-provoking situations in his life. Situations fell into several categories, ranging from thinking about germs or illness, to watching others touch things or people, to Jack touching things or people.

Because Jack had identified a SUDs level of three as "manageable," the situations at levels One and Two were likely to be fairly easy for Jack to enter without resorting to handwashing. These first two levels thus provided early mastery experiences for Jack and helped him to establish a "habit" of touching items or people, thinking adaptively about his ability to touch, and not handwashing. During the first treatment session, after generation of the hierarchy, Jack was encouraged to try the first exposure task. Because this involved thinking about germs and illness, it was largely an imaginal task, conducted with Jack sitting comfortably in a reclining chair with the lights dimmed and his eyes closed. To ensure exposure, Jack recited his thoughts aloud to the therapist (e.g., "I'm thinking about the little germs that float in the air or land on tables and stuff."), and the therapist added details derived from prior assessment as necessary to keep Jack focused on the task. Jack participated for approximately five minutes, during which time he reported his current SUDs level every one-to-two minutes. Jack's SUDs level began at one briefly increased to two, but stabilized at one. This task was brief and very easy for Jack, but introduced the concept of continuing an exposure activity to allow habituation and a decline in SUDs ratings to baseline, or to a manageable anxiety level. Jack's homework for the week was to repeat this exposure task daily and to record the duration of the exposure, the beginning,

Table 13.1: Jack's Exposure Hierarchy.

1 thinking about germs and illness
2 watching others touch things
       a. Mom taking mail from mailbox
       b. Dad handing a videotape to Julie
       c. Therapist looking through papers
3 watching other people touch each other
       a. Dad shaking hands with a visitor
       b. Two peers rough-housing on the playground
4 touching things after long delay (and did not witness someone else touching)
       a. taking fruit from bin at grocery store
       b. touching public telephone
5 touching things after moderate delay
       a. picking up homework assignment left on desk one hour previously
       b. putting away clothes that Mom put on bed 1 hr before
6 touching things with short delay
       a. eating off plate placed on table five minutes before
       b. picking up homework assignment just put on desk
7 taking things directly from people
       a. taking exam from teacher
       b. playing catch with classmate
8 being touched by other people – brief contact
       a. teacher patting Jack on back
       b. Mom adjusting Jack's coat
9 touching others – brief contact
       a. shaking hands with friend of Dad's
       b. punching peer in arm (playfully)
10 touching others – more intimate contact
       a. hugging family members

peak, and ending SUDs ratings, any compulsive handwashing that followed the exposure, and any problems that occurred during the task.

The response prevention component of treatment involved having Jack modify his ritual handwashing. Because the therapist wanted to encourage Jack to take charge of treatment rather than having the therapist or a parent "police" Jack's handwashing, it was considered impractical to require Jack to totally prevent handwashing. Rather, Jack and the therapist discussed ways that he could disrupt the ritual. For example, Jack agreed to refrain from washing his hands during or immediately after exposure activities. At the beginning of treatment, "immediately after" was defined as within ten minutes of the exposure activity, but over the course of treatment, this delay from exposure to handwashing was lengthened to several hours. However, it was important that Jack made sure to not schedule his exposure activities immediately before a time when he would need to wash his hands, such as before a meal or right after going to the restroom. Jack agreed to take care of restroom needs before beginning any exposure task. In addition to delaying handwashing, other response prevention activities involved changing the duration or form of the compulsive behavior. For example, Jack's normal routine was to wash for approximately ten minutes using a generous squirt of liquid hand soap every minute or so. Over the course of treatment Jack's goal was to shorten the duration of hand-washing to no more than ten-to-fifteen seconds and to use only one small squirt of soap.

Session Two. This involved: (1) reviewing homework, (2) introducing anxiety management (AMT) techniques, and (3) moving to level Two of the exposure hierarchy. Homework review involved examining Jack's notes about exposure duration and success, graphing peak SUDs levels and handwashing frequency to give Jack a visual depiction of his progress, and discussing any problems encountered during the exposure assignments. Jack completed his homework with ease each day with no hand-washing within ten minutes of the exposure task, athough he reported that it got boring by the end of the week. This increased boredom was matched by a decline in peak SUDs ratings over the course of the week. The therapist probed the content and duration of Jack's exposure tasks to make sure that the boredom and decreased anxiety could not be accounted for by avoidance of the task, but this did not seem to be the case. Instead, Jack seemed to have habituated to this mildy anxiety-producing task.

Next, the therapist described an array of AMT techniques that children often found useful in decreasing their anxiety and "talking back" to the negative thoughts from OCD, including diaphragmatic breathing, progressive muscle relaxation, and cognitive coping. Because Jack reported few physical symptoms of tension and was less enthusiastic about the "boring" progressive muscle relaxation, this technique was covered only briefly. Jack practiced tensing and relaxing his hands, arms, and legs so that he could "loosen up" before engaging in exposure tasks. The benefit of using such procedures before athletic or other performance events was also noted to facilitate generalization of the anxiety management technique to include other relevant situations. The therapist and Jack also practiced diaphragmatic ("deep") breathing and discussed when this technique might be useful. Finally, Jack generated several cognitive coping statements that he could use to "talk back" to the OCD. These included pointing out the illogic of obsessive thoughts (e.g., "I'm not gonna get sick from catching that ball; no one else does"), exaggerating or mocking the thoughts (e.g., "oh, I'm gonna croak right here! Yeah, right"), and expressing positive, self-efficacy thoughts (e.g., "I can handle this"). Jack made a written list of these thoughts, which was photocopied so he could keep copies in his bedroom, backpack, and other places where he might need reminders about cognitive coping statements. Jack was instructed to use these statements, reading them from the list if he could not remember them, when entering and participating in exposure tasks and other daily activities where his obsessive thoughts and urges to handwash were present.

The newly learned AMT techniques were then used during in-session exposure practice. Hierarchy levels Two and Three involved Jack watching other people touch things and people, so he and the therapist took a walk though the clinic and Jack practiced his breathing and cognitive coping (aloud, so the therapist could monitor) while watching the therapist touch papers, doorknobs, and so on, and shake hands with colleagues. Jack's baseline SUDs level was one, but rose to four/five where it stayed for approximately 15 minutes before decreasing to two. Of note is that this in-session exposure combined two levels of the hierarchy. This was because Jack anticipated manageable levels of anxiety for both steps, and because of a desire to move to steps involving Jack touching (versus merely observing) as soon as possible. However, Jack's between-session homework involved completing level. Two exposure tasks before moving to level Three. Jack completed homework for both levels within one week.

Sessions Three to Eleven. Subsequent treatment sessions continued review of Jack's homework, with problem-solving as necessary for difficulties encountered in compliance or successful completion, and in-session practice of AMT and E/RP for each hierarchy level. As exposure tasks began to involve situations and people who could not be present at treatment sessions (e.g., playing soccer with peers), in-session work was primarily imaginary. Jack and the therapist constructed imaginary scenes together and then Jack closed his eyes, reclined in a comfortable chair, and reported SUDs levels while the therapist described the imagined scene. As much as possible, however, in-session practice involved *in-vivo* exposure to facilitate generalization to Jack's homework assignments (usually *in-vivo*) and to identify and address potential problems in the upcoming homeworking tasks.

The total number of sessions depends on the child's rate of progress through the hierarchy. For Jack, progress was rapid through the first five hierarchy levels, taking just three sessions. However, progress slowed during later hierarchy levels. In particular, Jack became "stuck" on the level Seven homework assignment, which required taking things directly from people. He attempted the task one day, but ended the exposure task quickly, before his SUDs level declined, and spent 15 minutes washing his hands. Further examination of this level indicated that taking things from strangers or casual acquaintances was actually easier for Jack than taking items from his family, around whom the initial homework assignments had been designed. This hierarchy level was divided into two steps, with taking items from acquaintances, such as classmates, occurring in the first step, and taking items from family in the second step. Forward progress resumed and exposure tasks from hierarchy levels 7-a and 7-b were completed successfully over a two-week period.

Throughout treatment, Jack was largely compliant with exposure tasks, both in session and at home. As mentioned, progress slowed or stalled occasionally, but this was addressed successfully by dividing a hierarchy level into smaller steps and reviewing AMT techniques. Sessions were usually individual, although family members were included occasionally during exposure activities. Jack's parents were also involved in supporting his efforts and progress, by praising his session attendance and homework completion, and by providing occasional special rewards and privileges (e.g., taking him to a movie he wanted to see) when they noticed that Jack had completed a particularly challenging exposure task or for Jack's sustained efforts. Systematic contingency management, such as a behavioral contract of rewards and punishments, was not used because Jack's self-praise, increased comfort, and other natural contingencies were effective in maintaining his treatment involvement.

Termination and Follow-up

The bulk of treatment was accomplished in eleven sessions beyond the initial assessment and psychoeducation sessions. As Jack mastered the scheduled exposure tasks, he was encouraged to use his AMT skills to handle situations that arose in daily life. Over the course of treatment, he reported increasing comfort with these situations, and by the end of treatment, Jack was routinely touching objects he encountered in daily life, was not shrinking away from touch from others, and was beginning to initiate appropriate physical contact with others (e.g., slapping a peer on the back). He had recently hugged his parents for the first time in three years. His handwashing had decreased to an appropriate frequency and duration; Jack washed his hands for approximately five seconds after using the restroom three to four times per day, and occasionally before eating. He also scored in the non-clinical range on both the CY-BOCS and the NMIH Global Obsessive-Comuplsive Scale.

Two wrap-up sessions were used to address relapse prevention and termination issues. For example, the therapist explained that OCD symptoms might very well "pop up" in the future, perhaps during a stressful time in Jack's life. Jack and the therapist discussed ways he could use his AMT and E/RP skills to deal with the symptoms before they were able to "gain a foothold" in his life again. The therapist emphasized that such minor relapses were not uncommon, but could be relatively minor for people who had completed treatment successfully. At the therapist's suggestion, Jack chose to create a small notebook for his OCD coping tools, where he inserted copies of his hierarchy, his cognitive coping list, written descriptions of muscle relaxation and deep breathing that he requested from the therapist, and copies of his treatment progress charts, also requested from the therapist. Jack reported that he could use all of these notes to study in case OCD came to "test" him in the future. Finally, Jack requested a copy of the therapist's business card in case he wanted help coping with OCD in the future. Of note was that Jack had taken a very active role in his treatment by this time, and was spontaneously suggesting many of the relapse prevention strategies that the therapist would have suggested. Jack was also cautiously optimistic about his ability to cope successfully with OCD in the future. These were considered very positive prognostic signs,

A booster session was conducted one month post-termination. At that time, Jack had maintained treatment gains and was feeling increasingly comfortable with physical contact with objects and people. He reported rarely worrying about germs.

Alternative Conceptualization – Family Dysfunction

In the initial conceptualization and treatment program, Jack's OCD was considered primarily an "uncomplicated" neurobehavioral disorder, requiring little attention to other potential conceptualizations to design and implement successful treatment. Jack's family was considered to have contributed the initial genetic predisposition and to have modeled some anxious thoughts and behavior. They were also involved in supporting Jack's treatment efforts. However, family dysfunction was not considered to play a major role in Jack's illness.

An alternative conceptualization, implicating family dysfunction, might be warranted if certain family characteristics were suspected or observed during assessment or treatment. For example, Jack's mother admitted excessive worries, particularly during Jack's hospitalization, but denied exposing him to these worries. However, it can be easy to expose other people to one's fears and worries, even inadvertently, and Mrs. Sprague's worries may have been obvious to Jack and instrumental in the development and maintenance of his OCD. In particular, in addition to modeling germ-related concerns, it is possible that Mrs. Sprague also reinforced such concerns in her son by acknowledging or agreeing with his statements about possible contamination, providing reassurance when Jack expressed such concerns, and supporting his attempts to avoid contamination. As an example of Mrs. Sprague's support, both Jack and his mother noted that she would cooperate with his insistence that she place the dinner plate on the table rather than handing it directly to him. She also facilitated his handwashing by making sure that he always had a ready supply of liquid hand soap, as well as hand cream that he could use when his handwashing became painful due to chapped skin. Even if Jack's mother did not explicitly agree with the validity of his beliefs about contamination, her accommodation of his avoidance and compulsive behavior would support and maintain Jack's OCD. Other family members also acknowledged cooperating with Jack's OCD. For example, all family members avoided touching Jack or handing him things directly. The family had also taken over most tasks that involved touching "unclean" items, such as picking up the mail and opening doors. Even Jack's younger sister participated in these enabling behaviors.

Jack's family had found a reasonably comfortable routine for managing Jack's obsessive-compulsive symptoms. It is possible that in a family with a worrying mother and a perfectionistic father, a treatment-induced disruption of the status quo might be more painful and disruptive than the OCD itself. This is a particular concern given that exposure often creates distress before resulting in increased comfort and adaptive functioning. In this case, the family might sabotage treatment by missing appointments, allowing Jack to skip homework assignments, or even creating situations in which Jack could not complete E/RP tasks (e.g., keeping him too busy or ordering him to wash his "dirty" hands). In this manner, Jack's mother could avoid having to see Jack "suffer" through treatment and thus worrying herself. Likewise, Jack's father could avoid disruption, distress, and conflict in the orderly and predictable life that he preferred. This hypothesis suggests that although the OCD may be perceived by the family to be dysfunctional and distressing, the distress anticipated or encountered during treatment out-weighs any perceived benefit of treatment.

It is also possible that Jack's OCD serves some function in the Sprague family and that even smooth, successful reduction of Jack's symptoms would disrupt the status quo of the family in a negative way. For example, it is possible that Jack's avoidance of touch allowed one or both of his parents to avoid intimacy. A distancing parent would not only have a good reason to avoid contact with Jack, but with his/her spouse as well, given Jack's distress even when observing other people touch each other. Alternatively, Jack's symptoms may have diverted attention from another problem in the family, such as a poor marital relationship, or depression, or substance abuse in one parent. For example, if Jack's parents were experiencing low marital satisfaction, Jack's illness may have served to draw attention and energy to Jack, thus limiting the time that his parents had to interact as a couple.

Although the initial assessment revealed no evidence of significant family dysfuntion, there were some hints of family characteristics that might be problematic. First, as mentioned above, Jack's family engaged in several actions that enabled his compulsions and avoidance. Second, Jack reported that it was more anxiety-provoking for him to take items touched by family members than by strangers. This seems counterintuitive, given that strangers would be more likely to have unknown germs. One could hypothesize that Jack feared the increased contact and intimacy that his family might expect as they witnessed his treatment gains. Because family dysfunction is frequently somewhat hidden, it is entirely possible that problems in Jack's family would not become apparent until later in treatment. Signs of such dysfunction might include a failure to progress in treatment, sudden setbacks, or an increase in other family distress as treatment gains are made.

Alternative Treatment for Family Dysfunction

At the most basic level of family involvement, Jack's initial treatment program provided psychoeducation to Jack and his parents, and enlisted parent support of Jack's between-session exposure assignments. Although treatment progressed relatively smoothly, some of the issues discussed above could have impeded treatment progress. Such roadblocks to successful treatment could be addressed with various forms of family therapy.

As a first step in increasing family involvement, treatment might involve Jack and his mother both learning anxiety management techniques. Mrs. Sprague could use relaxation, breathing techniques, and cognitive coping to manage her worries, thus helping her to avoid modeling anxious thoughts and reinforcing Jack's obsessions. A decrease in Mrs. Sprague's anxiety could also increase her ability to resist enabling Jack's avoidance or compulsive behavior. For example, Mrs. Sprague may need to use diaphragmatic breathing and think, "Jack can do this; this is really going to help him" when Jack's homework assignments involve taking an item directly from his mother.

If straightforward anxiety reduction techniques with Jack and his mother are not successful, then the possible functions of Jack's OCD within the family should be explored. Based on the hypothesis that intimacy is threatening to family members, treatment may focus on identifying and remedying reasons for discomfort with intimacy. For example, it is possible that Jack's family members share few common interests or positive memories of shared activities, values, or feelings. Instead, their interactions may be characterized by disagreement and dissatisfaction, which in a conflict-avoidant family, could lead to disengagement and distancing. Thus, therapy may focus on increasing shared positive activities and communication.

It may be useful to view intimacy as a feared stimulus for the family and to employ graded exposure and anxiety management techniques. For example, the therapist and family could discuss shared activities that are common, easy, and enjoyable (i.e., low hierarchy items) and those that are perhaps desirable but relatively uncommon in the family (i.e., high hierarchy items). After discussion of existing family communication and interaction patterns, the therapist can identify an intimacy hierarchy and begin to assign family interaction exercises designed to foster increased comfort with intimacy. These exercises should be rewarding to involved family members. For instance, early assignments may involve Jack and Julie deciding on a birthday gift for their father (no physical contact, does not involve the potentially conflicting marital relationship) or a family evening of pizza and a video (requiring physical proximity but little sustained communication). Later assignments may involve lengthier decision-making discussions about an upcoming outing or physical intimacy, such as hugs. The therapist can model coping and efficacy thoughts by emphasizing each family member's input into family interaction decisions and their ability to interact in a satisfying manner. As the family becomes more comfortable with intimacy and feels increased control over the extent of interaction and intimacy, there should be less need for the family to use Jack's OCD to avoid intimacy. Of note is that at least some members of Jack's family may consider the lack of intimacy due to lack of desire ("I'm comfortable with the way things are") or necessity ("that's just how we do things in this family") rather than to fear. Thus, the therapist may not share this conceptualization with the family. Instead, he/she may focus on the benefits of increased closeness for understanding and supporting Jack as he recovers from his OCD, and the benefits of helping the family to adjust to Jack's new attitudes and behavior.

During therapy sessions and interaction exercises, Jack's family may display significant deficits in their ability to communicate and interact effectively. Shared activities may become sidetracked by arguments over the specifics of the activity (e.g., which movie to see), or family members may fail to listen to one another, may name-call or ridicule each other, or may simply not know what to say. In this case, training in communication and problem-solving skills (c.f., Silverman & Kurtines, 1996) may be helpful. Family members can learn to express their thoughts, opinions, and emotions with clear and direct "I state-ment" language, to listen actively, and to avoid blaming or off-topic communi-cation. They can also learn to identify problems so that they are solvable, to brainstorm and evaluate multiple solutions, and to cooperate in selecting solu-tions.

It is possible that some family impediments to successful treatment cannot be addressed fully in family therapy. For example, Jack's mother's anxiety may be severe enough to warrant individual treatment. Alternatively, marital therapy may be indicated if Mr. and Mrs. Sprague display extreme difficulty in communicating effectively or participating in shared activities. Depending on the severity of problems, these adjuncts to Jack's treatment may be conducted by his primary therapist in a few separate sessions, or may be referred to another therapist for a full course of treatment.

Conclusions

Integrated Treatment

Although Jack's was a relatively uncomplicated case of OCD that responded well to straightforward treatment, neither the conceptualization nor the treatment was simplistic. The initial conceptualization combined attention to neurological and environmental factors. The resulting treatment thus incorporates education about the hypothesized etiology and maintenance of Jack's OCD, behavioral procedures to break the links among anxiety-producing situations, obsessive thoughts, and compulsive behavior, with cognitive-behavioral anxiety management procedures to address physiologic and cognitive symptoms. However, even though family dysfunction was not hypothesized to be a major factor in Jack's OCD, family involvement was included as part of comprehensive treatment. As explored later in the chapter, more significant family problems would indicate more extensive incorporation of the family into treatment, with attention to communication training, problem solving, relationship enhancement, and so on. Given the current conceptualizations of OCD as a neurobehavioral disorder, combined with the fact that every child lives in the context of family, such integrated treatment seems optimal.

Of note is that a pharmacological approach was not included in Jack's treat-ment plan. The use of medication would have been consistent with the neurobe-havioral view of OCD, as well as appropriate based on studies of pharmacological treatment of child/adolescent OCD (March, *et al.*, 1995). However, medication alone is not optimally effective and its utility often lies in its ability to decrease symptoms to a level where clients can participate fully in psychological treatment. Because Jack was able to engage successfully in cogni-tive-behavioral treatment, medication was considered unnecessary. In cases where children are unable to accomplish even initial hierarchy exposure tasks, medica-tion would be indicated.

Summary

This chapter presents the case of Jack, a twelve year old boy with obsessive compulsive disorder involving a fear of germs and contamination and compulsive handwashing.

Jack's illness was conceptualized as a neurobehavioral disorder, with a likely genetic predisposition and a strong environmental component. Because Jack was maintaining a minimally adequate level of functioning at home and school and both he and his parents seemed motivated for treatment: outpatient cognitive-behavioral therapy was employed. Jack learned anxiety management techniques and participated in imaginal and *in vivo* graded exposure and response prevention. Therapy, including initial assessment and psychoeducation sessions, treatment sessions, wrap-up/termination, and one-month follow-up, involved 17 sessions over a six-month period. After treatment, Jack reported only occasional thoughts of germs and no excessive handwashing. In addition, Jack was not avoiding contact with objects and people and was engaging in age-appropriate academic, athletic, and social activities. Although Jack's family was appropriately supportive of Jack's treatment and improvements, it was possible that some of the family issues (e.g., mother's anxiety, family's enabling of Jack's symptoms, low intimacy) could have represented more significant family dysfunction that would impede successful treatment. Thus, an alternative view was suggested, which provided a conceptualization of the role of family dysfunction in Jack's illness and suggested family-focused treatment to address these issues. Finally, the importance of comprehensive treatment, integrating all relevant approaches, was discussed.

References

American Psychiatric Association. (1994). *Diagnostic and Statistical Manual of Mental Disorder* (4th ed.). Washington, D.C.: Author.

Flament, M. F., Whitaker, A., Rapoport, J. L., Davies, M., Berg, C. Z., et al. (1988). Obsessive compulsive disorder in adolescence: An epidemiological study. *Journal of the American Academy of Child and Adolescent Psychiatry 27*, 764–771

Lenane, M. C. (1991). Family therapy for children with obsessive-compulsive disorder. In M. T. Pato & J. Zohar (eds) *Current treatment of obsessive-compulsive disorder*. Washington DC: American Psychiatric Press. 103–113.

Leonard, H. L., Goldberger, E. L., Rapoport, J. L., et al. (1990). Childhood rituals: Normal development or obsessive-compulsive symptoms? *Journal of the American Academy of Child and Adolescent Psychiatry, 29*, 407–412.

March, J. S., Leonard, H. L., & Swedo, S. E. (1995). Obsessive-Compulsive Disorder. In J. S. March (ed.) *Anxiety Disorders in Children and Adolescents*. New York: Guilford. 251–275.

March, J. S., & Mulle, K. (1998). *OCD in Children and Adolescents*. New York: Guildford.

March, J. S., Mulle, K., Herbel, B. (1994). Behavioral psychotherapy for children and adolescents with obsessive compulsive disorder: An open trial of a new protocol-driven treatment package. *Journal of the American Academy of Child and Adolescent Psychiatry, 33,* 333–341.

Rettew, D. C., Swedo, S. E., Leonard, H. L., Lenane, M. C., & Rapoport, J. L. (1992). Obsessions and compulsions across time in 79 children and adolescents with obsessive compulsive disorder. *Journal of the American Academy of Child and Adolescent Psychiatry, 31,* 1050–1056.

Rutter, M., Tizard, J., Whitmore, K. (1970). *Education, Health, and Behavior.* London: Longmans.

Silverman, W. K., & Kurtines, W. M. (1996). *Anxiety and Phobic Disorders: A Pragmatic Approach.* New York: Plenum.

Swedo, S. E., Rapoport, J. L., Leonard, H., Lenane, M. C., & Cheslow, D. L. (1989). Obsessive compulsive disorder in children and adolescents: Clinical phenomenology of 70 consecutive cases. *Archives of General Psychiatry, 46,* 335–341.

Part V

Eating Disorders

Chapter 14

Anorexia Nervosa

Mary J. Sanders

> Her name is Deceit
> for plotting against the image of reality.
> Her name is Parasite
> for slowly sucking the blood from this innocent body.
> Her name is Religion
> for the prayers demanded of a youthful soul.
> Her name is Possession
> for claiming the ribcage meant to protect internal vitality.
> Her name is Carnivore
> for tearing and consuming the tenderness and rawness of beauty.
> Her name is Territory
> for claiming ownership without permission.
> Her name is Grief
> for burying motherhood under layers of helplessness.
> My name is Amy
> for I am enough.
>
> *Identity Crisis* by Amy Williams

Anorexia Nervosa strikes millions of women each year, usually between the ages of fourteen to 40 years. The course of illness is protracted, extremely costly, with high morbidity and mortality rates (Herzog, *et al.*, 1993). Prevalence in males is much lower but does occur. For simplicity sake, the female gender will be used, as this is the gender most affected by eating problems. The diagnosis of Anorexia Nervosa is given to someone who refuses to maintain adequate weight, weighs less than 85 percent of what is expected, has an intense fear of weight gain, and absence of menses in postmenarcheal females. If the individual has not regularly engaged in binge-eating (out-of-control overeating within a specific time period) or purging behavior, she would be considered to be "restricting type." If the person regularly engages in binge-eating, or purging (including vomiting, and misuse of laxatives or diuretics), she would be considered to be "binge-eating/purging type" (American Psychiatric Association, 1994).

Handbook of Conceptualization and Treatment of Child Psychopathology, pages 291–310.
Copyright © 2001 by Elsevier Science Ltd.
All rights of reproduction in any form reserved.
ISBN: 0-08-043362-6

Associated Clinical Features

Individuals who meet criteria for Anorexia may also meet criteria for other disorders as well, especially depressive and anxiety disorders. Some of the symptoms of depression, such as irritability, depressed mood, and insomnia, may be secondary to malnutrition and may resolve with adequate nutrition. However, others may experience depressive symptoms beyond the resolution of Anorexia Nervosa. Also associated with Anorexia Nervosa are obsessive compulsive features and other anxiety symptoms.

Developmental Considerations

Adolescence is the peak age period for the onset of eating disorders. There are several theories that address why puberty may be a factor in the development of eating problems during adolescence. One formulation involves inner conflict over developmental issues. As preadolescents move towards puberty, they may experience fears about sexuality and identity concerns. Furthermore, conflict may develop around the tasks of individuation and separation from their families. In an effort to gain a sense of mastery, adolescents may attempt to control their bodies. By halting physical development they have solved the issues of further individuation or sexual development.

Adolescents are also vulnerable to cultural messages that foster the "thin ideal." Developmentally, they are searching for acceptance from their peers and attempting to establish an identity. Thus they may begin to engage in weight loss as a means of gaining acceptance and self-esteem in their peer group. Prospective studies (Attie & Brooks-Gunn, 1989) found body dissatisfaction to be a significant predictor of eating disturbance. Pubertal changes resulting in fat accumulation placed girls at greater risk for increased body dissatisfaction and increased eating disturbance. Thompson, *et al.* (1995) found that level of obesity and teasing history were significantly related to body image and eating disturbance. Obesity did not have a unique impact on body image, but was mediated by reported teasing history. Both teasing and negative body image may lead to increased restrictive eating. Bulimic symptoms sometimes follow restrictive eating.

Multifactoral Model of Anorexia Nervosa

Figure 1 presents a pictorial view of the factors that may influence the child and Anorexia Nervosa as a problem. Both sociocultural and genetic influences have an impact on families. The specifics regarding genetic influence on eating problems is not known, but there is evidence of a higher prevalence of subclinical eating disorders, major depression, and obsessive personality traits in first degree relatives of individuals who develop Anorexia Nervosa (Lilenfeld, *et al.*, 1998). Furthermore, there may be genetic transmission of body type, timing for pubertal changes,

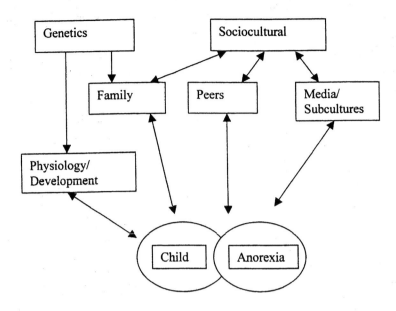

Figure 14.1: Multifactoral Model of Anorexia Nervosa.

physiology, and perhaps, temperament, all of which may influence the occurrence and maintenance of eating issues. The double-ended arrow indicates that Anorexia also affects the child's physiology and development via malnutrition and weight loss.

The family is a mediator of culture. The cultural ideal of "thinness" influences all members of the family. In a recent study, we asked children (third through sixth graders) who they heard talk about dieting and food issues. Seventy percent identified family members as the source of their information regarding dieting (Schur, *et al.*, 2000). Likewise, these messages may be embedded in the culture, thus influencing peers. As mentioned earlier, the perception of having been "teased" by peers has been associated with eating problems in individuals. Certainly in Western culture the media promote the message that "thin is in." This ideal is also promoted in certain subcultures of which children may be members, such as gymnastics, figure skating, and dance. Again the double-ended arrow indicates a hope that the recognition of serious eating issues in children may have some effect on media messages. The realization that Anorexia Nervosa has led to the death of some child athletes (Ryan, 1995) will hopefully have some effect on the promotion of thinness in some performance sports as well.

The interlocking circles of the child and Anorexia represent the child's experience of being "taken over" by the Anorexia. In this model the Anorexia is seen as separate from the child and the child is encouraged to recognize that she is "more" than the Anorexia. Initially the child may have difficulty differentiating her own thoughts from those of Anorexia. As she is able to separate herself somewhat from the effect of Anorexia, she becomes more aware of the ways in which Anorexia "tells" her what to do and invites her to feel anxious if she does not follow the directives of Anorexia, such as increased dieting and exercise. The goal of treatment is to decrease the overlap of these two circles or to help the child regain her life outside of the influence of Anorexia.

Assessment

This model suggests that the occurrence of Anorexia is multi-determined and thus requires a comprehensive approach to assessment and treatment. In the Stanford Child Psychiatry Program, there is a multidisciplinary team consisting of Adolescent Medicine, Nursing, Nutrition, and Psychological services that sees each child and family.

Medical Assessment

The patient is initially seen medically and has her heart rate and blood pressure taken to assess vital signs. If she is unstable or at imminent risk of becoming unstable due to food refusal, she would then be admitted to an inpatient treatment facility. One of the indications for instability is a weight less than 75 percent of Ideal Body Weight (IBW) (Sanders, *et al.*, 1998). If she is stable, she would continue to be followed on an outpatient basis.

Nutritional/Weight Assessment

The Nutritionist assesses the patient's weight and body fat. A diet and exercise history is also taken. The patient is informed about her current percentage of ideal body weight and current body fat percentage. If she has lost her menses, she is also informed of the weight she will probably need to attain in order to regain her menses as well as her ideal weight.

Psychological Assessment

A Psychologist, Psychiatrist, or Social Worker interviews the patient and asks about her desires regarding her health. Many times patients struggling with Anorexia do not wish to gain weight despite the information they receive about the need to do so. Even if they are informed that they have lost bone density due to malnutrition, the desire to maintain a low body weight is more powerful than the fear of continued bone loss. Thus, the challenge for the treatment team is how to help the patient regain and maintain health when this may not be a primary motivation for the patient.

Medical/Nutritional Treatment

The initial focus of any treatment of Anorexia must be restoration of health through weight gain. There is a strong indication that the act of dieting alone affects behavior and cognition which tends to promote a further desire for dieting and fear of weight gain. Counteracting the effects of malnutrition is extremely important in preventing permanent physical damage, such as bone loss and stunted growth (Sanders, *et al.*, 1998). Furthermore, malnutrition is associated with decreased cognitive ability and depression, which reduces the child's ability to fight the negative effects of the eating disorder.

Thus, obtaining adequate nutrition appears to be one of the most important treatment goals. The treatment team must present the patient with information regarding nutrition and the amount of weight gain necessary. It is important for the patient and the family to have information regarding the short- and long-term effects of decreased weight on health and development. Unfortunately this information alone does not usually lead to behavioral change, thus indicating the need for psychological treatment.

Treatment Settings

Optimally, children and their families struggling with Anorexia should have access to a flexible continuum of care which offers inpatient, day treatment, and outpatient care in order to meet the child's changing needs over time. The Stanford treatment program is outlined below.

Hospital treatment. Frequently, patients struggling with Anorexia may have to be hospitalized in order to regain medical stability. When this occurs, patients are placed on a protocol in which they are slowly refed, usually with a complete liquid nutrition that is more easily digested, and they are medically monitored as they regain stability. Sometimes this requires medical bedrest until they are stable enough to stand up without falling due to blood pressure changes. Patients are placed on a behavioral program in which their calories are observed and they are closely monitored. Monitoring by the hospital staff decreases as patients are able to take on more responsibility for their health. The weight gain that occurs in the hospital is often emotionally difficult for the patient. Thus, patients also receive support through individual, family, and group therapies. Many times patients have stated that they experience less anxiety with food intake in the hospital because they "know they have to eat." They have identified that it is more difficult for them to continue to eat outside the hospital because no one is monitoring their calories on an outpatient basis.

Partial Day Treatment. If a patient is not medically unstable or does not require a hospital setting but could benefit from a more intensive outpatient setting, admission to our partial day hospital treatment may be recommended. The patient comes in mornings, obtains weights and vital signs, and takes in daily meals on site. This program includes similar treatment groups, individual and family therapy, and school as is provided in inpatient settings. However, the patients go home at the end of the day and have a chance to integrate normal routines, such as eating dinner with their family and seeing friends. If they have difficulty with the program and become unstable, they may be hospitalized.

Outpatient Treatment. This may include individual, family and group therapies as well as medical check-ins. In the Stanford program, the children may attend twice weekly medical clinic visits, where they have their weight and medical vital signs checked. They also consult with a Nutritionist in order to continue progress with weight gain or maintenance. As they progress, the patients attend the clinic less often.

Psychological Treatments

Any psychological treatment of Anorexia Nervosa must have the restoration of health as an initial and ongoing focus. There are no identified effective treatment methods other than refeeding during the initial acute stages of the illness (Walsh & Devlin, 1998). The addition of medications to psychological treatments has not been found to be especially helpful. Family therapy has been found to be more effective than individual therapy with patients with early onset Anorexia (less than or equal to 18 years old) compared with older patients. Older patients (older than 18 years old) seem to benefit more from individual therapy. For those with early onset and whose illness lasted more than three years, treatment outcomes are poor regardless of treatment modality (Eisler, *et al.*, 1997).

Psychological therapists have differed in their ideas about underlying etiology of eating disorders. This affects the focus of intervention. A case study will be presented followed by two treatment approaches. First will be the Narrative/Constructive approach, which focuses its intervention on the co-construction of meaning with the acknowledgment of the importance of cultural beliefs, especially as they are mediated within families (Freedman & Combs, 1996). The second approach will be the Cognitive-Behavioral approach, which emphasizes the importance of irrational thoughts and the patient's perceived need for self-control as the focus of intervention.

Case Illustration

Amanda is a Caucasian female who presented at age fourteen with a two-year history of weight loss. She had been amenorrheic since having her first menses at age thirteen. Her diet consisted of very low fat foods and she was eating a very limited variety of foods. She denied diuretics and laxative use. She had attempted to purge once but felt unable to do so. Her exercise consisted of walking and numerous sit-ups daily. Amanda had lost weight to 75 percent of her IBW upon admission to the hospital. Her bone density test revealed that she had suffered significant bone loss; she also had very dry skin and brittle hair.

Assessment Findings

Medically, Amanda's temperature upon admission was 35.8 C, and she was orthostatic. Physical examination revealed a very cachectic girl. Tanner staging was IV for breasts and pubic hair. The physical examination was otherwise unremarkable.

Psychiatrically, on admission Amanda appeared appropriately dressed and groomed. She was quite tearful and endorsed depressive symptoms. Amanda was oriented and her thoughts were linear and goal-directed. Cognitively, she was intact, but appeared a bit slowed in her responses. She denied suicidal or homicidal ideation.

Inpatient Medical Treatment

Amanda was admitted 15 times to the inpatient service due to medical instability over an eight-year period. She spent more than 500 days inpatient over this time period. She was also admitted once to the Partial Day Hospital Program for a month following her last hospitalization. Amanda was hospitalized each time due to low body weight and medical instability. She was placed on the clinic's regular protocol that includes strict medical bed rest with continuous cardiac monitoring until she had regained vital sign stability for 24 hours. A complete liquid food supplement was given, with close observation by staff during feeds. Initial caloric intake was set at a level no greater than 500 calories more than what Amanda had been eating before her admission. Calories were increased by increments of 100–200 calories/day, whenever daily weight gain fell below 0.2 kg. A fluid maximum close to maintenance requirements was established, to avoid fluid overload. When her vital signs eventually stabilized and she reached 75 percent of ideal body weight, she was gradually advanced to a solid food diet, increasing solid food intake by 25 percent a day while decreasing the liquid supplement to maintain equivalent calories. Her initial hospitalization discharge criteria were to attain 75 percent of Ideal Body Weight, advance to solid food, and gain 0.2kg for two consecutive days. Subsequent admissions included increased requirements for obtaining "Exercise Weight," or a weight in which it would be safe for her to exercise without becoming unstable. Later admissions also included the criteria that she be able to plan her meals and eat unobserved while being able to maintain weight gain for a specified amount of time. Psychiatrically, Amanda received daily individual therapy and group therapies. She received weekly family therapy and attended the hospital school.

Partial Day Treatment

Amanda attended the Partial Day Program (PHP) following inpatient treatment as a means of returning to her normal routine. After her last hospitalization she utilized the PHP to work toward managing her caloric intake while reintroducing her sport back into her life.

Outpatient Medical Treatment

Amanda attended an outpatient Eating Disorder Clinic where her weight and vitals signs were monitored and she received medical and nutritional information at least once a week when she was out of the hospital. She attended individual and family therapy weekly when outpatient as well.

Narrative Approach: Treatment of Anorexia

Narrative/Constructivist approaches have emerged from postmodern and feminist influences. This approach is based on the idea that reality is socially constructed and individuals develop "stories" or understandings of themselves within the context of family and culture. Thus, the importance of messages in the culture, especially as they are mediated through families, may be very influential on the adolescent's behavior.

The Narrative model recognizes the importance of cultural messages to young women, which invite them to "disappear" and to not have their own voice. Thus, Anorexia may provide a sense of self to these young women. By abiding by the cultural ideal that it is important to be thin and to place their needs second to others, they may begin to diet. They tend to receive support for healthy eating and for weight loss from others, which may boost their self-esteem. However, in their attempt to win approval, gain control, and carve out a sense of self, they find themselves eventually opposing those from whom they may have originally sought approval. Thus their emerging identity as an "anorexic" may create a sense of self in opposition to the approval of others as well as give them a sense of structure.

Consulting the Adolescent Regarding her Story

An important premise of the Narrative model is that the child is the "expert" regarding her experience, and she alone may best articulate that experience. The therapist's job is to encourage this expression by being empathic and curious. As noted above, it may be a new experience for the adolescent to tune into her emotional life and explore her desires as well as her experience of Anorexia. Through the exploration of the child's experience, this bolsters a sense of self, counters the cultural idea that children are not knowledgeable, helps them explore how they experience the effects of Anorexia, and allows them to feel "heard" and acknowledged by the therapist.

Consulting the Family Regarding their Story

Just as it is important to obtain the adolescent's story regarding her experience, it is also important to obtain the family's experience of the effects of Anorexia on them and their relationship with the child. Families may have interactional styles that may contribute to the problem and/or they may develop interactional styles as a result of the problem. Frequently, families that have children struggling with Anorexia tend to engage in self-blame. Families sometimes receive cultural messages that if their children have a problem, they may be held responsible for poor parenting. As a result of these cultural messages, as well as their fears regarding their children's health, parents may find themselves engaging in self-blame that invites power struggles with their children to eat. The pressure the parents feel to protect and nurture their child tends to be at odds with the pressure Anorexia puts on the child to restrict or purge.

By eliciting the family's story, the members may also "be heard" and explore ways in which they would like to interact with each other. The family also provides an important "audience" to the child's story of herself and her struggle with Anorexia. Through these conversations, the child and family begin to develop an understanding of how Anorexia is "separate" from the child. They also may find that they are then able to unite in their struggle to fight the negative effects of this problem without being in conflict with the child herself.

Separating Self from the Problem

As adolescents explore their experience of self and their experience of Anorexia, we begin to talk about the Anorexia as a separate entity. By the time the girls come to treatment, they tend to have incorporated their experience of Anorexia as totalizing. For simplicity sake, reference will be made to the inner dialogue adolescents experience that tells them to restrict their diet and over exercise as the voice of Anorexia. In order to help the adolescents separate from the problem and find their own voice, they are encouraged to engage in externalizing conversations about the Anorexia. For example, they are asked about their experience and they will begin (using their words) to name the problem and ask about the influence of the problem on their lives. Then an exploration begins of how they may be separate from and "more" than merely the voice of Anorexia. The poem introducing this chapter was written by a young woman regarding her externalized experience of Anorexia.

Often the girls are quite hesitant about separating from the voice of Anorexia because they feel that if they do, they will no longer be "safe." Often too, patients are very "protective" of their eating disorder and feel that the treatment team is attempting to take away their only friend. They may also feel afraid of "crossing" the "voice" of Anorexia despite its tyranny and state they feel "safer" abiding by its rules. Through externalization of the Anorexia and exploring the negative and positive effects of the Anorexia on their lives, the struggle moves to one between the individual and the problem, rather than between the individual and the treatment team.

Exploring the Positive and Negative Effects of the Problem

As adolescents begin to separate themselves from the Anorexia, exploration begins of the positive as well as the negative effects of the problem on their lives. The girls are able to describe many positive effects, such as feeling powerful and having increased self-esteem. Initially it tends to be more difficult to identify negative effects. However, as they explore these questions they frequently state that the Anorexia does take up more time than they would like, gets in the way of relationships with others, pulls them from their activities and sports, and takes them out of the life they would like to have.

Exploring the Medical Effects of Anorexia

The adolescent needs to be informed about the physical effects of Anorexia on her health and development. The medical team and therapists must provide the information regarding the possibility of bone loss leading to higher risk of fracture, delayed growth, syncope due to unstable vital signs, hair loss, dry skin, brittle hair, growth of unwanted body hair (lanugo), and possibility of death. This information is given, not as a scare tactic, but to inform the adolescent regarding the known negative effects that dietary restriction has on her body.

"Unique Outcomes" and Alternative Stories

When adolescents have been able to identify the negative effects of the problem and begin to fight these negative effects, it is helpful to explore with them the times they have been able to do this. "Unique outcomes" is a term used to describe those situations in which an individual manages to escape the dominant story. For example, an adolescent may report that she is able to feel positive about weight gain when that has not been true for her in the past, or she has been able to go out to dinner with a friend, etc. Thus, these are times in which the adolescent has been able to fight the negative effects of Anorexia and also provides evidence of an alternative story of health.

Strategies for Reclaiming Lives and Becoming more Visible

When these unique outcomes are noted, the adolescent is asked how she was able to fight the effects of the eating disorder and take back more of her life. The strategies she found helpful in order to work toward increasing the alternative story of health are then explored. Initially the strategies employed may be utilizing thoughts such as, "If I don't eat, I will have to come back to the hospital." Sometimes the girls have asked others to encourage them to eat and some have continued to utilize the nutritional plan they began in the hospital. Through implementation of these strategies, the adolescents begin to discover their "selves" as separate from the problem and begin to make more of an appearance in their own lives.

Narrative Treatment of Amanda

Conceptually, Amanda reported feeling better about herself only if she was losing weight. Initially, she reported feeling that she and the Anorexia "were one" and that there were no aspects to her other than her experience of Anorexia. She indicated that the Anorexia was a totalizing experience and that this was the dominant story of who she was in her life. The therapy focused on encouraging Amanda to separate herself from the Anorexia and recognize that she was "more" than just Anorexia. Thus, the therapy worked to separate the overlapping circles of the Anorexia and her experience of herself.

Consulting the Adolescent Regarding her Story. Amanda explored and described her experience of the Anorexia through discussion in her therapies and through art and written work as well. She described the Anorexia as being like a nagging voice that was never satisfied. The Anorexia had numerous rules for her to follow and ways to measure if she were "safe" or not, depending on her weight and body fat content.

Consulting the Family Regarding Their Story. Amanda's family consisted of a father, mother, and younger sister. The family sessions focused on their experience of the Anorexia and its effect on their lives. They discussed their concern that Anorexia had taken Amanda out of her life at school and away from the family as she was hospitalized frequently. The younger sister expressed anger at having to come to therapy, although she had also lost weight and was treated in another facility. The two sisters also acknowledged their competition with each other and the desire to be the best at having Anorexia.

Separating Self from the Problem. Initially Amanda adamantly denied that she was separate from the Anorexia, feeling that they were one and the same. However, as she was able to see that she was separate from the Anorexia, she identified feeling caught in the middle between Anorexia and the treatment team. She described the desire to hold onto the problem and fight the treatment team's attempts to "take" it from her. Despite Amanda's desire to get out of the hospital and return to school and dance, she felt quite unable to fight the Anorexia. She frequently engaged in practices to make certain that she did not take in food, such as hiding uneaten food from the staff or drinking large quantities of water to appear as if she had gained weight without raising her calories.

Exploring the Positive and Negative Effects of the Problem. It was much easier for Amanda to identify the positive effects of Anorexia on her life. She felt that the imposed structure of Anorexia (i.e., the rules regarding eating and exercise) made her feel that she was in control of her life and thus empowered. Over time, Amanda could identify what Anorexia had taken from her, including her high school experience, friends, and something she valued very highly, her dance. As she was able to identify the negative effects of the Anorexia, she was more able to see that she was separate from it and attempt to fight the negative effects on her life.

Exploring the Medical Effects of Anorexia. Amanda was able to see that the medical effects of the Anorexia were negative. She did not like the loss of her hair and the fact that both her hair and skin became dry. She had previously had very beautiful long hair, which had become brittle and dull due to her malnutrition. Even more concerning to Amanda was her significant bone loss. This was especially concerning to her as it affected her ability to engage in high impact exercise due to fear of fractures. This impeded her ability to re-enter her dance. However, as she became weight rehabilitated, she was able to regain some bone density and thus able to take dance back in her life.

Unique Outcomes and Alternative Stories. As Amanda was able to separate herself from the Anorexia and begin to fight its negative effects on her life, she began to recognize that there was an alternative story about her life, one which did not include Anorexia. Initially, she was able to focus on craft projects and made some beautiful pottery that she sold at craft fairs. She was also able to go to college and make a few friends. After college, Amanda was able to move out on her own. She made some very close friends, dated, and continued to dance. Each new step toward her life was seen as unique and contributed to the alternative story of health in her life. The therapist and Amanda explored how she was able to take each step, whether it was a positive or negative step, and how she wanted to continue to make further steps toward health.

Strategies for Reclaiming Lives and Becoming more Visible. As Amanda explored her progress toward health the alternative story of becoming more visible in her life was acknowledged. Just as Anorexia had attempted to remove her from her life, she was attempting to make a comeback, especially in her desire to make friends and to dance. As she took each step, the strategies she used were explored. Initially, as she was able to approach a friend, she realized that the Anorexia attempted to keep her from feeling worthy of friendship. She was able to engage in some cognitive statements acknowledging her desire to make friends and not allow the Anorexia to take that from her. As she gained success with friends and could see that they enjoyed her and did not focus on any physical features, she was able to (somewhat) lessen her own focus on her physical features

Cognitive-behavioral Therapy: Treatment of Anorexia

Cognitive-behavioral therapy (CBT) has been found to be useful in the treatment of Bulimia Nervosa. However, although more helpful than drug therapies alone, CBT has not been found to be superior to other forms of psychotherapy in the treatment of Anorexia Nervosa (Wilson & Fairburn, 1993).

Fairburn, *et al.* (1999) have recently proposed a new cognitive behavioral theory that focuses on the patient's need for control of eating behavior. They propose a model which suggests that the individual has long-standing low self-esteem, a sense of ineffectiveness, perfectionism, and a strong need for self-control. The individual thus engages in dieting behavior and finds it to be very rewarding, especially in regard to increased feelings of self-control. It is also suggested that the controlled eating of the individual has a strong effect on the family in which there is likely to be a pre-existing dysfunctional relationship. It is further suggested that the occurrence of Anorexia in puberty may be a means of putting puberty "on hold," which is another means of controlling what may feel out of control. Finally, this theory recognizes the importance of the Western societal message that thinness and control are valued in the culture. The authors propose that the successful control of eating becomes highly rewarding and may be especially resistant to change.

Originally the goal of CBT was to help the patient overcome her dysfunctional thinking around body image and to replace restrictive dieting with healthy eating. As is true for most models of treatment on Anorexia, the psychological treatments are integrated with medical monitoring and the involvement of the family with younger (under 20 years of age) patients.

The new CBT maintenance model has self-control as the main focus of treatment. Within this model the use of eating as an indicator of self-control and self-worth, the frequent weight checks, disturbed eating, and low weights are addressed. Formerly, CBT also addressed low self-esteem, interpersonal functioning, family issues, and difficulty with emotional expression. However, in the maintenance CBT model, it is suggested that these latter issues be addressed only if they present obstacles to change. In both models, however, the family is involved with younger patients regarding the issues of self-control.

The patient's need for self-control must be redirected and moderated, which may be done both directly and indirectly by encouraging other activities and demonstrating that controlled eating does not provide what they are really seeking. This need for self-control is cognitively restructured and integrated into all stages of treatment as they progress with weight restoration.

Garner, *et al.* (1997) offer a slightly different, more comprehensive CBT approach. They suggest that therapy progresses in stages or phases.

Phase One:

Initially the therapist builds trust and creates an environment of acceptance for the patient. Depending on the patient's medical needs, she may require hospitalization or ongoing medical monitoring. The therapist provides education aimed at supplying corrective information and changing beliefs in accordance with the motivational state of the patient. Patients are encouraged to increase intake and implement self-monitoring of weight, intake, and compensatory behavior (e.g., exercise, use of diuretics, laxatives, and purging). As the patient goes through this process, dysfunctional cognitions begin to emerge.

Increasing Cognitive Dissonance. As the patient states her dysfunctional thoughts, the therapist attempts to create cognitive dissonance by helping her look at how the disorder is not consistent with higher-order goals, such as having a successful life. Some common dysfunctional beliefs include a desire to get better without having to gain weight, fear of loss of control, fear of change of shape, and unusual food beliefs (e.g., one gram of fat in food will turn into one gram of body fat).

Increasing Motivation. The therapist must be aware of the level of motivation the patient has to change her behavior, and recognize that motivation will fluctuate over time. The therapist must accept the patient's beliefs as valid to her and help her analyze the pros and cons regarding the maintenance of her disorder. The therapist further helps her recognize that maintaining her disorder is likely to interfere with her long-range life goals.

Determining Family Involvement. If the patient is living with her family, there should be some family involvement in the assessment and therapy. Parents should be educated that while family interactions may contribute to the patient's disorder, there is no empirical support for the idea that parents cause eating disorders.

Phase Two

During the second phase of treatment there is greater emphasis on expanding the issues from merely weight to include the meaning of "thinness" in the lives of these patients. The goal is to find how maintaining the disorder is functional to the patient and learn more adaptive means of meeting those needs. The issues addressed by Garner, *et al.* (1997) in Phase two may be similar to those that Fairburn and colleagues (1999) see as most important, especially the issue of self-control.

Identifying Dysfunctional Thoughts and Patterns. The therapist helps the patients notice that they have personal frames of reference from which they organize data. For those patients suffering from Anorexia Nervosa, the frame of reference for self-evaluation becomes one of weight. These personal schemas tend to be resistant to change. The goal of the therapy is not to remove these schemas but to create alternative ones.

Cognitive Restructuring. Once dysfunctional thoughts are identified, patient is encouraged to evaluate and challenge these beliefs with a more realistic framework. Frequently the patient engages in dichotomous reasoning and holds beliefs such that certain foods are "good" or "bad" or that if they allow themselves to eat a "bad" food that all self-control will be lost. Anxiety and fear are underlying emotions that are avoided by engaging in weight loss practices. The therapist must help the patient challenge her dysfunctional beliefs and engage in healthy behavior while struggling with this underlying anxiety.

Modifying Self-concept. Decreased self-esteem and the idea that self-worth is based on body shape are important contributors to the maintenance of Anorexia Nervosa. In helping the patient to modify these beliefs the therapist may first encourage the patient to recognize how much time she takes in self-evaluation. The basis for negative self-evaluation is then explored. Patients are often able to see that they do not make negative evaluations of others based on body shape or accomplishments. However, it is difficult for them to allow themselves to accept self-worth that does not contain these variables.

Phase Three

This phase emphasizes consolidating gains and preventing relapse. This includes reviewing progress and recognizing the need to continue to keep in practice strategies which promote health. It is important to be aware of areas of vulnerability and specific warning signs or triggers for possible relapse. Plans should be made regarding when it would be helpful to return to treatment if future problems arise. This should be promoted as a positive move and not one that implies failure.

Cognitive-behavioral Treatment of Amanda

Conceptually, Amanda reported feeling very anxious when not dieting. She identified the structure that her cognitions provided as allowing her to feel "safe" and in control. If she challenged these cognitions and allowed herself to eat she felt that she was being weak and even sinful. Within the hospital setting, Amanda utilized the cognition, "I have to eat here," which allowed her to participate in the program without feeling guilty. Amanda was able to recognize that by restricting her caloric intake she was frequently becoming unstable, hospitalized, and unable to participate in her dance.

Phase One

Increasing Cognitive Dissonance. The therapist explored with Amanda the cognitions which led her to feel "safe." She was able to articulate that her goal to become thin (even to become the "thinnest") was not consistent with her desire to engage in her dance. However, she also acknowledged that this goal and the "safety" she felt when she dieted were far stronger than the negative medical and emotional consequences of discontinuing the dieting.

Increasing Motivation. Amanda's initial motivation to achieve health was minimal. She was able to list the pros and cons of dieting. Since she denied the importance to her of medical consequences and admitted to not wanting to go to school or make friends outside the hospital, her only negative consequence of dieting was missing out on her dance. The positives of feeling in control and "safe" far outweighed any negative consequences.

The therapist worked toward helping Amanda move toward the one aspect of her life that she listed as a "con" of the Anorexia, that of losing her dance. The therapy focused on ways in which to regain this part of her life while continuing to feel in control.

Determining Family Involvement. As is usual for families who have a member struggling with Anorexia, they often became quite frustrated with Amanda. They tended to alternate between anger and withdrawal due to their levels of frustration and fear that she would not survive. In the family sessions, Amanda was able to articulate her cognitions regarding her need to be thin or else feel that she was worthless. Her family attempted to reassure her that these cognitions were unfounded in reality; however, they continued to feel frustrated when Amanda was unable to "believe" them. Over time Amanda was able to see that her family was supportive of her because they continued to nurture and encourage her despite her difficulty in letting them do so.

Phase Two

Identifying Dysfunctional Thoughts and Patterns. Amanda was able to identify the dysfunctional thought she had that, "I am worthless unless I weigh 60 pounds." If she discovered that she had gained weight (no matter how slight), her mood would change dramatically from being happy and pleasant to extremely sad, angry, and sometimes suicidal. She would then do anything she could to lose weight and felt she needed to do so in order to survive. It was extremely difficult for Amanda to recognize that she had worth beyond her body image.

Cognitive Restructuring. Once Amanda's dysfunctional thoughts and patterns were identified and the therapist had built a trusting and caring relationship with her, Amanda could begin to challenge these beliefs. She was able to see that the other girls in the inpatient unit, the staff, her therapist, and her family did value her irrespective of her body size. With the support of the staff and therapist, she was able to cooperate with the behavioral program on the inpatient unit and thus eat and gain weight. However, once outside the support of this setting, it was difficult for Amanda to maintain her weight. She required several hospitalizations to be able to reach a safe weight and maintain it over time.

Modifying Self-concept. Amanda was able to see that she judged herself more harshly than she did others. However she was also able to admit that she did judge others on the basis of body image, contributing to her feelings of negative self-worth, as she felt that she "shouldn't" do this. Amanda was also able to see that she spent an inordinate amount of time engaging in negative self-evaluation. Gradually, she was able to allow herself to notice the positive features that others saw in her.

Phase Five

Amanda has been weight rehabilitated for several years and is functioning quite well in her life. She lives independently, holds a full-time job, has many friends, and still enjoys her dance. Despite her progress however, she continues to experience feelings of negative self-worth and continues to judge herself largely by body image. She is able to recognize the progress she has made over the years and has identified useful strategies to battle these thoughts. For example, she continues to try to "see herself" through the eyes of friends when she feels especially self-loathing. She has also come to appreciate the strength of her body through her dance. Amanda has identified that while she would like to lose weight, this is a dangerous trigger which could lead to too much weight loss. Her desire to maintain her current independent life and her dance help her to remain healthy.

Comparison Between Narrative and CBT

There are many similarities between these two approaches. Each recognizes how tenacious Anorexia is in the lives of girls and their families and the importance of a swift restoration of health through behavioral change. Perhaps globally the difference between the two approaches is that the Narrative focuses on the adolescent's experience within the context of family and culture, while CBT focuses more exclusively on what appears to be the adolescent's need to feel in control. Additional similarities and points of divergence are also present.

Role of the Therapist

In both approaches, the relationship between patient and therapist is extremely important. The patient must trust and feel that the therapist cares about her progress. In the Narrative approach, the therapist is a collaborator with the patient in her exploration of her experience and provides an "audience" to her story. In both models the therapist helps the patient pay attention to personal data. In the Narrative model, the therapist encourages the patient to explore how the problem is situated in her family and cultural experience and how it may be affecting her life. The CBT therapist provides corrective information to the patient with the goal of changing her beliefs and fears as they relate to her behavior.

Definition of the Problem

The Narrative model emphasizes a non-pathologizing approach in which the adolescent is recognized as the expert. The problem (Anorexia) is seen as separate from the child, with the goal of therapy to increase this separation, recognizing that the child is not the problem. Within the Narrative model, the adolescent is asked to describe her individual experience of Anorexia and define for herself how it is a problem in her life. The CBT approach defines the problem as a dysfunctional or irrational cognition which fulfills the patient's need for self-control.

Role of the Family

Both approaches recognize that family members may be at risk of blaming themselves for the problem. Within the Narrative approach, the therapist asks family members to describe their experience of the problem, encourages them to engage in externalizing conversations about the problem, recognizing that the "problem is to blame" and not the child or the parents. They are encouraged to explore how the problem has affected them and to work toward decreasing the negative effects of the problem on their lives and their relationships with each other. In the more recent CBT maintenance model, Fairburn and colleagues (1999) suggest that family issues should be addressed only as they present an obstacle to the desired behavioral change of the adolescent.

Role of Cultural Influence

Both models recognize the importance of cultural messages. The Narrative has a very strong emphasis on the exploration of the child's experience in the context of her family and culture. This model highlights the idea that the adolescent can take back power in her life and question these cultural messages. The CBT model encourages the patient to explore how cultural messages have contributed to her belief system, especially in regard to the need to be in control.

Goals of Therapy

Certainly both models have the goal of helping the adolescent achieve and maintain health. Perhaps a secondary goal of the Narrative model is to help the adolescent recognize an alternative story of power in which she is competent and instrumental in bringing about change in her life.

Treatment Outcome Research

Due to the seriousness of the medical complications which arise as a consequence of decreased weight, treatment usually focuses initially on weight restoration, followed by individual and family intervention. No treatment, however, has been demonstrated to promote long-term recovery in all patients. Although there are many similarities in the course of the illness, individuals and families who suffer from Anorexia are quite diverse. It may be that there are components or guidelines for treatment that may be generally useful, but specific interventions need to vary in accordance with the needs and strengths of each family.

A ten to 15 year follow-up study of patients struggling with Anorexia Nervosa indicates that 14 percent did not recover 10 percent had a partial recovery and 75 percent had a full recovery within 80 months. Those patients who recovered fully did not do so before 70 months. Factors associated with poor prognosis were low initial weights and longer duration of these low weights, presence of bulimic symptoms such as binge/purge cycles and laxative abuse, and poor family relationships (Strober, *et al.*, 1997).

Summary

Anorexia Nervosa affects approximately one percent of females and is an extremely protracted and deadly disorder. This chapter presents a multifactorial model that indicates the need for diverse treatments that address biological, intrapsychic, familial, and cultural factors. Of utmost importance is the timely restoration of health. The central difficulty in the treatment of Anorexia is that of motivating adolescents to decrease their drive for thinness and increase their motivation to attain health, an extremely difficult proposition.

Psychological therapists have differed in their ideas about the underlying etiology of the eating disorder that directs the focus of intervention. Two treatment approaches are described: (1) the Narrative/Constructive approach, which focuses its intervention on the co-construction of meaning, with acknowledgment of the importance of cultural beliefs, especially as they are mediated within families, and (2) the Cognitive-Behavioral approach, which emphasizes the importance of irrational thoughts and the patient's perceived need for self-control as the focus of intervention. A case is presented for utilizing these two approaches. The goal of treatment for both of them is behavioral change and helping the adolescent regain her life outside the influence of Anorexia.

References

American Psychiatric Association. (1994). *Diagnostic and Statistical Manual of Mental Disorder.* (4th ed.). Washington, DC: Author.

Attie, I., & Brooks-Gunn, J. (1989). Development of eating problems in adolescent girls: A longitudinal study. *Developmental Psychology, 25(1),* 70–79.

Eisler, I., Dare, C., Russell, G. F., Szmukler, G., le Grange, D., *et al.* (1997). Family and individual therapy in anorexia nervosa: A 5-year follow-up. *Archives of General Psychiatry, 54,* 1025–1030.

Fairburn, C. G., Shafran, R., & Cooper, Z. (1999). A cognitive behavioral theory of Anorexia Nervosa. *Behavior Research and Therapy, 37(1),* 1–13.

Fairburn, C. G., Welch, S. L., Doll, H. A., Davies, B. A., & O'Connor, W. E. (1997). Risk factors for Bulimia Nervosa. *Archives of General Psychiatry, 54,* 509–517.

Freedman, J. & Combs, G. (1996). *Narrative Therapy.* New York: W. W. Norton.

Garner, J. M., Vitousek, K. M., & Pike, K. M. (1997). Cognitive-behavioral therapy for anorexia nervosa. In D. M. Garner and P. E. Garfinkel (eds) *Handbook of Treatment for Eating Disorders, (2nd Ed.).* New York: The Guilford Press.

Herzog, D. B., Sacks, N. R., Keller, M. B., Lavori, P. W., von Ranson, K. B., *et al.* (1993). Patterns and predictors of recovery in Anorexia Nervosa and Bulimia Nervosa. *Journal of the American Academy of Child and Adolescent Psychiatry, 32,* 8345–842.

Lilenfeld, L. R., Kaye, W. H., Greeno, C. G., Merikangas, K. R., Plotnicov, K., *et al.* (1998). A controlled family study of Anorexia Nervosa and Bulimia Nervosa. *Archives of General Psychiatry, 55,* 603–610.

Ryan, J. (1995). *Little Girls in Pretty Boxes.* New York: Doubleday.

Sanders, M. J., Kapphahn, C., & Steiner, H. (1998). Eating disorders. In R. T. Ammerman and J. V. Campo (eds), *Handbook of pediatric psychology and psychiatry.* Boston: Allyn & Bacon. *I,* 287–312.

Schur, E., Sanders, M. J., & Steiner, H. Effects of belief system on body dissatisfaction and dieting in elementary school children. *International Journal of Eating Disorders.* In press.

Strober, M., Freeman, R., & Morrell, W. (1997). The long-term course of severe anorexia nervosa in adolescents: Survival analysis of recovery, relapse, and outcome predictors over 10–15 years in a prospective study. *International Journal of Eating Disorders, 22,* 339–360.

Thompson, J. K., Coovert, M. D., Richards, K. J., Johnson, S., & Cattarin, J. (1995). *International Journal of Eating Disorders, 18(3),* 221–236.

Walsh, B. T. & Devlin, M. J. (1998). Eating disorders: Progress and problems. *Science, 280,* 1387–1390.

Williams, A. (1996). *Identity Crisis.* Unpublished poem.

Wilson, G. T. & Fairburn, C. G. (1993). Cognitive treatments for eating disorders. *Journal of Consulting and Clinical Psychology, 61,* 261–269.

Chapter 15

Bulimia Nervosa: An Overview of Coping Strategies Therapy

David Tobin

Therapeutic Choices

A common choice of interventions among therapists includes the instruction of coping skills. In fact, those who treat patients with Bulimia Nervosa rely heavily upon altering coping strategies of these individuals. The most empirically studied treatment for Bulimia Nervosa, cognitive-behavior therapy (CBT) (Fairburn, 1985), teaches coping skills that are intended to directly impact the mediating thoughts and behavior of bulimic symptoms. However, CBT for Bulimia may be too narrow in focus, such that it only partially targets some of the skills deficits of those with this disorder. There are alternative psychotherapy approaches that address other types of skills deficits via the instruction of skills for a variety of problems. Two approaches that have received increasing attention are interpersonal psychotherapy (IPT) (Fairburn, 1997), and dialectical behavior therapy (DBT) (Linehan, 1993). IPT teaches interpersonal skills, and DBT teaches a variety of skills related to managing emotions, crises, and interpersonal relationships. These interventions may hold promise in the treatment of Bulimia Nervosa and have been the subject of some empirical study. CBT has been shown to be an effective treatment for many, but not all patients with Bulimia Nervosa benefit from this approach. While IPT has also been shown to be effective, it is unclear which patients are best served by these disparate approaches. Those with borderline personality disorder have benefited from DBT, which is believed to be a promising strategy for Bulimia Nervosa patients who also have a personality disorder.

In addition to IPT and DBT, there are other treatments that address some of these same coping skills, particularly interpersonal and crisis management skills. These include brief (Strupp & Binder, 1984) and long-term psychodynamic treatments (Kernberg, *et al.*, 1989), feminist treatments (Kearney-Cooke and Striegel-Moore, 1994), and systemic treatments (Humphrey & Stern, 1988). While feminist, psychodynamic, and systemic approaches have not received much empirical study, they remain popular with many clinicians.

Considering the emphasis on empirically tested treatments by researchers, it is ironic that there has been little attempt to develop an empirical process in constructing psychotherapies for Bulimia, or to integrate the findings from empirical studies of psychotherapy process and mental health systems. While there is some

Handbook of Conceptualization and Treatment of Child Psychopathology, pages 311–326.
Copyright © 2001 by Elsevier Science Ltd.
All rights of reproduction in any form reserved.
ISBN: 0-08-043362-6

literature to support the use of CBT for Bulimia Nervosa, this literature is scant, and CBT only addresses some aspects of coping. Despite the emphasis on coping skills, training in cognitive and behavioral therapies and the emphasis on skills process in other approaches, there has been little integration of the empirical literature on coping in models of psychotherapy. One approach that tries to integrate empirical findings of coping and psychotherapy process literature is Coping Strategies Therapy (CST) (Tobin, 2000). CST uses three empirically based literatures to organize a more encompassing approach to psychotherapy. They include: (1) dose/effect theory (Howard, et al., 1986), (2) The Transtheoretical Model (Prochaska, 1979), and coping theory (Tobin, 2000). It should be noted that while using empirically tested constructs and empirically tested interventions in it's construction, CST outlines an integrated treatment approach that has not yet been the subject of systematic empirical study.

The therapeutic activities in CST are organized around the types of coping behavior most appropriate for a particular dose of therapy. CST divides treatment into four doses, ranging from two to hundreds of sessions. Patients are assessed to determine a particular CST. The required dose is ascertained by the patient's stage of readiness for change and the extent of co-morbid psychopathology, both of which have an easily administered, empirically-based algorithm for assessment (Tobin, 2000). Co-morbid psychopathology can be estimated from scores on a depression screening measure, such as the Beck Depression Inventory, and the presence or absence of paranoid/schizoid or psychotic symptoms. Stage of change can be assessed by asking patients how soon they might be able to change bulimic behavior. If their answer is more than six months, they are in the precontemplation stage. If their answer is less than six months but more than thirty days, they are in the contemplation stage. If their answer is within thirty days, they are in the preparation stage, and if they have already stopped their bulimic behavior, they are in the action stage. Each stage of change is associated with a particular set of change processes, or coping activities. According to the Transtheoretical Model, patients in the precontemplation and contemplation stages require experiential processes such as the use of interpersonal therapy, psychodynamic therapy, or cognitive therapy, and persons in the preparation and action stages need active behavioral processes such as cognitive-behavioral therapy.

Coping theory identifies dimensions of coping that correspond to these change processes (Tobin et al., 2000). These coping dimensions are arranged hierarchically, beginning with eight primary factors: problem solving and cognitive restructuring (problem engagement), social support and expressed emotions (emotion engagement), problem avoidance and wishful thinking (problem disengagement), and social withdrawal and self criticism (emotion disengagement). These are followed by four secondary factors, including a problem-focused and an emotion-focused factor for each of the two tertiary factors, engagement and disengagement. These coping strategies are organized into the doses of CST in the following way (Tobin, 2000):

Dose 1 involves a diagnostic stage of one to two sessions; some patients' symptoms may remit as soon as the symptoms are diagnosed and they are given some basic education about eating disorders. It is not unheard of for some Bulimia Nervosa patients to stop their disordered eating habits as soon as they make an appointment, even before attending the first session. Patients who respond to Dose 1 are usually in the action stage and are ready to employ problem-solving and cognitive-restructuring forms of coping.

Dose 2 involves the introduction of basic self-management skills training, such as self-monitoring and structuring meal patterns; this occurs in about three to eight sessions. Patients are usually in the preparation stage and ready to engage in problem-solving and cognitive-restructuring forms of coping. Approximately one-third to one-half of Bulimia Nervosa patients may remit following completion of this stage of treatment.

Dose 3 involves a variety of different interventions that are designed to teach coping skills related to interpersonal difficulties and self-esteem. These include cognitive, focal dynamic, and relational approaches to body image, emotional expression, interpersonal problem solving, and self-esteem, and may take up to 20 visits to accomplish. Though some studies have indicated that as many as 90 percent of patients remit by Dose 3, most indicate that about two-thirds of samples improve.

Dose 4 involves the resolution of deeply ingrained emotional dysregulation and maladaptive interpersonal patterns, and takes anywhere from 50 to hundreds of sessions. Here, treatment targets a broader array of coping deficits, disengaged coping, and environmental difficulties than in earlier stages, and usually involves focus on the therapeutic relationship as well.

A core construct of this CST psychotherapy model is the premise that both process and content change over the "dosage" of treatment, which requires the use of different interventions. The briefer the dosage, the more it is likely to reflect a cognitive or behavioral focus on symptoms and to involve very active and specific suggestions, as in Doses 1 and 2. Somewhat longer doses of therapy are likely to focus on environmental contingencies that shape and maintain symptoms, particularly interpersonal cues and patterns of behavior, as in Doses 2 and 3. Still longer doses of therapy include a direct focus on the patient-therapist relationship, as a kind of in vitro coping skills training on interpersonal relationships and mood regulation, as in Doses 3 and 4. While these shifts in process and content reflect the traditional differences between behavioral and psychodynamic models of treatment, the distinctions are much less pronounced with the advent of brief psychodynamic models of treatment and longer-term behavioral and cognitive models. Dose 3 probably offers the greatest degree of overlap between competing psychotherapy models.

It should be underscored that dosage of therapy discussed above refers to a guideline and not the absolute prescription of intervention strategies. For example, it is possible to analyze the transference and countertransference in Dose 2 treatment. Moreover, the longer dosages include coping strategies of the earlier dosages. Thus, problem-solving and cognitive-restructuring exercises must eventually be provided to patients in Dose 4, but only after they have reached the preparation stage of readiness. The different doses of psychotherapy are more of a teaching tool or guideline for approaching the problem of how to manage care than a rigidly prescribed sequence of approaches. The remainder of the chapter will outline examples of treatments at each of the four doses.

Working with Adolescents

Several important considerations must be noted with regard to applying CST to adolescents. The first is to consider the impact of developmental issues on the onset and maintenance of Bulimic symptoms. Adolescents face intense pressures from both maturational and environmental demands, often with a rapid pace of change. What is a problem one month, may or may not be a problem the next. Alternatively, new stressors can suddenly emerge that exacerbate symptoms (e.g., when someone leaves home to start college). It is also important to consider the direct impact that family environment has on the onset or maintenance of symptoms. This is particularly important in the context of diagnosing personality disorders, as the strong affects associated with personality disturbance may be a more direct result of family crises than of the patient's internal conflicts, deficits, and/or personality structure.

Because families can both be a cause and a cure for adolescents with Bulimia Nervosa, the family should typically be involved in the treatment process, if only to assure both the patient and the therapist that the parents support and understand the process of the child's recovery. Sometimes adolescent patients will have the maturity and motivation to engage primarily in individual treatment. Other times, they will require the family's continued involvement during treatment in order to recover. When parents are motivated to maintain a patient's symptoms, sacrificing their daughter's or son's well being as a pathological form of compensating for their own difficulties, treatment is very challenging. In these instances, it is important to attempt to engage parents in their own treatment. It is vital for the therapist to understand the dynamics of the family system and how it serves to impede or promote recovery of the adolescent with Bulimia.

Choosing a Treatment Focus

Treatments that involve families can have a different type of focus than individual treatments, as the focus of treatment shifts from the patient's bulimic symptoms to systemic (family-wide) issues. CST can accommodate this shift in the same way that it accommodates the need to focus on a patient's comorbid difficulties. If either family problems or comorbid symptoms are too compelling, a patient will not be able to work effectively on managing bulimic symptoms. To the extent that family issues are benign, and comorbid symptoms (e.g., depression) are relatively absent, then treatment can be focused more immediately on bulimic symptoms. To the extent that family problems or comorbid symptoms are quite severe, therapy may have to begin with serious threats to physical safety. The second most serious concern involves threats to the treatment process. Thus, the targets for treatment in CST are organized according to a hierarchy of concerns that include the following:

1) Physical safety;
2) Emotional safety, both in and out of treatment (e.g., reducing therapy interfering behavior);
3) Reducing symptom maintaining behaviors (e.g., self-injury, social isolation, abusive relationships);
4) Development of interpersonal skills;
5) Development of the self;
6) Self-management of eating difficulties.

When patients need only to focus on eating difficulties, they may require only Doses 1 or 2. When patients have some comorbid or interpersonal problems that are not catastrophic, they are most likely to require Doses 2 or 3. Suicidal or para-suicidal behavior, severe dissociative symptoms, or severe personality disorders usually require Dose 4. The following reflects a more thorough description of the doses:

Dose 1: One to Two Sessions

Dose 1 is the smallest dose of CST, lasting one to two visits. Patients who require only Dose 1 of CST are usually in the action stage. They are already making some kind of behavior change before they come in for their first appointment. Their difficulties are circumscribed; they tend to have no comorbid diagnoses. Sometimes, just making the phone call to arrange evaluation motivates these patients into action. Dose 1 is called "remoralization" in Howard et al.'s model (1986), and is most similar to the early phases of cognitive-behavioral treatments, with an emphasis on psychoeducation. It is also possible to make a very focal cognitive or behavioral intervention in Dose 1 (e.g., a single suggestion about stabilizing a patient's meal pattern, single session relaxation, or cognitive therapy (Tobin, *et al.*, 1989). For patients who are already changing their symptomatic behavior, information or advice is likely to be received by the patient as helpful and supportive. Prochaska and his colleagues (Prochaska, *et al.*, 1984) identify the processes of change which are most helpful to persons in action as active behavioral. The techniques of Dose 1 can be more like health education than psychotherapy or even behavioral therapy (Tobin, 2000).
　The key components of Dose 1 are to:

1) diagnose both eating disordered and comorbid symptoms;
2) determine the resources for recovery (e.g., family support and dynamics, psychological mindedness);
3) assess stage of readiness for change.

It is important to increase the patient's awareness of their symptoms, the societal factors that promote disordered eating, and any idiographic circumstances that influence the patient to maintain disordered eating. If a behavioral intervention is introduced in Dose 1, it must be very specific, simple, precise, and easily accomplished. The most basic intervention is to assist the patient in constructing a meal plan and to encourage monitoring of their eating and bulimic symptoms. However, the patient must be ready to incorporate these suggestions or the treatment must move to the second dosage. Some patients may benefit from the provision of a self-help manual in the first visit, and using the second visit for a follow-up appointment for a primarily self-administered treatment.

Case Example, Mary

Mary was a 16 year-old girl who presented with a brief history of Bulimia Nervosa (less than six months) but no comorbid symptoms and no history of abuse or trauma. She had learned about binging and vomiting from a friend, which they practiced together for a short time as a way of managing their weight. The patient's bulimic behavior was discovered by her mother, and it was the mother who called for her daughter's appointment at the clinic. The patient stopped her Bulimia the day her mother made the appointment. Therapist and patient talked about her concerns about her weight, the influence of friends, and her decision to quit engaging in bulimic behavior. She was seen twice, once for an initial evaluation and once for a follow-up visit. Her mother was included for part of both visits. As both patient and mother were satisfied about the recovery process by the second visit, the treatment was terminated and the patient invited to recontact the clinic if problems persisted.

Dose 2: Three to Eight Sessions

Dose 2 is the next larger dose of therapy, and lasts from three to eight visits. Howard calls this dose "remediation" because it involves direct efforts to alleviate a patient's symptoms. Patients likely to benefit from Dose 2 are in the preparation stage; they are feeling ready to initiate changes in behavior that may impact their symptoms. This dose of therapy is most consistent with cognitive-behavioral therapies that directly target behavioral symptoms and symptom-related cognitions. The interpersonal theme that is most prominent here involves the therapist as listener, expert, healer, and to some extent, teacher or trainer. Prochaska (1979) describes the processes of change most helpful to persons in preparation as active behavioral. In Dose 2, psychiatric symptoms must be accurately targeted and specific advice given on how to overcome them, as in self-management training and CBT (Tobin, 2000).

Using the same diagnostic process as Dose 1, patients who are most appropriate for Dose 2 will have little, or at least very circumscribed comorbid anxiety or depression. They will usually not have personality disorders or significant trauma history. Like Dose 1, interventions need to be focused and specific. Psychoeducation about the patient's symptoms, instruction in self-monitoring, and constructing a meal plan are the primary coping skills. However, in Dose 2 patients can take more time to prepare themselves for the change process than in Dose 1. In addition to the above goals, there may be time for one or two additional goals specifically designed to impact the patient's symptoms. These are typically constructed in a collaborative fashion with the patient by examining the self-monitoring sheets. Behavioral goals can include:

1) overcoming dieting and food avoidance (e.g., dieting causes hunger which triggers binge eating which leads to purging);
2) stabilizing the meal plan;
3) cue control strategies (e.g., removing binge foods from the house, eating with others, etc.);
4) planning alternative coping responses to stress (e.g., relaxation training, Tai Chi, seeking social support).

If there are comorbid symptoms, they may have to be targeted before the patient will feel ready to address bulimic symptoms. For example, if the patient binge eats in response to a depressed or anxious mood, symptoms may need to be directly addressed. However, in order to successfully address comorbid difficulties in Dose 2, they must be circumscribed and unrelated to severe personality or trauma disorders. Patients with depression can be encouraged to engage in more activities, particularly more social activities. Patients with anxiety can be taught relaxation skills, or instructed to take classes in yoga or Tai Chi. Patients with depression or anxiety may also benefit from a pharmacologic intervention, such as with serotonin specific reuptake inhibitors (SSRIs), as they are approved in the treatment of anxiety, depression, and Bulimia Nervosa. Therefore a referral medication evaluation should be considered if there is difficulty in achieving symptom remission.

Case Example, Tanya

Tanya was a 16 year-old, Caucasian female who was referred for evaluation of Bulimia Nervosa. Though she did not meet full DSM-IV criteria, she was diagnosed with eating disorder not otherwise specified (American Psychiatric Association, 1994). The patient was vomiting once or twice per week, which had been discovered by her aunt when she left a bag of vomit under her bed. The vomiting began in her freshman year of high school and had exacerbated during the six weeks before evaluation. It was evident that she did not really binge eat, but probably ate too much refined sugar in candy. The patient's weight was 109 pounds and she was 5'1" tall. She stated that she did not want to lose weight. Tanya was not depressed, did not report any difficulties with anxiety or PTSD, and denied using substances. She did report being emotionally and physically abused by her mother and her mother's boyfriends, though she denied sexual abuse. Her mother had had difficulties with alcohol and other substances, and had died of AIDS four years before. Tanya was currently living with an aunt with whom she had spent much of her earlier childhood because of her mother's chaotic lifestyle. This attachment may have left Tanya with greater ego strength and better relational attachment than might have been expected. Despite the chaos and loss in her life, she was an honor student and very involved with athletics.

Tanya was motivated to focus directly on her eating and vomiting. We set initial goals to (1) regulate her meal pattern, (2) monitor her eating, and (3) gain five pounds (which she wanted to do). She began monitoring her eating by the second visit and had already stopped her vomiting. She continued to be successful in these activities by the third visit, despite being "stressed out" because of some frustration with her aunt. The week leading to the fourth session was more diffi-cult for her as she continued to feel "stressed," and she relapsed, vomiting three times. This was resolved by the fifth session, when she began to "look forward to the summer." She was again no longer vomiting, and had improved her eating to the point that she had gained five pounds. The possibility of some family work with her aunt was discussed, and she agreed to talk to her aunt about this. Her aunt came in for the sixth visit, and some of their conflicts, which seemed develop-mentally normative were addressed. Her eating had continued to remain improved, and she did not return for a seventh scheduled visit.

The length of time, six visits, and the primary emphasis on eating symptoms, make this case a fairly typical Dose 2 treatment. Despite her chaotic and serious abuse history, the patient presented no significant comorbidity and was clearly in the preparation stage (ready to address the eating problems) during her initial eva-luation. She moved to the action stage of change by the second visit. Also typical for Dose 2, therapist and patient were able to generate one additional treatment focus, which in her case was trying to define and manage some conflict with her aunt. The treatment culminated in a single family therapy session, which can often have the impact of many individual visits, if the family members are motivated to be responsive to each other. Unfortunately, this is not always the case, which, as described in Dose 4, can greatly complicate the treatment process.

Dose 3: nine to 20 sessions

Dose 3 lasts for about eleven sessions, which Howard, et al., (1986) describe in terms of teaching new coping skills. However, these skills are not initially targeted on bulimic symptoms as in Doses 1 and 2, but on the problems and concerns that often precipitate bulimic symptoms (e.g., interpersonal difficulties and self-esteem). When patients require Dose 3, it usually means they are in contemplation; they are considering change sometime in the next six months but need motivational support, increased self-efficacy, and new ways of coping. In teaching patients to be more emotionally engaged, both interpersonal difficulties and self-esteem issues are prioritized. Dose 3 psychotherapy components include brief psychodynamic, feminist, and cognitive-behavioral interventions that focus on self-esteem and interpersonal concerns. The dimensions of coping that are most likely to move patients from contemplation to preparation and action involve emotional expression and interpersonal engagement. Prochaska (1979) identified the processes of change most helpful to contemplators as experiential; they can be also described as interpersonal. Interpersonal and experiential psychotherapies are linked together under the coping dimension of emotional engagement.

Again using the same diagnostic process as Dose 1, patients who are most appropriate for Dose 3 often have comorbid symptoms, and may not be immediately ready to target eating-related difficulties until their comorbid anxiety or depression is at least partially addressed. However, patients who are likely to respond to Dose 3 will usually not have severe personality disorders or an extensive trauma history. As in the earlier doses, interventions still need to be focused and specific but are more likely to involve interpersonal or self-esteem difficulties. The success of Dose 3 depends upon the therapist's ability to summarize the patient's difficulties in a focal, circumscribed way. At some point in the treatment, the therapist must be able to move the patient to the more specific behavioral goals of earlier doses, although some patients may do this on their own as their self-esteem or interpersonal difficulties begin to resolve.

There are a number of models for developing a circumscribed interpersonal or self-esteem goal (for review (Tobin, 2000), which are very similar. A typical approach is to examine a patient's difficulties for (1) an unsatisfied wish or desire, (2) the patient's efforts (or lack of efforts) to achieve the wish, (3) response to the patient's efforts from other people, and (4) the patient's response to that of others. The goal is to find a repeating interpersonal pattern that bothers the patient. Once the therapist has an understanding of these features, he/she should attempt to construct a focal problem, usually by about the third visit. A rule of thumb for achieving a good focal problem is that it should be about the length of a long sentence (or perhaps two or three short sentences).

As in Dose 2, if there are comorbid symptoms, they may have to be targeted before the patient will feel ready to address bulimic symptoms. For example, if the patient binge eats in response to depressed or anxious mood, these symptoms may need to be directly addressed. However, while these symptoms may be more severe than patients who respond to Dose 2, they must be largely unrelated to severe personality disorders or severe trauma. As in Dose 2, patients with depression can be encouraged to engage in more activities, particularly more social activities. Patients with anxiety can be taught relaxation skills, or encouraged to take classes in yoga or Tai Chi. However, there may have to be at least some progress on the focal problem before patients will be motivated to engage in these more behavioral goals. For patients with significant depression or anxiety, a pharmacologic evaluation for SSRIs may be considered, particularly if there is difficulty in symptom remission and there is no contraindication.

Case Example, Pete

Though most patients with Bulimia Nervosa are female, Pete was an 18 year-old male. The patient was vomiting most of his meals, about three times per day. He was also binge eating about once per day. He was 5'7", and weighed 130 pounds. His highest weight was three years ago at 190 pounds, and he was currently at his lowest weight. The patient also presented with major depression, including difficulties with sleep, depressed mood, and poor concentration and memory. In addition, he had symptoms of anxiety, which had both generalized and social features. He had recently been "dumped" by his girlfriend because he "didn't want to have sex." He initially denied being gay or having concerns about his sexuality, but stated that his friends wondered if he was gay. Pete seemed uncomfortable and embarrassed to discuss sexual matters. He had conflicts with his parents, particularly his mother, whom he described as cold and critical. Pete had a warmer relationship with his father, who was the only one to attend family meetings.

The most pressing conflict in the family involved the patient's desire to quit his high school swim team. He was afraid of his parents' reaction, particularly his mother's, who he thought would call him a quitter. Because of the severity of the patient's bulimic symptoms and the extent of his comorbid depression, a treatment plan was developed that involved Dose 3 of CST. In addition to examining the extent of the patient's comorbidity, there was an exploration of Pete's interest and ability to engage in behavioral eating goals. He was interested, but demonstrated more enthusiasm and motivation for focused eating goals after addressing his concerns about his family and the swim team. This was accomplished in a single family visit with his father, who assured Pete that it would be no problem if he decided to quit the team. Pete was then able to engage more actively in managing his eating symptoms. The therapist and patient constructed a food plan (e.g., three meals a day), and he began to self-monitor his eating. He was able to quickly reduce his vomiting to once a day and was binge eating only a few times a week. This was accomplished by about the fourth or fifth visit.

During visits five through about ten, there was an effort to become more focused, but it achieved minimal success with no more than a general focus on stress management. Pete complained about his parents and some conflicts at school. He was taught a relaxation exercise, and additional stress management strategies were discussed. During the tenth visit, Pete initiated a discussion about his sexuality, and stated that he believed he was gay. He had already begun "hooking up" with a gay friend, who after a brief affair, terminated the relationship. Though this experience challenged his self-esteem, his ability to accept his sexuality was very empowering, and he made significant progress on his Bulimia symptoms, binging and vomiting with much less frequency (about once per week).

During the next six visits, sessions focused on a number of developmentally appropriate issues, his feelings about his brief involvement with a gay lover, his parents' concerns about his sexuality, and his going away to college. This primary focus of treatment (i.e., the acceptance of his sexuality) was minimally addressed in the beginning of the treatment, but had enormous impact on the patient's mood, anxiety, and Bulimia. Pete felt enough acceptance and gained enough confidence during the treatment to come to some resolution regarding his sexuality, which reduced his anxiety and depression, and bolstered his self-esteem.

The patient interrupted treatment when he began college, even though he did not leave the geographic area, because he didn't have a car. He became very involved with new gay friends whom he met at a restaurant where he worked as a waiter. He became more involved with the restaurant than he did with school, resulting in a somewhat unstable and unfocused lifestyle. He slept away from his dorm at least three nights a week and let his studies and his grades slip. As a result, he became more depressed and his Bulimia relapsed. He attended a couple of therapy sessions over winter break, and was able to make some decisions that helped him become more focused. In addition, Pete finally agreed to try an antidepressant, which he had been reluctant to consider when treatment began.

This case illustrates an important aspect of working with adolescent patients, which is that role transitions and developmental challenges can arise at a very rapid pace, presenting the patient and the clinician with very different sets of circumstances from month to month or even week to week. Some of these circumstance will be normative (e.g., starting college) and others will be more idiosyncratic to the patient's own developmental struggles (e.g., accepting his sexuality in the context of the dynamics in his family). The more normative the stressors, the more likely dosage can be brief. The more idiosyncratic and challenging the stressors, the more likely dosage will be long.

Dose 4: 21 to 100 + Sessions

Dose 4 lasts from about 21 to hundreds of sessions, which Howard, *et al.*, (1986) describe in terms of "rooting out the disease at its source." However, these skills do not directly target symptoms as in Doses 1 and 2, and patients are often too self-destructive to work immediately on more satisfying interpersonal relationships or self-esteem. Treatment must focus initially on reducing negative or disengaged coping. When patients require Dose 4, it usually means they are in precontemplation, they are not considering change in the next six months. These patients see the cons of change greatly outweighing the pros and have little in the way of motivation or self-efficacy to engage in active change processes. Patients who need Dose 4 have severe comorbid difficulties, usually with personality disorders, trauma disorders, or both.

The psychotherapies most reflective of Dose 4 include psychodynamic psychotherapy and cognitive-behavioral therapies for personality disorders, feminist treatments for trauma, and treatments for dissociation. Prochaska (1979) identified the processes of change most helpful to precontemplators as experiential. However, CST conceptualizes that experiential therapies are most appropriate for contemplators, and patients in precontemplation with severe comorbidity need to focus on their disengaged coping. This includes problem avoidance, wishful thinking, social withdrawal, and self-criticism.

Again using the same diagnostic process as Dose 1, patients who are most appropriate for Dose 3 often have comorbid symptoms and may not be immediately ready to target eating related difficulties until their comorbid anxiety or depression is at least partially addressed. However, patients who need Dose 4 usually have personality disorders and/or significant trauma histories. Unlike the earlier doses, there may be many behavioral and symptom targets, which must be prioritized according to level of risk. The first focus is always on the patient's safety, followed by the safety of the treatment. Then the focus can gradually be moved to more interpersonal and self-esteem issues, as in Dose 3. At some point in the treatment, the therapist must be able to move the patient to the more behavioral goals of the earlier doses, although some patients may do this on their own, particularly if the self-esteem or interpersonal difficulties are sufficiently resolved.

Even more importantly than in Dose 3, in Dose 4 comorbid symptoms usually have to be targeted before the patient will feel ready to address bulimic symptoms. If binge eating and vomiting are conducted to manage catastrophic anxiety or profound depression, then patients will have little motivation to stop bulimic behavior until these other symptoms are reduced. Often these comorbid symptoms are themselves multifaceted, with anxiety, depression, behavioral, and interpersonal components. For example, one comorbid diagnosis usually requiring Dose 4 is dissociative identity disorder (DID). Though the DSM-IV diagnostic criteria for DID are succinct (APA, 1994), patients with DID usually have severe depression, anxiety, PTSD, self-injurious behavior, medical complications, substance difficulties, and interpersonal dysfunction. As described in Tobin (2000), Dose 4 treatment must first address the most self-destructive (i.e., disengaged) behavior (e.g., promiscuity, prostitution, substance abuse, etc.), which can then reduce PTSD, anxiety, and depressive mood states, which in turn reduce the need for bulimic behavior. Unlike the earlier doses, comorbid difficulties are rarely circumscribed, and treatment may have to address every aspect of a patient's life. To help organize treatment, the hierarchy of concerns described above should be considered.

Dose 4 combines use of active suggestion to eliminate negative, self-destructive behavior, with use of insight gained by analyzing the patient's history and the patient/therapist relationship. Contrary to what some theorists hypothesize, the analysis of transference is an ego building process. Since patients are already acting out primitive, regressed behavior when they come into treatment, interpreting the motivation for engaging in negative behavior helps the patient develop motivation for stopping it. Though analyzing the transference is most thoroughly described in psychodynamic models of treatment, it is an accepted practice among the cognitive-behavioral and feminist practitioners who treat personality disorders and trauma, including Linehan (1993) and Beck. It is important to emphasize that patients need to significantly reduce their disengaged coping before the introduction of engaged coping. However, it is important for the patient to understand why he/she was so disengaged in the first place. This involves analysis of the transference, creating the links between the patient's previous history and current experiences. It is this writer's clinical experience that simply reducing disengaged coping is usually not a sufficient platform for introducing engaged coping skills. Introducing engaged before disengaged coping is thoroughly understood and interpreted, can risk regression and relapse.

After patients have reduced their disengaged coping activities, and have sufficient insight to protect against relapse, they can be introduced to engaged coping activities, including the targeting of their bulimic symptoms as in Doses 1 and 2. Like the earlier doses, patients with depression can be encouraged to engage in more pleasurable activities, particularly more social activities, and to improve their social skills or self-esteem. Patients with anxiety can be taught relaxation skills, or encouraged to take classes in yoga or Tai Chi. Patients who need Dose 4 should probably be evaluated for a pharmacologic intervention. However, this writer's clinical experience is that medications may be less than fully effective when there are pronounced difficulties with personality disorders, trauma disorders, or both.

Case Example, Linda

At intake, Linda, a 19 year-old woman was bingeing and purging at least once per day, sometimes after every meal. She weighed 140 pounds and was 5'10". Linda was given the initial diagnosis of Bulimia Nervosa, dysthymia, and borderline personality disorder. She did not have an extensive history of sexual abuse, but had been sexually approached by an elderly neighbor when she was about thirteen years old. The patient was emotionally abused by both parents and had been physically assaulted by her mother on at least one occasion.

Linda's eating difficulties had begun when she was about 16 years old after some male classmates teased her about her body size. She dropped her weight from 155 to 132 pounds. At the same time, she struggled to get attention from her very passive father, who was only interested in her athletic activities. When Linda's athletic performance dropped because her weight dropped, he again reduced his involvement. Linda also struggled hard to please her mother. She chose a career in nursing, which her mother had always wanted for herself. This not only had the effect of arousing her mother's envy, but actually precipitated her mother's direct competition with Linda by also entering college, threatening the family's ability to pay for the patient's college and her treatment. Linda had had one boyfriend whom she had seen for about five years. They had a satisfactory sexual involvement, but she broke things off with him because according to Linda, he was too similar to her father, passive, quiet, and unemotional except when angry.

Treatment began on a twice weekly basis and focused on eating difficulties with a standard package of cognitive behavioral skills training, as the patient reported being ready to make specific behavioral changes. Linda was encouraged to begin a regular meal pattern, which helped to increase her calories, reduce eating binges, and reduce her vomiting. She was responsive and optimistic about the treatment, complying fully with self-monitoring and efforts to establish a regular meal pattern. The patient made considerable progress during the first three months until the therapist took a vacation. At this point Linda completely relapsed in her restriction, her bingeing, and her vomiting. At the same time, she met a sociopathic man whom she initially idealized, but who greatly disappointed her, confirming her belief that "all men are scum." Efforts to interpret the parallel between her experience with this man and her disappointment with either the therapist's absence ("it didn't bother me"), or gender ("you are not my type"), were met with denial.

Because the patient lived at home, and because her parents were such a regular part of her concerns, family therapy was initiated. Family meetings occurred once a week for about a year, with little progress. One dynamic that was explored in the family therapy was how Linda's mother felt abused and exploited by *her* mother, and the extent to which this might be re-enacted with her daughter. At one point it was suggested that the mother's mother be invited into treatment, which brought howls of laughter. The therapist also suggested that the mother seek her own treatment, but this was not pursued. Unfortunately, it was never possible to increase the mother's insight into her own behavior, and she remained rageful and envious towards Linda throughout the treatment. After more than a year, it became apparent that the family's dynamics were unlikely to change, and the family treatment was discontinued.

Linda's eating symptoms remained severe for the next two-and-a-half years, as she binged and vomited on at least a daily basis. She maintained her weight close to 130 pounds and would periodically use laxatives. Following the initial honeymoon phase of CBT, the therapy shifted back and forth between the patient's eating symptoms, her relationship with her family, and her relationship with the therapist. After several years of this work, usually meeting twice per week, Linda was finally able to see the futility of pleasing her mother, and gradually achieved a greater sense of autonomy. She realized and accepted that she would probably never gain her mother's acceptance or become more than a receptacle for her mother's anger and disappointment.

Themes of separation and abandonment also emerged in the transference as Linda alternated between trying to please the therapist and becoming enraged with the therapist for not helping her enough. Efforts to interpret this to the patient were met with stiff resistance, though there was constant reference to this in the parallel process of the sessions, in that Linda would rarely address her feelings for the therapist directly, at least until the end of therapy. Many sessions were spent trying to show her how her concerns about other people reflected her concerns about the therapist. When the therapist was finally able to point this out to Linda, it became clear that she predicated any feeling of connection to the therapist on condition that the therapist would be immediately accessible to her, as her mother insisted Linda be towards her, and the patient's grandmother insisted the mother be towards her. Such unreasonable demands left Linda feeling unconnected and depressed, or abused and depressed, both of which she experienced in relation to the therapist, and which was examined many times in session. This marked the full emergence of the transference into the process of treatment.

The growing realization on Linda's part of the therapist's importance to her and of her lack of omnipotent control over the therapist precipitated a major depressive episode near the end of the third year of treatment. She was evaluated for medication at that time, which she refused, and shortly thereafter was admitted to the hospital because her weight, vomiting, and laxative abuse had become so severe. She felt that her behavior represented an effort to commit suicide and realized the need to do something to correct this. Linda and the therapist collaboratively decided she should be admitted to hospital. This was very useful in allowing her to explore both the feelings of rage she had toward her mother, and the feelings of closeness she had for the therapist. This culminated in one extremely emotional session in which Linda expressed intense anger toward the therapist, leaving him speechless and feeling humiliated and inadequate. Though neither the countertransference nor the transference was interpreted at that time, the therapist was at least able to act out his feelings and retaliate in some way. This allowed the patient to make her own interpretation, that she was feeling too close to the therapist, and was struggling with how not to push him away or feel threatened by the closeness. This had the immediate impact of reducing her depression and allowing her to remit her bulimic symptoms.

She consolidated around these experiences over the next 18 months, remaining symptom free, until the therapist had to terminate treatment because of leaving the area. She was transferred to another therapist whom she saw for about six more months, before terminating treatment completely.

This case is rather typical of Dose 4 in that there was significant family disturbance, abuse history, and comorbidity in the patient's presentation of bulimic symptoms. It is important to point out that though cognitive-behavior skills were introduced early in the treatment, they were not fully utilized until almost three years of therapy had been conducted. The patient had significant relational issues to resolve before feeling motivated enough to give up her bulimic behavior. Furthermore, these relational issues could not simply be addressed on an intellectual or cognitive level, but had to be fully experienced and significantly worked through in the context of the relationship between the patient and therapist (e.g., the analysis of the transference). The patient thus learned to reduce her disengaged coping behavior in the context of her relationship to the therapist.

Summary

This chapter describes Coping Strategies Therapy (CST) for Bulimia Nervosa, an integrative psychotherapy. The treatment is organized around Howard, *et al.*'s (1986) dosage model, Prochaska's (1979) Transtheoretical Model, and coping theory. Though therapists often discuss what they do in terms of teaching coping skills, this is one of the few descriptions of treatment that uses an empirical model of coping as a basis for organizing treatment.

There are four doses of CST, consistent with Howard's description, and an empirically-based, clinically practical model for helping the therapist decide what dose a patient needs. And while there are empirically tested treatments that can be adapted for each of the doses, the hierarchical structure of coping also helps to identify psychotherapies that have had little or no empirical study but which may be very appropriate and effective treatments for some patients. In addition to being a widely encompassing model of care that can meet the needs of many patients, CST also helps the practitioner negotiate the reality of modern behavioral health practice, by identifying who needs what kind of treatment. By offering a wide range of treatment approaches, the therapist can more effectively argue that he/she is suggesting an effective and economical approach. Finally, although this approach has not yet been systematically tested as described here (and in Tobin, 2000), many of the components have been tested in a variety of studies. Unfortunately, there are no studies that have yet considered the clinical complexity of Bulimia Nervosa or attempted to match treatment to clinical presentation of comorbidity or stage of readiness. Hopefully, there will be such studies in the future.

References

American Psychiatric Association. (1994). *Diagnostic and Statistical Manual of Mental Disorder.* (4th ed.). Washington, D.C.: Author.

Fairburn, C. G. (1985). Cognitive behavioral treatment for Bulimia. In D. M. Garner and P. E. Garfinkel (eds) *Handbook of Psychotherapy for Anorexia Nervosa and Bulimia.* New York: Guilford. 160–192.

Fairburn, C. G. (1997). Interpersonal psychotherapy for Bulimia Nervosa. In D. M. Garner & P. E. Garfinkel (eds) *Handbook of Treatment for Eating Disorders.* New York: Guilford Press. 2nd ed., 278–295.

Howard, K. I., Kopta, S. M., Krause, M. S., & Orlinsky, D. E. (1986). The dose-effect relationship in psychotherapy. *American Psychologist, 41,* 159–164.

Humphrey, L. L., & Stern, S. (1988). Object relations and the family system. *Journal of Marital and Family Therapy, 14,* 337–350.

Kearney-Cooke, A., & Streigal-Moore, R. H. (1994). Treatment of childhood sexual abuse in Anorexia Nervosa and Bulimia Nervosa: A feminist psychodynamic approach. *International Journal of Eating Disorders, 15,* 305–320.

Kernberg, O. F., Selzer, M. A., Koenigsberg, H. W., Carr, A. C., Appelbaum, A. H. (1989). *Psychodynamic Psychotherapy of Borderline Patients.* New York: Basic Books.

Linehan, M. M. (1993). *Cognitive-behavioral Treatment of Borderline Personality Disorder.* New York: Guilford.

Prochaska, J. O. (1979). *Systems of Psychotherapy: A Transtheoretical Analysis.* Homewood, IL: Dorsey Press.

Strupp, H. H., & Binder, J. L. (1984). *Psychotherapy in a New Key: A Guide to Time Limited Psychotherapy.* New York: Basic Books.

Tobin, D. L. (2000). *Coping strategies Therapy for Bulimia Nervosa.* American Psychological Association Press.

Tobin, D. L., Holroyd, K. A., Reynolds, R. V., & Wigal, J. K. (1989). The hierarchical factor structure of the Coping Strategies Inventory. *Cognitive Therapy and Research, 13,* 343–361.

Part VI

Substance Use Disorders

Chapter 16

Alcohol and Drug Abuse

Eric F. Wagner, Holly B. Waldron and Adam B. Feder

The Clinical Syndrome, its Features and Development

This chapter provides a theoretical rationale and practical suggestions for inter-vention with teens experiencing alcohol and other drug problems. The first section provides background information on substance use and abuse among adolescents; the second describes the theoretical rationale for two different treatment models; the third presents a case example; the fourth describes how treatment might unfold using both treatment models; the final section discusses how the treatment models might be integrated in a broader intervention package. Throughout the chapter, many of the unique features of teen substance abuse treatment are high-lighted from a biopsychosocial perspective.

Epidemiological data indicate continuing high rates of alcohol and other drug use among adolescents, a small but significant proportion of whom will develop substance use problems. In the 1999–2000 class of U.S. high school seniors, 73.8 percent reported alcohol use, 43.1 percent reported illicit drug use during the past year, and 34.6 percent reported cigarette smoking during the previous month. Furthermore, 6.0 percent reported daily marijuana use, 3.4 percent reported daily alcohol use, 30.8 percent reported one or more episodes of binge drinking during the past two weeks, and 13.2 percent reported smoking at least half a pack of cigarettes daily. While males have historically outpaced females in rates of adoles-cent substance use and abuse, a number of researchers have noted increasing gender convergence.

Procedures and criteria for the diagnosis of substance use problems among adults are fairly well developed. This is not the case with teenagers. While criteria based on the Diagnostic and Statistical Manual of Mental Disorders – Fourth Edition (DSM-IV) (American Psychiatric Association, 1994) are often used with adolescents, a number of these criteria may be inappropriate for teens (Martin & Winters, 1999). In comparison to adult substance abusers, adolescent substance abusers are less likely to suffer from the progressive nature of the disorder, medical complications, and other consequences of protracted use. Furthermore, teens sent for treatment may use a greater number or different types of substances than adults, resulting in more complicated withdrawal and dependency patterns than suggested by the DSM-IV (APA, 1994). An additional difference between

Handbook of Conceptualization and Treatment of Child Psychopathology, pages 329–352.

adult and adolescent substance abusers is that adolescent substance use occurs in the context of rapid developmental changes, which may mimic or exacerbate drug effects. It should be noted that substantial proportions of teens with substance use problems seem to "outgrow" patterns of substance use/abuse by early adulthood without formal intervention or treatment.

It is well known that adolescents with substance use problems are a heterogeneous group, with individual differences such as the anticipated effects and consequences resulting from substance use, the context and motivations in which use occurs, and the factors that contribute to or accompany substance use involvement (Wagner & Kassel, 1995). Such individual differences may account for why some adolescents demonstrate clinically significant problems with substance use while others show few problems or spontaneous remission. These differences also may help explain why some substance-abusing adolescents respond to treatment, while others do not. Individual difference variables likely to affect treatment response have been labeled "amenability to treatment" or "matching" factors. Very few studies have examined the differential amenability of adolescents to various treatments, though several ongoing studies are examining possible amenability to treatment factors such as psychiatric comorbidity, alcohol expectancies, social support, delinquency, motivation to change, history of abuse or maltreatment, family conflict, and parental substance use (Wagner, Brown, Monti, Myers, & Waldron, 1999).

Scant research has examined the role of ethnicity as it relates to clinical outcomes in psychotherapy trials with children and adolescents. This applies especially to studies that have examined the effectiveness of substance abuse intervention with teenagers. While existing studies offer some support for the effectiveness of interventions for adolescent substance use problems, research to date has been plagued by inadequate attention to issues related to race and ethnicity (Williams, Chang, the Addiction Centre Adolescent Research Group, 2000). Clearly, adolescents from different racial and ethnic groups differ in risk factors for and rates of substance use/abuse; they also may differ in responsiveness to various treatments. Currently, the important question of whether adolescents from certain racial and ethnic groups are best treated by certain types of programs remains unanswered.

Two of the key developmental issues that must be considered when treating adolescent substance abusers are peer groups and identity formation. During adolescence, the peer group influences behavior and plays an important role in the development and maintenance of drug use. Teens with poor self-confidence and low self-esteem tend to be more dependent on peers, who are often more influential than parents. The social resources of teens are prognostic of clinical course once abusive patterns have developed. Most identity development occurs in adolescence; consequently, its process is significantly based within the social context. Healthy, close friendships play a crucial role in helping teens develop a sense of their own identity. The perceived acceptance of a teen by friends functions to bolster self-confidence and self-esteem, which are factors related to treatment success.

General Description of Individual Cognitive-behavioral Treatment and Functional Family Therapy

In an attempt to address substance use and abuse among adolescents, multiple intervention approaches have been developed. Unfortunately, little is known about which of these approaches is most effective for which individuals. Clinical demand for adolescent substance abuse prevention and treatment programs has been overwhelming and has outpaced empirical research evaluating their effectiveness. While a small number of investigators are currently conducting controlled clinical trials of various adolescent substance abuse interventions (Wagner, *et al.*, 1999). the vast majority of available substance abuse interventions has not been adequately evaluated as to effectiveness. The strongest conclusions that can be drawn about the effectiveness of different interventions are (a) that some intervention is better than none, and (b) that no particular intervention is superior to any other (Williams, *et al.*, 2000).

Individual behaviorally-oriented therapy and family therapy are two common forms of adolescent psychotherapy; individual behaviorally-oriented therapies have received a great deal of empirical support and are used widely, while family therapies (despite a strong rationale based in the notion that families are a key context for adolescent development) have much less empirical support despite their wide clinical usage (Kendall & Morris, 1991). Currently, there are very few controlled studies examining what specific form of treatment is most effective for each specific type of adolescent problem (Kendall & Morris, 1991), an empirical gap that is especially pronounced in the areas of alcohol and other drug (AOD) problems. Kendall and Morris (1991) suggest the comparison of individual therapy with family therapy as a necessary first step toward understanding what are the most effective interventions for specific adolescent problems. Hence, we have chosen individual cognitive-behavioral therapy and functional family therapy as the focal treatments for this chapter.

Rationale for Individual Cognitive-behavioral Therapy

A cognitive-behavioral approach to treatment is based in a social learning theory conceptualization of the development of substance abuse. Simply put, this perspective recognizes the contribution of many domains to the emergence of alcohol and drug use problems (i.e., the biopsychosocial model), but focuses on the role of environmental influences and learned beliefs and behavior. Behavior related to alcohol and drug use are believed to emerge as a result of modeling by family members, peers, and society. In the process of observing the use of alcohol and drugs within the context of family, peers, and society/culture, individuals develop beliefs regarding the influence or effects of substances. It is these beliefs about the anticipated effects of alcohol and drug use that are often found to predict later involvement. To the extent that teens anticipate that use of alcohol or drugs will provide them with stress-relief, facilitate social interactions (e.g., allow them to be seen as "cool" and accepted into a peer group), or produce feelings of euphoria (i.e., "high"), they may begin to engage in alcohol and drug use. While some adolescent experimentation with alcohol and drugs is normative, teens with poorly developed skills to manage negative moods, to engage in comfortable social interactions, to generate positive feelings in the absence of alcohol and drug use, or to effectively manage social pressures for substance involvement are at greater risk for developing substance use problems.

Skills-based approaches to substance abuse treatment suggest that effective treatment must provide skills for altering situations and conditions that give rise to substance use, and teach alternative means of achieving reinforcing experiences other than the effects of alcohol and drug use. Additionally, coping skills for managing social pressures to use alcohol and/or drugs have been found to play an important role in successful outcome following treatment for teen substance abuse. In particular, concern with the negative consequences of substance use and strategies that provide specific means for maintaining abstinence in the face of pressure to use are associated with better outcome following treatment for teen substance abuse.

Rationale for Functional Family Therapy

The family has long been recognized as a primary source of influence in the theoretical and empirical literature concerning the development and maintenance of adolescent substance use problems. Treatment literature has documented that the family can play a major role in influencing changes in an adolescent's substance use. Preliminary results from a controlled trial of family therapy for adolescent substance abuse indicate a 45 percent reduction from pretest to posttest in the number of days during which any substance was used (Wagner, et al., 1999). Thus, there is growing evidence that family involvement may yield positive effects in the treatment of adolescent AOD abuse.

The Functional Family Therapy (FFT) model (Alexander & Parsons, 1982) presented here represents an integration of family systems and behavioral perspectives for addictive behavior (Waldron & Slesnick, 1996). Family systems perspectives view problem alcohol and other substance use as maladaptive behavior expressed by one or more family members, but reflecting dysfunction in the system as a whole. The essential core and distinguishing feature of family systems models, then, is that the locus of problem behavior is relational, transcending the individual, and therefore the focus of treatment should also be relational. The FFT model goes beyond systems theory, however, integrating and conceptually linking behavioral and cognitive intervention strategies to the ecological formulation of the family disturbance. The cognitive-behavioral techniques used in FFT are designed to effect change in a number of substance use risk and protective factors, including parent and sibling drug use, ineffective supervision and discipline (monitoring), negative parent/child relationships, and family conflict. In general, however, changing family interactions and improving relationship functioning is key to reducing adolescents' involvement with alcohol and other drugs.

Description of Sample Case

Daniel was a 17-year-old male with a two-year history of polysubstance abuse, including marijuana, alcohol, and hallucinogens. He was referred for treatment to an outpatient substance abuse treatment program for adolescents by his probation officer, following a charge of possession of marijuana found in his locker at school. He attended the intake interview with his mother, who described school problems stemming back to his freshman year of high school: parent-adolescent conflict, curfew violations, and other problem behavior at home, including physical aggression toward his younger brother, age 15. Since Daniel had started his senior year two months before, he had missed ten days of school and he was not turning in homework. He received an intake diagnosis of Conduct Disorder.

The program routinely conducted an assessment at pre-treatment, including the Personal Experience Screening Questionnaire (PESQ; Winters, 1991), and Daniel scored above PESQ problem severity cut-off criteria (for age and gender) indicating the need for additional substance abuse evaluation. PESQ validity scale scores indicated no reason to suspect false or careless responding, so a more comprehensive substance abuse evaluation was conducted. Daniel was interviewed using the Teen Addiction Severity Index (T-ASI: Kaminer, *et al.*, 1993), and results indicated polysubstance involvement severe enough to warrant additional diagnoses of alcohol abuse and marijuana dependence. During the month before treatment, Daniel reported using marijuana almost every day, smoking cigarettes daily, drinking alcohol five times, using LSD once, and using mushrooms twice. He had started using alcohol and tobacco at age 13, marijuana at age 14, and LSD and mushrooms at 15. Other noteworthy findings from the T-ASI concerned Daniel's legal, family, academic, and psychiatric functioning. During the past year, he had been arrested twice while intoxicated, had experienced increasing difficulties getting along with his family members, and had demonstrated a marked decline in academic performance. Despite the assessment findings, Daniel initially denied that his substance use was problematic in any way.

Treatment of Adolescent Substance Abuse

Assessment. A good assessment of any adolescent problem is grounded in sound theory with an appreciation for developmental factors. We believe that adolescent substance abuse problems are best conceptualized as biologic, psychologic, and social phenomena. Failure to consider the role of any of these dimensions in the development and perpetuation of substance abuse may result in a worse clinical course. Thus, ideally, teen substance abuse assessment should include evaluation of each of the following areas:

1) the substance use behavior itself;
2) the type and severity of psychiatric morbidity that may be present and whether it preceded or developed after the substance use disorder;
3) cognition, with specific attention to neuropsychological functioning;
4) family organization and interactional patterns;
5) social skills;
6) vocational adjustment;
7) recreation and leisure activities;
8) personality;
9) school adjustment;
10) peer affiliation;
11) legal status;
12) physical health.

The biopsychosocial conceptualization of adolescent substance abuse also suggests the need for a broad-spectrum assessment process. Whenever possible, information should include teens' self-reports (gained through self-monitoring, clinical interview, and/or structured reporting forms), significant others' reports (e.g., parents, teachers), psychometric testing, direct observation of the adolescent's behavior, and biological measures. In actual clinical practice, however, reports of the adolescent and her/his parents are often the only data available to the clinician.

Overview of Substance Abuse Treatment with Adolescents. As mentioned above, heterogeneity in factors such as the anticipated effects and consequences resulting from substance use, the context and motivations in which use occurs, and the factors that contribute to or accompany using behavior characterize teenage substance abusers. As a result, interventions must be carefully tailored to meet the specific needs of each adolescent. The following are some suggestions for developing effective treatment plans based upon comprehensive assessment of teens in need.

Clients show greater improvement with interventions matched to their cognitive style and level. This is an important consideration in treatment, as adolescents vary in their level of cognitive development. As much as possible, interventions for this population should first consider level of cognitive functioning. Other client matching factors to consider include:

1) severity of substance use problem;
2) concurrent psychopathology;
3) adequacy of available support systems (home environment, school, etc.);
4) severity of problem behavior;
5) intrapersonal characteristics: (i.e., aggression; impulsivity; self-esteem);
6) interpersonal skills and functioning;
7) physical health;
8) academic functioning.

Rather that focusing solely on substance abuse, treatment goals should be developed for each of the teen's identified difficulties. Sensitivity to the teen's own perceptions of core problems is important. "Rolling" with initial resistance (i.e., empathizing with, rather than challenging, adolescent perceptions of why they ended up in treatment) can help reduce opposition and build rapport. Providing choices to the adolescent client during the process of treatment is also important for optimal clinical outcomes. Allowing teens to be active participants in selecting a treatment may be effective in increasing motivation, commitment, and compliance, and may help reduce resistance.

Individual Cognitive-behavioral Therapy: Techniques

Several common tools and techniques comprise individual cognitive-behavioral treatment (CBT), but the core techniques are functional analysis and role-plays. These techniques, as well as some useful general guidelines for implementing the treatment, are described below.

Functional analysis refers to examining the role of substance use in the teen's life (i.e., how is the adolescent reinforced by using alcohol or drugs; primary/secondary gains?). Functional analysis relies on the *behavior chain,* which is presented to the adolescent as a series of events that determine substance use.

The first three events in the behavior chain are classified as antecedents of behavior. *Trigger* is defined as an event that precedes alcohol and drug use. It is a stimulus to which the individual may react with an overt response (drinks in front of others to "appear cool") or covert response (thinks about taking a drink or drug upon presentation of a trigger). *Thoughts* are responses to the stimulus (trigger), which can be positive or negative. They are generally reflective of the individual's perception and interpretation of the context in which the trigger is presented. *Feelings* are another type of internal reaction to a thought or perception of a trigger. In the cognitive-behavioral model, emphasis is placed on thoughts in relation to how they precede feelings.

Behavior is an action generated secondary to antecedents. Behavior is identified as a response to the thoughts and/or feelings generated by the trigger, as well as resulting thoughts and feelings. In the current context, the focus will usually be on the behavior of substance use.

Consequences resulting from this behavior are divided into positive and negative. It is important to acknowledge that teens partake in alcohol and drugs because of positive consequences they associate with using. Likewise, raising awareness of the negative consequences ultimately incurred is important in promoting understanding of the personal costs of alcohol and drug use. The behavior chain is useful because it provides a concrete means for examining and understanding the antecedents to and consequences of substance use behavior. The schematic overleaf outlines the behavior chain.

Role-play is an important tool in treating adolescent substance abusers because it promotes identification of maladaptive behavior and immediate reframing. Furthermore, it is a therapeutic method effective for providing guided opportunities for adolescents to practice skills learned in treatment. Rehearsal of

Behavior chain Event	Definition	Examples
TRIGGER	Event preceding drug or alcohol use	Can be a person, place, situation, or combination. Does not cause, but may facilitate use.
THOUGHTS	POSITIVE/NEGATIVE – Internal response to presentation of trigger	"What will they think if I say no?" "Maybe, I'll look like a mama's boy"
FEELINGS	Internal reaction to trigger	Anxiety, craving, anger, etc.
BEHAVIOR	Action/Response to trigger	Alcohol or other drug use.
CONSEQUENCES	POSITIVE – Reinforcing; increases future likelihood of behavior NEGATIVE – Punishing; decreases the future likelihood of behavior	POSITIVE – felt euphoric, decreased stress, partied with friends (usually occur close to behavior) NEGATIVE – hangovers, DUI, trouble with parent (usually occur distant from the behavior)

behavioral skills through role-play is an essential part of skills acquisition, and gives teens a chance to hone their skills before attempting them in the real world. The focus should be on working through role-plays rather than engaging in discussion of problem situations and strategies.

Asking teens to participate in role-plays may provoke resistance and discomfort; therefore, clinicians should anticipate the need to employ certain strategies to facilitate performance. To "break the ice," the clinician might start by asking the client, Daniel, to relate a relevant personal experience, which will be used as the basis for a future role-play. It is important to initially create role-play scenarios of moderate difficulty, with a plan to practice and improve, before moving on to more challenging scenarios. To help Daniel generate role-play scenarios, we recommend:

1) asking for a recent situation in which the target skill would have been helpful but was not utilized;
2) asking for a situation that might occur in the future where the skill would be helpful;
3) suggesting situations based on our knowledge of Daniel and his presenting problems, including information from the behavior chain.

Following each role-play, Daniel would be reinforced for participating, and would discuss reactions to the performance with the therapist. Feedback is provided by the therapist on role-play performance, including praise for improvement and participation, along with constructive criticism about areas that need improvement.

General Guidelines for Individual Cognitive-behavioral Treatment

CBT sessions are designed to be structured. Typical sessions begin with a review of material discussed in the previous session, and reinforcement for successful utilization of skills presented. Successes in incorporating skills learned in previous sessions are built upon, and problems are addressed. When introducing new material in a session, it is always prefaced with a rationale and, in Daniel's case, would be explained in the context of his personal behavior chain. The explicit goal of all sessions is to maximize the likelihood that through skills training, maladaptive behavior and cognitions are replaced with more appropriate (positive) behavior and cognitions.

Handouts are useful, as they make esoteric aspects of the intervention more concrete by providing a visual image of the material. A form presenting the behavior chain may be especially helpful, and handouts with outlines of skills, examples, and other materials also may be useful. Lecturing for extended periods is to be avoided; it would be important to involve Daniel and solicit his input and ideas throughout the session. This latter approach will help to maintain his attention, bolster his self-esteem, and help him develop a sense of responsibility, directing his own efforts at behavioral change.

Homework assignments are important for practicing and acquiring skills, and should be part of each session. Daniel would be provided with a rationale for homework such as: "Using the techniques we will discuss in treatment do not always come naturally in the real world. Therefore, they require practice. The assignments we develop will help you learn and become comfortable with these ideas and behavior. How successful you'll be in changing your behavior is directly related to how much effort you put into practicing these changes."

Finally, alternative (non-substance involved) activities should be encouraged as opportunities for Daniel to build self-esteem and form healthier peer networks. Planning and engaging in alternative activities such as hobbies, sports, and organized groups play important roles in determining adolescents' success in changing their substance use behavior.

Cognitive-behavioral Coping Skills Training: Treatment Outline

Functional Analysis. After establishing rapport with Daniel, the session began by presenting the rationale for a skills training approach, including functional analysis. The behavior chain was explained, emphasizing the relatedness of antecedents, substance use behavior, and consequences. Possible resistance or fears Daniel had about the demands of treatment were assuaged by letting him know that the goal of treatment was not immediate perfection. Rather, treatment is about learning, practicing, and improving behavior over time. Metaphors may be used, like exercising regularly to develop muscles/skills over time.

The therapist introduced each element of the behavior chain, beginning with the antecedents. A sample trigger to illustrate each level of the chain aided Daniel's understanding of the model. Next, the therapist solicited a trigger from him by asking for an interpersonal situation where Daniel was uncomfortable or unhappy. The therapist and Daniel then worked through the behavior chain together. Once he understood the behavior chain and how it illuminated ways to change behavior, substance use became the primary target. When focusing on this, the therapist examined the kind of triggers used by Daniel. He was asked about his specific social/interpersonal triggers, as these are idiosyncratic for substance use. Again, the therapist used the behavior chain and focused on the thoughts and feelings that occured between the trigger and behavior.

After identifying an appropriate trigger and working through the antecedents, the consequences of substance use (positive and negative) were elicited. This was followed by an exploration of alternatives (i.e., what else could achieve the same positive consequences without the negatives?). Daniel was oriented to the components of treatment and his specific triggers were discussed. It was important to acknowledge that individuals differ in their triggers, but that the components discussed are commonly important for teens. He was allowed to prioritize those elements according to perceived importance. It was emphasized and explained how the various components of treatment might be helpful in improving Daniel's ability to communicate effectively with others, cope better with negative feelings, and consequently change his substance use behavior.

As homework, Daniel was asked to work on behavior chains for triggers related to interpersonal situations. These were not necessarily related to substance use, but included situations that resulted in negative feelings (angry, anxious, uncomfortable, sad, lonely, etc.), as these emotions, similar to boredom, often preceded his substance use/abuse.

Interpersonal Skills: Assertiveness Training. The therapist began by providing Daniel with a rationale for assertiveness training. He was told that assertiveness involves standing up for yourself, while respecting the rights of others. Assertiveness training can ultimately lead to increased self-esteem, which in turn builds resistance against artificial methods of escape from social stresses such as drinking and using drugs. A by-product of these changes is noted by dramatic improvements in relationships with others. Good relationships, as opposed to negative peer groups, are yet another tool for eliminating use and abuse.

Daniel was assisted in verbally listing and elaborating upon the following human rights:

1) to decide things and make one's own decisions;
2) to have one's own feelings;
3) to have one's own thoughts and opinions;
4) to express one's own thoughts and opinions;
5) to say "yes" or "no" to requests;
6) to be healthy and safe and not be abused physically, emotionally, or sexually.

The therapist then elicited defined, and discussed different patterns of social behavior:

1) Passive—respects others' rights but not one's own;
2) Aggressive—respects own rights but not others';
3) Assertive—respects own and others' rights.

At this point, the therapist used homework from the "triggers" section, and asked Daniel for personal examples involving passive and/or aggressive behavior. The therapist then defined and discussed assertiveness guidelines, included the following:

1) We can only control our own, not others', behavior. You can ask others to change, but they can say no;
2) Know what you want from a situation;
3) Be specific about what you want;
4) Pay attention to body language consistent with what you want;
5) Timing is important (e.g., if you're mad take some time to calm down before confronting someone);
6) Use "I" statements, and avoid words like "should" and "never;"
7) Criticize the behavior not the person;
8) When criticizing, use the "sandwich" technique; first say something positive about the issue/person, then give criticism, then end with something positive;

9) Be prepared to negotiate (plan what you are willing and unwilling to compromise).

The therapist then returned to triggers involving passive and aggressive behavior and engaged in role-plays using the above guidelines for assertive behavior. The therapist tried to work through two examples until Daniel demonstrated comprehension and improvement. For homework, Daniel was asked to select a relatively non-threatening situation in which to practice his assertiveness skills. He was also asked to work on behavior chains for triggers relevant to current or upcoming topics (daily experiences are good for providing concrete examples and increasing awareness of behavior).

Interpersonal Skills: Criticism, Expressing Feelings. Daniel was asked to generate situations in which he has had difficulty giving or accepting criticism or expressing feelings (positive or negative), particularly, but not necessarily, related to substance use. The therapist helped Daniel go through the behavior chain for selected triggers, and focused on ways of changing the behavior by altering the antecedents and generating alternatives to achieve the desired consequences. Selected examples were role-played. For homework, Daniel selected a relatively non-threatening situation in which to practice these skills and was also asked to identify behavior chains for triggers relevant to current or upcoming topic.

Interpersonal Skills: Dealing with Conflict (Anger and Frustration). Daniel was asked to present situations in which he has had difficulty dealing with conflict, particularly, but not necessarily, related to substance use. The therapist helped Daniel go through the behavior chain for selected trigger(s), and focus on ways of changing the behavior by altering antecedents and identifying alternative behavior to achieve the desired consequences. Selected examples were role-played. For homework, Daniel selected a relatively non-threatening situation in which to practice assertiveness skills and was also asked to identify behavior chains for triggers relevant to current or upcoming topic.

Intrapersonal Skills: Managing Emotions. A variety of strategies were discussed with Daniel to allow him to match skills with his particular circumstances and style. In addition to the interpersonal skills previously described, he was instructed on methods for managing mood, including relaxation training or meditation (for anxiety, tension, and anger management), involvement in pleasant activities (for depression, boredom), and cognitive strategies focused on identifying and changing negative or "irrational" thoughts.

Initially, it was helpful to elicit from Daniel his own experiences with negative feelings and, using the behavior chain, work through the elements of identified experiences. He was assisted in identifying and selecting the types of negative feelings that were most problematic. Once a particular feeling had been chosen, he was provided with a description of strategies for managing feelings and how they fit into the behavior chain. As in previous sessions, rehearsal and practice were important elements of successful mood management training. It was also important to point out how the interpersonal skills previously learned functioned to manage negative feelings (e.g., assertiveness, expressing feelings, etc.). Homework assignments depended upon the specific strategies selected for mood management. With these homework assignments, there was less focus on behavior chains, though emphasis remained on identifying potential triggers related to negative feelings.

Relapse Prevention. It was important to prepare Daniel for possible negative feelings and thoughts that may come if he lapses into previous patterns of substance use. The therapist emphasized that a slip was not a total failure, but rather a signal to examine what is going on and concentrate efforts to avoid the next slip. High-risk situations are those previously associated with substance use or which pose a risk for substance use, and must be identified for each individual. The triggers discussed throughout previous sessions provided many examples of high-risk situations. The availability of appropriate/adequate coping skills for managing them reduces the likelihood of relapse. Self-efficacy enhancement was crucial to the successful utilization of coping skills. It was important to draw on Daniel's previous success in using the skills, and to reinforce his sense of being able to cope successfully in high-risk situations.

After discussing the idea of relapse prevention with Daniel, work started on identifying high risk for relapse situations. First, the therapist described the types of situations/circumstances associated with relapse. For teens, high-risk situations typically involve the presence of peers: social pressure to use is the most common relapse situation. After Daniel identified personal high-risk situations, he was assisted in assessing his perceptions of risk of using and ways to cope with various situations identified. When Daniel has trouble coming up with high-risk situations, he was reminded of previously discussed triggers, and returned to functional analysis in suggesting high-risk situations. With this material, homework assignments involved having Daniel (a) make a list of high-risk situations for the present, the next two weeks, and the next month, and (b) work on behavior chains for one or two situations, coming up with alternative behavior and other strategies for avoiding relapse.

Further Skills Building. After the identification of high-risk situations, sessions focused attention on situations likely to be particularly problematic. Such situations are examined using the behavior chain. As before, the individual generates alternatives that accomplish the same result as substance use. In addition to alternative behavior, coping strategies focus on changing feelings and thoughts in response to a trigger. Discussion of refusal skills is particularly important. Assertiveness skills and role-play situations in which the adolescent might be pressured to use are reviewed and homework assignments focus on having fun without substances.

Daniel rehearsed a number of possible coping alternatives for identified high-risk situations. For each alternative, he discussed execution, consequences, possible reactions, and confidence. It was important for him to pre-plan a coping response before he was confronted with the situation. Treatment targeted anticipation and accurate appraisal of risky situations for each major problem area and reviewed upcoming events and identified potentially difficult situations. Plans were made for coping with a potential slip, framing this as a learning experience.

As Daniel became more skillful, he practiced new coping skills in increasingly more difficult situations. Avoidance of high-risk situations is useful early in treatment, but will not provide for lasting effects on confidence and preventing relapse. External aids should be used to help ensure success in homework assignments. Daniel was encouraged to make self-attributions with respect to treatment gains, and to reduce and ultimately fade out avoidance (within reason) and external supports as the end of treatment neared. Homework for this material involved having Daniel (a) work on plans for coping with high-risk situations, (b) practice skills, initially in easy, safe settings, and progress gradually to more difficult situations, and (c) role-play refusal methods in simulated high-risk scenarios.

Personal Risks, Alternative Activities. In addition to focusing on specific relapse prevention skills and strategies, a more global focus on developing activities that will provide reinforcement and non-substance abusing environments is important. This task can be conceptualized as goal setting and time set aside to discuss what types of activities or pursuits the teenager might enjoy. A variety of domains should be considered including hobbies, recreational activities (e.g., sports), social activities, employment opportunities, etc. These types of pursuits provide an avenue for successful resolution of substance abuse problems for many teens.

Functional Family Therapy: Techniques

FFT involves two major phases. The first one focuses on readiness to change and involves creating the context in which behavior change can occur. The therapist's aims in this phase are to:

1) engage the family in therapy;
2) enhance the family's motivation for change;
3) assess the relevant aspects of individual and family functioning to be addressed in treatment.

Although the elements of Phase I are conceptually distinct, therapists typically alternate between engagement, motivation, and assessment, or engage in all tasks simultaneously. For example, interrupting a hostile exchange to elicit information for assessment purposes can also serve to disrupt a family process inhibiting collaboration. The second phase focuses on establishing and maintaining behavior change both at the individual level and for the family as a whole. In this behavior change phase, the motivational framework created and the assessment data obtained in the first phase are used to guide the selection and implementation of specific behavioral techniques. FFT requires that Phase I be successfully completed before moving to Phase II to focus on long-term behavior change.

Developmental factors such as age of the family member with drug or alcohol problems, the cognitive functioning level of family members, and phase of the family life cycle must be considered in determining the strategies to be used for behavior change. Increasing parental supervision might be an appropriate intervention for a 13-year-old referred for drinking and smoking marijuana, for example, but increasing parental support would be more appropriate for an older adolescent like Daniel. Contingency management would be appropriate for adolescents of all ages, but the specific contingencies would differ with maturity. Different strategies might also be required with a family in the exiting phase of the life cycle versus a family whose adult child was temporarily reintegrating into the household after a failed marriage. In addition, the level and sophistication of therapist language and the complexity of interventions should also be tailored to the needs of the family on the basis of the levels of cognitive functioning of family members.

Treatment Engagement. The importance of engaging families in treatment is underscored by the realisation that without successful engagement, families cannot benefit from treatment. The process of engaging families relies primarily on creating positive expectations for therapy. A host of variables can influence treatment expectancies, including characteristics of the service delivery system (e.g., reputation, location, friendliness of staff), family attitudes and beliefs, and therapist characteristics (e.g., age, gender, ethnicity, cultural sensitivity, education level, experience, interpersonal warmth). In this relatively transitory period, the family members' perceptions that the therapist can help them are more important than any specific technique the therapist could employ. From first contact with the therapist, families are attuned to aspects of therapy important to them, such as the therapist's confidence that their problems can be solved, ability to listen and validate their feelings, or use of humor. Therapists can make some adjustments to maximize credibility (e.g., adopting the language system used by the family) but can also anticipate challenges to credibility and respond to them directly (e.g., "No, I haven't ever raised a teenager, but we've had a lot of families come in here and beat this thing, and I think the program can work for your family, too.").

Enhancing Motivation. Daniel's family would likely enter therapy with strong ideas about what the problems were and who was at fault, with blaming attributions centered on his traits or dispositions. Parents often portray adolescents as "disrespectful," "irresponsible," or with other negative characteristics. Family members often view therapy as a way to "fix" the member who is seen as causing the problem. At the same time, family members often do not have positive expectations for therapy, having given up on finding a solution to the problem or expressing anger and resentment at having been remanded to treatment with the referred adolescent by the school or legal system. Motivational enhancement is designed to effect cognitive changes compatible with systemic change by offering families alternative, less negative, relationship-based definitions of the problem.

Relabeling and relationship focus are the two main strategies for effecting short-term cognitive changes in families. To enhance motivation and set the stage for long-term change, therapists focus on changing the meaning of family members' behavior, with particular emphasis on decreasing negative attributions, and helping families develop a relational view of behavior. Daniel's family would be helped to consider their behavior as motivated and maintained by variables other than individual malevolence (e.g., "they don't know how to show their affection;"

"expressing anger is really demonstrating concern"). This would result in the family being more motivated to change, and increase their ability to see change as possible. Similarly, helping families develop an appreciation for how their thoughts, feelings, and behavior are related to those of the other family members can give them a context for suspending their blaming behavior and participating in the change process. The therapist's use of warmth, empathy, and humor in responding contingently to family members is vital to the success of motivational enhancement with them. Each participant should feel cared for and sided with while also experiencing their share of responsibility for the family's problems in the safety of the therapeutic environment.

Relabeling or reframing problem behavior is considered one of the core cognitive techniques in FFT used to affect a shift in the family's perspective about their problems. Relabeling changes the meaning and value of a negative behavior by casting it in a more benign, or even benevolent, light. Morris, *et al.* (1988) proposed that relabels may operate by:

1) suspending the automatic negative thinking and response patterns in families;
2) requiring them to search for new explanations of family behavior;
3) offering a cognitive perspective that opens the door to more effective communication and expression of feelings, and reconnects families with their underlying love and caring for each other.

If family members can be helped to consider that their own and others' behavior is motivated and maintained by variables other than individual malevolence (e.g., anger reflects underlying hurt or worry), they are more likely to see change as possible and are more motivated.

Reframes may take various forms. Some may focus on motives (e.g., "So Daniel, what feels intrusive to you is when your Mom tries to take every precaution to keep you safe from harm. It sounds like you're ready to start taking some responsibility for your own safety. What would that look like and how would your Mom know you're doing a good job?"). Others may emphasize a common experience shared by all family members (e.g., "A lot of times things don't get said in this family because everyone is protecting someone else, although in different ways. Daniel clowns around and diverts attention whenever things get too hot, Mom gets quiet and keeps her pain to herself, and Marisa steps in and offers herself as the focus of the fighting. Even though it feels frustrating when it's happening, it's almost as if you all have some investment in keeping it this way.") The therapist uses knowledge about the family, inferences, and guesswork in relabeling the family and persists for as many sessions as needed, until the negativity is reduced and family members have adopted the shift in perspective.

In disturbed families, individuals do not usually see their behavior as contributing to their current difficulties in an interdependent fashion. Rather, they view their own behavior as a necessary reaction to the misbehavior of other members. Part of the therapist's job is to point out the interactions between family members so they become aware of how they affect each other, and how the relationship affects their behavior. In the case of Daniel, his older sister, Marisa, is a straight 'A' student who is frequently praised by her parents. This is in contrast to Daniel, who started stealing to buy "weed." Their therapist can shift the focus from Daniel's "problem" by helping the family understand his need for attention and his feelings of inadequacy when compared with his sister. This shift in no way discounts that Daniel's behavior is unacceptable, but can facilitate the family's adopting a more cooperative, supportive outlook that would allow them to participate more fully in the change process that should ultimately eliminate drug use.

The therapist can facilitate a relationship focus by asking questions and identifying sequences of behavior that focus on the relational impact of family behavior, thoughts, and feelings and guide the family away from discussions of the adolescent's problem behavior. For example, when Daniel's Mom complained about his misbehavior, the therapist might turn to the grandmother, who lives with the family, and ask where she was during the last argument. Focusing on the relationship would "take the heat off" the referred family member (i.e., Daniel), lower defensiveness, and increase willingness to change with the rest of the family.

Actively interrupting families during hostile exchanges is often necessary to avoid an escalation of the kind of interactions families typically experience at home and allows the family to experience a change, albeit brief, in the usual outcome. Relabels or relational comments may be inserted into the family process to disrupt aversive interactions and inhibit blaming behavior. Process comments, described below, can also be used. Or, the therapist may interrupt the process specifically to slow down the pace of therapy, using reflective listening or summary statements to moderate the rate of exchange.

The FFT model proposes that confronting family members by challenging them directly about their behavior and their need to change serves to elicit resistance to the therapeutic process. Maintaining a non-blaming tone lowers defensiveness and allows the possibility of changing without forcing family members to admit fault for previous failures. The FFT model specifically prohibits judging family members, arguing with them, or attempting to persuade them to accept responsibility for their behavior. These strategies are viewed as counterproductive to inducing motivation. Instead, the therapist must take care to remain non-judgmental, use relabels, remain relationship focused, and use other strategies to shift the emphasis away from problem behavior. Care must also be taken to avoid forming a coalition with one family member at the expense of another. Establishing a positive focus can also help to establish a non-blaming tone in therapy. By inviting family members to reflect on aspects of family life that are working well for them or asking them to recall happier times, pleasant events, and rewarding family activities can emphasize strengths, raise expectations that family life can be better, and help motivate them to pursue more positive interactions.

Process comments, like summary statements or relational comments, can also slow the pace of therapy and help disrupt a negative cycle before it escalates. A therapist could say, for example, "Did you notice what just happened here? I asked Mom what would be helpful to her today and the two of you wanted to make sure I knew about the incident after school. Daniel, rather than get back into the discussion about the disagreement you all had, I wonder if you could share with Mom what you were thinking and feeling when you heard her say she was needing some 'down time' today." Process comments can also focus on the meaning family members ascribe to others' behavior, can be used to dissect or analyze the points at which interactions become negative, and can be used to interconnect the affect, behavior, and cognitions of family members.

Assessment. Family therapists often observe that families engage in the same interactions over and over again, even when they can articulate that their behavior (e.g., parents lecturing and sending teenagers to their rooms) is not having the effect they intended (e.g., youth repeatedly engage in the same misbehavior). The concept of function helps the therapist understand some of the resistance to change encountered when working with families by examining the ways each family member attempts to regulate relationships within the family and the interpersonal outcome or payoff the maladaptive behavior and patterns achieve. Analyzing interpersonal functions also reveals aspects of the relationships that family members are unable to tell the therapist. Assessment, in the FFT model, then, requires the therapist to look beyond the apparent problem and refocus on all relationships and the interpersonal impact of repetitive or problematic behavioral sequences.

According to the FFT model, all behavior can be viewed in terms of the interpersonal relatedness or interdependency they allow each family member to achieve with each other (Alexander & Parsons, 1982). To understand the interpersonal function of behavior that characterizes the relationship between family members, the therapist considers the outcome of the behavior. If a behavior is associated with repeated interactional patterns in families that result in family members experiencing significant physical or psychological separation from one another, then the outcome (i.e., function) of the behavior is distance. By contrast, if the outcome of behavior is that family members experience greater connection or interdependency, then the function of the behavior is closeness. Some relationships are characterized by marked distance and closeness, with the blending referred to as midpointing.

The functional states of closeness and distance represent separate dimensions, with the magnitude of each dimension varying from little to large amounts. While certain behavior more commonly produces certain functions (e.g., the state of drunkenness produces distance), a particular behavior must never be assumed to create a specific function. For example, Daniel's drug use created considerable distance from other family members, in that he spent the majority of his free time with other drug-abusing peers. Alternatively, drug use may have initiated a repeated behavioral sequence in Daniel's family that routinely resulted in increased closeness when mother and father rallied around him, in a renewed effort to support him. Or, drug use may have involved a mix of both closeness and distance when Daniel alternated messages expressing "cries for help" with messages that rejected his parents' attempts to help. Thus, an entire behavioral sequence must be examined and the final result determined so that an accurate functional assessment can be inferred for each family member.

Moreover, functions are unique to each relationship and any given behavior may simultaneously produce one function in one dyad and another in a different dyad. For example, Daniel's drinking invoked a family ritual of protracted discussions with his recovering alcoholic father (i.e., closeness), while at the same time produced distance between himself and his mother. The mother and father would later draw closer to one another in intense discussion about their son's problem, with their separating and merging best characterized as midpointing. Daniel's behavior, then, allowed a context for father and son to merge, mother and son to separate, and father and mother to moderate their merging and separating.

Although our society typically stereotypes closeness or intimacy as desirable in relationships and distance as undesirable, valence is not attached to functions in this approach. "Smothering" or enmeshed relationships represent maladaptive expressions of closeness, while maintaining distance from other people may facilitate the development of independent thinking and a sense of autonomy and competence. Midpointing can also be expressed in either adaptive or maladaptive ways. For example, Daniel may at times exploit his drug use as a way of escaping from the family and at other times use it as a way of connecting with them (e.g., "I lost my license because I was driving under the influence of alcohol, so you need to drive me to work."). There can also be non-pathological expressions of midpointing, such as the teenager who remains active in the family's affairs but also participates extensively in the school drama and music programs and spends prosocial time with friends. Both of these contexts create a balance of contact and distance, albeit in very different ways. Behavior is the target of change, not the functions themselves. The identification of the functions for each dyad in the family allows the therapist to develop a change plan that will target maladaptive behavior while preserving each family member's functions with others and in so doing increase the likelihood that behavioral changes will be more readily instituted and maintained.

Behavior Change. The primary goal of the behavior change phase is to establish new behavior and patterns of interaction that will replace old ones, preventing maladaptive patterns from reappearing and producing long-term change in the family. During the treatment readiness phase, techniques are used to change the meaning of behavior, the attributions family members have about one another, and family members' motivations. While such changes are important prerequisites to long-term change, changes will not be maintained by themselves unless interaction patterns follow a specific plan.

In the behavior change phase, therapists draw from a menu of treatment strategies and behavior change techniques, such as communication training, contingency management, negative mood regulation, and increasingly rewarding shared activities. This is done in order to achieve the objectives for change with each target behavior in the treatment plan. The particular selection of activities or techniques and how the techniques are applied in changing interactional patterns and behavior depend upon several considerations. An understanding of interpersonal functions is key; intervention attempts can lead to rapid change or resistance, depending on how well the intervention strategy has been fitted to each family member's interpersonal function with each other member's. Even when the behavior change strategy is technically correct and well developed, resistance will arise if the intervention implemented is inconsistent with one or more family members' interpersonal functions. For example, Daniel's substance use may enable him to achieve considerable distance from his parents, while at the same time creating a context for his father's merging function with his mother. That is, the son's substance use allowed the couple to draw closer as they discussed their concerns and attempted to problem solve how best to help their son. Attempts to move Daniel into more interdependent and intense interactions with his parents would be incompatible with the family's relational functions and non-compliance would have been the likely result.

An early goal in the behavior change phase is to enhance the family's experience of positive change. The therapist strives to help the family initiate new and positive interactions, heightening their experience that such interactions are possible (Alexander & Parsons, 1982). Throughout the behavior change phase, interactions are highly structured, and the therapist is active and directive. By maximizing the success experiences of families, the positive momentum and family motivation established in the treatment readiness phase will continue.

When change attempts do go awry, several sources for the problem should be considered. For example, the therapist may not have been sufficiently clear, directive, or otherwise informative for family members to be able to carry out the change plan. Another possibility is that the family's functions have not been met by the behavior change plan. Or, the therapist may need to cycle back to the treatment readiness phase to focus further on motivational enhancement. When compliance with change attempts does occur, the therapist should steadily decrease assistance as each behavior change technique is implemented and each target problem is addressed.

The specific techniques introduced by the therapist in the behavior change phase can include any strategies or devices capable of changing behavior and accomplishing these goals. The FFT model has not created a new set of techniques for changing behavior since many excellent cognitive and behavioral treatment manuals are already available. The most commonly applied modules for changing families are communication skills training, problem-solving and conflict resolution skills, strategies to increase pleasing behavior and rewarding activities, parenting and contingency management skills, the use of technical aids to facilitate family process, and relapse prevention skills. Optional modules also implemented with some families, depending on their particular needs, include emotional regulation (i.e., anger, depressed mood), relaxation training, self-esteem building, assertiveness training, contingency contracting, or methods of self-control.

The unique contribution of the FFT model is its emphasis on the application of techniques in the context of the assessment of functional payoffs in the family, and their tailoring to each set of family relationships. For example, the manner in which the therapist incorporates communication or problem-solving skills into family interactions may range from instituting nightly, formal, family meetings (high contact, low distance) to occasional, informal, "as needed" check-ups between family members or even the use of written notes to convey messages and solve problems (low contact, high distance). Similarly, community-based approaches, such as Alcoholics Anonymous, could be incorporated into treatment, with a father and son with drinking problems attending meetings together or attending different meetings on alternating nights of the week, again depending on their assessed relationship functions.

Families with addictive behavior problems also often have limited access to community resources that reduce the risk for alcohol abuse. Later in the behavior change phase, extrafamilial resources can be identified and contacts made to further support the treatment gains made in therapy. For example, the appropriate time to address other family problems that commonly occur would be after Daniel's substance use has decreased and family interactions have improved. Concerns about the marital relationship and parental drinking are common. The therapist should discuss these issues with the parents and, if they desire, continue treatment to work on such problems. Therapy in these cases should proceed with the marital dyad alone.

As behavioral changes are established in the family, the focus of sessions shifts toward maintenance of change and establishing the family's independence from the therapist. To develop independence, the therapist gradually takes a less active role in intrafamily processes. As family members experience short-term changes, they are helped to consider alternative ways to continue positive change. Gradually, the family is encouraged to develop techniques that might work for them on their own and the interval between sessions is extended.

Another area of emphasis related to generalizing behavior change is the focus on multiple system issues. Many extrafamilial factors cannot be changed, such as neighborhood crime or institutional racism. However, other factors may be modifiable for a family, such as responsiveness of school personnel. The therapist may interact directly with legal and educational systems on behalf of the adolescent and his/her family, particularly during the later stages of therapy when a family is about to complete. The therapist should also help families interact more effectively with extrafamilial influences. This may be addressed through enhancing communication and problem solving skills or other family processes. In addition, the therapist may help the family anticipate stressors and problems, exploring solutions to those future difficulties. For example, the therapist may engage Daniel in a role play, taking the role of the school principal, while Daniel practices positive assertive behavior in order to be allowed back into school. Parents in turn may be helped to learn how to facilitate such behavior.

Therapy moves toward termination when: (1) drug and alcohol use and other problem behavior is reduced or eliminated; (2) adaptive interaction patterns and problem solving styles have been developed and are occurring independent of therapist's monitoring and prompting; and (3) the family appears to have the necessary motivation, skills, and resources to maintain a positive clinical trajectory without the support of ongoing services.

Summary: Integration of CBT and FFT Strategies

One concern in choosing to implement either CBT or FFT over the other is that critical components necessary for establishing and maintaining change may not be included in the intervention. A major strength in integrating the two treatments is that dysfunctional family interactions that fostered the development and maintenance of substance abuse and dependence can be addressed, but the unique features of alcohol and drug use (e.g., reinforcing properties of the substance itself) that operate independently of the family can be taken into account in the context of treatment as well (Waldron, *et al.*, in press). The integrative approach would target the multiple influences affecting substance use and allow for change to be supported throughout a number of systems affecting the problem behavior, including the intrapersonal system of the individual adolescent, the interpersonal systems of family and peers, and the extrapersonal systems of school and the community.

An integration of CBT and FFT would focus on completing a core series of *therapeutic interventions*, rather than on completing a specific number of family or individual sessions. While the cognitive-behavioral and family treatments hold differing perspectives on the development and maintenance of substance use disorders, there is some procedural overlap between family and individual approaches. For example, both models may incorporate communication skills training or focus on dyadic relationship enhancement, albeit with differing rationales and foci. However, an integrative approach would allow for the flexible use of overlapping therapeutic interventions in a manner that is responsive to the needs of clients. Therapists could schedule family and individual sessions as clinically appropriate to enhance positive outcomes.

Integration would incorporate the following therapeutic intervention strategies:

1) utilizing treatment engagement strategies that create a positive expectation for change;
2) relabeling the meaning of behavior in the family to emphasize the relational nature of behavior and disrupt negative attributions using specified cognitive techniques;
3) conducting a family assessment that identifies consistent interaction patterns with each family dyad;
4) conducting an individual functional analysis of an adolescent's substance use with the intent of identifying antecedents of and reinforcers for those behaviors;
5) selecting from a menu of behavioral skills to be flexibly implemented in a number of possible ways within the family, to enhance interpersonal relationship functioning, individually with the adolescent as a means of fostering intrapersonal skill development, both individually and in the family context, or with some relationship dyad of significance to the adolescent.

The authors recommend meeting these objectives in three distinct phases. The first phase focuses on both the family and the individual. Initial sessions engage the family in treatment, enhancing the family's motivation for change, assessing aspects of family relationship to be targeted for change. The initial individual session with the adolescent involves a functional analysis of behavior and then using the functional analysis to guide the identification of targets for skills training. At this early juncture, a menu of options for individual sessions is discussed with the adolescent, and intervention components are selected and incorporated into the treatment plan tailored to the adolescent's needs and treatment goals. The middle phase of therapy focuses primarily on establishing behavioral changes in the family, but is designed so that parts of each session are spent with the adolescent to reinforce implementation of newly acquired skills. The last phase of therapy focuses on application of new family and individual behavior to the natural environment, with an emphasis on independent problem-solving within the family and substance abuse relapse prevention.

Preliminary support has been found for integrating CBT and FFT. Waldron, *et al.* (in press) conducted a randomized clinical trial comparing the efficacy of CBT, FFT, and combined CBT/FFT for treating substance abusing youth. Findings suggest that while adolescents benefited from CBT alone or FFT alone, only those who received the combined intervention reduced their use from pre- to post-treatment and maintained those gains three months later. These results underscore the potential for combining the two interventions, and suggest that treatment response may be improved when the treatment package includes CBT for adolescents and FFT for adolescents and their families.

References

Alexander, J. F., & Parsons, B. V. (1982). *Functional Family Therapy: Principles and Procedures*. Carmel, CA: Brooks/Cole.

American Psychiatric Association. (1994). *Diagnostic and Statistical Manual of Mental Disorders* (4th ed.). Washington DC: Author.

Kaminer, Y., Wagner, E. F., Plummer, B. A., & Seifer, R. (1993). Validation of the Teen Addiction Severity Index (T-ASI): Preliminary findings. *The American Journal on Addictions, 2*, 250–254.

Kendall, P. C. & Morris, R. J. (1991). Child therapy: Issues and recommendations. *Journal of Consulting and Clinical Psychology, 59(6)*, 777–784.

Martin, C. S., & Winters, K. C. (1998). Diagnosis and assessment of alcohol use disorders among adolescents. *Alcohol Health & Research World, 22*, 95–105.

Morris, S., Alexander, J. F., & Waldron, H. (1988). Functional Family Therapy: Issues in clinical practice. In I. R. H. Falloon (ed.) *Handbook of Behavioral Family Therapy*. New York: Guilford. 107–127.

Wagner, E. F., Brown, S., Myers, M., Monti, P. M., & Waldron, H. B. (1999). Innovations in adolescent substance abuse intervention. *Alcoholism, 23*, 236–249.

Wagner, E. F., & Kassel, J. D. (1995). Substance use and abuse. In R. T. Ammerman & M. Hersen (eds) *Handbook of Child Behavior Therapy in the Psychiatric Setting*. New York: John Wiley and Sons.

Waldron, H. B., Brody, J. L., & Slesnick, N. Integrative behavioral and family therapy for adolescent substance abuse. In P. M. Monti, S. M. Colby, T. A. O'Leary (eds),

Adolescents, Alcohol, and Substance Abuse: Reaching Teens Through Brief Interventions. In press.

Waldron, H. B., & Slesnick, N. (1998). Treating the family. In W. R. Miller and N. Heather (eds) *Treating Addictive Behaviors: Processes of Change.* (2nd ed.) New York: Plenum. 271–285.

Waldron, H. R., Slesnick, N., Brody, J. L., Turner, C. W., & Peterson, T. R., *Four- and Seven-month Treatment Outcomes for Substance-abusing Youth. Journal of Consulting and Clerical Psychology*, in press.

Williams, R. J., Chang, S. Y., & Addiction Centre Adolescent Research Group. (2000). A comprehensive and comparative review of adolescent substance abuse treatment outcome. A comprehensive and comparative review of adolescent substance abuse treatment outcome. *Clinical Psycholology: Science and Practice, 7,* 138–166.

Winters, K. C. (1991). *The Personal Experience Screening Questionnaire.* Los Angeles: Western Psychological Services.

Part VII

Special Topics

Chapter 17

Firesetters: Treatment of PTSD Following a Residential Fire Fatality

Russell T. Jones, Audra K. Langley and Carrie Penn

Prevalence

Firesetting has become a major problem among juveniles in the United States. Even though more juveniles are arrested for arson than for any other crime (Office of Juvenile Justice and Delinquency Prevention (OJJDP), 1997), little attention is given to the seriousness of the problem. Rate of juvenile arson reports are continuing to increase while other crimes such as murder and aggravated assault are on the decline for juveniles (Federal Emergency Management Agency (FEMA), 1998). From 1990 to 1994, the rate of juvenile arrest for arson increased 35 percent (OJJDP, 1997). In 1995, 52 percent of arson arrests were children under 18 (OJJDP, 1997).

It is estimated that at least 100,000 fires are set by children yearly (FEMA, 1998). In reality, this number could be considerably higher due to the fact that many fires go unreported or are dismissed as accidents. Among juveniles, prevalence of firesetting is higher for males than females. There is a higher incidence rate of fire setting between the ages of 12 and 14 (FEMA, 1998). Among psychiatric samples, Kolko (1999) found that outpatients and inpatients had a higher prevalence for both matchplay and firesetting.

As with any fire, fires set by children cause severe property damage and even fatalities. In fact, the leading cause of death among preschoolers is fireplay (Kolko, 1999; Hanson, *et al.*, 1995). It is impossible to ignore the increasing prevalence of firesetting among our youth. The need for more research in this area is essential.

Developmental Considerations

As noted earlier, many fires are dismissed and viewed as unintentional based on the belief that young children often start fires accidentally or out of curiosity. One possible explanation for why so many young children start fires is they are curious about fire and how it works.

When considering where adolescents are developmentally, we find many factors that help us to better understand why there is such a high frequency of firesetting among this group. Adolescents are at a point in their lives when they are

Handbook of Conceptualization and Treatment of Child Psychopathology, pages 355–378.

"attempting to assimilate into an adult world" (FEMA, 1998) and are struggling to develop their autonomy and independence. These individuals are also going through extreme transition periods in their lives both physically and mentally. As a result, powerlessness and anxiety are common and have been found to be key symptoms of crisis in firesetters (Richardson & Pinsonneault, 1996). Also, given that peers have a strong influence over behavior during this stage of development; delinquent firesetting is often the result of peer pressure or rebellion.

Clinical Syndrome

Defining the Disorder:

The term firesetting has been used interchangeably with fireplay, arson, fire interest, and matchplay throughout the literature, which leads to confusion and contradiction when defining firesetting. Through the course of this chapter firesetting will be used to refer to any involvement with fire in the broadest sense. Two subgroups will be identified. We will first describe the differences between fire interest, fireplay, firesetting, and arson. These differences have been best explained through a developmental perspective.

Kolko (1999) best distinguishes fire interest, fireplay, firesetting, and arson. **Fire interest** is used to describe a child's curiosity with fire by showing interest and asking questions concerning fire. This curiosity is considered to be "natural" and developmentally appropriate. Gaynor and Hatcher (1987) suggest that a natural curiosity about fire manifests around three years of age and that by the age of six a child will have acquired either fire safe or fire risk behaviors. Fire risk behaviors include fireplay and firesetting.

Fireplay is fire interest with actual experimentation with fire that results in an actual firestart and is associated with low recidivism (Kolko, 1999). An individual who is at low risk of recidivism typically displays no major problems or disorders and has positive surroundings (e.g., positive relations with peers and family). Although both fire interest and fireplay are usually dismissed as accidents and nonpathological, research suggests that fireplay in very young children may be the result of underlying psychosocial problems in either the child or family (Hanson, *et al.*, 1995).

Firesetting includes intentional firestarts with an underlying motive. High recidivism (e.g., definite and extreme risk) is associated with firesetting (Kolko, 1999). Definite risk of recidivism is indicated by some psychological problems in the individual and/or family and by those who set the fire for attention-seeking purposes. Individuals at extreme risk typically have more extensive behavioral and emotional problems, parental pathology and other family stressors, greater peer rejection, and longer histories of firestarts. **Arson** is simply fire starts with malicious and willful intent that meet the legal definition of the state. Many states will look at the criminal history and firesetting behavior before convicting a child of arson.

Gaynor and Hatcher (1987) refer to six behavioral factors that help to distinguish fireplay from firesetting: history, method, ignition source, target, and behavior. History refers to whether the firestart was a single or a recurrent event. The method of firestart refers to whether the event was planned or unplanned. Ignition source gives reference to whether the firesetter used available material or flammable/combustible material that was collected and/or found. The target refers to what the firesetter chose to burn, specifically whether the firesetter burned paper based products or animate objects and whether it was their own property. Lastly, the behavior following the event refers to whether the firesetter put the fire out or let it burn, or if he/she got help or ran away.

The OJJDP (1997) defines child involvement with fire in terms of age. Fires started by children under seven are typically the result of accident or curiosity. Children ranging from eight to 12 years typically show more underlying psychosocial conflicts that result in the form of fire starts. Finally, children between the ages of 13 and 18 have a longer history of undetected firestarts that are the result of a psychosocial conflict or simple criminal behavior.

It is also important to distinguish firesetting from pyromania. As defined in The Diagnostic and Statistical Manual of Mental Disorders-Fourth Edition (DSM-IV) (American Psychiatric Association, 1994), pyromania is an adult impulse-control disorder that involves multiple and deliberate firesetting (Criterion A). Other criteria include tension or arousal before the act; a fascination, curiosity, or attraction to fire and its situational contexts; pleasure, gratification, or relief in setting fire or watching it burn; when not done for monetary gain, as an expression of socio-political ideology, to cover criminal activity, to express anger, to improve one's living circumstances; as the result of delusion or hallucinations or impaired judgement; and that the firesetting can not be better attributed to conduct disorder, a manic episode, or antisocial personality disorder. The DSM-IV makes it clear that there is not an established relationship between juvenile firesetting and pyromania in adulthood, and that the age in which pyromania typically occurs is unknown.

When considering subgroups of firesetters, there are generally four types commonly discussed. These are **curiosity, crisis-precipitated** or cry for help, **delinquent**, and **pathological** (Humphreys, Kopet & Lajoy, 1994; Kolko, 1999).

Neither curious nor pathological firesetters have typically been discussed at length in the majority of research. Curious firesetters are simply seen as young children who have shown interest or set a fire as the result of a natural interest/curiosity. However, new evidence found by Hanson *et al.*, (1995) suggests that fireplay in young children may be the result of underlying psychopathology in either the child or family. A more serious form of firesetting, pathological firesetting, is extremely rare among juveniles and is therefore omitted from further discussion. However, crisis and delinquent firesetting is much more common among juveniles.

Crisis-precipitated firesetters are typically seeking attention through their firestarts and are therefore also termed cry for help firesetters. These children use fire to express their need for attention as the result of a recent crisis (e.g., parental divorce, loss of friends, moving, change of schools). Lack of coping and communication skills also set these children apart from those children who do not participate in firestarts (Richardson & Pinsonneault, 1996). Fires set by these children are more likely to occur in their own homes or schools (FEMA, 1998).

Table 17.1:   A Proposed Model of Risk Factors of Fireplay and Fire Setting

1   Learning experiences and cues
   a. Early modeling (vicarious) experiences
   b. Early interest and direct experiences
   c. Availability of adult models and incendiary materials

2.   Personal repertoire
   a. Cognitive components
     (1) Limited fire-awareness and fire-safety skills
   b. Behavioural components
     (1) Interpersonal ineffectiveness/skills deficits
     (2) Covert antisocial behavior excesses
   c. Motivational components

3.   Parent and family influences and stressors
   a. Limited supervision and monitoring
   b. Parental distance and uninvolvement
   c. Parental pathology and limitations
   d. Stressful external events

Delinquent firesetters typically set fires as the result of boredom, anger, peer pressure, or defiance (Richardson & Pinsonneault, 1996). Although firesetting by females is relatively rare, there is a higher frequency of female firesetters in this group than in others. Because peer pressure plays an important role in this category, there is a higher prevalence of group involvement in the firestarts. Another defining characteristic is that the majority of fires are set outside the home (FEMA, 1998).

In a conceptual model devised by Kolko and Kazdin (1986), risk factors for fire setting are identified (see Table 17.1). The lack of social competence and difficulties in interpersonal situations are identified as key risk factors. Parental psychological adjustment and marital satisfaction have also been correlated with juvenile fire setting. Such behavior is posited to be a later stage of progression of antisocial symptoms.

Associated Disorders

Disorders associated with firesetting include Conduct Disorder, Attention-Deficit Disorder and Adjustment Disorder (DSM-IV) (1994).

General Description of Two Treatments

Treatment Approach 1

While there have been a variety of approaches taken toward the assessment and treatment of firesetters, perhaps the most empirically-based program of research has been that carried out by Kolko and his colleagues.

The cognitive-behavioral approach has been employed in targeting the enhancement of fire safety/prevention knowledge, reduction of curiosity about or interest in fire-related stimuli, and the elimination of involvement with fire. Following an objective assessment of individuals' pretraining level of knowledge and skills related to fire, both children and parent(s) are engaged in a brief session to discuss the extent of the problem and treatment goals. A group intervention strategy is then implemented. Treatment consists of instructions, practice in fire safety concepts and prevention activities using didactic presentation, role-playing, self-instructions, modeling, and reinforcement. Results from an initial study of 24 inpatients ranging in age from 4.3 to 8.1 years showed a significant reduction in contact with fire-related toys and matches in analogue tasks and an increase in fire safety knowledge. Several of these positive findings were evident at a six-month follow-up.

Treatment Approach 2

An alternative approach to the treatment of firesetters is proffered by Richardson and Pinsonneault (1996). Here, it is first important to specify characteristics of the firesetter as viewed by these authors so as to place this strategy in a proper context. Their opinions are based on direct experience with some 2,500 children and adolescent firesetters who have obtained treatment based on their model. They begin by differentiating firesetting from pyromania, and from serious psychiatric or sociopathic disorders. They maintain that the firesetter's behavior frequently has underlying motives and seldom comes to the attention of criminal justice systems or mental health clinics. The firesetter's actions are hypothesized to be a function of issues related to power, anger, peer relations, control, inadequate communication skills, distrust of authorities, and abuse and neglect. Because many of these individuals have not been held accountable for their actions, they state that intervention from the criminal justice system is an essential component to any successful intervention strategy. An axiom for such intervention is that "firesetters must be held accountable for their actions."

Regarding treatment, Richardson and Pinsonneault maintain that regardless of motives for firesetting behavior, the most important component for effective intervention is accepting responsibility for the behavior and its consequences (both potential and real). Criminal prosecution is a key feature of this mode of intervention. The authors state that while specialized juvenile firesetter treatment is often a vital component of an effective treatment package, it should never be used to replace criminal prosecution. The treatment of the firesetter must employ an "all or nothing model." Management and control of one's own behavior as well as gaining insight into underlying motives for firesetting are fundamental aspects of this approach. Also, identification of "warning signs" is a crucial component. Additionally, key components to this treatment package include structured psycho-educational skills building, supervised community service as well as a specialized group-counseling course. These components are to be accompanied with an authoritative, supportive confrontation network of rules and contracts. Evaluation is also an important aspect of this strategy. To date, no publication has emerged documenting the impact of this intervention.

Sample Case and Conceptualization[1]

Duncan is a 15-year-old Caucasian male who resides in a small urban area with his mother and younger sister, Suzy (age 12). He was referred for services by a court mandate after being detained in a juvenile detention facility for setting a destructive home fire which resulted in the death of his three and a half year old brother.

Duncan started the fire by placing plastic bags, clothing, and boxes into a baseboard heater in the basement of his home while his mother was taking a nap. By the time the smoke detectors went off and woke her, the blaze had grown out of control. Duncan's half-brother, unable to escape the fire, which had started below his bedroom where he was also taking a nap, suffered significant burns to 95 percent of his body and subsequently died. Additionally, the fire caused $60,000 in damage. Some time after the fire, Duncan admitted that he was frustrated and angry, with his mother for her lack of attention toward him, and for his increased household and childcare duties, for which he did not feel properly acknowledged.

Kazdin (1989) revealed that Duncan had a long history of fire interest and firesetting. His mother reported that he had been fascinated with fire trucks, fire fighters, media coverage of fires and explosions since he was approximately two years of age. Prior to Duncan's starting school, she had noticed signs of his covert fire play in forms of burnt matches, singed household items and melted crayons on stove elements. In that his mother smoked cigarettes Duncan had shown an ongoing interest in smoking from a young age. On several occasions, she had found him with her cigarettes and matches, attempting to smoke. His fireplay continued during his pre- and early-school years despite his mother's efforts at education and prohibition. She noted that Duncan had never appeared frightened by his firestarts nor by other dangerous behaviors (e.g., hanging out of windows, running into the street without looking). At age six, Duncan set his sister Suzy's pajama top on fire with his mother's lighter. She extinguished it before it harmed her daughter. When he was 10 years old, Duncan set his mother's bed sheets on fire while she slept. Fortunately, the heat of the fire awoke her even before the smoke alarm went off. She was able to put the fire, out confining it to the bed and the surrounding carpet. She reported seeing Duncan staring into the flames, seemingly unafraid.

Duncan admitted to several other fire incidents, most of which occurred when he was alone. He reported having set a series of dumpsters on fire several weeks prior to setting his home on fire. Other intentional fire incidents included a grass fire, dismantling fireworks and making homemade fireworks, and burning paint thinner in his kitchen sink. Recently, he sprayed lubricant into a glass bottle, then

[1]While several portions of the case described above were based on data from the authors' lab, the actual case is fictitious.

held a lighter to the end of the bottle. The vapor ignited and burned his thumb. He stated that he found fire very intriguing.

A psychological assessment carried out approximately four weeks following Duncan's release from the juvenile facility indicated that firesetting was only one of his many problem behaviors. Duncan was administered the Diagnostic Interview for Children and Adolescents (DICA-R-C; DICA-R-A) (Reich & Welner, 1990), Youth Self Report (Achenbach, 1991), Children's Reactions to Traumatic Events Scale (CRTES) (Jones, 1996), March Anxiety Scale for Children (MASC) (March, *et al.*, 1997), and the Child Depression Inventory (CDI) (Kovacs, 1990). Duncan's mother described him as argumentative, aggressive, and impulsive, and was therefore administered the Parent Version of the DICA-P (Reich & Welner, 1990) and a Child Behavior Checklist (CBCL; Achenbach, 1991). Her endorsements on the CBCL placed him in the clinical range on several Externalizing and Internalizing scales. Duncan's teachers were asked to fill out the Teacher Report Form (TRF) (Achenbach, 1991), which showed similar levels of elevation. Based on the results of this thorough assessment, Duncan met DSM-IV criteria for Attention Deficit Hyperactivity Disorder (ADHD), Conduct Disorder (CD), and Post Traumatic Stress Disorder (PTSD) as a result of the fire he had set. Duncan had also been diagnosed with a learning disability (LD) and had consistently struggled in school, despite special classroom assistance. His teachers described him as non-compliant and lacking peer relationships. To obtain a measure of general and religious coping, the How I Coped Under Pressure Scale (HICUPS) (Ayers, *et al.*, 1996) and God Help Me scale (Pargament *et al.*, 1990) were also administered.

Duncan's strengths include: average intelligence, good physical health, and a normal early neurodevelopmental history. According to the fire risk assessment guidelines published by the Federal Emergency Management Agency (FEMA), Duncan would be considered to be at definite to extreme risk for firesetting recidivism due to his other psychological problems as well as parental problems (poor discipline and supervision, maternal depression), peer rejection, school problems, and family stressors.

A thorough developmental history of the family revealed that Duncan was the product of an unplanned, but uncomplicated pregnancy. He was born two weeks premature, but required no extensive hospitalization. His mother reported no alcohol or drug use during pregnancy; however, she smoked throughout her pregnancy. She described her marriage to Duncan's father as chaotic with considerable discord. She reported that they were divorced when Duncan was three years old, right after the birth of his sister Suzy. Duncan has had sporadic contact with his biological father, whom he describes as an alcoholic.

His mother reported always being overwhelmed when attempting to supervise Duncan. From a very young age, he required virtually constant supervision to prevent him from climbing on countertops, into the medicine cabinet, etc. Despite successful toilet training at age two, Duncan became encopretic and enuretic after the birth of his sister, urinating in heating ducts and smearing feces on the wall. She had sought behavior management assistance from a mental health center and a child welfare agency when he entered kindergarten. Mental health counselors at both agencies did not find Duncan's fire-related behaviors to be of "immediate protection concern." By the time he was in first grade, she stated that she "gave up" on attempting to control his behavior.

Working off and on as a bookkeeper, Duncan's mother often left he and his sister unsupervised. When Duncan was 11 years old his mother married her boss. Duncan described his relationship with his stepfather as distant. His mother stated that they "never had much to do with each other" during the three years he lived with them. A year after the marriage, Duncan's half brother was born. When Duncan was 14, his mother and stepfather separated. Subsequently, his mother vacillated between unemployment and working night shifts as a stock clerk. She reported experiencing symptoms of depression for much of the last year.

To obtain insight into Duncan's sister's and mother's psychosocial functioning, Suzy was assessed for depression and PTSD and was found to meet criteria for both. His mother was then administered a stressful life events questionnaire, parent stress index, and family environment scale, all of which indicated elevated levels of discord and distress. Assessments for depression and anxiety resulted in diagnostic levels of major depression and PTSD.

Conceptualization (Cognitive Behavioral)

Duncan's increased impulsivity and negative outlook on life had manifested itself through a series of externalizing behaviors. From a cognitive-behavioral perspective, his long history of fireplay, opposition, aggressive and impulsive behaviors, low self-esteem, ineffective parental supervision, unstable and negligent family environment and access to ignition materials had all played a role in his current pathological status.

Concerning the etiology of Duncan's firesetting behavior, it is posited that modeling played a significant role. His mother's ineffective parental supervision and management skills left a myriad of opportunities for Duncan to be unsupervised over the years. Despite her knowledge of his fire interest and repeated firesetting in the past, Duncan not only observed his mother smoking, but had unsupervised access to cigarette lighters, cigarettes, and matches at a very young age. Over time, he also had access to flammable chemicals, firecrackers, etc. As his firesetting behavior evolved, individuals or their personal property became targets. Thus, it is apparent that his mother lacked child behavioral management skills in general, and the specific skills needed to modify his firesetting behavior.

Several environmental stressors were seen as antecedents to Duncan's recent fire-setting episode; in particular, his sense of parental neglect and the added responsibility placed on him following his stepfather's departure. Since his mother's remarriage and the birth of his half brother, Duncan felt increasingly neglected by his mother. With the recent separation from his stepfather and his mother's subsequent depression, Duncan had to manage more household responsibilities while also caring for his siblings. His mother's depression served to increase her unavailability to his needs. This increased stress, along with his comorbid impulsivity, low self-esteem and school problems, led to an escalation of his conduct and firesetting behaviors. His firesetting served the functions of both getting his mother's attention, and entertaining his fascination with fire. Thus, based on Kolko's (1996) conceptualization of types of firesetters (see Table 1), Duncan fits into the "crisis-precipitated type."

Duncan's motive for firesetting is related both to his social skills deficits and his lack of assertiveness skills for directly expressing his needs. His difficulty with anger management and appropriate emotional expression exacerbates these problems. Additionally, given his mother's history of depressive symptomatology, it is likely that Duncan's acting out had historically served to "draw her out" of her depression by increasing their interactions, however negative that may be.

Cognitive Behavioral Treatment 1

While Duncan served as the primary target for therapy, his mother and sister were also treated. I conceptualized the therapeutic framework from a system's perspective, where each family member as well as the family unit was targeted. Treatment consisted of two phases. Phase 1 where only Duncan was treated, targeted the symptoms of ADHD, CD, LD, social skills deficits, and lack of assertiveness, while during phase 2, all family members were treated for PTSD. Because the treatment of PTSD is less well known than other problems areas, greater detail will be provided in this phase. While this case will be conceptualized within a systems perspective, in that an entire family was affected by Duncan's firesetting behavior and the subsequent fatal fire, only treatment for the firesetter (Duncan) will be detailed. It should be noted, however, that the literature suggests that the presence of PTSD in one family member can perpetuate and exacerbate a dysfunctional family system; their actions may even inadvertently help to maintain PTSD conditions that may cause additional stessors and maladaptive coping patterns. Hence, all three family members were assessed and treated for PTSD.

Pre-Post Assessments

Assessments across each behavior for Duncan, his mother, and sister were objectively and reliably carried out prior to the beginning of treatment. Assessments were readministered at the conclusion of treatment in order to ensure effectiveness of treatment efforts in reducing symptomatology described earlier.

Phase 1

Duncan's treatment consisted of the following five components:

1) contingency management to address his firesetting and aggressive behaviors;
2) behavioral training in social skills to increase his peer interactions, assertiveness skills and his self-esteem;
3) anger management to reduce negative interactions, problem solving, and to increase the implementation of non-destructive behavioral alternatives;
4) cognitive restructuring to target his thinking errors and the role they play in his

externalizing behaviors as well as his anxious and depressive symptomatology, both of which were exacerbated by the death of his half brother;

5) parent training, impulse control and Ritalin to lessen his ADHD symptomology.

Initially, contingency management procedures were implemented to discourage Duncan's involvement with fire and to reinforce contact with non-fire materials, including social interaction and other appropriate interests or hobbies. To increase consistency, Duncan's contingency plan was implemented in the home and at school. His probation officer, primary teacher, and guidance counselor were made aware of all intervention components in order to assist the implementation of various aspects of the program and consequently enhance generalization.

The therapist made several school visits to obtain the commitment of his teachers and guidance counselor in assisting Duncan in the implementation of the contract, as well as to explore opportunities for appropriate attention and social interaction with peers. Behavioral contracts were agreed upon and signed by Duncan, his mother, his teachers, and his therapist, all of whom had a role in the implementation of the contingency procedure.

In addition to taking Ritalin on a daily basis, specific instructions were given to his mother and teacher to enhance his level of compliance to requests. Across both home and school settings, skills to enhance impulse control were also targeted.

Duncan's desire for maternal attention was integrated into his contingency plan, in that he was reinforced for positive behavior by spending one-on-one time with his mother. During these times, topics and issues of concerns to both Duncan and his mother were discussed. Problem-solving and the planning and scheduling of certain events also took place during these times.

Cognitive-behavioral training in social skills, anger management, and problem-solving were implemented to address Duncan's motives for setting fires. This included cognitive-behavioral skills that promoted assertiveness, self-esteem; non-destructive problem solving including appropriate coping skills, relaxation training to gain a sense of control over his physiological reactions to the trigger events, and cognitive restructuring to obtain an understanding of the role of his thinking errors in relation to his anger, and possible social anxiety. Duncan was given an opportunity to practice anger management, problem-solving, and social skills in session and assigned to "practice" them throughout the week at home and school. Duncan's improved ability to express his emotions, needs, and wishes appropriately and assertively led to decreases in his displaced aggression.

During this phase, treatment for Duncan's mother consisted of the following components:

1) parent training and behavioral contingency strategies to address her difficulties with behavioral management and lack of supervision;
2) referral for services targeting her long-lasting depressive symptomatology.

She was trained in effective parental management strategies. Parent training consisted of his mother reading, observing, role-playing, and implementing techniques of attending, positive reinforcement, proper command-giving, and appropriate restriction as punishment. Additionally, she was made aware of the role of modeling and the importance of removing possible igniters from the home, including being very cautious in storing cigarettes, matches, and lighters. In fact, she reduced the time she smoked in front of both children, and removed all flammable items from the garage. Duncan's mother assisted in a plan to reorganize Duncan's responsibilities such that they were reasonable for his developmental level and current capabilities. She was encouraged to solicit the help of extended family both in supervising Duncan and his sister and in providing social support for the family. Finally, his mother was encouraged to seek therapy to address her depressive symptomatology.

Phase 2

Since the PTSD, symptoms of nightmares, flashbacks, difficulty sleeping and poor adjustment were voiced by Duncan, Suzy and Mother, treatment of distress levels resulting from the fire and the death of the youngest child was implemented. The intervention was a cognitive-behavioral treatment package, consisting of Systematic Desensitization and Rehearsal-Plus (R+). Each component will be detailed below. Based on our work in the area of assessing the impact of residential fire on children, it was determined that the Jones and Ollendick (in press) model was most applicable in conceptualizing this phase of treatment (see Figure 17.1).

Since Duncan's mother was extremely resistant to beginning this phase of treatment because of the anticipated negative consequences of "talking about the fire again," as well as the fear of her son being "punished more severely," we decided to provide her with our reasoning for this decision.

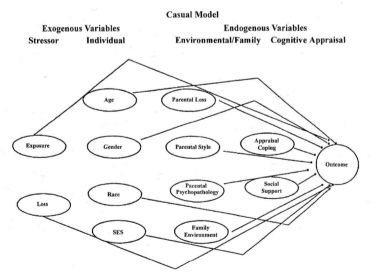

Figure 17.1: Stress and Coping Model

At the outset of treatment, we met with the family to introduce them to this phase of training as well as my reasoning for using this approach. Given the mother's busy schedule, and the families' recent relocation due to the fire, we thought it important to explain our rationale for treatment in hopes of facilitating a greater level of compliance on the part of each participant.

More specifically, we began the session by stating that she and each of her children met the criteria for PTSD. We then discussed the major criteria for PTSD as the experience of a sudden, unpredictable event outside the normal range of experience that involves actual or threatened death or serious injury, or a threat to the physical integrity of self or others; continuous re-experiencing and intrusive memories of the traumatic event (i.e., nightmares, flashbacks); persistent avoidance of disaster-related activities (i.e., psychic numbing); and increase levels of arousal (i.e., difficulty concentrating, somatic complaints). Because Duncan and Suzy were at different developmental levels, we took time to state that symptoms often differ across development level. Younger children tend to withdraw from others and exhibit attachmental behavior because of fear of separation, while older adolescents may do poorly in school. We went on to state that children also express their symptoms through repetitive, and post-traumatic play. However, a few symptoms are common across all developmental ages, such as sleep disturbances.

We shared with the family that a number of studies had examined the mental health impact of fires on adults and children in relation to the extent of damage or loss incurred. Several studies found that the level of adjustment of both mother and child was significantly related to the amount of loss incurred, and that the highest levels of psychopathology were related to the number of disaster-related deaths. We also noted that the second variable effecting levels of psychopathology was the amount of time since the disaster had occurred. Greater time since disaster was associated with lower levels of psychopathology.

We informed the family, particularly the mother, that additional assessments would be carried out to verify significant levels of pathology had resulted from the fire, and also to identify factors which may contributed to these elevated levels. We indicated that additional areas to be assessed included premorbid psychopathology as well as distress during and following the fire. We informed the mother of the need to actually further assess children's reaction to the fire as well as her's, because parents often underestimate the level of distress experienced by their children.

We went on to point out to her that we were using a conceptual model to guide our work with her and her children. More specifically, we explained that the Stress and Coping Model (Jones & Ollendick, in press), includes four primary factors, which interact to determine short-term and long-term adjustment to a traumatic event. These factors are:

a) characteristics of the stressor (i.e., loss, life threat);
b) individual characteristics (i.e., age, sex, race, SES);
c) characteristics of the environment (i.e., reactions of family members, community response);
d) cognitive processing of the event (i.e., appraisal, coping style).

We explained that each of these factors would be examined at varying levels within our multidimensional approach. At the completion of this session, we asked the mother to be thinking about our plan for treatment and informed her that we would discuss it in more detailed during the following session.

At the beginning of the next session, Duncan's mother informed us that she felt the intervention would be helpful in lessening her and her children's PTSD symptoms. She stated that one reason for her decision was " to help other families who may experience such trauma." Because of her stated interest in this intervention, we actually provided her with several factors found to be important in the development of PTSD as well as factors that may affect one's recovery from trauma. More specifically, we walked the mother through each of the following four characteristics while explaining the implications of them.

1) Exposure to the Traumatic Event

We explained that exposure has often been defined in reference to proximity to the event, degree of displacement resulting from the event, amount of physical disruption, and degree of life threat. Additionally, we stated that bereavement had been shown to be correlated with heightened levels of psychological distress. We told her that we thought the impact of exposure on her and her children would be significant given the death of her son and the loss of material items and disruption of her normal routine. We informed her that we would objectively assess its impact with the Fire-Related Traumatic Experiences (FRTE) which was designed by Jones and Ollendick (in press). Measures for these instruments would be obtained from her, Suzy, and Duncan. Additionally, a broader measure of loss would be obtained to include additional losses such as property, money, time, and friends. Justification for this assessment of "comprehensive loss" was to determine its addictive impact on levels of distress.

We explained that we felt that an individual's perception of the stressor had a significant impact on their functioning and that a comprehensive definition of "loss" was needed. Therefore, within the Conservation Resource Model (COR) of loss, resources are conceptualized as tools that facilitate successful interaction with the environment. If certain resources are unavailable, acute negative emotional experiences result. Additionally, prolonged emotional distress will occur if losses are not effectively compensated through individual, social, and community-wide efforts. She was told that loss would be objectively assessed using a modified version of the Resource Loss Scale (Freedy, 1992). She and both of her children's level of loss would be obtained. It was hypothesized that the extent of loss would be related to psychological distress.

2) Cognitive Processing of the Stressor

She was told that cognitive processing of the event is viewed as a primary factor that is hypothesized to impact both short-term response and long-term adaptation to the event. The three major aspects of the "stress response" consist of input from the environment (an event), perception and the immediate appraisal of the event, and reactions to the event (outcome). We informed the mother that the perception and the immediate appraisal of the fire and death of her son by her, Suzy, and Duncan would have a major impact on their respective levels of distress.

We then informed the mother that we would be examining the style of coping that she and her children engaged in and that it would influence reactions to the fire. In response to her question "which styles have been found to lead to the best recoveries?" I stated that problem-focused coping, an active coping strategy, had been found to facilitate adjustment and lead to less distress. In contrast, we stated that using avoidance strategies and other negative coping strategies, such as anger and blame, were the best predictors of PTSD symptomatology. Since we have found that parents' level of distress affects that of the offspring, she was informed that her coping style would also be assessed. It was predicted that greater levels of positive coping would be correlated with greater levels of post-fire adjustment

3) Pre-existing Adolescent Characteristics

The mother was told that reactions to traumatic events vary across age where younger children exhibit regressive behaviors, impulsivity, traumatic anxiety reactions, destructiveness, drops in school performance, and depression. Adolescents' overall level of symptomatology is more similar to that of adults than to younger children; trauma-specific fears all represent symptoms characteristic of this age group. While these patterns typically hold, there have been exceptions in that some studies have failed to find differences among youths of varying developmental levels. Furthermore, Terr (1983) reports that distress may be relatively independent of age, at least when the stressor is chronic and prolonged. By examining her symptoms as well as Suzy's and Duncan's, we told her that we would be able to determine the extent to which the expression of PTSD symptomology is similar across developmental levels represented by Suzy and Duncan. We will also be able to examine the impact of her (parental) distress on her children's adjustment. She found this information to be potentially quite beneficial for those families she hoped to share it with in the future. No hypotheses were made given that Duncan (an adolescent) had actually started the fire.

4) Characteristics of the Environment

With respect to the potential impact of her reactions on each of her children, mother was provided the following rationale for studying this factor. Because of the growing literature concerning parental reactions to traumatic events, the role of the family support following stressful events would be examined. Findings suggesting that children's reactions to traumatic events may be more a function of their parents' reactions (typically the mother) than the event itself, strongly support the need to examine this relationship. The examination of parents' impact on their offspring's functioning has focused primarily on preschool and school-aged children. While the data for younger and middle-aged groups are in line with previous findings, the adolescent data are not. Most studies have shown that adolescents undergoing stress are less affected by parental psychopathology than are their preschool and middle-aged counterparts. We informed her that adolescents may be more influenced by their parent's functioning than their middle-aged siblings because they "bear the brunt of parental reactions if parents are functioning poorly" under disaster conditions. Duncan may react more negatively than Suzy, in part due to this phenomenon. Of course, the most salient reason as to why Duncan may respond more negatively to the fire was because he caused it as well as the death of his brother. It is hypothesized that Duncan's level of psychologic distress would be positively correlated with her level of distress.

We further informed the mother that support from family members, friends and peers had been found to affect children's rate of recovery. Therefore, we would objectively assess the influence of social support through the use of Dubow and Ullman (1989) social support scale. It was hypothesized that social support following the residential fire would be correlated negatively with Duncan's and Suzy's level of psychological distress.

The impact of previous stressful life events would also be examined. We were viewing life stressors as a "characteristic of the environment" inasmuch as they may serve to buffer or potentiate the current stressor (fire). We informed the mother that studies point to the need to examine further the impact of prior disaster experiences (stressful life events) on children's and adolescents' post-disaster functioning. We told her that we predicted that heightened stressful life events would be associated with increased distress in Duncan.

We reiterated to the mother that the purpose of this phase of treatment was to determine the systematic impact of the fire on her as well as her children. Employing standardized assessment instruments, objective assessment of symptom expression was ascertained. We also informed them that we would be testing out the following predictions:

a) higher levels of distress would be related to higher levels of loss (as measured by the Resource Loss Questionnaire);
b) higher levels of distress would be related to higher levels of exposure (as measured by the Fire Related Trauma Events Scale, the Anxiety Disorder Inventory Schedule, ADIS, and the Brief Symptoms Inventory, BSI);
c) levels of appraisal and coping would be associated with the degree of exposure to the fire (as measured by the Stress and Coping Scale);
d) greater levels of premorbid distress would be related to greater levels of distress (as measured by the DICA-R, and DICA-P).

Deep Muscle Relaxation and Systematic Desensitization

Symptoms of intrusion, avoidance, and over-arousal were targeted. More specifically, intrusive symptoms including distressing dreams, feelings that the fire was reocurring, and distress during exposure to internal and external cues resembling the fire were targeted. Concerning avoidance symptoms, efforts to avoid a fire-related stimuli, including fear of returning to the destroyed home, or conversation about the fire were treated. The arousal symptoms targeted included: hypervigilance, difficulty concentrating, sleeping difficulties and anger outbursts. Also, general anxiety surrounding fire-related stimuli portrayed on television, hearing of sirens en route to and from school, and executing fire drills at school were targeted. More specifically, a thematic hierarchy consisting of 18 scenes was devised with Duncan over a three-week period targeting the aforementioned symptoms. The subjective units of distress scale (SUDS) was employed to obtain ratings prior to and following treatment.

Prior to the implementation of systematic desensitization proper, Duncan was trained in deep muscle relaxation over a three-week period. His mother was also taught to carry out this procedure to facilitate Duncan's mastery of it. More specifically, she was given the homework assignment to practice the relaxation procedure at least four times a week with Duncan, so that he could become an "expert in relaxing." It was determined that the best practice time was following dinner each day.

During the implementation of systematic desensitization, Duncan was first relaxed and presented with scenes from the previously constructed hierarchy. This phase of treatment extended for two sessions. SUDs ratings indicated that a high level of effectiveness was achieved with this procedure.

Rehearsal-plus (R+)

Prior to describing the components of R+, a brief history of this procedure will be provided. The conceptual model upon which this work has been based was devised by Jones and McDonald (1986) that identified the appropriate steps to take when attempting to conceptualize behavioral and cognitive behavioral interventions with those at-risk for unintentional injuries. This complementary model was designed to enhance the quality and efficacy of existing methods in treating those who suffer from childhood injuries. This model integrated behavioral, community and prevention conceptual frameworks. More specifically, the prevention framework guided our thinking concerning the timing of intervention, the behavioral framework served as the foundation for the actual identification and modification of behaviors and cognitions , and the community framework was employed to assist in the widespread dissemination and implementation of these strategies. The key components of this model consists of:

1) documenting the need for intervention;
2) deciding what skills to teach and validating them;
3) deciding how to teach emergency skills;
4) determining when to teach emergency skills;
5) selecting change agents and training setting;
6) obtaining community-wide involvement.

This integrative model has been helpful in having a more dramatic impact on those at risk for injury.

Rehearsal-plus (R+) focused in on 1) cognition, where cognitive reprocessing of the event was carried out, and 2) behavior, where fire evacuation skills were taught. The rationale for the cognitive component was primarily based on Duncan's report that he had "feelings of guilt for setting the house on fire and not being able to save his brother and not knowing what to do after starting the fire." Shortly after starting the fire, he stated he "totally lost it and ran out of the house screaming." He said he totally forgot about his little brother who was asleep in his room. Once he realized that he was in the house, he felt totally helpless with respect to saving him.

Hence, during the initial two sessions Duncan was encouraged to discuss the event in detail as well as his feelings and perceptions of various aspects of it (i.e., inability to save his brother, not knowing what to do during the fire) This discussion assisted him in processing the event at a developmentally appropriate level. He was then taught how to identify symptoms as well as the triggering cues. Meaningful ways of coping with the resulting trauma were then targeted (i.e., prayer, relaxation, self-instruction). A goal of the cognitive component was to provide him with valid ways of thinking of (processing) the event (i.e., it's okay to be upset, you should not continue to feel guilty for actions during the fire, it's okay to discuss your feelings). He was also encouraged to visit his home and help with the repair process, and to discuss the incident and resulting trauma with his mother, sister, school counselor, teacher, and minister.

With regards to the behavioral component of R+, it was reasoned that mastery of fire evacuation skills would enable him to function more appropriately in the event of another fire, and would greatly enhance his sense of coping efficacy. Thus, Duncan was taught the steps necessary to evacuate a burning house spelled out by Jones, Kazdin, and Haney (1981) (see Figure 17.2).

Following a behavioral demonstration of each step, Duncan was allowed to behaviorally practice them and educated on the rationale. This procedure is spelled out in detail in earlier reports (Randall, *et al.*, 1994) (see Appendix). Training took place over four sessions.

Objective pre, post, and follow-up test data were obtained to document mastery of these skills. During this assessment phase both behavioral and verbal data were obtained regarding what he would do if confronted with another fire in their home. In a simulated situation he was asked to show and tell what he would do to safely evacuate the burning house.

Results of this treatment showed a significant decline in SUDS ratings obtained immediately following each session of SD, as well as a significant drop in symtoma-tology on the CRTES and PTSD portion of the DICA-R. Concerning the R+ component, as expected, a significant increase in both appropriate behavior and knowledge was obtained. This increase in behavior and knowledge also led to increase in his coping efficacy. The use of SD to treat specific symptoms of intrusion, avoidance, and arousal was also most beneficial with Duncan.

Desired levels of functioning as assessed by each instrument were found to be maintained at the 6-month follow-up. Long-term therapy was recommended to assist Duncan in dealing with feelings of guilt and loss concerning his brother's death as well as damage to the home and distress incurred by his sister and mother because of his actions. In a similar strategy carried out for Suzy, several significant gains were obtained. Duncan's mother was treated for grief, depression and PTSD during 15 weekly, 50-minute sessions. Objective pre- and post-test data were obtained to document the positive impact of treatment.

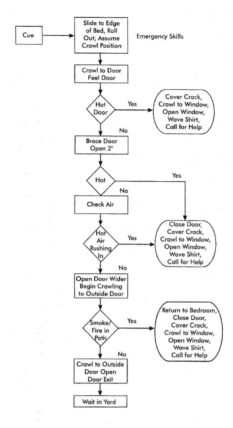

Figure 17.2: Emergency Escape Skills

Alternative Conceptualization

An alternative approach to the treatment of firesetters proffered by Richardson and Pinsonneault (1996) was introduced earlier. They maintained that factors which place certain adolescents at-risk for firesetting behavior include the transition period across several dimensions of functioning (i.e., social, moral and sexual) which contribute to anxiety, defensiveness, and powerlessness. These feelings are hypothesized to lead to powerlessness and lack of control which are classic characteristics of the crisis firesetters.

Behavior of the delinquent firesetters who engage in such behavior within group settings often stems from the developmental need to achieve independence and autonomy. The desire to impress peers is also an important component of this activity. This type of firesetting is not thought to be a function of wanting to observe or experiment with fire, but a result of peer dominance and poor judgment.

Regarding treatment, these authors maintain that regardless of motives for firesetting behavior, the most important component in treatment is accepting responsibility for behavior and its consequences (both potential and real). Criminal prosecution is a key feature of this mode of intervention. While specialized juvenile firesetter treatment is often a vital component of an effective treatment package, it should never be used to replace criminal prosecution. The treatment of the firesetter must employ an "all or nothing" model. Management and control of one's own behavior as well as gaining insight into underlying motives for firesetting are fundamental aspects of this approach. Identification of "warning signs" is a crucial component of this prevention-focused strategy. Key components in this treatment package include structured psycho-educational skill building, supervised community service, as well as a specialized group-counseling course. These components should be accompanied with an authoritative, supportive confrontation network of rules and contracts. Evaluation is also an important aspect of this strategy. Each component of this model will be briefly described below:

Educational Interventions

Skills building to address deficiencies regarding knowledge, behavior, values, and judgment is an essential component of this strategy. This component is entitled: "Think About It." Twelve self-contained educational workbooks providing exercises are employed to objectively enhance critical thinking and higher level cognition. Issues related to safety, survival, decision-making, fire science, responsibility, and communication skills are presented in hour-long units. A degree in fire science is not required for educators to carry out this strategy.

Community Service

This component provides a concrete way to address the consequences endured by society resulting from the firesetter's behavior. For individuals to totally appreciate the hardships endured by members of society resulting from their actions, time and energy in community service is essential. Since monetary restitution is not always feasible, given that many adolescents do not have access to paying jobs, this mode of punishment is viewed as effective given that it is very tangible and undeniably aversive. Such tasks are accompanied by an explanation as to their educational and behavioral significance.

Specialized Group Counseling

This component consists of weekly or bi-weekly group meetings designed to enhance issues related to self-esteem, generalized powerlessness, faulty thinking, and impaired judgment. It is believed that long-term treatment of this nature will curb inappropriate behavioral patterns associated with firesetting. Several forms of supervision, including probation support, secure residential or correctional facilities, and tracking and diversionary programs, have been found to be successful.

Groups consisting of six participants have found to be the optimal number for successful short-term treatment.

Within this all or none approach, change-agents are viewed as educators and confrontational adversaries rather than comforter, nurturer, or guide as is often the case in more traditional approaches. They liken this approach to the once controversial treatment for sex offenders. Primary justification stems from two assumptions, namely, both behaviors result from issues of power and control in the offender. When such control is lacking, structure imposed by this form of treatment is warranted. Given that the program provides clear and concrete guidelines, practical exercises, precise and strict rules, it has been reported to produce internal controls and safeguards for firesetters.

Strategy Based on this Approach

A detailed treatment strategy for this case would consist of a number of steps. The initial step is to carry out an intake where formal assessment is obtained from Duncan and his mother. This assessment, which is primarily educational, consists of the following sections: demographic and background information, school and work related experiences, families and friends, preferences of the client (Duncan), and the fire incident. A consent form is signed by both Duncan and his mother prior to the beginning of this interview. A pre-test assessment package is given to Duncan to assess his level of knowledge regarding fire-related information such as frequency of home fires, science of fire, motivation for firesetting and number of deaths resulting from fire. Additionally, ascertainment of what to do in potentially dangerous fire situations is obtained. An open-ended questionnaire designed to assess personal characteristics about Duncan as well as his feeling concerning firesetting and potential consequences of this behavior follows. Lastly, definitions of relevant terms including alarm, fire, and responsibility are requested as well as a short essay detailing Duncan's account of the crime he committed.

Authorization for the release of all information rendered by Duncan and his mother is obtained along with an acknowledgment of non-confidentiality and waiver. An intervention contract is then signed by Duncan that states that he agrees to be completely honest with program staff and parent regarding his firesetting offenses. He must also consent to attend all sessions of the intervention strategy.

Unit One of the intervention, consisting of a decision-making lesson, will require Duncan to learn a five-step decision-making process through a series of activities including evaluation of positive and negative influences (internal and external), critical evaluation of the decision-making process, ascertaining urgency and significance of decisions as well as short and long-term goals. Lastly, the ability to determine consequences of various decisions will be presented and mastered. Several homework assignments will be given to ensure that the proper mastery of each concept is attained. Duncan will also be required to evaluate his own performance.

Unit Two will focus on fire science. Duncan will be taught the definition of the "fire triangle" and generalize this knowledge to the processes of combustion, starting, and extinguishing fire. Through development of 14 fire scenarios, ways of beginning and preventing fire will be acquired. Duncan will also be required to evaluate real-life fire situations, employing the fire triangle and chain reaction concepts to determine areas of cause, effect, prevention, and costs.

In Unit Three, responsible use of fire will be presented using a series of fact sheets discussing the history of the art of "cookery," ways of distinguishing responsible from irresponsible use of fire, and the development of guidelines for the responsible use of fire. Materials used to convey this information will include a dictionary, reference materials on the history of fire, and activities including cooking and candle making. Segments from popular television shows and movies will be employed to demonstrate responsible and irresponsible fire-related behaviors.

Unit Four will provide Duncan with the necessary skills to engage in personal safety, responsibility and prevention of fire. "Ten Rules to Live By" will be mastered through the presentation of several worksheets and activities. The ability to distinguish between "Excuses" and "Explanations" as well as rule for appropriate fire involvement will be acquired.

Unit Five, entitled "Fire Prevention," will enable Duncan to differentiate between the concepts of "accident" and hazard, provide and describe examples of six types of home fire hazards, carry out a room by room inventory of his home, identify potential hazards, and provide explanations as to how he would correct the problem. Lastly, Duncan will be required to complete a "Home Fire Prevention" encyclopedia. Duncan's mother will be required to sign each page of his homework assignments to ensure the proper mastery of each objective.

Alarm Devices will be the topic of Unit Six. Through the use of a workbook, Duncan will learn the characteristics of the "social contract" or the Golden Rule and relate this concept to public alarm systems. The basic design and function of the alarm system including the maintenance and benefits of 10 distinct systems will be presented. Different types of smoke will be discussed as well as local fire and building codes as they relate to smoke alarm systems. Duncan will be required to research local fire/building codes through a series of phone calls or trips to the city hall. He will also be required to complete a survey form on local codes. These objectives will be obtained with the use of a dictionary, smoke detector and description of local codes related to fire alarm systems.

In Unit Seven, Fire Survival, Duncan will be taught how to recognize serious fire situations and actually survive life-threatening emergencies. Knowledge of oxygen deficiency, toxic gases, elevated temperatures, smoke, fire survival time, and fire survival planning will be obtained. Actual plans of how to evacuate a burning house will be developed by Duncan with the use of video tape presentations.

Within Unit Eight the concept of victimization will be taught. Duncan will acquire the definition of "victim," differentiate "victims of crime" from "victim of circumstance," "victim of natural disasters," and "victim of manmade catastrophe" in terms of preventability and responsibility. Consequences of arson to its victims will be discussed as well as community assistance for arson victims. Ways in which individuals are victimized by arson will also be presented. Topics of empathy and responsibility as they related to arson situations, as well as ways to demonstrate each will be learned. Each of these objectives will be achieved through the presentation of a series of worksheets, videos, statistic sheets, and visits from Red Cross personnel.

Unit Nine, consisting of information on burns prevention, will require Duncan to describe the architecture and function of the skin organ, evaluate the strengths and weaknesses of this organ, categorize burn injuries by heat sources, explain the physical effects of burns of the skin, describe the process of rehabilitation from severe burn injuries, and identify ways to prevent common burn injuries. Through the use of cut-away drawings, burn injury reports, flash cards, magazines, catalogs, and videotapes this information will be acquired.

In Unit Ten, communication, Duncan will acquire the ability to explain the "communication" process. Various modes of communication including verbal, non-verbal, direct, and indirect will be obtained. The identification of each with the use of television and video equipment will also be acquired. Explanation of the "talking hand" system as well as the five communications styles (the Finger Pointer, the Brush-off, the Pleaser, the Escape Artist, and Thumbs Up) will be made and Duncan will be required to identify and compare and contrast each. He will be required to keep a communication diary documenting both effective and ineffective communication styles.

At the completion of the activities described in each of the 10 Units, Duncan will be given a post-test to evaluate his level of mastery. He will then be required to carry out a community service project which will underscore the fact that firesetting is a serious and wrong action which demands an equally serious response.

Summary of the Integration of Conceptualization and Treatment Strategies

While both of the above discussed approaches have merit (pre- and post-test assessments, objective definitions of target behaviors) each has shortcomings. For instance, although our approach has several important components, shortcomings include the limit of external validity and brevity of treatment that may not ensure maintenance of treatment gains. On the other hand, the Richardson and Pinson-neault method may be too comprehensive in its scope and does not provide the level of assessment necessary to insure the internal validity of components. Perhaps the best method to treat firesetters, and those most likely to be affected by any fire, would be a combination of these approaches.

References

Achenbach, T. M. (1991). *Manual for the Child Behavior Checklist/418 and 1991 Profile.* Burlington, VT: University of Vermont, Department of Psychiatry.

Ayers, T.S., Sandler, I.N., West, S.G., & Roosa, M.W. (1996), "A dispositional and situational assessment of children's coping: Testing alternative models of coping". *Journal of Personality, 64*, 923–958.

Diagnostic and Statistical Manual of Mental Disorders (4th ed.) (1994). American Psychiatric Association.

Dubow, E. F., & Ullman, D. G. (1989). Assessing social support in elementary school children: The survey of children's social support. *Journal of Clinical Child Psychology, 18,* 52–64.

Federal Emergency Management Agency (FEMA) (1998).

Freedy, J., Shaw, D., Jarrell, M., & Masters, C. (1992), "Towards an understanding of the psychological impact of natural disasters: An application of the conservation resources stress model". *Journal of Traumatic Stress, 5,* 441–454.

Gayner, J., & Hatcher, C. (1987). *The Psychology of Child Fire-setting: Detection and Intervention.* New York: Brunner/Mazel.

Hanson, M., Mackay, S., Atkinson, L., Staley, S., & Pagnatiello, X. (1995). Firesetting during the preschool period: Assessment and intervention issues. *Canadian Journal of Psychiatry, 1(40),* 299–303.

Humpreys, J., Kopet, T., & Lajoy, R. (1994). Clinical considerations in the treatment of juvenile firesetters. *The Behavior Therapist, 17,* 13–15.

Jones, R.T., Kazdin, A. E., & Haney, J. I. (1981). Social validation and training of emergency fire safety skills for potential injury prevention and life saving. *Journal of Applied Behavior Analysis, 14,* 249–260.

Jones, R. T. (1996). Children's reaction to traumatic events scale (CRTES): Assessing traumatic experiences in children. In J. P. Wilson & T. Keane (eds). *Assessing Psychological Trauma and PTSD.* New York: Guilford Press.

Jones, R. T., & Ollendick, T. H. (in press). The impact of residential fire on children and their families. In A. La Greca, W. Silverman, E. Vernberg, & M. Roberts (eds). *Helping Children Cope with Disasters: Integrating Research and Practice.* Washington, DC: APA Books.

Jones, R. T. & McDonald, D. (1986). Childhood injury: A prevention model for intervention. *Education and Treatment of Children, 9,* 307–319.

Kolko, D. J. (1999). Firesetting in children and youth. In V. Van Hasselt & M. Hersen (eds), *Handbook of Psychological Approaches with Violent Offenders.* New York: Plenum Press.

Kolko, D. J., & Kazdin, A. E. (1986). A conceptualization of firesetting in children and adolescents. *Journal of Abnormal Child Psychology, 14,* 49–62.

March, J. S., Parker, J., Sullivan, K., Stallings, P., Conners, K., (1997), "The Multidimensional Anxiety Scale for Children (MASC): Factor structure, reliability, and validity". *Journal of American Academy of Child Adolescent Psychiatry, 36,* 4.

Office of Juvenile Justice and Delinquency Prevention (OJJDP) (1997).

Pargament, K. I., Ensing, D. S., Falgout, K., Olsen, H., Reilly, B., Van Haitsma, K., & Warren, R. (1990), "God help me: (I) Religious coping efforts as predictors of the outcomes to significant negative life events". *American Journal of Community Psychology, 18,* 793–823.

Randall, J., & Jones, R. T. (1994). Teaching children fire safety skills. *Fire Technology, 29,* 268–280.

Reich, W., & Welner, Z. (1990). *Diagnostic Interview for Children and Adolescents Revised.* CITY: Washington University.

Richardson, J., & Pinsonneault, ? ? (1996*). Think About It! An Intervention Curriculum for Adolescent Firesetters.* Unpublished manuscript. Fire Solutions, Inc.

Terr, L. (1983). Chowchilla revisited: The effects of psychic trauma four years after a school-bus kidnapping. *American Journal of Psychiatry, 140,* 1543–1550.

Appendix

Situation One ("Nothing blocking your path") was taught on day one, followed by Situation Two ("Hot air rushing in" on day two. On day three, Situation One and Two were reviewed during the first 30 minutes of training.

During the first 30 minutes of training on days one, two, and three, the trainer first verbalized and modeled the fire safety steps depicted in Figure 2. While the trainer verbalized steps, children performed them individually. The trainer corrected each child's performance and gave feedback contingent upon correct response. When a child made an error, he or she was stopped immediately and told to watch as the trainer demonstrated the step correctly. The child then received an opportunity to perform the step a second time. If the child again made an error, the trainer modeled the step correctly one more time and instructed the child to perform it again. If the child made another error, the trainer simply verbally corrected it and instructed him or her to move on to the next step in the sequence.

During the second 30 minutes of training on days one, two and three, the trainer paired self-instruction statements with specific fire fear stimuli. That is, the trainer told the children: "Now I am going to teach you some ways to help you reduce your fears of some events that might occur during a fire. We will do this by talking to ourselves. Okay? We will ask ourselves five questions, and we will answer each question. We will ask ourselves first, what is happening? Second, how do I feel? Third, why? Fourth, what do I need to do? And fifth, how am I doing? Okay?"

The children then received mastery modeling. The trainer said, "Now I want you to pay very close attention to questions that I ask myself and the answers that I give because, later on, I will want you to give two of the same answers. Okay? Let's pretend we hear a fire alarm." Here the trainer held up a picture of a fire alarm and modeled the correct verbal responses to this item for the children.

The trainer then went on. "The first question I will ask myself is 'What is happening?' I answer 'I hear a fire alarm.' This was one of the 18 items from the Fire Fear items inventory.

"The next question I will ask is 'How do I feel?' I answer, 'I am not afraid.' The next question I will ask myself is 'Why?' I answer, 'Because I know what to do in a fire emergency.' The next question I ask myself is, 'What do I need to do?' I answer, 'I should relax and think before I act.' The last question I ask myself is, 'How am I doing?' I answer, 'I am doing well.'"

Chapter 18

Pediatric Trichotillomania: Conceptualization and Treatment Implications

Martin E. Franklin, Donald A. Bux and Edna B. Foa

Clinical Syndrome

Trichotillomania (TTM) is a chronic impulse control disorder characterized by pulling out of one's own hair, resulting in noticeable hair loss. The syndrome has been described in the psychiatric annals as far back as the 19th century, yet research on its epidemiology, psychopathology, and treatment remains scarce, particularly with respect to pediatric samples. According to the DSM-IV (APA, 1994), a diagnosis of TTM requires:

1) recurrent pulling out of one's hair resulting in noticeable hair loss;
2) an increasing sense of tension immediately before pulling or when attempting to resist the impulse;
3) pleasure, gratification or relief when pulling;
4) not better accounted for by another mental disorder and not due to a general medical condition (e.g., dermatological condition);
5) clinically significant distress or impairment in social, occupational, or other important areas of functioning.

A cardinal feature of TTM codified in DSM-IV is that TTM patients find hair-pulling pleasurable, satisfying or relieving, even if they feel badly about the negative emotional and physical consequences of pulling. Thus, TTM is thought to be maintained by positive rather than negative reinforcement, which is one of the ways to distinguish it from obsessive compulsive disorder (OCD). Notably, the few small-scale adult TTM epidemiology studies that have been conducted suggest that approximately one in 200 adults meets full diagnostic criteria for TTM, while approximately twice that number pull out their hair but do not meet the full diagnostic criteria. However, the relationship between this subthreshold pulling and DSM-IV TTM in regard to psychopathology and response to various forms of treatment has yet to be explored.

Most of the TTM-related research published to date has used adult samples, but the data on age of onset collected in these studies clearly indicate that TTM typically emerges during adolescence. Given that in clinical samples most adults with

Handbook of Conceptualization and Treatment of Child Psychopathology, pages 379–398.

TTM report that their pulling began during childhood, logic would suggest that the development of effective pediatric TTM treatments may ultimately reduce adult morbidity. There has been discussion in the literature about very early onset hairpulling (before age five) that may represent a qualitatively different and more benign form of the disorder, yet longitudinal data to support this contention are lacking.

The dearth of research in pediatric samples requires review of the adult literature in order to describe the psychopathology of TTM in sufficient detail. In adults, scalp hair appears to be the most common pulling site (Christenson, 1995; Lerner, *et al.*, 1998), with eyelashes and eyebrows representing the next most frequently reported site. However, all body hair is potentially vulnerable, as some TTM patients pull from pubic areas, trunk, arms, legs, beard, nipples, etc. Notably, over one third of this clinic's mixed adult and pediatric clinical sample reported pulling from multiple sites (Lerner, *et al.*, 1998), which is consistent with other reports. Patients have also reported pulling from multiple sites, but not simultaneously; these patients may pull scalp hair exclusively for a period of time, then move to exclusive pulling at other sites (e.g., eyelashes). Hairs are almost always pulled one at a time, although a recent adolescent patient described a progression from pulling one at a time close to the root to what she calls "batch pulling," in which she grabs several hairs at the ends and pulls them simultaneously.

A majority of adult patients describe searching for hairs with certain textural qualities; fewer pull in response to visual cues such as hair of differing length than the majority of hair, gray hair, etc. For patients with strong visual cues or who pull from sites unlikely to be exposed in public forums (e.g., pubic hair), time spent isolated in bathrooms is particularly risky, especially for patients with pre-pulling visual inspection rituals who have access to brightly lit bathrooms. Patients often describe touching or stroking their hair before pulling, and although most pull individual hairs with thumb and index finger, some patients use implements such as tweezers. Once a hair is pulled, patients vary with respect to additional behavior such as manipulating the hair in their hands, placing it in their mouths, inspecting the hair and its root, or eating the hair (trichophagy). Some patients simply discard the pulled hair and quickly continue pulling additional hairs. Most patients can identify high risk situations for pulling such as isolated time in the bathroom, talking on the phone, watching television, driving, reading, or immediately before falling asleep. Certain affective states can also serve as cues for pulling, such as boredom, frustration, anxiety, and sadness. Clinically, it can be helpful at intake to describe to patients the typical clinical picture of TTM. Provision of such information helps them overcome the embarrassment and shame they feel in discussing the details of their pulling behavior.

Less information is available on how TTM presents in children and adolescents, but the little that has been published suggests similarity to adult hair-pulling. As with adults, the scalp is the most common pulling site in children and adolescents, followed by eyelashes and eyebrows (Reeve, 1999). The absence of body hair on younger children precludes pulling from certain sites, but this clinic's work with adolescents appears consistent with adult data in that pulling from sites other than the face and scalp is also common. For example, one 14 year-old girl reported intentionally switching from her greatly preferred scalp hair to less satisfying arm hair on a temporary basis in an attempt to cope with strong urges to pull her scalp hair.

Approximately 75 percent of adult TTM patients report that most of their hair-pulling behavior takes place "automatically" or outside awareness (i.e., unfocused hair pulling); the remaining 25 percent describe themselves as focused primarily on hair-pulling when they pull (i.e., focused hair pulling) (Christenson & Mackenzie, 1994). Some have postulated that TTM patients who engage primarily in focused hair-pulling are more "OCD-like" and also may be more responsive to pharmacologic interventions found effective for OCD (Christenson & O'Sullivan, 1996). However, the distinction between focused and unfocused "pullers" is complicated by the fact that at least some patients engage in both types of pulling behavior. Clinical observation finds that patients who engage in both types of pulling often progress from unfocused pulling of a few hairs (which strengthens the urge to pull) to focused pulling. Assessment of both types of pulling behavior is imperative before beginning a cognitive behavioral treatment (CBT) program because clinical intervention strategies will differ depending on whether focused or unfocused pulling is primary.

As children get older there appears to be a fairly predictable association between hair-pulling and relatively sedentary activities (Reeve, 1999); hair-pulling then is also characteristic of unfocused pulling in adults. Psychiatric comorbidity appears to be common in adult and pediatric TTM, and the nature and severity of the comorbid disorder must be taken into account when making treatment recommendations to patients and their families.

Perhaps even more so than with adult patients, it is extremely important to describe typical TTM behavior to children and adolescents before querying them about the specifics of their own pulling and related behavior. Talking with unfamiliar adults can be daunting for some children, let alone discussing the intimate details of a problem as delicate as hairpulling. Pediatric patients should be assured that many people their age engage in similar habits, that these habits are actually quite common, and that discussion of the specifics of hair-pulling will assist the therapist in helping to reduce it. With younger patients, it can also be helpful to have a stuffed animal or doll with hair and ask the child to indicate where he/she typically pulls from by using the toy to demonstrate. This technique may allow the clinician to delay the direct inspection of pulling sites until greater rapport with the child has been achieved. For example, one pediatric patient recently described her initial TTM intake at another center as extremely anxiety provoking because the clinician insisted on seeing the alopecia patches on her scalp within the first few minutes of the visit. As is always the case, sensitive interviewing helps the clinician to maximize the amount of data that the patient is willing to provide, especially early on in treatment.

TTM is often associated with significant psychological and medical problems. In addition to the time spent on hair pulling itself, many sufferers spend considerable time concealing large resultant bald areas, and experience guilt, shame, and low self-esteem. The disorder can also lead to avoidance of activities in which hair loss might be exposed (e.g., swimming), avoidance of activities that may lead to direct physical contact with others (e.g., intimate relationships, sports) and, in more extreme cases, social isolation. Significant medical complications may include skin irritation and infections. When patients ingest pulled hair (trichophagia), serious gastrointestinal problems stemming from the presence of trichobezoars also can occur. Although thought to be very uncommon, complications of trichobezoars include gastric or intestinal bleeding, perforation, intestinal obstruction, acute pancreatitis, and obstructive jaundice.

Although careful empirical study of the impact of TTM on children and adolescents is lacking, collective clinical wisdom suggests that pediatric TTM can be highly disruptive to social and academic functioning, self-esteem, and the development of close friendships. Because TTM usually strikes during sensitive developmental years, it can be especially disabling. Children and adolescents who develop TTM often become extremely self-conscious of the effects of hair pulling on their appearance, and go to great lengths to avoid many typical childhood activities in order to maintain secrecy about the disorder. Sometimes this avoidant strategy results in their receiving fewer invitations to participate in future activities, compounding their sense of isolation. Moreover, when evidence of pulling is discovered inadvertently by their peers, these youngsters often experience a great sense of shame and embarrassment that clearly impacts social relationships. Adolescents are particularly vulnerable to negative feedback from their peer group, and discovery of a secret such as TTM can feel devastating to them. Hence, the development of empirically validated treatment programs is sorely needed in order to reduce the suffering of children and adolescents with TTM.

Description of Treatments

Many psychosocial therapies have been utilized to treat TTM, including psychodynamic approaches, hypnosis, family interventions, and a wide variety of behavioral and cognitive-behavioral procedures. Pharmacotherapy has also been used, with reports of controlled trials of fluoxetine (Christenson, *et al.*, 1991), clomipramine (Swedo, *et al.*, 1989), and naltrexone (Christenson, *et al.*, 1994) in the outcome literature. In general, existing data on TTM treatments in adults are limited by small sample sizes, lack of specificity regarding sample characteristics, non-random assignment to treatment, paucity of long-term follow-up data, reliance on patient self-report measures instead of clinician-rated interview data, or other more objective dependent measures such as photography ratings, and lack of information regarding rates of treatment refusal and drop-out. The treatment approaches that have been more carefully studied are cognitive-behavioral approaches involving habit reversal techniques and pharmacotherapy with serotonin reuptake inhibitors. Again, all of the available controlled studies have been conducted with adult samples; pediatric TTM treatment research remains in its infancy, which substantially limits conclusions that can be drawn about which forms of treatment youngsters with TTM should receive.

Cognitive-Behavioral Ttreatment

Adult Samples. The most extensive literature on the treatment of TTM pertains to the efficacy of CBT. A variety of specific techniques have been applied, including self-monitoring, aversion, covert sensitization, negative practice, relaxation training, habit reversal, competing response training, and overcorrection. Although successful outcomes following some of these interventions are reported, the vast majority of the literature consists of uncontrolled case reports or small case series. Programs involving habit reversal (HR) appear to have met with the most success, although awareness training and stimulus control procedures are also typically included in these multi-component interventions. This treatment team views HR, awareness training, and stimulus control as core interventions that comprise CBT for pediatric TTM, with other intervention strategies such as cognitive techniques used on an as-needed basis

In the only randomized group study comparing behavioral treatments for TTM (Azrin, *et al.*, 1980), habit reversal (HR) was found more effective than negative practice, with habit reversal patients reporting a 99 percent reduction in number of hair pulling episodes compared with a 58 percent reduction for negative practice patients. The authors report that the habit reversal group maintained their gains at 22-month follow-up, with patients reporting 87 percent reduction compared with pre-treatment. A significant limitation of that study is that efficacy was established solely by patient self-report, raising concerns about biases in reporting. A second problem is that only a subset of HR patients (twelve of 19) was available for the follow-up assessment, so long-term outcome data reported in the study may overestimate long-term benefit. Additionally, a treatment manual was not utilized so procedures cannot be readily replicated. Moreover, because the study was conducted before development of DSM nosology for TTM, the sample's diagnostic status is unclear. For example, at least one patient treated in this study reported only hair twirling, which would not meet current diagnostic criteria.

Since Azrin, *et al.*'s (1980) study, several additional case reports and small comparison studies have supported the efficacy of HR and related interventions in the treatment of TTM. In a small placebo-controlled trial, Rothbaum and Ninan (1996) found CBT involving HR superior to CMI and pill placebo at post treatment. However, follow-up data were not reported. Mouton and Stanley (1996) found that four out of five patients who received HR treatment in a group format experienced substantial TTM symptom reduction at post-treatment; however, two of the four responders relapsed substantially. The problem of relapse was further underscored in a recent study conducted in which patients received nine sessions of CBT involving HR (Lerner, *et al.*, 1998). Twelve of 14 patients were classified as responders at post-treatment (>50 percent NIMH-TSS reduction), yet only four out of 13 met this criterion an average of 3.9 years post-treatment.

In summary, of the three studies cited above that have included follow-up data, two (Lerner, *et al.*, 1998; Mouton & Stanley, 1996) suggest relapse in the long run, whereas one (Azrin, *et al.*, 1980) reported maintenance of gains. It is important to note that both of the studies that indicated relapse used independent assessment of TTM symptoms via semistructured interview, whereas Azrin, *et al.*'s study relied on unstandardized patient self-report. Single case reports are also generally mixed on whether patients maintained their treatment gains. Moreover, there is a "file drawer" effect to consider when reviewing the treatment, given a general bias toward publishing positive findings. Clinically, several TTM treatment experts have observed that patients often experience reoccurrence of hairpulling after treatment, especially in response to external stressors. Additional attention may therefore be needed to extending awareness training and use of competing responses to maximize long-term outcome.

Pediatric Samples. Single case studies examining the effects of a variety of cognitive-behavioral procedures for pediatric TTM have suggested the efficacy of treatment, but methodological problems render the findings inconclusive (Reeve, 1999). In two recent multi-case studies of CBT, children and adolescents appeared to respond to treatment initially yet some relapse was evident at follow-up. Vitulano, *et al.*, (1992) found maintenance of initial treatment gains at twelve week follow-up in two of three children and adolescents who received behavior therapy involving habit reversal. Similarly, Rapp, *et al.*, (1998) found that two of three children and adolescents treated with habit reversal and occasional booster sessions maintained their treatment gains from 18 to 27 weeks post-treatment. These studies suffer from the same methodological limitations raised previously with respect to adult treatment outcome studies, including the use of small samples, lack of treatment manuals, and lack of control treatments. They did, however, improve upon the measurement of TTM severity in that both used independent assessment of photographs of patients' alopecia. As noted above, there appears to be a significant link between sedentary activities and pulling in children with TTM, especially as they move into adolescence. Thus, awareness training is likely to be a critical intervention in treatment for children and adolescents who engage primarily in unfocused pulling, but less so with focused pullers. CBT for TTM must be sufficiently flexible to address the various forms of hair-pulling, including focused and unfocused types.

Pharmacotherapy

A detailed account of the hypothesized neurobiology of TTM is beyond the scope of this chapter. However, surface similarities between TTM and OCD clearly influenced the investigation of serotonergic treatments for TTM, as these compounds have been found efficacious in the treatment of OCD. Other non-serotonergic pharmacotherapies have also been tested on TTM, including a recently published study (described below) which examines the efficacy of naltrexone, an opioid blocking medication. Despite the presence of biological theories of TTM, evidence for the efficacy of resulting pharmacotherapies for adult TTM has been equivocal, and controlled pharmacotherapy research has yet to be conducted in exclusively pediatric samples. Randomized controlled trials have indicated that fluoxetine (Pigott, *et al.*, 1992), and clomipramine (Swedo, *et al.*, 1989; Pigott, *et al.*, 1992) have each been found superior to placebo at post-treatment. However, several other studies have yielded negative findings with respect to serotonergic medications versus placebo (Christenson, *et al.*, 1991), and another study indicated that most of a small sample of CMI patients lost their treatment gains even while being maintained on a previously therapeutic dose of the drug (Pollard, *et al.*, 1991). Intriguingly, naltrexone (Christenson, *et al.*, 1994), which is an opioid blocking compound thought to decrease positive reinforcement by preventing the binding of endogenous opiates to relevant receptor sites in the brain, has also been found superior to placebo in reducing TTM symptoms. However, no additional studies of naltrexone's effects on TTM have been published.

Available treatment literature strongly suggests that there is neither a universal nor complete response to any treatments for TTM. Given that monotherapy with CBT or pharmacotherapy are likely to be only partially effective in reducing TTM symptoms in the long run, these therapies may yield superior improvement when combined. Moreover, clinical recommendations of some treatment experts support the notion that combined treatment is best. Unfortunately, the absence of any controlled studies examining the efficacy of CBT treatments involving HR, pharmacotherapy, and their combination weakens this claim considerably.

Case Example

A physician working at a local medical center referred Ellen, a twelve-year-old girl for treatment. Ellen had been under the care of her physician for several years for congenital vision problems that required regular surgeries. During her last hospital stay, the physician noticed that a bald patch approximately the size of a quarter had developed on the left temporal region of the patient's scalp. Initially, the treatment team believed the spot to be of medical origin, possibly a dermatological condition, but upon further inquiry it was discovered that the patient had been pulling the hair from this region for several weeks. Upon intake, it was determined that Ellen met full diagnostic criteria for TTM and not for any other Axis I disorder. Ellen also had some relatively mild intellectual impairments related to her congenital medical condition, although she had been mainstreamed successfully in her public school setting with some special education assistance. Cognitive-behavioral treatment for TTM was discussed with Ellen and her mother, and the family agreed to enter the CBT program, which consisted of weekly treatment sessions held over nine weeks followed by regular booster sessions.

Theoretical Overview

According to cognitive-behavioral theory, chronic hair pulling is thought to originate as a normal response to stress that often escapes personal and social awareness, but that, with time, gradually increases in frequency and severity. Thus, hair pulling becomes associated with a variety of internal and external cues through conditioning mechanisms, and is maintained primarily by positive reinforcement. Hair pulling urges that are reinforced by pulling beget stronger urges to pull, resulting in a perpetuation of the behavioral cycle. At this clinic (the University of Pennsylvania Center for the Treatment and Study of Anxiety), there is also a focus on cognitive components in conceptualizing this disorder, incorporating cognition and affective states as cues and consequences of the behavioral sequence. For many patients there are emotional states that tend to precede pulling behavior, such as frustration, boredom, or anxiety. In some cases negative cognitions about the pulling habit itself (e.g., "kids at school will notice my bald spot and think that I'm weird") also may play a role in the perpetuation of pulling, as such cognitions result in increased negative emotion which in turn may increase urges to pull. Additionally, patients sometimes worry that urges to pull will never go away or will get stronger until they pull, despite their being able to provide ample evidence to the contrary from their own experience with urges. Cognitive restructuring can be used to highlight this discrepancy between actual and feared consequences of resisting urges, and these exercises may help patients feel better prepared for the occurrence of such thoughts.

We agree with the DSM-IV conceptualization of TTM as an impulse control disorder, rather than as a variant of obsessive-compulsive disorder. Many have likened TTM to OCD, given the apparent similarity between the repetitive and uncontrollable nature of hair pulling with that of other compulsions. However, unlike the repetitive and intrusive nature of obsessions in OCD, TTM is not characterized by persistent and intrusive thoughts regarding hair pulling. The nature of the repetitive behavior in TTM is generally limited to the topography of hair pulling, whereas compulsions in OCD often consist of a variety of behavior performed to alleviate anxiety. Moreover, individuals with OCD describe their compulsions as unpleasant, whereas most with TTM describe hair pulling as pleasurable or satisfying in some way. Thus, OCD is maintained by negative rather than by positive reinforcement. This difference in conceptualizing OCD and TTM has critical implications for treatment that lead to the use of disparate treatment strategies for each disorder. In CBT for OCD, individuals are encouraged to remain in anxiety-provoking situations (e.g., sitting on contaminated floor) to facilitate habituation, which typically occurs within 90 minutes. Alternatively, those receiving CBT for TTM are more successful when they exit a high-risk situation for pulling. This is because behavior maintained by the experience of pleasure is less likely to extinguish in the way behavior maintained by anxiety reduction would. The key concept to get across to the patient is that urges to pull are strengthened by pulling, which produces pleasure or satisfaction. Therefore, in order to weaken urges to pull, the patient must learn not to reinforce urges. This is accomplished by increasing awareness of pulling (awareness training), setting up the environment to make it less conducive to pulling (stimulus control), and acquiring an alternative set of pleasurable activities that provides positive reinforcement formerly gained by pulling (habit reversal). The strength of the urges to pull, which at present may be experienced as overwhelmingly powerful, is weakened with successful implementation of these procedures and passage of time. The relationship between external stressors and TTM must also be accounted for in the treatment, because when these stressors are increased the urges to pull might reemerge. Thus, the patient must also be taught to be on guard against reinforcing pulling urges when under duress.

Contributing Factors

The influence of external stressors on chronic hairpulling has been noted repeatedly in adult and pediatric TTM clinical literature. In children and adolescents, academic pressures, social difficulties, and family problems have each been thought to lead to increased urges to pull in some pediatric TTM patients. In Ellen's case, the stress of her surgery may have precipitated the pulling behavior that caused the initial bald spot observed by her physician. She reported that the frequent medical procedures she had to endure to improve her sight were very difficult for her, and that pulling her hair became a more regular habit when she was relatively unoccupied in the hospital, especially when she was watching television in her room without any family members being present. She could not recall when she first began pulling hair, although she did notice that the more she pulled the more satisfying the pulling became. Certainly in Ellen's case the high levels of stress associated with surgery and with hospitalization contributed to the pulling. Notably, even after she recovered from the surgery and was back at school for months the pulling persisted at a comparatively high rate. Occasionally it has been reported that skin irritations, cuts, etc. have led to picking skin from the scalp which then evolves into hairpulling, but there was no evidence that Ellen's pulling was precipitated by any injury to the skin on her scalp.

Sociocultural Factors

Although the epidemiological data cited above suggest that TTM may be a more common problem than was once believed, there does not appear to be widespread public knowledge about TTM and its effects. Lack of information about TTM, as well as misinformation about its meaning may serve to increase the desire of sufferers to keep the disorder secret or to minimize its consequences to those in the environment who have learned about the patient's pulling. Within a given family or social circle these influences can be even stronger; families that are very concerned about outward appearances and about being judged by others may have particular difficulty in emotionally supporting a child who has TTM. Often this problem is even more pronounced in the families of girls who pull when great emphasis is placed in the home on looking one's best at all times. In the present case, the family appeared to be appropriately concerned about the pulling but supportive of the child; it did not appear that Ellen's family was exacerbating the problem by reminding her how awful she looked, that everyone would think she was strange, or that she was ruining her appearance, and that nobody would want to be with her, as is unfortunately often heard from family members of other patients. Families especially vulnerable to feelings of shame about these kinds of problems may need additional psychoeducation about TTM and about managing questions that are posed by others regarding their child's noticeable alopecia.

Core Features of CBT

As mentioned earlier, CBT for TTM involves several core procedures as well as additional techniques to be used on a case by case basis as clinically indicated. The core procedures include awareness training, stimulus control procedures, and habit reversal. Children who have many negative thoughts about their pulling and its implications may require cognitive training to reduce the contribution this thinking makes to negative emotions. Specialized social skills training has also been included to assist patients who are asked many questions about their alopecia or who are teased by classmates about their pulling and its consequences.

Awareness training involves self-monitoring and other methods designed to help the patient become more aware of urges to pull and of pulling behavior. This is needed because most pulling takes place when the patient is engaged in other demanding activities, and lack of awareness serves as an impediment to intervening. Some athletically inclined pediatric patients have been told that stopping hair-pulling without detailed knowledge of when you are doing it is like trying to hit a dark baseball in the middle of the night, and that light needs to be shed on the pulling by self-monitoring in order to figure out how to reduce it. The degree of emphasis on awareness training depends largely on the degree to which the patient is unaware of pulling. Many if not most pediatric hair pullers at least begin an episode of pulling in an "unfocused" manner, usually while engaged in other activities such as talking on the phone, studying, or watching television. In order to intervene effectively, children must become aware not only of every hair pulled but of the response precursors, such as every time they put their hand on their heads. Training in these procedures should be tailored to the particular needs of the child. For older children awareness training can be facilitated by using elaborate self-monitoring forms that include information regarding the time, setting, preceding emotional state, negative thinking before pulling, number of hairs pulled, etc. Clearly this level of detail will be difficult to match with younger children, but creative solutions may help the clinician gain some basic information about pulling, such as saving pulled hairs, transferring marbles from one pocket to another each time a hair is pulled and counting them later, etc. Notably, self-monitoring methods also serve as a subtle stimulus control method, as the child who has pen in hand or is moving marbles from one pocket to another has an object between thumb and forefinger, at least temporarily. When the self-monitoring efforts have yielded sufficient information to determine the high risk places and times, the child can be engaged in the creative process of making reminder signs and pictures to place in these sites in order to decrease the chances of unfocused pulling. Signs can be developed "in code" that are meaningful only to the child so that reminders can be used in more public settings, such as the school library. A recent patient left Chicago Bulls stickers on his school notebooks to serve as reminders not to pull in class; he used these because of the rhymes with pull and because the stickers would be viewed as innocuous by classmates unaware of his habit.

Stimulus control methods can be used to reduce the chances of a patient being able to engage freely in pulling behavior in situations determined to be "high-risk" during self-monitoring. For instance, patients might put band-aids on the tips of their thumb and index finger when they are alone in their rooms studying, as this would serve as an impediment to gripping hairs to pull at a time when many pediatric TTM patients might be tempted. These "speed bumps," as they are called, may allow patients to delay pulling long enough so that they can reach for the various tools they have surrounded themselves with in order to do habit reversal. Because much of pediatric TTM takes place outside conscious awareness, stimulus control methods may prevent the patient from "priming the pump" by pulling out a few hairs. Once a few hairs have been pulled, urges to pull more are often reported to be much greater, so the prevention of the first few hairpulls may serve to prevent a much more prolonged and damaging "binge." Children can be engaged in the creative process of making signs for their rooms, bathrooms, television sets, etc., depending on where they are most likely to start pulling. More subtle signs can be made for use at school or in other places in which the child might worry about others discovering their "secret." One intervention found especially useful for unfocused pullers is to have the child put the TV clicker away in a "trich warning box" so they cannot put the television on without first being reminded of the need to be aware of pulling risks.

In and of themselves, however, stimulus control methods are unlikely to be effective because urges to pull are unlikely to be reduced sufficiently simply by resisting. Again, the core maintaining factor in TTM involves the positive reinforcement gained from hair pulling, and substitution of an alternative satisfaction may be needed in order to break the habit. In the same way that having carrot sticks nearby as a snack food to replace cookies is likely to assist with weight reduction, the TTM patient may need to surround him or herself with "fiddle toys" to utilize instead of engaging in hair pulling. Habit reversal procedures essentially serve to provide the patient with alternative pleasurable physical stimulation, preferably involving the same motions and muscle groups employed in hairpulling. Patients vary widely in the types of stimuli they "switch to" in HR: koosh balls, pieces of bath mats, clay, Playdough, sunflower seeds, and other such objects have been used successfully by patients instead of hair pulling when urges are high. It is imperative to spread these throughout the home and school area so they are easily accessible – reliance upon a single object will likely result in "poor coverage" if that object is forgotten for a day.

Assessment

The foundation of effective CBT for pediatric TTM is a detailed assessment of the problem, and this assessment should be completed before intervention strategies are agreed upon with the patient and family. Assessment should include information regarding response description, detection, precursors, high-risk situations, and consequences. Once antecedents to hair pulling are identified, information regarding hair pulling behavior and disposal of hair should be investigated, as well as other consequences. Ideally, this information is collected from multiple sources that include reliable and valid clinical measures and tailored self-monitoring sheets, in addition to clinical interviews with the patient and family members.

Response Description. Information regarding the number of hair pulling incidents, number of hairs pulled, the topography of hairs pulled, and bodily movements should be collected to gather as much information as possible about the circumstances of hair pulling incidents. The entire sequence of hair pulling should be gathered in detail, as hair pulling is a complex sequence of events that vary widely between individuals. Some have a rigid sequence of preparatory rituals, such as twirling hair at crown, searching for target hairs, pulling one hair at a time, etc. The method of discarding the hair must also be described. Some individuals report examining the hair or the hair root, while others chew on the hair or root, or swallow the hair (trichophagia). An example of a hair pulling sequence might be tingling sensation on scalp, lifting arm by the shoulder to head, bending wrist, twirling hair around forefinger, grasping a coarse hair with thumb and forefinger, pulling out, examining root, biting off root, and swallowing hair.

Response Detection. The circumstances in which an individual senses an urge, the strength of the urge, attempts to resist the urge, and the outcome of the urge to pull one's hair should be assessed, as this information influences treatment procedures.

Response Precursors. Assessment of external and internal cues to hair pulling identifies precursors to establish a context within which hair is pulled. External cues include setting (e.g., family room, kitchen, car), activities (e.g., watching television, working on the computer), and implements (e.g., mirror, tweezers). Internal cues include affective states, cognition, and sensations. Anxiety, boredom, frustration, or even excitement are common affective states associated with TTM. Cognition might involve thoughts of "evening out" hairs, pulling "just one more," or thoughts that urges will continue to strengthen indefinitely until pulling occurs. Qualities of the hairs that might provide sensory stimulation include visual (e.g., gray hair, split ends), tactile (e.g., curly, oily, coarse hair) and physical (e.g., tingling scalp) sensations.

High-risk Situations. A valuable part of assessment includes identifying high-risk situations in which hair pulling occurs. Situations often reported as problematic for individuals with TTM include watching television, reading, talking on the telephone, working on a computer, and driving a car. Identification of high-risk situations helps the individual become aware of potential patterns in hair pulling, heightens awareness for monitoring TTM during these activities, and serves as a cue for the individual to implement treatment procedures.

Consequences. Reinforcement of the behavior should be outlined. Consequences may include creation or reduction of physical sensations at the site of pulling, such as tingling, pleasure, or invigoration; relief from negative emotional states, such as stress, boredom, or negative affect; and the creation of symmetry, such as even hairlines.

Hair Loss. Additional assessments to utilize when evaluating TTM include photographs and measurement of alopecia. This serves as a document of severity of hair loss, as well as a motivator to practice treatment strategies. Measuring patches of alopecia in millimeters serves as an outcome measure of treatment.

Standardized Measures. Unfortunately, a single "gold standard" measure of TTM does not currently exist. Client selfmonitoring regarding information outlined is invaluable in preparing treatment plans. Several interview measures for TTM do exist, with varying degrees of psychometric support. Measures at this clinic include adapted NIMH severity and impairment scales, and a semi-structured clinical interview to assess the severity of TTM and comorbid conditions as a part of routine evaluations. The NIMH Trichotillomania Questionnaire (Swedo, et al., 1989) consists of two clinician-rated scales: the NIMH Trichotillomania Severity Scale (NIMH-TSS) and the NIMH Trichotillomania Impairment Scale (NIMH-TIS). The NIMH-TSS consists of five questions regarding average daily time spent pulling hair, time spent in this activity the day before the evaluation, resistance to urges, distress regarding hair pulling, and interference with functioning due to hair pulling. Scores range from 0 to 25. The NIMH-TIS rates the severity/impairment of hair pulling on a scale from 0 to 10. Higher scores indicate greater severity on both scales. The NIMH-TSS and NIMH-TIS have been shown to be sensitive to treatment outcome (Lerner, et al., 1998).

Implementing CBT with Ellen

Early Sessions. Ellen was determined to be a good candidate for the clinic's weekly CBT program, and she was scheduled for her initial treatment session. In advance it was agreed that Ellen would be seen on a weekly basis for approximately eight to ten sessions, depending on how she was doing in accomplishing treatment goals. The first two sessions were devoted to gathering sufficient information to conduct a functional analysis of the hairpulling, which would then enable the development of a tailored treatment plan specific to Ellen's needs. From that analysis it was noted that, like most pediatric and adult hairpullers, Ellen used her thumb and index finger to pull out hairs one at a time. Pulling was almost always preceded by an "urge" or an "itch," which was then followed by Ellen's searching with her thumb and index finger for a "good" hair to pull. She was unable to articulate exactly how she determined whether a hair was "good" for pulling, although it appeared that if she was unable to separate the hair quickly from other hairs she moved on to another spot. Notably, most of her pulling was being done in four situations : on the schoolbus, in classes that required focused concentration, at home while watching television, and while she was sitting on the toilet. Additionally, Ellen appeared to prefer pulling with her left hand, although it was discovered shortly afterwards that this was only the case in settings where her right hand was occupied, namely the classroom while holding a pen. Ellen also reported that her urges to pull appeared to be lower when her hands were busy. Unlike some pediatric TTM patients, Ellen did not have significant embarrassment or shame about pulling – she viewed it as a habit, and thought her friends wouldn't care much if they knew. Perhaps her frequent eye surgeries and their effects on her appearance served as a protective factor in respect of concerns about what others would think of her. Despite many obstacles in her life, Ellen appeared to be a confident child who was not especially swayed by the opinions of her classmates.

Ellen's pulling behavior appeared to be primarily unfocused, positively reinforcing, scalp hair exclusively, and occurring in a few circumscribed settings. She expressed an interest in stopping, although she was concerned that the task would be hard because "once I've pulled a few I feel like I want to pull a lot." In the second session, Ellen was trained in self-monitoring of hair pulling. A grid was created in which the four pulling situations were listed by days of the week, and Ellen was simply to make a mark for each hair she pulled in these settings. She was engaged in the process of creating the self-monitoring sheet (e.g., drawing a school bus) because this is helpful in the process of treatment collaboration, especially in treatment. While more elaborate detail on the self-monitoring sheet (e.g., thoughts preceding pulling, strength of urges) could have been requested, the child's age and intellectual capacity made this inpractical. An important tenet in creating a monitoring sheet is to not make it so complicated that the child cannot provide the information. Ellen's first sheet was used in the third session to review the "hot spots" and to reinforce her efforts to monitor. In light of her intellectual limitations her mother and her regular teacher were also asked to provide additional estimates of pulling behavior. Ellen appeared to be engaged in figuring out how to reduce her pulling, and her interest in this process was further reinforced.

Stimulus Control Methods. With the self monitoring in place, stimulus control methods for use in the "hot spots" were introduced in the third session. Ellen had tried gloves on her own in the past but found that she would frequently take them off because "my hands would get hot" or because the gloves significantly impaired her ability to pick up objects, write, etc. With this in mind, it was suggested she use small band aids placed on her left thumb and index finger; this would decrease sensitivity for "good" hairs if she began searching for hairs and would interfere with her grip if she began pulling. Also, the school granted permission for Ellen to begin wearing hats to class, which would further interfere with the initial search for good hairs. During this same session Ellen began working on devising signs for the settings in which she pulled, and tailoring these signs particularly to the settings in which she was concerned about being discovered by classmates. Ellen had reported in the second session that when she had something in her hands that her pulling and her urges to pull were reduced. As a result, a plan was implemented whereby she had a pen and another object of her choosing for her to carry onto the school bus and to keep in hand for the duration of the ride. She was asked if she believed other students would be conscious of this behavior and would give her a hard time about it, but she denied that this would pose an impediment to implementing the plan. During the week after this session, Ellen even put the initials FHPH ("Free hands pull hair") on her bookbag to serve as a further reminder not to pull while on the schoolbus, and sat with it in her lap on the bus.

Habit Reversal. Inspection of her self-monitoring sheets and the report of her mother and teacher suggested significant improvement already, which indicated that she could move on to habit reversal methods in session four. If compliance with monitoring and stimulus control methods had been poor, addition of new strategies would have been postponed in order to explore possible reasons for non-compliance. This is especially important for children such as Ellen who have intellectual impairments that could interfere with the learning of the new techniques. Notably, Ellen's mother reported that things at home had been going well, and that her older sisters were "rooting for her" to reduce her pulling rather than becoming irritated by the behavior as they had from time to time in the past.

Habit reversal practice was initiated in the session by having Ellen select from among several "fiddle toys" gathered over the years in working with TTM patients. Ellen gravitated towards a koosh ball in the shape of a Sesame Street character, and she was taught the principles of HR during the session. She was instructed to use the koosh ball several times a day for several minutes at a time, once on the school bus on the way in to school and later at home while watching television. Ellen borrowed the toy for a week and was asked to buy several others so she had enough to go round, at least one for the book bag, one for her room (to be placed on top of the box the TV clicker was now housed in), and one for the bathroom when she was using the toilet. The placement of these implements coincided with identification early on of the high risk pulling situations. Ellen particularly enjoyed pulling the single strands of rubber on the koosh ball, which isconsistent with the HR procedure of using the same muscle groups for HR as were used previously for pulling. Children sometimes have preferences for other objects, or objections to the use of certain strategies for reasons that are difficult to anticipate – one boy failed to use the rubber ball he selected initially because after a while it, "made my hands smell weird." In HR it is important to experiment, as the first selection may not automatically be accepted by the child or, as is often the case, an obtrusive looking implement that works fine at home is unacceptable for use around friends or classmates. It is important that relevant school personnel be informed of the treatment strategies at this point, as confiscation of treatment tools at school poses both a threat of stigmatization and a barrier to compliance.

As is true of all treatment sessions, session five began with a review of self-monitoring and a report from Ellen's mother regarding reduction of hairpulling and implementation of HR strategies in designated places. Her mother reported that she had selected several koosh balls for use in HR, some of which were smaller and more easily concealed for use at school and on the bus. Other children were interested in sharing the koosh balls at school, and Ellen was having only partial success in getting the balls back when borrowed. Whether this was a problem of assertiveness or a fear of being "discovered" by the other students was explored in session, and Ellen reported that it was more a matter of forgetfulness on her part. It was decided to add a "back-up" koosh ball to her bookbag to decrease the amount of time she would be without one. The successful use of the hat and the band-aids in school continued, and Ellen's self-monitoring sheet indicated that pulling in school had virtually ceased, down from approximately 100 hairs per day at intake. The main place that pulling appeared to be persisting was in the bathroom at home. Gaps in stimulus control methods (e.g., taking her hat off before sitting on the toilet) and in having a fiddle toy readily reachable from the toilet may have contributed to the persistence of the behavior in this setting. Ellen was re-instructed about methods by which she could reduce this pulling as well, and began work on unobtrusive signs she could use in the bathroom to remind herself not to pull.

Sessions six and seven consisted of reviews of self-monitoring, critiquing the use of stimulus control and HR strategies over the weeks, and reinforcement for efforts and for successes achieved. The last five minutes of each session are typically engaged in activities that the child finds reinforcing, and Ellen routinely selected Nerf basketball in the therapist's office for her "fun time activity." These activities are kept in place so that therapy remains fun for the child, and it also serves as a time to discuss other non-TTM related activities going on in the child's life. Knowledge of this information may assist therapists in anticipating new stressors on the horizon and to plan for possible lapses. By session seven Ellen's pulling behavior had been reduced by over 90 percent, although some pulling remained. In session seven, discussion started on the maintenance of gains, which led on to how to eliminate the remaining 10 percent of hairpulling. Ellen was able to recognize that by this point she was more likely to pull at home than at school, and that incomplete preparation played a large role in the persistence of the behavior. Situations in which Ellen reported pulling in the previous week were focused on, and strategies devised that would be more likely to be effective, such as switching to a bandana from a hat when lying in bed reading because the hat would inevitably come off, and keeping something in her left hand when reading in her room and holding the book open with her right hand. The use of HR strategies appeared to have been helpful, as Ellen now reported that the koosh ball was almost as satisfying to play with as her hair used to be. Thus, a combination of strategies appeared to be useful: awareness training, stimulus control, and habit reversal, with each strategy intertwined with the others.

Relapse Prevention and Booster Sessions. Sessions eight and nine involved review of the previous week and relapse prevention. For Ellen the fading of the therapy proved to be somewhat distressing, as she had forged a strong relationship with the therapist and was afraid that her gains would be compromised without weekly reminders. In light of her concerns, a brief scheduled telephone contact was scheduled once per week between session nine and her first booster session, which had been scheduled for three weeks later. The scheduling of these telephone contacts eased the pressure Ellen reported regarding "having to do it alone," and the contacts themselves served to be particularly brief since Ellen and her mother reported no pulling at each call. Booster sessions were held monthly for three months, at which point Ellen's treatment was suspended until such time that she felt the need to come back in. Indeed, approximately nine months after the final booster session Ellen's mother called to report a temporary setback, with her mother citing a significant increase in family distress that probably contributed to the increase. A single booster session was held followed by a scheduled telephone contact, which appeared to result in the cessation of the relapse.

Biological Approach and Pharmacotherapy

Findings regarding pharmacotherapy for TTM have not proven to be especially compelling in adult samples, and no controlled research has been conducted with exclusively pediatric samples. Nevertheless, many pediatric TTM patients receive pharmacotherapy, usually with selective serotonin reuptake inhibitors (SSRIs). SSRIs have received FDA approval for the treatment of adult and pediatric OCD, and the selection of pharmacotherapy strategies for TTM has been influenced by the theoretical argument that TTM is an OCD-spectrum disorder, perhaps with shared biologic underpinnings. The use of SSRIs with TTM is further influenced by their apparent efficacy in reducing symptoms of impulse control problems such as anger. Thus, pharmacotherapists have support on several fronts to try SSRIs with pediatric TTM, despite the lack of clear evidence for their efficacy in that condition. At present, pharmacotherapists considering a trial typically begin with either sertraline (Zoloft) or fluvoxamine (Luvox), although paroxetine (Paxil) and fluoxetine (Prozac) may also be used. A non-selective serotonergic compound, clomipramine (Anafranil), has been found superior to desipramine for TTM, but psychiatrists tend not to use clomipramine as a first-line treatment because of its less favorable side-effect profile and because of increased risk for seizures and cardiac conduction problems as compared to the SSRIs. There has been little formal research on SRI augmentation with OCD much less with TTM, so it is difficult to say what the pharmacotherapist should do if the initial SRI trial does not substantially reduce pulling.

Some experts have suggested that disorders that are substantially aversive are more likely to respond to SRI pharmacotherapy than those that involve substantial reward or positive reinforcement such as gambling. As mentioned above, TTM is thought to be maintained more by positive reinforcement, and therefore may not be as likely to respond to SRI pharmacotherapy. One study found naltrexone superior to placebo for adult TTM (Christenson, *et al.*, 1994). A growing body of research now suggests that naltrexone reduces drinking in alcoholics, apparently by reducing the subjective pleasurable effects of alcohol (O'Brien, *et al.*, 1996). By extension, then, it is plausible that naltrexone could be acting similarly in TTM, although further controlled studies of this medication would clearly be necessary to establish its safety, tolerability, and mechanism of action in pediatric TTM.

Integration of Case Conceptualization and Treatment

As noted previously, conceptualization of the psychopathology of a disorder should dictate the treatment strategy to be employed. Thus, the cognitive behavioral conceptualization of TTM as a learned habit maintained by the reinforcing properties of the pulling behavior leads logically to a treatment strategy that involves preventing the reinforcement of urges to pull by interrupting the precipitant behaviors (e.g., touching head, identifying preferred hairs for pulling) in the behavioral chain, and finding alternative sources of positive reinforcement that are similar functionally to the pulling. The degree to which anxiety or other negative emotional states can be linked to the pulling behavior will further dictate the inclusion of additional treatment strategies to improve effective coping and thereby decrease the contribution of stress on the target behavior. This general conceptualization is used as a guide, but must be further modified depending on the function of the behavior for the particular child who is being treated. For example, if a child's self-monitoring data reveal clear links between family arguments and subsequent pulling behavior, intervention strategies may be needed to ensure that the child does not retreat to his/her room alone after such negative interactions.

A problem with pediatric TTM is that there has been insufficient experimental study of the psychopathology of the disorder, which results in gaps in understanding of the factors that maintain the behavior. Moreover, TTM appears to be a heterogeneous disorder, which serves as a further barrier to comprehensive understanding and thereby hinders the development of treatment strategies. For example, no studies of pain tolerance at the pulling site have been conducted, which limits knowledge of whether the unfocused pulling often seen in pediatric TTM is mediated by an increased tolerance (and thus decreased awareness). Such studies could also help clarify what role, if any, is played by endogenous opioids in TTM. Progress in the development of effective treatments is hampered by the absence of experimental psychopathology data upon which to build theory. This can be said of the development of pharmacotherapies and psychosocial approaches alike, as a firm understanding of what a condition is will facilitate intervention strategies.

In the case presented above, it was clear that major stressors (e.g., surgery, family stress) preceded the initial onset of TTM and the temporary lapse that Ellen experienced after treatment had been terminated. According to functional analysis of the behavior, Ellen's pulling appeared to be maintained by positive reinforcement she experienced from the pulling. Developmental and sociocultural factors also warranted consideration in Ellen's case, although cognitive-behavioral conceptualization of TTM as a learned habit maintained by reinforcement of pulling urges dictated the clinical decision to remain focused on the non-reinforcement of urges rather than to shift the therapy to a more family-oriented approach, or to engage in extensive stress management training. Clearly, therapists with different theoretical views would approach the problem from a different vantage point, and the absence of experimental study of pediatric TTM and the resultant dearth of knowledge about this problem does not offer sufficient evidence upon which to dictate an approach. The absence of controlled outcome research clearly demonstrating the efficacy of any particular therapeutic approach further contributes to the confusion about how best to think about and to treat pediatric TTM. More work is needed in these areas in order to help sufferers overcome this difficult and apparently intractable problem.

References

American Psychiatric Association. (1994). *Diagnostic and Statistical Manual of Mental Disorders*. (4th ed.). Washington, D.C.

Azrin, N. H., Nunn, R. G., & Frantz, S. E. (1980). Treatment of hairpulling (trichotillomania): A comparative study of habit reversal and negative practice training. *Journal of Behavior Therapy & Experimental Psychiatry, 11*, 13–20.

Christenson, G. A. (1995). Trichotillomania: From prevalence to comorbidity. *Psychiatric Times, 12*, 44–48.

Christenson, G. A., Crow, S. J., & MacKenzie, T. B. (1994). A placebo controlled double blind study of naltrexone for trichotillomania. In *New Research Program and Abstracts of the 150th Annual Meeting of the American Psychiatric Association.* Philadelphia, PA, NR597.

Christenson, G. A., MacKenzie, T. B., Mitchell, J. E., & Callies, A. L. (1991). A placebo-controlled, double-blind crossover study of fluoxetine in trichotillomania. *American Journal of Psychiatry, 148*, 1566–1571.

Christenson, G. A., & O'Sullivan, R. L. (1996). Trichotillomania: Rational treatment options. *CNS Drugs, 6*, 23–34.

Lerner, J., Franklin, M. E., Meadows, E. A., Hembree, E., & Foa, E. B. (1998). Effectiveness of a cognitive-behavioral treatment program for trichotillomania: An uncontrolled evaluation. *Behavior Therapy, 29*, 157–171.

Mouton, S. G., & Stanley, M. A. (1996). Habit reversal training for trichotillomania: A group approach. *Cognitive and Behavioral Practice, 3*, 159–182.

O'Brien, C. P., Volpicelli, L. A., & Volpicelli, J. R. (1996). Naltrexone in the treatment of alcoholism: A clinical review. *Alcohol, 13*, 35–39.

Pigott, T. A., L'Heueux, F., & Grady, T. A. (1992). Controlled comparison of clomipramine and fluoxetine in trichotillomania. In *Abstracts of Panels and Posters of the 31st Annual Meeting of the American College of Neuropsychopharmacology.* San Juan, Puerto Rico. 157.

Pollard, C. A., Ibe, I. O., Krojanker, D. N., Kitchen, A. D., Bronson, S. S., *et al.* (1991). Clomipramine treatment of trichotillomania: A follow-up report on four cases. *Journal of Clinical Psychiatry, 52*, 128–130.

Rapp, J. T., Miltenberger, R. G., Long, E. S., Elliot, A. J., & Lumley, V. A. (1998). Simplified habit reversal treatment for chronic hair pulling in three adolescents: A clinical replication with direct observation. *Journal of Applied Behavioral Analysis, 31*, 299–302.

Reeve, E. (1999). Hair pulling in children and adolescents. In D. J. Stein, G. A. Christenson, & E. Hollander (eds) *Trichotillomania* Washington, DC: American Psychiatric Association Press, Inc. 201–224.

Rothbaum, B. O., & Ninan, P. T. (1996). *Behavioral Versus Pharmacological Treatment of Trichotillomania*. Unpublished manuscript.

Swedo, S. E., Leonard, H. L., Rapoport, J. L., Lenane, M., Goldberger, E. L., *et al.* (1989). A double-blind comparison of clomipramine and desipramine in the treatment of trichotillomania (hair pulling). *New England Journal of Medicine, 321,* 497–501.

Vitulano, L. A., King, R. A., Scahill, L, & Cohen, D. J. (1992). Behavioral treatment of children and adolescents with trichotillomania. *Journal of the American Academy of Child and Adolescent Psychiatry, 31,* 139–146.

Chapter 19

Enuresis/Encopresis

Michele L. Ondersma, Steven J. Ondersma and C. Eugene Walker

The Condition

Enuresis is defined in the *Diagnostic and Statistical Manual of Mental Disorders-Fourth Edition* (DSM-IV; American Psychiatric Association, 1994) as repeated voiding of urine in inappropriate places (e.g., clothes, bed). The behavior may be voluntary or involuntary and must:

1) be by a child with a chronological or developmental age of at least five years;
2) occur at least twice a week for at least three consecutive months or cause clinically significant distress or impairment in social, academic, or other important areas of functioning;
3) be unrelated to the direct effect of a general medical condition.

In addition, description of the wetting as nocturnal, diurnal, or both is required by DSM-IV.

Children who meet the diagnostic criteria for enuresis are frequently embarrassed and fearful of the reaction of others (e.g., peers, parents, teachers) to their difficulties and frustrated by their apparent inability to "grow up." Feelings of embarrassment, fear, and frustration increase with age as the enuretic child becomes more aware of the social stigma associated with the disorder. Additionally, these children often believe that they are the only ones among their peers with urinary incontinence. This belief fosters feelings of shame and isolation; enuretic children will avoid social activities such as sleep-overs or summer camps for fear they will wet the bed. In spite of this, however, a number of enuretic children will present with seeming indifference to the wetting. This indifference can often add to parental views of their child's enuresis as willful, and can necessitate significant work on the part of therapists in order to establish a positive and supportive atmosphere at home.

A great number of approaches to the treatment of enuresis have been documented. Only those treatments that comprise the current standard of care will be presented in this chapter.

Handbook of Conceptualization and Treatment of Child Psychopathology, pages 399–416.
Copyright © 2001 by Elsevier Science Ltd.
All rights of reproduction in any form reserved.
ISBN: 0-08-043362-6

Medical Treatment

While initial surveys suggested that primary care physicians overwhelmingly preferred pharmacologic treatments to other options, more recent research indicates a
growing preference for the use of behavioral techniques. However, at least half of
primary care physicians still regularly prescribe medication for children with functional enuresis.

Physicians most often use one of two medications in the treatment of enuresis.
The tricyclic antidepressant imipramine (Tofranil) was until recently the universal
first-line choice. Imipramine generally results in a decrease in enuretic episodes;
unfortunately, complete or nearly complete reduction in wetting episodes with the
use of imipramine is only approximately 50 percent (Gross & Dornbusch, 1983).
Further, nearly all patients relapse after the medication is discontinued.

More recently, the synthetic anti-diuretic hormone DDAVP (Desmopressin) has
been selected as the drug of choice for the treatment of enuresis. Administered
intranasally, DDAVP acts by concentrating urine and thereby reducing the
amount produced by the kidneys. This drug has been shown to be reliably more
effective than a placebo; unfortunately, as with imipramine, DDAVP does not
often result in complete dryness, and most children return to their previous
wetting frequency after discontinuing the medication (Moffat, et al., 1993). Interestingly, DDAVP may be more effective in children with a family history of
enuresis than in those without such a history.

Behavioral Treatment

Behavioral methods offer a well-studied alternative to the use of pharmacological
agents in the treatment of enuresis. Historically, urine alarm systems used in the
treatment of nocturnal enuresis consisted of a pad upon which a child slept; the
presence of wetness on the pad would complete an electrical circuit and cause a
loud alarm to go off. In place of the traditional pad, current urine alarm systems
utilize a small absorbent strip that is placed into the child's pajamas or underwear.
Both classical (i.e., Pavlovian) or operant (i.e., Skinnerian) conditioning paradigms
can be used to describe the mechanism by which such devices reduce enuresis. The
classical one suggests that awakening and/or contraction of the muscles of the
pelvic floor (conditioned response) occurs in response to a full bladder (conditioned stimulus) as a result of pairing the full bladder and the loud alarm (unconditioned stimulus). The operant paradigm rests on the principle of punishment;
under this model, children learn to retain urine until morning or to awaken in
response to a full bladder in an effort to avoid the aversive stimulus of the loud
alarm. In a meta-analysis, Houts, et al. (1994) reported the overall effectiveness
rate (complete dryness) for urine alarms alone to be 59 percent. As with medication, rates of relapse for urine alarm treatments (as high as 40 percent) remain an
issue, but are much lower than with pharmacologic treatment. Subsequent reconditioning, the use of intermittent rather than continuous schedules of alarm use,

and over learning (challenging the child's mastery through increasing levels of liquids before bedtime) have all proven effective in reducing relapse (Ondersma & Walker, 1998).

Use of additional behavioral procedures with the urine alarm is relatively simple and has been shown in some studies to speed acquisition of dryness and reduce relapse. Two such multicomponent packages have been published and evaluated. *"Dry Bed Training"* (Azrin, *et al.*, 1974) consists of a urine alarm plus a waking schedule (regular wakings during the night to check for dryness), retention control training (learning to hold increasingly large amounts of urine), positive practice (repeated trials of rapid awakening and appropriate toileting), and cleanliness training (making the child responsible for helping clean up after accidents). Full spectrum home training (Houts & Liebert, 1984) consists of a urine alarm, retention control training, over learning, and cleanliness training.

Other Treatments

Hypnosis, individual psychotherapy, and family therapy have all been utilized in the treatment of enuresis. Although only a few reports exist in the treatment literature, hypnosis may be a promising intervention. In contrast, individual or family therapy without the use of behavioral techniques have not been an effective treatment for enuresis.

Case Study, Annalies

Annalies was an eight year-old-female who had never completely achieved night-time urinary continence. She typically experienced urinary accidents an average of two nights per week; however, after a motor vehicle accident in which Annalies suffered significant abdominal injuries and the death of her mother, her urinary incontinence increased to an average of eight times per week. No other significant behavior problems were present; however, marked emotional distress (e.g., crying, fear, restless sleep, decreased appetite) was present. Her developmental history was unremarkable, other than repeated urinary tract infections and a family history of enuresis.

During the evaluation, Annalies' father reported that both he and his now deceased wife had regarded the urinary incontinence as something she would eventually out grow. Both parents were sympathetic and non-punitive in their approach; they would change the sheets when they were wet, gently restrict Annalies' fluids before bedtime, and comfort her while helping to change her bedclothes subsequent to a wetting accident. However, in the midst of his mourning, Annalies' father had become less tolerant with the wetting. He now had less time to deal with the near daily changing of wet sheets and clothes and had made those tasks Annalies' sole responsibility. Additionally, he began removing privileges as punishment for the enuretic episodes. Further assessment which included Morgan

& Young's (1975) scale of parental perceptions of enuresis revealed that it had become a significant source of distress for Annalies' father and that confusion as to how to deal with it was exacerbating the situation.

Conceptualization

A physician must always evaluate enuresis before psychosocial interventions are attempted. In some cases, a urinary tract infection is present; in a portion of cases where such an infection is present, the wetting ceases after treatment with antibiotics. However, nocturnal enuresis typically does not have a clear medical cause. This was true of Annalies, whose pediatrician evaluated her and found no evidence of a medical cause for her ongoing incontinence.

We viewed Annalies' nocturnal enuresis in learning theory terms as a simple skill deficit: whereas the majority of children learn to contract the muscles of the pelvic floor and/or awaken in response to the sensations of a full bladder while sleeping, Annalies had not. Learning to monitor bladder sensations while sleeping and to either awaken or contract key muscle groups is a relatively complex skill. However, evidence suggests that people do screen stimuli for relevance while sleeping, as when new mothers may sleep through very loud noises but awaken immediately to the sound of their infant's cry. The meta-analysis by Houts, *et al.* (1994) suggests that the urine alarm, which specifically teaches the skill of contraction/awakening in response to bladder sensations while sleeping, is the single most important treatment component in working with enuresis, and that psychological interventions without the urine alarm are much less effective.

A range of factors may have contributed to Annalies' enuresis. First among these is genetics: studies have shown greatly increased risk for enuresis in children whose parents were also enuretic as children. While the mechanism by which genetic risk is manifested is not known, it may have to do with relatively weak nighttime surges in anti-diuretic hormone, or vasopressin. It may also have to do with relative difficulty scanning stimuli for relevance during sleep; many clinicians and parents will report that enuretic children are extremely deep sleepers, but evidence does not appear to support this theory, and depth of sleep may not be related to ability to scan stimuli for relevance. The fact that children sleep much longer than adults (typically nine to ten hours per night) further taxes their ability to retain urine until morning awakening. The trauma that Annalies had recently experienced also appears to be a contributing factor. However, in this learning theory conceptualization, the trauma is seen as disrupting Annalies' ability to carry out what for her is a poorly developed and difficult skill, rather than as directly causing the wetting. The fact that her enuresis predated the trauma is consistent with this hypothesis. The trauma may also be affecting her toileting through her father's increased stress, as he may be less consistent in limiting fluids or helping her to use the toilet prior to bedtime. It is important to note that while the above factors are important to recognize in working with this family, none are seen as crucial in making treatment decisions specifically in reference to the enuresis.

Treatment

A crucial first step in working with Annalies and her father was to alleviate the distress and confusion surrounding her enuresis. The involuntary nature, prevalence, and difficulties associated with the wetting was explained in detail in order to help them view their situation as common and understandable, and to remove distressing feelings of responsibility. It was explained to Annalies and her father that bladder control is a complex and difficult skill, much like riding a bike without training wheels. "It's difficult enough at normal times," she was told, "but especially when you're upset and distracted by sad things." Second, the family was provided with a clear rationale for why behavioral interventions can effectively treat the problem. (See Appendix 1 for methods of explaining enuresis and its treatment to children and parents.) In this case, Annalies and her father were told:

> "Right now, Annalies, your brain doesn't think much of it when it notices the feeling of a full bladder at night. We need to teach it to make a really big deal out of the feeling of a full bladder. To help it, we use an alarm that makes a loud noise every time you start to wet the bed. After hearing the loud alarm enough times, your brain starts to learn that having a full bladder is something that it should pay attention to. Pretty soon, it starts to either tell your body to hold it or to wake up when it notices that your bladder is full."

Third, the family was given a description of what treatment would be like: that it would start with simple monitoring of wet nights, that the treatment with the urine alarm itself could take up to twelve weeks or even longer, that initial improvement often takes up to five weeks, and that it was likely Annalies would have temporary lapses in success.

After an evaluation phase in which wet and dry nights were recorded on a calendar, several relatively simple and non-intrusive behavioral methods were implemented. First, a series of simple rewards for dry nights was developed. Relatively inexpensive, commonplace rewards were recommended, such as stickers, pieces of gum or candy, coins, small gifts or toys (e.g., flavored lip balm, beads), or a meal or dessert of her choosing. Any dry mornings were to be marked with a sticker on the special calendar used for evaluation, and a reward was to be administered. Wet nights were to be handled without rewards or reprimands, but Annalies would be required to help change her own sheets. Finally, a series of positive practice exercises was implemented: before each bedtime, Annalies was to repeatedly li.e. in bed, imagine herself asleep but with a full bladder (actually having a full bladder would be ideal), and jump up to go to the bathroom. Liberal praise following each "success" was recommended.

After several weeks, Annalies' wetting had decreased significantly. Simple techniques such as those being used often are sufficient, especially when children have been continent previously. However, Annalies' prior history of enuresis (never

having reached continence) and her incomplete response to the more simple procedures led to a decision to utilize a urine alarm. Several factors were stressed to
Annalies' father:

1) The importance of ongoing use of the calendar to record wet and dry nights;
2) the need to practice, while awake, the process of turning the alarm off, going
   immediately to the bathroom, and changing the sheets when the alarm sounds;
3) the importance of having Annalies herself turn the alarm off when it sounds;
4) the likelihood that Annalies would not at first awaken when the alarm sounded,
   and that she would eventually learn to wake up to it if her father woke her up
   and had her turn the alarm off (rather than vice versa);
5) the importance of having Annalies' father sleep close enough to hear the alarm
   initially so that he could help her to wake up to the alarm;
6) that use of the alarm is often difficult and disruptive initially, but that this
   decreases with time;
7) the importance of not greatly limiting fluids before bedtime while using the
   alarm;
8) that the system of rewards for dry nights should be continued.
   (Urine alarms are available from Palco Laboratories, 8030 Soquel Avenue,
   Santa Cruz, CA 95062; 1-800-346-4488).

All of these factors were reviewed extensively with the family before implementation of treatment with the urine alarm. Special attention was paid to the system
of rewards for dry nights, and any concerns that the father had in using rewards
were discussed. Commonplace rewards which are relatively inexpensive such as
those mentioned above were suggested. The importance of having Annalies change
her own sheets after wetting episodes was emphasized, as was the practice of
appropriate voiding after any wetting episodes. A reward was suggested contingent
upon even partial voiding in the toilet during these exercises.

Once Annalies showed a significant decrease in wet nights (e.g., one wet night
per week), over learning could be initiated as a means of preventing relapse. Based
on the system described by Scott, *et al.,* (1992), Annalies should drink four ounces
of water 15 minutes before bedtime. This amount is then increased by two ounces
for every two consecutive dry nights, up to a maximum of nine ounces. Upon
reaching the criterion of 14 consecutive dry nights, treatment can cease. Subsequent re-treatment with the same procedures used initially for children who experience lapses in dryness may be necessary; fortunately, successful reconditioning
typically occurs much more quickly than during the initial treatment phase.

Alternative Conceptualization

The above case could also be seen solely in biological terms. Although enuresis by
definition is inappropriate voiding which is unrelated to a general medical condition, some researchers have hypothesized that much wetting is the result of a

distinct medical cause not yet widely recognized. As noted above, enuresis is clearly heritable: Bakwin (1973) reported that, of children whose parents had no history of enuresis, 15 percent could be diagnosed as enuretic; in contrast, 44 percent of those children with one parent and 77 percent of those with two parents with histories of enuresis met diagnostic criteria for enuresis. Biological theories of the etiology of enuresis include broad implications of genetic factors and suggestions of specific abnormalities in hormonal fluctuations, arousabilty, bladder capacity, and developmental maturity. Given the family history of enuresis present in the case sample above, conceptualization on the basis of biology warrants consideration. DDAVP is a safe medication with few side effects that is especially effective in children with a family history of enuresis.

Summary

Enuresis is clearly a treatable disorder; however, rates of relapse or failure to respond to treatment can be significant. Etiological theories of the disorder fall into three general categories: learning, emotional, and biological. Treatment strategies are closely tied to the etiological conceptualization. Learning theory lends itself well to behavioral/psychological intervention whereas biological theory dictates the use of medication. Although comorbid emotional symptoms may warrant treatment, treatment based on emotional theory is unlikely to be effective as a means of reducing or eliminating the enuresis. There are two sources of information regarding how medical and behavioral treatment compare: (1) the meta-analysis by Houts, *et al.*, (1994), in which both treatments were equal at post-treatment but urine alarm treatment was significantly more effective at follow-up (i.e., relapse was significantly lower with the urine alarm); and (2) a direct comparison by Wille (1986) who also found the two treatments comparable at post-treatment, but not at follow-up when the lesser relapse rate of urine alarm treatment resulted in significantly fewer wet nights. For very short-term needs (e.g., sleep over, vacation, summer camp), DDAVP may be a very useful intervention.

Encopresis

The DSM-IV (APA, 1994) defines encopresis as the passage of feces in inappropriate places (e.g., clothing, on the floor). This fecal elimination may be voluntary or involuntary and must:

1) be by a child with a chronological or developmental age of at least four years;
2) occur at least once a month for a minimum of three months;
3) be unrelated to the direct effect of a general medical condition;
4) indication of the presence or absence of constipation with overflow incontinence is also required by the DSM-IV.

Although not included in the DSM-IV, Walker (Ondersma & Walker, 1998) identified three general subtypes of encopresis: retentive (resulting from constipation and overflow incontinence), manipulative (intentional soiling for secondary gain), and stress-related (anxiety-induced and diarrhetic). It is estimated that 80-95 percent of children who meet the criteria for a diagnosis of encopresis are chronically constipated and are classified as having constipation with overflow incontinence (i.e., retentive encopresis). Rather than the result of diarrhea, as most parents assume, this form of encopresis is the result of serious constipation. Children may become constipated for any number of reasons, including genetics, poor diet, and voluntary withholding. In some constipated children, the resulting pain associated with bowel movements leads to further withholding and avoidance of bowel movements. In time, the bowel can become progressively less sensitive to the presence of large amounts of formed stool, while simultaneously becoming stretched, flaccid, and progressively less able to eject that formed stool. Through this process a large amount of formed stool can become impacted in the colon. Subsequently, loose waste pools above the impaction and leaks around the impacted material through the now flaccid and insensitive colon, resulting in soiling (see Figure 19.1). Manipulative and stress-related encopresis can be seen as subtypes of encopresis not related to constipation with overflow incontinence.

Encopresis occurs during the day more often than at night and is often accompanied by a strong odor; thus, encopresis is markedly more socially evident and stigmatizing than enuresis. The distress experienced by children and their parents as a result of encopresis is evident in terms of both self-esteem and behavior/

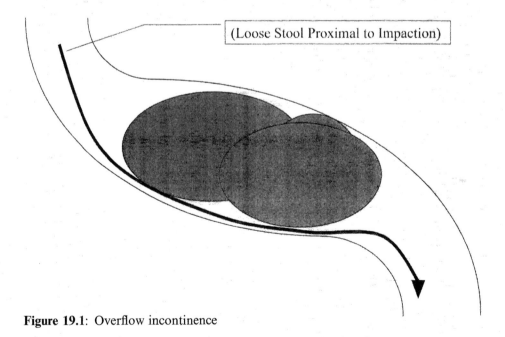

(Loose Stool Proximal to Impaction)

Figure 19.1: Overflow incontinence

emotional problems. Parents may present as overwhelmed and frustrated and often feel that their child could be continent if he or she desired; therefore, punishment for soiling episodes is common. Encopretic children, in contrast to their parents, often present as indifferent to their soiling, despite the fact that a majority are eager to be continent. These children are often unaware of the foul odor they carry and insist that they have little or no control over their bowel functions (which is often true).

The typical soiling episode involves relatively small amounts of a yellowish, pasty, and foul-smelling material, but occasionally involves huge amounts of very dark stool. In addition, encopretic children tend to have infrequent bowel movements that are hard, dark, and often bloody, and many show reluctance to use the toilet.

Research on effective treatments for encopresis lags behind that of enuresis. However, three primary treatment methods and combinations thereof have been shown to be effective.

Medical Treatment

A commonly used form of treatment for encopresis is laxative and purging therapy, the goal of which is to remove any impacted fecal material and establish regular bowel movements. Oral laxatives are sometimes ineffective in removing impaction and instead cause pain and increased overflow incontinence. Purgatives (e.g., enemas, suppositories) are often used with severe impactions. Once an impaction is cleared, stool softeners and laxatives (e.g., mineral oil, dietary fiber) are used for one year or longer before gradual fading. Mineral oil should be taken one to three hours after meals because of its tendency to inhibit absorption of fat-soluble vitamins; additionally, vitamin supplements should be added to the diet. Evidence suggests that the occurrence of laxative dependence following such treatment is low, and the nutritional safety of such programs has been documented.

Studies of the efficacy of medical treatments alone are limited. Several such studies report initial success rates ranging from 38–84 percent with most averaging approximately 70 percent (Abrahamian & Lloyd-Still, 1984). Abrahamian and Lloyd-Still conducted the only long-term follow-up and reported that 47 percent of the children treated remained symptom-free five years later; 36 percent had only minor symptoms which were controlled with intermittent use of laxatives.

Behavioral Treatment

Behavioral treatment of children with retentive encopresis has included education regarding the constipation-impaction-soiling cycle, positive reinforcement for appropriate toileting, mild punishment, scheduled toilet sittings, cleanliness training, and/or regular pant checks. Reinforcement is provided contingent upon appropriate toileting and/or clean pants; mild punishment is provided contingent upon soiled pants. The literature includes various case studies that report cessation of soiling using these behavioral techniques. Nolan, *et al.* (1991) conducted the only group study and found that 36 percent of children diagnosed with retentive encopresis and treated with behavioral methods alone were free of symptoms at twelve months.

Combined Behavioral & Medical Treatment

A multitude of studies have assessed the efficacy of a combined behavioral and medical treatment intervention. Most of them include an initial clean-out phase followed by education, scheduled toilet sitting, diet modifications, rewards, and laxatives or suppositories. Overall, such interventions appear to be highly effective with retentive encopresis; success rates ranged from approximately 79 percent to nearly 100 percent. Further, children who initially failed to respond to other methods of treatment have been shown to frequently become continent when treatment using combined methods is employed. Little research has been conducted to determine which components of combined treatment interventions are most effective. Houts and Abramson (1990) suggest that positive reinforcement for appropriate toileting is an important component of most treatment packages. In addition, most research and extensive clinical experience suggests that clearing of the colon using either diet or laxatives, along with behavioral interventions, is necessary for effective treatment.

Other Treatments

A few investigators have reported successful treatment of encopresis with hypnosis (Tilton, 1980). Various individual and family therapies have also been explored as interventions with encopretic children. Individual (non-behavioral) psychotherapy has proven to be no more effective than not intervening, and family therapy has proven ineffective without the addition of behavioral, dietary, and/or medical components.

Biofeedback has also been used to successfully treat retentive encopresis, although most studies using it are among children with fecal incontinence secondary to a medical condition. Recent research has suggested that biofeedback may be a useful additional component to behavioral treatment with encopretic children.

Case Study, Owen

Owen was a nine-year-old boy who had been soiling at least once per day for years, and who had never been completely continent. His parents reported that the frequency of his soiling increased noticeably during times of separation from his mother (e.g., in the morning when leaving his parents for school, during overnight stays at his grandparents' home). Despite frequent prompts from parents and teachers throughout the day for him to use the toilet, the frequency of his soiling did not decrease. Owen's medical history was unremarkable; a work-up by a pediatric gastroenterologist showed his sphincter strength and physical examination to be in the normal range. However, an unusual amount of fecal material was present in his colon, which did not appear to be a full impaction. Overall, the pediatrician was confident that all possible medical causes of the child's current constipation and soiling had been ruled out.

Although the soiling had begun to impact Owen's social functioning and self-esteem, no significant behavior problems were present and his knowledge of toileting skills was adequate. However, symptoms of generalized anxiety (e.g., fidgeting, nail biting, crying, somatic complaints, difficulty sleeping) were present. Additionally, Owen was experiencing significant anxiety and pain with toileting. Owen and his mother reported that both were becoming very frustrated and upset, especially as there appeared to be no real reason for the soiling.

Conceptualization

It was concluded that Owen had retentive encopresis, which could be conceptualized by learning theory. His learned avoidance of defecation was seen primarily as a result of pain during bowel movements due to his chronic constipation; this avoidance could also be related to unsanitary or less than private school bathrooms, a lack of confidence in toileting skills, a diet low in fiber and high in dairy products, or simple unwillingness to stop a more reinforcing activity in order to relieve oneself. Owen's avoidance was believed to be further strengthened by two factors: (1) the large and painful nature of the infrequent bowel movements that followed his prolonged withholding, and (2) the gradual inability of his stretched and flaccid colon to either sense or expel fecal material. Rather than seeing the increase in soiling during unique situations (visits to grandparents, during school) as indicative of a direct association with stress, this was seen as simply the result of greater unwillingness to use the toilet appropriately in unusual situations where bathrooms were not familiar.

Treatment

The principles of learning theory would suggest that Owen had learned to retain stools and fear toileting because of early experiences with large and painful bowel movements; further, the continued practice of withholding prevented extinction of the fear. Treatment, then, should be based on keeping the colon as clear as possible to allow it to regain its usual size, muscle tone, and sensitivity. In order to achieve this goal, a combination of medical management (to achieve initial removal of any impacted stool) and behavioral methods (to facilitate regular toileting, appropriate diet, and use of laxatives) was seen as necessary.

The first step in treatment with Owen was to help him and his parents understand the above conceptualization of his soiling, and to attempt to reduce blaming and anger. A key feature of this latter goal was emphasizing the non-voluntary nature of soiling once impaction or severe constipation had taken place. Secondly the family was given an explanation of treatment: that it would begin with a two-week period in which soiling was carefully tracked using a daily diary, that a physician would be asked to help with laxatives and perhaps an initial "clean-out" of his colon, that afterwards he would be helped to try to defecate regularly so that he did not become constipated again, and that there would be some changes to his diet, also to help prevent constipation. The extreme importance of consistency with this protocol was emphasized to his parents.

The pediatric gastroenterologist agreed that Owen appeared to be chronically constipated, even though a clear impaction was not present. She recommended a high-fiber, high-fluid diet in which dairy products were avoided and mineral oil was taken a few hours after meals. The physician provided the family with a list of suggested high-fiber foods (e.g., popcorn, fruit, beans, grains, bran cereal) and dairy products to be avoided (milk, cheese, ice cream, etc.).

In addition to the medical intervention, a behavioral program was developed according to the protocol suggested by Calkins, *et al.* (1994). A list of reinforcers was developed with Owen's help. These included such items as small toys (e.g., toy cars, airplanes), pieces of candy and/or gum, coins, and gift certificates. The rewards were wrapped and placed in a basket in the bathroom. Owen was told he would earn one prize each time he produced a bowel movement at any of four daily regularly scheduled toilet sittings.

Clothing checks were also included in the behavioral program. At the end of each day, Owen's clothing was to be examined for soiling. Under this program, if he is soiled, he must actively participate in cleaning himself and his clothes. If he has not soiled, he should be provided with a reward. Owen's success or failure at the toilet sittings and clothing checks was charted daily, with Owen himself being heavily involved in the charting process. Therapist monitoring of progress occurred via weekly return visits and/or phone contacts. The behavioral program was continued until Owen was able to demonstrate eight consecutive weeks of appropriate toileting (i.e., absence of soiling).

Alternative Conceptualization

Given the non-conclusive results of the physician's examination, Owen's encopresis may not be primarily retentive in nature. It is possible that his soiling is indeed primarily related to stress: while stress-related encopresis is less common, it is certainly not rare. Thus, Owen might lack either appropriate control over the sphincter muscles that inhibit defecation, or he might have very limited stress coping skills, or (more likely) some combination of both.

Treatment techniques for children who soil in response to stress have not been systematically evaluated. However, a combination of decreasing diarrhea (if present), increasing anal sphincter control, and reducing the effects of stress on the child appears indicated (Ondersma & Walker, 1998). Some studies have reported success using systematic desensitization, stress inoculation training, relaxation training, and assertiveness training. The specific treatment techniques selected should vary depending on the particular characteristics of the case; in this particular case, treatment for symptoms of anxiety (particularly separation anxiety) would be the focus.

Summary

Although the etiology of encopresis has yet to be clearly defined, it can be conceptualized as the result of genetic predisposition, learned patterns of toileting, and/or maladaptive environmental contingencies. Additionally, encopresis may develop in combination with stressors such as a poor diet and/or emotional factors. Comprehensive behavioral treatment programs which include medical interventions for the clean-out phase and psychotherapeutic techniques to address comorbid emotional features have been shown to be safe and highly effective, when the presence of a general medical condition has been ruled out.

There is a dearth of research related to clarifying subtypes of encopresis and dismantling strategies to isolate which aspects of treatment are most effective, when, and for whom. Such research will be crucial in the attempt to increase treatment effectiveness, reduce relapse, and decrease length of treatment.

Appendix 1

Simplified Format for the Explanation of Treatment Principles

A very high level of skill is needed before the bladder can be properly controlled during sleep. Some children find it difficult to learn to swim or to ride a bicycle. It is perhaps not surprising that some children do not learn bladder control as infants, or easily lose their ability to control the bladder at night – it should perhaps be more surprising that so many do manage to learn such a complicated skill.

Some children who wet the bed have other problems, while others have few difficulties apart from their bedwetting. In either case it is usually possible to help the child to overcome the bedwetting problem.

It is likely that unpleasant experiences make the learning of bladder control more difficult, and often a child who has already become dry may begin to wet again after some disturbing event. Whether a child has been wet all his/her life, or has more recently lost bladder control, he/she needs special help with the difficult task of gaining control. The child will usually be examined first by a physician in case there is a physical cause for bedwetting, although this is rare. A sample of urine will also be taken for examination.

When a child wets the bed, it seems that his/her brain is not properly aware of the amount of urine in the bladder, allowing it to empty automatically during sleep. The child cannot help this.

A device known as the "enuresis alarm" has been developed to help children overcome the problem of bedwetting, Basically, the alarm is made up of a pair of detector mats on the bed, connected to a buzzer next to the child's bed. As soon as the sleeping child begins to wet, the buzzer sounds. The sound of the buzzer normally has two effects: Firstly, the muscles that have relaxed to allow urine to pass contract once more, stopping the stream of urine that has already started (it may have been noticed that loud noises will often interrupt the stream of urine). Secondly, the sound of the buzzer awakes the child.

The use of the alarm produces these two actions – stopping the stream and waking – whenever the child's bladder begins to empty automatically during sleep. Gradually the child's brain learns to connect these two actions with the feeling of a full bladder. After a time, the brain becomes aware of the amount of urine in the child's bladder, and itself begins to take the two actions. As the brain's control over the bladder becomes stronger, it's apparent how the actions learned from the alarm are used; wet patches become smaller as the child's muscles are contracted more quickly, and when the bladder is really full the child begins to awaken before passing any urine at all. Eventually, the child is able to sleep without wetting, waking up on his/her own if he/she needs to use the toilet at night. (Morgan, R.T.T. (1974). *Enuresis and the enuresis alarm: A clinical manual for the treatment of nocturnal enuresis.* University of Leicester School of Social Work, unpublished manuscript.)

Alternative Explanations of how the Enuresis Alarm Works

Right now, the human brain doesn't think much of it when it notices the feeling of a full bladder at night. It has to be taught to make a really big deal out of the feeling of a full bladder. To help it, an alarm is used to make a loud noise every time bedwetting starts. After hearing the loud alarm enough times, the brain starts to learn that having a full bladder is something that should get its attention. Pretty soon, it starts to either tell the bladder to hold it or to wake up when it notices the bladder is full.

Some people have very quiet bladders, and some people have loud bladders. Sometimes, if a bladder is too quiet, the brain can't hear it when it says it's full at night. This alarm is a special way to make quiet bladders really, really loud. After using the alarm for a while, children's bladders learn to be loud enough to wake them up if they have to go the bathroom at night. At first it won't be loud enough and it will only wake the child when it is too late. Pretty soon, though, it learns to be louder and louder until it will make the child either hold it or wake up.

Appendix 2

Treatment record sheet

In the first column, write a "W" if the child was wet at all during the night, a "D" if he or she was completely dry.

Night	"W" or "D"	Time of wetting	Patch size (small/ medium/large)	Did the alarm wake the child?	Did the child wake without the alarm to use the toilet during the night?
Monday					
Tuesday					
Wednesday					
Thursday					
Friday					
Saturday					
Sunday					

Source: Morgan, R.T.T. (1974). *Enuresis and the Enuresis Alarm: A clinical manual for the treatment of nocturnal enuresis.* University of Leicester School of Social Work, unpublished manuscript.

Appendix 3

Encopresis - Conservative Protocol Calkins, Walker, & Howe, 1994)

1) If the child is severely impacted, it may be necessary to administer one or two children's enemas to thoroughly evacuate the bowel;
2) Implement a high-fiber diet that includes fresh fruits and vegetables, fruit juices, and fiber; sprinkle raw bran and wheat germ on or cook it into dishes; and decrease but do not eliminate dairy products (milk, cheese, and ice cream). Stool softeners may also be required, and some, such as Colace, are available without prescription;
3) Institute a system of regular attempts to produce bowel movements (two to four times per day) and small rewards for daily bowel movements without soiling. Involving the child in the selection of rewards will increase the likelihood of success.

Rewards and Punishments

1) The selection of rewards is a critical component of the treatment program. The chosen rewards must be tailored to the individual child, as that which is rewarding to one child may not capture the interest of another. The value of reinforcers to the child must also be sufficiently powerful to motivate the child;
2) Two levels of rewards are required for three desired behaviors. The largest reward is given when the child defecates in an appropriate place without the aid of a cathartic. One approach is to fill a "treasure chest" with wrapped rewards such as small toys, money, or personal notes of encouragement that include privileges such as permission to stay up an extra 30 minutes before going to bed. A smaller reward (e.g., a piece of gum or candy) is given if the child defecates after a glycerine suppository is administered. A reward is also given if the child does not soil his or her underwear during the day. Giving the child 20 to 30 minutes of individual attention by one or both parents has been found to be quite useful and has the added potential for improving the parent-child relationship. Allowing the child to choose how to spend the time increases the motivational power of this reward;
3) The punishment given for soiling underwear needs to be something the child wants to avoid; however, it must not be excessively severe. A punishment that has been shown to be effective is to have the child sit in a chair for ten to 15 minutes. The chair needs to be in a place where the child has no interactions with family members or other distractions. Physical punishment such as spanking is not recommended;
4) Chart the child's behavior on a daily basis. Involving the child in maintenance of the behavioral chart is recommended. Results should be shared with the therapist by phone or in person on at least a weekly basis;

5) Improvement is typically evident within two to three weeks and the problem is generally eliminated within twelve to 16 weeks;
6) A "graduation" ceremony can be planned for the child after eight weeks of appropriate toileting without an accident. This provides the opportunity to compliment the child for gaining control, to terminate the reward system, and to provide a special event for completion of the program. Activities such as going to a movie, eating out, and taking a trip to the zoo are examples of excellent termination events. Continuance of dietary changes beyond this point is recommended.

References

Abrahamian, F. P., & Lloyd-Still, J. D. (1984). Chronic constipation in childhood: A longitudinal study of 186 patients. *Journal of Pediatric Gastroenterology and Nutrition, 3*, 460–467.

American Psychiatric Association (1994). *Diagnostic and Statistical Manual of Mental Disorders*. Fourth ed. Washington, DC: American Psychiatric Association.

Azrin, N. H., Sneed, T. J., & Foxx, R. M. (1974). Dry-bed training: Rapid elimination of childhood enuresis. *Behavior Research and Therapy, 12*, 147–156.

Bakwin, H. (1973). The genetics of enuresis. *Clinics in Developmental Medicine, 48–49*, 73–77.

Calkins, D. L., Walker, C. E., & Howe, A. C. (1994). Elimination disorders: Psychological issues. In Olson, R. A., Mullins, L. L., Gillman, J. B., & Chaney, J. M. (eds) *The Source-Book of Pediatric Psychology*. Boston: Allyn and Bacon. 46–54.

Gross, R. T., & Dornbusch, S. M. (1983). Disordered processes of elimination: Enuresis. In M. D. Levine, W. B. Carey, A. C. Crocker, & R. T. Gross (eds) *Developmental-behavioral Pediatrics*. Philadelphia: W.B. Saunders. 573–586.

Houts, A. C., & Abramson (1990). Assessment and treatment for functional childhood enuresis and encopresis: Toward a partnership between health psychologists and physicians. In S. B. Morgan, & T. M. Okwumabua (eds) *Child and Adolescent Disorders: Developmental and Health Psychology Perspectives*. Hillsdale, NJ: Lawrence Erlbaum Associates, Publishers. 47–103.

Houts, A. C., Berman, J. S., & Abramson, H. (1994). Effectiveness of psychological and pharmacological treatments for nocturnal enuresis. *Journal of Consulting and Clinical Psychology, 62*, 737–745.

Houts, A. C., & Liebert, R. M. (1984). *Bedwetting: A Guide for Parents and Children*. Springfield, IL: Thomas Books.

Moffat, M. E. K., Harlos, S., Kirshen, A. J., & Burd, L. (1993). Desmopressin acetate and nocturnal enuresis: How much do we know? *Pediatrics, 92*, 420–425.

Morgan, R. T. T., & Young, G. C. (1975). Case histories and shorter communications. *Behaviour Research and Therapy, 13*, 197–199.

Nolan, T., Debelle, G., Oberklaid, F., & Coffey, C. (1991). Randomized trial of laxatives in treatment of childhood encopresis. *Lancet, 338*, 523–527.

Ondersma, S. J., & Walker, C. E. (1998). Elimination disorders. In T. H. Ollendick and M. Hersen (eds) *Handbook of Child Psychopathology*. Third edition. New York, New York: Plenum.

Scott, M. A., Barclay, D. R., & Houts, A. C. (1992). Childhood enuresis: Etiology, assessment, and current behavioral treatment. In M. Hersen, R. M. Eisler, & P. M. Miller (eds) *Progress in Behavior Modification.* Sycamore Publishing Company. *28*, 83–117.

Tilton, P. (1980). Hypnotic treatment of a child with thumb sucking, enuresis, and encopresis. *American Journal of Clinical Hypnosis, 22*, 238–240.

Wille, S. (1986). Comparison of desmopressin and enuresis alarm for nocturnal enuresis. *Archives of Disease in Childhood, 61*, 30–33.

Chapter 20

Conceptualization and Treatment of Childhood-onset Schizophrenia

Martha C. Tompson and Joan R. Asarnow

This chapter is dedicated to the memory of Michael J. Goldstein. He contributed both to understanding how families could assist in the treatment of their mentally ill relatives and to training a generation of researchers investigating the causes and impact of psychosis.

> *"In first grade I was in the top reading group . . . By the third grade I was in the bottom reading group."*
>
> *"All of a sudden I couldn't read or write or do math anymore. Everything was so confusing because I couldn't understand what was going on around me."*
>
> *"I certainly heard voices. . . . At first the voices were friendly; then they got mean and scared me to pieces."*
>
> Anonymous, 1994

Introduction

Schizophrenia is the most severe of functional mental disorders. Individuals suffering from schizophrenia experience deficits and dysfunctions in cognition, affect, behavior and interpersonal relations. Studies indicate that in most developed countries approximately one percent of the Gross National Product is spent on treatment of mental disorders, and in the US these direct service costs have been rising over the last few decades. Treatment of individuals with schizophrenia makes up the majority of this expense. Indirect costs, such as lost productivity for patients and their family members, have been estimated at many times these mere direct costs (Souetre, 1997). While schizophrenia with onset before age 14 is rare, it may be particularly costly to society due to its early onset, potential for severe dysfunction over a longer time period, and greater direct and indirect costs. However, despite extensive treatment studies for schizophrenia in adults, there is little empirical data on treatment strategies for youth with schizophrenia. This chapter presents a hypothetical case description and conceptualizes a comprehensive treatment strategy based on current knowledge of both developmental outcomes

Handbook of Conceptualization and Treatment of Child Psychopathology, pages 417–435.

among children with schizophrenia and empirically-supported treatments for
adult-onset schizophrenia.

Schizophrenia: The Clinical Syndrome

Diagnosis

In the DSM-IV (APA, 1994) children are diagnosed using the same criteria for
diagnosing adult-onset forms of schizophrenia. These criteria require:

1) at least a one-month period in which psychotic symptoms are present (delusions, hallucinations, disorganized speech, grossly disorganized or catatonic
   behavior, and negative symptoms);
2) disturbance in one or more areas of functioning (i.e., school, work, interpersonal relationships, self-care);
3) continuous signs of illness for at least six months.

Additionally, if mood symptoms are present they must be brief in comparison
with symptoms of schizophrenia; the symptoms must not be the direct result of
substance use or a general medical condition; and if the individual has a history of
a pervasive developmental disorder, prominent hallucinations and/or delusions
must be present for an additional diagnosis of schizophrenia to be given. While
diagnostic criteria have expanded and contracted since DSM-II (Kendler, 1991),
the present criteria represent a narrow definition of schizophrenia, excluding
individuals with prominent affective symptomatology, predominant negative
symptoms, or time-limited psychotic process.

Associated Clinical Features

Schizophrenia in childhood is frequently accompanied by inadequate scholastic
achievement and academic adjustment, poor peer relationships, and restricted
interests (Asarnow & Ben-Meir, 1988; Asarnow, et al., 1994). Thus, children with
schizophrenia most often demonstrate deficits in a wide range of functional activities. They also frequently present with a plethora of associated symptoms.
Children with schizophrenia often have histories of language and motor delays,
poor muscle tone, hyperactivity, and poor social responsiveness (Watkins, et al.,
1988). Common comorbid diagnoses include attention deficit disorder, learning
disorders, disruptive behavior problems (conduct and oppositional disorders), and
depression (Asarnow, et al., 1994; Werry, et al., 1991). Indeed, the frequency of
depressed mood and suicidal behavior among children with schizophrenia makes
the differential diagnosis of bipolar disorder a particularly difficult, but important,
issue in deciding on appropriate treatment (McClellan & Werry, 1992). Additionally, research has consistently indicated that childhood-onset schizophrenia

presents with significant premorbid impairment and an insidious, rather than an acute, onset, making determination of the precise time of onset challenging. Indeed, it is often difficult to determine whether additional problems were precursors or comorbid conditions. For example, should one interpret the frequent presentation of symptoms of attention deficit hyperactivity disorder (ADHD) before and during schizophrenic episodes as a precursor state, early manifestation of the schizophrenic illness, or as a co-occurring condition? Future work is needed to understand the role of comorbity in children with schizophrenia.

Developmental Considerations

Although schizophrenia in childhood is diagnosed using adult diagnostic criteria, developmental issues arise in both the diagnosis and treatment of youth. Schizophrenia is often difficult to assess and diagnose in childhood and evaluation requires a thorough understanding of developmental progression and a firm knowledge of schizophrenic pathology. Treatments which are effective in adults require adaptation for the unique developmental needs of children.

In diagnosing schizophrenia in youth, five prominent issues arise. First, due to limitations in both cognitive and language development, younger children are often poor reporters of both chronology and their internal states than older individuals. For this reason it is important to use additional informants (parents, teachers), as well as observation, in diagnosing children with schizophrenia. Second, hallucinations, delusions, and thought disorder are rare and difficult to diagnose before age seven. The clinician must distinguish between psychotic symptoms, such as delusions, and elaborative fantasy play typical of childhood. "Imaginary friends" and creative fantasies, which are usually recognized by even elementary school-aged children as pretend and do not tend to impair functioning, should not be confused with psychotic symptomatology. Third, thought disorder, a core psychotic symptom, is difficult to evaluate in young children due to overlap between developmentally immature speech and "thought disorder." Play often provides a context for evaluating thought and communication processes. For example, Caplan, *et al.*, (1989) have developed the Formal Thought Disorder Story Game to allow structured evaluation of thinking disturbance, providing both a means of eliciting speech and a system for scoring. Fourth, while adults with schizophrenia often show a deterioration in their psychosocial attainment and skills, children with schizophrenia have often not developed cognitive and self-care skills at the time of onset, and the symptoms of schizophrenia impede the development of such skills. Indeed, the DSM-IV stipulates that when the onset is in childhood or adolescence, failure to achieve expected level of interpersonal, academic or occupational achievement may be evidence of social/occupational dysfunction (APA, 1994, p. 285). Finally, children presenting with psychotic symptoms require careful evaluation for potential general medical conditions that may produce similar symptoms (e.g., cerebral tumor). Organic factors should be carefully excluded before entertaining a schizophrenia diagnosis.

In treating schizophrenia in childhood, it is important to consider developmental level. First, children reside within larger systems which impact development. Family, school and peer group influence the child's acquisition of skills, development of interpersonal relationships and overall adjustment. Effective treatment must address the child's problems in multiple systems. Second, early adaptation influences later development (Sroufe, 1979) with later skills built on a platform of earlier competencies and experiences. The child with schizophrenia often fails to develop skills across a range of domains. Treatment must actively promote the acquisition of capacities in order to encourage optimal development.

Course and Outcome

Effective intervention must consider the natural history and course of the pathology in question. While much is known about the course and outcomes of adult-onset schizophrenia, there is only limited data on the natural history of childhood-onset schizophrenia. Although longitudinal studies of schizophrenia among youth have often involved small samples, four prospective studies have been completed and underscore the frequent chronic nature of early onset schizophrenia and the poor psychosocial adjustment among its victims.

In the first study, Werry, et al., (1991) followed 30 schizophrenic youth for an average of five years (range one to 15 years). Severe impairment in this sample was evident at follow-up, when 90 percent had either chronic schizophrenia or at least two psychotic episodes, only 17 were either full-time workers or students, and the average rating of Global Adaptive Functioning (GAF) was 40. Fully one-third of the patients demonstrated poor compliance with psychiatric care.

Second, Eggers and Bunk (1997) completed an exceptional long-term follow-up study of 44 individuals with child- and adolescent-onset schizophrenia. Remarkably, 35 were personally evaluated and relatives of the other nine were interviewed over an average of 42 years after initial diagnosis. Approximately one-third of the sample had onset of psychosis before age twelve. Using a three-category outcome rating, 25 percent of the sample had achieved complete remission of symptoms, 25 percent were in partial remission (showing some ongoing symptoms and moderate impairment in functioning), and 50 percent of the sample were either in poor remission, chronically psychotic or had developed severe residual symptoms. Insidious onset was more common in earlier onset cases and was strongly associated with poor remission.

Third, Asarnow, et al.'s (1994) presentation of two to seven year follow-up data on a sample of 18 children is remarkably consistent with the findings of Eggers and Bunk (1997). Twenty-two percent of the children demonstrated substantial recovery (GAF scores over 60) by the end of the follow-up period; whereas 44 percent of this sample showed either minimal improvement (GAF scores consistently less than 50) or a deterioration in functioning. When those children diagnosed at follow-up as having schizoaffective disorder were excluded from the sample, eight (50 percent) of the 16 remaining cases demonstrated minimal improvement or deterioration.

Finally, Remschmidt, *et al.*, (1994) examined 61 youth with schizophrenia, eleven of whom had onset before age 14 (very early onset). Compared with youth whose onset was after age 14, this very early onset group demonstrated a longer period of negative symptoms before full manifestation of the disorder. Of these eleven very early onset cases, 100 percent showed a continuous course of schizophrenic symptoms. This group of children had demonstrably worse outcomes than are evident in the Eggers and Bunk (1997) or Asarnow, *et al.*, (1994) studies but similar outcomes to those children studied by Werry, *et al.*, (1991).

In summary, findings from the few longitudinal studies of schizophrenia in youth indicate poor outcome for a substantial proportion of youth with schizophrenia. It is important to note, however, that while most children in each of these follow-up studies received psychotropic medication, only one study systematically evaluated the role of medication (Remschmidt, *et al.*, examined Clozapine). Even so, in this study few very early onset cases were examined, leaving questions about the potential role of antipsychotic medications in the treatment of early-onset schizophrenia. With careful medication management, outcomes may be improved. However, the numerous impairments shown by these children underscore the need for comprehensive and effective treatment strategies.

Treatment Conceptualization

Model

The vulnerability-stress model has been proposed as an heuristic for understanding factors influencing schizophrenic onset and course (Nuechterlein & Dawson, 1984). Three central factors that are emphasized across various vulnerability-stress models include:

(1) **Vulnerability factors** refer to characteristics that predispose an individual to develop the disorder and are assumed to be present in individuals at risk and to comprise an enduring characteristic of individuals who suffer from schizophrenic episodes. Both constitutional and environmental vulnerability factors have been posited, including genetic factors, central nervous system damage resulting from obstetric and birth complications, limited information processing capacity, autonomic arousal, dopaminergic dysfunction, schizotypal personality traits, inadequate learning opportunities, and exposure to deviant family communication patterns. Some vulnerability factors may be specific to schizophrenia, whereas others may be associated with general risk for psychiatric disorder. For example, genetic loading for schizophrenia might represent a specific risk factor for schizophrenia; whereas, malnutrition might represent a general risk factor associated with increased risk for psychiatric disorder.

(2) **Stressors** are hypothesized to lead to an increased likelihood of a schizophrenic episode. They may include major life events such as death of a family

member, as well as more chronic life stressors and problems. Major life events (e.g., death of a parent) may also become increasingly chronic as time progresses (e.g., living in a home with a bereaved parent). The presence of such stressors may also impair the development of effective coping responses and competencies, leading to increased experiences of stress.

(3) **Protective factors** refer to favorable characteristics of the individual or environment that are associated with a reduced risk of symptoms among at-risk individuals. These protective factors may include use of effective coping strategies, consistent use of antipsychotic medication, effective family communication and problem solving, and involvement in supportive psychosocial treatment.

Vulnerability factors, stressors and protective factors are hypothesized to interact in determining both the onset and course of schizophrenia. Those with the greatest exposure to stress and/or highest vulnerability are viewed as most likely to develop schizophrenic episodes and to have the most malignant outcomes. Alternatively, lower loadings on vulnerability factors and lower levels of stress exposure are hypothesized to lead to more favorable outcomes. However, hypotheses addressing the nature of the interaction between vulnerability factors, stressors, and protective factors vary across models. Whereas some models postulate additive relationships in which posited factors are presumed to act relatively independently, transactional models emphasize environment interactions over time. Transactional models, thus, focus on the question of how genetically transmitted predispositions are expressed at various developmental stages and interact with care-giving environments to determine whether individuals develop schizophrenia as well as their levels of psychosocial functioning. Vulnerability-stress models suggest that effective treatment for schizophrenia will focus on reducing vulnerability factors, decreasing stress, and increasing available protective factors in the environment.

Alternative Model

Theories of schizophrenia positing that dysfunctional family processes could cause it have been discredited, theories such as the one proposing that development of schizophrenia was a result of severely dysfunctional family communication. Specifically, Bateson, *et al.*, (1956) advanced the "double-bind" theory, in which they argued that parents of individuals with schizophrenia communicated conflicting messages to their offspring. For example, the spoken content may have conflicted with the unspoken (body language), as in saying "I love you" while pushing away. This communication confuses the developing child, who eventually retreats into a psychotic state. In such a model, reducing contact with the pathogenic family or engaging in family therapy addressing the dysfunctional family system are the preferred treatment strategies. Unfortunately, intensive systemic family treatments may be disorganizing and precipitate an exacerbation of psychotic symptoms in individuals with schizophrenia. More contemporary work with families of schizophrenic individuals has not supported the double-bind theory. There are some data that indicate that parents of schizophrenic individuals are more likely than parents of depressed individuals to demonstrate communication difficulties, including subclinical thought disorder and trouble maintaining a "shared focus of attention." These communication difficulties may represent a manifestation of the genetic predisposition to schizophrenia, but may also represent a psychosocial risk factor that might exacerbate underlying cognitive and perceptual vulnerabilities for schizophrenia (Asarnow, *et al.*, 1988; Tompson, *et al.*, 1997; Tienari, *et al.*, 1987; Miklowitz & Stackman, 1992). Treatments based on this model include an emphasis on improving family communication to address such difficulties.

Other models of schizophrenia, both in adults and children, posit that it is a brain disease, specifically effecting dopaminergic systems (Weinberger, 1994). Interventions based on this model support the reliance on biological treatments such as medication. However, recent evidence suggests that (1) the course of illness among individuals with schizophrenia is influenced by the environment, including life events (Norman & Malla, 1993) and the emotional climate of the family (Butzlaff & Hooley, 1998), and (2) medication effects are enhanced by the addition of psychosocial treatments (Bellack & Mueser, 1993).

Stages of Treatment

Although reviews of the therapy literature reveal no controlled treatment trials of psychosocial interventions for youth suffering from schizophrenia, adult treatment literature, the vulnerability-stress model, and results of naturalistic studies of the lives of schizophrenic youth, highlight some major issues with respect to treatment. First, treatment of schizophrenia is a long-term process which can be conceptualized as three-phases (e.g., Goldstein & Miklowitz, 1995): (1) the **acute** phase which utilizes a combination of medication and inpatient care to bring acute psychotic symptoms under control, (2) the **stabilization** phase which employs outpatient pharmacologic and psychosocial interventions to further reduce symptoms, and (3) the **maintenance** phase which emphasizes a multimodal treatment approach to help youth with schizophrenia maintain a stable clinical state and improved psychosocial functioning. This discussion will focus on psychosocial treatment strategies during the stabilization and maintenance phases of treatment. Second, in addition to active and residual symptoms, individuals with schizophrenia suffer from family stress, poor peer adjustment, academic dysfunction, and impairments in social interaction and motivation. Given that schizophrenia impacts a wide range of domains, it is essential that treatment be multimodal, ameliorating symptoms and assisting in the rebuilding and development of skills.

Third, the current emphasis on treating youth within the least restrictive setting and reducing hospitalizations and residential care have resulted in many more youth with schizophrenia being treated within their families and communities. Therefore, effective treatment must involve these systems. Fourth, research has shown that attributes of the family may have an impact on illness course. Expressed Emotion (EE), a measure of critical, hostile, and/or emotionally overinvolved attitudes on the part of family members toward a mentally ill patient (as expressed in a clinical interview), has been found to be a potent prospective predictor of relapse in adults with schizophrenia (Butzlaff & Hooley, 1998). Interestingly, the only study examining expressed emotion in families of children with schizophrenia found very low rates of high EE, comparable with children having no mental illness and far lower than in families of children with depression (Asarnow, *et al.*, 1994). This underscores the potential dangers of generalizing from adult research as well as the importance of understanding the needs of families with youth suffering from schizophrenia. Clearly, families need support managing the child's disorder and enhancing his/her ability to develop competencies. In summary, optimal psychosocial treatment for childhood-onset schizophrenia varies with the phase of disorder, involves a multimodal treatment approach with numerous targeted behaviors, and integrates the family and larger systems in intervention. Given this need for an integrated multimodal approach, treatment of childhood schizophrenia will almost invariably include a team of treatment professionals. Psychiatry, psychology, social work, special education providers all have a role to play.

Three empirically supported intervention strategies for adult-onset schizophrenia include: (1) individual therapy, (2) family-based treatments, and (3) behavioral skills building interventions. A combination of these treatment strategies can provide a basis for interventions among children with schizophrenia.

Hypothetical Case Example

John is a 13-year old Caucasian male. He is the eldest child in an intact family with two younger siblings, Angie age eight and Cory age six. He was recently discharged after a two-month inpatient hospitalization for schizophrenia and is being treated with Haloperidol. Although John's parents appear well-adjusted and have never sought mental health services, his paternal uncle was diagnosed with paranoid schizophrenia ten years ago and is currently on disability, and his maternal great aunt was hospitalized several times for "nervous breakdowns" when John's mother was a child.

John was born prematurely at 34 weeks gestation and demonstrated poor muscle tone and a weak sucking response. He was somewhat delayed in reaching developmental milestones. Given poor speech development and immaturity his parents did not place him in kindergarten until age six. He demonstrated difficulty adjusting to the classroom in the first grade, frequently wandering around the classroom, hiding under his desk, and crying easily. He was diagnosed with Attention Deficit Disorder in second grade and briefly placed on stimulant medication. However, after he developed eye blinks the stimulants were discontinued. John continued to be inattentive and was often oppositional in the classroom and at home. His father and mother frequently argued about the best strategies for controlling John's behavior and briefly sought behavior therapy for managing his temper outbursts. While this intervention was effective, the parents felt overwhelmed by the demands of all three children and discontinued the intervention shortly after the end of treatment.

In the third grade he was placed in a special class for children with learning and emotional problems. He did not develop friendships and was rejected by his classmates who considered him "weird." At this time his parents began to notice that his speech was often difficult to understand, as he used peculiar logic and had a tendency to drift from one topic to another without warning. Around sixth grade he developed a strong interest in space aliens, which he could talk about for hours on end. He quickly became obsessed with anything having to do with space travel. His mother found it increasingly difficult to manage his behavior. He often refused to bathe, was aggressive with his younger siblings, and was performing poorly in school. Around the winter holiday he claimed that the aliens wanted him to join them and would kill him if he did not. He made a suicide attempt by dodging in front of a moving car and was hospitalized following this incident.

During the hospitalization he was frequently fearful and suicidal and demonstrated a number of psychotic symptoms, including hallucinations (hearing aliens' voices), ideas of reference (believing events were messages from the aliens), and paranoia (believing the aliens were trying to find and kill him). His speech was tangential and illogical, his affect flat, and his mannerisms bizarre. He participated in a structured inpatient program and was placed on Haloperidol. His symptoms gradually improved and after a two-month stay he was discharged to his family home.

He currently attends the local middle school, where he is placed in a special classroom for emotionally disturbed children. While his speech is easier to follow and he seldom speaks about the aliens, he continues to express belief in them when asked, demonstrates blunted affect, and is frequently socially withdrawn. At home he is often distractable, fights with his siblings, fails to complete tasks which his parents assign him (including homework), and demonstrates poor hygiene (often refusing to bathe).

Conceptualization

John's symptoms can be understood within a vulnerability-stress framework. There is evidence from his family history and his own developmental history of vulnerability. First, there is a family history of mental disorders John's uncle, and possibly his great aunt as well, experienced schizophrenic symptoms. Thus, genetic vulnerability for schizophrenia may clearly play a role in this case. John demonstrates many of the characteristic early deficits experienced by children with schizophrenia, including developmental delays, attention deficits, and difficulties adapting to the academic environment. These developmental difficulties reflect neuro-cognitive vulnerabilities which might place John at increased risk for the development of psychosis. These deficits also limit John's ability to cope with stressors as they occur, contributing further to maladaptation. John has a history of family conflict and peer rejection, both acting as stressors in the vulnerability-stress model. Despite parental conflict over discipline, his supportive, intact family and access to a supportive school environment represent potential protective factors. With support these strengths increase the probability of a more favorable outcome.

John displays typical onset with thought and language disturbances followed by hallucinations and delusions. While active symptoms of his disorder have abated during the acute phase, he continues to experience some psychotic symptoms and to demonstrate significant psychosocial impairment.

Detailed Treatment Strategy: Goals

In this case, a number of foci for intervention present, including residual positive and negative symptoms, parental conflict over behavior management strategies, sibling conflict, and poor social skills. Using the vulnerability-stress model to conceptualize John's symptoms and problems, the treatment should take a "two-prong" approach: (1) **Medication management** focusing on the amelioration of personal vulnerability factors; this intervention can be conceived as a "specific" treatment in that it is aimed at altering the symptoms which comprise the particular disorder. (2) **Psychosocial interventions** aiming at decreasing stressful family interactions, improving coping skills, and increasing both effective family communication and problem-solving. These interventions can be viewed as "general" in that they address ongoing needs of the child and family in managing the disorder (McClellan & Werry, 1994).

Treatment of schizophrenia is a long-term process with goals shifting as the patient demonstrates improvement and shows evidence of relapse. Table 20.1 lists goals and strategies for each phase of treatment.

During the stabilization phase, once the diagnosis of schizophrenia has been confirmed, three tasks immediately confront the treatment team: (1) further reduction of characteristic symptoms, (2) building a therapeutic alliance with both the parents and the child, and (3) evaluating the child's current level of psychosocial functioning. During the maintenance phase four different tasks present: (1) maintaining a stable clinical state, (2) managing potential psychiatric crises, (3) reducing stress, and (4) improving the child's psychosocial functioning.

Phases of Treatment: Stabilization

Further Reduction of Symptoms. During the stabilization phase, the medicating physician adjusts medication to increase efficacy and reduce side-effects. Coordination between the psychosocial intervention team and the medicating physician must be ongoing with the efforts of each informing an evolving treatment approach. The medicating physician provides the team with important information on the process of stabilization, current strategies for addressing residual symptoms, and medication changes that may impact on functioning. Such

Table 20.1: Treatment for Childhood-onset Schizophrenia: Goals and Strategies.

Phase	Goals	Strategies
Acute	Reduction of acute psychotic symptoms	Medication trials Structured inpatient setting
	Complete diagnostic and social evaluation	Observation and psychological testing
Stabilization	Further reduction of symptoms	Adjust medication dosage Address medication side effects
	Building therapeutic alliance with child and family	Begin parental psychoeducation Begin psychoeducation with child Supportive psychotherapy with the child
	Evaluation of ongoing deficits	Regular evaluation of skills
Maintenance	Maintaining stable clinical state Managing crises	Continue maintenance medications Address issues of medication compliance Psychoeducation focusing on identification of prodromal symptoms Treatment team availability
	Reducing Stress	Family communication/ problem-solving
	Improving psychosocial functioning	Social/life skills building and stress management with child Behavior management with parents

information allows clinicians to construct a treatment plan that accommodates the child's current level of functioning and provides strategies for coping with residual symptoms. The psychosocial intervention team reciprocates with additional reports of and side-effects that are apparent during treatment sessions. Frequent communication between treatment providers lays the foundation for an integrated and comprehensive treatment approach.

Building a Therapeutic Alliance

In building a therapeutic alliance with the family important strategies include supportive psychotherapy with the child and parental psychoeducation. Given that a child who has recently been discharged from hospital after a psychotic episode may be particularly vulnerable to overstimulation and may have difficulty processing complex information, it is recommended that initial psychoeducation sessions involve the parents alone. Child sessions at this early point may involve play and conversation but should focus on building an alliance between the clinician and child.

In conducting psychoeducation with parents, clinicians must recognize that parents vary considerably in their knowledge of schizophrenia so treatment should be targeted at the knowledge level of each family. Parents also vary in their desire for specific information. For example, some parents may be satisfied in understanding that their child has a "chemical imbalance" in the brain which underlies symptom expression, whereas other parents may want more specific information on the nature of the dysfunction. The clinician should not assume that parents who claim to understand the problem do not need education. Parents may be confused about the need for psychosocial intervention and concerned that they will be blamed for the child's difficulties. Effective psychoeducation both facilitates a therapeutic alliance and provides a rationale for treatment. First, in facilitating a therapeutic alliance psychoeducation should be conducted in a "no fault" environment where the clinician conveys an understanding of the parents' experiences and frustrations. The process of psychoeducation confronts parents with difficult realities about the nature and course of schizophrenia in childhood, and parents need a safe environment in which to express their fears, grief and loss. The provision of such an environment can contribute to the development of a strong therapeutic alliance and a commitment on behalf of the parents to the treatment process. Second, psychoeducation based on the vulnerability-stress model provides a rationale for the integrated treatment. Explaining that treatment of both the vulnerability (through medication) and the stress (through psychosocial strategies) are essential for optimal recovery helps parents appreciate the need for both.

Goldstein and Miklowitz (1995) describe five critical issues in psychoeducation with the families of individuals who have psychosis and suggest strategies for addressing each of these issues. While the strategies are modified here for application to schizophrenic youth, the issues remain essential. First, the parents must integrate the psychotic experience. The clinician initially reviews the signs and symptoms of the disorder, encourages both parents to share their experience of the phenomenology of psychotic experiences, reviews the nature of life events that could have served as triggers for the most recent episode, and presents the vulnerability-stress model as a system for understanding how psychosis comes about. In addition, the clinician may need to describe the experience of psychosis from the child's perspective, noting how differences in family members' perceptions of these experiences come about. With parents who have difficulty understanding the child's psychotic behavior, this may lead to a greater appreciation of the extreme fear and anxiety that may follow from psychotic experiences.

Second, parents need to accept that their child is vulnerable to future psychotic episodes. The clinician can present data on the probability of recurrence and help parents to express feelings and concerns about this probability. It is often helpful to use analogies with other chronic medical disorders to reduce stigma and to help parents to identify risk factors in the child (e.g., poor coping skills) and environment (e.g., school stress, overstimulating environment) as well as protective factors (e.g., medication compliance, social support). Helping parents to see how they can assist in their child's recovery by controlling modifiable risk and protective factors, for example, supporting the child in taking medications, is also useful.

Third, the parents, and eventually the child as well, must accept the child's need to take psychotropic medications for controlling and reducing the risk of recurrence. Strategies for addressing this issue include presenting information on neurotransmitter models of psychosis (dopamine hypothesis), explaining how drugs reduce vulnerability by modifying problematic neurotransmitter states, encouraging discussion of negative side- effects and ways of managing them, and encouraging the parents to help in promoting medication compliance. Fourth, the clinician helps parents understand the significance of life events as stressors for psychotic relapse. Strategies for addressing this issue include reviewing the stressful life events presaging each prior episode, having parents rank their impact and significance, attempting to identify categories into which they might fit (e.g., losses, interpersonal difficulties), helping parents predict which life events are likely to recur, and engaging in anticipatory planning to address these stressors.

Finally, parents must try to distinguish ongoing personality traits and styles from signs and symptoms of schizophrenia. This is particularly difficult in childhood-onset schizophrenia where early, insidious onset and poor premorbid functioning strongly impact on both the development of personality and the perceptions of others. Clinicians can assist parents in identifying functional aspects (strengths) of their child, in discriminating normal variations in mood and behavior from prodromal signs, and in distinguishing between residual psychotic states and individual personality traits.

Research has indicated that providing families of adult-onset schizophrenics with a one time educational session is inadequate for information retention (Cozolino, *et al.*, 1988). Psychoeducation needs to be an integrated, ongoing process across the course of treatment. Psychoeducation with the child should begin only after the clinician has formed an alliance with the child. Information should be presented slowly to the child and adjusted to his/her developmental level. As John is only 13 years old, he is unlikely to benefit from extensive explanations of the potential neurobiological substrates of schizophrenia. However, a conceptual framework can facilitate his understanding of his current difficulties and treatment regimen. Some central information to impart early includes:

1) signs and symptoms of schizophrenia;
2) the notion that these symptoms represent an illness;

3) the illness is not a deadly one (younger children may be particularly prone to these fears);

4) the treatment team and medication can help the child to continue to get better.

For John, this preliminary information provides a scaffold on which to build an effective treatment strategy and an evolving understanding of the disorder and its management. Children often have limited insight into their behavior, and psychoeducation continues as the child's cognitive development allows for greater understanding of educational material.

Evaluating Ongoing Deficits

In evaluating the child's psychosocial functioning and ongoing deficits, the clinician is exploring targets for intervention. Regular feedback from classroom teachers provides invaluable data on the child's daily functioning. The child with schizophrenia often has multiple deficits, and the clinician must work with the child and his/her parents and teachers to prioritize goals. For example, in the case of John, important targets for intervention include reducing his task-related behavior, improving his hygiene, and helping the parents work together to find strategies for affecting his behavior.

Maintenance Phase

Maintaining a Stable Clinical State and Managing Crises. For treatment of residual symptoms and prevention of relapse, antipsychotic medications should be continued after the stabilization phase. Relapses may occur during this phase. Careful monitoring of prodromal symptoms, frequent contact between clinician and parents, and treatment team availability help improve the probability of early intervention impeding relapse and reducing the likelihood of difficult and costly hospitalization. Psychoeduction with both the parents and the child focuses increasingly on identifying potential prodromal symptoms, which can then be carefully monitored over time. John's earlier psychotic episode, presaged by an increasing interest in space aliens, may represent an early prodromal or "warning" sign that John and his parents can discuss with the treatment providers. Other prodromal signs, such as sleep disturbance or affective changes, may provide additional information.

Frequently the maintenance phase of treatment is the time during which medication compliance issues first begin to surface. Non-compliance may occur for many reasons, including a child's difficulty in taking pills, side-effects, fear of blood tests, denial of the disorder, and conflict between family members. It is not always the case that these are the child's issues. For example, one parent may deny the reality of the disorder, leading to conflict between the parents and to inconsistent medication administration. It is essential that the clinician explore non-critically the reasons for the non-compliance. If the child has difficulty taking pills, medication may often be prescribed in liquid form; if medication side-effects are problematic, dose adjustments, medication changes or additional medications targeted at reducing side-effects may be appropriate.

Particularly among adolescents, medication may become an arena around which battles for autonomy are waged. Escalating cycles of conflict and non-compliance result when power struggles between the parents and adolescent become focused on treatment. Compliance problems may become further exacerbated when family members have different attributions about the adolescent's behavior. For example, if the adolescent dresses oddly the parents may convey that this behavior "is because he has an illness which leads to poor decisions," whereas, the adolescent believes "I'm just being myself and my parents don't understand me." As the parents and the adolescent become more polarized in their positions, these conflicts may culminate in medication non-compliance – the adolescent's final message of independence. With these issues in mind, three strategies for addressing non-compliance may be particularly important for adolescents with schizophrenia. First, it is essential that youth as well as parents understand and accept the treatment plan. Reframing can be used to decrease the polarization between parents and adolescent. For example, the clinician can reframe the non-compliance as a message from adolescent to parents and discuss with the family other ways for the adolescent to communicate his/her increasing autonomy. Second, problem-solving can help families arrive at concrete solutions for addressing medication non-compliance. For example, if the child/adolescent often forgets to take the nightly dose of medication, problem-solving can help the family arrive at a solution in which the child can be reminded but not feel "nagged." Third, early in the course of psychoeducation, the clinician can predict that non-compliance will occur at some point, normalize this behavior and encourage family members to discuss it with the treatment team should it occur. In presenting non-compliance as part of the treatment process, the clinician can reduce family conflict around the issue and increase the likelihood it will be discussed early with treatment providers.

Reducing Stress in the Environment

In reducing environmental stress, the clinician should work individually with the child, with the parents alone, and with the family as a unit. In sessions with each, the goal is to identify potential sources of stress and develop strategies for reducing it when possible and coping with it when necessary. Family interventions have been shown to be particularly effective in adults with schizophrenia (Goldstein & Miklowitz, 1995), and these strategies can be adapted for the families of children. In addition to psychoeducation, these family approaches generally involve working with families to build communication and problem-solving skills.

Schizophrenia presents many challenges to child and family and improved communication and problem-solving help them all to better manage these challenges.

First, both adults and children with schizophrenia show a variety of information-processing deficits, particularly with selective attention and vigilance (Asarnow & Asarnow, 1995). Family communication training aims at helping parents provide simple yet consistent feedback to the child. Second, family conflict and parental criticism may increase stress and subsequent relapse risk. Family skills building, including training in communication and problem-solving, can assist parents and children in reducing disagreements, developing conflict resolution skills, and reducing family stress. In family sessions, John and his parents can work together on communication skills, including active listening, giving positive and negative feedback, and making positive requests for change in one another's behavior. Communication training includes role-playing, rehearsal, and homework assignments that will require John and his parents to work on the skills between sessions. In implementing this training, it is essential that the clinician gives positive feedback to all members as they attempt these new skills, provides concrete examples of how these skills can be used in daily life, and adjusts the sessions to the developmental needs of the child. Family members can also learn problem solving techniques, including identification of specific problems, brainstorming of solutions, and evaluation and implementation of self-selected solutions. Problem-solving should first be geared toward relatively easy problems; the more difficult problems can be faced as family members develop confidence in the problem-solving skills. Problem-solving can be used in individual sessions with John's parents to help them establish agreement over rules and expectations for John's behavior and for disciplinary strategies. John and his family should also be assisted in using their developing skills to complete a "relapse drill" in which problem-solving focuses on planning a family-wide response should John's symptoms increase.

Improving Psychosocial Functioning

The child with schizophrenia often presents a number of problem behaviors, including positive symptoms that persist despite appropriate medication management, poor concentration and attention, lack of motivation, and agitation. Parents may be taught behavioral skills for managing behavior at home. John's limited on-task behavior and poor hygiene may all be the focus of behavioral strategies. Contingency management, for example, could be used to address his poor hygiene. The clinician may assist the parents in establishing a system of reinforcers for appropriate grooming activities. It is discovered that John enjoys playing videogames. Thirty minutes of evening videogames is made contingent upon him bathing.

A number of skills building approaches have been used with adult schizophrenics. Skills training approaches employ behavioral techniques to teach individuals with schizophrenia requisite skills for establishing interpersonal relationships and living in the community (Liberman & Kopelowicz, 1995). Specific skills that have been the focus of attention include social skills (e.g., conversational) and self-management skills (e.g., hygiene, medication management). Skills building approaches, which can be implemented in groups or using an individual format, have focused goals and specified behavioral techniques, and emphasize in vivo practice to facilitate generalization. Behavioral techniques for implementing skills building include modeling, role playing, reinforcement and rehearsal of skills. Complex social skills are broken down into teachable pieces, rehearsed extensively, and finally practiced in more complex sequences.

John needs to work on his social skills, particularly starting conversations with others, making eye contact, asking appropriate questions, and ending these interactions. Each of these topics can be introduced and practiced during individual sessions with John. Further practice in family sessions helps reinforce the skills, increasing generalization to the home environment. As John grows and develops he may focus on skills that help increase his autonomy. For example, he may be taught skills for managing his own medication.

Summary and Integration of Conceptualization and Treatment

Schizophrenia with onset in childhood and adolescence presents with significant psychosocial impairment, multiple associated symptoms, and a high societal cost. Although some research has been conducted on the correlates, course, and outcome of child- and adolescent-onset schizophrenia, inferences about its neurobiology, the psychosocial factors predicting outcome, and strategies for effective treatment are generally downward extrapolations from the adult schizophrenia literature. Childhood- and adult-onset schizophrenia appear to represent the same illness or set of illnesses. However, limited data are available on biological and genetic variables in the childhood-onset forms (Jacobsen & Rapoport, 1998). Further research is needed to determine the significance of the atypical childhood-onset, including whether it represents one end of the distribution in age of onset or a more severe variant of schizophrenia with a stronger biological vulnerability.

Investigators have begun to examine the efficacy of psychotropic medications for childhood-onset schizophrenia (McClellan & Werry, 1994), but research on psychosocial interventions has lagged behind. Therefore, there is no child schizophrenia treatment literature to provide a basis for interventions. Examination of treatment efficacy studies with adult schizophrenics, research on course in childhood-onset schizophrenia, and conceptualization using vulnerability stress models provide some guidance for developing treatment approaches with this population.

The vulnerability-stress model provides an heuristic for understanding factors that impact outcome and for designing comprehensive treatment interventions for children with schizophrenia. Vulnerability factors, stressors, and protective factors all provide foci for treatment. An integrated intervention package based on this model would combine psychotropic medication to reduce acute symptoms and vulnerability and psychosocial interventions to reduce stress and build coping strategies. Effective treatment takes place on multiple levels and across multiple contexts, recognizes the impact of developmental level on the treatment process, requires skills in working with family members and school systems, and represents a long-term process. Given the frequent comorbidity in this population, attention must be paid to associated symptoms as well. Management of schizophrenia in youth generally requires a range of resources and treatment providers.

Information from long-term follow-up studies of youth with schizophrenia and literature on treatment for adult-onset forms of this disorder provide some promising therapeutic approaches; however, much work remains to adapt treatments for youth, examine treatment efficacy, and provide integrated interventions for this difficult population. Ultimately, these interventions must address the unique needs of the individual child and family. Important questions to address include:

1) What factors are associated with improved course in childhood onset schizophrenia?
2) What interventions are effective in reducing symptoms and improving psychosocial functioning?
3) What factors might moderate these treatment effects?
4) How can pharmacotherapy and psychosocial interventions be combined for maximum effectiveness?

Finally, research on etiology and prevention must proceed.

References

American Psychiatric Association (1994). *DSM-IV: Diagnostic and Statistical Manual of Mental Disorders.* 4th ed. Washington, DC: The Association.

Anonymous (1994). First person account: Schizophrenia with childhood onset. *Schizophrenia Bulletin, 20(4)*, 587–590.

Asarnow, J. R. & Asarnow, R. F. (1995). Childhood-onset schizophrenia. In E. N. Mash & R. A. Barkley (eds). *Child Psychopathology.* New York: Guildford Press.

Asarnow, J. R. & Ben-Meir, S. (1988). Children with schizophrenia spectrum and depressive disorders: A comparative study of onset patterns, premorbid adjustment, and severity of dysfunction. *Journal of Child Psychology and Psychiatry, 29*, 477–488.

Asarnow, J. R., Goldstein, M. J., & Ben-Meir, S. (1988). Parental communication deviance in childhood onset schizophrenia spectrum and depressive disorders. *Journal of Child Psychology and Psychiatry and Allied Disciplines, 29(6)*. 825–838.

Asarnow, J. R., Tompson, M. C. & Goldstein, M. J. (1994). Outcome in childhood-onset schizophrenia-spectrum disorders. *Schizophrenia Bulletin, 20(4)*. 599–617.

Asarnow, J. R., Tompson, M. C., Hamilton, E., Goldstein, M. J. & Guthrie, D. (1994). Family expressed emotion, childhood onset-depression, and childhood-onset schizophrenia spectrum disorders: Is expressed emotion a nonspecific correlate of child psychopathology or a specific risk factor for depression? *Journal of Abnormal Child Psychology, 22(2)*. 129–146.

Bateson, G., Jackson, D. D., Haley, J., & Weakland, J. (1956). Toward a theory of schizophrenia. *Behavioral Science, 1*, 251–264.

Bellack, A. S. & Mueser, K. T. (1993). Psychosocial treatment for schizophrenia. *Schizophrenia Bulletin, 19(2)*. 317–336.

Butzlaff, R. L. & Hooley, J. M. (1998). Expressed emotion and psychiatric relapse. *Archives of General Psychiatry, 55(6)*. 547–552.

Caplan, R., Guthrie, D., Fish, B., Tanguay, P. E. & David-Lando, G. (1989). The Kiddie Formal Thought Disorder Rating Scale: Clinical assessment, reliability, and validity. *Journal of the American Academy of Child and Adolescent Psychiatry, 28(3)*, 408–416.

Cozolino, L. J, Goldstein, M. J., Nuechterlein, K. H.; West, K. L., *et al.* (1988). The impact of education about schizophrenia on relatives varying in expressed emotion. *Schizophrenia Bulletin, 14(4)*. 675–687.

Eggers, C. & Bunk, D. (1997). The long-term course of childhood-onset schizophrenia: A 42-year followup. *Schizophrenia Bulletin, 23(1)*. 105–117.

Goldstein, M. J., Miklowitz, D. J. (1995). The effectiveness of psychoeducational family therapy in the treatment of schizophrenic disorders. *Journal of Marital and Family Therapy, 21(4)*. 361–376.

Jacobsen, L. K. & Rapoport, J. L. (1998). Research update: Childhood-onset schizophrenia: Implications of clinical and neurobiological research. *Journal of Child Psychology and Psychiatry and Allied Disciplines, 39(1)*. 101–113.

Kendler, K. S. (1991). Mood-incongruent psychotic affective illness: A historical and empirical review. *Archives of General Psychiatry, 48*, 362–369.

McClellan, J. & Werry, J. (1994). Practice parameters for the assessment and treatment of children and adolescents with schizophrenia. *Journal of the American Academy of child and Adolescent Psychiatry, 33*, 616–635.

Mikowitz, D. J. & Stackman, D. (1992). Communication deviance in the families of schizophrenic and other psychiatric patients: Current state of the construct. In E. F. Walker, R. H. Dworkin, & B. A. Cornblatt (eds) *Progress in Experimental Psychopathology Research.* New York: Springer-Verlag. *15*, 1–46.

Norman, R. M. & Malla, A. K. (1993). Stressful life events and schizophrenia. I: A review of the research. *British Journal of Psychiatry, 162*, 161–166.

Nuechterlein, K. H., Dawson, M. E., Ventura, J., Gitlin, M., Subotnik, K. L., *et al.* (1994). The vulnerability/stress model of schizophrenic relapse: A longitudinal study. *Acta Psychiatrica Scandinavica, 89 (382, Suppl)*. 58–64.

Souetre, E. (1997). Economic evaluation in schizophrenia. *Neuropsychobiology, 3(2)*. 67–69.

Sroufe, L. A. (1979). The coherence of individual development: Early care, attachment, and subsequent developmental issues. *American Psychologist, 34(10)*. 834–841.

Tienari, P., Sorri, A., Lahti, I., Naarala, M., *et al.* (1987). Genetic and psychosocial factors in schizophrenia: The Finnish adoptive family study. *Schizophrenia Bulletin, 13(3)*. 477–484.

Tompson, M. C., Asarnow, J. R., Hamilton, E. B., Newell, L. E., & Goldstein, M. J. (1997). Children with schizophrenia-spectrum disorders: Thought disorder and communication problems in a family interactional context. *Journal of Child Psychology and Psychiatry, 38(4)*, 421–429.

Watkins, J. M., Asarnow, R. F., & Tanguay, P. (1988). Symptoms development in childhood onset schizophrenia. *Journal of Child Psychology and Psychiatry, 29*, 865–878.

Weinberger, D. R. (1994). Biological basis of schizophrenia: Structural/functional considerations relevant to potential of antipsychotic drug response. *Journal of Clinical Psychiatry Monograph Series, 12*, 4–9.

Werry, J. S., McClelan, J. M., & Chard, L. (1991). Child and adolescent schizophrenic, bipolar, and schizoaffective disorders: A clinical and outcome study. *Journal of the American Academy of Child and Adolescent Psychiatry, 30*, 457–465.

Chapter 21

Sleep Disorders in Children and Adolescents

Ana I. Fins and William K. Wohlgemuth

Introduction

Sleep in infants, children and adolescents differs greatly from that of adults. Furthermore, there is great variability in sleep requirements and in the presence of sleep disorders across the developmental span of children and adolescents. By age five, approximately half of a child's life will have been spent in sleep, thus making sleep a very important component of a child's life (Lin-Dyken & Dyken, 1996). Although this chapter will focus on one particular sleep disorder, delayed sleep phase syndrome in adolescents, it is important to note that several different sleep disorders exist across childhood and adolescence. As such, a brief overview about sleep and some of the sleep disorders with which children and adolescents may present will first be provided.

Development of Sleep

Newborns typically spend approximately 18 hours a day sleeping. The amount of time spent sleeping, however, is quickly reduced, so that by the time an infant is six months old, he/she is only sleeping approximately 13 hours in a 24-hour period. During this time, an infant's sleep is also becoming better consolidated so that the time spent sleeping occurs without as many awakenings, and a large proportion of that sleep is occurring at night. By 24 months, toddlers are sleeping approximately 12 hours between their night-time sleep period and daytime naps. Usually children by four years of age will be sleeping between 10 and 12 hours per day, this amount gradually decreases throughout childhood so that by late adolescence the time spent sleeping is closer to that of adults, approximately eight hours (Mindell, 1997).

Common Sleep Disorders

When children present with sleep problems, it is important to complete a comprehensive evaluation that takes into consideration the developmental stage of the child (Mindell, 1997). In addition to a psychiatric history, a thorough history of

Handbook of Conceptualization and Treatment of Child Psychopathology, pages 437–448.

the sleep problem is necessary, which includes a review of the child's wake/sleep cycle (e.g., daytime naps, activities during early evening and at bedtime, time to onset of sleep, nighttime behavior, frequency and duration of awakenings, wake times, daytime sleepiness) along with a family history of sleep disorders (e.g., narcolepsy). Furthermore, medical consultation is frequently necessary to rule out organic/physiological causes of the sleep complaint.

Infancy and Childhood

A commonly occurring sleep problem among infants and toddlers is insomnia, being expressed as either night awakenings, difficulty falling asleep at bedtime, or a combination of both. These problems are frequently observed in children between the ages of one and three (Anders & Eiben, 1997). Treatment often includes behavioral interventions and family guidance (Ferber, 1985; Rickert & Johnson, 1988).

Starting at approximately 18 months and through six years of age children may experience sleep terror disorder. With an etiology clearly different from nightmares, children with night terrors will awaken approximately one to two hours after sleep onset vocalizing distress while simultaneously being inconsolable, disoriented, and difficult to arouse. In addition, no specific dream content can be recalled upon awakening. There are physiological concomitants to the disorder which include irregular respiration and increased heart rate. Frequently they will have no recollection of the event in the morning. Commonly used treatments include psychoeducation, stress reduction and implementation of afternoon naps (Anders *et al.*, 1997).

Sleepwalking can also frequently occur in children, usually between the ages of four and twelve. About 15–30 percent of children in this age group have at least one sleep walking event. However, recurrent attacks are not as common (Carlson & Cordova, 1999). As with sleep terrors, sleep walking occurs shortly after sleep onset and its treatment may consist of education about the nature of the disorder, suggestions for making the environment safe, attempts to reduce fatigue and stress via relaxation therapy and mental imagery, timed awakenings before the time of the usual sleepwalking event, incorporation of a late afternoon nap, and pharmacotherapy (Lin-Dyken, *et al.*, 1996).

Anders and Eiben (1997) have also reported another common sleep problem among toddlers and young children, sleep apnea. Behavioral complaints associated with sleep apnea include daytime tiredness and/or inattention. Among toddlers a concomitant problem may be growth retardation, similar to the failure-to-thrive syndrome. Treatment for sleep apnea is often surgical in nature and entails removing tonsils and adenoids.

Adolescence

Narcolepsy is a sleep problem which usually begins during adolescence. Its symptoms consist of excessive sleepiness during the day or sleep attacks, loss of muscle tone (cataplexy) for brief periods of time that can be precipitated by strong affective states and hypnagogic hallucinations, vivid images which occur while the individual is awake (Carlson, *et al.*, 1999). Treatment usually includes an educational component for the adolescent, as well as family members and teachers, sleep hygiene procedures which build in regularly scheduled naps, and use of psychopharmacologic agents such as psychostimulants to increase alertness (Dahl, *et al.*, 1994; Lyn-Dyken, 1996).

Insomnia also occurs in adolescence, and it is important to determine if any underlying factors are responsible for the poor sleep. For example, caffeine, nicotine, and alcohol use increase during adolescence, and these substances may interfere with sleep onset and maintenance. Also, depressive or anxiety disorders may be causing poor sleep. Treatment frequently consists of stimulus control and sleep restriction.

A common sleep problem which has recently received media attention due to impact on adolescents (Ellison, 1999) may appear at first to be sleep onset insomnia. Adolescents with circadian rhythm sleep disorder, specifically delayed sleep phase syndrome, present with complaints of daytime sleepiness, difficulty awakening in the mornings, late sleep onset and sleeping longer on weekends. Although not well documented, prevalence of circadian rhythm sleep disorder has been estimated at seven percent (Anders, *et al.*, 1997). There are several factors which may play a role in the development of this problem including puberty, circadian rhythms, parental influence, curfews, school schedules, and jobs (Carskadon, 1990). Given the wide impact this sleep disorder may have on adolescents, including relationships with parents, academic performance, job performance, and even the farther-reaching social implications that have been proposed, including altering school schedules, we have chosen this particular disorder as the focus of this chapter. Thus, further description of the syndrome as well as treatment approaches will be discussed below.

Clinical Syndrome

Adolescence is a period during which significant changes in sleep patterns occur. Typically during this stage, adolescents begin to delay their bedtimes. Carskadon, *et al.*, (1998) have attempted to explain this tendency by proposing that the biological need to sleep, or sleep pressure, that builds throughout the day is slower in older adolescents than in younger ones, thus allowing for older adolescents to stay awake later. In addition, it has been established that sleep needs are not reduced during adolescence (Wolfson & Carskadon, 1998). Instead, what is observed is a phase delay, where there is a tendency to fall asleep later and wake up later.

In addition to this circadian rhythm phase delay, there is one significant environmental constraint which decreases available sleep time for adolescents: earlier school start times. To compound these effects, other developmental considerations exist. Frequently, adolescents take afternoon jobs or become more involved in extracurricular activities after school, reducing the chance of obtaining afternoon naps. The combination of a later bed time, a forced earlier wake time, and afternoon/evening jobs and activities results in a reduction in the amount of total sleep obtained during the week. Thus, these adolescents may be unable to awaken in the mornings, be late to school, be unable to concentrate, and may fall asleep in class, creating a tendency for poorer school performance. Family arguments may ensue as parents or other family members struggle to awaken the adolescent either in the morning or after daytime naps. Frequently these young adults will "make up" the sleep debt by delaying their wake times on weekends, sometimes until the early afternoon. However, these attempts to catch up on lost sleep are not very successful and can further disrupt the biological clock (Anders, *et al.*, 1997).

Treatment Approaches

Education is an important component of treatment in working with adolescents who have delayed sleep phase syndrome as well as with their parents. The importance of keeping a regular schedule needs to be highlighted and the consequences of this behavior should also be addressed (e.g., vulnerability to accidents, mood and behavior problems, increased vulnerability to drugs/alcohol, academic difficulties, etc.) Behavioral contracts are frequently used to maintain regular bed times and wake times in conjunction with teaching stress management and priority-setting skills. In mild cases of delayed sleep phase syndrome, the combination of education, behavioral contracts, and prioritizing may be sufficient to improve the symptoms.

Often, however, adolescents with delayed sleep phase syndrome do not present to a health care professional until they have experienced serious consequences, such as expulsion from school. In these cases, a more rigorous approach to changing bedtimes and wake times is required. Chronotherapy, a method for resetting the biological clock, has been used to treat the syndrome. This approach consists of either delaying or advancing sleep and wake times every day until the desired schedule is reached. In phase delay chronotherapy an individual is instructed to delay bed time and wake time by one or two hours, although some professionals recommend delaying these times by as much as three hours. This approach gradually shifts the bed time around the clock until eventually it reaches the desired bed time (e.g., 10:30 p.m.). Although adolescents like this method because they can delay their bed times more every night, it is very difficult to implement during the school year because the adolescent is required to sleep during the day for part of the intervention, as the bed times and rise times get further delayed. Often this intervention requires inpatient hospitalization in order to reduce interference from environmental factors.

Phase advance chronotherapy combined with exposure to bright lights appears to be an effective and less disruptive method of treating delayed sleep phase syndrome. With this intervention, the adolescent is required to advance wake time by 15 to 30 minutes every two days until the desired wake time and bedtime are reached. At the time of awakening the adolescent is also required to have at least 30 minutes of exposure to either sunlight or bright lights. Sometimes, sun exposure is not possible due to the time of year and/or the geographical location. In these instances special lights with particular specifications (e.g., must give off 10,000 lux) can be used instead of sunlight exposure.

Strict behavioral contracts during and subsequent to the completion of either phase delay or phase advance treatment must be implemented to avoid a progressive shift back to the delayed sleep phase schedule. The sleep hygiene rules that need to be followed rigorously include: maintaining a regular schedule on weekdays as well as weekends, no napping, strict bed times, and wake times, no caffeine, no activities after bedtime (e.g., no reading, talking on the telephone, etc.)

After successful completion of phase realignment and two or three full weeks of maintaining the strict schedule, a maintenance protocol can be adopted. This allows some deviation from the original schedule, for example, for a weekend activity or vacation. However, sleep hygiene rules should continue to be followed and, if there is one night where the bed time is delayed, the adolescent should still get up within one hour of regular wake-up time (i.e., no sleeping in) and must not take a nap on the following day.

Successful treatment of delayed sleep phase syndrome must address the biological etiology as well as the psychological and social factors associated with the disorder.

Case Example 1

M. A., a 17-year-old boy, presented to a Sleep Disorders Center because he had difficulty falling asleep at night as well as getting out of bed in the morning. This problem had been occurring for a few years but was currently troublesome because M. A. had been late for class five times. He attended a selective, residential magnet school and if he arrived late for class one more time he would be expelled. Both M. A. and his mother were concerned about the problem and expressed some urgency in resolving it.

Sleep History. M. A. reported experiencing this sleep difficulty for approximately four years with a gradual worsening over the past few years. The patient's mother confirmed this pattern and added that M. A.'s sleeping problem created significant tension in the home. Both parents were school teachers and became quite frustrated and angry that M. A. would not awaken easily in the morning. M. A. typically would go to bed between 10 and 11 p.m and reported that it would take him between 30 minutes and three hours to fall asleep. Notably, once he fell asleep, he was able to sustain a consolidated sleep pattern. He claimed to be very sleepy in the morning but this sleepiness dissipated throughout the day and by the afternoon and evening he would feel wide awake and alert. He reported falling asleep in class in the morning and as well as struggling to stay awake while driving in the morning. His mother confirmed this pattern of sleepiness in the morning and increasing alertness throughout the day.

M. A. denied reading, watching TV, eating or working in bed, but he worried in bed approximately four times per week. Such worrying had become more common recently as M. A. had become increasingly concerned about being expelled from school. He reported great difficulty relaxing his body and turning off his mind at bedtime. M. A. claimed that his roommate often studied until late at night and this noise made falling asleep more difficult. During the four days before the interview, M. A. kept a record of his sleep. His bedtimes ranged from 10:30 to 11:30 and it took him from 50 minutes to 2.5 hours to fall asleep. During the four-day period he woke up once during the night for one minute. His waketimes ranged from 7:00 to 10:00 am. The time that he spent in bed ranged from 7.5 hours to 12 hours. His total sleep time ranged from 5.5 hour to 10.5 hours, and the average over these four days was approximately eight hours. On each of these days he rated the quality of his sleep as above average and felt well rested.

The patient's mother reported that M. A. had never been observed snoring or stopping breathing while asleep nor had leg twitches been observed. M. A. denied symptoms associated with other sleep disorders (e.g., restless legs syndrome, narcolepsy, night terrors, sleep walking).

Medical/Psychiatric History. M. A. had no current medical or psychiatric problems nor was he taking any prescribed medication at the time of the evaluation. He denied depressive symptoms and did not feel overburdened by his academic workload. He reported slightly increased anxiety due to concern about his sleep problem. At time of intake he was taking melatonin each night to help him fall asleep, but said it was not working very well. He reported smoking about twelve cigarettes per day, usually in the afternoon and drinking one cup of coffee in the afternoon.

Diagnosis. M. A.'s problem has been chronic and increasing in severity over the past several years, to the point where his attendance at a residential magnet school is threatened by inability to wake up in the morning and attend class. The patient's presenting symptoms offer no evidence of narcolepsy, sleep apnea, periodic limb movements of sleep, or restless legs syndrome. Once he falls asleep he is able to remain asleep. In addition, M. A. has a subjective impression that his sleep is restful and of good quality.

Based on the symptom picture, two diagnoses could be considered. The first is sleep onset insomnia and the second is delayed sleep phase syndrome. Difficulty falling asleep at bedtime in combination with increased physiological and cognitive arousal around bedtime are common complaints in sleep onset insomnia. However, the complaint of insomnia is usually accompanied by daytime fatigue, difficulty concentrating on work or school tasks, and irritability which remain consistent throughout the day. M. A. reported that he felt increasingly alert as the day progressed and school difficulties were limited to the morning hours. Furthermore, his sleep was of good quality and he felt rested upon awakening. The best diagnosis for this patient is delayed sleep phase syndrome. The timing of the onset and offset of M. A.'s sleep cycle occurs at a later time in the day than the average sleeper. That is, instead of feeling sleepy at 10:00 p.m. and waking up at 7:00 a.m., for example, M. A. would fall asleep at 1:00 or 2:00 a.m. and wake up at

10:00 or 11:00 a.m. This mismatch between M. A.'s sleep pattern and his school requirements were the cause of his presenting problem.

Case Conceptualization

To address the multifaceted nature of this disorder we have chosen a biopsychosocial perspective to conceptualize M. A.'s case. Engel (1984) has formulated a biopsychosocial model for medical disorders in an attempt to emphasize the importance of the psychological and social aspects of health and disease. Engel conceptualized the model as a series of systems. Each system is sufficiently organized so that each functions as an organized whole. Examples of these systems from smaller units to larger units include molecules, cells, organs/organ systems, nervous system, person, family, community, society, and so on. While able to stand alone, each system is a "component of higher systems" (Engel, 1984, p.47). So, for example, the system "cells" is a component of the "organs" system, "person" systems are components of the "family" system which, in turn, are components of the "community" system. There is a hierarchy of systems, with smaller systems being subsumed under larger, more complex systems.

Within this conceptualization, Engel states that health and illness can be viewed as either the function or disruption of the intra- and intersystemic hierarchy. Disruption can occur at any level of the hierarchy and, depending on whether that particular system has the capacity to handle or cope with the disturbance, it will be contained by that particular system or it may affect other systems as well.

Psychologists most often function within the systems that Engel labels as "person," "two-person," "family" and, at times, "community." However, psychologists working with individuals with medically-related disorders need to become familiar with lower-level systems (e.g., nervous system, organs/organ systems). how these may be affected and the impact they may have in creating disruption in the higher-order systems.

In the case of delayed sleep phase syndrome, there is a clear-cut disruption in biological systems. As was discussed earlier, it has been proposed that the biological sleep drive changes between childhood and adolescence, allowing older adolescents to stay awake later. However, since sleep needs are not reduced during this time, the result is a phase delay, where there is a tendency to fall asleep later and wake up later. This change, in and of itself, would not be considered problematic, if adolescents were allowed to set their own *ad lib* bed times and wake times. However, the "community system" creates a constraint whereby an adolescent needs to get up earlier to go to school. It is the "community system" of early rising that creates the disruption at the level of the biological systems, a disruption which cannot be effectively handled by these systems. In turn, the "person, two-person and family" systems may also be affected. Thus, the adolescent may have difficulty waking up in the morning, may have arguments with a parent about being late to school, may do poorly in school because of difficulty concentrating in class, etc. In addition, as in the case presented, the "community" system may also become involved. In this particular case, the school threatened to expel the adolescent for numerous unexcused tardies.

In terms of this conceptual model, delayed sleep phase syndrome must be approached by intervening at the "nervous system," "person," "family" and "community" systems levels. Bright light therapy is used to phase-advance the biological clock to the desired schedule. Prescription of bright lights, however, requires knowledge about circadian rhythm biology. For example, if bright lights are applied too early in the sleep period, a phase delay rather than a phase advance may occur. That is, the waketime may be pushed to a later time rather than an earlier time. It is important that the clinician be familiar with the phase-response curve so that application of bright lights occurs at the proper time within the sleep period (Kilduff & Kosida, 1999). In the case of M. A. the therapeutic goal is to advance the sleep cycle to an earlier time in the night so he is able to fall asleep and wake up earlier. The patient and his mother were informed about how and where to get a bright light box. M. A. was instructed to sit in front of the bright light at 7:00 a.m. for approximately 30 minutes each morning. He was informed that he was to sit near the lights (about an arm's length) and could read or engage in other similar activities as long as he would periodically look at the light source.

In addition to bright lights treatment, the individual must be educated about the facts of delayed sleep phase syndrome. Both M. A. and his mother were provided with information about the circadian rhythm of alertness and sleepiness as well as the sleep phase delay which occurs in adolescence.

It is also important to teach adequate sleep hygiene and sleep restriction skills, so that maladaptive behavior is extinguished and does not become a possible precursor for relapse (e.g., napping during the afternoon, sleeping late on weekends). At times, behavioral contracts may be incorporated to improve adherence to treatment. The time M. A. spent in bed varied greatly from night to night. Because his average total sleep time was eight hours, his time in bed was reduced to 8.5 hours. He was instructed not to spend more than 8.5 hours in bed on any night. This procedure facilitates more consistent nightly consolidation of sleep (Wohlgemuth & Edinger, 2000; Spielman, *et al.*, 1987). Also, M. A. was advised to decrease his cigarette smoking and avoid drinking caffeinated beverages after six p.m. to reduce external factors that are often related to delayed sleep onset.

Parents are often involved in treatment as well. They are offered information about the disorder and encouraged to reinforce positive changes the adolescent makes and problem-solve as treatment maintenance difficulties arise. M. A.'s mother was provided with information about the syndrome and was encouraged to positively reinforce treatment-related changes made by the boy.

Depending on the severity of the disorder, other systems (e.g., school) may be involved. In such cases, providing written materials or meeting directly with teachers, counselors, and school administrators to discuss the case can often help to ameliorate the situation until the student's biological clock can be reset and all of the systems can return to a homeostatic level. In the current case, the school counselor was contacted and informed about M. A.'s delayed sleep phase problem so that the prescribed treatment could be incorporated into the overall educational plan for M. A. This conversation also provided an excellent opportunity to give the counselor more information about the problem of delayed sleep phase syndrome in high school students.

Case Example 2

T. S., an 18-year-old male presented to the Sleep Disorders Center for "staying up all night and sleeping all day." This patient had graduated from high school but remained living with his mother. The patient's mother was very concerned about the possibility of a sleep disorder in her son because he had difficulty staying awake in the daytime. She urgently pursued an evaluation.

Sleep history. Because of the initial complaint of excessive daytime sleepiness, T. S. was evaluated for narcolepsy by a neurologist in the clinic. An overnight polysomnographic (PSG) study along with a daytime multiple sleep latency test (MSLT) were both performed. The overnight PSG was performed to determine if the patient had any respiratory pathology occurring during his sleep. The MSLT assessed the extent of the patient's physiologic sleepiness during the daytime. Both of these test results were negative, so the neurologist referred the patient to the psychologist in the clinic for evaluation and treatment of delayed sleep phase syndrome.

The patient was employed at a restaurant and typically worked until three or four in the morning. Upon returning home, he would talk to friends and watch movies until five or six a.m. He would then sleep until three or four in the afternoon. He would keep the same schedule on his days off. The symptom picture in this case was similar to the first one. There was no evidence of any other sleep disorder, neither did the patient complain of depression or anxiety or any other psychiatric disorder. He denied use of alcohol, caffeine, tobacco, and other substances. T. S. was slightly concerned about his difficulty waking up before noon when his schedule required. He also wondered if he had a physical problem that made getting up earlier a struggle. He said he was glad he did not have to get up before noon very often. He was receptive to the idea of advancing his sleep schedule to an earlier time. A schedule for the phase advance was developed, the patient was given information about getting a bright light box and return for follow-up was scheduled.

The patient returned to the sleep clinic one month later and was quite pleased with and appreciative of the success of his treatment. His mother agreed that the treatment was very effective and expressed relief that her son was on a more normal schedule. He was going to bed each night at approximately 11:30 p.m. and getting up each day at about 8:00 a.m without difficulty and feeling refreshed each day. However, approximately six months later, the patient's mother once again urgently contacted the sleep clinic because her son was once again "awake all night and sleeping all day." No appointments were available that day, but the patient's mother did not want to schedule an appointment for the following week. Neither the patient nor his mother have contacted the clinic again.

Case Conceptualization

This case demonstrates a failure in the treatment goal due to inadequately addressing some of the systems within the biopsychosocial model. The intervention at the "nervous system" and "person" level was quite effective and useful for T. S. in the shortterm. He expressed relief that he could wake up earlier and that his level of alertness in the morning was not totally out of his control. However, there were no interventions at either the "family" or "community" levels. In this case it appeared to be more important for the mother of the patient than the patient himself to remain on the daytime schedule. In addition, there was no discrepancy between T. S.'s sleep/wake schedule and his "community" (employment in a restaurant, late-night friends) so no conflict was created at this level for T. S. Thus, there was no incentive for T. S. to remain on a daytime schedule. It is likely that this patient reverted to his previous schedule because the "family" level and the "community" level were not adequately addressed.

Alternative Conceptualization

These two cases present opportunities to discuss alternate conceptualizations. In the case of M. A., focusing strictly on a behavioral regimen to attempt to shift the adolescent's regular wake-up time would have been possible. With strictly set wake times and bed times as well as behavioral contracts, the young man's sleep difficulties could have been improved. However, disregarding the biological functioning underlying the disorder and recommendations for bright light exposure may prolong reaching the desired effects. In the second case, it appears that the symptoms of delayed sleep phase were more problematic for the mother than the adolescent. In this case, although the adolescent initially responded to the treatment, T. S. reverted to his late night hours shortly after completing treatment. It was his mother who was again complaining about the relapse. Although initially T. S. was willing to follow the treatment recommendations, he did not appear to be highly distressed by an off-hour schedule which did not seem to interfere with many of his activities. In fact, he had developed a routine that fit his sleep-wake schedule. This presentation could have been taken into consideration at the initial intake and a recommendation for family therapy at that time may have been more successful than direct treatment of the delayed sleep phase syndrome. Clearly, the presenting problem was the sleep-wake schedule difficulties. However, family therapy may have been better able to address either control issues existing between mother and son or other family concerns not addressed by the selected approach to treatment.

Summary

Sleep disorders in children and adolescents are highly varied. This chapter has focused on just one of many sleep disorders that can present to a clinician.

Delayed sleep phase syndrome is a particularly interesting disorder because it highlights the importance of taking into consideration not only the psychological and social manifestations of the disorder but also the biological factors that lead directly to it. The choice was to conceptualize the syndrome using a biopsychosocial perspective that allows for the integration of these factors. It must be emphasized that this conceptualization allows the flexibility to address multiple components that may be affected. As such, treatment consists of changing the sleep-wake schedule of an individual by using bright light exposure. Concomitantly, the adolescent participates in modifying behavior that may contribute to maladaptive sleep habits and within the individual's social environment, educating family and school about the syndrome and enlisting them as support in order to enhance treatment outcome.

References

Anders, T. F. & Eiben, L. A. (1997). Pediatric sleep disorders: A review of the past 10 years. *Journal of the American Academy of Child and Adolescent Psychiatry, 36(1).* 9–20.

Carlson, C. R. & Cordova, M. J. (1999). Sleep disorders in childhood and adolescence. In S. D.Netherton, D. Holmes & C. E. Walker. *Child and Adolescent Psychological Disorders: A Comprehensive Textbook.* New York: Oxford University Press. 415–438.

Carskadon, M. A. (1990). Patterns of sleep and sleepiness in adolescents. *Pediatrician, 17,* 5–12.

Carskadon, M. A., Wolfson, A. R., Acebo, C., Tzischinsky, O. & Seifer, R. (1998). Adolescent sleep patterns, circadian timing, and sleepiness at a transition to early school days. *Sleep, 21(8).* 871–881.

Dahl, R., Holttum, J. & Trubnick, L. (1994). A clinical picture of child and adolescent narcolepsy. *Journal of the American Academy of Child and Adolescent Psychiatry, 33,* 834–841.

Ellison, A. (1999, June 2). Having trouble staying awake in class? You're not alone – and it might not be your fault. *The Miami Herald,* 8E.

Engel, G. L. (1984). Clinical application of the biopsychosocial model. In D. E. Reisier & D. H. Rosen (eds) *Medicine as a Human Experience.* (Rockville, MD: Aspen Systems Corporation. 43–60.

Ferber, R. (1985). *Solve your Child's Sleep Problems.* New York: Simon and Schuster.

Lin-Dyken, D. C. & Dyken, M. E. (1996). Sleep in infancy, childhood and youth. In A. Culebras (ed.) *Clinical Handbook of Sleep Disorders.* Boston: Butterworth-Heinemann. 345–374.

Kilduff, T. S. & Kushida, C. A. (1999). Circadian regulation of sleep. In S. Chokroverty (ed.) *Sleep Disorders Medicine.* Boston: Butterworth-Heinemann. 135–147.

Mindell, J. (1997). Children and sleep. In M. R. Pressman, & W. C. Orr (eds) *Understanding sleep: The Evaluation and Treatment of Sleep Disorders.* Washington, D.C.: American Psychological Association. 427–439.

Rickert, V. & Johnson, M. (1988). Reducing noctorunal awakening and crying episodes in infants and young children: A comparison between scheduled awakenings and systematic ignoring. *Pediatrics, 81,* 203–212.

Spielman, A. J., Saskin, P. & Thorpy, M. J. (1987). Treatment of chronic insomnia by restriction of time in bed. *Sleep, 10(1)*. 45–56.

Wohlgemuth, W. & Edinger, J. D. (2000). Sleep restriction therapy. In K. Lichstein & C. M. Morin (eds) *Treatment of Late-life Insomnia*. Newbury Park: Sage Publications.

Wolfson, A. R. & Carskadon, M. A. (1998). Sleep schedules and daytime functioning in adolescents. *Child Development, 69(4)*. 875–887.

Chapter 22

Dissociative Disorder

Joyanna L. Silberg

Treating a Young Teenage Girl with Maladaptive Dissociation

Clinical Syndrome

Since the mid-1980s, dissociation and dissociative disorders have been described with increasing frequency in the clinical and research literature. Controversies in the adult literature have revolved around whether the increased diagnosis of dissociative disorders, particularly DID (dissociative identity disorder). reflect an iatrogenic phenomenon (Lilienfeld, et al., 1999) or advances in diagnostic sensitivity (Gleaves, 1996). The applicability of adult dissociative disorder criteria has been questioned for children and adolescents who seem to present with dissociative features which often appear distinct from adult descriptions (Putnam, 1997). Controversy has also surrounded the recommended treatment approaches for children, as critics have warned of iatrogenic dangers for children of a prescriptive treatment model (Donovan, 1997).

Because a comprehensive understanding of the complex processes involved in maladaptive dissociative symptoms is still lacking, the importance of theory and treatment conceptualization is especially important. Recommended treatments for dissociative disorders, particularly DID, have often been tied to a very specific theoretical model that posits the onset of these pathogenic processes in early childhood, with the fragmentation of identity as a coping tool in the face of overwhelming trauma. This theoretical model dictates that treatment should involve the integration of fragmented identity states, and the integration of dissociated traumatic experiences (Kluft, 1999). When dealing with children and adolescents a treatment model based on adult retrospective report is particularly fraught with difficulty. Presentations of dissociative symptoms are different in children, and they may be particularly susceptible to potential iatrogenesis. Furthermore, the treatment of children and adolescents is a complex endeavor, which involves an appreciation of the multiple domains – school, home, and peers – in which children grow and develop. It is important that case conceptualizations for children and adolescents address all of the dysfunctional behavior that interferes with mastery of the important developmental tasks and challenges that await them in all their domains.

Handbook of Conceptualization and Treatment of Child Psychopathology, pages 449–474.
Copyright © 2001 by Elsevier Science Ltd.
All rights of reproduction in any form reserved.
ISBN: 0-08-043362-6

Cross-cultural case studies (Zoruglu, *et al.*, 1996) and clinical reports from a variety of academic (Jacobsen, 1995). hospital-based (Hornstein & Tyson, 1992). and rural settings (Klein, *et al.*, 1994) describe the dysfunctional behavior that children with dissociative disorders and symptoms display as including "black-outs," trance states, or other anomalies of continuous consciousness, belief in imaginary internal worlds or identities, fluctuating states or moods, and inconsistent access to autobiographical or other needed information.

These symptoms often have been accompanied by a variety of self-harming behavior, somatic symptoms, problematic aggressive behavior, and post traumatic symptoms (Hornstein & Putnam, 1992). A history of child abuse has been documented in many described cases (Coons, 1996). as well as histories of exposure to war violence (Cagiada, *et al.*, 1997). kidnapping and torture (Coons, 1996). repeated illnesses or surgical procedures (Dell & Eisenhower, 1990). and in cases of depersonalization or fugue states, extreme family conflict (Dollinger, 1983; Venn, 1984). Maladaptive dissociative processes have also been described in children without histories of severe environmental trauma, but children whose experiences have led them to idiosyncratic traumatic beliefs about their world (Donovan & McIntyre, 1990).

A pattern of behavior with some similarity to adult dissociative identity disorder has been documented in preschool children (Putnam, 1997). but it is not yet known what type of developmental course these disorders may take if left untreated. The presumption of much of the adult theoretical literature, which is often based on patient retrospective report, is that dissociative identity disorder may be a lifelong condition, intensifying in adulthood. Yet, there is evidence that some severe dissociative conditions may have their onset in adolescence after exposure to extreme stress, and rapid remission of cases in childhood has also been described (Kluft, 1984).

The treatment model described here takes a comprehensive and multifaceted view of maladaptive dissociation that appreciates its complex origins influenced by multiple etiological pathways. No simplistic causal relationship between trauma and dissociative symptoms is posited by this model. This case also highlights that trauma is an idiosyncratically defined concept based on the perceptions of the individual in reaction against a specific environment.

This chapter will illustrate how the treatment of a young adolescent girl with maladaptive dissociative behavior helped her achieve a positive outcome. This case history presents a 14-year-old who came to treatment after displaying severely regressed behavior which she and her family viewed as her "becoming a three year old." When entering this regressed state, she showed a consistent pattern of language, facial, and gait changes; she initially denied memory for her behavior in this state. The treatment involved helping her integrate contradictory feelings and attitudes, improving her sensitivity to internal affective changes, identifying the function of the regressed behavior, and determining alternate communication and coping strategies.

Environmental strategies are described which include showing the family how they inadvertently reinforce the regressive behavior, and teaching the parents to work together to facilitate the young girl's growth towards maturity. This case presentation provides abundant material for speculating about the etiology of dissociative states, including the roles of iatrogenesis, suggestive family influences, and the idiosyncratic meaning of trauma for an individual.

The treatment approach, termed the integrated developmental model, is contrasted with two approaches to dissociative disorder treatment, one in which traumatic experiences are considered the focus of treatment, and one in which the dissociative presentation is ignored completely.

Theoretical Conceptualization of Dissociation and Dissociative Disorder

One of the difficulties of the burgeoning literature on dissociation is multiple definitions of what dissociation is and what in fact therapists are attempting to treat when dealing with a dissociative disorder. Some authors have stressed the normative functions of dissociation as useful coping tools for avoidance of stressful situations or as a cognitive facility to do multiple tasks at once. Newer theories have stressed that even multiple self-states are normative phenomena and that dissociative patients are unable to manage the inevitable conflicts between these self-states or roles (Rivera, 1996; Bromberg, 1998). Pathological dissociation has been seen as a maladaptive overreliance on normal coping tools, or as a failure of the integration of a cohesive sense of self across state shifts (Putnam, 1997).

This discussion introduces the integrated developmental treatment model, in which pathological dissociative processes are viewed as a complex, multi-determined outcome for certain children with predisposing capacities and vulnerabilities in an environment which is viewed as threatening. This coping style then becomes reinforced through moment-to moment interactions in the child's world, as well as the larger social context of meanings and expectations which may promote dissociative coping in direct or indirect ways.

While "dissociativity" has been viewed as a predisposing trait for the development of a dissociative disorder, children who are at risk may have a unique composite of traits and abilities including symbolic skills, fantasy-proneness (Rhue, *et al.*, 1995). empathic perceptiveness, and social traits such as social compliance or high attachment needs that are related in part to capacity for trance induction (Silberg, 1998). One might speculate that the threatened child, unable to feel safe due to conflicting messages about attachment for which she is particularly sensitively attuned, learns a pattern of disavowal and disconnection from threatening information, facilitated by skill at trance-induction and using fantasy for escape and coping. This pattern becomes habitual over time, in environments that discourage the resolution of these threats. Finally, unconscious enactments or role plays can arise which symbolically display the disavowed information and these can be reinforced and strengthened by social feedback. This model suggests that a full treatment approach must help identify for the child the sources of threat in the environment and work towards resolving these, as well as work on the shaping contingencies which sustain dissociative role enactments. Finally, the child must learn a new pattern of attention to internal cues so that the habit of dissociating information is replaced with attending to important emotional, cognitive, or perceptual information that will promote a more healthy adaptation.

Imagine an airplane on autopilot that does not have the self-regulatory mechanism to override autopilot when new and unique incoming data are received. While the autopilot feature is convenient for expected situations, it is inadequate for unique or unanticipated events and may cause the plane to crash if not circumvented with more appropriately flexible strategies. Similarly, the individual who has learned to automatically disregard important information of a perceptual, emotional or cognitive nature, may be missing cues that would help regulate appropriate transitions between states, and guide personal "navigation" more successfully. Siegel (1999) has similarly described an integrated developmental model that heavily emphasizes the interpersonal factors that promote the development of healthy consciousness, and emphasizes the transition moments between states as the key moments for promoting integrated experience. These ideas are consistent with Janet's early conception of dissociation which similarly highlighted the maladaptive feature of dissociation as lack of attention to reading internal signals that help regulate action (van der Kolk & van der Hart, 1989). This conception is also consistent with contemporary neurobiological views of consciousness (Damasio, 1999). Damasio (1999) regards the experience of emotional awareness as a foundation of autobiographical consciousness, which is viewed as a survival-based homeostatic tool for the regulation of behavior. Ignoring their own feelings, which are the basic building blocks of continuous consciousness, may lead these children to adaptations in which they are highly susceptible to parental projections and other pathological family expectations.

In pathological environments, the avoidance of important feedback may become a learned habit that promotes pathological adaptation. For example, in an abusive home, if pain is continuous, and in fact associated with increased attention, a child might learn to disregard perceptual cues that signal pain, important cues that in normal circumstances lead to adaptive, biologically driven escape responses. Such built-in capacities to disconnect from usually important feedback are probably rooted in human biology as well, as animals in situations of extreme threat do enter a state of analgesia for pain (Nijenhuis, *et al.*, 1998). Emotional feedback mechanisms can similarly become compromized in families in which children are confused by conflicting emotional signals. A child might be faced with intense but contrasting emotions, which signal opposing behavioral repertoires – such as fear and love – in abusive families. Finally dissociation from relevant cognitive information may be commonplace for children in families which demand that children protect family secrets (Donovan & McIntrye, 1990). Further failures of integration can lead to ongoing disconnections from self and identity when these various forms of dissociation are practiced and reinforced in environments in which children must conform to contradictory expectations, and internalize parental misattributions that unconsciously support familial pathology.

The integrated developmental model takes very seriously the potential suggestive social influences that affect behavior, as stressed by the socio-cognitive critique of

DID therapy (Lilienfeld, *et al.*, 1999). However, rather than emphasize the therapy as the only source of these suggestive influences, the family environment is viewed as a place where dissociation is reinforced both through conscious and less conscious pathways. Children who are at risk for dissociative disorders are, in fact, viewed as more suggestible and susceptible to this kind of environmental reinforcement because their needs for attachment have been frustrated; they are context dependent, and have not developed the internal self-regulation that would allow them to resist the expectations of powerful others. As a result, the therapy must emphasize how to develop autonomy, self-direction, and resistance to suggestion, while the environment is shaped, as well to avoid the pressures that have led to this kind of coping.

While the critics of DID therapy have stressed that the diagnosis is a sociological construction that serves to promote a certain societal myth about women's roles (Acocella, 1999). dissociative behavior is viewed as a family construction which similarly supports certain myths about the child and his/her role. If this disorder can be created by a therapist-client role enactment as the socio-cognitive model suggests, how much more invasive might it be for families to support and embellish conflicting attributions about their children in the suggestive and powerful domain of family life? Thus, the family myths and expectations that sustain a particular view of the child and his/her role in the family need to be understood and explored in the treatment.

While the traumatic roots of these dysfunctional patterns are appreciated, in this treatment approach, dwelling on traumatic memories is not as important as changing the patterns of dissociative responding in the here and now. The therapist works to create a safe and stable relationship where the strengths of the child can be reinforced. The therapy setting becomes an opportunity to learn that avoidance of knowledge about one's life and one's past carries more risks than facing them and developing a full integration of self. The integrated developmental approach emphasizes learning about the moments when the child tries to cope by use of dissociative "switches" so that the information (cognitive, emotional, or perceptual) that is being dissociated can be explored more directly. This approach also emphasizes the environmental stressors that make a dissociative strategy adaptive for that individual, and attempts to minimize these in the child's environment.

Case Summary

Allison was fourteen when she began to display "sleepwalking" behavior. She got out of bed in the morning with her eyes still closed, and batted at objects and bumped into things. She was brought to an emergency room on two occasions for this behavior, but on both occasions "woke up" before she got to the emergency room and was sent home.

This behavior escalated and began to occur routinely just before it was time to leave the house for school. Allison began to talk like a baby, roll around on the floor, and throw her sister's stuffed animals on the floor. Attempts to disrupt her by calling her name or tapping her were unsuccessful and led her to be aggressive. Her mother identified Allison's behavior as resembling what Allison had been like at three. Allison was taken to outpatient psychotherapy where she talked about routine high school difficulties. Her therapist advised the family that by talking about stress, this other behavior would go away and that there was no need to attend directly to her disruptive morning behavior. The behavior continued to escalate, Allison was missing more days of ninth grade than she was attending, and the behavior began occurring during the day and not only on waking. Finally, the family could not disrupt her from her three year old behavior for a whole day, took her to the emergency room again, and was referred to the author, known for specializing in childhood dissociative disorders.

On initial assessment, Allison appeared a mature and self-composed girl who denied awareness of the disruptive morning behavior that led her to school avoidance. She claimed she was angry about it and in fact wanted to go to school, as she would never amount to anything otherwise. She was embarrassed when her parents talked about the behavior in front of her, and tried to hold her ears to avoid listening. Later, alone in the session, when asked further questions about the behavior, Allison's eyes suddenly closed and she began to breathe deeply and rhythmically as if in a trance. When she opened her eyes again, her jaw was slackened, her limbs held awkwardly and she spoke in a whiny babyish voice. She spoke about her fear that if she went to school her mommy would leave her there like she always did, forget to pick her up, and the teachers would yell at her for having such a bad mommy. I reassured her that she must have pretty important reasons for not wanting to go to school and that we would work together to figure these out. Allison again closed her eyes and again displayed her 14 year old composed manner. She talked about some of the stresses of her home life, including her maternal grandmother's recent deterioration with Alzheimer's disease, her perception that her mother had abandoned grandmother, and her desire for her parents to break up so that she would not have to hear their chronic fighting. She also mentioned disappointment at how she was doing in ninth grade, and teachers who did not seem to understand her and whose demands seemed unreasonable and arbitrary. On further inquiry, she was able to recall the stress she had experienced in preschool when her mother was chronically late in picking her up, but didn't think that was relevant to her problems now. She also described being upset about having many baby hamsters that died because they were attacked by their mother, and that her father would not allow her to purchase separate cages for them. She also discovered that her father had killed some of them himself, as he stated there were too many for them to take care of.

Psychiatric history revealed that Allison had four previous therapists, and one psychiatric hospitalization. Her pattern since fifth grade, was to have onset of some symptoms interfering with school in the early fall, to see a therapist until winter, then resume school attendance in early spring. Allison would claim to dislike the therapist, state the therapist was not helping her, and the parents would assume all was well, until the following fall when the pattern would be repeated. Every year she had months of absences, but was apparently bright enough to pass each year. The previous year, she had been diagnosed with seasonal affective disorder and had spent a week in a psychiatric hospital for suicidal ideation. Prior diagnoses included obsessive compulsive disorder and generalized anxiety disorder. In addition to these psychiatric diagnoses, Allison had been diagnosed with rheumatoid arthritis at age 13, which was generally controlled with methotrexate, although she experienced flare-ups of severe pain and even incapacitation on occasion.

Evaluation further revealed that despite these problems, Allison was accomplished in many ways. She was an award-winning equestrian, played piano with great skill, and had always received A's and B's in school, despite many absences. She had friends, who were mostly younger, as she did not share the interests of her age mates. She had not yet had the onset of menses, and had no interest in boys, clothes, or other more typical teenage concerns.

Family history revealed that Allison had one sister two years her elder who was functioning well and perceived by parents as a normal teen. Parents described a marriage characterized by constant conflict. Mother had accommodated to the father's demanding and authoritarian style and resorted to sneaking behind his back to buy things he would not approve. The parents were in chronic disagreement about how to help Allison, with father believing that mother tended to accommodate to all of her regressions, and that the problem was actually mother's. Mother in turn, felt it was her job to protect Allison from a demanding and perfectionist father, and did not support his attempts to let Allison be more responsible and made excuses for her about doing chores in the house. Father had an episode of severe depression and violent and suicidal behavior for which he had been hospitalized when Allison was two-and-a-half. In a rage, he had kicked in a door of their house. This episode followed a job disappointment and eventually father was diagnosed with bipolar disorder, released, found other employment, and returned to his previous level of functioning. He stopped taking any medication after a time, and refused continued psychotherapy. Marital counseling ended unsuccessfully as both agreed their problems were too big for them or anyone else to solve. Nonetheless, when the children were not discussed or in the way, they described an occasionally satisfying relationship.

Allison's three-year-old presentation was viewed as a way to communicate information about the sources of stress in her life that she could not articulate directly. Allison was encouraged and required to tune into this knowledge to help her problem solve. Family interventions included helping to get Allison out of the middle of conflict between her parents, helping the parents develop a common goal to work together for Allison's benefit, and helping Allison articulate her feelings. Mother was helped to see how to avoid reinforcing the three-year-old presentation in her interactions with Allison.

As Allison had become hopelessly behind in ninth grade, she was put on temporary home teaching through a public school program. This allowed Allison to describe, free from pressure, the problems she was experiencing in the school setting so a program could be worked out for her that minimized these. Allison returned to school within two months after treatment began, with a mildly revised school program that emphasized her strengths and interests. Over the course of the next year, Allison displayed the three-year-old behavior with increasingly less frequency, until it was confined only to her bedroom at night, and finally disappeared altogether. However, at times of increased stress, new dissociative or conversion behavior emerged, such as inability to move her legs, or repetitive fainting. These were solved by reminding Allison to attend to the wisdom of her body's message and solve the conflict these symptoms were avoiding. The parents had minor improvements in their relationship, which continued to improve as Allison improved, and father was able to express more directly his appreciation for her accomplishments. After two years of treatment, Allison used therapy only on an as needed basis for support in helping her cope with the more mundane stresses of high school. She managed a part-time job as a veterinary assistant, continued her hobby of horseback riding as a manager of a "pony club," and achieved A's and B's in advanced classes. She managed the next two falls, without her typical pattern of regression, further hospitalizations or switches of therapist. Relations with both parents improved as they became proud of her accomplishments, and the parental relationship improved as well. In addition, the frequency of arthritis flare-ups decreased, and her doctor began to wean her off of methotrexate. When Allison did experience some joint swelling in her fingers, she calmly asked for more time on her tests, and avoided regression, withdrawal or avoidance, her previous coping pattern. She began to discuss her feelings about her arthritis more openly with disappointment, but also gratefulness that her symptoms were generally well managed.

Formulation

The complex history presented by Allison reveals clearly how psychiatric diagnosis is only a cloudy window through which to view ongoing issues and concerns that lead a child to seek psychiatric treatment. Her diagnosis changed conveniently from year to year, as she tried to find a way to communicate her feelings that the environment she was in was intolerable. As her problems compounded with the diagnosis of her juvenile rheumatoid arthritis, she presented with the dissociative symptomatology seen in the initial presentation.

The dissociative symptomatology that she eventually hit on was a convenient solution for her for a variety of reasons. For one thing, it allowed her to compartmentalize her deepest fears about growing up safely in her home, which she could not express directly, and allowed a way to disavow responsibility for her avoidant and angry behavior. She could at once dissociate the physical pain of her arthritis, and the awareness of it, deal with her confusing emotional world, and achieve a new sense of power through keeping her parents off balance and unable to manage her.

It served to involve the mother in a gratifying and indulgent role with her, and also served to preserve two extremely contradictory identifications – with her perfectionist father, with his own "secret" about his past dysfunction, and her indulgent but sometimes irresponsible, and forgetful mother. It also served pragmatically to help her cope with the pain of arthritis and dissociate her anger and frustration from awareness of the limitations imposed by this disability.

While no specific traumatic events such as physical or sexual abuse were ever uncovered in the course of a long history and intensive family work, Allison's own perceptions of the limitations imposed on her by her illness, and the contradictions and pain in her environment were indeed a source of threat to her. Mother's inability to be "on time" which upset her greatly as a three year old in preschool was enhanced by the teacher's blaming mother for this, and her father's constant and continuing disparagement of her mother. While she felt little sense of security about the stability of care for her as a three-year-old, these feelings were reactivated when her own grandmother became ill. Allison feared that her own mother would die, and was frightened by the family's neglect of the grandmother, which further convinced her that parental care was unstable and undependable. Allison's experience with the dying baby hamsters further confused her about the reliability of parental care and left her with considerable rage and fear of her father. Allison's sense of safety was further compromised after she was diagnosed with juvenile arthritis, and the problems in her life began to feel increasingly insurmountable. Allison wondered if she could grow up to be responsible and mature, or if that meant only pain for her and abandonment by her mother. Once she grew up, would her mother and father be there for her? And if she grew up to be the perfectionist ideal that her father suggested, would that also be an abandonment of her mother? Could she grow up at all, or was she destined to be limited by her illness in accomplishing all of the things that she loved to do?

Her role enactment preserved loyalty to both parents and expressed anger at them simultaneously. By not being who either of them wanted her to be, she resisted the contradictory expectations, but in effect gave them both. By giving dad more ammunition against mom, she showed loyalty to him. By regressing, she got from mom the soothing attention she was seeking to protect against the loss of attachment that she feared maturity entailed. By letting herself be this regressed child whom dad rejected, she helped dad preserve his own perfectionist self-view, while still painfully reminding him that all was not "perfect" in their family. Her regressive behavior also served to soothe her mom, who seemed to enjoy the regression, and protect her mom from dad's rejection and disparagement. The dissociated childlike state seemed at once to encapsulate all of this turmoil and allow their expression without solution.

Her role enactment further preserved her own conflicts about identity – her late onset of menses leading to feelings of "differentness" and childishness compared with other students at school, and her arthritis which challenged her belief in her future potential. Thus in her regressed state, she was young and incompetent, portraying her biggest fears about who she really was.

On another level, this dissociative state became self-perpetuating as an instant stress reliever. As Allison disavowed stress whenever she encountered it, she converted her perception of the threat of this stress into a signal for the customary

458 Joyanna L. Silberg

regression. Allison in fact described "getting addicted" to her retreats into three-year-old behavior in which she could successfully put out of her mind the difficulties of mature responsibilities, and the pain of her arthritis. The self-reinforcing quality of this self-soothing hypnotic retreat became-one of the most difficult things to eliminate.

This assessment leads to a plan of intervention that must proceed on two fronts, simultaneously. The tasks of therapy on an individual level include promoting self-acceptance and self-awareness, decompartmentalizing the feelings and attitudes contained in the dissociated state, understanding the threats that elicit transitions between states and minimizing them, tolerating, tuning into, and regulating emotions and perceptions, and finding more direct means to communicate and to provide self-soothing. The environmental level of intervention includes changing the contingencies which concretely support the dissociative behavior, and working with the parents to free Allison from the conflicting messages that have supported this maladaptive coping style. Through these interventions the dissociation of perception, cognition and emotion can all be counteracted as Allison learns to cope more effectively with her life's challenges.

Treatment Approach

Therapeutic Importance of the Relationship

While theoretical views and treatment techniques deriving from them are important to outline, the quality and nature of the therapeutic relationship is the essential vehicle for the delivery of any healing interventions. Without attention to developing a therapeutic relationship, no treatment techniques can be effective. The attitude conveyed by the therapist to this young girl was one of intense belief in her potential, genuine caring, and respect. This attitude may not always be fostered in typical psychiatric settings for severely disturbed children, in which psychiatric labels often serve to distance helping professionals from a truly empathic stance towards these children. Certainly a child with a complex history such as this may elicit an approach of diagnostic scrutiny which is antithetical to really listening to the child's view of what is wrong.

Allison made it clear from the beginning that she did not like therapists, was impatient with the way they asked questions, thought that they generally followed a textbook of what to ask, and were usually wrong in their assumptions about her. Also, she made it clear that she could not stand people telling her the same things twice as she learned things quickly, and that most therapists did not know when to "shut up." She also made it clear that she saw the fact that she was in therapy as a sign of great personal weakness, feared the therapist's judgements about her, and when possible preferred to handle things on her own.

Allison was often able to cleverly encapsulate her disregard for therapy and the therapist in her images. At one point, the therapist patted her back while she was coughing and she broke into a diatribe stating forcefully, "That is what is wrong with all therapists. They think they are doing something when all they are doing is making themselves feel good. You can't help me by patting my back. Unless I am really choking, than you need to do the Heimlich maneuver. Our bodies have natural means to expel foreign objects. You are useless to help my cough. Similarly, it is only me that can help my problems. I must deal with them alone." The therapist agreed with her image but suggested to her that there were people she could rely on who could facilitate these natural processes.

The therapist supported Allison's need to handle things independently, was sensitive to her fears of being judged, and let her set the pace and frequency of visits later in treatment as she was progressing. This approach seemed to secure her trust enough that she was willing to continue seeing me rather than switch therapists as she had done so frequently. Later when scheduled therapy had terminated, she even initiated calls for as needed sessions when she was having a particularly stressful moment. Of all the healing affects of the therapeutic relationship, it is probably the sincere belief that the child can master her current difficulties that serves as a guiding force to propel the child to achieve what she can. This is the backdrop against which all interventions in the area of home and school need to be understood.

Concerns about Iatrogenesis

While Allison's enactment of the three-year-old was a compelling experience to witness, as she changed her face, her gait, her voice quality, and mannerisms, it seemed important from the beginning to avoid reinforcing this regressive behavior by undue fascination. Although never asked to "switch" into this behavior, Allison even in the first session was comfortable showing it off. Very aware of how changes in the therapist's response to her in this state might subtly reinforce it, an effort was made to maintain the same even calm whatever behavior she showed, trying to gently point out stresses that might have led to a sudden change in behavior. It was considered important for Allison herself to learn immediately what the natural precursors were that elicited these switches, and if the therapist were to become the one controlling this, she might lose the sensitivity of determining herself how this behavior had emerged and what function it served. As one of the goals of therapy was to make Allison more in charge of herself and her functioning, eliciting the childlike state would interfere with her attempts to be the one to gain central control of this. In addition, eliciting these switches might provide physiologic rehearsal for the neural pathways involved in this behavior, thus making it easier to engage in this maladaptive behavior over time.

It was made it clear from the beginning that the therapist was certain that in time she would have no need to engage in this behavior any longer and that fourteen year olds could find ways to do everything they needed without this kind of stereotyped regression. It was stressed that in time she would learn to engage in age-appropriate regression seamlessly (watching silly movies, laughing with friends) and this would be a real achievement. I also stressed that she would never lose whatever important ideas, feelings, or skills she felt she had in her three-year-old state. The therapist continually put the expectation on her that she would learn to manage this, but never took over this process for her by telling her to "act fourteen." An effort was made to model acceptance of the feelings expressed by the regressed behavior, so that she herself could learn to accept these in herself, leading to increased awareness and control.

Promoting Self-acceptance

Initially, the therapist helped Allison accept that this was indeed her behavior and that we would get nowhere unless she began to understand it and own it. She was educated that bodies and minds have wisdom that we ourselves are not always in touch with, but that we can be healthier if we learn the full extent of the wisdom we hold within us. She was told that it would be her job to begin to try to tap into that wisdom, that the three-year-old behavior had a reason, and that missing school, or telling her parents something seemed to be a very important goal. At first she claimed she did not know and could not tell at all what it was about, but she was gently reassured that if she let herself tune in to this information, it would be there for her. By the third session, Allison no longer reported any amnesia for her behavior and was able to tune in to a voice in her mind that helped her understand the three year old behavior. She began to see the three-year-old behavior as her protection from stress, as information that she needed a break, needed to play, or could not handle responsibilities. The therapist helped her to begin to notice those feelings before switching into the three-year-old behavior and finding other ways to articulate those needs. It was also stressed that whatever skills, knowledge, or attitudes that three year old knew about and that she valued were essentially her own.

Self-acceptance most importantly involved helping Allison focus on the positive aspects of her identity, her skills and talents, and the fact of her unfortunate illness and its impact on her. As Allison became better at accepting her real self fully, there was less need for the dissociated sense of identity that prevented her from true awareness.

Breaking Dissociative Barriers

The therapist immediately encouraged a bridging between the two states of presentation – competent, joyless, driven perfectionist Allison, and the playful emotional, irresponsible Allison. She was told that both of these were important parts of her identity and that she would not be a whole person without including the playfulness and emotionality along with her driven perfectionist achievement standards. There was no effort to try to rid her of the three-year-old self, but to help her become more in charge of accessing what she needed when it was appropriate. She was assured that there were times everyone needed to be less mature and more emotional and she needed to pick those times appropriately. On the way to school in the morning clearly was not one of those times. Thus, she was encouraged to build in more fun-filled relaxed time in her schedule and her mother and father were asked to monitor that she did in fact do this.

While encouraging her to be more three-year-old-like in her mature state, she was also encouraged to find ways to access more mature capacities while she was regressed. For example, while drawing a picture in the office during one of her three-year-old enactments, Allison asked how to spell her name. The therapist stated gently that this was information that she had, and she could find that out herself. Rather than indulge her view of herself as a three-year-old, she was encouraged to find a way to build bridges to her mature capacities no matter how she presented.

Allison was urged to be both of her identities at the same time, and not to alternate between them as she was doing, because both were her and both were needed. As Allison did learn to do this, a new playfulness in her approach to life was noted, as she would reach for toys in the office and play with them while talking about a fourteen-year-old's problems, something she initially had never done.

Highlighting Transition Moments

Helping Allison understand what prompted her transitions between these states was viewed as essential for Allison to develop mastery and internal regulation. Whenever mom reported that a switch to the three-year-old had occurred at home and led Allison to avoid something, she was asked to role play a new way to handle the stress that did not involve the regression. These switches were usually initiated during a parental argument, mother being angry or upset with her, or Allison feeling overwhelmed by homework. Identifying each of one these moments became an opportunity for the family and Allison to identify the feelings and conflicts stimulated and to develop a new more direct coping strategy. In therapy, Allison was encouraged to express directly whatever the difficult feeling was that had gotten stimulated at the time of these switches – anger at the mother, fear about her abilities, worry about not completing her work. As Allison matured physically and began to menstruate, switches to the three-year-old presentation also occurred when she noticed the blood at the onset of menstruation. Her difficulties with menstruation became an opportunity to have Allison discuss in therapy her dislike of the teenagers in her school, her fears about what being a "teenager" meant and her fears about not fitting in.

Similarly, when a switch occurred in the office the therapist tried to help trace back what the signal of stress was that Allison was responding to and discuss with her other ways to express it. She was not permitted to use the switches to avoid entirely difficult conversations in therapy, but if a switch happened in the middle of a discussion, the therapist would point out "Talking about your history teacher must be very upsetting to you. Maybe you can tell me more about how upsetting this really is, or why you have just tried to avoid this conversation entirely. What are you trying to tell me?" Thus, Allison was encouraged not to use this dissociative form of communication but to be direct about what she was feeling and to express it. Sometimes, Allison would use this as an opportunity to say, "I am trying to say I hate therapy or I want to go home," and she was encouraged for her ability to be direct.

There were only two occasions in which Allison reported switching into her three-year-old state outside home or therapy. One of these times was while waiting for her turn at a piano recital. Allison became very frightened about the fact that she had done this and that she might have done it during the performance. This served as a motivator to work harder on treatment to deal with behavior which began to feel out of control. The other time was in an art class at school, and Allison was told that it was nothing to worry about, as art is a natural time to feel regressed, and she knew what skills she needed for the harder subjects. The feelings stimulated by these two events seemed related to Allison's fear of losing control of her hands because of her arthritis. Expressing these fears served in part to help her believe she could gain control of her three-year-old behavior even if she could not completely control the arthritis. The therapist did not express to her concern about the switching behavior itself, but assumed that Allison's own motivation and mature consciousness would serve to regulate her. In time, Allison became confident that it was really she who was in charge of her behavior, and became eager to discover immediately the meaning behind a particular regression. Allison, who was very interested in science, had many neurobiological questions about how her brain was doing this. She was encouraged to do her own neurobiological research one day.

Tuning into Feelings

Allison was educated about the importance of feelings using the metaphor of road signs. Without road signs, we would have trouble safely getting where we are going. Similarly, our feelings help us navigate by telling us what to approach, what to avoid, and helping us learn what to expect when we encounter new things that are similar to what we once experienced. Allison was taught to try to tune in to these, rather than her usual habit of ignoring them until they found a way to express themselves in a somatic form or in dissociative states. Allison learned to notice when she was feeling tired or overworked, frightened, angry, or overwhelmed, as these often became signals for her to switch states. She also had difficulty when faced with competing feelings, such as a drive to succeed and a fear of rejection or failure. "Facing the conflict," "solving the war," and "watching the road signs" became handy slogans to remind Allison of how to use her feelings more productively. By identifying the feeling, its cause, and ways to express it, she could solve the problem. As this was explored, it became clear that Allison had learned the habit of dissociating physical pain as an initial strategy for coping with the pain of her arthritis. She described that she could do things in the three-year-old state that would hurt her when she was in her regular fourteen-year-old state. Her rheumatologist concurred that Allison's pain tolerance was unusually high, and he marveled about her ability to persist in activities that others with her symptoms would have abandoned.

Allison felt a loss when she was no longer able to dissociate from the pain of her illness by regressing, but she was helped to see that the pain served as a signal not to stress her body in certain ways, but to seek other medical consultation to address the symptomatology more directly. By the end of treatment, Allison herself initiated calls to her doctor when in need of more pain management, and talked to her teachers directly about getting more time for written work.

Alternative Strategies for Communication and Self-soothing

The three-year-old enactment was seen as goal directed behavior, and so it was very important to find alternatives for accomplishing the same goals. Foremost, the behavior was seen as a form of communication with the family. Allison was helped to communicate directly with her parents about her needs and feelings during family therapy. As switch times were often when parents were arguing or Allison perceived that her mom was unhappy, having Allison describe to them how that felt became an important goal. Sometimes Allison was more comfortable writing her feelings in letters to her father, and this activity was encouraged as well.

Sometimes parents and child were given specific assignments of topics to talk about at home, like how each of them deals with stress. As Allison became better at expressing her fears about her grandmother's deterioration and the family's abandonment of grandmother, Allison and mom worked out a schedule for visiting. It was suggested that even if Grandma could not recognize them, just as Allison's mature self could hear even when she was acting three, so Grandma could hear them on some level and know they were there even if she could not respond.

Allison's regressive behavior also served as a form of self-soothing, so Allison needed to learn alternatives to comfort herself as well. She was taught how to use fantasy images for positive coping and self-relaxation. When faced with parental conflict, Allison was encouraged to walk away to her room and close her door, write in a journal, or turn up her music, rather than regress and stay in the room with the conflict. Her entrance into the three-year-old state just before bedtime persisted for quite awhile, and Allison was taught to use self-relaxation, self-hypnosis, and imagining positive scenarios for the next day, to help undo the day's stress and get to sleep. Finally, the last self-reinforcing element of the three year-old faded away after a year and a half of treatment. By this time, Allison had been attending school regularly, and functioning in all aspects of her life in an age-appropriate fashion.

Family Interventions

While the dissociative behavior had become a new problem to solve, clearly Allison was telling people for several years that she was experiencing many problems before she began to display this particular symptom. Relieving her of some of the pressures of her conflict-filled family became an essential component of treatment. On one level, Allison was torn between expectations of perfection from her father, and the belief held by her mother that she was ill, impaired and very dependent. It was important to help the parents see that they were both right about their interpretations of Allison's behavior; that she *could* master being a normal 14-year-old (dad's view)) but she also *could not* (mom's view) do all the things they wanted. She was stuck in this no man's land, and only by their extricating her from the battle between them could she prove to herself what she could accomplish. She would never live up to her full potential unless they could get her out of the middle of their struggle. This took constant reminders, but both were committed enough to Allison to work on this.

As one strategy, parents were encouraged to attempt a role reversal with Allison, so that dad was the one to tell her to take a break in the middle of her homework and mom was the taskmaster. When the parents did this, Allison was enormously pleased, but they were never able to sustain this role reversal for too long.

The therapist also wanted to help the family understand how the three-year-old's behavior could be seen in a normalizing way and possibly something she shared with the whole family. The family was asked to engage in a task of identifying what they want to preserve in themselves from the time that they were three-year-olds. This gave the parents a chance to talk about healthy regression in their own lives and to normalize the experience of regressive needs. The family was also helped to see that all of them had the desire at times to escape from responsibility and stress.

At times, mother was seen individually to work on bolstering her esteem, clarifying her views about what she wanted in the marriage, and encouraging her to take a stand to get her needs met more directly. During this work, mother was helped to see that Allison's father had many sensible points about Allison's ability and that his high expectations and demanding manner were not simply a rejection of Allison. Mother was also helped to appreciate in a gentle way how her own struggles to be "grown up" and take mature responsibility for her life and her marriage might be echoed in Allison's regressed behavior. Dad was frequently unavailable and it was difficult to get him to come in, but occasional phone calls kept him informed about the treatment plan. The sister was included in therapy on occasion to reinforce the idea of not indulging or becoming overly fascinated with her sister's aberrant behavior, which she was prone to do, and to deal with issues of sibling rivalry.

Allison was also given many concrete rewards for following through on school attendance, and the family was shown how to develop a clear behavioral program. One of these involved letting her take care of a neighborhood dog that she loved, when she successfully attended school that day.

Avoiding Reinforcement of Three-year-old Behavior

Mom had gotten into a pattern of indulging, excusing, and allowing these regressions, so they had become a very handy way for Allison to avoid school, family dinners out, and other kinds of stressors. The family immediately responded to Allison's behavior, and Allison was temporarily off the hook. The family was encouraged to change this approach. For example, when Allison regressed into her three-year-old state in the middle of homework, mom was encouraged to believe that she could finish the work herself, that Allison did have access to the information needed. Mom was helped to see that Allison was not actually a three-year-old, and it was inappropriate to treat her as such. Over time, mom noticed that she could do her homework even as her face changed and she adopted the characteristic childlike gait and immature language. Soon, Allison was switching back between the two states fluidly in and out of conversations. Mom was told to take no notice as this was Allison's way of learning to be both of these at once. It would be most helpful for mom to simply ignore this and let this be Allison's problem to manage. As mom continued to ignore this, the changes in state became so fluid that they eventually became undetectable, and she achieved the fluidity of state transitions that normal consciousness allows.

Illustrative Family Session

A turning point came for Allison and her relationship with this family when her beloved grandmother neared death. Allison and her mother came into the session very fearful of how to proceed. Allison was afraid of seeing how regressed Grandma had become, but felt guilty about not wanting to go. She was encouraged to go so she could say goodbye to her grandmother and support her mother through this difficult time. Allison was asked to write a poem for her grandmother about what she had meant to her, which she later read aloud. She movingly described memories about her Grandma' slife, and while she read it, her mother began to cry. Suddenly, Allison switched into identifiable three-year-old behavior, picked up the poem and ripped it into pieces. "It is bad," she said, "because it made my mommy cry." Mother looked on helplessly while witnessing this. The therapist said, "No, the poem was not bad, what you just did was hurtful to your mommy and was a bad thing to do. You took something meaningful to your mother and ripped it up. That is way more sad, and would make your mother cry even harder. Do you know how you could make your mommy feel better? Take this tape and tape it back up so that mommy has the beautiful poem that you wrote." At first she resisted, but her mother was asked to encourage this behavior. This was new for her mother, as she was accustomed to feeling helpless and unable to impose limits during Allison's regressions. With mom's encouragement, Allison taped the poem and soon switched back to her 14-year-old demeanor. That night they went directly to grandma and she died while they were talking to her. Allison felt very proud of herself for going, for having communicated with her grandmother in her final moments, and for supporting her mother. Allison's ability to mourn this loss along with her family, and to say goodbye the way she needed to, helped her to more readily accept the inevitability of facing her own maturity. This incident became an important symbol to Allison and the family that regression would not help Allison and the family avoid all pain, nor would following her into that regression help mother avoid the inevitable pain of loss.

Mother and daughter could both gain by accessing their mature coping resources. In addition, during this period of mourning, father was supportive of mother in a way he had not been earlier, so that the dynamic of a normal family was approximated for all of them during the time of grandmother's death, and it became a healing time for the family. Grandmother's nursing home gave Allison a dog that had been a companion for grandmother. Allison's care for this pet helped illustrate in a concrete way that the legacy of love for her grandmother was the mature ability to provide loving care. Even father embraced this new pet, which became a meaningful symbol for the family of new possibilities for Allison and the whole family.

School and Peer Interventions

As a sensitive perfectionist and demanding student, Allison was frequently angry at her teachers and worried about minor details that made little sense to her. Her dislike of school resulted from feeling constantly frustrated at not getting the answers to her questions, feeling annoyed that she had to comply with silly rules she did not feel furthered her education, and finding little sensitivity to the limitations she had due to her occasional arthritis flare-ups.

The initial removal of Allison from school and her placement on home teaching, immediately disrupted the angry and avoidant pattern Allison had gotten into over the last five years of school attendance. By essentially "prescribing the symptom," the conflicts between Allison and her family about school attendance were instantly removed and Allison was given the opportunity to focus on her own motivations and plans. In addition, Allison had gotten so far behind so quickly in ninth grade, that this home schooling provided the stress-free space she needed to "dig herself out of the hole." During this initial period, Allison freely expressed frustrations about her teachers and concerns and dissatisfactions about the curriculum. Within two months, Allison expressed the desire to return to school. When she did return to school, she was encouraged to be assertive in appropriate ways to get assignments clarified further, and to follow her own instincts on assignments with overly rigid direction. Allison became more skilled over time in learning how to balance her perfectionism with the realistic demands of a challenging high school.

Sometimes, even after Allison no longer regressed with her stereotyped three-year-old behavior, she would resort to further dissociative behavior or physical manifestations of her stress while encountering the maze of demands, expectations, and contradictions in her high school. Her need to live up to her own perfectionist standards often came into conflict with her need to please and satisfy her teachers, thus mirroring her home difficulties. As supporting Allison's independence and mastery was an important treatment goal, she was encouraged to disengage from teacher demands that felt silly or unnecessary and handle projects in the way that made sense to her.

At one point, Allison came into the office carried by her mother and stated she could not walk. She begged the therapist to lift her feet up on the couch for her as she stated she had no ability to move her legs. She was told that her body was telling her that there was a good reason she could not move or go forward, and that the reason would be uncovered. If her legs were moved for her, than there would be less information about what was preventing her from finding her motion and will. Eventually, Allison lifted her legs up onto the couch herself and she was able to describe her fear and anger about a teacher's comment, her desire to avoid the class because of it, but her interest and motivation about the subject matter. A discussion ensued about a way for her to address both sides of the conflict, her motion returned, and she walked out of the office without problem.

Occasional contacts with Allison's school were for the purposes of normalizing her school functioning as much as possible. No information was provided that would further isolate or pathologize her. She was given an exemption from physical education requirements during arthritis flare-ups, and she was allowed extra time to finish tests when her writing was slow.

Allison felt that she was different from many of the students in her high school and, at first, pointedly avoided many school social events. In therapy she discussed her dislike of the superficiality of students in her class, which often covered her fears of being accepted and her worries about being different due to her illness and other problems. Allison was encouraged to participate in a girl's social skills group and quickly became one of the most assertive, helpful members of the group, providing insight and advice to the others. This experience helped build her feelings of social competence which continued to grow as therapy progressed, and she became more positive about her identity as a teenager. As Allison further tested her social competence outside the group, she began to try harder to fit in with school activities, attended dances, and even became involved in planning these activities.

During the course of treatment, Allison was diagnosed with an allergic sensitivity to formaldehyde, which resulted in anaphylactic shock and a rescue by medics in the nurse's suite at school. Thus, the trauma of this frightening experience was added to the stressors in Allison's life, and further promoted her view of herself as "different" from other students. However, this extremely frightening event did not result in further regressions or retreats into dissociative behavior. It did result in a conditioned fear response of hyperventilation and muscle contracture as she approached science class, which lasted for several weeks following the incident.* Nonetheless, Allison's ability to cope without dissociation at this point allowed her to recover from this rather frightening event without significant regression.

---

* Author's note: Allison's "allergy" to formaldehyde was eventually diagnosed as paradoxical vocal cord dysfunction, a stress-induced conversion symptom resulting in vocal cord constriction and respiratory distress. This was successfully treated with vocal exercises and stress management techniques.

Discussion

The treatment described involved eliminating dissociation through an individual approach that helped Allison develop more mature methods for dealing with emotion and internal conflict, and a family approach that helped facilitate a more nurturing and less conflict-filled environment. This case raises many interesting questions about dissociation and dissociative disorders. How did this three-year-old state emerge? Was it a suggestive effect of therapy, a suggestive effect of family expectation, a manipulation on Allison's part, or was it a hidden traumatic fragment that Allison had harbored since she was three?

Traditional DID theory might suggest that this three-year-old had been there in a split-off form and unavailable to awareness since the traumatic time at three when her father had been violent, and she had repeatedly been picked up late from preschool. If this were the case, than fully integrating the traumatic elements of these experiences might be seen as the correct approach. This hypothesis was not given much support, as Allison did not describe these traumas at length, and the difficulties of her life in the present seemed of greater significance. Instead, it seemed that current stressors elicited this regressive state, and that this state came to provide over time a protective function against current stress.

The onset of her diagnosis of arthritis five months before her dissociative presentation and the associated pain in her fingers was a traumatic event for which dissociation became a convenient coping tool. In fact, Allison's rheumatologist commented that Allison seemed almost immune to her pain, and was surprised at how much she could accomplish despite it. Allison was also able to articulate that she felt no pain when she was in her three-year-old state and this was one reason why it became very resistant to extinction even when it was no longer reinforced by her family.

Might this have just been a conscious manipulation on Allison's part to avoid school and other responsibilities? This explanation is highly unlikely as Allison complained often about her feeling of lack of control when the three-year-old state emerged, at least in the initial phase of therapy. Given the time it took for this behavior to finally evaporate, her distress and conflict about it, and her frequent development of other somatic and conversion symptoms, it would be difficult to interpret her behavior as a conscious manipulation.

Was this behavior simply an artifact of therapy for a dissociative disorder? While the behavior certainly had presented before her entrance into this therapy, it is possible that it became elaborated and intensified through the family's knowledge that she had a dissociative disorder and was in treatment for it. This might have made mother more willing to accept the behavior, excuse it, and indulge the desires of the three-year-old. While such an explanation is possible, it should be noted that the therapist worked immediately on combating the reinforcing elements of the environment and did not encourage or indulge the three-year-old presentation in therapy. However, the therapist, having witnessed the behavior, did convey an acceptance of the existence of the behavior that might have given a subtle message that this behavior was appropriate in some ways. A strict behavioral approach, on the other hand, might have set clear limits on her regression and more quickly extinguished the behavior. Such an approach was not used here because of the belief that the meaning of the behavior could only be fully appreciated by helping Allison tune into the message she was trying to communicate, and that she needed to attend to its meaning for her. Given Allison's desperation and creativity, it is difficult to imagine that a simple behavioral approach might have been fully successful. She may have developed even more dysfunctional behavior to call attention to her difficulties, as she had done with her previous psychiatric symptoms during the preceding years. One would expect that she could easily have found other dysfunctional symptoms to express her conflicts if this one avenue had been stifled.

The explanation proposed here is that Allison, a girl with clearly identified dissociative predispositions, was susceptible to the development of this kind of dissociative symptomatology. Allison displayed many anomalies of consciousness including falling asleep easily at the dinner table and suddenly fainting when hearing stressful information; she seemed to have a very low threshold for conditioned responses. Allison showed the fantasy-proneness, trance-inducing abilities, symbolic skills, empathic perceptiveness, and attachment conflict characteristic of many dissociative patients.

At first, Allison seemed to utilize the twilight state of consciousness in sleepwalking as a way to avoid responsibility for school which was producing great conflict in her. With mom's labeling of this behavior as "like a three-year-old," Allison was able to unconsciously embellish this, then this regressed state seemed to coalesce and begin to take on a life of its own. Allison's aptitude for trance and altering her consciousness aided her development of this unconscious enactment within this context. Allison's clear conflict about her loss of choice in moving her body when she had an arthritis flare-up might have further led to this dissociative symptom where she truly experienced "no choice." It is often the criticism leveled against therapists (Acocella, 1999; Lilienfeld *et al.*, 1999) that suggestible, fragile and hypnotizable patients can develop these kind of enactments in an unconscious way through a therapy which has high expectations of these phenomena. In this case, it would appear that the embellished role enactment is more related to the unconscious dynamics within Allison and supported within the family, that served to facilitate the pathological development of this symptom in a context even more powerful than therapy.

What role did a traumatic etiology play in this symptom? While Allison's home life was indeed traumatic due to the chronic arguments, discrete events of physical and sexual abuse were absent in this case. One clear traumatic precursor was the ongoing pain from juvenile rheumatoid arthritis, and the pain of her worry about the diagnosis and its implications. It was noted, in fact, that Allison walked on her toes both in the child-state and when her arthritis was particularly severe. However, it is important to note that the arthritis was a late developing phenomenon, at age thirteen, and so chronic pain of this type had not been an ongoing developmental factor when she was a child of three. It was most likely a combination of all of the compounded stressors in her life, the parental conflict, her illness, her pain, and her fears about growing up that led to this habitual pattern of avoidance that the dissociative behavior perpetuated.

Although in some ways this case is unique compared with cases of dissociative disorders often presented in the literature, this author's experience suggests that the subtle processes described here involving the family's unconscious reinforcement of dissociative pathology may be generally applicable to other children with severe dissociative symptomatology as well.

Alternative Conceptualizations and Discussion

The integrated developmental model described here differs in a variety of ways from traditional dissociative treatments described in the literature. In this approach, the dissociative behavior is viewed as a developing phenomenon, that has originated through a complex interplay of family and individual psychological factors. The integrated developmental approach presumes that sensitivity to both these internal and external factors will be necessary to promote recovery. In contrast, dissociative disorders have often been seen as more static phenomena that are individual responses to early traumatic events. In this view, the trauma must be identified and processed in order for the dissociative state to be integrated into the whole personality (Kluft, 1999). This traditional treatment involves the identification and description of the dissociated alternative states. Direct communication with the alternatives is encouraged in order to have each describe itself fully, and negotiation and bargaining is conducted for the parts to learn to operate together as a whole. In this approach, the ongoing problems in Allison's life might be viewed as secondary to the manifestation of the traumatic memories from her early years.

The traditional approach might have led to different interventions from the earliest moments in therapy. More of an emphasis might have been placed on Allison's early history, the father's out of control early behavior, and inquiry into the possibility of ongoing abuse in Allison's life. An attempt might have been made to determine if any more dissociated identities existed, and Allison might have been encouraged to think about this question and explore this possibility. In fact, during one part of treatment, mother did state that she thought a new alternate identity had emerged that could not talk, and one that represented Allison at five rather than three. At the time, this observation was largely ignored, as it seemed to present a new way for Allison to avoid communication. In the traditional approach, attempts might have been made to engage this other "five-year-old state" and determine what it represented about Allison's early life. Psychological testing measures may have been utilized to identify other dissociative features that Allison might have had.

As tools to work with these alternative states, the therapist might have asked Allison to draw pictures of them and talk about the formation of their identities, their traumatic histories, and their current goals and jobs. It is possible that the therapist might have asked directly to interact with these alternate states for the purpose of negotiating their conflicts. Allison might have been required to talk to her mother in these alternate states and in those states tell her mother the things that made her sad from her early years. For example, she might have been asked to talk about her disappointment at being picked up late as a three-year-old and asked to have her mother apologize to her in this state. As new traumas became associated with these other states, Allison would then talk to her mother about each of the feelings associated with each of these states. Over time, Allison would be expected to integrate all of the identities after the traumatic processing of feelings within these alternate states.

In this approach, art and play therapy might have been encouraged with Allison making models of her child states and even rocking a model of her child state to allow her to "grow up" (Waters & Silberg, 1996). Attachment might have been seen as impaired and Allison's need for attachment to her mother as a three-year-old might have been emphasized and reinforced. During the session, when Allison switched to the three-year-old and ripped up the poem, the therapist might have treated Allison more like the three-year-old she was enacting and asked her to talk to her mother about how she felt about her mother crying, and why it was so unsettling. The emphasis would have been more on understanding the feelings in the dissociated part of the self, rather than encouraging Allison to develop immediate mastery for this regressive coping.

Many underlying assumptions distinguish this traditional approach from the integrated developmental model described earlier. The integrated developmental approach encourages immediate mastery of dissociated feelings and ideas, with no automatic assumption that the dissociation is necessary at that moment. The traditional approach moves more cautiously at disrupting dissociative barriers that are viewed as protective against information that may be too intolerable for the individual to handle. The traditional approach assumes that the dissociated identities formed suddenly and does not presume that they are constructed over time. The integrated developmental approach assumes that these are multi-determined phenomena that are constructed through an active process by which they develop into learned patterns of communication, avoidance, and self-soothing. The traditional approach assumes that awareness during dissociated states is more limited and outside the individual's control. In contrast, the integrated developmental model assumes that awareness is constantly being constructed and that the therapist maintaining an assumption of awareness will help ongoing awareness develop more quickly. The integrated developmental approach assumes that at each instance of dissociation an alternative, more direct means could exist for communication, awareness, or coping. The traditional approach assumes that only over time with the exploration of dissociated content can an integrated self emerge. On the other hand, the integrated developmental approach assumes that an integrated self is in the process of construction at each moment in time, and overemphasis on the content of what is dissociated might interfere with this ongoing process.

The integrated developmental approach is very sensitive to the ongoing interpersonal dynamics that support and embellish the dissociative behavior, and requires that there be interventions in the environment. This approach recognizes that the therapist becomes an integral part of the interpersonal environment who can help shape awareness, coping, and mastery of dissociation. The traditional approach pays less attention to the ongoing shaping influences of the switching and role enactments that may be encouraged in the therapy itself.

The author believes that the integrated developmental approach presents many advantages over a traditional approach, and presents a departure in some ways from the views presented in her own previous writings (Silberg, 1996). One major concern is that a traditional approach may have led to iatrogenesis, with more identities proliferating and Allison perceiving that her regressions were validated. By allowing communication about feelings of insecurity to occur primarily in the regressed state, Allison may not have been able to master ownership of these feelings in her more mature state. By encouraging the expression of attachment needs in the dissociated states alone, it might have served to inadvertently reinforce dissociation rather than curb it. In so doing, it is possible that for a suggestible child like this, memories might have been suggested, dissociated identities might have proliferated and further dysfunction incurred. The integrated developmental approach is viewed as being more cautious, in that only the dissociative behavior in direct evidence was addressed, no search for other alternates or memories was conducted, and iatrogenic factors and family reinforcement factors were attended to immediately.

There is some overlap between these two approaches. Both emphasize that an integrated self involves, in part, the inclusion of dissociated identity fragments represented in the other states of awareness. Risks would be seen as resulting from an approach that completely ignored the dissociative presentation. If Allison were told, for example, not to regress in the office and never to show that immature behavior, it might have been very difficult to get to the level of connection with Allison in which she could finally own that the regressed Allison had important feelings that were indeed her own. In fact, this is what had occurred in a previous therapy in which Allison discussed the stresses of her life but never owned her regressed behavior and the meaning of her school avoidance. In addition, an approach which completely ignored the dissociation might have missed the important opportunity to help Allison's parents understand the messages of Allison's regressed behavior, and change their manner of relating to her.

The integrated developmental approach of this chapter is a middle of the road approach between these two extremes. While the dissociative behavior is attended to and attempts made to understand it, the content of the dissociated constructions is not reinforced or supported. Yet, the dissociated behavior is understood to reveal important information about Allison's struggles with identity in her conflict-filled world.

The case presented here illustrates that a dissociative presentation could be seen as a form of language that symbolically communicates what cannot be said directly. Through her "three year old" presentation Allison was telling her family that mature responsibility was too much for her, that she feared growing up, that she felt she needed escape, and that she longed for the dependency of a young child. Through listening to this, one could learn about the perfectionist standards that Allison had set for herself, as well as the very real impediments to Allison trying to get her needs met – the insecurity resulting from her parents' chronic conflict, and the reality of her physical impairment. Listening to Allison involved hearing the messages contained in the three-year-old presentation without making the vehicle of this communication more prominent than the message it contained. In addition, Allison's use of this stereotyped regression as associated with feeling avoidance became an opportunity to teach new skills involving feeling identification, expression, and integration of painful information about her identity, her illness, and her disappointment in her parents.

If the dissociative symptoms are the child's symbolic language of resistance in an untenable environment, the language and ritual of a stereotyped dissociative disorder's treatment could be turned by a misdirected therapy into a new language of imprisonment. The dangers of this could be overwhelming for children, particularly these children who are seen as suggestible, context-dependent, and desperately seeking attachments.

Controversy will no doubt continue about how best to help children and adolescents manifesting dissociative symptoms. While all of the answers to the many controversial questions raised by this case are not yet in, it is hoped that this case presentation will serve to further stimulate the discussions of practice that can help us be most successful with these patients.

References

Acocella, J. (1999). *Creating hysteria*, New York: Jossey-Bass.

Bromberg, P. (1998). *Standing in the Spaces, Essays on Clinical Process, Trauma, and Dissociation*. Hillsdale New Jersey: The Analytic Press.

Coons, P. M. (1996). Clinical phenomenology of 25 children and adolescents with dissociative disorders. *Child and Adolescent Psychiatric Clinics of North America, 5,* 361–374.

Cagiada, S., Camiado, L, Pennan, A. (1997). Successful integrated hypnotic and psychopharmacological treatment of a war-related post-traumatic psychological and somatoform dissociative disorder of two years duration (psychogenic coma). *Dissociation 10,* 182–189.

Damasio, A. (1999). *The Feeling of What Happens*. New York: Harcourt Brace & Company.

Dell, D. F. & Eisenhower, J. W. (1990). Adolescent multiple personality disorder: A preliminary study of eleven cases. *Journal of the American Academy of Child & Adolescent Psychiatry, 29(3),* 359–366.

Dollinger, S. J. (1983). A case report of dissociative neurosis (depersonalization disorder) in an adolescent treated with family therapy and behavior modification. *Journal of Consulting and Clinical Psychology, 51(4),* 479–484.

Donovan, D. M. (1997). Why memory is a red herring in the recovered (traumatic) memory debate. In J. D. Read & D. S. Lindsay (eds) Recollection of trauma: Scientific, research & clinical practice. New York: Plenum. 403–416.

Donovan, D. M. & McIntyre, D. (1990). *Healing the hurt child: Developmental-contextual approach.* New York: W. W. Norton.

Gleaves, D. H. (1996). The socio-cognitive model of dissociative identity disorder: a reexamination of the evidence. Psychological Bulletin, 120, 42–59.

Hornstein, N. L. & Putnam, F. W. (1992). Clinical phenomenology of child and adolescent dissociative disorders. *Journal of the American Academy of Child and Adolescent Psychiatry, 31,* 1077–1085.

Hornstein, N. L., & Tyson, S. (1991). Inpatient treatment of children with multiple personality/dissociation and their families. *The Psychiatric Clinics of North America – M.P.D.,* 631–648.

Jacobsen, T. (1995). Case study: Is selective mutism a manifestation of dissociative identity disorder? *Journal of American Academy of Child and Adolescent Psychiatry, 31,* 1077–1085.

Klein, H., Mann, D. R., Goodwin, J. M. (1994). Obstacles to the recognition of sexual abuse and dissociative disorders in child and adolescent males. *Dissociation, 7,* 138–144.

Kluft, R. P. (1984). M.P.D. in childhood. *Psychiatric Clinics of North America-MPD, 7,* 121–134.

Kluft, R. P. (1999). Current issues in dissociative identity disorder. *Journal of the Practice of Psychiatry and Behavioral Health, Jan.* 9–19.

Lilienfeld, S. O., Lynn, S. J., Kirsch, I, Chaves, J. F., Sarbin, T. R., et al. (1999). Dissociative identity disorder and the sociocognitive model: recalling the lessons from the past. Psychological Bulletin.

Nijenhuis, E. R. S., Vanderlinden, J., & Spinhoven, P. (1998). Animal defensive reaction as a model for trauma-induced dissociative processes. *Journal of Traumatic Stress, 11,* 243–260.

Putnam. F. W. (1997). *Dissociation in Children and Adolescents.* New York: Guilford.

Putnam, F. W., Hornstein, N., & Peterson, G. (1996). Clinical phenomenology of child and adolescent dissociative disorders: Gender and age effects. *Child and Adolescent Psychiatric Clinics of North America, 5,* 303–442.

Rivera, M. (1996). *More Alike than Different.* Toronto: University of Toronto Press.

Rhue, J. W., Lynn, S. J., & Sandberg, D. (1995). Dissociation, fantasy and imagination in childhood: A comparison of physically abused, sexually abused, and non-abused children. *Contemporary Hypnosis, 12,* 131–136.

Siegel, D. (1999). *The Developing Mind.* New York: The Guildford Press.

Silberg, J. L. (ed.) (1996). *The Dissociative Child: Diagnosis, treatment, and management.* Baltimore: The Sidran Press.

Silberg, J. L. (1998). Afterword. In J. L. Silberg (ed.) *The Dissociative Child.* (2nd ed.). Lutherville, MD: The Sidran Press.

Van der Kolk, B. A. & van der Hart (1989). Pierre Janet and the breakdown of adaptation in psychological trauma. *American Journal of Psychiatry, 146,* 1530–1540.

Venn, J. (1984). Family etiology and remission in a case of psychogenic fugue. *Family Process, 23,* 429–435.

Waters, F. W. & Silberg, J. L. (1996). Promoting integration in dissociative children. In J. Silberg, The Dissociative Child: Diagnosis, Treatment and Management. 167–190; Lutherville.

Zoruglu, S. Yargic, I.. Tutkun, H. Ozturk, & V. Sar (1996). Dissociative identity disorder in childhood: Five Turkish cases. *Dissociation, 9,* 253–260.

Author Index

Subject Index

ADHD, see Attention Deficit/Hyperactivity
   Disorder
Alcohol abuse, see Substance Abuse
Anorexia Nervosa, 291–310
   associated features, 292
   developmental considerations, 292
   multifactoral model, 292–294
   assessment, 294
      medical, 294
      nutrition and weight, 294
      psychological, 294
   medical and nutritional treatment,
      295–296
   psychological treatment, 296
   case illustrations, 296–298, 301–302,
      305–307
   narrative therapy, 298–302
   cognitive-behavioral therapy, 302–307
   treatment comparisons, 307–308
   treatment outcome research, 308–309
Attention Deficit/Hyperactivity Disorder
   (ADHD), 21–32, 77–104
   toddlers and preschool children, 21–22
      precursors, 22–24
      treatment, 24–26
   middle childhood, 26–32, 89–102
      symptoms, 26–30
      treatment, 30–32
      case illustrations, 89–102
   description and diagnosis, 78–79
   comorbidity, 79–80
   impairment, 80–81
   etiology, 81–82
   underlying mechanisms, 82–83
   treatment, 24–26, 30–32, 83–89
      behavioral/psychosocial, 24–25, 30–31,
         84
         direct contingency management,
            84–85
      clinical behavior therapy, 85

cognitive based interventions, 85–86
      social skills interventions, 86
   stimulant medications, 25, 31–32,
      86–88
   combinations, 32, 88–89
   case illustrations, 89–102
Behavioral Family Therapy (BFT), 162–170
BFT, see Behavioral Family Therapy
Bulimia Nervosa, 311–326
   treatment choices, 311–314, 314–325
      coping strategies therapy, 312, 314–325
      case illustrations, 317–325
CBT, see Cognitive-Behavioral Therapy
Child Development, 9–38, 108–111,
      134–135, 268–269, 292, 355–356,
      419–420, 438–440
   developmental contexts of, 13–14
      parental psychopathology, 13
      parent–child attachment, 13–14
   risk and protective factors of, 15–17,
      case illustration, 19–21
   and attention deficit/hyperactivity
      disorder, 21–32
   and depression, 108–111
   and dysthymia, 134–135
   and obsessive compulsive disorder,
      268–269
   and anorexia nervosa, 292
   and schizophrenia, 419–420
   and firesetting, 355–356
   and sleep disorders, 438–440
Classroom Behavior Management, 50–52
Cognitive-Behavioral Family Therapy,
      202–208
Cognitive-Behavioral Therapy (CBT), 63,
      111–116, 120–127, 155–157, 214–215,
      233–236, 259–262, 269–272, 302–307,
      311–312, 331–332, 335–342, 362–372,
      383–384, 385–387
Conduct Disorder, 57–76